THOMAS JEFFERSON

A Reference Biography

The life portrait of Jefferson painted in Philadelphia early in 1800 by Rembrandt Peale. COPYRIGHTED BY THE WHITE HOUSE HISTORICAL ASSOCIATION; PHOTOGRAPH BY THE NATIONAL GEOGRAPHIC SOCIETY.

THOMAS JEFFERSON

A Reference Biography

MERRILL D. PETERSON

EDITOR

CHARLES SCRIBNER'S SONS
NEW YORK

A list of sources and credits for the design ornaments that are reproduced
above each chapter title appears in the back of this volume.

Copyright © 1986 Charles Scribner's Sons

Library of Congress Cataloging-in-Publication Data

Thomas Jefferson: a reference biography.

 Bibliography: p.
 Includes index.
 1. Jefferson, Thomas, 1743–1826. 2. Presidents—
United States—Biography. I. Peterson, Merrill D.
E332.T43 1986   973.4′6′0924 [B]   86–6736
ISBN 0–684–18069–3

Published simultaneously in Canada
by Collier Macmillan Canada, Inc.
Copyright under the Berne Convention

1 3 5 7 9 11 13 15 17 19 Q/C 20 18 16 14 12 10 8 6 4 2

PRINTED IN THE UNITED STATES OF AMERICA

The paper in this book meets the guidelines for permanence and durability of
the Committee on Production Guidelines for Book Longevity of the Council
on Library Resources

Editorial Staff

NORMA S. FRANKEL, *MANAGING EDITOR*

JONATHAN G. ARETAKIS, *Assistant Editor*

JOHN F. FITZPATRICK, *Associate Editor*

LAURA D. GROSS, *Editorial Assistant*

SANDRA D. KNIGHT, *Administrative Assistant*

LELAND S. LOWTHER, *Associate Editor*

ANJU MAKHIJANI, *Production Manager*

BETH ANN McCABE, *Production Assistant*

W. KIRK REYNOLDS, *Associate Editor*

PATRICIA FOGARTY, *Copyeditor*

ELIZABETH C. HULICK, *Proofreader*

HELEN JARDINE, *Proofreader*

JACK RUMMEL, *Proofreader*

G. MICHAEL McGINLEY, *DIRECTOR, REFERENCE BOOKS DIVISION*

Contents

Contents

Introduction

On the occasion of a state dinner honoring the Nobel laureates of the Americas, President John F. Kennedy called his assembled guests "the most extraordinary collection of talents that has ever been gathered together at the White House, with the possible exception of when Thomas Jefferson dined alone." The third president of the United States was indeed a "most extraordinary collection of talents," not only a statesman but a scientist, architect, philosopher, agriculturist, philologist, ethnologist, educator, inventor, geographer, man of letters, and more. This multifaceted genius, this "American Leonardo," led the footsteps of the infant American republic into the paths of civilization. Rising to fame as a leader of colonies in revolt against an empire, penning the charter of American independence in his thirty-fourth year, Jefferson embodied the new nation's aspirations for freedom and enlightenment, and throughout a long life was intellectually and politically engaged in the affairs of a nation and a world swept by war and revolution.

His was a life of seemingly bewildering conflicts and contradictions. By birth, taste, and training, Jefferson was a Virginia aristocrat, yet his principles and politics placed him in the vanguard of American democracy. One of the first Americans to give authentic expression to the nation's ideals and aspirations, to the extent of being called the Apostle of Americanism by one biographer, he nevertheless appeared more at home in Parisian salons than in the rude American world and was more cosmopolitan than national in thought and feeling. For his home he built a Palladian villa reminiscent of old Rome on a mountaintop looking toward the Appalachian frontier—"a portico facing the wilderness," in John Dos Passos' felicitous phrase. He was both a philosopher and a politician. Although highly successful in a career in politics that began in the Virginia House of Burgesses in 1769 and ended in the American presidency forty years later, he often cursed the fate that yoked him to the labors of government rather than to the infinitely more agreeable labors of the arts and sciences for which he believed he had been born. Jefferson was a man of theories and ideals; indeed, *visionary* was a favorite epithet of his enemies. Yet, on the evidence of his work, he was uncommonly disciplined, hardheaded, and practical. Even his dreams proved more substantial than the limiting realities so much insisted upon by more conservative men. Outwardly amiable, pleasant, open to all and sundry, a charming conversationalist, with a seemingly effortless talent for drawing people to him, he was nonetheless a man of almost impenetrable emotional reserve, "easy and delightful of acquaintance, impossible of knowledge," as Albert J. Nock observed. Almost every other American statesman, the historian Henry Adams wrote, could be portrayed with "a few broad strokes of the brush," but Jefferson "only touch by touch, with a fine pencil, and the perfection of the likeness depended upon the shifting and uncertain flicker of its semi-transparent shadows."

Adams' observation remains true, by and large, despite the outpouring of scholarly work on Jefferson in recent years. It remains true, in part, because of the intrinsic complexity of Jefferson the man and, in part, because of his unique relationship to the democratic experiment in America. Jefferson never reduced his thought to a system. He wrote but one book, *Notes on the State of Virginia,* which is the best single index to his mind. Much can be learned from his library or from architectural monuments. There are many state papers, reports, and similar documents. But for the most part the record of Jefferson's thought and activity must be pieced together, like a mosaic, from tens of thousands of his letters, which, in their freshness and variety, their literary grace and philosophy, are an inexhaustible treasure. Through his political career Jefferson would become identified, beyond any of his illustrious contemporaries, with the destiny of American democracy. In generation after generation his name, his doctrines, and his ideals were invoked in one cause or another, and he was therefore implicated in the successive crises of the democratic experiment. Indeed, in retrospect American history has sometimes seemed a protracted litigation—hearings, negotiations, trials, and appeals in endless number—on Thomas Jefferson. Through the fog of emotion generated by the political symbol, it has often been difficult to discern the historical personage.

Around what idea, motif, or formula, students of Jefferson have asked, may the crowded events, the intellectual strivings, and the moral passions of Jefferson's life be organized for comprehension? What is the figure in this richly embellished carpet? James Madison, after the death of his great friend, attempted to sum up Jefferson's genius and, in doing so, anticipated the judgment of posterity. He was, said Madison, a man of generous learning and versatile industry who left "the philosophical impress" of his mind "on every subject which he touched." But what especially distinguished all this activity, he continued, was "an early and uniform devotion to the cause of liberty, and systematic preference of a form of government squared in the strictest degree to the equal rights of man." In all the avenues of life, through all the shiftings and turnings of his mind, liberty was the ideal. It was emblazoned in the Declaration of Independence, and it came to have an almost religious power over him. "Rebellion to Tyrants is Obedience to God"—this was the motto Jefferson inscribed on his personal seal. "I have sworn upon the altar of God eternal hostility against every form of tyranny over the mind of man"—this was his noble vow, which today encircles the dome of the Jefferson Memorial in Washington, D.C. There are many and contrasting images of Jefferson, but the dominant one is that of the Apostle of Liberty, a figure of universal dimensions committed to the rights of man. In 1789 he hailed the French Revolution as "but the first chapter of the history of European liberty," and although disappointed in the sequel, Jefferson went to his death in the unshaken conviction, as he wrote in his last letter, that the achievement of the American Revolution had opened the eyes of the world to "the palpable truth, that the mass of mankind has not been born with saddles on their backs, nor a favored few booted and spurred, ready to ride them legitimately, by the grace of God."

Thomas Jefferson: A Reference Biography is dedicated to the proposition implicit in President Kennedy's witty remark to the Nobel laureates. And from the essays of twenty-five authors on different aspects and facets of Jefferson's genius, it is hoped that the figure in the carpet will emerge. The first contribution, by Dumas Malone, author of a magisterial six-volume biography, is a capsule life. It is, in fact, a thorough revision of the article Malone contributed to the *Dictionary of American Biography,* of which he was editor, over fifty years ago. The next half-dozen essays treat large themes in Jefferson's life and thought, particularly with regard to the founding of the American Republic. The essays that follow, from "The Classical World" through "Religion," focus on different facets of Jefferson's intellect and imagination—the architect, the educator, the scientist, and so on. The next group of essays deals with major chapters in his career as the leader of the Republican party in the 1790s and as president of the United States. Essays on the West, agriculture, the American natives, slavery, and Monticello round out the volume.

The final contribution—a particularly valuable one—is a comprehensive guide to Jefferson bibliography. This volume is a reference work. It has an index for convenient cross-referencing. It does not claim to be encyclopedic, however, and the essays are interpretive as well as informative. Although they are written for the general reader, they may also prove of interest to the serious student. The reader or student who wishes to extend his inquiries should consult the bibliography.

MERRILL D. PETERSON

The Life of Thomas Jefferson

DUMAS MALONE

Thomas Jefferson, statesman, diplomat, author, scientist, architect, apostle of freedom and enlightenment, was born on 13 April 1743, at Shadwell in what is now Albemarle County, Virginia, then on the fringe of western settlement. Whether or not the first Jefferson in the colony came from Wales, as the family tradition held, a Thomas Jefferson was living in Henrico County in 1679 and married Mary Branch. Their son Thomas, who married Mary Field, lived at Osbornes in the present Chesterfield County, where on the last day of February 1707/1708 Peter Jefferson was born. His father was a "gentleman Justice," but Peter enjoyed few educational opportunities and had largely to shift for himself. Becoming a surveyor, he moved to Goochland County, where by 1734 he was a magistrate. The next year he patented a thousand acres on the

Note: This is a revision of the article published in 1933 in Volume X of the Dictionary of American Biography.

south side of the Rivanna River and shortly thereafter, "for a bowl of punch," purchased from William Randolph of the plantation of Tuckahoe four hundred acres more. This contained the site north of the river upon which he erected a plain frame house in about 1741. Thither he brought his wife, and there Thomas, his third child, was born.

Jane Randolph, who became Peter Jefferson's wife at nineteen, first cousin of William of Tuckahoe and the eldest surviving child of Isham Randolph of Dungeness and his wife, Jane Rogers, connected her husband with one of the most distinguished families in the province and assured the social standing of his children. Peter Jefferson's career closely followed that of Joshua Fry, under whom he served as deputy surveyor in Albemarle, with whom he completed the boundary line between Virginia and North Carolina and made the first accurate map of Virginia, and whom he succeeded as burgess and county lieutenant. Thomas Jefferson had great respect for his father's map and from him may have acquired his zest for exploring and drawing and his liking for untrodden paths. From him he inherited a vigorous, if less powerful, body and perhaps his fondness for mathematical subjects. Of the ten children of Peter Jefferson, eight survived him. He left Thomas, the elder of his two sons, about five thousand acres of land and an established position in the community.

Seven of the first nine years of Jefferson's life were spent at Tuckahoe, on the James a few miles above the present Richmond, whither his father moved in fulfillment of a promise to William Randolph to act as guardian of the latter's son. Here Thomas began his education at the "English school." The red hills of Albemarle became his permanent home, however, at the age of nine and held evermore an unrivaled place in his affections. Soon thereafter he began the study of Latin and Greek under the Reverend William Douglas, who also introduced him to French. Of Douglas' abilities he later expressed a low opinion. After the death of his father, he studied with the Reverend James Maury, whom he later described as "a correct classical scholar." Jefferson gained an early mastery of the classical tongues and ever found the literature of Greece and Rome a "rich source of delight." In March 1760 he entered the College of William and Mary, from which he was graduated two years later. At Williamsburg, the provincial capital, he was able to view history in the making and government in practice. His chief intellectual stimulus while a student came from his association with William Small, who held the chair of mathematics and ad interim that of natural philosophy. Small aroused in him the interest in scientific questions that was destined to remain active all his life. Small introduced him to the "familiar table" of Governor Francis Fauquier and to George Wythe, most noted teacher of law of his generation in Virginia,

under whose guidance he prepared himself for practice.

During these years Jefferson was a recognized member of the close-knit social group that the children of the ruling gentry of Virginia constituted. He visited homes, made wagers with girls, gossiped about love affairs, served at weddings. Tall, loose-jointed, sandy-haired, and freckled, he was not prepossessing in appearance, but he was a skilled horseman, played on the violin, and seems to have been a gay companion. The strain of seriousness in his nature was soon apparent, however. It may have been accentuated by the unhappy outcome of his love affair with Rebecca Burwell, an "affair" largely carried out in his imagination. Before he became a prominent actor on the stage of public life, he had formulated for himself a stern code of personal conduct and had disciplined himself to habits of study as few of his contemporaries ever found strength to do. Some time after 1764, perhaps, he began to apply historical tests to the Bible, lost faith in conventional religion, though without questioning conventional morality, and for inspiration turned to the great classical writers. Finding these insufficient in later years, he found ethical guidance in the teachings of Jesus. That he prepared himself with unusual care for his profession, by the study of legal history as well as of procedure, is shown by the notebook in which he abridged his legal reading. He was admitted to the bar in 1767 and despite his dislike of court practice, was distinctly successful in the law until, on the eve of the Revolution, he abandoned it as a profession.

On 1 January 1772, Jefferson was married to Martha (Wayles) Skelton, then in her twenty-fourth year, the daughter of John Wayles of Charles City County and his wife, Martha Eppes. She was the widow of Bathurst Skelton and had borne him a son, who died shortly before her marriage to Jefferson. In the ten years of their married life she bore Jefferson six children, only three of whom survived her and only two of whom, Martha and Mary (or Maria), attained maturity. She is reputed to have been beautiful, and certainly her second husband lavished upon her notable devotion. The young couple began their married life in the only part of Monticello then finished, the southeastern pavilion. Jefferson had moved to his adored mountaintop after the house at Shadwell burned, together with his cherished library, in 1770, and had begun the building operations which were to extend over a generation. From the estate of his father-in-law he acquired in behalf of his wife, soon after his marriage, holdings roughly equivalent to his own. With them, however, went a huge debt from the effects of which he never entirely escaped. Throughout most of his mature life he was the owner of approximately ten thousand acres of land and between one hundred and two hundred slaves. Nothing if not methodical, he made periodical records of everything connected with his plantations—his slaves, his horses and cattle, the trees planted, the temperature at Monticello, the dates on which birds and flowers first appeared.

In 1770, Jefferson was appointed county lieutenant of Albemarle. In May 1769 he had become a member of the House of Burgesses, and he continued to be one until the House ceased to function in 1775, though he did not attend in 1772. He says he had been intimate for almost a decade with Patrick Henry, whose eloquence had enthralled him in his student days. Never an effective public speaker, Jefferson himself did greatest service in legislative bodies on committees, where his marked talents as a literary draftsman were employed. Identified from the outset with the aggressive anti-British group, he was one of those who drew up the resolves creating the Virginia Committee of Correspondence and was appointed a member of the committee of eleven, though not of the select committee of three. In 1774 he was one of the champions of the resolution for a fast day, on the day the Boston Port Act was to go into effect. This resolution led to the dissolution of the House. In 1775 he was on the committee appointed to draw up an address to the earl of Dunmore, the royal governor, rejecting Lord North's conciliatory offer, and he says that he drafted the address adopted. Prevented by illness from attending the Virginia convention of 1774, he sent a paper that was later published as *A Summary View of the Rights of British America.* This proved to be his greatest literary contribution to the American Revolution next to the Declaration of Independence, and it reveals, as perhaps no other document does, his point of view in that struggle. Though approved by many, it was not adopted because it was regarded as too advanced. Emphasizing the "natural" right of emigration exercised by the first English settlers in America as by the Saxon settlers in England, he denied all parliamentary authority over the colonies. He claimed that the only political tie with Great Britain was supplied by the king, to whom the colonists had voluntarily submitted. He believed that the assistance rendered by the mother country to the colonists had been solely for commercial benefit and was repayable only in trade privileges. This powerful pamphlet, distinctly legalistic in tone, reveals no adequate conception of the value of early English protection or of the contemporary British imperial problem. Throughout his career as a Revolutionary patriot he emphasized "rights as derived from the laws of nature," not a king; and here, as elsewhere, he strove for the "revindication of Saxon liberties."

Elected by the Virginia convention to serve in Congress in case Peyton Randolph should be required at home, Jefferson sat in that body during the summer and autumn of 1775. Though he drafted several papers, these were too strongly anti-British in tone to be acceptable while there was hope of conciliation. He was not present in Congress from 28 December 1775 to 14 May 1776. Probably called home by the illness of his mother, who died 31 March, and by the needs of his family, he also had duties to perform as county lieutenant and commander of the militia of Albemarle, to which office he had been appointed by the Virginia Committee of Safety on 26 September. Following the famous resolutions introduced into Congress on 7 June 1776 by Richard Henry Lee, Jefferson was elected four days later, with John Adams, Benjamin Franklin, Roger Sherman, and Robert R. Livingston, to a committee to draw up a declaration of independence. The reasons for the prominence in this connection of one so young as Jefferson have been much disputed. It was inevitable that a Virginian should be on the committee, and Richard Henry Lee had gone home. Now only thirty-three years old, Jefferson had been a "silent member" on the floor of Congress, though outspoken and decisive in committees. The "reputation of a masterly pen" stood him in good stead and opened to him the door of dangerous but glorious opportunity.

More changes in his draft of the Declaration were made at the instance of Franklin and Adams than he remembered, and some were made by Congress itself; but the most famous American political document as a composition belongs indisputably to Jefferson. The philosophical portion strikingly resembles the first three sections of George Mason's Declaration of Rights, itself a notable summary of current revolutionary philosophy. Jefferson probably availed himself of this, but he improved upon it. The doctrines are essentially those of John Locke, in which the more radical of the patriots were steeped. Jefferson himself did not believe in absolute human equality, and though he had no fears of revolution, he preferred that the "social compact" be renewed by periodical, peaceful revisions. He steadfastly believed that government should be based on popu-

lar consent and secure the "inalienable" rights of man, among which he included the pursuit of happiness rather than property, that government should be a means to human well-being and not an end in itself. He gave here a matchless expression of his faith. The charges against the king, who is singled out because all claims of parliamentary authority are implicitly denied, are in general an improved version of those that had already been drawn up by Jefferson and adopted as the preamble of the Virginia constitution of 1776. Relentless in their reiteration, they constitute a statement of the specific grievances of the revolting party, powerfully and persuasively presented at the bar of public opinion. The Declaration is notable for both its clarity and its subtlety of expression, and it abounds in the felicities that are characteristic of Jefferson's unlabored prose. It is eloquent in its sustained elevation of style and remains his noblest literary monument.

Desiring to be nearer his family and believing that he could be more useful in furthering the reformation of Virginia than in Congress, Jefferson left the latter body in September 1776 and, entering the Virginia House of Delegates on 7 October, served there until his election to the governorship in June 1779. While a member of Congress, he had submitted to the Virginia convention of 1776 a constitution and preamble, only the latter of which had been adopted. With the new constitution and government, which were marked by little change in law and social organization, he was soon profoundly dissatisfied. To him the Revolution meant more than a redress of grievances. Against the continuance of an established church, divorced from England, which the conservatives favored, he desired the entire separation of church and state. He was determined to rid his "country," as he called Virginia, of the artificial aristocracy of wealth and birth and to facilitate through education the development of a natural aristocracy of talent and virtue and of an enlightened electorate. He believed that the legal code should be adapted to republican government "with a single eye to reason, & the good of those for whose government it was formed." Because of his skill as a legislator, the definiteness of his carefully formulated program, and the almost religious zeal with which he pressed it, he immediately assumed the leadership of the progressive group. He deserves the chief credit not only for an unparalleled program but also for legislative achievements that have rarely been equaled in American history.

He struck the first blow at the aristocratic system by procuring the abolition of landholding in fee tail. On 12 October 1776 he moved the revision of the laws. Elected to the board of revisers with four others, of whom only George Wythe and Edmund Pendleton served to the end, he labored two years with scholarly thoroughness on his share of the revision, including the law of descent and the criminal law. The report of the board (18 June 1779) consisted of 126 bills, most of which were ultimately enacted in substance. Primogeniture was abolished in 1785. His Bill for Establishing Religious Freedom, presented in 1779 by John Harvie of Albemarle and passed, with slight but significant modifications in the preamble in 1786 when Jefferson was in France, was regarded by him as one of his greatest contributions to humanity. In its assertion that the mind is not subject to coercion, that civil rights have no dependence on religious opinions, and that the opinions of men are not the concern of civil government, it is indeed one of the great American charters of freedom.

Jefferson's educational bills, which represented the constructive part of his program, were unsuccessful. Of his extraordinary Bill for the More General Diffusion of Knowledge, which summarizes his educational philosophy, only the part dealing with elementary schools was acted on (in 1796), and a provision was inserted that defeated its purpose. His attempts to amend the constitution of his old college and to establish a public library entirely failed. During his governorship, however, he effected the abolishment of the professorships of Hebrew, theology, and ancient languages and the establishment of professorships of anatomy and medicine, law, and modern languages, the two latter being the first of their kind in America. Though he did not originate the idea of removing the capital to Richmond, he framed a bill for that purpose and the measure that was passed in 1779 included his preamble and provisions for handsome public buildings such as he had favored.

On 1 June 1779, Jefferson was elected governor of Virginia by the General Assembly. His term was one year, and he was re-elected for another. The qualities of mind that made him so conspicuous a planner and prophet were of slight avail to him as a war-time administrator. He had little power. Under the state constitution of 1776, he could not veto legislation, and his actions were subject to the approval of the Council of State, a body of eight men who were elected by the Assembly. He presided over this group but could vote only in case of a tie. He was not disposed to overstep his constitutional bounds, but his experience in this office caused him to oppose legislative dominance ever afterward.

This agricultural society suffered during the war from the loss of the British market for tobacco, and the wheat crop was almost wholly destroyed by drought in Jefferson's first year as governor. For money, the legislators turned to the printing press. By the time Jefferson left office, the currency was said to have had little more value than oak leaves. Under these difficult circumstances, he was unceasing in his efforts to meet the requisitions of the Continental Congress, to raise troops, and to procure arms and supplies.

In the autumn of 1780, weary and frustrated, he talked privately of resigning and certainly had no desire to serve a third year. Thus far, the state had been spared invasion; and its military resources had been drained to strengthen armies elsewhere. In the first days of 1781, Benedict Arnold made a surprise raid into the interior from the coast. He did little damage in Richmond, which had recently become the capital, but he set fire to the foundry six miles upstream, where arms were stored. After the governor was reliably informed that Arnold was coming, he was tireless in his effort to protect the property of the state, but he did not call the militia in time to oppose the invader, and he was afterward charged with slowness and indecision. The advance of Cornwallis from the south in the spring with an overpowering force was far more serious. This occasioned the precipitate flight of the entire state government and its virtual dissolution.

The legislators who gathered in Richmond on 10 May for their annual spring session adjourned to meet later in Charlottesville, seventy miles to the west; there on 28 May they attained a quorum. The election of a governor was scheduled for Saturday, 2 June, when Jefferson's second year would end, but unfortunately was postponed until Monday. That morning Lt. Col. Banastre Tarleton and a large body of British horsemen entered Charlottesville. Cornwallis had sent him to upset the Assembly. Jefferson had as guests at Monticello the Speakers of the two houses and other legislators. There could be no meeting of the Council of State, because there were not enough councillors, but he wrote some last official letters.

Before dawn on Monday, a gigantic horseman rode up the mountainside. Capt. Jack Jouett had made a heroic ride through the night to warn Jefferson and the Assembly. The aroused delegates met in Charlottesville, voted to adjourn to Staunton across the mountain, and fled precipitately in that direction. They did not wait to elect a governor. Jefferson sent his family to Blenheim, an estate in the southern part of the county. He himself remained at Monticello until he could actually see Redcoats through his telescope. Then he rode through the woods to Blenheim. Later he took his family to Poplar Forest, his place in Bedford County.

What was left of the General Assembly, meeting at Staunton, finally got around to the election of a governor. By choosing Gen. Thomas Nelson, the ranking officer of the militia, they joined the civil and military authorities. On the same day (12 June 1781) the House of Delegates adopted a resolution calling for an investigation of the conduct of the recent executive at the next session. No specific charges were made at this or any other time. Judging from what Jefferson learned from the author of the resolution, George Nicholas, during the summer, that delegate was not thinking of Tarleton's raid, which actually appears to have frightened the legislators more than it did Jefferson, but of the raid of Benedict Arnold. It was his official conduct in the earlier raid, not the later, that the former governor defended at the legislative session in the fall. By this time the invasion of the state by Cornwallis had ended with his surrender, and there was no need to blame anybody for the sufferings of the past.

On 12 December the committee appointed by the House of Delegates to inquire into the conduct of the recent executive reported that no information had been offered them except rumors, which they regarded as groundless. A week later, resolutions of thanks to Jefferson were adopted by both houses. Formally vindicated, Jefferson soon recovered his prestige in Virginia. His election as delegate to the Continental Congress at this session of the legislature—an election he declined—showed that he retained public confidence. The chief significance of the closing events of his ill-fated governorship lay in the relatively distant future, when he was involved in national contests. Then these events were distorted out of all reason in the effort of political enemies to show that he was unfit to be president of the United States. By then his skin appears to have become a little tougher than it was in 1781. Despite the handsome amends his fellow Virginians then made for unjust criticism, he was convinced that public service and private misery were inseparable. Accordingly he had retired to his neglected farms, his cherished books, and his beloved family, convinced that nothing could again separate him from them.

Jefferson took advantage of the leisure forced upon him by a fall from his horse to organize the careful memoranda about Virginia that he had made over a long period. Arranging these in the order of the queries submitted in 1781 by François de Barbé-Marbois, secretary of the French legation, he somewhat corrected and enlarged them during the winter of 1782–1783 and had them printed in France in 1785. The *Notes on the State of Virginia* went through many editions and laid the foundations of Jefferson's high contemporary reputation as a universal scholar and of his enduring fame as a pioneer American scientist. Unpretentious in form and statistical in character, this unusually informative and generally interesting book may still be consulted with profit about the geography and productions, and the social and political life, of eighteenth-century Virginia. With ardent patriotism as well as zeal for truth, Jefferson combated the theories of Buffon and Raynal in regard to the inferiority of animal and intellectual life in America, and he manifested great optimism in regard to the future of the country, but he included "strictures" on slavery and the government of Virginia. In 1783 he drafted another proposed constitution for his state, which was published in 1786 and ultimately bound with the *Notes* as an appendix.

But for the death of his wife on 6 September 1782, he might have remained in philosophic retirement. He lavished upon his motherless daughters extraordinary tenderness and solicitude, but he was now glad to abandon Monticello and seek relief from personal woe in public activity. Appointed peace commissioner to Europe on 12 November 1782, he was prepared to sail when, his mission having become unnecessary, his appointment was withdrawn. In June 1783 he was elected a delegate to Congress, and during six months' service in that body the following winter he was a member of almost every important committee and drafted an extraordinary number of state papers. Some of these were of the first importance, especially his notes on the coinage, in which he advocated the adoption of the dollar, to be divided into tenths and hundredths, and his successive reports on the government of the western territory. The reports of 22 March 1784 contained most of the features of the epoch-making Ordinance of 1787. If it had been adopted as Jefferson presented it, slavery would have been forbidden in all the western territory after 1800, and the secession of any part of that region would have been rendered indisputably illegal. Jefferson had earlier drafted a deed of cession of the northwestern territory that was claimed by Virginia, and he drew up a land ordinance that failed of adoption. Certainly he was a major architect of American expansion. He also drafted a report on the definitive treaty of peace that was eventually adopted. On 20 December 1783 he drew up a report that was agreed to as the basis of procedure in the negotiation of treaties of commerce and was himself appointed, on 7 May 1784, to assist Franklin and Adams in this work in Europe.

Joining them in Paris on 6 August, with his daughter Martha, he was appointed in 1785 Franklin's successor as minister to France and remained in that country until October 1789. Rightly regarded in France as a savant, he carried on the tradition of Franklin, but until the end of his own stay he was overshadowed by Franklin's immense reputation. Jefferson's attitude toward his predecessor, whom he regarded as one of the two greatest Americans (the other being George Washington), was one of becoming modesty without a tinge of jealousy. During his ministry he was somewhat overshadowed by Lafayette, who was regarded as the French symbol of American ideals and the protector of American interests. Jefferson took full advantage of Lafayette's invaluable cooperation and associated with him on terms of intimacy and affection, content to be relatively inconspicuous if he might be useful.

Though he later characterized his official activities in France as unimportant, he proved a diligent and skillful diplomat. He and his colleagues succeeded in negotiating, in 1785, a treaty of commerce with Prussia. Early in 1786 he joined Adams in London, but their efforts to negotiate a commercial treaty with Great Britain were futile. He took careful note of English domestic gardening and mechanical appliances, but of English architecture and manners had few kind words to say. He supported Thomas Barclay in the negotiation of a treaty with Morocco in 1787 but was convinced that the Barbary pirates could be restrained only by force and worked out a scheme for concerted action on the part of a league of nations. This was accepted by Congress but aroused no enthusiasm in Europe. He negotiated with France a consular convention, signed 14 November 1788, which was the first of the sort agreed to by the United States. Though he could not hope to make much of a breach in the wall of commercial exclusiveness, he gained some relaxation of French duties on American products and, by his arguments against the tobacco monopoly of the Farmers-General, made a definite impression on Vergennes and his successor, Montmorin. Jefferson left Europe with the belief that the French had granted all the commercial concessions possible at the time, that they had few interests in America, and that they had great sentimental attachment to the young republic. He was convinced that the

United States should be friendly to France, both because of gratitude and because of France's value as a counterpoise against the British, whom he regarded as hostile in sentiment and entirely selfish in policy. He gained the impression, however, that Great Britain and Spain would pay much for American neutrality if they should become involved in European controversy. The hope that the United States would ultimately gain great advantages from the troubles of Europe profoundly affected his subsequent foreign policy, predisposing him to ways of peace.

At a time when there was a flood of sentimental French writings about America, Jefferson endeavored to present the American cause adequately and accurately. These motives in part caused him to distribute his own *Notes on the State of Virginia* and the Virginia statute for religious freedom. Not only did he respond generously to inquiries about America, but he shared freely with his own countrymen the knowledge he himself gained of another world. To interested friends at home, he wrote about inventions in dozens of letters; and for Madison, Monroe, and others he continually purchased books. In 1787, on an extensive journey through the French provinces, he made a careful study of vineyards, and he went into northern Italy to see the machines used there for cleaning rice. He sent samples of upland rice seed to South Carolina and Georgia and forwarded information about the olive tree. At Nîmes he gazed for hours on the Maison Carrée, "like a lover at his mistress." For the new state capitol of Virginia, he sent a plan modeled on this temple and thus initiated the classical revival in American architecture. On a tour in 1788, he made numerous observations in Germany. This keen-eyed, reflective traveler purposed that his mission should prove educational to his fellow citizens as well as to himself and never lost sight of his obligation to be useful.

He was greatly impressed with the manners of the French though opposed to any aping of them by Americans, and he was attracted by French cuisine and wines. He found the French a temperate people but believed the life of the upper classes to be lacking in domestic happiness and rather futile on the whole. He was appalled by the poverty he observed among the lower classes. He thought little of the science of the French but was enthusiastic about their arts—architecture, painting, and music. Perhaps he valued music the more because a fractured wrist had ended his days as a violinist. Distressed by the oppression and inequality he observed in the Old World, he came to think less than ever of kings, nobles, and priests. His experience in France did not give him a new political and social philosophy. It confirmed the basic views he already had and stimulated his democratic faith. He shared the belief of the *philosophes* in the indefinite improvability of mankind and made a virtual religion of enlightenment. He also had a firsthand knowledge of the operations of representative government, which the French reformers lacked. He correctly perceived that this society was far from ready for self-government of the American variety, and he never ceased to fear that the reformers would attempt too much and promote a reaction.

The course of the French Revolution until his departure Jefferson followed closely and reported in detail. Though he strove to maintain strict official propriety, this skilled political architect privately suggested to Lafayette's aunt, Madame de Tessé, a desirable course of procedure for the Assembly of Notables, and to Lafayette himself he submitted a proposed charter for France. A meeting of the leaders of the Patriot party, arranged by Lafayette, was held at Jefferson's house in the effort to arrive at a compromise on the questions of the royal veto and the constitution of the Assembly. Jefferson commented on successive drafts of a declaration of rights by Lafayette and through him may have had some influence on the famous Declaration of the Rights of Man and the Citizens. He rejoiced in the adoption of this great charter of individual freedom and had high hopes that the revolt against tyranny in France would be followed by the establishment of a firm government. In revolutionary France, however, he was distinctly a moderate. He now believed that the reformers should be content with a limited monarchy, and he never ceased to regard the execution of Louis XVI (1793) as a crucial mistake. The French Revolution became a burning issue in American politics, and his discriminating attitude was not understood by many at that time and thereafter. Toward the end of his life, he said that nothing was immutable but the "inherent and inalienable rights of man." So long as the French Revolution served to support and advance these rights, he strongly approved of it. But he deplored the tyranny of Robespierre as well as that of Napoleon.

This counselor of moderation was strongly opposed to the counterrevolution, and he favored the adjustment of laws and institutions to the inevitable changes in human affairs. In a letter he wrote Madison shortly before his departure from France (6 September 1789), he denied the right of one generation to bind another. "The earth belongs always to the living generation," he said. In particular, he denied the right of a government, such as that of France, to transmit to posterity a heavy burden of debt. His objection to certain features of Alexander Hamilton's financial policy a few years later and his persistent effort to reduce the national debt after he became president were both grounded on what he regarded as a moral principle. He also asserted that any and every generation has the right to be governed by laws of its own making. He argued that constitutions should be revised every nineteen years. Cogent arguments against this impracticable procedure were duly presented to him by Madison, but he appears to have forgotten these, for he revived the idea when seeking to modernize the Virginia constitution in his old age.

Having been granted a leave of absence to settle his private affairs and to take home his two daughters, the younger of whom, Mary, had joined him in Paris in 1787, Jefferson sailed in October 1789 and arrived at Monticello two days before Christmas, to be welcomed tumultuously by his slaves. Soon after he landed, he received from President George Washington the offer of appointment as secretary of state, a post that was being temporarily filled by John Jay. Jefferson's dislike for publicity and shrinking from censure made him reluctant to enter the storm of politics, from which in France he had been relatively aloof, but on patriotic grounds he eventually accepted the eminently appropriate appointment. After giving his daughter Martha in marriage to her cousin Thomas Mann Randolph, Jr., he proceeded to New York, where, in March 1790, he became the first secretary of state under the Constitution.

Although he had kept in touch with American developments through extensive correspondence, Jefferson was not fully aware of the conservative reaction that had taken place in his own country while he was in the midst of political ferment in France. He had seen nothing threatening in the commotions that had marked the last years of the Confederation and, in any event, thought dangerous liberty distinctly preferable to quiet slavery. Despite the imperfections of the government, he had described it as "without comparison the best existing or that ever did exist." Nonetheless, he had viewed with favor the movement for strengthening the federal government and had given the new Constitution his general approval, objecting chiefly to the absence of a bill of rights, which was later supplied, and the perpetual reeligibility of the president. He had denied that he was of the party of Federalists but had stated that he was much farther from the Anti-Federalists. Before his retirement from office, he came to be regarded as the leader of the group opposed to the policies of Alexander Hamilton. To distinguish themselves from their opponents, whom they termed "monarchists," Jefferson and his sympathizers called themselves "republicans." Until the end of his life, he believed that his early fears of an American monarchy were warranted. Undoubtedly he was distressed by the change in the political atmosphere in which he found himself. In the aristocratic Federalist court, at first in New York and soon in Philadelphia, this accomplished gentleman was ill at ease.

With Hamilton, who was nearly a dozen years his junior and had already assumed the first place in the counsels of the government, he strove at the outset to cooperate. His subsequent statement that he was duped by his colleague in connection with the bill for federal assumption of state debts incurred by the Revolution is unconvincing. His contemporary letters clearly show that he believed at the time that some compromise was essential for peace and the preservation of the Union. When at length better provision for Virginia was made in the bill and the location of the federal city on the banks of the Potomac was agreed to, he gave his approval to the measure. While Jefferson may already have perceived that Hamilton was catering to a new moneyed group and was relatively indifferent to the agricultural interests, he had shown no particular disapproval of his colleague's financial policies as yet. He was always fearful of centralized government, but he was not yet fully aware that there was danger of the concentration of power in Hamilton's own person.

The first serious difference of opinion between the two men was over a question of foreign policy. Fully convinced that the British would not yield their posts in the Old Northwest or grant commercial privileges unless forced to do so, Jefferson favored the employment of commercial discrimination as a weapon against them. This policy, advocated in Congress by Madison, was opposed by Hamilton, who feared the loss of revenue from British imports. The movement in Congress for discrimination was strengthened by Jefferson's successive able reports on matters of commercial policy, but through the influence of Hamilton it was blocked in February 1791 and ultimately abandoned. Meanwhile, the secretary of the treasury had maintained a surprising intimacy with George Beckwith, the unofficial British representative (1789–1791), with whom the secretary of state properly refused to have anything to do.

Early in 1791, at the request of his chief, Jefferson drafted an opinion on the constitutionality of the measure creating the Bank of the United States. This had been passed by Congress at the insistence of Hamilton, but the power of the federal government to set up such a corporation had been denied by Attorney General Edmund Randolph and by Congressman James Madison. Jefferson agreed with them, holding that the powers assumed by Hamilton's bill were not among those enumerated as belonging to the federal government. Neither could they be properly derived from the general clauses, which he interpreted literally. While he believed that constitutions should be periodically revised, he insisted on their strict interpretation until formally modified. He granted little latitude to judges and was characteristically distrustful of strong government. In this instance, his fears were indirectly heightened by his growing distrust of Hamilton, who lusted for power and appeared to be interpreting the Constitution to suit himself. These objections were referred by Washington to Hamilton, who responded in a lengthy paper in which he ably championed the doctrine of liberal construction. After receiving this, the president signed the bill.

Despite his confidence in his own position, Jefferson had stated that, in deference to Congress, the president should not veto the bill unless thoroughly convinced of its unconstitutionality. Washington kept the opinions in his own hands, and they were not made public for many years. There is no reason to suppose he showed Hamilton's to Jefferson, and the conflict over the construction of the Constitution was far from over. It was clear that the aggressive secretary of the treasury had won another victory.

In the spring of 1791, Thomas Paine's *Rights of Man* appeared in America, with an extract from a private note of Jefferson as a preface. His statement that he was glad that something was to be said publicly against "the political heresies" that had sprung up was interpreted both as an approval of Paine, who was anathema to the Anglophiles in America, and as a reflection on John Adams, whose expatiations on the faults of democratic systems Jefferson had indeed had in mind. Jefferson's statement of regret that he and his old friend had been "thrown on the public stage as public antagonists" may be accepted as sincere by others, as it was by Adams, but the incident identified Jefferson with criticism of the aristocratic tendencies of the government and in the end was politically advantageous to him. Fortuitous circumstances thus served to make a popular figure of one who abhorred controversy, who preferred to work behind the scenes, and who lacked the personal aggressiveness commonly associated with political leadership.

In May–June 1791 he and Madison made a botanical trip to New England, during which they doubtless gave some thought to politics; and, on 31 October, Philip Freneau published in Philadelphia the first number of the *National Gazette,* in opposition to the *Gazette of the United States,* published by John Fenno. Jefferson, knowing Freneau to be an ardent republican, had given him the small post of translator in the Department of

State. Hamilton had already given Fenno the more lucrative printing at his disposal and was later to give him personal financial assistance. With the increasingly bitter criticism of Hamilton in Congress during the winter of 1791–1792 Jefferson afterward claimed that he had nothing to do, except that he expressed hostility in conversation with, and letters to, his friends. Madison was the major organizer but Jefferson had become the symbol of anti-Hamiltonianism, and although more scrupulous of proprieties than his colleague, he served to inspire forces that he did not now or ever essay to command.

Hamilton had established with George Hammond, who presented in November 1791 his credentials as British minister, an intimacy similar to that which Beckwith had enjoyed. Hammond, forced by Jefferson to admit that he had no power to negotiate a new treaty, unwisely undertook to debate with the American secretary of state the infractions of the treaty of peace. Jefferson's magnificent reply of 29 May 1792, which completely demolished the mediocre case of the Britisher, was submitted in draft to Hamilton and, with the latter's relatively minor criticism, to Washington, who heartily approved it. To Hammond, however, the secretary of the treasury lamented the "intemperate violence" of Jefferson and stated that the reply had not been read by Washington and did not represent the position of the government. Thus fortified by assurances that nullified Jefferson's arguments, the British minister submitted the matter to his superiors at home, who felt safe in ignoring it. The full extent of Hamilton's intrigue was not exposed until the twentieth century, but Jefferson was probably aware that he owed his undeserved defeat to his colleague.

By the summer of 1792 the hostility of the two men had become implacable. In the spring Jefferson had expressed in no uncertain terms to Washington his opinion that the causes of public discontent lay in Hamilton's policy, particularly in the "corruption" that had accompanied the financial measures of the latter and that had extended to the legislature itself. A formal list of the objections Jefferson had cited was submitted by the president to Hamilton on 29 July and was replied to by the latter three weeks later. In the meantime, Hamilton, smarting under the barbs of Freneau, had made an anonymous attack on the democratic editor and, through him, on Jefferson. Washington's letters to his two secretaries, deploring their dissensions within the government, elicited lengthy replies in which each man presented his case, not only to his chief but also to posterity. Washington did not succeed in stilling the troubled waters. During the autumn of 1792, Hamilton published in the newspapers a series of ferocious anonymous attacks on his colleague, with the definite object of driving him from office. Jefferson, with greater dignity or greater discretion, refrained from newspaper controversy, leaving his defense to his friends. He probably played a part, however, in drafting the resolutions of William Branch Giles, presented early in 1793, which were severely critical of Hamilton's conduct of the treasury.

Jefferson's hostility to Hamilton, apart from his justifiable resentment at the interference of the latter in the conduct of his department, was like that of a religious devotee to an enemy of his faith. In a letter to Washington of 9 September 1792, Jefferson said he was convinced that Hamilton's "system flowed from principles adverse to liberty, and was calculated to undermine and demolish the Republic, by creating an influence of his department over the members of the Legislature." Hamilton's hostility to Jefferson, apart from resentment that his own power had been challenged, was like that of a practical man of affairs who found specific projects impeded by one whom he regarded as a quibbling theorist. Washington valued both men and wanted both to remain in office, utilized both, and followed the policies of neither exclusively. The invaluable service rendered by each in his own field of activity vindicates the judgment of the patient president.

Yielding to the request of his chief, Jefferson remained in office until the last day of 1793, during a critical period of foreign affairs. Although the course of the revolution in France had been followed with growing concern by the conservative groups in America, popular opinion was still rather favorable to the French when the war in Europe was extended to Great Britain (1 February 1793) and a new French minister, Edmond Charles Genêt, came to the United States (8 April 1793). Jefferson was determined that his country should take no action that would imply opposition to the principles of the French Revolution or the repudiation of the French alliance, but he fully agreed with Washington and Hamilton that American neutrality was imperative. He successfully urged the avoidance of the word "neutrality" in Washington's proclamation, however, in order to offend the French as little as possible and in the hope of gaining commercial concessions from the British. He also prevailed upon Washington to receive Genêt without qualifications. Although Jefferson greeted Genêt kindly, rejoiced in the popular enthusiasm for democracy that the fiery emissary kindled, and, through a letter of introduction, came dangerously near conniving with the Frenchman in his projected expedition against Louisiana, he strove with diligence to maintain neutrality and bore with patience the immense labors that the American position imposed upon him. When Genêt persisted in offensive actions and criticisms, Jefferson lost patience with him. Agreeing with his colleagues that the man had become intolerable, he wrote a powerful letter asking Genêt's recall.

Although Jefferson protested vigorously against British infringements on American neutral rights during the war, he was unable as secretary of state to solve the problem of British relations. Jay's Treaty (1794), which was negotiated after his retirement under the influence of Hamilton, was regarded by Jefferson as an ignominious surrender of American claims. The negotiations instituted by him with Spain were equally unsuccessful during his term of office, but the American objectives that he had formulated were attained in Pinckney's Treaty (Treaty of San Lorenzo) of 1795. If in the heat of the controversy with Hamilton he was at times guilty of extravagant assertion, he performed an inestimable service to the republic by calling attention to the dangers of his colleague's policy, by formulating the chief grounds of opposition to it, and by inspiring the forces that were to effect its modification after it had achieved its most significant results.

Now in his fifty-first year, Jefferson believed that his second retirement from public life was final. Soon he resumed building operations at Monticello, following revised plans that had grown out of his architectural observations abroad. By a system of crop rotation he tried to restore his wasted lands. He experimented with mechanical devices, built a gristmill, set up a nail factory, and directed his large but relatively unprofitable establishment with characteristic diligence and attention to minute details. His renewed and increased enthusiasm for agriculture quite got the better of his love of study. At no other period of his mature life, perhaps, did he read so little and write so rarely. His days on horseback soon restored his health to the vigor that he feared it had permanently lost, and he brought some order into his tangled finances. During his years as a national officeholder he had largely lived on his small salary, yet the profits from his plantations and even sales of slaves and lands had been insufficient to rid him of the old Wayles debt, which in 1795 was increased by a judgment against the executors as security for the late Richard Randolph. Like so many of his fellow Virginians, Jefferson was unable to realize on his assets and was eaten up by interest to British creditors. Nonetheless, his personal generosity was unabated.

To Madison, whom he regarded as the logical Republican candidate for the presidency, he wrote on 27 April 1795 that the "little spice of ambition" he had had in his younger days had long since evaporated and that the question of his own candidacy was forever closed. He remained, however, the symbol and the prophet of a political faith. When the leaders of his party determined to support him in 1796, he did not gainsay them, but he was surprisingly content to run second to Adams, who was his senior and whom he perhaps regarded as the only barrier against Hamilton.

The vice-presidency provided a salary that Jefferson undoubtedly needed, enabled him to spend much time at Monticello, and afforded him relative leisure. The chief significance of his service as presiding officer of the Senate lies in the fact that out of it emerged his *Manual of Parliamentary Practice* (1801), subsequently published in many editions and translated into several languages and still the basis of parliamentary usage in the Senate. Despite the conciliatory spirit that marked his early relations with Adams, Jefferson played no part in the conduct of the administration, in which the hand of Hamilton was soon apparent.

As vice-president, Jefferson was characteristically discreet in public utterance, but his general attitude toward the questions of the day was undoubtedly well known; and he was inevitably the target of the Federalist press, which continued to regard him as the personification of his party. The publication in the United States in May 1797 of a private letter of his to Philip Mazzei (24 April 1796), which originally appeared in a Florentine paper and was somewhat altered in form by successive translations, gave wide currency to his earlier criticisms of the Federalists. It was interpreted by many as an attack on Washington. Jefferson made no effort to disavow a letter that was in substance his, suffering in silence while the Federalist press termed him "libeler," "liar," and "assassin."

He had approved of the conduct of James Monroe as minister to France, which aroused much hostile Federalist comment, and believed that the bellicose spirit which swept the country after the publication of the "XYZ dispatches" was aggravated by the Hamiltonians, with a view to advancing their own interests and embroiling the United States on the side of the British. He himself was sympathetic with Elbridge Gerry, the commissioner who proved more amenable than his colleagues to French influence, and suggested that Gerry publish an account of his experiences, but Jefferson had no enthusiasm for the existing order in France. He was glad to drop the disastrous French issue when, at the height of the war fever, the Federalists provided a better one by passing the Alien and Sedition Acts. Jefferson rightly regarded hysterical hostility to aliens, such as his friends C. F. Volney and Joseph Priestley, and attacks upon freedom of speech as menacing the ideals he most cherished. Since the Sedition Law was applied chiefly to Republican editors, partisan as well as philosophical motives were conjoined in his opposition to it.

His most notable contribution to the campaign of discussion consisted of the Kentucky Resolutions of 1798. (His authorship was not disclosed until years later.) The Virginia Resolutions, drawn by Madison, were similar in tenor though more moderate. The constitutional doctrines advanced by Jefferson—that the government of the United States originated in a compact, that acts of the federal government unauthorized by the delegated powers are void, and that a state has the right to judge of infractions of its powers and to determine the mode of redress—were much emphasized in later years. His dominant purpose, however, was to attack the offensive laws as an unconstitutional and unwarranted infringement upon individual freedom, a denial of rights that could not be alienated. The language of what was in effect a party platform was in the nature of the case extravagant, but Jefferson and Madison had no intention of carrying matters to extremes. More important from the practical point of view than any promulgation of constitutional theory was the vindication of the right of public discussion and political opposition.

Nominated by a congressional caucus for the presidency and by no means indifferent to the outcome as he had been four years earlier, Jefferson owed his success in the election of 1800 as much to Federalist dissensions as to any formal issues that had been raised. To the Republican victory, his running mate, Aaron Burr, made no small contribution. By fault of the electoral machinery, soon to be remedied, the two Republicans received an identical vote and the choice of a president was left to the House of Representatives. Despite the personal hostility to Jefferson of the High Federalists, who voted for Burr to the end, the opinion (to which Hamilton contributed) that Jefferson was the safer man of the two caused the House ultimately to yield to the unquestionable desire of the Republicans and to elect him.

Jefferson's diffidence and lack of spectacular qualities would have constituted in a later day a grave political handicap. His popular success was due in considerable part to his identification of himself with causes for which time was fighting—notably the broadening of the political base—and to his remarkable sensitivity to fluctuations in public opinion. As a practical politician, he worked through other men, whom he energized and who gave him to an extraordinary degree their devoted cooperation. His leadership was due not to self-assertiveness and imperiousness of will but to the fact that circumstances had made him a symbolic figure and

that to an acute intelligence and unceasing industry he joined a dauntless and contagious faith. The long struggle between his partisans and the Federalists has been variously interpreted as one between democracy and aristocracy, state rights and nationalism, agrarianism and capitalism. In retrospective old age, he referred to the "revolution" of 1800, comparing it to that of 1776. He may have exaggerated the importance of the victory of his party. At the least, however, it signified vindication of political opposition, the repudiation of a reactionary faction, and the accession of more representative leaders to power.

Jefferson, the first president to be inaugurated in Washington, had himself drawn a plan for the city, part of which survives in the Mall. As secretary of state, to whom the commissioners of the District of Columbia were responsible, he had suggested the competition for the new federal buildings and he was considerably responsible for the selection of classical designs. As president, he appointed Benjamin H. Latrobe surveyor of public buildings and fully cooperated in planning for the future development of a monumental city. In his day, pomp and ceremony, to which on principle and for political reasons he was opposed, would have been preposterous in the wilderness village. Remaining until the last at Conrad's boardinghouse, where his democratic simplicity was marked, he walked to the nearby Senate chamber of the uncompleted Capitol, to receive the oath of office from his distant cousin and inveterate political foe Chief Justice John Marshall. Although aware of the last efforts of the Federalists to entrench themselves in the judiciary, he believed that after the long "contest of opinion" the danger of monarchy was now removed, and in his benevolent inaugural he sought to make acquiescence in the will of the majority as easy as possible. Although he challenged the assertion that a republican government could not be strong, he defined its functions as sharply limited. It should restrain men from injuring one another, he said, but otherwise leave them to regulate their own concerns. He declared against special privileges and urged encouragement, not of industry, but of agriculture and of commerce "as its handmaid." He reiterated his conviction that the federal government should chiefly concern itself with foreign affairs, leaving to the states the administration of local matters.

Inaugurated in his fifty-eighth year, he made his official residence in the boxlike and incompletely plastered President's House, though he continued to spend as much time as possible at Monticello, where he was still directing building operations. His beautiful second daughter, Maria, now the wife of her cousin John Wayles Eppes, had also by this time made him a grandfather. (She was to sadden her father's life by her untimely death in 1804.) Generally deprived of adequate feminine supervision while in Washington, Jefferson lived there in sartorial indifference and dispensed generous but informal hospitality, as he was accustomed to do at home, to the consternation of diplomats jealous of precedence. After he had overcome his initial diffidence, his manners were easy. To hostile observers his democratic simplicity was a pose. To his friends it was the naturalness of one who had achieved and thought enough to dare to be himself. His loose gait and habit of lounging, together with his discursive though highly informative conversation, doubtless contributed to the common but erroneous impression among his foes that this most scholarly of statesmen was a careless thinker. "His external appearance," according to his ardent admirer Margaret Bayard Smith, "had no pretentions to elegance, but it was neither coarse nor awkward, and it must be owned his greatest personal attraction was a countenance beaming with benevolence and intelligence."

Chief in his harmonious official family were James Madison, the secretary of state,

and Albert Gallatin, who as secretary of the treasury was to carry out with considerable success his program of economy. Jefferson found the federal establishment completely dominated by Federalists and clearly recognized the desirability of attaining a balance. This could be done only by removals, for, as he said, vacancies "by death are few; by resignation none." Judicial officers were removable only by established process, but other civil officials were appointed at the pleasure of the president and were thus removable by him. Early in his administration Jefferson stated publicly that he would have to avail himself of this unquestionable authority and would appoint only Republicans to office. He had not fully restored the balance by the middle of his first term, but he then felt warranted in leaving the creation of vacancies to the course of nature. Although no nonpartisan policy was adopted and the Republicans eventually came to dominate the establishment as the Federalists had done, the standards of the federal service were fully maintained.

Jefferson abandoned the custom of delivering messages to Congress in person, and he carefully avoided the appearance of dictating to that body. Until almost the end of his administration, however, he maintained over Congress indirect and tactful but efficacious control. The Republicans were the majority in both houses, and despite occasional minor revolts, he fully maintained his leadership of the party. During most of his presidency, the floor leader of the House was recognized as his spokesman.

The repeal of the excise taxes early in 1802 redounded to the popularity of the administration. At this time the Western world was enjoying a temporary period of peace, and a reduction in military and naval appropriations seemed to be warranted. In 1802 the repeal of the Judiciary Act of 1801 followed Jefferson's recommendation. That act, which has been described as the last word of the Federalist system, was not without merit, but it was clearly designed to perpetuate Federalist dominance of the federal judiciary. In the case of *Marbury* v. *Madison* (1803), Chief Justice Marshall rebuked the president for withholding the commission of the justices of the peace appointed by John Adams in the last hours of his presidency. This rebuke attracted far more attention at the time than the declaration that a minor provision of an act of Congress was unconstitutional. In Republican opinion the motivation of the chief justice was suspect, and the transcendent authority of the judiciary over the legislative and executive branches of the government was not conceded. Jefferson undoubtedly regarded himself as authorized to judge of the propriety of his own conduct. His responsibility was to the people, not the Court.

In pardoning victims of the Sedition Act, Jefferson pronounced that statute unconstitutional, as he believed he was called upon to do. He approved of the use of the weapon of impeachment against Samuel Chase, a notoriously partisan justice, and deeply regretted its failure. Though the federal judges learned to observe the proprieties better, they did not cease to be political. Jefferson never receded from his position that the Federalists, from the battery of the immovable judiciary, were endeavoring to beat down the works of Republicanism and defeat the will of the people.

By the spring of 1802, Jefferson became alarmed by reports of the retrocession of the province of Louisiana to France by Spain. In a private letter of 18 April 1802 to Robert R. Livingston, the American minister in Paris, he said that the possessor of New Orleans was the natural enemy of the United States and that by placing itself there France would assume an attitude of defiance. He was now willing to ally himself with his old British foes if the mouth of the Mississippi should fall under the control of the nation that Napoleon had made the most aggressive in the world. The Spanish, who were weaker and more compliant, had granted to Americans, in Pinckney's Treaty of 1795, the right of deposit in New Orleans. The revocation of this by the Spanish intendant on 16 October 1802 created a crisis in the West. In fact, this was an independent action and was afterward reversed, but it was commonly blamed on the French. There was warlike talk in Congress, and Jefferson was not averse to the ultimate resort to force if necessary to keep the Mississippi open. But he still hoped to meet this crisis by diplomacy.

Early in 1803 he appointed James Monroe special envoy to France and secured from Congress an appropriation of $2 million. By secret agreement this fund might be used to purchase the "island" of New Orleans. The hopes of the administration extended to West Florida and, in lesser degree, to East Florida. The treaty that Monroe and Livingston signed on 30 April 1803 provided for the purchase of the entire province of Louisiana for approximately $15 million. They had achieved a diplomatic triumph of the first magnitude and made an extraordinary bargain, but the sheer size of the cession and certain provisions of the treaty created perplexities and problems.

Before dispatching Monroe, Jefferson, as a strict constructionist, had raised the question of the constitutional authority of the federal government to acquire territory. His colleagues, especially Gallatin, had assured him that because the United States was a sovereign nation, the federal government had that power. He dismissed his doubts at the time, but they were revived when he learned that his representative had not merely acquired the island of New Orleans but had doubled the area of the country. The treaty specifically required the incorporation of a vast region and the granting to its inhabitants all the rights and privileges of American citizens. This would ultimately effect a change in the Union which the fathers of the Constitution had not anticipated or provided for. Jefferson believed that a fresh grant of power in the form of a constitutional amendment was called for and made at least two attempts to draft one. None of his counselors and supporters appears to have seen any need for an amendment, however, and, while it was generally agreed that an amendment would have been readily adopted, there was not enough time to go through the prescribed procedure. To be effective, the treaty had to be ratified within six months. Furthermore, the report reached Jefferson that Napoleon now regretted having ratified the treaty and would tolerate no change in it. Jefferson's constitutional scruples were voiced in private to his own supporters. The treaty was approved and put into effect against the opposition of Federalist die-hards but with overwhelming public approval.

The Louisiana Purchase provides a striking example of Jefferson's pragmatic statesmanship. By means of it, he assured the physical greatness of his country and the future success of his party, as exemplified by his own triumphant reelection. Western discontent was largely stilled, and the Federalists were reduced to sectional impotence. For all of this, his momentary theoretical inconsistency seemed to his partisans a small price to pay and later historians have exaggerated its significance. The purchase served to facilitate the expedition for which he had already commissioned Meriwether Lewis. For this, he himself prepared elaborate instructions. No one rejoiced more than he in the discoveries made by Lewis and William Clark. He afterward wrote the best biographical account of Lewis, his former secretary.

Livingston and Monroe had bought a vaguely defined region that they soon persuaded themselves included West Florida. Jefferson subsequently embodied similar views in a pamphlet that determined the attitude of the administration and its supporters. The Louisiana revenue act that came to be known as the Mobile Act of 24 February 1804 assumed the acquisition of West Florida, but Jefferson, finding that the Spanish were not acquiescent as he had expected, practically annulled its offensive features by proclamation and sent Monroe on what proved to be a futile mission to Spain. The perplexing question of West Florida remained unsettled during Jefferson's administration, and his tortuous efforts to acquire this coveted region served only to weaken his position in Congress and his hand abroad.

His policy of peaceable negotiation did not extend to the Barbary pirates, to whom he applied more force than had any previous American president. Following the repudiation of a treaty by the bey of Tripoli in 1801, Jefferson dispatched against him a naval force, which blockaded his ports. Subsequently Jefferson employed naval force against the sultan of Morocco. The treaty at length negotiated with Tripoli granted the United States the most favorable terms yet given any nation by that piratical power.

Jefferson was slow in becoming alarmed by the mystifying movement of his former vice-president, Aaron Burr, in the West, but on 27 November 1806, he issued a proclamation of warning against an illegal expedition against the dominions of Spain. He was now convinced of the existence of a conspiracy and was aware that its objectives might extend to the separation of the trans-Allegheny region from the Union. In January, responding to a congressional resolution, he described the actions he had taken and communicated a copy of an incriminating letter from Burr to Gen. James Wilkinson that he had just received from the latter. Presumably with a view to justifying his own actions, Jefferson stated that Burr's guilt was unquestionable. Thus, he left himself open to the charge of prejudging the case. Furthermore, many people were highly distrustful of Wilkinson, who had been ordered to New Orleans to stop Burr's expedition if it got that far and had been guilty of high-handed and arbitrary actions there against individuals whom he suspected. News of these actions was received in Washington before the failure of Burr's enterprise was reported there. By order of Gov. Edward Tiffin of Ohio, boats and supplies that Burr had caused to be assembled were captured at Blennerhassett's Island in the Ohio River. Burr himself joined the remnant of the expedition at the mouth of the Cumberland, and it came to an inglorious end in Mississippi. Opponents of the administration, taking up the cause of Burr, claimed that the danger had been greatly exaggerated and that the prosecution of Burr was actually persecution at the hands of a vindictive president.

The trial of Burr for treason in Richmond before Chief Justice Marshall in the summer of 1807 was one of the most extraordinary in American history. Among its more notable features were the issuance of two subpoenas ordering the president to produce documents, the unmeasured denunciation of the president by Burr's counsel, especially by the "Federal Bulldog," Luther Martin, and the near escape of General Wilkinson from indictment. The grand jury indicted Burr for both treason and misdemeanor for causing the assemblage at Blennerhassett's Island. The chief justice, reversing the position he had recently taken in another case regarding treasonable conduct, now ruled that the physical presence of the accused at the scene of the crime was required. Burr had not been at Blennerhassett's Island, and Marshall did not allow the prosecution to present the evidence of his actions elsewhere. Burr's acquittal on both counts was thus made inevitable. Not without warrant did a prominent Republican say that the chief justice acquitted Burr. Marshall was critical of Jefferson throughout the extremely political proceedings. Jefferson believed that there had been a miscarriage of justice but had no thoughts of resorting to impeachment. He observed the proprieties better than Marshall did. He would not have done his duty

if he had not caused Burr to be prosecuted. He always believed that Wilkinson had done the country a service in revealing the conspiracy, but he went too far in his support of that tattered warrior.

The difficulties that Jefferson faced during his second term as the head of a neutral nation in a time of ruthless European war could probably have been successfully met by no American statesman. Until 1805 the British had in practice granted sufficient concessions from their commercial regulations to permit prosperity to the American carrying trade, but following the *Essex* decision of that year, they tightened their control of commerce and seized many American vessels. Also, the impressment of seamen remained a grievance, which the British would do nothing to remove. Then, in the battle between British orders in council and Napoleonic decrees, the neutral American Republic, unable to meet both sets of requirements and threatened with the confiscation of commercial vessels in case of violation, was placed in an intolerable position.

Of the possible courses of action open to him, war did not commend itself to Jefferson, who did not want to take sides with either of the European rivals. After the *Leopard* fired on the *Chesapeake* in June 1807, a declaration of war against the British might have been supported by the American people. Jefferson issued a proclamation that denied to British armed vessels the hospitality of American waters. He gave the British government the opportunity to disavow the outrage, but they responded to this by prolonged procrastination. He had previously sent William Pinkney to London to serve with Monroe on a mission extraordinary, and had tried to strengthen the hands of the negotiators by the Non-Importation Act of 1806, which was to become effective some months later. His reliance was on diplomacy, supplemented by the threat of economic pressure, and when diplomacy failed (as it did in the unacceptable Monroe-Pinkney treaty), he fell back on economic pressure.

Because of the intensification of the conflict between the two great powers and the increased infringement on American rights by both of them in the summer and autumn of 1807, some sort of governmental action seemed unavoidable. Jefferson recommended the embargo as the least evil of his options. Its immediate purpose was defensive—to keep American ships and seamen out of this conflict. It came to be regarded increasingly as an offensive weapon by means of which concessions could be gained. Adopted in December 1807, after an inadequate debate and by an overwhelming vote because of the dominance of Congress by Jefferson's party, the measure combined with the Non-Intercourse Act to bring about a theoretical suspension of foreign commerce without a specified limit of time.

The attempts to enforce the embargo involved an exercise of unexampled economic authority by the federal government and an inevitable and increasing infringement on individual rights, which were contrary to Jefferson's most cherished ideals. He and Gallatin, the chief enforcement officer, exercised no authority beyond what was granted by successive acts of Congress, and while regretting the hardships attributable to the provisions of embargo, Jefferson had expected them to be endured as they would have been in wartime. He had not anticipated the degree of resistance in commercial districts or the rank crop of corruption that sprang up. His political enemies undoubtedly made things harder for him and Gallatin, but he blamed them unduly for the failure of enforcement. He claimed, with considerable justification, that the embargo was not in effect long enough to attain its objectives, and it may well be that under other circumstances some measure of the sort might have proved an efficacious weapon. But in 1808–1809, employed by a weak power, it served chiefly to impoverish

the sections that supported Jefferson most loyally, to give a new lease on life to partisan opposition in New England, and to bring a memorable administration to an inglorious close. Forced to yield to a rebellious Congress, on 1 March 1809 he signed the Non-Intercourse Act, which replaced the embargo. Shortly afterward he turned the presidential office over to his friend and colleague James Madison with unquestionable relief. He described himself as a waveworn mariner approaching the shore, as a prisoner emerging from shackles, and declared that Nature had intended him for the tranquil pursuits of science, in which he found supreme delight.

During the past eight years this earnest advocate of the freedom of the press had been subjected to a flood of personal calumny. Long regarded in ecclesiastical circles, especially in New England, as the embodiment of French infidelity, he not unnaturally aroused a storm of indignation, soon after his first inauguration, by offering to Thomas Paine passage to America on a sloop of war and by expressing the hope that his "useful labours" would be continued. The following year an indefensible assault was launched by a disgruntled pamphleteer to whom Jefferson had previously made monetary gifts that he himself designated as charity but that could be readily interpreted as a form of subsidy. To the charges of personal immorality made in 1802 by James Thomson Callender in the Richmond *Recorder,* almost every discreditable story reflecting on Jefferson's private life can be traced. Given nationwide currency by the Federalist press, these were discussed in 1805 in the legislative assembly of Massachusetts, where a motion to dismiss the printers of the assembly for publishing in the *New-England Palladium* (18 January 1805) libels on the president failed of adoption. One only of these charges was admitted by Jefferson. This referred to improper proposals of his to the wife of his friend John

Walker, while he was yet a young man and single. For these he made restitution. The sensational story of his illicit relations with his slave Sally Hemings is without historical foundation and is wholly out of character. As Henry Adams said, Jefferson, a model husband and father, was "more refined than many women in the delicacy of his private relations."

For the wide acceptance, by persons of the better sort, of the extravagant charges of an unscrupulous drunkard, the sensitive president was disposed to blame his old theological foes, especially in New England. There his followers were assaulting the ancient alliance between church and state, for the final overthrow of which they deserve considerable credit. It may well be, as Henry Adams said, that Jefferson did not understand the New Englanders, but it is certain that they did not understand him. Though sanguine in temperament, he was as serious-minded and almost as devoid of humor as any Puritan, and had he lived a generation later, he would have been more at home in liberal religious circles in New England than anywhere else in America. At many times he paid grateful tribute to Epicurus and Epictetus, but as early as 1803 he began to select from the Gospels the passages that he believed to have come from Jesus. Toward the end of his life this amateur higher critic placed parallel texts, in four languages, in a "wee-little book," which he entitled *The Life and Morals of Jesus of Nazareth*. This was not published until the twentieth century. He regarded himself as a "real Christian," since he followed what he believed to be the teachings of Jesus.

During the last seventeen years of his life, Jefferson did not leave Virginia. The embargo and its aftermath were ruinous to him, as to many Virginia planters, and because of the demands of incessant hospitality, he could not live as simply as he desired. After the War of 1812, however, the sale of his library of some sixty-five hundred volumes

to the government, for the Library of Congress, served to relieve his financial burdens somewhat; and his grandson, Thomas Jefferson Randolph, took over the management of his lands. Laborious correspondence occupied a disproportionate amount of his time, but he enjoyed exchanging ideas with John Adams (with whom his old friendship was beautifully restored), with Lafayette, Pierre-Samuel Du Pont de Nemours, and many others. In the letters of these years he has left a mine of treasure. He gave his counsel to Madison and Monroe when they asked it; and some of his expressions on public policy, as on the Missouri Compromise and on the attitude of the United States toward Europe and the Latin American republics, are notable.

The chief public problem to which he addressed himself was that of education in Virginia, which he continued to call his "country." He never ceased to advocate a comprehensive statewide system of public education, such as he had proposed in 1779. "Enlighten the people generally," he wrote Du Pont de Nemours on 24 April 1816, "and tyranny and oppressions of both mind and body will vanish like evil spirits at the dawn of day." Popular education he regarded as more than a defensive weapon and a guarantor of freedom. His proposals of 1779 had been marked by a unique provision whereby youths of great promise were to be advanced from one grade of instruction to another without cost, and he hoped that these "geniuses . . . raked from the rubbish" would serve as statesmen or would enlarge the domains of human knowledge. He formulated, as perhaps no other American of his generation, an educational philosophy for a democratic state; and in his last years he declared himself in favor of a literacy test for citizenship.

Having failed in his earlier efforts to transform the College of William and Mary, by 1800 Jefferson had hopes of establishing in the more salubrious upper country a university on a broad, liberal, and modern plan. Whatever interest he may have had, during his presidency, in the creation of a national university contingent upon the amendment of the Constitution, Virginia was central to all his thoughts after 1809. Indeed, his regret that so many of his "countrymen" went to be educated among "foreigners" (as at Princeton) or were taught at home by "beggars" (northern tutors) was partly due to the fear that their political principles were being contaminated. His representations may have stimulated Gov. John Tyler to send to the Assembly in 1809 his strong message on education, which resulted in the establishment, the following year, of the Literary Fund. Jefferson regarded this as an inadequate provision for general education, but it later made possible the creation of an institution of higher learning.

By happy chance, Jefferson in 1814 became associated as a trustee with the unorganized Albemarle Academy. Transformed into Central College, this became the germ from which the University of Virginia developed, under his adroit management at every stage. His letter of 7 September 1814 to Peter Carr, outlining in masterly fashion his views of a state system, may have inspired the resolution adopted by the General Assembly on 24 February 1816, which required a report on a scheme of public instruction. Shortly thereafter, Jefferson himself drafted a bill that contained most of the features of his more famous proposal of 1779 and included a provision for a university. This was rejected, and for a time it appeared that after an appropriation for elementary schools no funds would be available for a higher institution. At length, in 1818, by a compromise, appropriations were authorized for elementary schools (though not for intermediate schools) and for a university.

Jefferson was appointed a member, and became chairman, of the Rockfish Gap Commission, empowered to recommend a site. By skillful use of geographical arguments,

he gained the victory for Central College in August 1818. The report, which he had drafted beforehand, incorporated his ideas of what a university should be and remains one of his greatest educational papers. After a legislative battle in which he acted only behind the scenes, the report was adopted, and in 1819 the University of Virginia was chartered. It opened its doors in 1825. Though the services of Joseph C. Cabell and John H. Cocke in launching the institution were invaluable, Jefferson, who was inevitably appointed a member of the first board of visitors and elected rector, remained until his death the dominant factor in its affairs. He received architectural suggestions from Benjamin H. Latrobe and, to a lesser extent, William Thornton, but the plan of an "academical village" was his own. Many of the specifications were drawn up by him and the "pavilions," "hotels," dormitories, colonnades, and arcades were constructed under his supervision. At his death, only the Rotunda, modeled by him on the Pantheon at Rome, was incomplete.

Upon the organization of the institution, he left his most characteristic impression perhaps in the establishment of independent, diploma-conferring "schools," in the provision for entire freedom in the election of courses, in the complete disregard of the conventional grouping of students in classes, and in the provision for a rotating chairmanship of the faculty, without a president. Despite his insistence that Republican, rather than Federalist, principles be taught, to a remarkable extent he freed the institution from hampering restriction and made it in spirit a university. Though he was disappointed in his full hopes of drawing from the Old World to the faculty "the first characters in science," the mission of his young friend Francis Walker Gilmer to Great Britain to procure professors was measurably successful. The new institution had from the outset a flavor of cosmopolitanism, and several of the first professors achieved distinction. The "Old Sachem" lived to see the university opened in 1825 and for more than a year in operation.

During his lifetime, Jefferson received not only American but also international recognition as a man, and as a patron, of learning. Elected president of the American Philosophical Society on 6 January 1797, he remained the head of this notable organization until 1815 and actively cooperated with it in the advancement and dissemination of knowledge. By introducing to his colleagues, on 10 March 1797, his megalonyx he fired the "signal gun of American paleontology." To them he read on 4 May 1798 a description of a moldboard of least resistance for a plow, for which invention he received in 1805 a gold medal from a French agricultural society. In due course he became associated with an extraordinary number of important societies in various countries of Europe, as he had long been with the chief learned, and almost all the agricultural, societies of America. On 26 December 1801 he was elected a foreign associate of the Institute of France. This signal honor, which during his lifetime was shared by no other man of American birth and residence, may best be attributed to his reputation in France as the most conspicuous American intellectual. He himself interpreted it as "an evidence of the brotherly spirit of Science, which unites into one family all its votaries of whatever grade, and however widely dispersed throughout the different quarters of the globe." He corresponded throughout his life with an extraordinary number of scientists and philosophers in other lands, as well as in America, and sought to make available in his own country the best of foreign thought and discovery.

Modern scholars have recognized Jefferson as an American pioneer in numerous branches of science, notably paleontology, ethnology, geography, and botany. Living before the age of specialization, he was for his day a careful investigator, no more credulous than his learned contemporaries, and notable among them for his effort in all fields to attain scientific exactitude. In state papers he is commonly the lawyer, pleading a cause; in the heat of political controversy he may have compromised his intellectual ideals and certainly indulged in exaggeration at times; but his procedure in arriving at his fundamental opinions, the habits of his life, and his temperament were essentially those of a scholar. As secretary of state, he was in effect the first commissioner of patents and the first patent examiner. He himself invented or adapted to personal uses numerous ingenious devices.

At home in French, Italian, and Spanish, as well as Greek and Latin, he wrote *An Essay Towards Facilitating Instruction in the Anglo-Saxon and Modern Dialects of the English Language* (published in 1851); and during a generation he amassed a large collection of Indian vocabularies, only to have them cast upon the waters by thieves in 1809. He owned one of the best private collections of paintings and statuary in the country, and he has been termed by Fiske Kimball "the first American connoisseur and patron of the arts." Besides the Virginia state capitol, Monticello, and the original buildings of the University of Virginia, he designed wholly or in part numerous Virginia houses, among them his own Poplar Forest, Farmington, and Barboursville. Before the advent of professional architects in America, he began to collect books on architecture and discovered Palladio, from whom his careful and extensive observations abroad never weaned him. He did more than any other man to stimulate the classical revival in America. His own work, while always ingenious, is academic, precise, and orderly, but because of the fortunate necessity of using brick and wood, the new creation was a blend, with a pleasing domesticity. He created a definite school of builders in Virginia; sought to establish formal instruction in architecture; stimulated and encouraged, among others, Charles Bulfinch and William Thornton; and, except for the fact that he accepted no pay for his services, was as truly professional as they. It is probably no exaggeration to say with Kimball that he was "the father of our national architecture."

Few other American statesmen have been such careful and unremitting students of political thought and history as Jefferson was, or more concerned with ultimate ends. Yet he has left no treatise on political philosophy, and all general statements about his theoretical position are subject to qualification. He was always more interested in applications than in speculation, and he was forced to modify his own philosophy in practice. But, despite unquestionable inconsistencies, his major aims and the general trend of his policies are unmistakable. A homely aristocrat in manner of life and personal tastes, he distrusted all rulers and feared the rise of an industrial proletariat, but more than any of his eminent contemporaries, he trusted the common man, if measurably enlightened and kept in rural virtue. Though pained and angered when the free press made him the victim of its license, he was a passionate advocate of human liberty and laid supreme stress on the individual. Though he clearly realized the value of union, he emphasized the importance of the states and of local agencies of government. An intellectual internationalist, he gave wholehearted support to the policy of political isolation and anticipated the development on the North American continent of a dominant nation, unique in civilization. A philosophical statesman rather than a political philosopher, he contributed to democracy and liberalism a faith rather than a body of doctrine. By his works alone he must be adjudged one of the greatest of all Americans, while the influence of his energizing faith is immeasurable.

By the very contradictions of his subtle and complex personality, of his bold mind and highly sensitive nature, Jefferson has both vexed and fascinated all who have attempted to interpret him. As Henry Adams said in his *History of the United States,* "Almost every other American statesman might be described in a parenthesis. A few broad strokes of the brush would paint the portraits of all the early Presidents with this exception . . . ; but Jefferson could be painted only touch by touch, with a fine pencil, and the perfection of the likeness depended upon the shifting and uncertain flicker of its semi-transparent shadows."

The last years of this most enigmatical and probably most versatile of great Americans were marked by philosophical serenity in the face of impending financial disaster. Ruined by the failure in 1819 of his friend Wilson Cary Nicholas, whose notes for $20,000 he had endorsed, he tried vainly to find a purchaser for his lands and secured legislative permission, in the last year of his life, to dispose of most of them by the common method of a lottery. The public strongly protested against this indignity to him and some voluntary contributions were made, so the project was ultimately abandoned. Jefferson died believing that his debts would be paid, fortunately not realizing that Monticello was soon to pass from the hands of his heirs forever. A beloved and revered patriarch in the extensive family circle, he retained extraordinary intellectual vigor and rode his horse daily until almost the end of his ordered and temperate life. His death occurred, with dramatic appropriateness, on the fiftieth anniversary of the Declaration of Independence, shortly after noon and a few hours before that of John Adams. His daughter Martha Randolph, with ten of her children and their progeny, and his grandson Francis Eppes survived him. On the simple stone over his grave in the family burial ground at Monticello, he is described as he wished to be remembered, not as the holder of great offices, but as the author of the Declaration of Independence and the Virginia statute for religious freedom, and as the father of the University of Virginia.

The American Revolution

RICHARD R. BEEMAN

IN 1760, twenty-two-year-old George III was crowned king of England, succeeding his grandfather, George II, who had ruled the British Empire for thirty-three years. Thomas Jefferson was seventeen at that time, and he too was contemplating an important new stage in his life. In the winter of 1760 Jefferson left Shadwell, his family's home in Albemarle County, and headed for Williamsburg, where he was to enroll at the College of William and Mary. The young man traveled to Williamsburg carrying with him both substantial material wealth and impressive connections. He stood to inherit two thousand acres and more than one hundred slaves when he turned twenty-one, and as the oldest son in the family he would eventually inherit much more. His father, Peter Jefferson, had accumulated over five thousand acres of land and, perhaps more important, had risen in the esteem of his neighbors, achieving the rank of colonel in the county militia and, in 1754, gaining election to the House of Burgesses. Jefferson's mother, Jane Randolph, provided for her son even more impressive connections. She

was a Randolph, and the world that her kin inhabited was a far-flung and influential one. Thus, when the young man arrived in Williamsburg he found that the doors of the colony's first citizens—Peyton Randolph, the king's attorney in Virginia, George Wythe, the colony's leading jurist, and the Royal Governor, Francis Fauquier—were open to him.

THE SCHOOLING OF A REVOLUTIONARY STATESMAN

The individual in Williamsburg with the most immediate impact on Jefferson was not, however, a politician, but a teacher, William Small, the Scottish professor of mathematics at the College of William and Mary. Small was at that time the only non-clergyman on a badly depleted and generally unimpressive college faculty, and though his formal teaching responsibilities were supposed to center on the subjects of mathematics, physics, and metaphysics, he gave Jefferson his basic instruction in ethics, rhetoric, and belles lettres as well. Garry Wills, in his provocative reading of the intellectual sources of Jefferson's revolutionary political thought, gives Small a central position in that story, claiming even that "We have enough evidence of [Jefferson's] reading, and of his conclusions from that reading, to establish that the real lost world of Thomas Jefferson was the world of William Small, the invigorating realm of the Scottish Enlightenment at its zenith."

It is not necessary to accept all of Wills's conclusions about the Scottish origins of Jefferson's political thought to acknowledge Small's important place in his intellectual upbringing. Jefferson himself, later in life, would write that his connection with Small was "what probably fixed the destinies of my life." Small was more than Jefferson's intellectual mentor, for he also introduced the young man to others who would come to have an important influence on both his intellectual and social development. Through Small, Jefferson was brought under the tutelage of Wythe, and through him he was drawn into a small coterie consisting of such eminences as Peyton Randolph, Edmund Pendleton, and Francis Fauquier.

Fauquier was in Jefferson's opinion the ablest of Virginia's royal governors; he was a man who combined a mastery of classical learning with wit and social grace, and as an amateur natural scientist he shared with Jefferson a curiosity about all manner of natural phenomena around him in Virginia. Together Fauquier, Wythe, Small, and Jefferson frequently "formed a partie quaree, and to the habitual conversations on these occasions [he] owed much instruction."

The very fact that these four were on such cordial terms suggests that Williamsburg society on the eve of the Revolution was rather different from that of many other capitals of provincial government in America. In Boston, for example, royal governors and provincial leaders often viewed one another with deep suspicion; royal officials like Thomas Hutchinson and Francis Bernard were likely to hold themselves aloof from provincial leaders, and for their part men like James Otis, the Adamses, and John Hancock tended to resent the power and privilege of those who found themselves in the king's patronage.

In prerevolutionary Virginia, however, those divisions were not so readily apparent. Not everyone in the province had access to high royal officials like Fauquier and not all governors were as gracious, congenial, and convivial as Fauquier, but the overall level of harmony prevailing among provincial leaders and royal officials in Virginia was nevertheless striking. On an official level, royal governors only rarely found themselves at odds with the House of Burgesses, and on a personal level, the men upon whom royal governors came to rely for advice as well as friendship—men like Wythe, Randolph, Pendleton, and even the young Jefferson—were the very ones who stood high in the esteem of the provincial elite as well.

This brief glimpse of Jefferson's youth and early training should make it clear that he was—by birth and training—hardly the most likely candidate to challenge the traditional order of things. He had, both as a youth and as an adult, profited enormously from that traditional order. His inheritance in 1764 would grow to more than five thousand acres and two hundred slaves within a decade; as he continued to build that estate, the projects into which he poured most of his energy and money were those that reflected his genteel values. The man who built Monticello was hardly one who wished to change the fundamental structure of the society that had been so kind to him and his forebears.

Yet over the course of the American revolutionary era Jefferson would display a radical temperament that was often quite at odds with his traditional upbringing. Many of his most extreme statements—his comment, for example, that "the tree of liberty must be refreshed from time to time with the blood of patriots and tyrants"—can perhaps be passed off as reflecting only the passions of the moment, but running through his career one does see a streak of radicalism. The central core of that radicalism was Jefferson's concern about "liberty," a commodity that he believed was as much the birthright of ordinary people as it was of wealthy gentlemen like himself. Nowhere, perhaps, are the contrasts—and the contradictions—between Jefferson's traditional and radical inclinations more noticeable than during the period of the Revolution, for it was then that the young, affluent, and well-connected Virginian was forced to confront the multiple meanings of liberty for the first time.

THE IMPERIAL CRISIS

The events of the American Revolution would strain and ultimately destroy the spirit of congeniality and conviviality that existed between Virginia's provincial and royal officials; indeed, Jefferson's years as a student in Williamsburg would be the last in which anything like a "normal" atmosphere of political relations prevailed. Beginning in 1763, the English Parliament, led by George Grenville, would begin a program of imperial organization that would reverse previous policies of "salutary neglect" and eventually place royal officials and American colonists in nearly constant conflict with one another. Jefferson had spent the years from 1760 to 1762 as a student at William and Mary and then stayed in Williamsburg for nearly four more years while he pursued his legal studies. His mentor Wythe had been instrumental in drafting a set of resolutions in December 1764 objecting to a proposal then being debated in Parliament for a stamp tax to be levied on the colonies. Those resolutions, which anticipated the

subsequent and more famous set drafted by Patrick Henry in May 1765, asserted that it was "a fundamental Principle of the British Constitution, without which Freedom can no Where exist, that the People are not subject to any Taxes but such as are laid on them by their own Consent," and then concluded that "your Memorialists are therefore led into an humble Confidence that your Lordships will not think any Reason sufficient to support such a Power in the British Parliament, where the Colonies cannot be represented."

Governor Fauquier, trying to remain on good terms with the House of Burgesses while at the same time retaining the confidence of his superiors in London, was obviously discomfitted by the resolves. He reported back to the Lords of Trade that the language of the resolutions was "very warm and indecent," but also assured them that leading burgesses were anxious to "mollify them, and they have Reason to hope their is nothing now in them which will give the least offence." Though Jefferson did not leave behind any written commentary on the resolves, he was probably more in sympathy with Wythe than with the royal governor, but neither he nor Wythe allowed the matter to interfere with their personal friendship with Fauquier. They continued to enjoy the pleasure of his table at the Governor's Palace, and it was during this time that Jefferson, Robert Carter, and Fauquier performed regularly in a series of informal concerts (with Jefferson playing the violin) in the ballroom of the palace.

The following spring, in May 1765, Patrick Henry would present to the House of Burgesses a set of seven resolutions that, in ascending order of vehemence, claimed that Americans possessed the same rights as Englishmen in England and denounced the English attempts to tax the colonies as a violation of those rights. Jefferson, then a twenty-two-year-old law student, listened outside the capitol building to a "most bloody" debate on Henry's resolves. In the end, five of the resolutions—amounting to a denial of parliamentary authority to tax the colonies—were passed, and the sixth and seventh—calling for outright resistance to the Stamp Act—were defeated. Henry had, however, by the boldness of his oratory in defense of his resolves, made a dramatic entrance onto the public stage in Virginia.

We can only speculate on how the young law student, so well versed in the classics and in English common-law precedent but so awkward and uncomfortable in a public forum, reacted to Henry's pyrotechnics. Jefferson would remain dedicated to the rule of reason over passion throughout his public life, and though he would soon join the cause that Henry was so instrumental in igniting, he would also come to disdain the very skills that Henry displayed in such abundance.

Governor Fauquier would ultimately fail altogether to enforce the Stamp Act in Virginia. On 30 October, Virginia's provincial leaders succeeded, through "mob" action, in insuring the resignation of Colonel Hugh Mercer, the individual charged with distributing the government stamps. Fauquier, writing to the Lords of Trade, gives a striking impression of the genteel character of the Virginia insurgents: "This Concourse of people I should call a Mob did I not know that it was chiefly if not altogether composed, of, Gentlemen of property in the Colony some of them at the Head of their Respective Counties, and the Merchants of the Country, whether English, Scotch or Virginians for few absented themselves."

On 1 November, Virginians, in common with Americans in virtually every colony, were steadfast in their opposition, to the Stamp Act, choosing either to refuse to transact any of the business requiring the stamps or simply to go ahead and do that business without the stamps. And the British Parliament, faced with this unexpected but nevertheless implacable resistance, finally capitulated, repealing the Stamp Act in March 1766.

Jefferson continued his law studies in Williamsburg until late 1765 or early 1766, when he returned to Albemarle County. He had by that time attained his majority, thus obtaining the rights of his inheritance from his father's estate. Settling himself at Shadwell, along the Rivanna River, he quickly began to stake his claim to all of the prerogatives and responsibilities to which his inheritance entitled him. He evidently spent most of his time during his first few years at Shadwell attending to the business of the plantation, for he did not seek formal admission to the bar of the colony until 1767, when he was twenty-four. From 1767 until 1774, when for all intents and purposes he retired from active legal practice, Jefferson combined the duties of plantation manager and lawyer, gaining valuable experience in both arenas and steadily enlarging the circle of people who were acquainted with his considerable talents.

Jefferson's wealth and family background assured him some influence in the local politics of Albemarle County, but to rise to a position of political prominence within the colony at large one needed more than a patrimony. When he gained election to the House of Burgesses in 1769 at the age of twenty-six, he did so without having served the customary apprenticeship as a justice of the county court. The details of the election are obscure; we do not know whether the incumbent burgess, Edward Carter, retired voluntarily or whether he was unseated by Jefferson in a contested election. We do know that Jefferson had already gained considerable respect for his efforts in persuading the House of Burgesses to facilitate the clearing of the Rivanna River, making that river an important artery of transport for the tobacco produced in Albemarle County. He may therefore have already established himself not only as a young man of unusual intelligence, but of some practical effectiveness as well.

When Jefferson traveled to Williamsburg to take his seat in the Burgesses in May 1769, he encountered a political situation significantly different from that prevailing during his student years. Francis Fauquier had died in the spring of 1768 and was replaced in the governorship by the Right Honorable Norborne Berkeley, Baron de Botetourt. Like Fauquier, Botetourt would win the affection and respect of many of Virginia's provincial leaders, but the political waters that he was charged with navigating were far more treacherous than those of his predecessor. The Stamp Act had been followed by the Townshend Acts—a series of taxes on a long list of goods imported into America—and the American opposition to British policy, already fueled by the earlier protests against the Stamp Act, was building in intensity. In addition, events in other colonies had served to undermine relations between royal officials and provincial leaders still further. In New York the governor had dissolved the legislature as punishment for its refusal to cooperate in the quartering of British troops in the homes of the colony's residents, and in Massachusetts the legislature was actively agitating for an intercolonial boycott of British goods as a means of opposing the Townshend duties. In a fit of overreaction, England's secretary of state for the colonies, Lord Hillsborough, had ordered the royal governors to dissolve any colonial legislature that supported the boycott proposal of the Massachusetts legislature. Thus, when Jefferson began his legislative career, the stage was set for a confrontation between the representatives of royal and provincial authority.

The May 1769 session of the House of Burgesses began cordially enough, with an amicable greeting to the assembly from Botetourt. The burgesses then appointed a committee to draft a reply to the governor's message. The person initially selected to compose the draft was the twenty-six-year-old freshman legislator from Albemarle, but to Jefferson's chagrin a number of burgesses were unhappy with the draft and substituted a version written by Robert Carter Nicholas. It was not an altogether auspicious beginning for Jefferson, but he would soon be involved in matters of much greater substance. On 16 May the burgesses passed resolutions asserting once again their right to petition the king for redress of grievances, their exclusive right to levy taxes upon themselves, their opposition to plans to try Americans accused of crimes in English courts, and perhaps most serious in light of the recent edict by Lord Hillsborough, their right to unite with other colonies to seek a redress of their grievances. Governor Botetourt, following the mandate contained in his instructions from Hillsborough, promptly called the burgesses into his chambers and pronounced: "I have heard of your resolves, and augur ill of their effect. You have made it my duty to dissolve you; and you are dissolved accordingly."

Thus it was that Jefferson and his colleagues found themselves, after only nine days in session, without a legal forum in which to conduct their business. This did not deter them, however, for upon hearing Botetourt's pronouncement they marched over to the Apollo Room of the Raleigh Tavern and there adopted the essential proposal contained in the Massachusetts Circular Letter—a nonimportation agreement stipulating that Virginians would not import any of the items taxed under the terms of the Townshend Acts. Similar agreements were being adopted by merchant associations in the major port cities of the North, but the actions of the burgesses in their extralegal session in the Raleigh Tavern would set at least one precedent: it was the first time that a continental colonial legislature, acting outside of its official capacity, had engaged in an act of purposeful defiance of British policy. And it would not be the last.

The renewed determination of the American colonists to boycott English goods until the Townshend duties were repealed soon had its effect in England. As British merchants complained about the harmful effects on their trade and as English politicians realized that the revenues from those boycotted goods had almost ceased to exist, the English ministry began to back down. Lord Botetourt, anxious to repair the breach caused by his dissolution of the House of Burgesses in May 1769, called the legislature back in session in November. Jefferson, who evidently gained reelection with no difficulty, was on hand to hear Botetourt issue a call for conciliation and announce that the English Parliament was preparing to bring forward a bill repealing most of the duties imposed by the Townshend Acts. And indeed, in March 1770, after the death of Charles Townshend and the ascendancy of Lord North as the chief minister in Parliament responsible for colonial policy, all of the Townshend duties except the one on tea were repealed. In most of the colonies the partial repeal of the Townshend duties, together with a growing suspicion that the mobs of Boston were pushing America into an unwanted confrontation with England, caused a marked diminution in the level of colonial protest against British policy. In Virginia, Jefferson joined with a group of burgesses and merchants to reaffirm their determination to boycott British goods until all of the unconstitutional tax levies had been repealed, but this turned out to be only a gesture, for the collapse of nonimportation in other colonies made it impossible to enforce a boycott anywhere in America. Jefferson, in his own personal conduct, kept the spirit of the boycott alive at least for a while. This was no easy task, for it was at just this time that he was most actively involved

in building his home at Monticello, a project that called for a wide range of English-made materials. Writing to his English agent, Thomas Adams, on 20 February 1771, Jefferson laid out a list of articles he wished to purchase, adding:

> You will observe that part of these articles (such as are licensed by the association) are to be sent at any event. Another part (being prohibited) are only to be sent if the tea act should be repealed before you get home. If it is not you will observe a third class to be sent instead of those which are prohibited.

The years from 1771 to 1773 would be for Jefferson a time of relatively slight political involvement. Although he stood successfully for reelection to the House of Burgesses in the fall of 1771, he missed the following session of the legislature. By 1773 he was back in the legislature where—along with a group that included Richard Henry Lee, Patrick Henry, and Dabney Carr—he sought to revive some of the flagging opposition to the mother country by introducing into the Burgesses resolutions calling for the establishment of "committees of correspondence" charged with the task of coordinating and publicizing the opposition to British policy. These committees, which were springing up in nearly every colony at about the same time, seemed to the new royal governor, John Murray, earl of Dunmore, to threaten his authority and, accordingly, he prorogued the assembly after it had been in session for only eleven days.

This was only the beginning of Dunmore's troubles, for relations between royal officials and provincial leaders would go rapidly downhill in virtually every colony from that point on. Following the passage of the Tea Act, and Boston's rebellious reaction to it, the lines of opposition between Great Britain and America hardened. By May 1774, news of the passage of the Coercive Acts—Great Britain's program of retaliation against Boston—had reached the colonies, and nearly everywhere the response was one of support and sympathy for Boston. The Virginia House of Burgesses' initial action was to appoint 1 June 1774 as a day of "fasting, humiliation, and prayer" in support of Boston, but even this mild gesture infuriated Governor Dunmore, who promptly dissolved the assembly for its action. The burgesses, in what was becoming routine practice, reconvened in the Raleigh Tavern, agreed to send delegates to the recently called Continental Congress in Philadelphia, and supported the radical proposal from Massachusetts for a thoroughgoing boycott of all English goods to protest the Coercive Acts.

On 1 August the Virginia Convention, the body that would take the place of the House of Burgesses (now forced into permanent adjournment by Governor Dunmore) met for the first time. Jefferson fell ill on his way to the convention and was not able to attend, but he forwarded a draft of some proposed instructions to the Virginia delegation to the Continental Congress. That draft would ultimately be rejected in favor of a much more cautiously worded draft, but Jefferson's twenty-three-page version, which was later reprinted in both Philadelphia and England under the title *A Summary View of the Rights of British America,* would gain for the young Virginia lawyer an instant reputation both as an elegant stylist and as an early advocate of what amounted to virtual independence from British rule.

Jefferson's *Summary View* is an excellent example of the conflicting strains of temperamental radicalism and intellectual traditionalism in his character, for it alternately displays an angry and belligerent tone while at the same time utilizing a line of legal argument based on a careful and meticulous reading of ancient English history. The essential line of argument pursued by Jefferson in his *Summary View* marked a sharp break from traditional Whig thinking respecting the rights of the colonies. Even America's most sympathetic Whig supporters in England clung to the belief that Parliament did have ultimate legislative authority over the colonies; their hope was that that issue could be finessed—that wise parliamentary ministers would refrain from exercising that authority, and that moderate and temperate American provincial leaders would refrain from antagonizing English officials. Jefferson, however, was one of the first individuals on either side of the Atlantic to deny categorically Parliament's authority over the colonial legislatures.

In Jefferson's view, the Americans, "before their emigration . . . were the free inhabitants of the British dominions in Europe." As such, there was never "any claim of superiority or dependence asserted over them by that mother country from which they had migrated." Following this logic, Jefferson went on to assert both the complete independence of the various colonial legislatures from all parliamentary authority and to admit only the legitimacy of the king of England as the "central link" connecting the several independent and autonomous political components of the empire.

Running through the *Summary View* were descriptions of British behavior that was ill calculated to conciliation and well suited to revolution. Describing the British attempts to establish admiralty courts in England for the trial of Americans accused of violating customs laws, Jefferson proclaimed that "the cowards who would suffer a countryman to be torn from the bowels of their society in order to be thus offered a sacrifice to parliamentary tyranny, would merit that everlasting infamy now fixed on the authors of the act!" And, speaking of the efforts of royal governors to harness the colonial legislatures, he denounced the king for the "trifling reasons" used to veto colonial legislation.

Ever the lawyer, Jefferson sought to prove

the truth of his contentions by a careful analysis of ancient Saxon legal precedent. The essence of that argument was that the Americans'

> Saxon ancestors had, under this universal law, in like manner left their native wilds and woods in the north of Europe, had possessed themselves of the island of Britain . . . and had established there that system of laws which has so long been the glory and protection of that country. . . . And it is thought that no circumstance has occurred to distinguish materially the British from the Saxon emigration. America was conquered, and her settlements made, and firmly established, at the expence of individuals, and not of the British public. Their own blood was spilt in acquiring lands for their settlement, their own fortunes expended in making that settlement effectual; for themselves they fought, for themselves they conquered, and for themselves alone they have right to hold.

By the spring of 1775, after news of the battles of Lexington and Concord had reached Virginia, the state of relations between royal officials and provincial leaders was continuing on its downhill course. Patrick Henry remained the most eloquent and outspoken in demanding firm measures to combat what he was now openly terming British "tyranny," but Jefferson, though refraining from Henry's pyrotechnic oratorical displays, was nevertheless of one mind with his colleague from Hanover County. Jefferson supported Henry's resolutions calling for the colony to be put in a state of defense and was the primary author of a response to Lord North's offer of "conciliation" to the colonies. In a proclamation of February 1775, North had reiterated England's right to tax the colonies, but had stated his intention to avoid doing so if the colonies would promise to tax themselves in order to meet the revenue requirements of the mother country. Jefferson rejected North's proposal out of hand, stating that it

only "change[d] the form of oppression, without lightening its burthen." And, in a concluding paragraph that left little room for optimism, he proclaimed:

> For ourselves, we have exhausted every mode of application which our invention could suggest as proper and promising. We have decently remonstrated with Parliament; they have added new injuries to the old: we have wearied our King with supplication, he has not deigned to answer us: We have appealed to the native honour and justice of the British nation; their efforts in our favour have been hitherto ineffectual. What then remains to be done?

The answer, not long in coming, was hardly likely to comfort those favoring conciliation. By June 1775 Jefferson found himself in Philadelphia—only the second time he had been out of Virginia (the first having been nine years earlier, when he had gone on a tour of the northern colonies). Peyton Randolph, the leader of the Virginia delegation to the Continental Congress, had been called back to Virginia to preside over the Virginia Convention, and Jefferson, who was the first alternate in the balloting for delegates to the Congress, was sent to Philadelphia in his stead. At thirty-two he was one of the youngest members of that body and though he would, as always, stay in the background during the debates in the Congress, he would almost immediately establish his reputation as one of the most effective committee members in that body. According to John Adams, though Jefferson was "a silent member of Congress, he was so prompt, frank, explicit and decisive upon committees and in conversation, not even Samuel Adams was more so, that he soon seized upon my heart."

The 1775 session of the Continental Congress met in the immediate aftermath of the battles of Lexington and Concord, and Jefferson's first important assignment there was to draft a set of resolutions justifying the Declaration of the Causes and Necessity for Taking Up Arms. This effort, like the *Summary View,* drew from Jefferson another spirited denunciation of British policy and intentions and, apparently, a good many felt that it went too far. According to William Livingston, another member of the committee charged with drafting the resolutions, Jefferson's draft "had the faults common to our Southern gentlemen. Much fault-finding and declamation, with little sense of dignity. They seem to think a reiteration of tyranny, despotism, bloody, &c., all that is needed to unite us at home." In fact it was not simply a tendency toward "fault-finding and declamation" that caused some to oppose Jefferson's version of the resolutions. As in his *Summary View,* he argued in these new resolutions that Parliament had never had any authority over the colonial legislatures, and many members of the Congress were simply not yet prepared to travel that far down the road of legislative independence. As a consequence, a much milder version of the *Declaration of the Causes and Necessity for Taking Up Arms,* drafted by John Dickinson and refraining from a complete denial of parliamentary authority over America, was ultimately adopted by the Continental Congress.

Jefferson would soon have other opportunities to shape the American response to British policy. Having already drafted the Virginia House of Burgesses' response to Lord North's plan for "conciliation," Jefferson was selected to draft the Congress's response as well. His draft, which followed along the lines of the Virginia version, again displayed some of his militant temper. He denounced the "wicked administration" in the British Parliament, vowed to resist those " 'cowardly' sons of America" who counseled "unreserved submission," and rejected Lord North's proposal emphatically.

The young lawyer who had retreated to Monticello in order to marry and begin a family in the peace of Albemarle County would from this point on have little time to devote to his private life. With the recess of the Continental Congress in August, Jefferson came home via Richmond, where he attended the Virginia Convention and was reelected to the next session of the Continental Congress. Soon after his arrival home his second daughter, Jane Randolph, died, and within a few weeks of that tragedy he was again on his horse bound for Philadelphia and the Continental Congress. Though Jefferson himself may have been nearly ready to support a final break from England, the months between the fall of 1775 and the summer of 1776 would see delegates from other colonies—particularly those from New York and Pennsylvania—move only gradually and fitfully toward that conclusion.

Jefferson's own mood at the time was perhaps best summarized in a letter to the colony's former attorney general, John Randolph, in November 1775. Randolph, after painful reflection, had decided to cast his allegiance with the Crown and had sailed to England. Jefferson, like most of Virginia's provincial leaders, continued to like and respect Randolph, but he also obviously felt some need to justify his current sentiments to him. Reviewing the events of the previous months, Jefferson pronounced King George III "the bitterest enemy we have," claiming that "ignorance or wickedness somewhere controuls him." "There is not," he concluded, "in the British empire a man who more cordially loves a Union with Gr. Britain than I do. But by the god that made me I will cease to exist before I yeild to a connection on such terms as the British parliament propose and in this I think I speak the sentiments of America."

Jefferson took leave of the Congress in late December 1775 in order to return home, to look after family affairs. He did not remain aloof from the imperial struggle, however; soon after he arrived at Monticello he was at work on a pamphlet seeking to justify independence. The occasion for his action was a speech delivered by George III to Parliament in which the British monarch appealed for an end to all American rebelliousness and recounted the "tenderness," "industry," and "expense and treasure" with which England had nurtured her colonies. Seeking to refute the king's claims about the beneficial aspects of British rule, Jefferson embarked on a lengthy history of the British colonization of America, beginning with the attempts of Sir Humphrey Gilbert and Sir Walter Raleigh to settle the colonies and continuing up through the various charters issued to the Virginia Company of London. The point of his argument was that the Crown had given great latitude and scant assistance to all of those early adventurers and, thus, that the settled colonies were more the result of the initiative of the early colonizers than they were the product of a benevolent imperial power. The exposition, as far as it went, was too overloaded with historical precedent and too narrowly argued to have the effect that its author wished for it, and thus it was wisely filed away in his personal papers, never to be used in the conflict that was so soon to reach a climax.

The period between late January 1776, when Jefferson made his effort at a general justification of American independence, and the middle of May was one when the natural momentum of the armed conflict between England and America, given further acceleration by the publication of Thomas Paine's *Common Sense,* carried the colonies closer to the brink of secession from the British Empire. Jefferson took his seat in the Second Continental Congress on 14 May, and the next day in Williamsburg the delegates to the Virginia Convention voted to instruct their delegates to the Congress to "propose to that respectable body to declare the United Colonies free and independent states, absolved from all allegiance to, or

dependence upon, the crown or parliament of Great Britain." On 7 June, Virginia's Richard Henry Lee introduced that resolution onto the floor of the Continental Congress and, after nearly a month of debate, on 2 July, the Resolution of Independence was adopted.

As befitted his personality and temperament, Jefferson's crucial role in this enterprise came not in the debate on the floor of the Congress, but in the work of the committee appointed—on the same day that Lee introduced the resolution for independence —to prepare a declaration and justification of independence. How Jefferson, at age thirty-three, came to be appointed to such a distinguished committee—the other members were Benjamin Franklin, John Adams, Robert R. Livingston, and Roger Sherman —and how it came to pass that he would be the principal draftsman of the Declaration remains a matter of speculation. John Adams' frequently quoted recollection of the matter, though perhaps uncharacteristically modest, probably still comes closest to the mark. According to Adams, Jefferson approached him and suggested that the Massachusetts lawyer make the draft. Adams, in turn, demurred, suggesting instead that Jefferson take primary responsibility. When asked for a justification, Adams replied: "Reason first—You are a Virginian, and a Virginian ought to appear at the head of this business. Reason second—I am obnoxious, suspected, and unpopular. You are very much otherwise. Reason third—you can write ten times better than I can."

All of those reasons have at least some validity. It was indeed important that a Virginian, or at least a southerner, play a principal hand in the business in order to dispel the impression that the movement for independence was simply a plot engineered by a few New England fanatics. Indeed, Adams' image as "obnoxious, suspected, and unpopular" was less the consequence of his own personal crankiness than it was of a general suspicion of the Massachusetts "radicals." And Jefferson, by his previous committee work in the Congress, had already earned a well-deserved reputation as a careful and elegant stylist.

This reputation for literary grace may have been the most important reason why Jefferson was selected over other, more senior members of the Virginia delegation, but, as Garry Wills has pointed out, Jefferson also occupied an important "middle" position within his delegation. Although he was, by temperament, on the side of radicals such as Patrick Henry and Richard Henry Lee, he was also, by training and social connection, a representative of the more cautious views of the recently deceased Peyton Randolph, as well as George Wythe and Edmund Pendleton. As Wills puts it: "Jefferson in Philadelphia looked like a rising star of the James River oligarchy. Fastidious, youthfully grave in his powdered hair, his slaves attending at the State House door, he must have suggested a younger Edmund Pendleton, studious of his elders and patrons, preparing himself to replicate their achievements."

The specifics of the actual drafting of the Declaration have been laid out in lucid fashion by Carl Becker in his classic book, *The Declaration of Independence* (1922). There can be no doubt that the work was overwhelmingly Jefferson's. Beginning sometime in the third week of June, Jefferson composed the rough draft of the Declaration, and then submitted that draft to Adams and Franklin for their editorial advice. Though he later claimed that he did not rely on any other written materials in making his composition, it seems certain that the preamble of the Virginia Declaration of Rights, drafted by George Mason and in circulation in Philadelphia by mid-June, had some influence on his own preamble for the Declaration of Independence. The phrases of Mason's Declaration of Rights—"that all men are born equally free and independent, and have certain inherent natural rights . . . among which

are, the enjoyment of life and liberty, with the means of acquiring and possessing property, and pursuing and obtaining Happiness and safety"—are so strikingly similar to the memorable second paragraph of Jefferson's Declaration that to call it a coincidence strains the laws of probability.

Though the influence of Mason's Declaration of Rights seems well established, historians have differed sharply over the more general intellectual sources for Jefferson's Declaration. The most frequently argued position—one adopted both by Carl Becker and by most of Jefferson's early biographers—is that Jefferson's Declaration owed the most to John Locke. By Jefferson's own testimony, Locke stood with Sir Isaac Newton and Francis Bacon as his intellectual heroes, and much of the articulation of natural rights in the second paragraph of the preamble is a paraphrase of sections of Locke's *Second Treatise on Government.* More recently, Wills has advanced a strikingly revisionist hypothesis that the John Locke whom Jefferson admired was the Locke of the *Essay Concerning Human Understanding* and not of the *Second Treatise on Government* and that, indeed, the primary intellectual sources for the Declaration are to be found not in London, "Philadelphia, or Paris, but [in] Aberdeen and Edinburgh and Glasgow." In support of that contention, Wills traces a line of intellectual influence beginning with Jefferson's friend and teacher William Small at William and Mary and continuing on to the Scottish moral-sense philosophers Henry Home Kames, Thomas Reid, and Francis Hutcheson.

Wills's explication of the Scottish sources of Jefferson's revolutionary thought is an intellectual tour de force—meticulous, erudite, and elegantly argued—and after reading his account historians will never again be able to assert blithely that the ideas embodied in the preamble of the Declaration were simply paraphrases of Locke's *Second Treatise.* On the other hand, the claim that the ideas embodied in the preamble are preeminently those of the Scottish moral-sense philosophers seems equally dubious, for there is simply too much evidence—both in the text of the Declaration itself and in Jefferson's own intellectual background—indicating that Jefferson, like most provincial Americans of his generation, was powerfully influenced by the English Whig political theorists.

Still other historians, such as Daniel J. Boorstin, have been impressed by what they discern to be the "conservative" and "legalistic" quality of the Declaration. For Boorstin, the evidence for that contention is to be found in Jefferson's list of specific grievances against the king, a list that comprises more than three-quarters of the document as a whole. That recitation of American grievances, aimed at proving that the king had forfeited the colonies' allegiance by his "long train of abuses" against American liberty, persuades Boorstin that "the more the Declaration is reread in context, the more plainly it appears a document of imperial legal relations rather than a piece of high-flown political philosophy."

Ultimately, none of these interpretations arguing for a single, or even a dominant path of influence into Jefferson's revolutionary thought is entirely persuasive. The sources of Jefferson's thought—emanating from the classical worlds of Greece and Rome, from England, Scotland, and to a lesser extent France—were all filtered through an experience that was quintessentially American and even more pointedly, provincially Virginian. As Merrill Peterson, following the lines of interpretation laid down by Bernard Bailyn, has argued, American revolutionary ideas were, in their broadest sense,

> founded on the ideas of the Enlightenment. But these ideas had a traditional base in English law and government, which facilitated the transition. Moreover, in America, the ideas were virtual mirror images of emerging social and political realities only dimly perceived before the birth of revolutionary consciousness. As liberal ideas called attention to these native realities, so did they enable Americans to release the substance of English liberty from its corrupted and constricted forms. The patriots did not invent these ideas, but they organized and condensed them into a revolutionary ideology, then proceeded to put it to work in the civil life of the new nation.

It was the ability to distill this complex combination of classical, continental, and English political and legal thought into a statement that resonated with the reality of the American experience that made the "truths" uttered by the Declaration so "self-evident." And unlike most of Jefferson's earlier literary efforts, where his explication of the history of Anglo-American legal and political precedents was both detailed and at the same time tedious and technical, the Declaration succeeded in doing that in concise and uncluttered fashion. As he himself was later to recall, the purpose of the Declaration was

> not to find out new principles, or new arguments, never before thought of, not merely to say things which had never been said before; but to place before mankind the common sense of the subject, in terms so plain and firm as to command their assent, and to justify ourselves in the independent stand we are compelled to take. Neither aiming at originality of principle or sentiment, nor yet copied from any particular and previous writing, it was intended to be an expression of the American mind, and to give to that expression the proper tone and spirit called for by the occasion.

THE REVOLUTION AT HOME

The Declaration of Independence, far from marking a climax, was in fact merely the beginning of Thomas Jefferson's career as a revolutionary statesman. For Jefferson, as for virtually all of America's revolutionary leaders, the decision for independence carried with it substantive obligations for the building of a new society. Not only were Americans claiming the right to "alter or abolish" their existing governmental connections, but they were at the same time seeking "to institute new Government, laying its foundation on such principles and organizing its powers in such form, as to them shall seem most likely to effect their Safety and Happiness." It seems appropriate here to sketch out the broad outlines of this constructive phase of Jefferson's career as a revolutionary statesman and to note his contribution to the "new government" of Virginia.

Having completed his work in the Continental Congress, Jefferson would return to Virginia, where he would work for nearly the entire period of the Revolution to establish the principles of republican government in his home state. His efforts as a builder of Virginia's new polity would reveal him once again to be a man of extraordinarily complex instincts, a political leader who combined in his thought and behavior the attributes of a revolutionary, a reformer, and a defender of tradition.

By his presence at the Continental Congress at the crucial moment of independence, Jefferson would be deprived of the opportunity to play an influential role in another crucial moment in the political history of his colony, for all through the month of June 1776, Jefferson's legislative colleagues in Virginia, gathered in their extralegal convention, drafted a new constitution for their newly independent commonwealth. Indeed, there is some indication that Jefferson may have regarded this work as more important than his own in Philadelphia, for he wrote Thomas Nelson on 16 May that the work of framing a new government was "the whole object of the present controversy; for should a bad government be instituted for us in future it had been as well to have accepted at first the bad one offered to us from beyond the water without the risk and expence of contest." Anxious to play a part in that all-important act of erecting Virginia's new government, Jefferson composed three different drafts of a constitution and sent the final one of those to the Virginia Convention for consideration. Historians have differed over both the degree to which Jefferson's proposals influenced the final outcome in Virginia and over the direction in which Jefferson's proposals might have moved the Virginia government had they been adopted. Most historians continue to credit George Mason with being the principal architect of the Virginia Constitution while acknowledging that Jefferson's draft did, in the later stages of the constitution's drafting, serve as a source for some amendments to Mason's frame of government. Julian Boyd, however, in *The Papers of Thomas Jefferson*, has concluded after a meticulous analysis of all of the many sources for the Virginia constitution, that Jefferson's contribution was much greater than anyone has realized and, indeed, that the convention in its closing moments turned to it and incorporated "considerable part[s]" into the final draft.

The various drafts of Jefferson's version of the Virginia constitution, together with his later comments on the final form of that constitution, suggest once again that Jefferson's blueprint for his state's political future contained in it a complicated mixture of the innovative and the traditional. In some respects—for example, in his proposal for the election of the upper house of the state legislature by members of the lower house (an electoral device that owed more to English notions of mixed government than it did to democratic forms)—his version was actually more conservative than the one eventually adopted by the Virginia Convention. In others—such as his proposal that prerevolutionary property qualifications imposed as a condition for suffrage be eased but not eliminated—his thinking suggests that he was interested in modifying, but hardly destroying, traditional definitions of who should have a right to take part in the civic polity.

These relatively conservative aspects of Jefferson's constitutional thinking are, however, not necessarily representative of the general direction of his thought. Indeed, Boyd, in his elaborate introductory note to the three drafts of Jefferson's proposals for the constitution, has argued that those drafts

> contain . . . most if not all of the leading principles to which Jefferson's entire career was dedicated: the people as the source of authority; the protection of "public liberty" and of individual rights against authoritarian control; the widening of suffrage and an equalization of the distribution of representation in the legislative branch; the use of unappropriated lands for the establishment of a society of independent farmers . . . ; the just and equitable treatment of the Indians; the use of the western lands so as to remove friction with neighboring states and promote the cause of nationality; the encouragement of immigration and the lowering of barriers to naturalization, the elevation of the civil over the military authority; the abolition of privilege and prerogative; and so on.

While it is true that some of the provisions of the first draft of Jefferson's proposed constitution were more progressive than those in the version eventually adopted (for example, Jefferson's draft contained provisions that would have abolished primogeniture and entail and ended government support of religion), Boyd's claims for Jefferson's progressive and egalitarian vision are overdrawn. The specific character of Jefferson's reform proposals both at the time of the drafting of the Virginia Constitution and in the decade that followed show him to be an enlightened and energetic reformer, but the reforms he advocated were most often articulated within and tempered by a well-settled Anglo-American legal and political system for which Jefferson continued to have much respect. As Merrill Peterson has noted, Jefferson

> had none of the typical radical's rage against the past. . . . He was, at bottom, attached to Virginia society, wishing only to reform its abuses. . . . He would not go to radical lengths to achieve his objectives. And even his most progressive reforms were streaked with conservatism. If democracy was his destiny, he had yet to escape from the chrysalis of Whiggery in which he was born.

The issue occupying most of Jefferson's attention during the years immediately following the Revolution was legal reform. That issue itself encompassed the full range of Virginia's civil and criminal law, and Jefferson, as chairman of the committee of the postrevolutionary House of Delegates charged with the task of revision of the laws, threw himself into the work without hesitation. The essential question confronting Jefferson's committee was whether to scrap the English legal system that they had inherited and start from scratch or to "preserve the general system, and only modify it to the present state of things." In spite of some strong antipathies to particular parts of the English legal code, Jefferson and his fellow Virginians decided on the latter course.

One of the aspects of the English legal system that Jefferson most disliked was the collection of feudal laws restricting the descent of property. Attacking the notion of this "aristocracy of wealth," and seeking "to make an opening for the aristocracy of virtue and talent," Jefferson pressed for the abolition of laws of entail—which prevented the division of large estates among several heirs —and of primogeniture—which stipulated that estates of men who died intestate should automatically descend to the eldest son. He was successful in both of these efforts; entail was abolished by an act of the assembly in 1776, and in 1785 the feudal restrictions encouraged by primogeniture met the same fate.

The attacks on primogeniture and entail are excellent examples both of Jefferson's impatience with what he considered to be unjustifiable hereditary privilege and of the way in which his thinking conformed with the natural trend of thought and events in the America of his time. Virginians, living in a society with an expansive frontier and an even more expansive and highly mobile population, had already found ways around laws restricting the alienability and inheritance of land; the formal abolition of entail and primogeniture, while a decisive break with a European feudal past and an important recognition and codification of existing practice, was wholly consonant with the colonial experience of his fellow Virginians.

Along with a good many other progressive-minded individuals in America and Europe, Jefferson was determined to do something about his colony's chaotic and often barbaric criminal code. Most colonies had borrowed their system of punishing crime in haphazard fashion from English statutory and common law, and the result was a nearly universal ignorance of the law among lawyers, judges, and lay people, and a harsh and inconsistent regimen of punishment for those who found themselves on the wrong side of the criminal law. Having read the works of criminal-reform advocates such as Cesare Beccaria and William Eden, Jefferson had already arrived at the position—still relatively novel in the late eighteenth century—that punishments should be aimed at reform rather than vengeance. By and large, his plan for criminal reform—presented to the legislature in 1779 in the form of a Bill for Proportioning Crimes and Punishments —displayed that spirit. Believing that capital punishment should be "the last melancholy resource" of society, he advocated that the death penalty, previously applied to a long list of felonies, should be meted out only to those convicted of murder or treason. And, more generally, he advocated much greater consistency in the apportioning of punishments in order to combat the favoritism and inconsistency that marked the attitudes of many American judges toward punishing specific offenders.

At the same time, Jefferson's proposed revision of the criminal code showed that he was still a captive of older notions of punishment. His proposal that "whosoever committeth murder by poisoning, shall suffer death by poison" was obviously based on notions that had little to do with reform of the convicted felon. Similarly, he fashioned a whole series of punishments for crimes committed against persons that were governed by laws of retaliation and not reform. "Whosoever shall be guilty of rape . . ., with man or woman, shall be punished; if a man, by castration, a woman, by boring through the cartilage of her nose a hole of one half inch in diameter at the least"; and, in as literal a devotion to the principle of *lex talionis* as is likely to be found, Jefferson proposed that anyone guilty of disfiguring another, was to be disfigured in the same manner, "or if that cannot be, for want of the same part, then as nearly as may be, in some other part of at least equal value and estimation."

The entire text of Jefferson's bill on punishments was peppered with extraordinarily elaborate footnotes—excerpts from Anglo-Saxon, Latin, and English laws, citations to Beccaria and Charles de Secondat Montesquieu, as well as the standard English legal texts by Sir Edward Coke, Sir William Blackstone, and Henry de Bracton. In sum, what we can see at work in Jefferson's bill is not only the reformer, but the legal scholar, reveling in the accumulation of tradition and precedent and, as a consequence, unwilling or at least not wholly able, to free himself from some of the less benevolent constraints of that legal tradition.

Jefferson's proposed revisions for the criminal code were part of a much larger report issued by the Committee of Revisors, of which Jefferson was the chairman. Included among the 126 specific bills reported out of that committee was another one of Jefferson's pet projects, his **Bill for the More General Diffusion of Knowledge**. There is perhaps no other proposal from his pen that demonstrates more clearly both his disdain for the notions of hereditary aristocracy and his faith in the idea of an aristocracy of talent. The preamble to that bill was explicit in its belief that the best way to preserve the principles of republican liberty was "to illuminate, as far as practicable, the minds of the people at large." Toward this end, Jefferson believed "that those persons, whom nature hath endowed with genius and virtue, should be rendered by liberal education worthy to receive, and able to guard the sacred deposit of the rights and liberties of their fellow citizens, and that they should be called to that charge without regard to wealth, birth or other accidental condition or circumstance."

The proposal, in its specifics, called for a three-tiered system of elementary, secondary, and higher education. At the base of the system were to be one hundred wards, or local school districts, in which "all the free children, male and female . . . shall be intitled to receive tuition gratis, for a term of three years." From these local schools, a smaller group, including both those "in easy circumstances" who could afford to pay tuition and those less wealthy pupils whose academic performance earned them scholarships, would be sent to twenty grammar schools spread throughout the state. At those grammar schools there would be a progressive winnowing of talent, with the result being that "twenty of the best geniuses will be raked from the rubbish annually, and be instructed, at the public expense, so far as grammar schools go." Of those twenty, ten "of the best learning and most

hopeful genius and disposition" would be given scholarships to the College of William and Mary, which was meant to stand at the apex of Jefferson's educational meritocracy. Although Jefferson's plan for public education was in most respects more modest than similar plans already in operation in New England, the cadre of wealthy gentlemen who controlled the Virginia legislature considered it too costly and cumbersome to be implemented in their geographically diffuse, agrarian society. Content with an informal network of private academies and tutors for the instruction of their own children, Virginia's political elite would continue to deny the children of ordinary men and women in Virginia the right to "illuminate their minds." Indeed, it would be well after the Civil War before Virginia instituted a program of public education for all free citizens; the legacy of that delay—the perpetuation of social, political, and economic inequality, superstition, intolerance, and parochialism —would contribute to Virginia's decline from the birthplace of presidents to a cultural backwater.

Although many of Jefferson's "revolutionary reforms" were neither very revolutionary nor very successful in winning adherents within his home state, one of his postrevolutionary legislative proposals—his **Bill for Establishing Religious Freedom**—richly deserves the attention that historians have lavished on it. The principle of separation of church and state, though reasonably well established in an ethnically and religiously diverse colony like Pennsylvania, was, in most of America and certainly in most of the world, a genuinely revolutionary idea. Jefferson's articulation of that principle was, both in its eloquence and in its vehemence, an important milestone in the redefinition of the relationship between government and religion.

The Church of England in Virginia, though institutionally, intellectually, and spiritually weaker than its counterpart in England, was nevertheless still very much the church of choice of virtually all of the prominent planter-gentlemen who composed the political leadership of Virginia during the revolutionary era. Anglicanism was, however, rapidly ceasing to be the religion of choice among the ordinary people of Virginia. Between 1740 and 1776 evangelical religion—first manifested in the increase in the number of Presbyterians and then, more prominently, in the dramatic insurgency of the Baptists—had emerged as the most visible, and to some, visibly threatening, form of religious observance in Virginia. The evangelicals had expressed their uneasiness about the Anglicans' legally privileged position long before the Revolution had begun. In the first and most fundamental instance, they wished an explicit guarantee of their right to hold their religious services without disruption or intimidation, a right often infringed by zealous sheriffs and local officials. And more generally, as stated in November 1785 in a Petition to the House of Delegates from a Committee of Several Baptist Associations in Virginia, they believed that "as ministers are the Voluntary Servants of the Church, So every Church or Congregation should be left to reward them in such a manner as they think their services deserve," and thus wished to end all government support of the Church of England or, for that matter, any other religion.

It was to this cause that a few prominent Virginia Anglicans—James Madison, George Mason, and Jefferson—contributed their intellectual and legislative skills. To call Jefferson an Anglican is of course to mislabel his religious beliefs, for he certainly did not subscribe in any strict way either to the theology or the institutional structures of Anglicanism. He was, however, both by his social and legal position within his home country, very much a representative of what has been called an Anglican-gentry elite. What differentiated Jefferson and a few others like Madison and Mason from the great mass of

their fellow gentrymen was that they genuinely believed that the state had no authority over private matters of conscience. As he stated in his *Notes on Virginia:* "The legitimate powers of government extend to such acts only as are injurious to others. But it does me no injury for my neighbour to say there are twenty gods, or no god. It neither picks my pocket nor breaks my leg." Moreover, in looking back over the history of government attempts to impose uniformity of religion upon the citizenry, Jefferson noted:

> Millions of innocent men, women, and children, since the introduction of Christianity, have been burnt, tortured, fined, imprisoned; yet we have not advanced one inch towards uniformity. What has been the effect of coercion? To make one half the world fools, and the other half hypocrites. . . . Reason and persuasion are the only practicable instruments. To make way for these, free enquiry must be indulged; and how can we wish others to indulge it while we refuse it ourselves.

Since Virginians, by declaring independence, not only ended their political connection with England, but also their legal attachment to the Church of England, the opponents of established religion were in an advantageous position from which to mount their attack. The first battle in the campaign for disestablishment was led by George Mason, who included in his Declaration of Rights for the new Virginia Constitution the principle that "all men are equally entitled to the free exercise of religion, according to the dictates of conscience." This said nothing specifically about the privileged position of the Anglican church, but in the first postrevolutionary session of the Virginia legislature in December 1776 Jefferson managed to muster enough support to pass a bill exempting dissenters from paying taxes to support the church, temporarily suspending parish levies on church members, and leaving open the question "whether a general assessment should not be established by law, on every one, to the support of the pastor of his choice, or whether all should be left to voluntary contributions." This amounted in fact to a major revolution in church-state relations in Virginia, for just four years before, members of dissenting sects had been so much on the defensive that they were petitioning merely to be allowed to exercise their religion free of harrassment. By 1776 they not only had attained that freedom but were well on their way toward eliminating the privileged position of the Anglican church.

It would take another nine years, however, before Jefferson, aided immeasurably by a vigorous petition campaign by thousands of evangelicals, was able to institutionalize the principle of separation of church and state once and for all. His Bill for Establishing Religious Freedom, passed by the Virginia legislature on 16 January 1786, was a landmark piece of legislation not only for Jefferson's home state, but for the rest of the world as well. The text of that statute—particularly its preamble—is testimony to the intensity of Jefferson's feeling about the matter. In contrast to Jefferson's bill on crimes and punishments, which displayed the legalistic and scholarly bent of his intellectual training, the Bill for Establishing Religious Freedom revealed the passion of his commitment to the cause of freedom of conscience. Proclaiming it "sinful and tyrannical" to compel the taxpayers to support a religious doctrine to which they did not subscribe, Jefferson asserted that "truth is great and will prevail if left to herself; that she is the proper and sufficient antagonist to error, and has nothing to fear from the conflict."

Though the principles enunciated in Jefferson's Bill for Establishing Religious Freedom are, in the 1980s, taken for granted by most Americans, they were, in the eighteenth-century world that Thomas Jefferson inhabited, genuinely revolutionary. As Jefferson himself noted on many occasions, the eighteenth-century world was one in which countless men and women had languished in prisons and lost their lives in the name of a legally imposed religious orthodoxy. The twentieth-century world is of course not wholly free from those same impulses toward authoritarian and terroristic religious establishments, but Jefferson more than any other man in his country helped to free America from that danger. Moreover, unlike many of Jefferson's more progressive schemes for Virginia, this one not only was adopted by the Virginia legislature, but it would also have an immediate impact on the structure of religious life in the Old Dominion. The Anglican church, shorn of the involuntary support of Virginia's taxpayers, would decline precipitously in the years that followed; evangelical religion, freed from the restraints imposed upon it in the prerevolutionary years, would become the dominant religious force in Virginia.

If Jefferson's Bill for Establishing Religious Freedom is the best and most successful example of the radical bent of his mind and heart, then his thoughts and actions respecting Virginia's slave population are perhaps the best indication of the way in which his upbringing and social circumstance in the slaveholding society of Virginia constrained his revolutionary and egalitarian vision. In Jefferson's general attitudes toward slavery there are two facts that are beyond dispute. The first is that he had, from his first pronouncement on the subject to his very last, a genuine abhorrence of the institution, an abhorrence of both the cruel effect of slavery on those Africans involuntarily held within the system and of the effect of the system on the economy and social structure of Virginia. The second, equally indisputable fact is that Jefferson held slaves in large numbers all of his adult life and, in spite of his considerable anguish about the institution, did virtually nothing to free either himself or his society from dependence upon African labor.

If there ever were an opportunity for Jefferson and his fellow Virginians to live up to their revolutionary vision of liberty and equality, that opportunity came at the time of the Revolution, when Virginians, in the process of revising their legal code, confronted in the most obvious fashion the contradictions between their commitment to liberty and their reliance on African slavery. That Jefferson was aware of the contradiction is manifest, for he commented on it often. Yet his attempts at resolving that contradiction must be considered palliative at best. In his proposed Constitution for Virginia he sought to prohibit the importation of any slave from either Africa or any other part of America into Virginia. He also strongly endorsed a statute of 1778 that did end the trade in slaves from Africa to Virginia. But ultimately Jefferson was himself so bound up in the slave system—not only in the obvious, economic sense, but also culturally and intellectually—that he was powerless to take any meaningful steps either to eradicate the institution where it already existed or even to ameliorate the condition of the slaves. This failure of Jefferson's revolutionary and egalitarian vision was not merely his or Virginia's or the South's failure alone. As Winthrop D. Jordan has pointed out in his path-breaking study, *White Over Black* (1968), American racism did not emerge simply as a response to the needs of a class of southern slaveowners to justify their economic exploitation of Africans, but rather, out of a complex cluster of attitudes and beliefs—scientific, religious, and social—that were common to virtually all British Americans, North and South. In that sense, Jefferson's failure to extend revolutionary notions of liberty and equality to his black bondsmen and bondswomen placed him, tragically, squarely in the center of his nation's racial dilemma.

REVOLUTIONARY GOVERNOR

Though it pained him to be away so frequently from his home and family at Monticello during the years immediately preceding and following Independence, Jefferson was nevertheless a willing, even eager participant in both the decision to break from England and in the creation of a new government in his independent state. However, the final phase of his revolutionary career—his service as wartime governor of Virginia from 1779 to 1781—would bring him little satisfaction, for the structure of the office that he held and the nature of the problems he confronted combined to make his years in the executive mansion ones of great personal trial.

Jefferson had never liked the structure of the executive branch as it had been created by the Virginia Constitution of 1776. Elected by the legislature and deprived of a veto over the actions of that branch, Virginia's chief executive was further constrained by an eight-person Council of State, a situation that rendered the governor, in Jefferson's opinion, a "mere cipher." These limitations made decisive executive action difficult under the best of circumstances, but during the years of the revolutionary war—when the demands of both defense and finance were greatest—the effects of those structural weaknesses were particularly severe.

The Virginia General Assembly elected Jefferson governor on 1 June 1779, just a few months before the state moved its capital site from Williamsburg to Richmond, a plan favored by Jefferson. The new governor and his family would have to move their belongings from the elegant governor's palace in Williamsburg—the same palace in which the young law student had played his violin during Governor Fauquier's time—to temporary quarters in Richmond, for construction of the governor's residence had not even begun in the new capital town. For the first year and a half of his governorship Jefferson would be spared the burden of coping with actual warfare in his home state, for during that time the principal scene of action was to the south, in South Carolina. Large numbers of Virginia soldiers were engaged in that action, however, and the job facing the governor—the raising, equipping, and payment of troops—was a daunting one.

In Virginia that job was made particularly frustrating by a militia system that depended heavily on the compliance of individual counties both in meeting their quotas of "able-bodied freemen between the ages of sixteen and fifty" and in equipping those militiamen in adequate fashion. During the early years of the war, when patriotic fervor and optimism about a speedy American victory were high, the ranks of the Virginia militia were full, but by the time of the southern campaign of 1779–1781, enlistments had fallen, supplies were scarce, and Virginia's state finances were precarious.

In many respects the burdens imposed on Governor Jefferson were no more serious than those shouldered by every revolutionary governor in America, for the problems of providing men, materiel, and money for the war effort were common to every state. The fall of Charleston, South Carolina, in May 1780, followed by a devastating military defeat for the continental army in Camden in August, would, however, expose Virginia to new dangers. Midway into his second term as governor, in September 1780, Jefferson was thinking that he had had enough. Writing to Richard Henry Lee, he confided, "The application required to the duties of the office I hold is so excessive, and the execution of them after all so imperfect, that I have determined to retire from it at the close of the present campaign." He tried to persuade John Page to succeed him in the job, but Page was unwilling, counseling his friend to stay on both for the remainder of his second one-year term and then again for

another. "I know," he wrote, "the many mortifications you must meet with, but 18 months will soon pass away." Jefferson would take his friend's advice, but he would find the months ahead to be the most difficult of his public career.

The military threat facing Virginia in the fall of 1780 was not confined to that posed by Lord Cornwallis' troops in the South, for Virginia was also vulnerable to attack from the east, by sea. Indeed, Jefferson's basic military dilemma throughout this whole period was that any effort he made to strengthen General Nathaniel Greene's depleted continental forces in the South would inevitably increase the danger of invasion along the coast. Conversely, too great a preoccupation with coastal defenses would make a bad situation even worse in the South. Faced with these difficult prospects, Jefferson tended to be more concerned about Cornwallis' regiments in the South, hoping all the while that if the British made some effort on the coast America's French allies might ward them off.

As it turned out, there was probably no right decision, for British strength on both fronts was growing and Virginia's defenses, unaided by new support from the North, were declining. The immediate threat materialized in the east, where British forces under General Alexander Leslie landed near Portsmouth. This proved to be only a temporary foray, but more serious efforts shortly followed. On a Sunday morning, on the last day of 1780, Jefferson received word that twenty-seven ships had been sighted off the Virginia coast. Not knowing whose ships they were or where they were heading, Jefferson reacted cautiously, sending General Thomas Nelson with a relatively small force of men to investigate further. Unfortunately, it was not until Tuesday, 2 January, that it was confirmed that the ships were British and that the general in charge of the operation, Benedict Arnold, had advanced with his men as far as Jamestown.

At this point Jefferson acted decisively, calling the full available force of militia into action, but he was too late. Arnold's forces were the beneficiaries of some exceptionally lucky winds, which allowed them to sail up the James River unmolested and land some fifteen hundred men at Westover, the Byrd family estate. Jefferson himself best expressed the extent to which Arnold's boldness had surprised the Virginians; he noted ruefully: "Winds favoring them in a remarkable degree, they almost brought the first news themselves of their movements."

From that point on there was virtually nothing that Jefferson could do to stop Arnold's advance. By early afternoon on 4 January, Arnold and his troops entered the capital in Richmond. The next few days were frantic ones for Jefferson, overseeing a partial evacuation of government arms, supplies, and records, making certain that his own family was safely out of the town, and then going back to the outskirts of Richmond where he had a view of enemy troops occupying the Virginia capital.

Within a week the worst of the invasion was over. Arnold retraced his steps back to the coast and by the middle of January was safely encamped with his men behind barricades at Portsmouth. In fact, the actual losses suffered by the Virginians as a result of Arnold's raid were relatively slight, but the humiliation was enormous. Arnold had proven how porous the Virginia defenses really were and, in the process of their ineffectual attempts at repelling him, the Virginians had been forced to divert valuable troops and supplies from General Greene in the South, thus strengthening Lord Cornwallis' hand in that theater of the war.

The damage to Jefferson's reputation, both then and subsequently, has been considerable. He was blamed for his initial delay in reacting to the sighting of the ships, for his failure to station lookouts on the coast in the first place, for the lack of fortifications up

the James River, and for what seemed to some a precipitous flight from the capital. Looking back on the specific events of the invasion, it seems clear that Jefferson is undeserving of blame for either cowardice or incompetence; given the circumstances of Arnold's landing, the Virginia governor probably acted as conscientiously and courageously as could be expected.

Understandably touchy about the criticism of his handling of the invasion, Jefferson was himself consistently reluctant to admit any error at all, but that attitude too seems unwarranted. Dumas Malone, certainly sympathetic to Jefferson's plight, perhaps sums it up best:

> It would have been better if he [Jefferson] had admitted the unvarnished truth: Arnold had caught him off his guard. It would have been better if he had erred on the side of self-reproach and had assumed more than his proportionate share of blame, just as he had shouldered more than his share of labor. Neither civil nor military officials often do that, but such an attitude would have been in character with the high-minded and personally disinterested public official that he was.

Jefferson had more than his reputation to worry about in the winter and spring of 1781, for Arnold's raid had exposed the weakness of the Virginians' defenses. Over the course of the next several months, Jefferson, working with General Greene and the Prussian general, Baron Friedrich Wilhelm von Steuben, sought to prevent a replication of the events of early January. The Virginia governor and the two generals worked together conscientiously, although their correspondence indicates that the history of friction between American civilian and military leaders in times of war goes back at least as far as the Virginia campaigns of the American Revolution. In spite of their conscientious efforts, the British forces both to the east and to the south again proved too strong for Virginia's defenses. In late April the British once again sailed up the James. Though they stopped short of Richmond, the Virginia Assembly, which was due to meet in early May, decided to move its session to Charlottesville. Jefferson, his term as governor less than a month away from ending, moved west with them, taking up residence at Monticello. Shortly after the Virginia government evacuated westward, the British forces from the coast rendezvoused with Cornwallis' southern forces at Petersburg, and the worst of Jefferson's fears were realized.

The last days of Jefferson's governorship would be bitterly disappointing. The British continued their march westward and the Virginia government continued its retreat. Warned by Jack Jouett, a Virginian version of Paul Revere, Jefferson alerted the assembly to the British advance and the government moved west again, to Staunton, on the other side of the Blue Ridge Mountains. Jefferson's term as governor had actually expired two days before, on 2 June, but since the assembly had been in perpetual flight it had not had time to appoint a successor. From 4 June, until 12 June, when the assembly elected General Thomas Nelson, Virginia operated without a governor.

It seemed an ignominious ending to a revolutionary career that had been otherwise so splendid. And it seemed even more humiliating when the Virginia Assembly, in July, proposed an inquiry into Jefferson's conduct as governor. Though Jefferson himself would remain despondent over the debacle for many months, Virginia's circumstances and his own reputation would both recover rapidly from that nadir. Cornwallis' army—tired, sick, and overextended—pulled back into Yorktown, and in October the American army would extract its revenge. And the Virginia Assembly, meeting on 19 December 1781, would back off from its censure of Jefferson, passing a resolution stating: "The Assembly wish in the strongest manner to declare the high opinion which they entertain of Mr. Jefferson's Ability, Rectitude, and Integrity as chief Magistrate of this Commonwealth, and mean by thus publicly avowing their Opinion, to obviate and remove all unmerited Censure."

In temporary retirement at Monticello, Jefferson must have taken some comfort, though hardly unrestrained glee, at the assembly's pronouncement. Although he was at that time determined to spend the rest of his days with his family and neighbors in Albemarle, his talents and his ambitions would both be too great to confine him to Monticello. His service to the cause of the American Revolution may have ended, but more than a quarter of a century of service to the independent American nation awaited him.

The Enlightenment

HENRY F. MAY

THE ENLIGHTENMENT

THE *Enlightenment* is a term used by nineteenth- and twentieth-century philosophers and historians to describe the principal movement of thought in eighteenth-century Europe. Often more a mood or a style than a set of fixed principles, the Enlightenment was so various that it is hard to define. Only two propositions seem to have been common to all enlightened Europeans. First, men of the Enlightenment believed, and the term itself implies, that the present is better than the past—better informed, freer, and altogether more promising. Usually they expected this improvement to continue into the future. Second, they believed that we can best understand nature and man, the two most important objects of study, not through faith or tradition or sudden illumination, but through the use of our own mental faculties. Just how to use these was a subject of incessant debate, but for most enlightened people careful scientific inquiry was the principal means by which we had moved out of the medieval darkness into the present age, an age whose achievements promised to equal or surpass those of the universally admired classical era of Greece and Rome.

About the sources of the Enlightenment there has been much discussion. The most obvious was the long series of scientific achievements culminating in the staggering achievements of Sir Isaac Newton, who, it seemed, had explained for all time the relations among the bodies that make up the universe and the cause of their regular movements. Another contributing cause of Enlightenment emphasized by contemporaries was the recovery and careful study, especially in the past two or three centuries, of the Greek and Latin authorities. A third cause perceived by many was the weakening, since the Reformation, of the repressive power of the church, though the relation between the Reformation and the Enlightenment was and is a difficult problem. Another cause cited by some writers of the time and some later historians was the increased contact, through exploration and settlement, with non-European civilizations and the

47

consequent beginnings of anthropological study.

Aside from these intellectual sources of Enlightenment, social historians have pointed to the increasingly orderly, predictable, and prosperous lives of the European middle and upper classes. It was among these classes that the Enlightenment flourished. The large majority of Europeans who worked on the land lived lives of little comfort or predictability, and seldom were they attracted by enlightened ideas. The beginning and early flowering of the Enlightenment took place when the Industrial Revolution was only starting in England and was not yet under way in France. It can perhaps best be seen as the climax of the intellectual history of early modern Europe, taking place just before the vast transformations that ushered in the nineteenth century. There is much argument as to whether the French Revolution was the culmination of the Enlightenment, its death-agony, or both.

Americans, because their own revolution and their relatively democratic political reorganization took place during the late Enlightenment, sometimes find it hard to realize that in much of the Enlightenment democracy played no part. The moderate British Enlightenment of the first half of the eighteenth century, reacting to the violence and upheaval of the British seventeenth century, placed its highest value on balance and order. The British government, perfected by the gloriously moderate revolution that ended Stuart tyranny in 1688, seemed to perpetuate a miraculous equilibrium in which king, lords, and commons each had their place—"commons," of course, meant that propertied minority represented in Parliament. The balance of forces in the Newtonian cosmos was recapitulated in British institutions and also in human nature, forever balanced between reason and passion.

The French thinkers of the mid-eighteenth century, with some British allies like David Hume, pushed beyond this complacent and invincibly moderate British Enlightenment into a deep-going skepticism. Prevented from undertaking political reform by a decadent but still-dangerous alliance of absolute monarchy with an intolerant church, they pushed their speculations as far as they dared, often arriving at materialist conclusions in natural philosophy and agnosticism or atheism in religion. These conclusions were sometimes expressed in satirical tales and witty aphorisms. Disbelief in the official political and religious doctrines became widespread among the French upper classes. Hope for the future was a more difficult matter, since most of the French thinkers found it impossible to believe that the agrarian masses could ever become enlightened. Some said openly that monarchy and Catholic dogma were best for the people, even though neither could any longer be taken seriously by the cultivated minority.

In about the 1760s, however, a third form of Enlightenment arose in both England and France, a revolutionary Enlightenment calling for drastic social change to reflect the new knowledge and embody the new intellectual freedom. Many of the first spokesmen of this new kind of Enlightenment were idealistic aristocrats who wanted to help those beneath them; others were attorneys, merchants, artisans, and writers who lived by their wits. The teachings of the revolutionary Enlightenment proved everywhere to bring to the surface currents of popular resentment and discontent that had long been present just beneath the aristocratic surface of European civilization, often briefly breaking through it in rebellions, riots, and popular sectarian movements. Some of these barely suppressed democratic feelings were associated in England with the memory of the seventeenth-century Commonwealth. It was the combination of these memories with the last phase of Enlightenment that led some people to believe that the time had come at last drastically to alter not only old ways of thinking but all institutions, making human life immediately happier and more rational.

There is no question that Thomas Jefferson was completely a man of the Enlightenment, taking the term in its broadest sense. He believed devoutly that the human mind, which had made such great advances already, was destined for further progress. Any argument that the past was superior to the present or future was a cowardly device of tyrants and reactionaries. In ringing phrases he proclaimed again and again that truth is great and will prevail.

Of the three kinds of Enlightenment briefly discussed above—the Moderate Enlightenment, the Skeptical Enlightenment, and the Revolutionary Enlightenment—Jefferson was influenced by the first and third, but not at all by the second. In his youth in Virginia he was steeped in the doctrines of the moderate English and Scottish thinkers. Both his experience of the American Revolution and his residence in France during the first, idealistic phases of the French Revolution made him a warm advocate of the Revolutionary Enlightenment. However, he did not follow this movement into its most radical phase, that which led some democrats clear out of the Enlightenment and into romantic democracy.

Even though his tastes, interests, and way of life were similar to those of the European aristocrats of the earlier phases of the Enlightenment, Jefferson was different from them for two main reasons. The first difference arose from his Virginian and American environment. The Virginian upper class, from which he came, thought of itself as aristocratic, but it was far less luxurious and leisured than the English gentry and aristocracy that served as its models. America was less urban, more open to expansion, and less rigidly class-divided than Europe, though care must be taken not to exaggerate these qualities and make the continent into a frontier utopia. With all that was hopeful about Jefferson's beloved country, it contained one tragic paradox: the institution of slavery. Jefferson, a slaveholder and a libertarian, struggled unsuccessfully all his life to come to grips with this terrible contradiction.

The second set of reasons why Jefferson was different from his European (or, indeed, his American) contemporaries lay in his temperament and personality. Jefferson was above all and always serious. He once said that a grave man could play the fool only when playing with children. A man of lofty virtue and carefully disciplined passion, he could not tolerate frivolity, moral skepticism, pessimism, undisciplined emotion, or unresolved paradox. Despite his Parisian residence, he was repelled by the skeptical part of the French Enlightenment. He had no touch of Voltaire's often rueful wit, of Hume's ultimate doubt about the reliability of human reason. Nor was he capable of Benjamin Franklin's earthy ribaldry or John Adams' playful tendency to speculate along really dangerous lines. He could never have suggested even in fun, as Adams did once in a letter to him, that this planet might turn out to be the Bedlam of the universe. His style reflects the man: whether in public documents or in private letters to his close friends, his daughters, or his favorite nephew, he was always serious, lofty, disciplined, and elegantly organized.

Without being a scientist or philosopher of real originality, Jefferson was more variously gifted than almost any of his contemporaries. An extremely versatile man in a versatile age, he was deeply interested in all fields of human learning except theology and metaphysics. It was almost the end of the time when such universal mastery was possible. To understand further his relation to the Enlightenment, it is necessary to see him briefly in terms of a number of his main fields of interest, some of them covered more intensively in other chapters of this book.

PHILOSOPHY

Perhaps Jefferson's most consistent intellectual passion was for philosophy, a term that in the eighteenth century covered many modern fields of knowledge. Metaphysics he thought a waste of time. His ideas about political and natural philosophy will be discussed later. For him what was most important was moral philosophy, the central arena for enlightened argument.

Always an ardent student and delighted reader of the most enlightening Greek and Roman authors, Jefferson was deeply affected by the two schools of Stoicism and Epicureanism. The peculiarly Roman stance of the Stoic, calmly and nobly facing the inevitable vicissitudes of life, gave dignity and gravity to Jefferson's generally optimistic styles of thought and conduct. It helped him face a series of devastating personal blows, including the early loss of his wife and the later death of his favorite daughter. It informs his brief, compassionate, and dignified letter to Adams on the death of the latter's wife. Epicureanism to Jefferson was far from a program for indulgence. As explained by Pierre Gassendi in the early sixteenth century, it was rather a program for the pursuit of happiness through disciplined tranquillity of mind and body. The ancient thinker Jefferson disliked the most was Plato, to him the fountainhead of meaningless mysticism.

As for his choice among modern thinkers, Jefferson once said to Alexander Hamilton that his trinity of the greatest men who had ever lived consisted of Bacon, Newton, and Locke. These were to him, and to many, the founders of the Enlightenment. The work of Bacon was the starting point for the scientific revolution, that of Newton its fulfillment. Locke's *Essay Concerning Human Understanding* was for Jefferson, as for all well-educated people of the eighteenth century, a taken-for-granted starting point for discussion of the mind, its various faculties, and its possibilities. In addition, Jefferson called Locke's *Second Treatise on Government* perfect as far as it went, and he closely echoed some of its sentences in the Declaration of Independence. Long excerpts from Locke's *Letter Concerning Toleration* were copied into Jefferson's early Commonplace Book.

Throughout his life Jefferson was powerfully influenced by the Scottish thinkers who formed one major part of the moderate British Enlightenment. Some of these he studied at the College of William and Mary under his Scottish teacher William Small. In this period he admired the political and moral essays (not the skeptical epistemology or the Tory-leaning history) of David Hume, and the writings on moral philosophy of Henry Home, Lord Kames, Adam Smith, and especially Francis Hutcheson, the founder of the Scottish school. Hutcheson, following Shaftesbury and others, taught that a moral sense was implanted in all human beings, enabling them instantly to detect good and right actions through a favorable emotional reaction. In this Hutcheson was followed by Hume, Kames, and Smith. In Europe, Jefferson met and admired Dugald Stewart, one of the last major figures of the Scottish Enlightenment, who taught another variety of moral-sense theory derived from his teacher Thomas Reid.

It is difficult to overstate the central importance for Jefferson of the universal moral sense. As he well knew, without it his intellectual world would have been chaotic and his democratic optimism impossible. He explained this in a letter of 10 August 1787 to his nephew Peter Carr:

He who made us would have been a pitiful bungler if he had made the rules of our moral conduct a matter of science. For one man of science, there are thousands who are not. What would have become of them? . . . State a moral case to a ploughman and a professor. The former will decide it as well, and often better than the latter, because he has not been led astray by artificial rules.

When Jefferson went to Paris at the age of forty-one he carried the Scottish philosophers in his mental baggage. In the French capital, on the eve of the great Revolution, he was confronted by a dazzling display of talent. Jefferson delighted in French architecture, music, and natural science, and he was by no means indifferent to the charm of French society. He had little use, however, for the destructive and cynical wit that flourished in the last days of the Old Regime and usually chose as his friends those who were hopeful that the progress of Enlightenment would bring improvement to human society.

Jefferson's closest friend among the French thinkers was the marquis de Condorcet, a high-minded aristocrat who believed that the revolution he foresaw would usher in the complete triumph of mankind over misery, disease, and even death itself. Jefferson also approved and translated *The Ruins* by Count Constantin de Volney, who also prophesied a new dawn of liberty and justice on the ruins of monarchy and the church. He was personally friendly with the two radical abbés, Gabriel Bonnet de Mably and André Morellet, though he never followed them in blaming private property for human evil.

The American visitor was fascinated from time to time, but he was not entirely sympathetic with the doctrines of Claude Adrien Helvétius and the baron d'Holbach, the radical materialists of the last days of the Old Regime. Later, however, he was to follow with excitement the experiments on the brain by Georges Cabanis and others, who were working toward a physiological psychology. Jefferson rejoiced that Cabanis had struck hard blows against the "spiritualists," believers in an immaterial soul. He cited these experiments, however, to help establish the puzzling mixture of moralism and materialism that is discussed below as part of his religion.

Finally, in his old age Jefferson came increasingly to admire the work ,of A. L. C. Destutt de Tracy, whom he considered "unquestionably the ablest writer living on abstract subjects." Tracy was the founder of the science of "Ideology," an ambitious attempt to analyze and classify the operations of the mind on the basis of a more radical empiricism than Locke's. He was an enemy not only of traditional religion but also of the new, anti-empirical romanticism derived from Jean-Jacques Rousseau, a writer who held little interest for Jefferson. Jefferson admired Tracy's libertarian political economy and his naturalistic psychology. Above all he approved the boldness of his reasoning and the clarity of his style.

It is not altogether easy to put together in a system the philosophers Jefferson most admired: Epicurus, Hutcheson, Locke, Stewart, Condorcet, Tracy. This statement would not greatly trouble Jefferson, usually no friend to vast philosophical systems. What his favorite philosophers had in common is that they were useful—useful as guides to the moral conduct of life and the construction of a republican polity. For what was not useful, Jefferson usually had little taste.

POLITICAL THEORY

For Jefferson, as for most enlightened thinkers, political philosophy could never long be separated from moral philosophy; the nature of government depended on the nature of man. Jefferson's political theory, like his moral philosophy, was eclectic and not always consistent, except for its humane and liberating purposes and its premise that mankind was, on the whole, rational and benevolent.

Jefferson began as a matter of course with the standard republican theory, which was based on the classics and had developed throughout European history. Republican theory came to fruition in the seventeenth century in the work of Hugo Grotius, Samuel von Pufendorf, and Locke, and was carried on in the eighteenth century by Cesare Beccaria, Jean-Jacques Burlamaqui, and many others. The central content of this theory consisted of two related principles: natural rights and the social contract. Underlying both these ideas was the assumption of a rational universe: government existed for certain clear purposes and therefore its powers must be limited by those purposes. Jefferson rejected all assumptions that made any kind of government prescriptive or sacrosanct. He abhorred Thomas Hobbes' view that man's greedy and violent nature justifies all existing power structures, and he detested Edmund Burke's romantic glorification of the kind of government that has slowly and naturally evolved through the centuries.

His belief in unalienable natural rights may have sat a bit uneasily with his historical relativism: rights endure but everything else must change. The earth, Jefferson insisted, belongs to the living; no generation must bind its successor either by public debts or unchangeable constitutions. He once calculated that a generation lasts nineteen years; at the end of this time, every constitution should expire.

From the great writers of the end of the Roman Republic, from Cicero, Pliny, Sallust, and especially Tacitus, Jefferson drew evidence that frugality is necessary to the survival of republics. The simple, sturdy life of the farmer nourishes virtue; the corruptions of urban wealth destroy it. Like a great many other American thinkers in all periods, Jefferson was divided between his belief in noble and primitive simplicity on the one hand and his commitment to science and progress on the other.

A final major ingredient in his political thought was the tradition of balanced government drawn from Aristotle and Polybius. In its original form this theory taught that each of the three classic forms of government—monarchy, aristocracy, and democracy—had its own virtues, faults, and dangers. Through the centuries, many theorists had concluded that safety lay in a careful mixture of the three. In his youth Jefferson tended to accept the view of most literate Englishmen, interpreted for the world by Montesquieu, that the existing British government constituted a correct and admirable balance. Well before the American Revolution he became convinced that this balance had been perverted and corrupted and needed to be radically redressed in the direction of rule by the people. Here he was completely in accord with the Radical Whig tradition that had precariously survived in England, especially among religious dissenters, ever since the seventeenth-century Puritan Commonwealth. Jefferson did not feel exactly the same nostalgic passion for the Cromwellian Commonwealth that pervaded New England, since he did not share the religious views that sanctified this part of the past. Yet nobody admired more fervently the great heroes of the Commonwealth, especially John Milton, the theorist of intellectual liberty, and Algernon Sidney, the martyr of republican freedom. Jefferson, like a great many Americans, admired and quoted *Cato's Letters,* a collection of pamphlets by John Trenchard and Thomas Gordon that called for an end to oppression, corruption, and bribery.

On the basis of both Radical Whig interpretation of the future and late-Enlightenment French visions of the future, Jefferson became the great spokesman of democracy, a believer in the essential wisdom of the people and the safety of entrusting them with government. Yet this unchanging theoretical commitment was considerably qualified in practice: Jefferson was an eighteenth-century democrat, not a nineteenth- or twentieth-century egalitarian. The best form of government, he told Adams in a letter of 28 October 1813, was that which stripped away artificial distinctions and permitted government by the natural aristocracy, "the most precious gift of nature."

RELIGION

In religion Jefferson, a believer by temperament, began with a rejection, common enough in the Virginian upper class, of orthodox revealed Christianity. He particularly disliked those he considered mystics or "Platonizers" and those who seemed to him to preach the immoral paradoxes of predestination. In this category he included John Calvin, St. Augustine, and St. Paul. A believer in religious toleration, he sometimes sounded as though he based tolerance on indifference. In his *Notes on Virginia,* for instance, he made a statement that was often quoted against him: "The legitimate powers of government extend to such acts only as are injurious to others. But it does me no injury for my neighbour to say there are twenty gods, or no God. It neither picks my pocket nor breaks my leg."

More typical and far more eloquent was his preamble to the Virginia Statute for Religious Freedom, in which he attacks religious coercion as impious, tyrannical, and tending "to corrupt the principles of that very religion it is meant to encourage." To Jefferson religion was a private affair between a man and his god, for knowledge of whose existence and nature he must rely on the findings of reason alone. He was willing to respect religious organizations that were tolerant themselves, but he detested those that were not, including the Roman Catholic church and the established Congregational churches in New England. The New England clergy returned his hatred with interest, organizing against him in the election of 1800 and accusing him of being a deist or infidel. In that election, however, he received the support of a great many Baptists and Methodists, who differed with him on most religious matters but shared his hatred of establishments.

During most of his life Jefferson was a serious deist. For some men of the Enlightenment deism was a halfway house on the journey toward agnosticism or an affair of occasional conventional phrases. To Jefferson, however, a just and benevolent creator and ruler was an essential intellectual need, the source of both the law of nature and the moral sense. In his youth he read with approval the works of the English deists of the early eighteenth century. He especially admired the scholarly Conyers Middleton and, oddly, the Tory aristocrat Lord Bolingbroke.

Refusing to follow all the way the intriguing doctrines of the French materialists, Jefferson drew his own kind of materialism from a chance remark of Locke and the works of his friend Dr. Joseph Priestley, an advanced English Unitarian. The creator, according to Locke, Priestley, and Jefferson, could perfectly well have endowed one form of matter—man—with the power of thinking, just as he had endowed the sun with the power of attraction.

During his presidency Jefferson, again following Priestley and influenced also by another friend, Dr. Benjamin Rush, became far more sympathetic toward what, in a letter to Priestley of 21 March 1801, he called "the Christian philosophy,—the most sublime and benevolent, but most perverted system that ever shone on man." He was sure that careful study of the Gospels could rescue the original teachings of Jesus from the perversions and additions of the Platonizers. Reverently and painstakingly, Jefferson set about this task, confident that it would be as easy as finding "diamonds in a dunghill," hopeful that his purified Christianity could serve to unite sensible people. He produced two drastically revised and shortened versions of the Gospels, one of which was published long after his death, the other lost. Jefferson's Jesus, to judge by the surviving version and a recent reconstruction of the other, was an inspired moral prophet, teaching universal benevolence with sublime eloquence, making no claims to divinity, and founding no church. The mature Jefferson

53

may fairly be called a Unitarian Christian, radical and completely sincere. In his old age he rejoiced in the triumph of Unitarianism among his old political enemies in Eastern Massachusetts and was mistakenly confident that this rational and enlightened faith would soon become the religion of the entire republic.

SCIENCE AND THE ARTS

Jefferson's devotion to science, like his religion, reflected the commitments of the optimistic part of the Enlightenment. He once suggested, almost wistfully, that nature had intended him for "the tranquil pursuits of science," and he said several times that science was more important than politics. Involved most of his life in political pursuits that were anything but tranquil, he gave science what time he could. He is, so far, the only person to serve simultaneously as president of the United States and of the American Philosophical Society, then the nation's leading scientific organization.

Like most enlightened virtuosos of science, Jefferson placed no special value on overarching theories as against practical results. He had little interest, for instance, in contemporary arguments about the age of the earth or whether fire or water had played the greater part in its formation. Jefferson preferred to assume that the world had come into being in its present form, designed by a benevolent creator. Our task was to learn all we could about the creation in order to understand its manifold uses to mankind.

In science, as in everything, Jefferson was interested in what was useful. He cared passionately about agricultural methods; he studied plant husbandry, soil composition, and drainage and invented a new model plow. In a scientific spirit he concerned himself with currency, weights and measures, Anglo-Saxon grammar, and Indian dialects. For a new country, one of the most useful

forms of science was the discovery and classification of new life forms, from the moose to seashells. Jefferson gave a great deal of energy to refuting the opinion of some European scientists that all plants and animals degenerate in America. He argued patriotically that the very opposite was true, that New World animals were larger and more vigorous than their European counterparts. He was especially interested in the huge bones of the mammoth and the giant sloth, and was sure that these species must exist somewhere in the wilderness. For them to have been created and then extinguished would make no sense and serve no purpose.

In his ventures into literary and artistic pursuits Jefferson tried to follow his enlightened preference for cool reason and sober usefulness, but he was sometimes overcome by aesthetic passion. He probably loved architecture more than either science or politics and was the greatest American architect of his day. Like Voltaire and many other major figures of the Enlightenment, he was an epitome of correct classical taste. Gothic cathedrals were survivals of barbarism; the Georgian buildings that surrounded him in Virginia were of no interest. But, as he wrote a Parisian friend, when he encountered at Nîmes in southern France a small but perfect Roman temple, he stood gazing at it for hours, "like a lover at his mistress."

In his own architectural work, Jefferson meticulously followed the precepts and proportions of the Roman writer Vitruvius, as interpreted in the sixteenth century by Andrea Palladio. His building and rebuilding of Monticello was perfectionist to the point of fanaticism; it exhausted his fortune and left a supreme model of Palladian taste, none too comfortable to live in. Perhaps his chef d'oeuvre was the University of Virginia, where a careful presentation of all the major classical modes and an exact scale model of the Roman Pantheon were designed to inculcate in young Virginians a taste for classical greatness.

In Jefferson's literary tastes again we find

aesthetic passion struggling with utilitarianism. His love for classical historians, philosophers, poets, and dramatists went well beyond an appreciation of their moral utility. Outside these, however, he thought fiction and drama something of a waste of time unless they reinforced the moral sense. *Macbeth,* for instance, might make us hate wickedness more than a moral treatise. In his youth Jefferson was somewhat attracted by the melancholy preromantic strain in British poetry, and like his contemporaries he admired Ossian, the celebrated Celtic bard (who was later found to be a fake). He came to think, however, that poetry should be indulged in sparingly. When he tried to write some, he concluded that he was deficient in imagination. As he got older he stuck more and more to Virgil and Homer and, finally, especially to Homer.

Jefferson had a cultivated and fairly conventional taste in music. He delighted in what he heard in Paris and would have liked to import a French orchestra. He saw sculpture as primarily a means of preserving the memory of great and virtuous men. In painting Jefferson had little more than a conventional interest.

POLITICS IN PRACTICE

Despite his longings for the tranquil pursuit of architecture or science or for time to meditate on classical philosophy, Jefferson was absorbed in practical politics for most of his life. This was for him the theater in which the Enlightenment had to be defended against its enemies. It is in his political career that his devotion to enlightened principles can best be seen and understood. Here as elsewhere his passionate commitments were usually under the control of disciplined reason.

To begin with, his absolutely sincere devotion to democracy was qualified by the belief that people should have no more rights or powers than they were equipped to han-

dle. As he wrote on 14 July 1807 to a French *philosophe,* Pierre-Samuel Du Pont de Nemours, "What is practicable must often control what is pure theory: and the habits of the governed determine in a great degree what is practicable." Above all, the people, to be trustworthy, must be educated. The educational system Jefferson proposed for Virginia, in his Bill for the More General Diffusion of Knowledge, was public, but it was hardly egalitarian. For all free children of both sexes, the state would provide three years of elementary education, emphasizing not the Bible but history and morals. From each school the best student would be selected for further education, which would also be available to those whose parents could afford it. Through a series of similar competitive screenings, a few would be chosen for university training. Thus, as Jefferson put it in his *Notes on Virginia,* "the best geniuses" would be "raked from the rubbish," to the benefit of society and the state. Literacy and the moral sense would qualify all to make the basic political decisions, but the government would be carried on by men of liberal education.

When Jefferson said that it was safe to trust the people, he meant primarily the small landowning farmers, believed ever since Aristotle to be morally superior to town dwellers. Horrified by his encounter with the cities of Europe, he hoped that America could remain rural, importing European manufactures but no European vices. Once he went so far as to say that he counted on diseases like yellow fever to prevent the growth of great cities in the New World.

The most drastic concession Jefferson made to practical limitations was in his long and agonized confrontation with slavery, which he fully recognized to be a degrading institution, utterly incompatible with his enlightened commitments to justice. In a famous passage in the *Notes on Virginia* he speculates awkwardly on the question of mental and moral differences among the races. Believing that history would make it impossible for the two races to live together in freedom, he proposed for Virginia a scheme of gradual emancipation and deportation. Full of regret, Jefferson refrained from pushing this through. "It was found that the public mind would not bear the proposition. . . . Yet the day is not now distant when it must bear it and adopt it, or worse will follow."

Jefferson was no friend to simple majoritarian democracy. His Federalist opponents believed in the necessity of checks and balances in order to put a brake on the majority. Jefferson believed quite as much in similar mechanisms, primarily to lessen the danger of aristocratic takeover. The central government should exist, he thought, primarily for foreign affairs, while most powers should remain in state and local control. Governmental oppression should further be prevented by specific reservation of rights to the people. Jefferson can no more be placed with believers in powerfully centralized government than he can with those who believe all government evil. Government at all levels must be limited, he thought, in accordance with its rationally determined purposes.

Finally, the nature and limitations of Jefferson's enlightened optimism can be seen best of all in his attitude toward revolution. In theory, he regarded frequent alterations of government as desirable, and his rhetoric is often that of a committed revolutionary. In practice, however, during a long life in a revolutionary age he usually took the side of moderation. He belongs to the Revolutionary Enlightenment, but to its practical and gradualist wing; he was much more like Condorcet than like Rousseau and had nothing in common with Robespierre.

The exception to Jefferson's moderation was his all-out commitment to his first revolution and the first of the enlightened age—the American struggle for independence. In his *Summary View of the Rights of British Amer-*ica, written in 1774, he took the advanced position of denying altogether the right of Parliament to legislate for the colonies, and he invoked the truly revolutionary and enlightened principle of natural rights. In 1776 he gave magnificent expression to the principle of the natural right to revolution in the most radical founding document possessed by any major state. If any government becomes destructive of the rights it was founded to defend, "it is the right of the people to alter or to abolish it."

This revolution triumphed, and Jefferson was always loyal to its principles as he understood them. His second revolution was less successful. This was his effort to turn his beloved Virginia into a modern enlightened society. He did indeed help to achieve a sweeping and complete separation between church and state, the first of modern times. His changes in the inheritance laws, designed to diminish aristocratic power in Virginia, failed to accomplish its end. The rest of his proposals—an enlightened revision of laws and punishments, a uniform, graded system of public education, a gradual abolition of slavery—all failed of adoption.

Jefferson's third revolution, perhaps the best model for the kind he believed in most wholeheartedly, was constituted by his legislation for the territories of the United States. Classical state names and arbitrary geometrical boundaries he easily abandoned, but not the great measures ensuring the future triumph of enlightenment in the vast empire of liberty: a gradual movement of the territories to the status of equal and self-governing states, and a commitment to the support of popular education. In the Northwest, at least, it proved possible to prevent the curse of slavery from ever getting started.

Jefferson, like all ardent believers in humane progress, was thrilled by the outbreak of the French Revolution. He expected and hoped for its spread throughout Europe, believing that its triumph would prevent America from reverting to the British monarchical system. Yet when he was consulted by his French friends as a visiting expert on revolutions, he gave them very moderate advice. He advocated settling for a two-house legislature presided over by the king. As he expressed it in his letter of 20 March 1787 to Madame La Comtesse de Tessé, the French people

> would thus put themselves in the track of the best guide they can follow; they would soon overtake it, become its guide in turn, and lead to the wholesome modifications wanting in that model, and necessary to constitute a rational government. Should they attempt more than the established habits of the people are ripe for, they may lose all, and retard indefinitely the ultimate object of their aim.

When Jefferson sailed for home in 1789 he was confident in both the permanence and the moderation of the French Revolution. Even after the September prison massacres of 1792 and the Jacobin seizure of power, he remained loyal to the great hopes of the Revolution. In a letter to William Short of 3 January 1793, Jefferson deplores the execution of some innocent and admirable people, but also states the principle of the omelet and the eggs in remarkably uncompromising terms. "My own affections have been deeply wounded by some of the martyrs of this cause, but rather than it should have failed I would have seen half the earth desolated; were there but an Adam and an Eve left in every country, and left free, it would be better than as it is now." Soon after he wrote this letter, however, the outbreak of the full-scale Reign of Terror forced Jefferson to conclude that the Revolution had gone wrong, a fact he usually blamed on the depravity of city dwellers. He supported Washington's policy of neutrality between the French Republic and its monarchical British opponent. Though his own sympathies were always with France and against England, this preference was not nearly as important as the preservation of America, increasingly the world's best and only hope for enlightened republican government. Jefferson detested Napoleon, for some the heir both of the Enlightenment and the Revolution, as a scourge and a tyrant. In 1802, faced with the possibility of Napoleonic control of New Orleans and potentially of the American West, he even contemplated, in a letter of 18 April to Robert Livingston, the possibility of "marriage with the British fleet and nation." Fortunately that desperate choice was averted by the Louisiana Purchase, securing the West and the future against all forms of European tyranny. An enlightened believer in progress for all nations, Jefferson was also an American nationalist.

Jefferson's final revolution was his own election as president in 1800. In the struggle that preceded it, when the hopes of the republic seemed at stake, Jefferson surprised and infuriated his opponents by showing superb skill and practicality as a political organizer, willing when necessary to make use of dubious instruments despite his lofty precepts. He called his election the Revolution of 1800, but as Henry Adams points out in his ironical and masterly history of the Jefferson administration, he made sure that no sweeping revolution took place. The disappointment of his most radical followers started with his inaugural address, a plea for unity and tolerance that demanded only a minimum of political change, mostly corrective rather than innovative. This fortunate country, Jefferson announced, needed only one thing more to secure its happiness: "a wise and frugal government, which shall restrain men from injuring one another, which shall leave them otherwise free to regulate their own pursuits of industry and improvement, and shall not take from the mouth of labor the bread it has earned." Taxes were lowered and repressive laws allowed to lapse; but Jefferson did not destroy the banking system he had often denounced, he did not revamp the legal system, he did not even set up structures for the systematic support of science by the government. The only doctrinaire act of this man, who was so violently denounced as a revolutionary dreamer, was the embargo on foreign trade in 1807, an emergency measure designed to keep the nation out of European war. With the same purpose in mind, Jefferson largely abandoned his longstanding hostility to manufactures. His strictures against governmental power were drastically modified in order to defend the Louisiana Purchase. To protect this action, the embargo, and his whole very moderate revolution, Jefferson was willing to consider drastic actions. Forgetting for a moment his most consistent lifelong commitment—his devotion to free speech—he even toyed with the idea of a few highly selective prosecutions of his most violent press critics.

The key to Jefferson's combination of revolutionary rhetoric and moderate action lies, I believe, in his central commitment to Enlightenment optimism. Human nature, he insisted, was essentially virtuous and susceptible of improvement. The people would make the right choices, insofar as they were free to do so and qualified by education and experience. The European revolution might go wrong, but in this fortunate country, with longstanding experience of free institutions and land enough for "the hundredth and thousandth generation," the Enlightenment would prevail. To protect it against oppression, reactionary conspiracy, and war, any number of inconsistencies were justified. Everything could be compromised but the freedom to build a better future. With proper safeguards for liberty, that future was bright. Even the bigots of New England would eventually be reconciled. Only slavery cast a deep shadow over the American future, challenging Jefferson's fundamental hopes, but surely the progress of enlightenment would somehow bring this curse to an end. Europe would some day be redeemed, as Jefferson wrote to John Adams on 12 September 1821:

> Should the cloud of barbarism and despotism again obscure the science and liberties of Europe, this country remains to preserve and restore light and liberty to them. In short, the flames kindled on the 4th of July, 1776, have spread over too much of the globe to be extinguished by the feeble engines of despotism; on the contrary, they will consume these engines and all who work them.

Jefferson did not find it easy to preserve these noble hopes. His personal life was too sad, and his political experience too broad and deep to allow him the easy cheerfulness of Voltaire's Dr. Pangloss. To believe in the moral sense and the enlightened future was absolutely essential to his equilibrium: his was a strenuous, at times almost a desperate optimism. This I think explains the unremitting seriousness of his style in speech and action: there was no room for frivolity when the stakes were so high and the struggle so tense.

In his old age Jefferson agreed with Adams that the eighteenth century, the century of revolution and enlightenment, was the most honorable to mankind. Neither he nor Adams was altogether comfortable with some major developments in the new century: reaction in Europe, and in America the revival of emotional, evangelical religion. He could hardly have approved the romantic populism that has dominated much of our politics, the business conservatism that has been its main opponent, or the conservative, literalist religion that has repeatedly asserted its power. Jefferson was and remains a man of the eighteenth century, a splendid representative of that century's Enlightenment at its most generous and useful.

Republicanism

JOHN HOWE

In a letter of 13 August 1777 to Benjamin Franklin, Thomas Jefferson observed that the people of Virginia "seem to have deposited the monarchical and taken up the republican government with as much ease as would have attended their throwing off an old and putting on a new suit of clothes. Not a single throe," Jefferson asserted, "has attended this important transformation." Jefferson may have exaggerated the ease with which Virginians exchanged monarchy for republicanism, but he was correct in pointing up the importance of the change, for along with national independence, America's successful adoption of republicanism gave the revolution its momentous importance.

Unlike more recent colonial rebellions in which Third World peoples have based their new identities on themes of racial and cultural distinctiveness from their European colonial masters, England's North American colonists turned to politics and constitutionalism for their major categories of self-definition. Most members of the revolutionary generation spoke English and guided their lives by variants of English custom, religion, and law. What set them unmistakably apart as a revolutionary people, in their own minds as in the minds of Europeans, was their commitment to republicanism. Not only did 1776 signify the creation of a new nation, but it represented the moment when republican theory became historical reality. Jefferson shared the drama and enthusiasm of that historic occasion.

For Jefferson, as for most of his contemporaries, the central principles of republicanism were clear: rejection of monarchical government and aristocratic privilege; an emphasis on individual rights and public liberty; a determination to limit governmental power; sensitivity to the intimate connections between republican forms of government and the underlying social order. The tasks of designing republican government and fashioning a republican society were anything but simple, for they involved constitutional structures, political arrangements, private and public morality, religion, economic values and behavior, and forms of social organization.

Members of the revolutionary generation disagreed—strongly and loudly—over such questions as how democratic their new republican governments should be; what balance was required between individual liberty and social obligation; and what mix between agrarian, commercial, and manufacturing activity was desirable. Those disagreements reflected differences of personal philosophy and interest, but they were rooted as well in regional patterns of historical experience. That was true of Jefferson, for his understanding of revolutionary republicanism was solidly grounded in the tangible, immediate experiences of Virginia life.

Jefferson was familiar with the major theorists of republicanism. As the imperial crisis with England deepened during the 1760s and early 1770s, he searched the writings of Sir John Harington and Sir Philip Sidney, John Trenchard and Thomas Gordon, as well as John Locke and Montesquieu for guidance on defending public liberty and controlling arbitrary power. Following independence, he read further in search of the universal truths on which republican government should be based. In classic Enlightenment fashion, he believed in an underlying system of natural laws that provided the essential logic of republicanism and was discoverable by human reason.

For Jefferson, however, republicanism was not primarily an abstraction; he sought republican truth, as he sought truth of all sorts, in the specific, concrete circumstances of life. Experience—tangible, immediate, vivid—was for him the essential key to understanding. Knowledge was above all situational; it emerged from the immediate circumstances of life.

The immediate, tangible character of Jefferson's republican thought was in part a function of his commitment to Newtonian science, with its emphasis on the empirical gathering and evaluation of evidence. Newton he thought one of the three greatest men who had ever lived. Throughout his life, Jefferson examined the world about him by measuring and recording, and thereby understanding it.

The experiential cast of Jefferson's thought derived as well from his close adherence to Lockean sense psychology. Jefferson believed that humans possessed from birth an innate moral sense, a conscience that enabled them instinctively to distinguish right from wrong. Knowledge, however, as Locke had argued, was not instinctive but acquired. It resulted from the mind's efforts to order the flood of sense impressions that encounters with the natural and social worlds produced. "The opinions and beliefs of men," Jefferson explained in his Bill for Establishing Religious Freedom, "depend not on their own will, but follow involuntarily the evidence proposed to their minds."

The situational character of Jefferson's republicanism also reflected his personal temperament. Jefferson took delight in the variety and multiplicity of nature. It stimulated his curiosity, gratified his aesthetic sense, and provided satisfying evidence of God's benevolence. He reached out eagerly to the world about him by acting as well as observing. Thus he learned the law not only by studying but by practicing it, and he mastered architecture through the long process of creating Monticello. More to the point, he grasped the true meaning of "revolutionary republicanism" by deep and continuing immersion in American public life.

Jefferson never found public service easy. Repeatedly, he lamented his absence from family and friends, bemoaned his financial sacrifices, and deplored the controversies that seemed inevitably to surround public office. Time and again, he declared his determination to exchange the travail of public politics for the tranquillity of private life. On several occasions—after his tempestuous term as Virginia's governor, when he returned in 1789 from an extended diplomatic mission in Europe, and again after four years in Washington's cabinet—he withdrew from public life, vowing never to take up the burdens of office again. In each case, however, he soon reneged, and returned to the political fray, drawn by a sense of public duty and a desire to understand better America's evolving experiment in republicanism.

Jefferson's republican thought was tied inseparably to the practical tasks of statecraft. His major writings—the *Summary View of the Rights of British America*, Declaration of Independence, draft of the Virginia constitution and revised legal code, reports as secretary of state, and presidential messages—were exercises in practical leadership. Even his correspondence reveals his fascination with praxis, that intimate, reciprocal connection between thought and action. To understand Jefferson's republicanism is to grasp its grounding in experience and its intimate association with the practical tasks of founding a republic.

The years between 1776 and 1783 were crucial to Jefferson's republicanism, for it was then that he fashioned his basic understanding of what American republicanism should be. During these years he was deeply involved in the affairs of the new American nation. He attended Congress, crafted the Declaration of Independence, and later, as war governor of Virginia, labored to meet Congress' urgent pleas for supplies and troops. The successful formation of a new nation was, he believed, essential to the protection of American liberty. Yet during these early years Virginia was his preoccupying concern, for Virginia drew his primary loyalties and there he spent most of his time. As a result, Jefferson's republicanism was shaped profoundly by the particular circumstances and revolutionary experience of his native state. It was his intimate knowledge of Virginia and its people that gave his revolutionary republicanism its vividness and distinctive meaning.

In the mid-1780s the focus of Jefferson's republicanism shifted from Virginia to the nation at large. The reasons had to do with changes both in his public career and in the nation. Responding to those changes, he refashioned certain elements of his republican belief—his attitudes toward central government, his views on political equality, and his understanding of the problems posed for American republicanism by economic and social development. Even so, he continued to draw heavily on the republicanism he had devised during the revolution. A clear understanding of Jefferson's republicanism must focus on those earlier years and the republican world view that he then created.

VIRGINIA'S WELL-ORDERED REPUBLIC

The focus of Jefferson's republicanism was government and the politics that surrounded it, for government exercised power, and power threatened republican liberty. Virginia was the setting in which power and liberty would have to be reconciled.

The Virginia Republic

Evidence abounds of Jefferson's commitment to Virginia: Monticello's hold on his imagination; the rich and lovingly crafted description of the state's topography and climate, flora and fauna, society and politics, laws and religion contained in his *Notes on Virginia;* and the constancy with which he served his state during the threatening years of revolution and war.

The reasons for that commitment are not hard to find. Virginia was what Jefferson knew and his social and personal ties were there. Prior to independence Jefferson had spent all but a few months of his life within the state's boundaries. Born at Shadwell in

Goochland County, Jefferson had lived at Tuckahoe on the James River near Richmond, in Williamsburg where he attended the College of William and Mary, and at Monticello, his mountaintop retreat near the crest of the Blue Ridge. Through the years he had traveled across the colony, practicing law, investigating nature, and coming to know the people. Prior to 1783, when he left Virginia to attend Congress and then go abroad, Jefferson was continuously immersed in revolutionary affairs within his home state.

Jefferson's intimate involvement with Virginia reflected his secure position as a member of the state's planter elite. By the time of American independence, he owned nearly fourteen thousand acres of land and over 135 slaves, had married the daughter of one of the colony's wealthiest families, and was firmly established in Virginia society. Already he had spent seven years in the House of Burgesses, consorted on familiar terms with a royal governor, and represented Virginia in the Continental Congress. In the years following independence, he served again in the House of Delegates and as wartime governor. Small wonder that he should value Virginia so highly and identify so closely with its people.

More than personal biography, however, focused Jefferson's attention on his home state. It was a central tenet of revolutionary belief that republics were viable only in small, contiguous areas where society was relatively homogeneous and government could be kept simple. The reasons for that were several. Only powerful governments, it was believed, could effectively administer large areas, and power was regarded as the bane of republics. The economic and social differences characteristic of large countries were understood to generate "factions," organized private interests that sought their own advantage at the expense of the public good. Faction was the cancer of republicanism, for it eroded people's sense of public

duty—their willingness to forego private interest, if need be, for the public good—and generated civic strife. "Public virtue" was the term for this self-sacrificing stance. In republics, where kings and aristocracies, armies and established churches—the traditional agencies of social control—were missing, such conflict easily spiraled out of control into civil war.

Republican theory, then, required that no area larger than an individual state could be encompassed by a republican system. Jefferson had to deal with that belief. The United States he regarded not as a republic, but an alliance of thirteen republics. America's republican experiment was to unfold within each of them, rather than in the nation as a whole. Jefferson shaped his revolutionary republicanism, then, with the special needs and circumstances of Virginia squarely in mind.

The Limits of Republican Reform

Immediately after independence, Jefferson turned to the task of building a republican order in Virginia. He was deeply impressed with the historical importance of the undertaking. America's revolution, he believed, represented a fundamental turning point in human history, for it signified the rejection of a past filled with social and political tyranny and the opening of a new era in which human liberty would flourish. Not only his liberty, but that of generations yet unborn, depended on what Jefferson and his contemporaries did. It was an awesome but exhilarating responsibility. And so Jefferson plunged headlong into the civic life of revolutionary Virginia, eager to seize the opportunity of building a republican future.

Jefferson never described the revolutionary task in language as breathtaking as Thomas Paine's. "We are now really another people," Paine exulted in 1776. "We have it in our power to begin the world over again.'' Still Jefferson knew that the challenges of republicanism would not be easily met, for the necessary changes would threaten deeply entrenched interests and long-standing ways of life. He challenged the institution of slavery, argued for religious freedom, proposed a system of public education, and spoke openly against social and political privilege. Perhaps most impressive of all was his open, embracing attitude toward change. Jefferson was oriented toward the future, not the past, toward a new world constantly changing, not an old world kept intact. He harbored no utopian visions, for he was too deeply embedded in the real world for that. But he struggled to free himself and his society from the constraining influence of tradition, and he believed passionately that human reason could fashion a better tomorrow.

At the same time, when Jefferson turned from rejecting British authority to the practical task of building a republican Virginia, he proved less the revolutionary than the careful reformer. Though independence irretrievably separated past from future, he was sensitive to the continuities that carried across that chasm. Virginia's republican order would be new, but it would emerge organically from what had existed before.

The explanations for his measured approach to republican reform are several. For one thing, his republicanism was ideologically moderate. Set against such adamant conservatives as the wealthy planter Edmund Pendleton, Jefferson looks radical indeed. Compared with the demands of many blacks for personal freedom and calls by frontier settlers and other ordinary folk for political democracy, however, Jefferson's reform program appears cautious and carefully limited. At no time did he reject Virginia's established social and political orders. Indeed, Virginia society and politics seemed to him already republican-like in essential ways. Important changes would be

made, but they would be accomplished gradually and would be designed as much to prevent antirepublican developments as to recast existing ways of life. Jefferson was optimistic about Virginia's republican future because he believed that it could flow so logically from Virginia's past.

Jefferson's moderation was a function of personal temperament as well. Order, balance, and restraint characterized everything that he did. The elegant symmetry of Monticello; his famous dialogue between Head and Heart; the balanced structure he proposed for republican government; the pastoral calm he offered as his social ideal; his conviction that nature, both physical and human, was ordered by stable, harmonious systems—all reveal his essential character.

Finally, Jefferson's strategy of reform rather than radical reconstruction derived from his own secure place in Virginia society and politics. His position as an insider gave him the authority and know-how to be politically effective. At the same time, his social and political commitments limited what he thought the scope of reform ought to be.

Abolishing Monarchy

Cleansing Virginia of monarchy was the essential first step in Jefferson's strategy of republicanization. Independence ended Virginia's political and constitutional ties with England but left the task of rooting out any lingering monarchical principles that Virginians might have absorbed during their long association with royal government.

Though Virginia lay thousands of miles distant from the English court, the institution and principles of monarchy loomed large in Jefferson's imagination. The revolutionary crisis had made brutally clear the disruptive force of royal power. More was involved than power, for the monarchy lay at the very center of Anglo-American identity. The great, defining events of English history

—Henry VIII's break with Rome, the accession and rule of Elizabeth, the English Civil War and Restoration, the Revolutionary Settlement of 1688—revolved around the monarchy, its authority, and attempts to constrain it. In provincial Virginia, laws had been passed and offices filled in the name of the king, while news of the English government was eagerly followed. In 1760, Jefferson had helped celebrate the accession of a new king, George III, to the English throne, while in 1763 he shared in the intense national pride generated by the great Anglo-American victory over the French in the Seven Years' War. That victory seemed clear evidence of the grandeur of England's monarchical order.

Rejecting the king's authority in 1776, moreover, was to commit treason and launch onto the uncertain seas of independence; few were able to take that step easily. The difficulties, psychological as well as constitutional, of breaking with the Crown explain the vehemence of the colonists' final attack upon it. For example, the scurrilous language of Paine's *Common Sense* was intended to destroy American respect for monarchical government while the long catalog of "repeated injuries and usurpations . . . having in direct object the establishment of an absolute tyranny" with which Jefferson charged George III in the Declaration of Independence were intended to demonstrate the king's unfitness "to be the ruler of a free people." The rhetorical power of both statements indicates how difficult and how important it was to destroy American loyalties to the monarchy and what it represented.

Jefferson made his rejection of monarchy explicit in the preamble of a 1776 bill he proposed for "new-modelling" Virginia's government. George III, he declared, had transformed "the kingly office in this government" into "a detestable and insupportable tyranny." It was thus necessary that the monarchy be "divested of all its privileges, powers, and prerogatives." "George III," he repeated so there could be no confusion about the matter, "hereby is deposed from the kingly office within this government."

Jefferson then proceded to delete all references to the monarch from the new, republican frame of government. In Bill No. 98 introduced in May 1779, public officials were to "renounce the character of subject or citizen of any Prince" and swear "to be faithful . . . to the said commonwealth of Virginia." References to the monarch were dropped as well from governmental ceremonies, while laws "inculcating principles inconsistent with republicanism" were expunged from the statute books.

Such changes in the public language of government were relatively easy to accomplish. It would be more difficult to eradicate from people's minds deep-seated principles long associated with monarchy, such as hierarchical authority, aristocratic privilege, and deferential attitudes toward governmental power. Jefferson, however, was confident that it could be done because monarchy was ultimately inconsistent with the basic conditions of Virginia life. Monarchical government was "artificial" and "unnatural," dependent for its continued existence on force, the deadening weight of tradition, and an aristocratic social order, none of which existed in Virginia.

Controlling Power

Purging Virginia of monarchy was important because it cleared the way for the more positive task of building a republican political order. During the years following independence, Jefferson turned to that task with eager determination.

Independence plunged Virginia into a constitutional crisis, for in breaking with the Crown, Virginians destroyed all existing bases of governmental authority. Their republican regime would have to be fashioned entirely anew. Even before independence, while he struggled in Congress with the deepening imperial crisis, Jefferson's thoughts turned homeward to the task of building the revolution in Virginia. In May 1776, he wrote from Philadelphia to his friend Thomas Nelson expressing his eagerness to return home. Establishing republican governments in the states, he declared, was "the whole object of the present controversy," and he was determined to have a part in it. In September, Jefferson left Congress, resumed his seat in the Virginia assembly, and plunged into the task of constitution-making. He brought with him a nearly completed plan for a new republican government. Over the next several years he labored (in large part unsuccessfully) to achieve his constitutional goals as well as to revise Virginia's laws and shape state politics. These efforts tell us a great deal about what he understood revolutionary republicanism to mean.

Nothing was more basic to Jefferson's republicanism than his fear of governmental power and his determination to contain it. Jefferson shared the conviction, broadly held among the revolutionary generation, that governmental power posed a continuing threat to human liberty. By "power" Jefferson meant the capacity of some individuals to control others. Liberty signified power's absence, that is, personal autonomy and independence or the ability to control one's own life.

Jefferson believed that continuing, inescapable tension between these two principles constituted the central theme of human history. That tension arose because power was expansive, always encroaching on liberty's domain. This happened because power worked destructively on human nature, stimulating selfish interests and exciting private ambitions. When possessed of power, individuals inevitably used it for their own advantage and at the expense of others' liberty. Republican theorists warned of power's danger. Harington and Sidney had done so in seventeenth-century England, and the essayists Trenchard and Gordon kept the theme alive a century later. The

conflict between power and liberty was real for the revolutionary generation; their desperate clash with powerful England persuaded them that the warnings were true. The central task of republican statesmanship, therefore, was to limit governmental power and nourish public liberty. Of that Jefferson was absolutely certain.

He understood that power was a necessary attribute of responsible government. Liberty itself, to say nothing of life and property, required protection by stable and effective government. As war governor of Virginia from 1779 to 1781, Jefferson despaired over the state's inability to protect its people from invasion or successfully administer public affairs.

War put an unusual and dangerous premium on governing power. "Necessity is law," warned Jefferson, "in times of war most especially"—reason enough for republics to avoid war whenever possible. The ongoing problem of republican statesmanship was not to enhance governmental power but to contain it, to find ways of controlling its restless tendency to expand. A written constitution, clear and exact in its definitions of what government could and could not do, was one essential weapon in that never-ending struggle.

Jefferson grounded his republicanism in the doctrine of a fundamental law, a written constitution existing prior to government and defining what government should be. The English constitution consisted of the Common Law, parliamentary statutes, judicial decisions, and sacred documents such as Magna Carta and the Revolutionary Settlement of 1688. Experience had proven, however, that England's constitution was too vague and inexact to protect American liberties. Virginia's fundamental law would place clear limits on governmental power, specify the liberties government was intended to protect, and be written down for all to see.

Jefferson began his constitutional draft with a long recital of George III's arbitrary behavior, then moved to a description of the "fundamental laws and principles of government [that] shall henceforth be established." After describing separate legislative, executive, and judicial branches, Jefferson came in Part IV to a delineation of "Rights, Private and Public" that government was not to infringe, including "full and free liberty of religious opinion," freedom of the press, and guarantees against a peacetime army.

His concern to "fence in" government also explains his emphasis on dividing it into distinct branches capable of standing watch against each other. "The Legislative, Executive and Judiciary offices," he explained, "shall be kept for ever separate, & no person exercising the one shall be capable of appointment to the others, or to either of them." Government's power centered in its capacity to pass legislation, so Jefferson provided for two legislative houses, "to wit a house of Representatives, and a house of Senators." The assent of both was required to make law.

The rule of law was another principle essential, in Jefferson's mind, to control governmental power and protect republican liberty. Monarchy's threat to liberty had come from its arbitrary, manipulative use of the law. Conspicuous among the crimes charged by Jefferson against George III was his misuse of the law:

> He has refused his Assent to Laws, the most wholesome and necessary for the public good. He has forbidden his Governors to pass laws of immediate and pressing importance. . . . He has called together legislative bodies at places unusual, uncomfortable, and distant from the despository of their public Records. . . . He has obstructed the Administration of Justice, by refusing his Assent to Laws for establishing Judiciary powers . . . [and] has made Judges dependent on his Will.

No wonder Americans rejected a monarch who used the law so blatantly against public liberty.

Laws clear in their meaning, just in their purposes, and equitably administered were the ligaments that held a republican order together. Thus in his constitutional draft Jefferson described how new laws were to be passed, provided a full complement of courts to insure the speedy and easy administration of justice, and stipulated that judges should hold office "during good behavior" rather than at the pleasure of politicians.

Jefferson sought in other ways as well to guarantee regular laws, regularly administered. The law's intent, he affirmed, should be clear, while punishments for its violation should be "strict and inflexible." A judge, he stated in a letter to Edmund Pendleton of 26 August 1776, should act as "a mere machine" so the law's protection would "be dispensed equally & impartially," not by "the eccentric impulses of whimsical, capricious designing man."

He also labored to reform Virginia's legal code. From 1776 to 1779 he served on a special legislative commission appointed to revise and consolidate existing colonial statutes and Parliamentary enactments into a uniform, republican code of law. Jefferson's goals in pressing so urgently for legal reform were several. One was to simplify existing laws so they could be more easily known and understood. Legal revision was also Jefferson's vehicle for republican social reform. His third purpose, as he later recalled in his autobiography, was to establish "a system by which every fibre would be eradicated of antient or future aristocracy; and a foundation laid for a government truly republican." "Our legislation under the regal government," he wrote, "had many very vicious points which urgently required reformation."

Jefferson and his associates quickly decided not to compile an entirely new legal institute, for such a task lay well beyond their time and competence. Nor did they recast ancient statutes in modern language, primarily because they feared that new language would call forth a flood of clarifying litigation. Instead the commissioners produced a selective revision of 126 bills, including statutes for establishing religious freedom, proportioning crimes and punishments, providing for the general diffusion of knowledge, and determining the criteria of citizenship. Jefferson correctly judged these revisions one of his major legacies.

Popular Sovereignty

Popular sovereignty was another fundamental principle of Jefferson's revolutionary republicanism. He meant two things by the term: first, that government had no existence apart from the people but derived its authority directly from them; and second, that government should be accountable to the people in its day-to-day operations. Together these concepts represented a profound change from the monarchical assumptions that had informed Virginia's provincial government.

In England's monarchical system, government and people were regarded as separate parties that contracted together, the people offering obedience in return for the Crown's protection. The English monarchy was far from absolute, especially with the limitations put upon it by the Revolutionary Settlement. But in both constitutional theory and political fact the Crown possessed extensive governing authority of its own. When Crown and Parliament acted together their authority was virtually absolute. Short of the people's ultimate right of revolution, sovereignty—that is, ultimate governing authority—lay with government, not the people. Such were the facts of English constitutionalism, and such had been the underlying logic of Virginia's provincial order.

In a republican system, the relationship between government and people was profoundly different. Republican government had no existence apart from the people, for it was created by them and derived its "just powers from the consent of the governed." Republican elections were to be held and government was to begin only after a constitution had been drawn. That constitution should be created by a convention elected by the people specifically for that purpose. To Jefferson's distress, Virginia's existing legislature, an extralegal rump assembly having no clearly defined authority, wrote the state's new constitution. If government can write a constitution, Jefferson warned, it can abolish it as well, and then what protection against arbitrary action would such a document be? Not until 1830 did Virginians choose a constitutional convention and re-create their fundamental law. To the end of his life, Jefferson believed that the foundation of Virginia republicanism remained insecure.

Popular sovereignty required not only that government be founded on the people's will but that it be continuingly accountable to them as well. Only if government was held responsible for its actions could public liberty be preserved. The colonists had learned that hard lesson when they discovered how ineffective their petitions to king and Parliament for relief from oppressive laws had been.

Virginia's written constitution contributed to the goal of accountability. The beginnings of English government were lost in the mists of the ancient past and its constitution had evolved gradually over many centuries. Virginia's republican constitution, by contrast, was the product of a single, purposeful act of creation. Its origins and principles were clearly known.

Accountability presumed the full and accurate flow of information about government officials and their behavior. Tyranny, Jefferson warned, lurked where government was shrouded in secrecy and misinformation. For Jefferson, freedom of speech and press were natural as well as constitutional rights. To constrain thought and expression was to violate human nature. It was in connection with the right of republican citizens to examine and criticize their leaders that issues of free expression came most alive for Jefferson. He was no absolutist on issues of speech and press. Still, he believed the open, untrammeled discussion of government was essential to the defense of republican liberty. "Printing presses shall be free," he wrote in his constitutional draft, "except so far as by commission of private injury cause may be given of private action."

Frequent elections were also essential to republican accountability. In his constitutional draft, Jefferson specified annual elections for Virginia's new House of Representatives and placed limitations on the number of terms that legislators could hold office. Elections, frequently held and broadly based, were essential protections against official misconduct. Not only did they provide regular occasions for evaluating official behavior, but voting stimulated civic consciousness among the citizenry, thus strengthening the ties between government and people. Jefferson proposed a bill requiring qualified voters who failed to participate in elections to pay a double portion of taxes the following year.

At the same time, Jefferson had no desire to institute government by popular impulse. The doctrine of popular sovereignty was intended by him to be prophylactic, a safeguard against arbitrary behavior rather than an instrument for shaping governmental action. In the context of the nineteenth century's more egalitarian, democratic politics, popular sovereignty would take on more positive dimensions; but not for Jefferson in revolutionary Virginia.

This concern to limit the impact of popular sentiment on republican government was consistent with the central task of republican constitution-making—to restrain governmental action, not facilitate it. Republican laws were to be few and "mild,"

not numerous and oppressive. Jefferson, moreover, had no experience with an activist government. Virginia's colonial regime had played only a limited role in people's lives. Its agenda had been narrow and its budget small.

There were limits, then, to Jefferson's doctrine of popular sovereignty. Those limits were closely tied to another of his republican principles, political equality.

Political Equality

Jefferson embraced the doctrine of political equality more fully than many of Virginia's revolutionary elite. All men, he affirmed, possessed the same natural rights and merited similar protection by government. He favored something very close to universal white male suffrage. Jefferson agreed with the standard eighteenth-century dictum that citizens should demonstrate a commitment to the community before being entrusted with the franchise, but he offered any number of ways of meeting that requirement: a freehold of a quarter of an acre in town or twenty-five acres in the country; payment of taxes the preceding two years; or simply evidence of residency over a two-year span. Jefferson even provided in his constitutional draft for free allotments of public land so that "every person of full age" could possess at least fifty acres "in full and absolute dominion." His point was clear: the franchise was an essential right of every republican citizen.

He also called for the strict apportionment of Virginia's new lower house according to the number of voters in each county. In a republic, he insisted, equal representation was "capital and fundamental." Each man's vote should count as much as any other's.

Not every Virginian, however, was to be the political equal of every other in Jefferson's republican scheme. Together with most of his male contemporaries, he imagined that men alone were qualified to participate in public life and thus take on political identity. American women, he advised Anne Willing Bingham from Paris in May 1788, should be "too wise to wrinkle their foreheads with politics." Their role was "to soothe & calm the minds of their husbands returning ruffled from political debate." Jefferson made the point unmistakably clear to his recently married daughter Martha in a letter dated 4 April 1790. After observing that her "new condition" would "call for abundance of little sacrifices," he reminded her that "the happiness of your life depends now on . . . continuing to please a single person," her husband.

Women, in Jefferson's judgment, possessed neither the economic nor the personal independence essential to political judgment. Their emotional nature further disqualified them for republican citizenship. They were suited instead to serve as republican mothers, cultivating the domestic virtues and nurturing future republican citizens.

Nor did Jefferson believe that black freedmen could meet the responsibilities of republican citizenship—to say nothing of black slaves whose condition so obviously disqualified them. Throughout his life, Jefferson wrestled with the philosophic and scientific dimensions of race. He examined evidence of black intellectual and cultural accomplishment, as reflected for example in the life of the black mathematician Benjamin Banneker, yet he remained persuaded that blacks had neither the innate capacities nor the experience to qualify them for republican self-government. That seemed to Jefferson clear from observing his own slaves at Monticello. The bill he introduced in 1779 describing "Who shall be Deemed Citizens of this Commonwealth" specified "white persons."

Jefferson was convinced that the two races could never live peacefully together. In part that was because of the "deep, rooted prejudices entertained by the whites," but also because of "ten thousand recollections, by the blacks, of the injuries they have sustained." Efforts to join the two people, he predicted grimly, would "produce convulsions, which will probably never end but in the extermination of the one or the other race." Jefferson thought slavery an abomination, urged its partial abolition, and called for an immediate end to the slave trade. However, he coupled those calls with proposals for the colonization of freed blacks outside Virginia. On that point he remained adamant.

Jefferson was more uncertain about Native Americans, largely because his attitudes toward them were less rigidly controlled by notions of racial inferiority. Throughout his life, Jefferson retained a fascination with American Indians and their potential for "civilized" behavior. He admired their courage, independence, and primitive innocence and believed them physiologically equal to whites. Concerning their intelligence and moral faculties, he was decidedly less certain. Jefferson entertained the possibility, even the hope, that over time Native Americans could be Christianized, civilized, and ultimately assimilated into white society. Even in his most sanguine moments, however, he placed that possibility far into the future. Never did he imagine that Native Americans, with perhaps rare individual exceptions, could in his own time exercise the responsibilities of republican citizenship.

Adult white males, then, constituted Jefferson's republican citizenry—not a surprising limitation given the cultural values of late-eighteenth-century Virginia. Even among those republican citizens, however, his definition of political equality was far from all-encompassing, especially when it came to matters of political leadership.

Jefferson opposed special property requirements for public office. "Every person . . . qualified to elect," he stipulated in his constitutional draft, "shall be capable of being elected." That did not mean, however, that every individual should have an equal voice in public affairs. He thought the voice of ordinary people was often virtuous; "The decisions of the people in a body," he affirmed in his letter to Pendleton dated 26 August 1776, "will be more honest and more disinterested than those of wealthy men." More virtuous, perhaps, but not more wise, for he thought popular actions were often neither rational nor well informed. The popular will, moreover, was subject to manipulation by ambitious demagogues. As much as he valued popular vigilance against official misconduct, Jefferson valued just as strongly the guiding role of a republican leadership elite, a "natural aristocracy" of wisdom and talent.

European aristocrats—with their immense wealth, political power, and privileges sanctioned by custom and law—Jefferson viewed with a deep and abiding distrust. Given the visible power of aristocratic classes throughout the Atlantic world in the eighteenth century, his fear of them is understandable. But Jefferson was careful to point out the differences between his republican aristocracy and the aristocracies of Europe. The first was based on "natural" qualities of judgment and ability, the second on "artificial" distinctions of family name and wealth. A republican aristocracy was replenished each generation as new individuals demonstrated their qualifications for it; an artificial aristocracy passed its privileges intact from one generation to the next. A republican aristocracy gained only the burden of public service, while traditional aristocracies used their power for personal aggrandizement.

Persons of talent and virtue, Jefferson emphasized, could be found in every social class, and he urged that leadership roles not be limited to the wealthy and well known. Leaders, he asserted in his Bill for the More General Diffusion of Knowledge, should be

"called to that charge without regard to wealth, birth, or other accidental condition or circumstance." Jefferson demonstrated his commitment to that principle by proposing in his bill a new system of public education that would provide all young men with basic literacy and progressively filter out a leadership elite.

Jefferson's aristocracy of talent, however, was not intended to be class-neutral. Male children of wealthy planters would clearly have special opportunities to develop the knowledge, self-confidence, governing experience, and personal independence so essential to republican leadership. Even Jefferson's educational scheme became decidedly less equal the higher up the educational pyramid youngsters climbed. Whereas every white child, male and female, would receive basic literacy in the local or "hundred" schools, if necessary at public expense, only one of the most promising "public foundationers" from each of the local "hundreds" was to be sent each year to the district grammar schools. By the end of the second year there, only the single best publicly supported scholar would be chosen to continue in each of the twenty-four district schools; the rest would be sent home. Finally, one of those remaining "seniors" would be selected each year to attend the College of William and Mary, "there to be educated, boarded, and clothed, three years" additionally at public expense. By contrast, his entire educational system would remain open to all qualified children whose parents could pay their way. The hundred schools, Jefferson explained in his *Notes on Virginia,* were intended to enable "the less wealthy people" to "understand their rights" and "exercise with intelligence their parts in self-government." That was sufficient for citizenship, but republican leadership required considerably more.

Jefferson sought in very practical ways to buffer Virginia's new republican government against excessive popular influences.

The lower house ought truly to represent the people; the senate, however, should not. In designing the upper house, as Jefferson explained to Pendleton in August 1776, he sought to accomplish two goals: insuring that the wisest men were chosen and making them "perfectly independent" once elected. "I have ever observed," Jefferson continued, "that a choice by the people themselves is not generally distinguished for its wisdom." It is instead usually "crude and heterogeneous." Far better to filter public sentiment by having senators chosen by the lower house. Jefferson further reinforced senatorial independence by giving them nine-year terms. Sufficient guarantees against their arbitrary behavior, he thought, could be provided by making them ineligible for reelection. This would "keep alive [their] regard to the public good" by returning them to "the mass of the people" where they would again "become the governed instead of the governor[s]." Senatorial independence was so important, Jefferson acknowledged to Pendleton, that he "could submit, tho' not so willingly to an appointment for life, or to any thing rather than a mere creation by & dependance on the people."

Jefferson's views on the nature of political representation also reveal his less than fully democratic sensibilities. Elections served to legitimize government and authorize representatives to act on behalf of the public good. They were not intended, at least in ordinary times, to serve as referenda either on public policy issues or the political judgment of public officials. Even the House of Representatives, Jefferson declared in his draft constitution, "shall be free to act according to their own judgment and conscience." Honesty, informed commitment to public liberty, diligent attention to the duties of office—these were the only obligations of Jefferson's republican aristocracy.

Jefferson distrusted the motives of politicians such as Patrick Henry who openly courted the people. Republican leaders should not seek public office but accept its burdens when thrust upon them. Jefferson seldom invoked the model of Cincinnatus when commenting on public service, but the image of selfless heroes stepping forward at times of crisis and then voluntarily melding back into the populace fit his ideals very well. It was also consistent with his personal distaste for political campaigning.

Above all, republican elections should not be organized in any party or factional sense, because such organization invariably served private ambitions rather than the public good. Lessons enough about the evils of electioneering could be found in England, where the king's ministers dispensed secret funds and royal favors while powerful economic interests competed for political influence. Republican citizens were to cast their ballots not at the urging of political managers or in response to candidates' blandishments, but independently, according to their own disinterested judgment.

Creating Republican Majorities

The distinctive, predemocratic character of Jefferson's revolutionary republicanism is evident, finally, in his doctrine of majoritarianism. Jefferson's commitment to majority rule was clear. "It is my principle," he declared in a letter to James Madison of 20 December 1787, "that the will of the Majority should always prevail." Only thus could republican liberty be preserved.

Jefferson had some revealing things to say, however, about how republican majorities should be formed. Adversarial, interest-based politics, Jefferson believed, was inconsistent with republican liberty, for it emphasized private ambition and blocked out consideration of the public good. He was quite aware that in the political world of revolutionary Virginia, speculators competed for public lands, politicians reached eagerly for power, Baptists and Episcopalians battled over religious freedom, and localities struggled to escape the burden of taxes and troops. The task of republican statesmanship was to mute such conflicts, dampen private interests, and build majorities based on a disinterested concurrence in the public good. Only in this way could the centrifugal forces of private interest be overcome and the common welfare sustained.

Factions, that is, politically organized private interests, threatened the stability of republican government, for little could be done to prevent faction's growth once it had begun. It thus became essential to reinforce the consensual, disinterested, virtuous pursuit of the general good.

Personal inclination as well as ideological belief pointed Jefferson toward consensus rather than conflict as the controlling principle of republican politics. His public life was filled with controversy; it could hardly have been otherwise, given the times in which he lived and his activist predispositions. Still, Jefferson found political conflict exhausting. Criticisms of his performance as war governor of Virginia, he admitted to Madison in a letter dated 20 May 1782, "inflicted a wound on my spirit which will only be cured by the all-healing grave." The reasoned exchange of opposing views Jefferson thought essential to republican freedom, but given the imperfections of human nature, political arguments too often degenerated into conflict and that, he believed, obscured rather than clarified understanding. Political consensus remained his republican ideal.

FASHIONING A REPUBLICAN SOCIETY

If republicanism had to do most obviously with matters of politics and government, it involved social issues as well. For republican government to flourish, a republican society was required.

The Importance of Social Reform

It was a truism of eighteenth-century thought that different forms of government took their character from distinctive, organizing principles—what Montesquieu called "the human passions" that set governments in motion. According to Montesquieu's formulation, despotism's organizing principle was fear and monarchy's honor. Republicanism found its organizing force in the doctrine of "public virtue."

Jefferson agreed that public virtue provided the essential spirit of republicanism. He never made as much of it as did New England republicans such as John and Samuel Adams, essentially because he did not share their Calvinist distrust of human nature or their belief in the American people's special, covenanted relationship with God. The Adamses, so unlike each other in many ways, saw in the colonies' troubles with England evidence of God's displeasure with America. Somehow the new American Israel had strayed from God's intended way and, in keeping with the covenant doctrine, had drawn his punishment. George III and Parliament were the agents of God's admonishing concern. Regaining God's favor required public repentance and renewed obedience to him. In the politically charged atmosphere of the revolutionary crisis, this meant an end to internal squabbling and selfish ambition, and dedication to the cause of republican liberty. A "Christian Sparta" cleansed of luxury and selfish ambition was what Samuel Adams sought for Massachusetts.

Lacking the Adamses' Calvinist convictions, Jefferson gave little thought to such notions as public sin, punishment, repentance, and moral reform. His God was more benevolent than the Adamses' and worked less directly in human affairs. While Jefferson took the doctrine of public virtue seriously, he was skeptical of the moral regeneration that the Adamses seemed to require. He found precious little Spartan behavior among his planter contemporaries, for they were worldly men, intent on improving their lot and living in the world, not apart from it. Not self-denial but moderation, self-restraint, and a harmonious balance between individual freedom and public concern were what public virtue meant to Jefferson. Moreover, he grounded those qualities not in religion, but in the social order. Political sociology rather than political morality was his concern.

The depth of a people's commitment to republican liberty, Jefferson believed, was in part a function of their political arrangements. Individuals could grasp liberty as an abstraction and long for it, but its true understanding came only through its practice. Jefferson was confident of Virginia's republican experiment in good part because generations of self-government had taught Virginians the value of ordered liberty.

Republican liberty was grounded just as importantly in the underlying social order. If liberty was to thrive, it had to be nourished by a republican society. Jefferson's social theory was much less trenchant than were his observations on government and politics, largely because social thought was relatively underdeveloped in the eighteenth century, but also because of the revolution's preoccupation with political and constitutional concerns. His categories of social analysis were broad and inexact. Nor did he always make clear just how social arrangements connected with political realities. Those connections, however, were terribly important to him and he had much to say about them.

Fashioning a republican society was, if anything, more difficult than forming republican governments, for governments could be changed—England had done so in 1648, again in 1660, and once more in 1688. Jefferson and his colleagues recast Virginia's constitution in 1776. Reconstructing societies was another matter. Social arrangements were deeply embedded in the very fabric of people's lives and could not be so easily changed.

Fortunately, the task of social reform seemed to Jefferson manageable, for he believed that Virginia already contained the essentials of a republican social order. Unlike governmental reconstruction, where the old monarchy had to be thrown out and a new regime begun, building Virginia's republican society required less wrenching change. Things could not simply stay as they were; during the decade following independence, Jefferson proposed an impressive array of social reforms. At bottom, however, he sought not to transform Virginia's existing social order but to perfect it.

The Agrarian Republic

Jefferson's confidence in the republican-like character of Virginia society derived above all from its agrarianism. The overwhelming majority of Virginians lived on the land, working it as farmers or planters. They thus enjoyed the economic independence so essential to republican citizenship. They also lived scattered across the landscape, apart from each other and in close communion with Nature. When people lived closely together, as in cities, competition developed, ambitions were aroused, and patterns of dependence emerged. In the countryside, people developed self-reliance and governed their lives by the ordered, rhythmic regularity of Nature.

Jefferson valued as well the moderate but pleasing prosperity he believed an agrarian republic could bring. His ideal citizen was a prosperous agriculturalist selling his tobacco or grain in outside markets. He feared an unrestrained commercial spirit, for that drove people into speculative ventures, turned them away from disciplined, productive labor, and focused their ambition on personal gain. Such behavior he thought characteristic of economies based primarily on manufacturing and overseas trade.

As a tobacco planter he understood the importance of the expanding market economy. Selling an agricultural surplus brought economic security and material comfort, important dimensions of "the pursuit of happiness" that Jefferson listed among men's inalienable rights. The possibility of economic security, he noted in a letter to Madison dated 28 October 1785, even for ordinary people, was one of the things that distinguished America from Europe, where "enormous inequality" produced misery for "the bulk of mankind." Producing a surplus stimulated habits of industry and self-discipline, crucially important private virtues among republican citizens, while a pleasing prosperity generated contentment and offered persuasive evidence of republicanism's blessings. Though persuaded that Virginia's agrarian order was preeminently suited for republicanism, Jefferson believed it needed improvement. He attempted that through an ambitious program of social reform.

The Problem of Social Class

Jefferson had no clearly developed theory of social class, but he recognized the dangers to republican liberty of class extremes and sought to moderate them. Social distinctions, even very substantial ones, he accepted as natural. He was deeply concerned, however, by what he perceived to be the emergence in the coastal Tidewater, Virginia's longest settled area, of an increasingly wealthy and closed planter elite, aping European behavior and transmitting its property and social position from one generation to the next. Such a development affronted his personal sensibilities, given his own family's recent entrance into the planter class, and clashed with his idea of what a natural, republican aristocracy ought to be.

His solution was not to attack the planter class itself or the economic and social arrangements essential to its survival. He was, after all, deeply embedded in that class and regarded its leadership as essential to the republic. His reforms actually threatened to disrupt the standing order very little, except perhaps at its most reactionary extreme. Jefferson entertained no thoughts, for example, of an agrarian law or other strategies for the forced redistribution of property. Property rights were among the most fundamental for which Americans had rebelled. His goal was to prevent the development over time of a rigid, entrenched aristocratic elite, one that represented not talent and personal accomplishment but inherited status.

One strategy was to prohibit the use of family titles. Virginia passed laws to that effect, as did the other American republics. Equally important, Jefferson proposed the abolition of primogeniture and entail, ancient legal instruments for the accumulation and transmission of family wealth across generations. He sought as well to restrict the activities of speculators who attempted, through political influence, to build fortunes out of public lands in the West.

Had Jefferson been free to implement such reforms at will, he might have adopted a bolder stance, for he feared the social consequences of the monopolization of property and detested the arrogance that inherited status produced. In fact, however, his approach was careful and deliberate. His reforms would not prohibit Virginians from transmitting their property intact or allotting double portions to eldest sons, but would make the process optional. Primogeniture and entail, moreover, had already come to be honored as much in the breach as in observance; the burgesses had approved countless petitions for exceptions from the law. The main effect of Jefferson's reform was to free individual families from the necessity of seeking legislative assent.

Jefferson's most direct challenge to the planter elite came from his proposals concerning slavery, for Virginia fortunes had been built on slave labor and plantation life was based on the master-slave relationship. He called for an immediate end to the slave trade, but that idea was not new. By the middle decades of the eighteenth century, Virginia's flagging tobacco economy and increasing shift to less labor-intensive grain crops had caused countless Virginians to question the wisdom of continuing to import blacks.

More revealing, Jefferson's proposals concerning slavery neither eased the restrictions on private slave manumissions—he freed only a few of his own slaves during his lifetime—nor provided for slavery's abolition, even in the distant future. His bill required that slaves brought into the state would be freed after a year's residence, but it explicitly excluded the offspring of existing slaves. Moreover, it continued the long-standing prohibitions against blacks keeping guns, pleading in court against whites, or leaving their masters' property without a pass. In addition, it provided firm punishments for "riots, routs, unlawful assemblies, trespasses and seditious speeches" by blacks or mulattos. The bill, Jefferson later recalled in his autobiography, was intended as "a mere digest of the existing laws" respecting slaves, "without any intimation of a plan for a future and general emancipation."

Jefferson claimed in his autobiography, as he did earlier in his *Notes on Virginia,* that he had prepared an amendment to his own bill providing freedom for all slaves born after a certain date once they reached a certain age. There is no reason to doubt him on the point, but the amendment was not introduced and no copy of it has ever been found. In the end, Jefferson agreed to leave slavery much as it was.

If Jefferson sought to blunt the development of an aristocratic Tidewater elite, he struggled to alleviate class extremes at the bottom of society as well. His strategy was to insure that every citizen was possessed of at least some land. The fact that he proposed a minimum of fifty acres rather than the twenty-five required for the franchise indicates that he had social as well as political concerns in mind.

Here again Jefferson sought not to recast the existing social structure but, by opening opportunity, to preserve it. He put no limits on the amount of land that individuals might accumulate, nor did he oppose slavery's spread west of the mountains and south of the Ohio.

Jefferson affirmed each individual's moral worth and showed neither animosity nor scorn for those less fortunate than he, but he was no advocate of social equality. His life was sheltered, cosmopolitan, and genteel. Monticello, after all, was his home, black slaves the source of his wealth, and Virginia's social and political elite his associates. Though he commented in fascinating detail on much of the world around him, his writings are devoid of commentary on the downtrodden, even though slaves, tenant farmers, and frontiersmen were increasingly evident in Virginia's population. Such people in the aggregate interested him as social issues, but they did not touch his imagination.

In Jefferson's republic, social distinctions blended seamlessly together. Different classes were connected not by opposing interests but through reciprocal and mutually reinforcing ties. Where Newton's mechanical universe served as a metaphor for his constitutional thought, Jefferson's social metaphor was biological. Societies, like individuals, passed inevitably through a life cycle of birth, growth, maturity, decay, and death. The image fixed his attention on the social whole and its passage through time, not on relationships among its parts.

Later in his career, Jefferson would worry about the implications of that life cycle for the national republic. During the years immediately following independence, however, he worried about it scarcely at all, for the Virginia republic was new and its society seemed harmonious and stable. Virginia's vast interior, with its land sufficient for generations to come, offered hope that the cycle of social development could be slowed and the ravages of time avoided. The agrarian society's expansion across geographic space would enable Virginians to surmount the perils of historical time by avoiding the growth of cities, the spread of commerce and manufacturing, and the development of social dependencies. Thus did Jefferson finally overcome the dogma that republics were viable only in small areas. In an agrarian republic, the law of territorial limits did not apply.

Not that Jefferson imagined the Virginia republic expanding indefinitely into the interior. Problems of communication across the mountains, to say nothing of interstate competition over western lands, would stand in the way. In 1784 he prepared for Congress his famous "Report on Government for the Western Territory" in which he outlined a scheme for organizing the region north of the Ohio into new republics and admitting them, "on an equal footing with the . . . original states," into the union. Virginia had earlier ceded all claim to those lands, but Jefferson could imagine new republics rising in Virginia's western territory as well. Whether as part of Virginia or not, the West contained the promise of America's republican future.

Seeking Cultural Unity

Finally, Jefferson thought Virginia preeminently suited to republicanism because of its ethnic and cultural homogeneity. As we know, his solution to the state's racial divisions was selective emancipation and colonization. Eventually, Jefferson's republic would be entirely white. Native Americans were to be kept physically apart until that far-distant day when they would cease being Indians and would come to think and behave like Anglo-Americans.

Jefferson's attitudes toward white ethnic diversity were more ambivalent. He believed firmly in the right of naturalization; individuals, he reasoned, should not be bound forever by the accidental location of their birth. In a bill of October 1776 for the naturalization of foreigners, he proposed significant inducements for Europeans to come and settle: twenty dollars apiece to help defray the costs of passage, fifty acres of free land, and immediate admission to citizenship upon a simple declaration of intent to reside in and obey the laws of the state.

There is no evidence, however, that Jefferson either expected or desired hordes of foreigners to emigrate. Though the American republics should offer asylum for the persecuted, Virginia, the most populous of the thirteen states, did not need a large influx of people. Jefferson, moreover, had doubts about most Europeans' readiness for republican self-government, doubts that were later powerfully reinforced by his experiences in Europe.

Inducements to emigrate, he thought, should be focused selectively on individuals who could make distinctive contributions to Virginia. He particularly favored people from southern Europe who could, he wrote to Richard Henry Lee on 30 August 1778, introduce "many useful plants, esculant, medicinal and for manufacture, and arts useful tho' as yet unknown to us." Such newcomers might also help open badly needed markets in their former lands for Virginia's exports: tobacco, wheat, and rice.

At the time of independence, Virginia's white population was ethnically uniform. As many as ninety percent of its white inhabitants were of British ancestry. That was the situation that Jefferson knew and valued. Far better, he thought, to depend for Virginia's growth on its already impressive rate of natural increase.

Jefferson's preference for social and cultural unity is evident even in his attitudes toward religious liberty. Jefferson was one of Virginia's most determined champions of religious freedom. He embraced that principle, though, not because it promised to produce a rainbow of religious sects, but because restrictions on religious belief violated natural rights, were impossible to enforce, and had historically been instruments of oppression.

Jefferson defended the right of Baptists, Methodists, and other "dissenters" to worship as they pleased. But he found their often noisome manner and extravagant theology distasteful. Religious freedom, he hoped, would mute religious enthusiasm, reduce religion's role in Virginia society, and bring Virginians of all persuasions together in a republican faith of rational, genteel morality.

THE EXPANDING NATIONAL REPUBLIC

Jefferson's political career did not end in 1783 when he left Virginia for Europe: in fact, its longest and best-known phase was yet to come. The republican principles he had developed in revolutionary Virginia continued to guide him, but they changed significantly in response to dramatic changes in both his own life and the life of the nation.

In the mid-1780s, the focus of Jefferson's career shifted from Virginia to the nation at large. Between 1785 and 1789, he served as United States minister to France. He returned to enter Washington's cabinet as secretary of state, was vice-president under John Adams from 1797 to 1801, and filled two presidential terms of his own from 1801 to 1809. The new, national context of his public life forced Jefferson to reconsider virtually every important principle of his revolutionary republicanism, for compared with Virginia the national republic was geographically vast, economically and socially diverse, and politically complex. Moreover, he was unfamiliar with many of its regions and people. The Virginia republic had been familiar and manageable; the sprawling, expanding national republic seemed much less so.

During the 1790s, the United States began the surge of economic and social development that in little more than fifty years would make of it a bustling, continental republic. Expanding overseas commerce, booming prosperity, the emergence of merchant capitalism, rapid occupation of the trans-Appalachian interior—all were beginning to redraw the very contours of economic and social life. In addition, the federal constitution created for the first time the basis for national electoral politics, while leaving unresolved how those politics should be conducted.

To complicate things still further, the new, national republic faced difficult problems of foreign relations: balancing the agrarian interests of the South against the commercial and manufacturing interests of the Northeast and, above all, dealing with the implications—ideological and political, as well as diplomatic—of the French Revolution, the international cataclysm that shook the entire Atlantic world.

During the 1790s and early 1800s, Jefferson struggled to adapt his Virginia-based republicanism to these dramatic, new realities. In most ways, his national republicanism represented a logical extension of his revolutionary faith. Certainly his overriding concerns remained the same—to expand republican liberty and contain arbitrary power. And yet amidst the sharply altered circumstances of post-revolutionary America, Jefferson's republicanism took on a significantly different cast.

For one thing, where Jefferson had earlier thought that the only central government consistent with republican liberty was a limited confederation of states, he now embraced the notion of a truly national government elected directly by and capable of acting on the people. Jefferson was in France when the Philadelphia convention met, but he endorsed the new federal constitution once he was assured that a bill of rights would be added. A more vigorous national government was now necessary, he was persuaded, to protect the nation abroad and maintain the union at home. If properly constrained, governmental power could serve as liberty's guarantor rather than its enemy. Effective constraints could be provided by a written constitution, strictly interpreted, and a federal system in which the states would guard against the abuse of national power. During the 1790s, Jefferson railed against the efforts of Alexander Hamilton and the Federalists to expand the central government's authority. As president, he set the national government on a more limited, properly republican course.

Beginning in the 1790s, Jefferson significantly expanded his commitment to the principle of political equality. His reasons were several. The French Revolution, exploding in violence in 1793, polarized political debate throughout the Atlantic world between the defenders of privilege and aristocracy and the advocates of individual freedom and equality. Jefferson doubted France's readiness for republican self-government, but supported its people's desperate struggle for political liberty. His experience in France during the 1780s had intensified his fear of aristocratic privilege and its threat to human liberty. The forces of counterrevolution, which gathered strength across Europe during the 1790s, worried him even further.

His fears were compounded by the Federalist party's denunciations of revolutionary France, aggressive assertions of political elitism, and increasing intolerance of political opposition. Federalist doctrines would have to be countered by more aggressive assertions of political equality.

Practical considerations also moved Jefferson in the direction of political equality. Defeating the Federalists would require mobilizing the people, persuading them that the future of republican liberty was at stake, and forming them into electoral majorities. Gaining political control of key mid-Atlantic states such as New York and Pennsylvania was essential to the growing Jeffersonian opposition; it would require marshaling the votes of farmers, artisans, and other working people—all among the most openly democratic Americans. By 1800, Jefferson the Virginia republican had become the national democrat.

In his new role as national statesman, Jefferson reexamined his assumptions about the social bases of republicanism as well. Here, however, he altered his revolutionary faith little, if at all. No longer could he simply assume American social and cultural unity. The diversity contained within the expanded national republic was simply too great to be ignored. How could Massachusetts sailors, New York artisans, Pennsylvania farmers, Ohio frontiersmen, and South Carolina rice planters be forged into one unified republic? More important, how was he to deal with the accelerating pace of economic and social development represented by America's surging overseas trade, intensifying commercial spirit, growing cities, expanding frontier, and increasing social inequalities? Such changes challenged some of the most fundamental assumptions of his republican belief.

Jefferson's response to the nation's growing socioeconomic diversity reveals the continuing hold of his original republican convictions, for he sought to minimize diversity and avoid change by projecting an endlessly evolving agrarian republic. Expansion across America's unlimited space would free the nation from the ravages of historical time.

A nation of yeoman farmers—living independently on the land, equal in economic and social condition—constituted his national republican ideal. As secretary of state and president, he pursued that ideal by seeking overseas markets for agricultural surpluses, limiting American manufacturing, moving Indians aside, and opening the West to white settlement. The purchase in 1803 of the Louisiana Territory, in one stroke more than doubling the nation's size, was the ultimate expression of his national republican faith.

Nothing expresses more vividly the essentials of Jefferson's national republicanism than his first presidential inaugural address of 1801. He began that remarkable testimonial by celebrating America's "rising nation, spread over a wide and fruitful land . . . advancing rapidly to destinies beyond the reach of mortal eye." What remained to realize that destiny?

First, the dampening of political conflict and restoration of "that harmony and affection without which liberty and even life itself are but dreary things." Offering his defeated Federalist opponents "their equal rights, which equal law must protect," he called on the moderates among them to set their past errors aside. "Every difference of opinion," he declared, "is not a difference of principle. We have called by different names brethren of the same principle. We are all Republicans, we are all Federalists." Those who still opposed American republicanism could be left "undisturbed as monuments of the safety with which errors of opinion may be tolerated where reason is left free to combat it."

What constituted the "essential principles" of the republican faith around which Jefferson urged his fellow citizens to rally? Above all "a wise and frugal Government" capable of restraining people from injuring one another but that would "leave them otherwise free to regulate their own pursuits of industry and improvement." Beyond that, "equal and exact justice to all men, of whatever state or persuasion, religious or political"; "commerce and honest friendship" with all nations, but "entangling alliances with none"; "support of the State governments in all their rights, as the most competent administrations for our domestic concerns and the surest bulwarks against antirepublican tendencies"; preservation of the central government "in its whole constitutional vigor, as the sheet anchor of our peace at home and safety abroad"; a "jealous care" of popular elections; "absolute acquiescence" in majority rule, the "vital principle of republics"; economy in public expense and the honest payment of public debts; the "encouragement of agriculture, and of commerce as its handmaiden"; diffusion of public information, freedom of religion and press, and guarantees of habeas corpus and jury trial. Taken together, these were the heart of Jefferson's mature political faith.

Guaranteeing that faith, preserving it against the ravages of historical time, were the republic's separation "by nature and a wide ocean" from "the exterminating havoc" of Europe and, most important, America's location in "a chosen country, with room enough for our descendants to the thousandth and thousandth generation."

It was an inspiring vision that Jefferson offered the nation in 1801. More than any other, it has guided the American republic from his day to ours, though not always clearly, for the vision in important ways attempted to deny the realities of historical change. As time would show, moreover, its language could be turned to un-Jeffersonian political ends. But its principles remain the most luminous guide to America's continuing republican experiment.

Political Theorist

A. J. BEITZINGER

IN American civil religion, Washington reigns as the creator-father, Lincoln as the sacrificial savior-son, and Jefferson as the informing spirit. Alexis de Tocqueville called Jefferson "the most powerful advocate democracy has ever had"; Lincoln stated that "the principles of Jefferson are the definitions and axioms of a free society"; and John Dewey hailed Jefferson as "the first modern to state in human terms the principles of democracy."

A reflective man of action, Jefferson wrote no systematic political treatise. His arguments and ideas must be gathered from the great revolutionary and state papers and laws that he drafted; his only book, *Notes on the State of Virginia*; and the many letters that he wrote in his long life as revolutionist, lawmaker, governor, diplomat, party leader, president, educator, and retired statesman. He wrote over years of great change in response to events and for particular purposes. These temporal and political factors, along with his eclecticism, gave rise to modifications, shifts in emphases, ambiguities, and inconsistencies in his thought. As a political actor he often used words that were at once effective rhetoric for the occasion and philosophical terminology with universal implication. Care must be taken neither to fault him as a political actor for philosophical insufficiencies nor to exempt him as a thinker from critical examination of his political use of philosophical terms or from scrutiny of the terms and arguments themselves.

PRINCIPLES OF JEFFERSON'S THOUGHT

Jefferson regarded the English empiricists Bacon, Newton, and Locke as the greatest men who ever lived. He scorned speculative thinkers such as Plato, whose mystical vision affronted him temperamentally and intellectually. He contemptuously identified metaphysics with acceptance of immaterial being. And yet, his own thought was rooted in a complex of interrelated naturalistic principles, the validity of which he, in good part, presupposed. Within this framework he could organize experience, interpret events, and influence practice. There is a discernible pattern of development in Jefferson's naturalism as it moved from a Lockean juxtaposition of moral rationalism and empiricism to an increasing emphasis upon empiricism.

Creator (Nature's God)

Jefferson rejected chance and blind necessity as ultimate cosmological principles. Because he saw around him order and design, he inferred an externally preexisting powerful, wise, and benevolent Creator, whom he described as "a fabricator of all things . . . a superintending power to maintain the Universe in it's course and order." Because from his youth he was attached to Epicurean materialism, he precluded as unreal all non-materiality or spirituality and regarded the Creator as a material being. Late in life he speculated that although we cannot know the Creator's essence, we might say that it is akin to mind. Because he regarded mind as a function of material brain, this speculation did not abridge his belief in the Creator's materiality. He simply equated matter and existence, as in his letter to John Adams of 15 August 1820. "To talk of *immaterial* existences is to talk of *nothings.*" His developed theistic materialism drew justification not only from the French Ideologists Pierre Cabanis and Antoine Destutt de Tracy and the Scottish common-sense realist Dugald Stewart, but also from Locke, whom he called a materialist on the improbable basis of Locke's concession that if the deity so pleased, he could endow matter with the power of thought.

Given an acceptance of the Newtonian framework as descriptive of reality, this material view of the Creator posed a difficulty: Matter alone can act on matter; God is the author of the laws of nature governing matter. Is God as material reality then subject to the laws governing the material reality that

He created? If so, the ultimate principle is not the Creator but the eternally existing laws of nature. God thus tends to become naturalized and nature deified. Jefferson never directly confronted the difficulty for three reasons. First, his materialism was essentially a common-sense empiricism. Second, his concern was less with inanimate than animate nature, in which growth and purpose are more readily evident. And third, his humanism brought him to posit, as equally basic with his materialism, the moral nature of man. In any case Jeffersonian theology proceeded from the notion of the will of the Creator as reflected in nature.

Nature

Jefferson envisioned the Creator as an architect whose intentions are written legibly in the visible world of nature. Nature is known through the senses by observation of "facts" from which empirical generalizations can be drawn. Jefferson's common-sense realism and naive materialism modified his Lockean sensationalism and protected him against skepticism. Thus, in his letter to Adams of 15 August 1820, he equated the world of tangible experience with the real world:

> "I feel: therefore I exist." I feel bodies which are not myself: there are other existencies then. I call them *matter.* I feel them changing place. This gives me *motion.* Where there is an absence of matter, I call it *void,* or *nothing,* or *immaterial space.* On the basis of sensation, of matter and motion, we may erect the fabric of all the certainties we can have or need. I can conceive *thought* to be an action of a particular organisation of matter, formed for that purpose by it's creator. . . . When once we quit the basis of sensation, all is in the wind.

Jefferson had anticipated the conclusion of this mode of reasoning earlier, in the *Notes*: "A patient pursuit of facts, and cautious combination and comparison of them, is the drudgery to which man is subjected by his Maker, if he wishes to attain sure knowledge."

The attainment of "sure knowledge," however, is complicated by the fact that Jefferson believed that men's minds, like their bodies, are differently shaped. This necessarily gives rise to variations in opinions: "Differences of opinion . . . like differences of face, are a law of our nature, and should be viewed with the same tolerance." Even though "every man's own reason must be his oracle," his opinions "are not voluntary." And yet, this is socially beneficial, because "difference of opinion leads to inquiry, and inquiry to truth."

Assuming the reliability of sense knowledge in the attack on practical problems, Jefferson thought that men, through cooperative inquiry, could arrive at useful, communicable truths. The term "opinion," as he used it, pertained to metaphysics, abstract theories, beliefs or dogmas of any kind. It was different with scientific theories; he regarded Newton's theory as proven by "reason and experiment." He also believed that certain political propositions, such as that man can govern himself and that a republic can be preserved in a large territory, had been experimentally elevated in America above mere "opinion" into "truth."

Thus within Jefferson's materialist monism there existed an implicit dualism. On the one hand he stressed variations in minds that necessarily give rise to different opinions. On the other hand he professed a belief in the objective reality of sensed evidence. Although he would not concede a universal standard of truth for the peculiar issues of idiosyncratic brains, he served his partisan purposes by measuring "opinions" hygienically. He wrote Lafayette on 4 November 1823: "The sickly, weakly, timid man, fears the people, and is a Tory [Federalist] by nature. The healthy, strong and bold, cherishes them, and is formed a Whig [Republican] by nature."

Daniel Boorstin concluded in *The Lost World of Thomas Jefferson* that Jefferson saved himself from the unfavorable consequences of this dualism by differently emphasizing its elements. In theology and politics, where sociability was the goal, stress was placed on the desirable diversity of ideas. Thus in the *Notes* Jefferson held that variety of opinions was particularly beneficial in religion where "the several sects perform the office of a *censor morum* over each other." In natural science, stress was put on the community and the objective reality of the evidence of men's senses.

Because Jefferson believed that nature concretely reflects the divine power, wisdom, and goodness, he concluded that conformity thereto is in compliance with the will of "Nature's God." Man's duty is to proceed not by inner reflection or contemplation but by striving to understand the Creator in his works, and to shape his own behavior and institutions accordingly.

Laws of Nature and of Nature's God

As Newton has shown, the laws of physical nature can be known by rational man. Jefferson's acceptance of the notion of a cosmos informed by intelligible laws brought him to deny the possibility of divine interventions such as revelation and miracles. Otherwise the Creator would have been a "bungling" workman. This view left no room for mystery, disorder, or inexplicable evil.

Unlike physical nature, which is describable in its regularity, and animate nature, which is describable in its life process, man, although subject to physical and biological nature, is a moral agent possessing reason and a freedom to choose between right and wrong. Consequently, insofar as nature indicates a moral law to man, human nature must be differentiated, if one is not to conclude that "whatever is, is right." The moral law of nature is predicated on the existence of an essential human nature with ends to be realized, entailing corresponding duties and rights.

Despite the nominalism implicit in his empiricism, in his emphasis on idiosyncratic minds, and in his disdain for abstract entities, Jefferson assumed the existence of a divinely created essential human nature. The moral law of nature constituted for him a discernible order of obligation, issuing from the will of "Nature's God," which transcends and measures custom, tradition, positive law, and institutions, and indicates the "right" that exists "independent of force."

Moral Law of Nature: Structure and Content

Almost fifty years after the event, Jefferson wrote to Henry Lee that his purpose in writing the Declaration of Independence was "not to find out new principles, or new arguments, never before thought of, not merely to say things which had never been said before; but to place before mankind the common sense of the subject, in terms so plain and firm as to command their assent." He intended it to be "an expression of the American mind," resting "on the harmonizing sentiments of the day." On the theoretical level the Declaration was a restatement of widely used, conventional English and colonial Whig ideas. These ideas constituted the document's major premise; the bill of indictment of the British king constituted the minor premise; and the declaring of independence constituted the conclusion.

Because Jefferson fully subscribed to the ideas he set forth in the Declaration, questions of his political use of philosophical terms and the logical structure and meaning he gave them are important to students of his thought. These questions are best addressed by reading the final draft in light of Jefferson's Rough Draft, where the underlying logic is more evident. The pertinent portion of the Rough Draft reads as follows. (The changes made in the committee draft —shown below with the deletions indicated in brackets and the revisions set in italics and placed next to them—were either made or agreed to by Jefferson. The only significant further change in the final draft involved deletion of the word "inherent" and addition of the word "certain" in reference to "unalienable rights.")

> We hold these truths to be [sacred and undeniable] *self-evident;* that all men are created equal [and independent, that from that equal creation they derive rights inherent and inalienable]; *that they are endowed by their Creator with inherent and unalienable rights, that* among [which] *these* are [the preservation of] life, [and] liberty, and the pursuit of happiness; that to secure these [ends] *rights,* governments are instituted among men, deriving their just powers from the consent of the governed; that whenever any form of government [shall become] *becomes* destructive of these ends, it is the right of the people to alter or to abolish it, and to institute new government, laying it's foundation on such principles and organizing it's powers in such form, as to them shall seem most likely to effect their safety and happiness.

The four "truths" are called "sacred and undeniable" in one draft and "self-evident" in the other. Self-evident truths are understood as immediately intuited or apprehended by reason. John Dickinson had called them "indubitable." Jefferson described them in his *Summary View of the Rights of British America* as "principles of common sense," and later, as "terms so plain and firm as to command assent." The English republican Algernon Sidney, with whose work Jefferson was acquainted, had earlier called them truths "which none could deny that did not renounce common sense."

Assuming that "undeniable" applies not only to principles but to conclusions from principles, the change to "self-evident" involved movement to a less inclusive term. Thus the interrelated propositions called self-evident in the revised draft must each have been immediately intuited or apprehended. On the other hand, the Rough Draft, after stating the principle, "equal creation," lists propositions that *derive* therefrom, implying the use of discursive as well as intuitive reason.

Read in light of the Rough Draft the theoretical portion of the Declaration can be understood as an exercise in the moral rationalism evidenced in Locke's *Second Treatise of Government*. This contention stands in contrast to that of Garry Wills who, ignoring the Rough Draft and using the committee draft, maintained in *Inventing America* that the theoretical portion of the Declaration should be seen in terms of the influence of Scottish communitarian thought on Jefferson. He argues that Jefferson, in dealing with the "self-evident" truths, drew from Thomas Reid's common-sense approach and Francis Hutcheson's moral-sense approach with the latter "in charge." If this is true, Jefferson was either attempting to bring together two incompatible epistemologies or he was incognizant of their incompatibility. Hutcheson differed from both Reid and Locke in arguing the existence of a noncognitive moral faculty and in opposing appeals to self-evident and deduced moral principles.

In his *Second Treatise* Locke wrote that there is "nothing more evident, than that Creatures of the same species and rank promiscuously born to the same advantages of Nature, and the use of the same faculties, should also be equal one amongst another without Subordination or Subjection." He restated this proposition in terms of the Law of Nature: "Reason, which is that Law, teaches all Mankind . . . that being all equal and independent, no one ought to harm another in his Life, Health, Liberty, or Possessions." Locke proceeded from the principle of the natural equality of all men to a practical moral principle that was self-evident to

him upon comparison of its terms—since men are equal and independent by nature they should not subjugate each other. Corresponding to this natural duty is the natural right of each man not to be subjugated.

Jefferson's formulation in the Rough Draft asserts the undeniability of the Lockean principle, "all men are created equal and independent." Given his equation of existence and matter, he could not have meant equality in the possession of an immaterial soul. Nor could the principle mean identity without differences. Instead it suggests a moral equality of all men in the possession of a common human nature, or in their unity as a species. Locke derived the right to preserve liberty from the duty to preserve liberty as implied in the natural equality of men; Jefferson derived from "equal creation" the "inherent and inalienable" rights to the preservation of life, the preservation of liberty, and the pursuit of happiness. In the process he implicitly assumed obligations.

Morton White has recently shown in *The Philosophy of the American Revolution* the significance of the eighteenth-century Swiss jurist Jean Jacques Burlamaqui, with whose work Jefferson was acquainted, as a key to interpreting the Rough Draft. Burlamaqui attempted to bring together Lockean rationalism and Hutcheson's moral-sense view in terms of the temporal priority of the latter and the logical superiority of the former. Applied to Jefferson this approach allows the relative influence of Hutcheson on his moral thought without peremptorily dismissing Locke, as does Wills.

Burlamaqui argued in his *Principles of Natural and Politic Law* that certain moral truths, such as "man ought to seek his own happiness," are just as evident in themselves as are scientific axioms. His moral rationalism and resemblance to Locke are evident in the following proposition: "Reason . . . informs us, that creatures of the same rank and species, born with the same faculties to live in society, and to partake of the same advantages, have in general an equal and common right." Burlamaqui examined the nature that God has given man and the states in which God has placed man. From this he inferred God's intentions regarding man, from which he further inferred what God has willed, while presuming throughout the process divine power, wisdom, and goodness. The movement is thus from the Creator to man's created essence, to man's ends, to man's duties as willed by the Creator.

White argues that Jefferson's statement that it is "undeniable" that the rights to preserve life, to preserve liberty, and to pursue happiness are derived from equal creation had the same logical standing as it had in Burlamaqui's system. Thus the statement can be understood not as self-evident but as an undeniable deduction from the following two presumed self-evident propositions: (1) because God has given man life as part of his essence, placed him in the same species and into society with his fellow men, and given him a desire for happiness, God has proposed at least three ends for man—the preservation of life, the preservation of liberty, and the pursuit of happiness; and (2) because God proposed three ends for man, he imposed on man three corresponding duties to attain these ends. From these propositions it is inferred that from God's equal creation of man as possessed of a certain nature and put in a certain state, there are derived the duties to preserve life and liberty and to pursue happiness. White then suggests that "by what Locke might have called a trifling step . . . Jefferson deduced his statement . . . that from equal creation man derives his *rights* to preserve life and liberty, and to pursue happiness." White concludes that whereas the rights to preserve life and to preserve liberty, as listed in the Rough Draft, are readily incorporated into Burlamaqui's system, the right of life and the right of liberty, as listed in the final draft, are not. This is so because the dele-

tions of "equal creation" and "preservation of life" and "preservation of liberty" prevent the seeing of the movement from created essence to the divinely willed ends, duties, and rights.

On the basis of both the Lockean and Burlamaquian interpretations it can be concluded that although Jefferson's Rough Draft stressed "rights," it presupposed correlative duties in accordance with the primacy of the law of nature. Besides a specific reference in the Declaration to the duty to overthrow unjust government, Jefferson in later years explicitly emphasized obligations. He wrote that "the laws of nature create our duties and interests" and the function of legislators is "to declare and enforce only our natural rights and duties." Similarly, he told Francis Gilmer in a letter of 7 June 1816 that "every man is under the natural duty of contributing to the necessities of the society," and further, that "no man having a natural right to be the judge between himself and another, it is his natural duty to submit to the umpirage of an impartial third." Projecting to the collective level, he wrote in a 1793 opinion on the rights of the United States in its treaties with France: "The moral duties which exist between individual and individual in a state of nature, accompany them into a state of society, and the aggregate of the duties of all the individuals composing the society constitutes the duties of that society towards any other."

Jefferson apparently assumed that duties to fulfill what Burlamaqui saw as the self-regarding ends indicated in man's nature (preservation of life and pursuit of happiness) precede and imply rights, whereas the duty and right indicated in man's relation to his fellows (preservation of liberty) follows upon recognition of their right not to be subjugated as implied in their equality. Consequently, Jefferson's political rhetoric, addressed to man in his social relationships, emphasized rights. Thus liberty, which presupposes life and is the condition of the pursuit of happiness, becomes politically central.

Natural Moral Sense

Quite evident in the unfolding of Jefferson's thought is an increasing emphasis on the moral sense, a faculty distinct from reason. The reasons seem to be political and philosophical. The democratic impulse pushed him to recognize the limited number of men who might through reason come to an adequate knowledge of the law of nature. With this in mind, he appealed to a universal, instinctual sense of right and wrong in men. This verifiable moral sense supplied a strong empirical foundation for his argument of "equal creation" and thus equal rights and democratic government. Similarly, unlike reason, a shared moral sense could better explain cooperative social participation of men with idiosyncratic minds. Thus Jefferson wrote to James Fishback on 27 September 1809: "The practice of morality being necessary for the well-being of society," the Creator "has taken care to impress its precepts so indelibly on our hearts that they shall not be effaced by the subtleties of our brain."

Surveying Jefferson's evolving thought on the point, as early as 1771 he remarked on the importance of "the moral feelings." In the *Summary View,* he referred not only to "the principles of common sense, but the common feelings of human nature." In the Declaration, he relied not on a moral-sense approach but on the stronger support of reason. In the *Notes on Virginia,* he opposed "sentiment" to "demonstration," with superiority apparently accorded to the latter. In 1786 he wrote in a dialogue between Head and Heart that because "morals were too essential to the happiness of man to be risked on the incertain combinations of the head," nature "laid their foundation therefore in sentiment, not in science." Nature afforded sentiment to all, "as necessary to all"; she gave science "to a few only, as sufficing with a few." His best-known statement on the point came in a letter to his nephew Peter Carr of 10 August 1787:

> He who made us would have been a pitiful bungler if he had made the rules of our moral conduct a matter of science. For one man of science, there are hundreds who are not. What would have become of them? Man was destined for society. His morality therefore was to be formed to this object. He was endowed with a sense of right and wrong merely relative to this. This sense is as much a part of his nature as the sense of hearing, seeing, feeling; it is the true foundation of morality. . . . It is given to all human beings in a stronger or weaker degree . . . . It may be strengthened by exercise, as may any particular limb of the body. This sense is submitted indeed in some degree to the guidance of reason; but it is a small stock which is required for this; even a less one than what we call Common sense. State a moral case to a ploughman and a professor. The former will decide it as well, and often better than the latter, because he has not been led astray by artificial rules.

White suggests that what Jefferson meant in the first sentence of this quotation was that God "would have been a pitiful bungler if he had made the rules of our moral conduct a matter of science *alone.*" He adds that when Jefferson also says that the moral sense is submitted to the guidance of reason, "he acknowledges the kind of superiority of reason that Burlamaqui and Locke had both asserted."

A year later, in a letter to Richard Price, Jefferson showed his ambivalence by writing that "we may well admit morality to be the child of the understanding rather than of the senses." And, in his opinion on French-American treaties in 1793, he referred to "the true fountains of evidence, the head and heart of every rational and honest man" in which "nature has written her moral laws, and where every man may read them for himself." Finally, on 13 June 1814, in a letter to Thomas Law he wrote that "the foundation of morality" is the "moral instinct," and not "truth" or "love of God" (although each of these is a "branch"), nor "taste" or "self-love." The word "foundation" might here be construed as indicating only temporal priority.

Concerning the relation of the moral sense to reason, Burlamaqui had taught that the moral sense provides "a first notice," whereas reason "verifies and proves it." Reason is thus logically superior. Insofar as it can be argued that the main thrust of Jefferson's thought, at least to the turn of the century, was that the moral sense is submitted to the guidance of intuitive and discursive reason, it can be concluded that he was consistent with Burlamaqui and remained a moral rationalist. Insofar as he moved on to render reason merely instrumental, he left both Burlamaqui and Locke and followed Hutcheson. That he never deserted rationalism is evident in his use of the syllogism, in his letter of 7 June 1816 to Gilmer, to establish the existence of a sense of justice, and in his labeling, in a letter of 24 September 1823 to Thomas Earle, as "self-evident" certain interrelated propositions concerning the rights of the living in the use of the earth.

In any case Jefferson regarded the moral sense as a social instinct, a faculty "necessary in an animal destined to live in society." Admitting its imperfection in some men as a departure from "health," Jefferson believed corrections could be made by education, appeals to expedience and interest, legal sanctions, exploitation of the desire to please others, and fear of divine punishment.

Jefferson saw happiness as the ultimate natural end for man. This entailed self-realization through the attainment of virtue. Believing, as did Hutcheson, that "every human mind feels pleasure in doing good to another," Jefferson concluded in a letter of 14 October 1816 to Adams that "the essence of virtue is in doing good to others." This was, he told Law, because "nature hath implanted in our breasts a love of others, a sense of duty to them . . . which prompts us irresistibly to feel and to succor their distresses." He looked to the stoicism of Epictetus and the refined hedonism of Epicurus for prescriptions for personal conduct. Concerning duties to others he found no teachings superior to those of the nondivinized Christ. He considered them simple and pure enough to be understood even by the lowliest. He could brook no double standard, declaring that he knew "but one code of morality for men, whether acting singly or collectively."

Jefferson came to qualify his moral-sense doctrine by considerations of utility. To Law in his letter of 13 June 1814, he wrote: "Nature has constituted *utility* to man, the standard and test of virtue. Men living in different countries, under different circumstances, different habits and regimens, may have different utilities; the same act, therefore, may be useful, and consequently virtuous in one country which is injurious and vicious in another differently circumstanced." He also talked of progressive development in the moral sense as exemplified in treatment of prisoners of war. He conceded that degradation is also possible; men can become debased as have the rabble in European cities. Favorable social conditions and institutions are requisite to the development and healthy functioning of the moral sense.

Natural Rights

Jefferson spoke of "inherent and unalienable" rights in the Rough Draft, specifying as basic the rights to preserve life, to preserve liberty, and to pursue happiness. Rights are "inherent" insofar as they are a part of man's nature as a moral being; rights are "unalienable" insofar as they are moral powers to perform actions requisite to the fulfillment of basic duties prescribed by the law of nature. Inalienable rights cannot morally be renounced, transferred, suppressed, or destroyed.

In speaking of an inalienable right of life, the final draft of the Declaration is challengeable inasmuch as there can be no right to what is God-given and to what man already possesses. The correct expression is the right to the preservation or continuance of life. Although morally inalienable, the right to preserve life does not contradict the mutual pledge by the Declaration's signers of their lives in its support. White remarks, "We may have an unalienable right to preserve our lives and yet not only have a *right* to risk them but an *alienable* right to risk them."

The inalienable right to preserve liberty presupposes the possession of liberty, which Jefferson, like Locke and Burlamaqui, declared to be a characteristic of "the equal and independent" natural state of man. The fact that men can be unjustifiably deprived of life and liberty may explain not only the change to the rights of life and liberty in the later drafts of the Declaration, but also that part of the passage in the Rough Draft (deleted by Congress) indicting the king for violating the "most sacred rights of life and liberty" in carrying others into slavery. In the case of involuntary servitude, the God-given inalienable right to lost liberty is retained, which implies a corresponding duty of man's fellows to restore it. Jefferson defined "rightful liberty" as "unobstructed action according to our will within limits drawn around us by the equal rights of others." He was convinced that man "has no natural right in opposition to his social duties."

A difficulty intrudes regarding Jefferson's assertion of a freedom "to believe" in his Bill for Establishing Religious Freedom. Therein he wrote that "the opinions and belief of men depend not on their own will, but follow involuntarily the evidence proposed to their minds." If men lack the power to will belief they then have no duty and no corresponding right to believe. White has shown that Jefferson attempted to escape this quandary by arguing that because God created the mind free and wills that it remain free, God has placed a duty on men not to attempt to change the fact that the opinions of men are necessarily produced by what they regard as evidence. That duty implies a right of all men to continue without restraint in so forming their opinions. This led Jefferson to include among "the natural rights of mankind" freedom of religious worship, freedom from restraint or burdens on account of "religious opinions and belief," and freedom to profess "religious opinions."

Jefferson departed from Locke in not listing "property" as a right in the Declaration. Although Jefferson regarded property in the sense of possession of goods and estates as a natural right, he did not and could not logically regard it as inherent and inalienable. Here again, as White suggests, he may have followed Burlamaqui, who distinguished between a primary and secondary natural law. Burlamaqui held that primary natural law issues directly from the divinely ordained constitution of men apart from any human act or establishment that secondary natural law supposes. The establishment of property in specific goods modifies the original common right of all men to earthly goods and accords with secondary natural law.

On 24 April 1816, in a letter to Du Pont de Nemours, Jefferson declared that the right to property is "founded in our natural wants, in the means with which we are endowed to satisfy these wants, and the right to what we acquire by those means without violating the similar rights of other sensible beings." This formulation follows his naturalistic penchant; each natural right issues from a basic want or need, the denial of which is a violation of nature's plan. This gave additional force to his earlier pronouncement in October 1785 to Madison that "whenever there are in any country uncultivated lands and unemployed poor, it is clear that the laws of property have been so far extended as to violate natural right." Finally, on 13 August 1813, dealing with the question of patent rights in a letter to Isaac McPherson, he precluded as exclusive property "the action of the thinking power called an idea." In this context he remarked that "it is a moot question whether the origin of any kind of property is derived from nature at all." The term "nature" should here be understood in the Burlamaquian sense of the original condition of man before any human act or establishment. It is important to notice that Jefferson's conception of property as an adventitious and not a primary right clearly allows for changes in its distribution.

By listing in the Declaration the three universal rights, Jefferson made the broadest appeal "to the opinions of mankind" for moral recognition and approval of the revolutionary cause. From such inalienable rights, reinforced by the argument from basic wants, as well as historical practices, he later articulated more specific claims. He spoke of rights involving motion, including freedom of movement, migration, assembly, communication, commerce, work and the enjoyment of its fruits, as well as legal "fences" such as equal protection of laws, trial by jury, habeas corpus, and the exclusion of ex post facto laws.

Natural Society

In the Rough Draft Jefferson stated that "all men are created equal and independent." Elsewhere, in a letter to Edward Carrington dated 16 January 1787, he wrote that "experience declares that man is the only animal which devours his own kind," and he divided men into "sheep" and "wolves." He further observed, in a letter to James Madison dated 1 January 1797, that civilization seemed to have no other effect on man "than to teach him to pursue the principle of *bellum omnium in omnia* on a larger scale" than in the natural state. Independent men with idiosyncratic brains, predatory instincts, and conflicting opinions can scarcely be said to possess the ties that communal life presupposes.

These passages should be understood in light of Jefferson's conception of the Creator's overall design. Predatory man serves a purpose in the economy of nature by aiding in the control of the numbers within the many species including his own. Nevertheless, Jefferson regarded the social conflict between men as secondary to their struggle with the environment. He saw the intention of the Creator as the healthy growth and prosperity of the species in the development of a continent unfettered with a feudal inheritance. In this view human institutions can never be regarded as primary shaping forces but at best as instruments facilitating nature's intention by reducing frictions in the exercise of free human energies.

Alongside Jefferson's pessimistic remarks on human nature must be placed his contention that man was "made for society" and "endowed with a sense of right and wrong relative to this," as well as social duties under the law of nature. Natural society is implicit in the common possession of the moral sense, which brings men together by attaching a pleasurable feeling to benevolent acts. Then, too, the challenge of the environment brings men together in the common pursuit, combination, and comparison of "facts" producing practical truths that in application issue in material prosperity, security, and happiness.

Jefferson regarded agriculture as the pursuit most in accordance with nature and productive of individual and social health; as he wrote to John Jay on 23 August 1785, "Cultivators of the earth are the most valuable citizens. They are the most vigorous, the most independant, the most virtuous, and they are tied to their country and wedded to it's liberty and interests by the most lasting bonds." In fact, he wrote in Query 19 of the *Notes,* "those who labour in the earth are the chosen people of God." In a letter to William Short dated 4 August 1820, he extolled the predominance of agriculture in the broad American environment by contrasting it to the European condition: "Here, room is abundant, population scanty, and peace the necessary means for producing men, to whom the redundant soil is offering the means of life and happiness." The ends for a "healthy" society are thus implicit in unencumbered nature.

The environmental factor as a societal influence was complemented by Jefferson's stress on what has been called "presentism" as the essential temporal factor. Proceeding again on biological lines but calculating mathematically, Jefferson posited "generations" (each lasting approximately nineteen years) as the natural vehicles of society; as he wrote to John Wayles Eppes on 24 June 1813, "We may consider each generation as a distinct nation, with a right, by the will of its majority, to bind themselves, but none to bind the succeeding generation, more than the inhabitants of another country." There are then no natural obligations between the present and the past. And the present generation owes to the future only the duty not to pass on any debt. Thus, Jefferson told Madison in a letter from Paris dated 6 September 1789, it is "self evident" that *the earth belongs in usufruct to the living"* and "no man can by *natural right* oblige the lands he occupied, or the persons who succeed him in that occupation, to the payment of debts contracted by him." And "what is true of every member of the society individually, is true of them all collectively, since the rights of the whole can be no more than the sum of the

rights of individuals." It follows that the present generation is never morally bound by traditions, inherited institutions, and ancient customs and practices, but can and should remake society as it wishes. With its limits and tasks set by the environment and its ends implicit in nature, the present generation constitutes the substance of society. The "natural law" of society is the "law of the *majority."* To be "rightful," however, the will of the generational majority must be "reasonable," that is, not violative of the inalienable rights of man.

Finally, nature provides each generation in society with a "natural aristocracy" grounded in "virtue and talents," as opposed to an artificial aristocracy of birth and property. In a letter to Adams dated 28 October 1813, Jefferson called the natural aristocracy "the most precious gift of nature for the instruction, the trusts, and government of society." He thought that "it would have been inconsistent in creation to have formed man for the social state, and not to have provided virtue and wisdom enough to manage the concerns of the society." To him, as to John Milton and Algernon Sidney before him, "the people" were a society led by a natural elite. He assumed that "the people" would readily defer to their natural leaders. Presumably the natural aristocracy is gifted not only with a "healthy" moral sense but with the "science" denied to the "ploughman"; this science ostensibly provides a reasoned and fuller understanding of the law of nature. The division between the natural aristocracy and the people at large can be seen as a social reflection of the dual epistemology Jefferson drew from Burlamaqui. The egalitarian basis is the common participation in the moral sense. The aristocratic basis is the further participation of the virtuous and talented in the logically superior corrective and guiding faculty of reason. The political link is the assumption that the people will defer to the elite in democratic choice.

JEFFERSON'S POLITICAL THOUGHT: THE EMPIRE FOR LIBERTY

Further illustrative of Jefferson's propensity to regard nature as model is his evaluation, in a letter to Madison dated 30 January 1787, of three main extant societies: those without formal government, exemplified in the American Indians; those under governments in which each person has a just influence and "a precious degree of liberty and happiness," exemplified to a limited degree in England, and to a great degree in the United States; and those with governments based on force, the rule of "wolves over sheep," exemplified in monarchies other than England and in most republics. Jefferson was "not clear" in his mind that the first condition "is not the best," although inconsistent with growth and a large population. He admired in it the control exercised by manners, social sanctions, opinion, and the moral sense. It was preferable to the condition in civilized Europe, which evidenced rule by "too much law."

Implicit in these statements is much of Jefferson's political thought. Convinced that man is a social animal, Jefferson seems to have entertained a strong doubt that nature intended man to be a political animal. His ideal appears to have been a healthy natural society without coercive government. Consequently he looked to political institutions that would least depart from the "free" natural state, while safeguarding the advantages of civilization and development, and protecting the sheep from the wolves. Contending against those who saw government under the Articles of Confederation as bad, he declared in a letter to John Rutledge dated 6 August 1787: "The only condition on earth to be compared with ours . . . is that of the Indians, where they have still less law than we."

Basis of Government: The Consent of the Governed

Jefferson expressed, in a 1790 opinion on the constitutionality of a residence bill, the belief that "every man, and every body of men on earth, possesses the right of self-government: they receive it with their being from the hand of nature." Self-government is a morally inalienable right of a "people." Jefferson defined a people vaguely as "a society or a nation." In the state of nature a people is a society of "equal and independent" individuals possessed of natural rights and moved legitimately by the rightful will of the majority. Formal government, established by majority consent, is not a substitute for nature but at best an institutional framework that, as Locke had contended, facilitates society by removing the "inconveniences" of the state of nature. Jefferson did not explicitly articulate a contract theory of state authority. The closest he came to this was in connection with his notion of the sovereignty of the present generation in the establishment of a constitution. Implicit in his thought, however, was the Lockean formulation. Concerning the form of government, he held, in a letter to Gouverneur Morris dated 30 December 1792, that a nation may "govern itself under whatever forms it pleases, and change these forms at it's own will." Jefferson thus pronounced the principle of political legitimacy and obligation as indicated by the law of nature—government established by "the consent of the governed," a consent that is not corporate but individual, and yet rendered conclusive by the majority.

End or Purpose of Government

A vexing ambiguity exists in the Jeffersonian writings concerning the purpose of government. This is graphically illustrated in the changes made in the drafts of the Declaration. In the Rough Draft Jefferson declared the "undeniable" truth that "to secure these *ends*" (the preservation of life and of liberty, and the pursuit of happiness) "governments are instituted among men." The revised draft substituted the word "rights" for "ends," so that the "self-evident" truth becomes "to secure these *rights*" (life, liberty, and the pursuit of happiness), "governments are instituted among men."

What is the significance of this change, along with the other changes? Following White's analysis it can be said that the word "secure," in its reference in the Rough Draft to "ends," is best understood as "attain." Government can then be understood to have as its purpose the positive task of aiding and abetting men in attaining their divinely ordained ends—the preservation of life, the preservation of liberty, and the pursuit of happiness. When the word "ends" was changed to "rights" (along with the change to the rights of life, liberty, and the pursuit of happiness), the verb "secure" lost the positive connotation of activity toward a goal or goals and becomes understandable if construed as "to make secure," "to protect" the inalienable rights.

On this reading the full range of changes from the Rough Draft to the final draft brought significant modification in the logical structure and meaning of the theoretical portion of the Declaration. White concludes that the changes "reveal a tendency on the part of Jefferson, or of others to whose wishes he acceded, to dilute the purpose of government to the point where it ceases to be an *abettor* of men in the active attainment of three Burlamaquian ends proposed by God and becomes only a *protector* of certain rights."

The revisions, however, might otherwise be explained in terms of a presumed decision by Jefferson (and the committee) to scale down, and thus enhance, the appeal to "the opinions of mankind" by stating only what could be held as universally valid and minimally required as moral justification of rebellion. This would preclude as unnecessary and irrelevant a broader statement of substantive ends. Thus government is justified minimally and universally under the moral law of nature insofar as it is founded by consent and works to realize the basic "ends," seen in the revised draft as the securing of the primary and inalienable rights.

Scholars Gilbert Chinard, Arthur M. Schlesinger, and Charles Wiltse, in contrast to White, have interpreted the final draft of the Declaration to mean that Jefferson espoused the view that government exists to attain the happiness of all its subjects. And most recently, Garry Wills argued from his examination of the committee draft that Jefferson applied the moral-sense theory, in its equation of benevolence and happiness, to "the *public* scale of political action" and consequently cannot be considered a Lockean individualist.

Later Jeffersonian pronouncements are either balanced or ambiguous enough to support any meaning that is inferred from them. On the one hand Jefferson wrote that "the legitimate powers of government extend to such acts only as are injurious to others," and that "it is to secure our just rights that we resort to government at all," and that the "true office" of legislators is "to declare and enforce only our natural rights and duties, and to take none of them from us." On the other hand he stated that "the care of human life and happiness, and not their destruction, is the first and only legitimate object of good government," and that "the only orthodox object of the institution of government is to secure [attain?] the greatest degree of happiness possible to the general mass of those associated under it." And, apparently sounding both notes, he wrote: "The equal rights of man, and the happiness of every individual, are now acknowledged to be the only legitimate objects of government."

The Rough Draft of the Declaration, construed in light of Burlamaqui, must be regarded as revelatory of important and neglected facets of Jefferson's thought, as well as instructive in interpreting the final draft. Without it we miss the linkage between his conception of natural rights and their derivation from duties to realize ends prescribed in the law of nature. In this light it belies Boorstin's charges that Jefferson was unable or unwilling to state explicitly moral ends to be served by government and that in Jefferson's natural-rights theory the Creator apparently prescribed no duties but only rights.

The arguments of scholars such as Wills notwithstanding, the later drafts are susceptible to such charges. It is difficult to argue that Jefferson and his cosigners, in referring to the purpose of government, meant more than the duty to respect, protect, and guard what John Dickinson had earlier called "the rights essential to happiness." On this reading the inalienable right to pursue happiness is afforded by the Creator to each individual to follow in the manner he sees fit, compatible with the equal rights of his fellows, and without governmental prescription of its content and assurance of its attainment. It would then again appear that, politically speaking, liberty is central in the triad of rights.

Jefferson best expressed his mind on the point in his First Inaugural Address: "A wise and frugal Government, which shall restrain men from injuring one another, shall leave them otherwise free to regulate their own pursuits of industry and improvement, and shall not take from the mouth of labor the bread it has earned. This is the sum of good government, and this is necessary to close the circle of our felicities." This objective was compatible with government providing not only legal conditions but removing obstacles to the full realization of material and intellectual development. In light of this must be seen Jefferson's efforts to effect equitable land distribution and easy access to the public domain, to establish a broad public system of education with advancement based on achievement, to eliminate feudal remains in the laws and artificial hierarchy in society, to circumvent schemes of land speculators, to free commerce, to prevent the building of a public debt, to work for the eventual end of slavery, to prevent central concentration of governmental and financial power, and to expand the territory of the United States to continental dimensions and develop its resources, especially the agricultural, with commerce as its handmaid, in an "empire for liberty."

Finally, for Jefferson to have arrived at a clear and distinct conception of a transcendent common good, indicating affirmative governmental implementation of clearly defined substantive ends, would have required him to have seen a "people" as more than the sum of its individual members in a mathematically calculated "present generation" moved by a numerical majority and loosely united by institutions that merely guard against the inconveniences of natural society. It would have demanded a revision of his belief that "the rights of the whole can be no more than the sum of the rights of the individual." Society, energized by the industry and cooperation of free and equal men, and not government, was to him the prime mover.

The Right of the People to Alter, Abolish, and Reinstitute Government

Jefferson proclaimed in the Declaration the "self-evident" right and duty of the people to change a government that acts in violation of its purpose—the securing of their natural rights. He carefully added that prudence dictates that long-established governments should not be changed for "light and transient causes." Using Lockean language he wrote that it is only "when a long train of abuses and usurpations pursuing invariably the same object, evinces a design to reduce them under absolute despotism," that action by the people becomes morally necessary. Thus the right of rebellion was asserted in highly qualified moral terms.

A difficulty arises concerning the questions who or what constitutes "the people" and how is the decision to take the fateful step to be made? It is obvious that Jefferson did not require unanimous consent; the moral engine of movement in natural society is the rightful majority. Nonetheless his retrospective approval of the "Glorious Revolution" of 1688, which David Hume remarked was the work of seven hundred men in a nation of ten million, indicated that he did not believe an active majority was a practical moral requisite. He probably thought that an active minority (the natural aristocracy), with widespread moral support, provided an adequate basis. It might be added that John Adams estimated that one-third of the American people in the Revolutionary period were loyal to the Crown, one-third were in rebellion, and one-third remained neutral.

A decade later Jefferson abandoned verbal restraint and emphasized the need for the recurrent exercise of the right of rebellion. In a letter to Madison dated 30 January 1787 he wrote: "I hold it that a little rebellion now and then is a good thing, and as necessary in the political world as storms in the physical. . . . It is a medicine necessary for the sound health of government." Referring to Shay's rebellion he commented in a letter to William Stephens Smith dated 13 November 1787: "God forbid we should ever be twenty years without such a rebellion. . . . The tree of liberty must be refreshed from time to time with the blood of

patriots and tyrants. It is it's natural manure." Rebellion was thus seen as purgative, bringing men back to the first principles of nature from which they can begin anew.

Because it is the living generation that alone possesses sovereignty and rights and because Jefferson calculated that a generation lasts approximately nineteen years, he concluded in his letter to Madison of 6 September 1789 that "every constitution . . . and every law, naturally expires at the end of 19 years. If it be enforced longer, it is an act of force and not of right." Joining the doctrine of rebellion to that of the present generation, it follows that each generation possesses not only a right but a duty to remove itself, by force if required, from the shackles of the past. James Madison interposed cogent objections in a letter dated 4 February 1790, asking whether a government so often revised would not "become too mutable to retain those prejudices in its favor . . . which are perhaps a salutary aid to the most rational Government," and maintaining that the title of the living extends only to the earth's natural state and that the improvements made by the dead constitute a charge upon the living who benefit by them. Jefferson's position can be characterized as an extreme expression of the classical republican doctrine of the recurrent need to return to first principles lest the accretions of time and privilege submerge them.

And yet Jefferson's remarks were the rhetoric of exaggeration. He was prudent in practice and cognizant of the fact that the general must be understood in terms of the particular. He could extol rebellion but admit that the peaceful making or amending of a constitution, as well as an election, served the purpose as well. Thus he regarded his election to the presidency in 1800 as a great revolution in the principles of government—as great as the revolution of 1776 was in the form of government. If the "wolves" know not only that the "sheep" are watching them but also that they have a constitutional means for change, backed up by the moral right to rebel, the inclination to mischief will be lessened. Jefferson's moderation is borne out by his statement in a letter to Samuel Kercheval dated 12 July 1816: "I am certainly not an advocate for frequent and untried changes in laws and constitutions. I think moderate imperfections had better be borne with; because, when once known, we accommodate ourselves to them, and find practical means of correcting their ill effects."

Republicanism

Jefferson thought that European nations with their feudal inheritances, class distinctions, and crowded cities were divided, "under pretense of governing," into two groups, "wolves and sheep." He considered America as not immune to such division because "human nature is the same on every side of the Atlantic, and will be alike influenced by the same causes." Although he would not agree "that fourteen out of fifteen men are rogues," he confessed that in matters of power and profit he "always found that rogues would be uppermost," unless strong safeguards are provided. The sheep must have power to check the wolves and preserve freedom.

To this end Jefferson prescribed popular sovereignty, democratic republicanism, and constitutional limitations. While not equating *vox populi* and *vox Dei*, he declared, in a letter dated 31 October 1823 to Monsieur A. Coray, that the people "are the only safe, because the only honest, depositories of the public rights, and should therefore be introduced into the administration of them in every function to which they are sufficient." He assumed that "in general they will elect the wise and good" (natural aristocracy), but above all he trusted not to their virtue but to their numbers, which precluded the possibility of their being bought.

Although the Declaration of Independence attests to Jefferson's adherence to popular sovereignty, his theory of republicanism is an affirmation of participatory democracy. "Purely and simply," he said of a republic in a letter to John Taylor dated 28 May 1816, "it means a government by its citizens in mass, acting directly and personally, according to rules established by the majority; and that every other government is more or less republican, in proportion as it has in its composition more or less of this ingredient of the direct action of the citizens." This pure form of republicanism, direct democracy, he saw as impracticable beyond the limits of a town. Beyond the town level he declared that republicanism shades off into types where the powers of the government, being divided, should be exercised each by elected representatives expressing the will of their constituents.

Like Madison, Jefferson broke with the classical doctrine expounded by Montesquieu that only small states are fitted to be republics. In happy accordance with his notion of an expanding empire for liberty, Jefferson conjectured, in a letter to François D'Ivernois dated 6 February 1795, that a just republic "must be so extensive as that local egoisms may never reach its greater part; that on every particular question, a majority may be found in its councils free from particular interests, and giving, therefore, a uniform prevalance to the principles of justice."

Jefferson's theory of an ascending series of republics illustrates not only his conception of how political man might approximate the natural order of freedom but how he brought together his ideas of direct and representative democracy, the territorial devolution of authority, and the feasibility and desirability of an extensive republic. At the base is the self-reliant individual who administers his own farm or property. These citizens participate directly and fully in the government of "wards." Each ward, covering five or six miles square, provides basic governmental services and election of governmental functionaries. On the next level, the county, government would be controlled by justices elected in the wards and would deal with matters of general concern to the county. Above this, the state government, a representative republic, would attend to "civil rights, laws, police, and administration of what concerns the State generally." Finally the national government, an extensive representative republic, would deal with defense and foreign and federal relations. Corresponding roughly to this hierarchy within the states, Jefferson prescribed free public education, with advancement beyond the elementary stage based on achievement, as necessary to free republican government and as a means to the identification of the natural aristocracy.

Jefferson's constitutional theory should be understood against this background. He saw a constitution as a compact deriving from the sovereign present generation. He thought that certain operational and structural principles, such as the provision for amendment, the separation of powers, and a bicameral legislature, were necessary to free government. He was as opposed to the tyranny of a legislative majority as to the tyranny of one man. He worked to implement the principle of equality in the form of equal districting and extension of the suffrage. In his draft of a constitution for Virginia in 1776, he included a provision to grant a fifty-acre freehold to every propertyless white male citizen. He turned away from the classical republican prescription of a balance of the few and the many in government and toward equal participation in limited democratic governments. Because he advocated limited government he insisted on inclusion of a bill of rights in constitutions. He sought the establishment of a secular state in which religion would have no public function but would be freed from all ties to government. This would permit its free and unrestrained exercise and propagation so

long as its principles did not "break out into overt acts against peace and good order." Similarly did he champion freedom of expression. On 16 January 1787, he wrote to Edward Carrington, "Were it left to me to decide whether we should have a government without newspapers or newspapers without a government, I should not hesitate a moment to prefer the latter."

In accordance with his advocacy of strong checks on government Jefferson fought for strict construction of the federal Constitution. Concerning the determination of the constitutionality of questions, he denied exclusive power to the judiciary by holding, in a letter to Judge Spencer Roane dated 6 September 1819, that "each department is truly independent of the others, and has an equal right to decide for itself what is the meaning of the Constitution in the cases submitted to its action; and especially, where it is to act ultimately and without appeal." Because he deemed the federal Constitution to be a compact between the states, he declared, in his draft of the Kentucky resolutions attacking the constitutionality of the Alien and Sedition Acts, that the federal government as a creature cannot be the final judge, in any or all of its branches, of the extent of its powers. He considered nullification a "natural right" of the states and the "rightful remedy." His overall attitude is best summed up in his words, "free government is founded in jealousy, and not in confidence."

The logic of historical events decided against Jefferson's notions of strict constructionism, limited judicial review, and nullification. His federal republic extended not only in territory but in powers, as evidenced in the broad assertion of authority he himself exercised while serving as president. His general theory of limited constitutional government remains, however, as a vital facet of the American political mind, although it frequently has been abused as a rationalization of more underlying interests.

SIGNIFICANCE OF JEFFERSON'S THOUGHT

Because he regarded man as the most exalted being in nature's realm, Jefferson focused on the liberty that he believed to be the precondition of each man's "pursuit of happiness." Because he was a lawyer with a deep knowledge of legal and constitutional history, he saw his ideas reducible to concrete, historical content. Thus the theoretical part of the Declaration of Independence is given substance in terms of the particulars in the indictment of the king. The "natural rights" that he extolled were given specificity and procedural guarantee in terms of the historic rights of Englishmen, which time and experience had verified to be in accord with the needs of free men. Likewise he hedged in pushing his ideas to their logical conclusion. Thus while he could speak of a "natural right" of the present generation to sever itself from the past and return to natural principles, he could also regard the organic common law (as expounded by Coke) as essentially worthy of retention. Also, while he exalted the law of the majority as the dictate of nature and a means by which "the wise and good" could rise to leadership, he advocated bicameralism, separation of powers, and constitutional limitations as restraints on the majority and the natural aristocracy. Finally, in practice, he not only generally operated with prudent moderation, but proceeded on his belief that what is practicable must often control what is pure theory and that no maxim can be regarded as applicable to all times and circumstances. Consequently as president he was undeterred by his principle of strict construction of the Constitution in his purchase of Louisiana, his retention of part of the Hamiltonian program, and in his establishment of a rigid embargo. And as a responsible statesman cognizant of the ubiquity of power he wrote to J. B. Colvin on 20 September 1810: "A strict observance of the written laws is doubtless *one* of the high duties of a good citizen. . . . The laws of necessity, of self-preservation, of saving our country when in danger, are of higher obligation."

Symbolic of Jefferson's approach was his proposal that the seal of the United States bear the faces of the children of Israel and the Anglo-Saxon chieftains Hengist and Horsa. He saw Americans as a chosen people who had recaptured their prefeudal Anglo-Saxon birthright with its pristine common law. The Saxon myth was a significant category in the Jeffersonian mind, referring to an earlier golden age ending with a fall brought about by the Norman imposition of feudalism. Above all, the myth symbolized the Anglo-Saxon cultural matrix, the source of Jefferson's basic aspirations and formation, in light of which should be understood his universalized ideas.

Jefferson's political thought was predicated more on man's relation to nature than to government. As such it entailed a major modification of classical republicanism by Lockean individualism domesticated in accordance with American conditions. Thus, the private virtues and interests of self-reliant, vigilant individuals in their independence and free association were afforded primacy over "public virtue" in service of a substantive republican common good beyond collective self-preservation and protection of individual rights. The democracy of equal political participation replaced the notion of government as a balance between the few and the many. The notion of control from the political center gave way to the idea of individual economic decision making and bartering. Finally, along with the central spirit of democratization went the notion of the expanding extensive republic as a most significant modification of the classical republican view.

Jefferson's thought was prehistoricist, asserting unchanging self-evident truths, a stable human nature, and a moral law of nature. The acids of modernity have corroded confidence in such approaches, without supplying viable substitutes. Despite philosophical insufficiencies and ambiguities, there is an abiding fundamental truth in Jefferson's approach that had to be relearned in the twentieth century. This truth is summed up by two statements of Jefferson that best capture the enduring spirit of his thought: "Nothing then is unchangeable but the inherent and unalienable rights of man" and "There exists a right independent of force."

Political Economy

DREW R. McCOY

VIRTUALLY everyone knows something about Thomas Jefferson and political economy. His ringing tribute to "those who labour in the earth" as "the chosen people of God" has resonated across the centuries to our own time, when it continues to express the yearnings of the disenchanted in postindustrial America. Nothing is more commonplace than the belief that Jefferson was an "agrarian" who detested crowded cities, noisy factories, and the unhealthy patterns of corruption they bred. His celebration of the farmer and rural life has, indeed, informed a cultural tradition in the United States that extols the virtues of social simplicity and personal independence. Moreover, there are few Americans today who are not equally familiar with Jefferson's idea of the "chosen" government, which he defined so eloquently in his first inaugural address. In this celebrated passage, Jefferson spoke of "a wise and frugal government" that would "restrain men from injuring one another" but "leave them otherwise free to regulate their own pursuits of industry and improvement" by not taking "from the mouth of labour the bread it has earned." Enemies of so-called big government—those who decry fiscal waste, high taxes, and bureaucratic regulation in general—have long rushed to embrace this venerable prescription for a low-profile federal government.

These two well-known images of Jeffersonian political economy would appear to mesh nicely. Taken together, they have in fact formed the dominant image of Jefferson as agrarian democrat, eager to protect the virtuous farmer and the ordinary citizen from the predatory schemes of privilege-hunting aristocrats who manipulate government to their own selfish, unproductive ends. Over the years many of the seemingly "wrong" people, including spokesmen for huge corporate interests actively working to undermine Jefferson's agrarian democracy, have trumpeted his laissez-faire slogans when it has suited their needs, but not even this grotesque incongruity has dispelled the composite portrait. In a very real sense the spirit of Thomas Jefferson, as political economist, still lives.

But the story is, of course, far more complex than superficial popular images would suggest. If the subject of Jefferson and political economy is to an extent familiar, it is also elusive and easily misconstrued. As with most simplifications, there is in this case enough historical truth behind the symbol to lend it both energy and some semblance of validity. Although some scholars in recent years have endeavored to turn conventional wisdom on its head, even going so far as to portray Jefferson as more of a friend to American manufactures than his adversary Alexander Hamilton, they have missed the point. The problem is not that people have gotten things backward, inventing a Jefferson who never existed, but rather that over the centuries a sense of the distinctively eighteenth-century context that shaped and gave meaning to his vision in political economy has been lost. To understand what Jefferson meant and why he believed what he did we must somehow bridge the vast cultural gap that separates us from what Daniel Boorstin has so aptly called "the lost world of Thomas Jefferson." It is clear, on one level, that the twentieth-century world of experience would be utterly foreign, even incomprehensible, to an eighteenth-century Revolutionary; that Jefferson lived in a world without automobiles, airplanes, computers, and all forms of modern mass communication goes without saying. But few outside the historical profession (and not all within) fully understand or appreciate just how much has changed since the eighteenth century concerning the ways in which people think about society, economy, and government. More than our society and day-to-day lives have changed. Our broader world of cultural experience has itself been radically transformed, and Jefferson's familiar preferences and beliefs in political economy take on a somewhat different and more intense meaning when they are properly rooted in his, and not our, paradigm of perception and discourse.

A related issue is worth noting here at the outset. Perhaps the most important statement Jefferson ever made pertaining to political economy is one that scholars alone are fond of quoting, no doubt because it lacks the felicitous resonance and conspicuous relevance of his more memorable quotes concerning farmers and small government. "In so complicated a science as political economy," he wrote in 1816, "no one axiom can be laid down as wise and expedient, for all times and circumstances, and for their contraries." Jefferson was reasonably well read in this science, as he was in most. He was familiar with the writings of Adam Smith, Jean-Baptiste Say, and T. R. Malthus, among others, and he even oversaw the translation and publication in the United States of Destutt de Tracy's *Treatise on Political Economy.* But he was also eminently practical and flexible in his approach to problems, intellectual and real, within the domain of these theorists, which is to say that neither rigid principles nor refined abstractions shaped his thinking or policies. Jefferson was not a doctrinaire political economist, and he never considered himself a formal disciple of any thinker or school, although some scholars have carelessly labeled him, among other things, a Physiocrat. Jefferson was well acquainted with the beliefs of this French circle of philosophical economists, and certainly there are enough surface similarities between his thinking and theirs to make the connection plausible. But there were significant differences as well, and more important, Jefferson's statecraft never proceeded from the coherent system of interlocking assumptions and principles that characterized the French *economistes.*

In this case as in most it simply makes no sense to approach Jefferson in terms of specific lines of intellectual influence. Historians are notoriously fond of playing the game of tracing Jefferson's ideas to this or that thinker (European, of course) who must have "influenced" him and therefore should be given credit for "shaping" his outlook. As a rule such direct or literal lines of influence never existed in the form such language suggests. Jefferson's was a richly informed and studious mind that cannot be understood, to be sure, apart from the broader texture of the transatlantic Enlightenment, but it was also a creative and eclectic mind that had, within that context, a discernable life of its own. His outlook was shaped as much by American experience as by any systematic reading in European sources. Congenitally averse to abstract metaphysical speculation, Jefferson approached political economy from a perspective best understood not in terms of specific sources or lines of influence, but only against the general backdrop of "enlightened" ideas that had their own distinctively eighteenth-century vocabulary, conceptual framework, and emotional context.

Other preliminary cautions are in order. In a superb examination of Jefferson's economic ideas and policies published in 1946, William Grampp persuasively suggested the dangers of assuming consistency and continuity over the long haul of his subject's fifty-year public career. That Jefferson adjusted to fresh developments and circumstances between the Revolution and his death in 1826 is indisputable, whether or not one accepts Grampp's specific formula of three distinct phases in his evolution as a political economist. But if Jefferson's specific policy recommendations shifted, sometimes reflecting changes in his thinking, these adjustments must not be exaggerated nor their significance overstated. They never overturned or significantly restructured the broader framework of assumptions and beliefs that guided his approach to political economy. One popular interpretation of Jefferson's later career, especially as president, is to view him as moving steadily toward acceptance of the policies and even the principles of his former Federalist adversaries, including Hamilton. As will be ex-

plained more fully later, this view misrepresents the evolution of Jefferson's political economy. In the minds of both Jefferson and his Republican colleague James Madison, the original expectations—and fears—that had shaped their understanding of America's republican revolution persisted intact into the nineteenth century. Jefferson's adjustments and accommodations were real, but they took place within a familiar paradigm of values and purpose—which is to say, they did not mark a capitulation to Hamiltonianism, modernity, or the exigencies of an Industrial Revolution.

In this connection, one of the greatest dangers in the attempt to comprehend Jefferson's political economy is a failure to distinguish the purposes of his policies from their actual consequences. It is all too easy to assume, uncritically, that Jefferson intended to bring about what his policies in fact produced. Yet as Henry Adams suggested a century ago, irony is central to any meaningful understanding of Jefferson's presidential administrations. Sometimes the adjustments that Jefferson was compelled to make in his later years were to circumstances that he had unwittingly helped create or that had resulted from the unacknowledged failure of his policies. To read into the short- and long-term repercussions of his programs purposeful intent, and to infer from them his "real" beliefs and principles, is a trap that invites both the unwary and those who wish to perceive Jefferson as more modern than he actually was.

THE BROAD VISION

Although Jefferson was not an ideologue with a systematic and coherent approach to political economy, his views and policies took shape within an intellectual universe of assumptions, values, and expectations that the student must first recapture and comprehend. Enlightened thinkers in eighteenth-century Europe and America generally conceived of social and economic development in terms of an evolutionary process with certain fixed stages. History suggested that all societies normally proceeded through several phases of organization from uncivilized simplicity to civilized complexity. Men first formed primitive groups of barbaric, wandering hunters—the "lowest and rudest state of society," according to Adam Smith—contemporary examples of which could be found among the native populations of eastern North America. At the next level men became herdsmen or shepherds, tending their flocks in a more settled, regularized existence. From there societies advanced toward a new plateau, an agricultural stage at which farmers actually began cultivating the soil without engaging in much commerce or manufacturing; to the extent that they had manufactures, they were of the simplest kinds, in the form of the rather crude and coarse household manufactures that rural families traditionally prepared for their own use. When societies moved beyond this agricultural phase, they were headed toward the highest stages of civilization, represented by the most advanced areas of eighteenth-century Europe, at which stage the development of commerce and the "finer" manufactures had progressed significantly. This final stage was modern commercial society, characterized by a highly developed division of labor (which permitted the more advanced forms of manufacturing) and great refinement in the manners and morals of men (often referred to as "polish" or, a more controversial term, "luxury").

This general framework for describing social and economic change highlighted a series of interrelated issues and concerns that stimulated spirited debate among eighteenth-century thinkers. As they pondered the progress of society through these recognizable stages, many, including Jefferson, tended to have a mixed or ambivalent opinion of the process. Few doubted that a more mature society had substantial benefits that ruder, younger societies did not—from the salient advantages of greater wealth and comfort to the advances in knowledge and technology that attended this enhanced refinement. To put it simply, civilized men were generally more peaceful and more humane as well as more comfortable. But the maturation or aging of a society also had a tendency to create unhealthy conditions, which included dangerous concentrations of wealth and power and the enervating corruption of morals that usually accompanied great affluence. The commercialization of society paradoxically both improved and debased men. The trick, it would seem, was to advance far enough in the cycle to enjoy the many advantages of commerce without moving so far as to begin an ominous descent into decay and corruption, powerful images of which were evoked by historical memories of ancient Rome.

As eighteenth-century observers scrutinized societies of both the past and present, they discovered examples of each stage and inferred that within any social system there was embedded a natural pattern of change that would normally manifest itself in time. What propelled societies through the stages? According to most accounts, population growth was the impetus for change, because it promoted first a quest for increased subsistence and eventually a search for new sources of employment to support the larger population. As Jefferson understood this dynamic of social evolution, demography was, indeed, the critical variable. When a society was pushed too far beyond the agricultural stage of development by the pressure of population growth on the available supply of land, the results were increasing inequality, poverty, dependence, and social misery. Those who could not own land in a mature society lost their independence and competence; eventually, they formed a class of degraded laborers, abjectly dependent on their propertied employers for a bare subsistence, in new forms of public manufacturing. In words that captured Jefferson's view just as well, Benjamin Franklin had tersely summarized the point some fifteen years before the American Revolution: "The natural livelihood of the thin inhabitants of a forest country, is hunting; that of a greater number, pasturage; that of a middling population, agriculture; and that of the greatest, manufactures; which last must subsist the bulk of the people in a full country, or they must be subsisted by charity, or perish." These social unfortunates, the surplus population of modern commercial society, were physically wretched, but their lack of independence made them socially and politically dangerous as well. As Jefferson so memorably phrased the matter in his paean to agriculture in the *Notes on Virginia,* such dependence "begets subservience and venality, suffocates the germ of virtue, and prepares fit tools for the designs of ambition."

Jefferson's invocation of the term *virtue* has larger resonance and significance than we might imagine. As he and the Revolutionary generation forged a commitment to republican government in the 1770s, they confronted several fundamental issues in political economy that emerged from this conceptual paradigm of social development. The neoclassical idea that republican government required an extraordinary degree of morality among the people—summarized in the notion of "virtue"—was not lost upon Jefferson, even though his conception of virtue was not as rigidly or intensely classical as that held by, say, the latter-day Puritan Samuel Adams of Massachusetts. The term had indeed taken on an elastic, even ambiguous meaning for many of the Revolutionaries. Originally it had signified the passionate devotion to the public good that arose from rigorous austerity and self-denial, but this classical definition made difficult sense in the more modern world of the eighteenth century. Often *virtue* referred simply to the general moral integrity of an individual and his ability to refrain from corrupt and socially dangerous behavior.

Above all, perhaps, American republicans, including Jefferson, emphasized the notion that the virtuous man was morally disciplined by his industry. A healthy republican citizen avoided the snare of idleness, which led inexorably to personal degradation and often to social and political corruption as well. Scholars have always been struck by Jefferson's methodical habits and his almost obsessive concern that he and all those dependent on his guidance remain busy. Just as he believed that personal discipline and industry were essential to individual health and happiness, he never doubted that on a larger scale a republican people, to be fit citizens rather than "fit tools for the designs of ambition," had to be active, industrious, and fully employed. No republic could long endure on the backs of idle, immoral men who lacked virtue; or, to put it a bit differently, republicanism was incompatible with the lowest stages of social development, where indigent savages prevailed, as well as with the highest stages, where civilized refinement turned suddenly to corruption.

Complementing this emphasis on industry as the essence of virtue, Jefferson believed that a republican society must have a certain structure—specifically, that property should be distributed widely and more or less equally among independent individuals. There must be, in other words, a measure of social and economic equality in a republic where ideally every man, by owning land, would have direct access to the productive resources of nature. When property became too narrowly distributed and large numbers of landless men depended for subsistence on an elite class of employers, republican government was in grave jeopardy. As economic power became concentrated in the hands of the few, political power would just as surely gravitate to them, and a republic would collapse into the monarchical or aristocratic forms that the Revolutionaries had risked their lives to escape. Thus, if the United States ever developed a social order like those found in England and Europe, Jefferson assumed its form of government would follow a comparably ominous path, away from virtue and republicanism toward corruption and monarchy. As he put it in more specific terms to James Madison shortly after the Revolution, "I think our governments will remain virtuous for many centuries; as long as they are chiefly agricultural, and this will be as long as there shall be vacant lands in any part of America. When they get piled upon one another in large cities, as in Europe, they will become corrupt as in Europe."

A republican America, in sum, would have to remain at a predominantly agricultural stage of development, a middle stage happily situated between the undesirable extremes of barbarous simplicity and corrupt maturity. What Jefferson envisioned as ideal was a nation of industrious, prosperous, and virtuous republican farmers, with its manufactures limited to the simplest, household types that every hardworking farm family would naturally produce for its own use. Artisans who were independent producers—that is, who owned their own shops and tools and produced valuable "necessaries" for a local market—could also be accommodated nicely to this republican mold; what could not was a system of public manufacturing that employed hordes of landless, dependent workers. That unfortunate system was to remain in the Old World, where it could conveniently offer Americans any "refined" manufactures they might want in exchange for their surplus produce.

One can infer from several of Jefferson's observations that he, like most enlightened thinkers of his time, attributed a certain grim inevitability to the customary pattern of social development. He did not doubt that eventually the United States would be swept up in the inexorable logic of social maturation and plunge into corruption. But Jefferson was an optimist, not a pessimist, because he thought it possible to postpone that moment for decades, indeed centuries, to come. As long as certain conditions were secured, America might flourish indefinitely at a republican stage of development. First and foremost, there had to be an ample supply of land to support the country's burgeoning population, because without land demographic pressures might force the development of a more complex economy with dangerous, unrepublican inequalities and dependencies. Thus vigorous expansion across space—the vast North American continent—was endemic to Jefferson's political economy, as his public career amply demonstrates.

Less obvious, perhaps, but just as significant, was Jefferson's principled commitment to the expansion of America's foreign commerce. Indeed, a second condition necessary for the republic's security was an adequate foreign demand for its agricultural surplus. Jefferson's farmers had to be disciplined and industrious in order to be virtuous; but in America, with its rich resources and tremendous productive potential, virtuous farmers created a surplus that, exceeding the collective demand of the home market, had to be exported to consumers abroad. Although Jefferson never explicitly stated the matter in these terms, republican farmers were in fact dependent on foreign markets to sustain their industry and full employment on the land; as a necessary cure for potential idleness and degeneracy, foreign commerce supported the virtuous character of America's rural population. Should sufficient markets for that surplus not be available abroad, Jefferson's republic was jeopardized from two potential directions: it faced the unenviable prospect, on the one hand, of declining into the state of uncivilized indolence that would accompany a primitive economy based on subsistence rather than commercial agriculture or, on the other hand, of being compelled to devise alternative incentives to industry and exertion including, perhaps, the advanced manufactures that might employ those who could not be profitably occupied on the land. Just as Jefferson's republican commitment to an ample supply of open land led directly to his policies of territorial expansion, his parallel commitment to an ample foreign commerce led directly to his policies in defense of free trade and a liberal international commercial order.

As the twin guarantors of Jefferson's republic, territorial and commercial expansion addressed problems in political economy posed by what he perceived to be a natural process of social development. It might be said that, understanding how America could grow old naturally by passing through the customary phases of social organization, he sought to throw space and foreign markets in the way of time. But Jefferson also believed that a society could be pushed prematurely into decay, and its natural predicament accelerated and aggravated, by the misguided operations of government. Indeed, given America's apparently vast resources of land, he tended to identify this artificial threat to the republic's potential well-being as both more immediate and more dangerous than the inevitable ravages of time. Jefferson's fear of meddlesome government and a corrupt political system reflects many strains of eighteenth-century concern, not the least important of which is the voluminous literature directed against what Adam Smith defined as "the mercantile system" and what we generally call "mercantilism."

Both Smith and the French Physiocrats were in the vanguard of a movement to combat a system of policy predicated on the belief that foreign commerce and manufactures were the most valuable sectors of a nation's economy and, as such, were deserving of political preference and artificial sup-

port. Their general complaint—one that Jefferson absorbed fully into his own outlook—was that such a system of administrative policy operated to the disadvantage of agriculture (always the most productive form of investment), in the process stifling overall productivity, encouraging the depopulation of the countryside, and promoting excessive and unnecessary social misery. Smith's memorable indictment of the mercantile system as antiquated, corrupt, and wasteful was not so much a blanket indictment of governmental involvement in the economy as it was an assault on a specific system of policy; as part of an age of "political economy" rather than pure "economics," both Smith and Jefferson assumed that to an extent the government was inextricably tied to the functioning of a country's economy and society. Indeed, Smith's classic formulation of the issue was part of a broader eighteenth-century debate over the precise relationship between government and social change—a debate that was closely linked to the simultaneous controversy about whether to interpret certain patterns of change as progress, corruption, or some curious amalgam of both.

Much of this debate in political economy can be understood as a response to the new activities and functions of governments in eighteenth-century Europe. Of especial relevance to Jefferson and other American republicans was the vehement reaction to the appearance in England of a modern fiscal system in the wake of the Glorious Revolution and the ensuing decades of war. The funding of the national debt, the creation of the Bank of England and other large moneyed companies, and the beginnings of a permanent stock and money market in the early eighteenth century were all part of a conspicuously new system of political economy, one that unleashed innovative patterns of speculation among the "moneyed men" and "stockjobbers" who suddenly appeared on the scene. Opposition to this system was intense, and it generally focused on the allegedly corrupt connection between the government and these new economic institutions.

The corruption was said to manifest itself, above all, in the ministerial manipulation of Parliament (which posed a profound threat to English balanced government and the preservation of liberty); the extension of privileges and favors to speculators in the public funds, and to other favorites; and an oppressive and unjust program of taxation that further subsidized personally lucrative but socially unproductive forms of economic activity. This "country" opposition to the "court" administrations of such early-eighteenth-century Whig leaders as Sir Robert Walpole formed part of an explosive ideology. While it attracted only a small, if vocal, minority in England who bemoaned the moral decay—reminiscent of ancient Rome —attending these changes, this ideology of opposition gained remarkably quick and significant influence in North America, where ultimately it shaped the ideology of American resistance and revolution in the 1760s and 1770s.

Jefferson's outlook, formed during these years, was in several obvious respects different in emphasis and approach from this English country tradition, but he absorbed directly from it a profound fear that this same corrupt system of political economy might somehow take hold in his own country. This fear expressed the essence of his opposition to Alexander Hamilton in the 1790s and contributed much to the formulation of his alternative, and ultimately triumphant, system of political economy. It is important to note as part of this introductory overview, however, that Jefferson's opposition was to a particular form of political intervention in the economy, one that he believed furthered unhealthy and unjust patterns of social change. In practice, if not explicitly in theory, Jefferson was to give ample evidence during his career of a willingness to use the power of government, when necessary, to secure the requisite conditions for his own vision of a republican economy and society.

JEFFERSON IN EUROPE

Jefferson's experience as a political economist began, in a sense, in the years immediately following the war for independence. As a delegate, briefly, to the Confederation Congress, then as minister plenipotentiary commissioned to negotiate treaties of amity and commerce with European nations, and finally as minister to France, his public career between 1783 and 1790 was inextricably tied to the critical issue of foreign commerce. As Merrill D. Peterson has noted, Jefferson gradually developed during these years a system of political economy that reflected a broader dimension of Revolutionary aspiration as well as the practical needs and interests of the new nation. The noble ideal of commercial liberty and the vision of a world of free trade, released from the unjust and illiberal restraints of Old World mercantilism, fired Jefferson's imagination as much as it had Adam Smith's. In words that might have been Smith's, Jefferson later summarized the appeal of this vision:

> Instead of embarrassing commerce under piles of regulating laws, duties, and prohibitions, could it be relieved from all its shackles in all parts of the world, could every country be employed in producing that which nature had best fitted it to produce, and each be free to exchange with others mutual surpluses for mutual wants, the greatest mass possible would then be produced of those things which contribute to human life and human happiness; the numbers of mankind would be increased, and their condition bettered.

This was heady idealism, but the stirring rhetoric also caught Jefferson's (and many Americans') shrewd sense of what might best serve the struggling economy of the

United States. America's economic future in the mid-1780s was problematic. Peace had brought an end to the disruptive effects and commercial uncertainty of a long war, but it had not brought the desired foundation for long-term prosperity. War-weary Americans rushed to consume British imports at a dizzying pace, buying much more than they could safely afford, and this orgy of consumption only exacerbated the difficulties they began to encounter in their export trade. During the flush years of almost boundless optimism in the mid-1770s, the Revolutionaries had talked confidently of expanding markets for their produce throughout the world. But the Revolution, in itself, unequivocally failed to produce even a rough approximation of their vision. Congress had adopted an ambitious "plan of treaties" in 1776 that by 1784 had met with only limited success in securing new American commercial privileges outside the traditional confines of the British Empire. Moreover, with independence Americans lost most of the advantages they had once enjoyed within that empire.

As early as July 1783 Parliament had moved to exploit the feebleness of the American confederacy and to keep the erstwhile colonies in a position of stark commercial dependency. The crucial measure in this program was an exclusion of American ships from the British West Indies, which delivered a devastating blow to an essential branch of the republic's commerce. In addition to undercutting shipping and the carrying trade, British orders-in-council jolted American farmers tied to the export trade. Together with the revival of old restrictions on American commerce with the Spanish and French colonies in the Caribbean, these British regulations dashed all naive hopes of a speedy ascent to the lofty world of prosperity and free trade.

Under these daunting circumstances the original plan of treaties was pursued with renewed vigor, and Jefferson found himself at the center of events. Prosecuting the war against mercantilism was, he believed, the best course of action, since the alternatives were rather sobering. In theory Americans might abjure an active foreign commerce and adopt the Chinese model of the hermit nation, and Jefferson was enough of a dreamer to ponder the possibility, if only to dismiss it as hopelessly impractical and shortsighted. Jefferson understood, above all, the essential role that an expansive export trade played in the workings of a virtuous agrarian republic. Moreover, he firmly believed that the United States had at its disposal a potentially effective means of gently coercing the removal of foreign barriers to its commerce. American trade itself was a formidable weapon, Jefferson reasoned, because it was in fact immensely valuable to those countries, including England, with whom the republic hoped to negotiate new, more liberal arrangements. The threat of American retaliation against those governments that stubbornly clung to the pernicious logic of mercantilism might work wonders; Jefferson was at least willing to give this more forceful approach a try. Appointed one of three American commissioners in May 1784, he took his ideas and ambitions to Europe, joining hands with John Adams and Benjamin Franklin in what proved to be an elusive quest for widening markets and economic salvation.

Congress had optimistically authorized sixteen treaties with various European states, but the yield proved paltry indeed. American idealism was generally spurned in the courts of Europe when it was noticed at all. Only a single treaty—with Prussia—was successfully concluded. By 1786, the general plan of treaties was a colossal failure, and Jefferson, now ensconced as the American minister to France, shifted his approach. With Britain as adamant as ever in its refusal to take seriously American overtures for commercial reform, Jefferson turned his energy to cultivating the logical counterpoise to that powerful nation—the United States' dearest ally, France. For several years he labored patiently to build a strong Franco-American commercial axis that would anchor his country's position in the postwar world. The strategy made a certain degree of sense, of course; for Americans, it promised an end to the British monopoly of their commerce and the humiliating dependency it fostered, while the French would be drawn to the prospect of stealing from their foremost adversary valuable new markets and sources of supply.

But the obstacles were formidable. Jefferson had to persuade the French that Americans were capable of shaking loose the British shackles, and even more he had to convince them to dismantle their own cumbersome system of monopoly and restriction that discouraged American efforts to trade directly and freely in the French market. As a Virginia planter Jefferson was familiar enough with the single most important American export—tobacco—and his diplomatic assault on French mercantilism appropriately centered on the Farmers-General monopoly of the right to import the American weed. But he was hardly indifferent to other important staples that reflected the needs of other regions; he promoted the interest of New England whale oil in French markets, and he went to remarkable lengths in support of rice exports from South Carolina and Georgia.

Altogether Jefferson's energy met with substantial but only limited success, and whatever progress he made was interrupted by the outbreak of the French Revolution in 1789. He succeeded to a remarkable degree in opening French markets to American exports, but his larger scheme of a Franco-American axis foundered on the inability of France to offer a viable alternative to American imports from Britain. To an extent Jefferson seemed blind to the fact that French producers were simply unable to compete with British manufacturers for the lucrative American market; for his planned system to work, trade between the two countries would have to be relatively equal and balanced. What Jefferson discovered, in sum, was that it was far easier to contemplate breaking British dominance of American commerce than it was to actually break it. Nevertheless, his quest to liberate his country's trade, and in so doing to safeguard the republic itself, was far from over. Following his return from France in late 1789, he became the first secretary of state in the new federal government created by the Constitution. From that position his career as a political economist entered a new phase, one in which his former endeavors in Europe became enmeshed in a much larger web of concerns.

THE QUARREL WITH HAMILTON

During the early 1790s Jefferson's commercial strategy became something it had not formerly been: the linchpin of an alternative system of political economy that was steadily pushed to the fringes of national policy. When he joined President George Washington's cabinet, he was optimistic that conditions favored more than ever the fulfillment of his aims. In theory, France's more liberal government should be ideologically receptive to the logic of commercial freedom, and the United States now had a federal government capable of coordinating and implementing a serious assault on British mercantilism. Along with his compatriot, Congressman James Madison, Jefferson assumed that one of the first acts of the new government would be to devise a program of commercial discrimination against foreign countries that had refused to negotiate reciprocity treaties with the United States. The two Virginians worked closely together, in vain as it turned out, to effect Jefferson's system of commercial retaliation and coercion. Their system was, ipso facto, anti-British and pro-French, which explains why it ran afoul of profoundly shifting conditions in Europe and, even more, the very different approach to political economy of the first secretary of the treasury, Alexander Hamilton.

Conventional wisdom has it that Jefferson's political economy in the 1790s cannot be understood apart from the ideas and policies of his legendary rival, and the point is well taken. Hamilton vigorously opposed —with consistent success—Jefferson's and Madison's program of commercial discrimination because it posed a direct threat to his own evolving system of political economy, which was pro-British in orientation and pointed toward a very different economic future. Everything depended on his fiscal system. Hamilton's primary purpose in funding the national debt, assuming the debts of the states, and incorporating the Bank of the United States was to stabilize the new national government and establish its credit. Beyond that, he aimed to facilitate the organization and investment of private capital. The primary source of the revenue that would ensure regular interest payments on the funded debt was foreign commerce, and the overwhelming bulk of the republic's imports were in the form of British manufactures. Hamilton disputed Jefferson's assumption that commercial retaliation against England would force quick concessions; in fact, he was sure it would provoke England into a commercial war with the United States, which would disrupt Anglo-American trade and therefore jeopardize the stability of his fragile fiscal system. Moreover, close commercial ties to England were necessary to supply the new nation with the credit and capital that would ignite the kind of economic growth Hamilton envisioned. As Jefferson soon realized, in sum, the secretary's system was predicated on accommodation of Britain and at least temporary acquiescence in her domination of American commerce. The world of free

trade would have to wait. Meanwhile, Hamilton urged appropriate adjustments in the domestic economy, including the aggressive development of native manufactures.

It is ironic that Hamilton's Report on Manufactures, presented to Congress in late 1791, has become the most famous of his state papers, because it had little direct effect on national policy or on the republic's economic development. Its immediate significance was nonetheless substantial: it provided vivid confirmation of Hamilton's cast of mind and thus intensified an emerging opposition to his system of political economy. What the report laid bare, in terms of the eighteenth-century paradigm of social change, was the secretary's belief that the young American republic should move ahead as quickly as possible into a higher stage of social development, both because conditions favored this advance and because he, unlike Jefferson, regarded it as inherently salutary and desirable. As the report revealed, Hamilton wanted large-scale, public manufacturing, not the primitive household industry dear to Jefferson's heart; he talked of exploiting the potentially productive labor of idle women, children, and the poor in the more densely populated regions of the country by placing them in factories; and he explicitly requested direct subsidies from the federal government (primarily in the form of "pecuniary bounties") to the appropriate entrepreneurs. If Hamilton's breathtaking report left any doubt as to his beliefs and intentions, his role in creating a huge corporation, the Society for Establishing Useful Manufactures, which was tied to his fiscal system and openly desirous of support from the federal government, dispelled it.

Since Hamilton deliberately set out to plant in America a British system of public finance that would promote the same kind of social and economic change that England had undergone since the Glorious Revolution, it is no wonder that scores of his countrymen, led by Jefferson, saw his program as nothing less than a repudiation of the American Revolution. As early as 1792 many of Hamilton's opponents came to fear a conspiracy to corrupt American government and society by imitating British forms, manners, and institutions. Drawing heavily on the country tradition of opposition groups in eighteenth-century England, this Jeffersonian opposition was profoundly ideological in character. Outraged republicans were soon hurling the epithet "Walpole" at Hamilton, for they perceived in him the image of the notorious British minister who had consolidated the financial system allegedly responsible for England's loathsome corruption and decay.

Jefferson was appalled by what he saw to be a corrupted legislature—the supposedly republican Congress of the United States—manipulated by Hamilton from his vantage point in the Treasury Department and slavishly beholden to the imperatives of his fiscal system. This system was dangerous and unjust in every respect. It encouraged reckless speculation and an unwholesome spirit of avarice in the society at large; it justified unduly heavy taxation of the republic's productive citizens for the benefit of scheming stockjobbers; it spawned an unnecessary and wasteful bureaucracy; it discouraged agriculture and westward expansion; it was preferential to the eastern commercial states, at the expense of the southern states; and it promised to expand the power of the new federal government in blatantly unconstitutional ways. Instead of viewing Hamilton's political economy as a forward-looking prospectus for economic growth and national integration, Jefferson perceived it as a blueprint for retrogression, as a falling away from the virtuous contours of republicanism itself.

Jefferson's battle against Hamiltonianism peaked in late 1793, shortly before he resigned his cabinet position, when he delivered to Congress his Report on the Privi-

leges and Restrictions on the Commerce of the United States in Foreign Countries. This report—a countermanifesto of sorts—eloquently summarized the logic of Jefferson's work of the previous ten years and served as a rallying point for Hamilton's adversaries in Congress, led by Madison, who moved quickly to implement its policy recommendations. If ever there were a time to mobilize Anglophobic energy, this appeared to be it. Madison tried to exploit a deepening diplomatic crisis with England, occasioned by the wars of the French Revolution, but his efforts were thwarted. The upshot of the 1793–1794 crisis was a stunning defeat of the Jeffersonian system. The desired commercial legislation failed to pass Congress, and the famous treaty that resulted from John Jay's negotiations in London only consummated Hamilton's triumph. By explicitly binding the United States to a renunciation of commercial discrimination against England for at least ten years, Jay's Treaty in effect outlawed Jefferson's system. To Jefferson, this treaty was indeed the fitting culmination of an American Walpole's attempt to spurn the vision of 1776 and strengthen the British connection that threatened to corrupt American government and society.

The events of the second half of this momentous decade threw Jefferson ever more on the defensive but also paved the way for his stunning electoral triumph in 1800. Under the leadership of President John Adams the Federalist administration carried the pro-British thrust of Hamiltonianism to a position just short of formal war against France. Although war was averted, the Federalists did succeed in creating something close to a parody of the Jeffersonian nightmare. In addition to attempting to silence political opposition in the infamous Alien and Sedition Acts, they raised taxes and increased government spending, enlarging both the army and the navy (even placing Hamilton in effective control of the federal army), the net result of which was an increase in the public debt and apparent confirmation of the Jeffersonian fear that the Federalists had no intention of reducing, much less eliminating, that debt. Viewed in broader terms of political economy, moreover, the Jeffersonians began to fear that America was developing a dangerously unbalanced posture, one thoroughly at odds with the "natural" order of economic development that Adam Smith, among others, so persuasively prescribed. As the French attacked ever more seriously the republic's mushrooming foreign trade and the Federalists appeared willing to go to great lengths to defend it, the Jeffersonians vehemently opposed aspects of the United States' recent commercial growth as well as the naval system that was designed to protect it.

Directing their fire at the wartime carrying trade—the sector of American commerce that transported goods neither produced nor consumed in the United States—Jefferson and his followers argued that the Federalists were foolishly promoting the least productive elements of the economy in a fashion reminiscent of mercantilist governments in Europe. Commerce merited government protection only to the extent that it was connected directly to agriculture, which was always the most productive application of labor; this carrying trade involved nothing more than the profits of a small group of recklessly speculative merchants. A truly republican political economy for America, Jefferson contended, involved neither this overgrown, extraneous commerce that was unrelated to the health and security of the great mass of republican producers nor the Federalist naval system that increasingly threatened to embroil the United States in unnecessary, expensive, and corrupting wars with the mercantilist powers of Europe. At the height of his despair in early 1800, Jefferson appropriately lamented that "we are running navigation mad, and commerce mad, and navy mad, which is worst of all." In a little over a year, however, in the

wake of his decisive defeat of the Federalists at the polls, he was catapulted into a position where he might hope to implement his alternative system of political economy.

JEFFERSON IN POWER

In itself, the electoral revolution of 1800 promised to remove the primary threat to Jefferson's vision that was posed by the machinations of a corrupt administration. Although Jefferson concluded with some dismay shortly after his election to the presidency that he could not safely dismantle Hamilton's entire fiscal system, he and his secretary of the treasury, Albert Gallatin, resolved to do everything possible to reduce its noxious influence. Extinguishing the national debt as rapidly as possible (the initial estimate was sixteen years), reducing dramatically government expenditures (especially on the military), and repealing the entire battery of Federalist direct and excise taxes became goals of Jefferson's administration, and his record of success in these areas became nothing short of brilliant. If one of his primary objectives was to purge the federal government of as much Hamiltonian fiscalism as he safely could, the so-called revolution of 1800 was as substantive as it was symbolic.

Securing a republican political economy required more, however, than merely displacing the Federalists and undoing their worst handiwork; it also necessitated the elimination of other dangers and the maintenance of certain vital conditions. Within the Jeffersonian framework of assumptions and beliefs, republicanism was predicated on unobstructed access to an ample supply of open land and a relatively liberal international commercial order that provided adequate foreign markets for America's flourishing agricultural surplus. During his two terms as president, Jefferson firmly pursued landed and commercial expansion; in these areas, however, his record of success was mixed and his legacy profoundly ambiguous.

The crisis over the Mississippi River that culminated in the Louisiana Purchase of 1803, undoubtedly the single greatest achievement of Jefferson's presidency, reflected some of his crucial and long-standing concerns. Although the pressure of America's burgeoning population on the available supply of land had always posed more of a theoretical than a real problem, Jefferson's optimism about the American future betrayed his assumption that the republic's western (and perhaps southern and northern) boundaries were not permanent and that future extension would provide the requisite supply of fresh land. But if that assumption were challenged, especially by a formidable foreign power, a theoretical problem might become a more immediate and practical one. This is, of course, what occurred in 1801 when France regained Louisiana from Spain. Jefferson handled a delicate situation quite shrewdly and through a stroke of good fortune resolved the Mississippi problem, once and for all, by securing American title to the vast territory in question. By gaining undisputed control of the river and the crucial port of New Orleans, Jefferson ensured that Americans emigrating into the trans-Appalachian West would not have their access to overseas markets obstructed by the threatening presence of any foreign power in the region. This active and secure commerce, Jefferson believed, was essential to the republican character of the West because it provided the necessary incentives for industry among a rural people who might easily succumb to indolence and savagery.

Even more important, the Louisiana Purchase doubled the size of the infant republic, and this addition of a vast reservoir of land west of the Mississippi held major significance for the future. Jefferson's republic would be able to continue expanding its people and institutions across space, escaping the corruption that came with a crowded society in which high population density forced movement into an older, more complex phase of social development. The pressures of corruption that would surely accumulate in the East could be relieved by diffusion into the West; or, as Jefferson cast the idea in memorable terms, "By enlarging the empire of liberty we multiply its auxiliaries, and provide new sources of renovation, should its principles, at any time, degenerate, in those portions of our country which gave them birth."

If the Louisiana Purchase was a fitting climax to the string of impressive triumphs during Jefferson's first administration, his second term brought renewed challenge in the familiar area of foreign commerce. The Purchase alone could not ensure the basis for a republican system of political economy. While it provided an abundant supply of open land for the future, and while it also afforded western farmers a safe route to the oceans, it did not guarantee Americans the unimpeded access to foreign markets they needed. The goal of free trade not only had remained on the agenda, it became ever more urgent after 1805, when the renewal and intensification of the Napoleonic Wars in Europe created an unprecedented crisis for the United States. Locked in a bitter struggle for supremacy in Europe, France and England preyed on the neutral trade of the young republic. Jefferson quickly identified England as the primary offender against the United States, especially when what had begun as a British assault on America's wartime carrying and reexport trades was extended by late 1807 to include restrictions on his country's direct trade with the Continent. Jefferson's response to these restrictions and the persistent threat of war was the great embargo of 1807–1809, a breathtaking trial of the theory and policy of commercial coercion that had long been dear to him.

Viewed from the perspective of political economy, the embargo's purpose was to liberate American commerce from devastating foreign restrictions in order to underwrite the long-term stability and prosperity of an agricultural republic. There can be no doubt that Jefferson expected his policy to encourage domestic manufacturing, but this indirect result was not his primary goal, nor did he intend to alter the predominantly agricultural character of American society. Above all, he expected the policy to succeed as a coercive measure, which in fact it did not. The unexpected duration and ultimate failure of the embargo gave added reason for Jefferson's interest in promoting manufactures, but it never resulted in a major reorientation of his beliefs in political economy. Upon closer inspection, indeed, Jefferson's attention to manufactures in this period actually supported, rather than supplanted, his traditional vision.

When Jefferson began to discuss the impact of his embargo on the economy, he gave clear evidence that he still thought largely in terms of very simple, coarse, household manufactures. One salutary consequence of the interruption in foreign trade, he argued, was that it encouraged Americans to produce crude manufactures "in our families" in greater abundance than ever before. Speaking of his own state of Virginia in early 1809, he affirmed "with confidence that were free intercourse opened again to-morrow, she would never again import one-half of the coarse goods" that she had prior to the embargo. "The economy and thriftiness resulting from our household manufactures" would never be laid aside, he boasted, so that when trade eventually resumed, Virginians and Americans everywhere would purchase far less from the British. If the embargo had thus finally persuaded his countrymen to realize their full potential in household manufactures, which he fervently believed it had, this momentous achievement would eliminate the chronically unfavorable balance of trade with Britain that had crippled the republic since the end of the Revolution.

Part of Jefferson's buoyant perspective involved his renewed contempt for America's swollen carrying trade; thanks to the embargo, he believed, the republic could look forward to a much healthier, more balanced economy than the one the Federalists had sought to advance. Economic independence was to be predicated on "an equilibrium of agriculture, manufactures, and commerce," and Jefferson even prescribed a formula in a letter to James Jay in April 1809:

> Manufactures sufficient for our own consumption, of what we raise the raw material (and no more). Commerce sufficient to carry the surplus produce of agriculture, beyond our own consumption, to a market for exchanging it for articles we cannot raise (and no more). These are the true limits of manufactures and commerce. To go beyond them is to increase our dependence on foreign nations, and our liability to war.

As a result of his embargo, in sum, Americans had substituted household manufactures for a dangerously bloated carrying trade and a perilous addiction to British imports.

Although Jefferson consistently emphasized the importance of coarse, household manufactures, he was not blind to the fact that his embargo, in large part due to its unexpectedly protracted duration, had also forced the transfer of capital from foreign commerce into large-scale manufacturing. He was not convinced, however, that the resulting development of public factories producing "finer" manufactures, especially in northern cities, was extensive, nor did he regard these new institutions as a permanent feature of the American landscape. When pressed by Du Pont de Nemours's fear that the republic was beginning to manufacture too much, Jefferson made his position abundantly clear:

> It is true we are going greatly into manufactures; but the mass of them are household

manufactures of the coarse articles worn by the laborers and farmers of the family. These I verily believe we shall succeed in making to the whole extent of our necessities. But the attempts at fine goods will probably be abortive. They are undertaken by company establishments, and chiefly in the towns; will have little success and short continuance in a country where the charms of agriculture attract every being who can engage in it.

In Jefferson's expansive agricultural republic, there was little likelihood that a permanent system of large-scale manufacturing of the kind Hamilton had dreamed of would arise, even with a boost from the embargo; Jefferson's other more successful policies, especially the Louisiana Purchase, had made sure of that.

Despite Jefferson's continuing emphasis on traditional household industry, his long-standing fascination with adapting advances in machinery to American manufactures intensified. As early as 1793, when he first heard of Eli Whitney's cotton gin, he had anticipated the potential success of such inventions "for family use." By 1812, he was boasting to Colonel Thaddeus Kosciuszko that the republic's manufactures were "very nearly on a footing with those of England," which, he averred, had "not a single improvement which we do not possess, and many of them better adapted by ourselves to our ordinary use." "We have reduced the large and expensive machinery for most things," Jefferson claimed, "to the compass of a private family, and every family of any size is now getting machines on a small scale for their household purposes." Even if we take into account that Jefferson's idea of a household could be stretched to include Monticello, with its thousands of acres and hundreds of bound laborers, it is still remarkable that he apparently had visions of literally domesticating the industrial revolution. In the United States, he argued, technological improvements were assimilated to

the traditional framework of domestic industry—he saw no necessary connection between the new machinery and the more advanced, large-scale forms of production that were alien to his conception of a republican political economy. By the end of the War of 1812 the ex-president proudly noted that "carding machines in every neighborhood, spinning machines in large families and wheels in the small, are too radically established ever to be relinquished."

Despite its colossal failure to coerce the European belligerents into acceding to a more liberal system of commerce (and, as it turned out, to avoid war), Jefferson chose to construe the embargo (and its unfortunate stepchildren, the Non-Intercourse Act of 1809 and Macon's Bill No. 2 of the following year) as a grand success. To acknowledge the measure of delusion that his perspective entailed is not to question the sincerity of Jefferson's self-serving belief that even some of the unintended consequences of his policies furthered, rather than undermined, his broader vision. What is surprising, perhaps, is the extent to which Jefferson's vision began to take on a utopian cast during what might appear to us, in retrospect, to have been a period of failure and even disaster. Once commerce was reopened and had assumed its altered form, he exulted, the republic would bask in the glow of its triumph. A predominantly agricultural America would continue to import in sufficient quantities for revenue purposes (thereby avoiding the need for odious direct and excise taxes) the finer manufactures that it was neither suited nor doomed to produce. Moreover, the tax on these imported luxuries would fall exclusively on "the rich" who consumed them, with the happy consequence that "the poor man in this country who uses nothing but what is made within his own farm or family, or within the U.S.," would not be taxed at all.

Indeed, when Jefferson thrust his gaze into the future and anticipated the extinction of the national debt, he foresaw a surplus of revenue accruing from this luxury tax, a surplus that might be used to finance all kinds of internal improvements. Writing in 1811, Jefferson summarized this heady vision: once revenues had been liberated by the discharge of the public debt and "its surplus applied to canals, roads, schools" and the like, the American farmer "will see his government supported, his children educated, and the face of his country made a paradise by the contributions of the rich alone, without his being called on to spare a cent from his earnings." Rather than burdening the citizen with oppressive obligations and regulations, American government would be a creative force in the improvement of everyone's lives. "The path we are now pursuing leads directly to this end," Jefferson promised, "which we cannot fail to attain unless our administration should fall into unwise hands."

A TROUBLED RETIREMENT

During the seventeen years between his retirement from the presidency in 1809 and his death in 1826 Jefferson's views on political economy matured and then regressed. His emphasis on the need for a balanced economy, including domestic manufactures, peaked after the Peace of Ghent. In what has become a famous letter to Benjamin Austin in early 1816, Jefferson acknowledged that he and all Americans now understood what they had not thirty years earlier, that "there exists both profligacy and power enough to exclude us from the field of interchange with other nations." Mercantilism had withstood the assault of insurgent liberalism and the revolutionary regime in North America; the United States could not anticipate with adequate assurance secure markets abroad, which meant that it should turn inward, exploit its boundless potential, and build an independent economy. This did not mean a

renunciation of foreign commerce and an adoption of the Chinese model, but it did mean that "we must now place the manufacturer by the side of the agriculturalist" rather than base an economy solely on the exchange of farm surpluses for European manufactures. Yet at no time did Jefferson's endorsement of a balanced economy approach acceptance of either the spirit or the substance of the Industrial Revolution. His approval of large-scale manufacturing was grudging at best, and even his limited concessions were invariably hedged. As Merrill Peterson has aptly noted, he never wholeheartedly or enthusiastically embraced anything beyond "the household-handicraft-mill complex of an advanced agricultural society." Similarly, while he was willing to support a moderate policy of public protection of America's infant industries, he never carried the logic of his revised political economy to the lengths that some younger Jeffersonians, even within his lifetime, were to do.

During the final decade of his life, in fact, Jefferson steadily retreated from optimism to pessimism and from the views of his mature years to those of his early career. He had given a hint of this shift during the War of 1812 when he noted that "in proportion as commercial avarice and corruption advance on us from the north and east, the principles of free government are to retire to the agricultural states of the south and west, as their last asylum and bulwark." After the war, and especially in the wake of the speculative orgy that culminated in the financial panic of 1819, Jefferson became increasingly wary of what he interpreted as the insidious schemes of northerners (especially New Englanders) to graft onto the republic unsound principles and systems in political economy. This growing tendency to view the United States in terms of stark regional differences was accompanied by a furious assertion of the most rigid agrarian-mindedness that he ever enunciated in his long career. Jefferson's somewhat frantic retreat to this sectional, narrowly agrarian perspective reflects both the influence of national trends and events and the quiet desperation of his own rapidly deteriorating personal situation. Burdened with debt and the vicissitudes of a plantation economy in depression and decline, Jefferson exuded an uncharacteristic and highly volatile mixture of fear, bitterness, and paranoia.

Jefferson's final years were marked, above all, by a return of his long-standing fear of corruption emanating from the chicanery and shenanigans of a politically ambitious clique. He came, once again, to see Federalists and crypto-Federalists lurking everywhere, now largely under the command of a fellow Virginian, his own kinsman, Chief Justice John Marshall. Back in the 1790s Jefferson had resisted Hamilton's conspiracy to subvert republicanism from within the Treasury Department; now he fixed on the machinations of the Supreme Court, a bastion of Federalism that sought to achieve through the judiciary what Hamilton had failed to bring about by other means. According to Jefferson, the Court threatened in its revival of the Hamiltonian heresy to impose a system of "consolidation" on the young agricultural republic, a system that would unduly centralize political power while implementing the selfish schemes of predatory merchants and manufacturers from the North. Now, once again, the security of Jefferson's republic demanded vigilant adherence to the principles of the opposition "country" tradition, and appropriately, if ironically, Jefferson found himself openly sympathetic to the views of country-minded ideologues, including John Taylor, who had not that long ago objected to Jefferson's own misuses of power and apparent change of heart.

In addition to castigating Marshall and the Court, Jefferson unequivocally opposed Henry Clay's formula of an "American System," which called for the creation of an integrated, balanced economy based on a national bank, a protective tariff for manufactures, and a program of federally sponsored internal improvements. To Jefferson, this bold system was thinly disguised Hamiltonianism, unmistakably linked to the larger consolidation conspiracy. President John Quincy Adams' famous message to Congress in late 1825, an even more ambitious statement of the American System idea than Clay's pronouncements, left Jefferson stunned and sputtering in rage. It is not difficult to understand why Clay, Adams, and many other Jeffersonian Republicans of the time conceived of and defended their American System as the logical fulfillment of mature Jeffersonian principles. There were ample precedents, in both Jefferson's policies and public statements, especially during his second presidential term, to make the linkages persuasive, and it is no coincidence that the Jeffersonian commitments of both Clay and Adams were forged during the embargo and its aftermath. But while this generation of Jeffersonians remained riveted to the mature vision of a balanced, independent, and self-sufficient economy, forged through the creative exercise of national power, their former leader finished his days reliving the 1790s.

One might be tempted to conclude that Clay and Adams, who emerged as leaders of the Whig party in the 1830s, were the voice of a Jeffersonian future. As it turned out, however, they were only one part of that future, because there were other latter-day Jeffersonians, calling themselves Jacksonian Democrats, who took their cue from a different Jefferson, of the 1790s and 1820s. Thus Jefferson's legacy in political economy proved ambiguous indeed.

Constitutionalism

RICHARD E. ELLIS

THE Declaration of Independence announced to the world the birth of the United States as a nation. It also provided in its eloquent second paragraph a national credo. But it did not create the constitutionalism that later became for many people almost an ideology in itself and that is at the very heart of the American system of government. Ideas about how government was to be structured and how it would operate had to be worked out in the years that followed separation from Great Britain in 1776. Jefferson recognized this period as a rare opportunity actually to implement his beliefs. "It is a work of the most interesting nature and such as every individual would wish to have his voice in," he observed in a letter to Thomas Nelson dated 16 May 1776. It was an awesome challenge, for the problem of how America was to be governed was at the very essence of the American Revolution. As Jefferson put it, "It is the whole object of the present controversy; for should a bad government be instituted for us in future it had as well to have accepted at first the bad one offered to us from beyond the

water without the risk and expence of contest."

These words, penned shortly before the issuance of the Declaration of Independence, clearly indicate that Jefferson understood the importance of the task. But he probably did not fully realize that in one form or another the problem of how Americans should govern themselves would preoccupy him for the rest of his life. The challenge was enormous in its dimensions. It involved dealing with such fundamental matters as the meaning of republicanism, the institutional structure of the state and national governments, the proper distribution of power in a federal system, and the protection of individual rights and liberties from the abuse of authority. This challenge was to involve various frustrations, defeats, mistakes, and missed opportunities for Jefferson. Often he did not fully think through the implications of some of his ideas, and more than a few times he changed his mind. In the end, however, many of his ideas proved to be of enduring importance, and as much as any member of the revolutionary generation, he shaped the constitutional values under which we live today.

Jefferson's first opportunity actually to implement the ideas of the American Revolution came in May 1776 when the Continental Congress called on the states to adopt new governments "under the authority of the people." Eager to participate in this important work, Jefferson requested permission to leave the Continental Congress and return to Virginia to help draft a state constitution. But the convention that governed Virginia at that time denied his request. Clearly disappointed, but undaunted, Jefferson prepared his own version of a constitution and a preamble with a list of grievances against the king. Only the latter was adopted by the convention.

Jefferson was very unhappy with the constitution adopted by Virginia in 1776. Thoroughly revolutionized by the preindependence debate with Great Britain, he believed the new state government should represent a more thorough break with the past. In particular, he advocated a more direct assault on the "artificial aristocracy," as he called it, that still ruled the Old Dominion. He believed it should be replaced by a natural aristocracy based on merit, virtue, and an informed electorate. He wanted to overturn the existing system of land tenure, which had its origins in feudal practices. He favored the elimination of an established church and a guaranty of complete religious freedom. And he proposed a state-supported system of public education to facilitate the upward mobility of the brightest white students, regardless of their class backgrounds.

As for the structure of the government created for Virginia in 1776, Jefferson agreed with the decision to reduce sharply the power of the executive branch. His opposition to placing too much power in the hands of a single person flowed naturally from the bitter debates of the 1760s and early 1770s, when royal governors were the leading spokesmen and chief enforcers of imperial policies. But Jefferson sharply disapproved of the manner in which the now all-powerful state legislature was elected. He desired to see property qualifications for officeholding eliminated, the suffrage broadened, and representation in the lower house based on white population rather than the existing system of two delegates per county (regardless of population), which was created deliberately to give a decisive advantage to the more numerous and smaller slaveholding counties in the eastern part of the state at the expense of the larger and more populous nonslaveholding counties in the west.

Although Jefferson wanted to see the Virginia Constitution more firmly grounded in the "consent of the governed," he was not as extreme as some proponents of democratic reform in 1776. The radical democrats who had gained control of the government-making machinery in Pennsylvania in 1776 had completely eliminated the executive branch and provided for a unicameral legislature and an elective judiciary. Jefferson was not prepared to go this far. In addition to favoring a relatively weak executive to administer the laws passed by the legislature, he also strongly believed in a bicameral legislature and had reservations about putting the government completely and directly under the control of the people. He believed the framers of the Virginia Constitution had committed a mistake by making both houses of the state legislature directly responsible to the electorate. Jefferson believed that the lower house should be elected by the people and that in turn it should select the upper house from among its most respected members. He justified this arrangement on these grounds, in a letter to Edmund Pendleton of 26 August 1776: "I have ever observed that a choice by the people themselves is not generally distinguished for it's wisdom. This first secretion from them is usually crude and heterogeneous. But give to those so chosen by the people a second choice themselves, and they generally will chuse wise men."

Like most Americans of his time, Jefferson had not worked out in 1776 the difficult problem of what role the judiciary should play in a republican form of government. In fact, it is doubtful that he ever fully came to terms with this problem, although he was to encounter it in various ways throughout his long public career. He did not advocate an elective judiciary, but he did indicate in the letter to Pendleton that a judge should "be a mere machine" in enforcing the will of democratically elected legislatures and that a judge's power to interpret the meaning of laws should be sharply limited.

Jefferson left the Continental Congress in September 1776 and won a seat in the newly created Virginia legislature, where he directed his energies to bringing about through ordinary legislation the reforms he advocated. He played a central role in revising many of the state's laws in order to create a "government truly republican." This included the abolition of landholding in fee tail and the elimination of the feudal practices of primogeniture and entail. More significantly, he initiated the political campaign that culminated in the Virginia Statute for Religious Freedom, finally enacted in 1786 after Jefferson had left for France. This law provides not only for the complete separation of church and state but also for complete religious freedom. Its underlying premise is that there should be no connection between the civil rights of the people and the manner in which they worship God. It is an extremely important piece of legislation, for it has served as the dominant model for church-state relations on both the local and federal levels of government in the United States. Jefferson considered it to be one of his greatest contributions to mankind.

He failed, however, to implement the other aspects of his reform program. A hu-

manitarian attempt to make the state's criminal code less bloody was rejected. His Bill for the More General Diffusion of Knowledge, premised on the belief that a truly republican government required a public system of education, also met defeat. A timid attempt by Jefferson to examine the relationship between slavery and republicanism came under sharp criticism, and he quickly retreated from it. He also could not get the legislature to broaden suffrage or adopt a more equitable system of representation. Virginia's failure to embrace the principles and opportunities of the American Revolution, as Jefferson saw them, distressed him for the rest of his life.

Jefferson became governor of Virginia in 1779. This was not a very happy experience. The war had been going badly for several years, and in 1781 the British invaded Virginia. Economic turmoil, the lack of adequate military supplies, and widespread desertion among the militia made effective resistance very difficult. The situation required strong, even arbitrary, leadership on the part of the executive, but Jefferson, as a true product of the Revolution, was not, at this point in his life, capable of providing it. He worked conscientiously but ineffectively within the framework of the weak governor's office created by the Virginia Constitution and only barely avoided being captured by the British himself. His opposition in the Virginia House of Delegates ordered an inquiry into his conduct of the war, and although he was eventually cleared, it was a humiliating experience. A significant result of what happened was that Jefferson began to rethink the issue of executive power.

Jefferson withdrew from public life for the next two years. During this self-imposed retirement, he wrote his only book, *Notes on the State of Virginia,* in response to a series of questions about Virginia and the New World posed by the secretary of the French legation in Philadelphia. Covering a range of topics, it included a substantial discussion of government in the Old Dominion as well as another draft of a proposed state constitution, which differed from his earlier draft of a constitution for Virginia on a number of key points. Jefferson now seemed to endorse the more traditional Whig view that the lower house of the legislature should represent the people, and the upper house, "the property of the state." Why he backed off from his earlier assertion that the upper house should consist of the wisest men in the state is unclear. He may have been impressed by the provision for an arrangement such as he now favored in the Massachusetts Constitution of 1780, which had been written by his good friend John Adams. At any rate, his strong belief in bicameralism further distinguished Jefferson from the more extreme proponents of constitutional democracy who had begun to emerge after 1776. Along the same lines, in his *Notes on the State of Virginia,* Jefferson was critical of the concept of legislative supremacy. He already was at odds with Patrick Henry, who opposed many of his reform measures and controlled the Virginia legislature, and his own experience as governor had clearly indicated what could happen if the legislature fell under the control of the wrong kind of leadership. He now realized that legislative supremacy was not an adequate check on arbitrary government for "173 despots would surely be as oppressive as one." The remedy, he now believed, was to build up the powers of the executive and judicial parts of the government as a way of checking the power of the legislature. "An *elective despotism,*" he wrote in Query VIII, "was not the government we fought for; but one which should not only be founded on free principles, but in which the powers of government should be so divided," among the different branches.

Finally, and perhaps most important, in the *Notes on the State of Virginia,* Jefferson elaborated on one of his major concerns about the Virginia Constitution of 1776 that he had only hinted at earlier. The idea behind a written constitution was to create a government of limited powers, one controlled by fundamental law. How was such a constitution to be created? Jefferson criticized the Virginia Constitution on the grounds that it had been written and adopted by an ordinary legislative body whose membership had been elected for a variety of reasons to carry on the ordinary business of the state. Like a growing number of Americans, Jefferson argued that for a constitution to be truly the fundamental law of the state and secure from legislative interference, it would have to be created "by a power superior to that of the ordinary legislature." It would have to be created by a special convention for the specific and sole purpose of writing a constitution, which was then to be submitted to the people for ratification. Only when formed in this manner could a constitution be called the highest or fundamental law of the state. Jefferson repeatedly urged the Virginia legislature to call such a convention, but to no avail.

Jefferson returned to active public life when he accepted an appointment to the Continental Congress in March 1783. He served little more than a year, but during this time he made one very major contribution. Jefferson chaired the committee that drafted the Ordinance of 1784, which created a national domain out of the area west of the Appalachian Mountains and established a system for surveying and selling the land that favored actual settlers over speculators. The ordinance, along with another adopted in 1785, provided a plan for territorial governments that stressed self-government for the settler. According to the provisions of the ordinances, when Congress opened part of the national domain for sale, the settlers within it were to form a temporary government and adopt the constitution and laws of any state in the Union they chose. When the population of a new area reached 20,000, a convention would be called and a formal constitution adopted. At this point the developing territory could also send a nonvoting delegate to Congress. As soon as the population of the new territory equaled that of the free inhabitants of the smallest of the original thirteen states, the new area could enter the Union as a state and equal partner. To do this, the new state would only have to consent to remain part of the United States, be subject to the laws of the central government, contribute its share to the payment of the national debt, maintain a republican form of government, and exclude slavery after 1800. Although various aspects of this plan were altered in 1787 and afterward, its basic spirit and emphasis on the need to create new, free, and equal self-governing states has determined the development not only of the Old Northwest but of all the territories in American history. Jefferson placed a great deal of emphasis on the importance of western development. He wanted to see America become a continuously expanding "empire for liberty." His stress on self-government and equal partnership stood in marked contrast to the European system of empire and imperialism.

During this time, Jefferson became interested in foreign affairs. He served on a special commission to negotiate commercial treaties with Europe, and in 1785 he succeeded Benjamin Franklin as minister to France. The development had a nationalizing effect upon Jefferson. Increasingly he had to deal with problems facing the United States as opposed to those of Virginia. He became more aware of the value of a strong central government that had the ability and the energy to require individual states to honor America's treaty obligations, to protect the country's vulnerable southern and northern borders and secure the allegiance of the area west of the Allegheny Mountains, to garner the respect of foreign countries, and to secure favorable treaties of navigation and commerce.

Jefferson did not play a direct role in the greatest single act of American constitutionalism: the writing and the debate over the ratification of the United States Constitution in 1787 and 1788. Still in France during these years, he recognized that the government under the Articles of Confederation was no longer adequate to maintain and strengthen the Union effectively and would have to be replaced by a more vigorous central government. But when he first saw the kind of central government that had been created in Philadelphia, he had serious reservations about it. Specifically, he feared that the perpetual reeligibility of the president was dangerous and had monarchist tendencies. He also believed it essential that the document contain a bill of rights guaranteeing the individual rights of citizens. Nonetheless, while Jefferson refused to align himself with the supporters of the Constitution, he indicated that he was much further from its opponents, the Antifederalists. Moreover, after Madison, the principal architect of the new government and one of Jefferson's closest personal and political friends, sent him a long letter of explanation, he softened his attitude toward the Constitution. But he remained adamant in his demand for some kind of bill of rights; this, along with the need to mollify the Antifederalists, was an important factor in convincing Madison to draft the first ten amendments to the Constitution.

Before Jefferson returned to the United States, the French Revolution occurred. At first he was wary that it might go too far and bring about a conservative reaction. But as it grew more radical, particularly with the adoption of the Declaration of the Rights of Man and Citizen, he was tremendously excited by the possibility of a major European country following the American example of overthrowing a monarchical government. Among other things, the actions of the French reinvigorated his faith in the yet only partially fulfilled republican promise of the

American Revolution. In this he differed with the growing political conservatism of many of the leading supporters of the adoption of the United States Constitution, who had become increasingly skeptical about the democratic implications of the principles of 1776.

At the urging of President George Washington and Madison, Jefferson accepted the position of secretary of state under the new government. When he returned to the United States, he found himself from the beginning opposed to the policies of Alexander Hamilton, who had been appointed secretary of the treasury. The split began on foreign-policy issues, but it quickly went beyond these and soon involved basic ideological and constitutional considerations. Hamilton favored closer ties with England and the centralization and vigorous enforcement of the federal government's power. Jefferson, on the other hand, wanted America to maintain close ties to France, whose aid after 1776 had been crucial in securing independence and whose own revolution he viewed as "the first chapter in the history of European liberty." Also, like many Americans, he feared the concentration of power in the hands of the national government, especially on domestic matters. The American Revolution, after all, was fought to deny the authority of a central government—the only one that the Americans had ever known, Great Britain. It was natural therefore to associate the idea of a central government with England's arbitrary actions during the 1760s and 1770s. Further buttressing and giving direction to this experience was the ideology of the Revolution, which stressed the tension between liberty and power. Hamilton, Jefferson believed, did not understand these precepts; in fact, given Hamilton's preoccupation with the accumulation and use of power, he showed outright hostility to them and was fully capable of betraying the principles of the Revolution.

Although Jefferson reluctantly went along with the funding of the national debt and the assumption of the state debts, he opposed Hamilton's proposal to establish a national bank. The measure had been adopted by Congress after a long debate and a close vote and had been sent to President Washington for his signature. The president asked Jefferson for a written opinion on the matter, which would be sent to Hamilton for rebuttal. Adopting a strict constructionist view of the Constitution and appealing to the Tenth Amendment, then in the process of being adopted, Jefferson argued that the incorporation of a bank was unconstitutional because it was not a delegated power. Nor could the bank be justified under any other grant of power to the federal government, for the "general welfare" clause was not an all-inclusive grant of power but a broad statement indicating the sum and purpose of the enumerated powers of Congress. With reference to the "necessary and proper" clause, Jefferson argued that the word *necessary* meant that the means to carry out delegated powers must be indispensable and not merely convenient. Any other interpretation would allow Congress "to take possession of a boundless field of power no longer susceptible to definition" and would shatter the rights of the states.

Although Jefferson's argument was to resonate throughout American history, it failed to convince President Washington, who gave his approval to the bank. Unhappy with the pro-English and what he viewed as excessively nationalistic policies of the administration under Hamilton's leadership, Jefferson found himself increasingly sympathetic to the growing opposition in Congress. This placed him in a difficult position, for not only was he opposed to the policies of the administration in which he held a prominent office, but like almost everyone else in his generation, he did not like the idea of political parties. Parties had not been anticipated by the framers of the Constitution, and no provision had been made for them. In fact, in the late eighteenth century the idea of a loyal opposition had not developed in America, and most people viewed an organized political opposition as dangerous and subversive. Jefferson tried to mitigate this somewhat by stressing his loyalty to President Washington even though he opposed Hamilton's policies. But it was not a satisfactory solution, and when his influence in the administration continued to wane sharply, he resigned his post as secretary of state, withdrew from politics, and retired to his beloved Monticello to put his private affairs in order.

President Washington's decision not to seek a third term in 1796 opened the way for the first contested election for the presidency under the United States Constitution. Reluctantly, and with some trepidation, Jefferson agreed to be the Republican standard-bearer against John Adams, who ran as a Federalist. This did not signify an acceptance on his part of the idea that political parties were a positive good. Rather, Jefferson justified his involvement with an organized opposition on the grounds that the Federalists had subverted the Constitution and strayed from the true principles of the Revolution. Adams was victorious, but Jefferson captured the vice-presidency. This result of the election of 1796 was a clear indication of how unprepared the framers of the Constitution were for the development of political parties. Under the original terms of the Constitution, they anticipated that the ablest man running would become president and that the second ablest man would become vice-president and heir apparent; they never expected that the two might represent antagonistic points of view.

Jefferson liked and respected Adams a great deal. He had worked well with him in the Continental Congress in the mid-1770s and in the diplomatic corps in the late 1780s, and he hoped they could cooperate now, in the best interests of both the country and the Constitution. But Adams' hostility to France quickly drove a wedge between the two men, and when, following the XYZ affair, Adams put the country on a war footing by building up the army and the navy, and moved through the Alien and Sedition Acts to suppress public criticism of his policies, Jefferson became alarmed. He feared, in particular, that the administration intended to use the military to crush its domestic opposition, and he believed the Alien and Sedition Acts were a violation of the First Amendment.

The question was how to oppose these measures effectively. It made no sense to go into the courts, since they were completely under Federalist control. Although throughout the country various Republicans denounced these measures in speeches, pamphlets, and newspapers, this kind of opposition was both ineffective and unofficial. Seeking to express their disapproval through a legally constituted forum, Jefferson and Madison secretly prepared two separate sets of resolutions to be submitted to, respectively, the Kentucky and Virginia legislatures, both of which were under Republican control.

These resolutions, which were adopted, not only denounced the Alien and Sedition Acts as unconstitutional but also put forward an elaborate theory of the Union. The federal government, they argued, was one of limited and specifically delegated powers and was a product of a compact made between the states in 1787–1788. The Kentucky and Virginia Resolutions also took issue with the Federalist claim that the United States Supreme Court was the exclusive and final arbiter of constitutional questions. As Jefferson argued in the Kentucky Resolutions, the Court was a creature of the Constitution and to give it the power of judicial review would be to make "its discretion, and not the Constitution, the measure of its powers." According to the Kentucky and Virginia Resolutions, should the federal

125

government assume a power not granted to it, each state, as a party to the compact, had the right to declare the law unconstitutional; and since Congress exceeded its constitutional powers when it adopted the Alien and Sedition Acts, the state of Kentucky declared these to be "not law" and "altogether void and of no force."

Of the two sets of resolutions, Jefferson's, for Kentucky, was the more extreme. He used the word *nullification* in his draft, although the Kentucky legislature omitted it when it formally passed the resolutions. The discovery of this in the 1820s allowed John C. Calhoun to link the states'-rights doctrine as promulgated in the Kentucky and Virginia Resolutions to slavery, secession, and nullification when he began to espouse it in the late 1820s and early 1830s. In the end, the question of whether a state or the United States was the final arbiter on constitutional questions would be settled by the Civil War.

The rhetoric of the Kentucky and Virginia Resolutions was a good deal more extreme than their reality. They were never meant to be a prescription for action. Even though both states declared the Alien and Sedition Acts to be unconstitutional, no official attempt was made to prevent the enforcement of the laws by federal officials within the boundaries of Kentucky and Virginia. The resolutions were issued for political effect: to rally the Republican opposition, to reaffirm the revolutionary tradition wherein the defense of personal and civil liberty was joined to states' rights, and to offer a theory of the origins of the national government that undercut the constitutional basis for the Federalist program of centralization. In this sense the resolutions were an enormous success, as they played an important role in helping Jefferson obtain the presidency in 1800.

The election of 1800 placed a severe strain on both the United States Constitution and the Union it created. The campaign was a bitter one, and while Adams failed in

his bid for reelection, he was only defeated by eight electoral votes. Moreover, the well-organized Republican electors each cast a vote for both Jefferson and Aaron Burr, the Republican vice-presidential candidate. This resulted in a tie, and it meant the election would have to be decided by the lame-duck Federalist-dominated House of Representatives, with each state delegation casting one vote. A deadlock ensued when a number of Federalists conspired to make Burr president. Outraged, some of Jefferson's supporters began to talk of resorting to military force to ensure that the will of the people be carried out. Finally, on 17 February 1801, after thirty-six separate ballots, Jefferson became the third president of the United States.

Jefferson's assumption of the presidency a short time later raised several significant constitutional and ideological problems. It was the first time that an opposition party had come to power under the United States Constitution. Did it mean simply a change in the policies and personnel of the new government, or did it mean a change in the government itself? To what extent was the Republican victory—which involved not only the presidency but both houses of Congress as well—a mandate to the new administration to do whatever it wanted? Was it obliged, after an especially bitter election contest, to take into consideration the feelings and interests of the defeated minority and to try to heal the wounds of the country? Further, how was Jefferson to reconcile his position as representative of all the people with the fact that he also now was a party leader? In the first decade of the nineteenth century, not all Republicans agreed on how to answer these questions. Many of Jefferson's followers wanted to see fundamental alterations made in the Constitution. Others, led by James Madison, who more than anyone else had helped create the Constitution, feared and opposed such changes.

Although Jefferson sympathized with the

concerns of the more radical wing of the party, he nonetheless opted for a policy of moderation and reconciliation. This was evidenced in his inaugural address when he asserted, "We are all republicans: we are all federalists." Jefferson refused to go along with any direct assault on the Constitution itself. The only explicit change he endorsed during his presidency was the Twelfth Amendment, which corrected the irregularities that occurred in the elections of 1796 and 1800 by providing that separate electoral ballots be cast for president and vice-president. No other amendments were adopted during his presidency. Jefferson did not engage in sweeping removal of Federalist officeholders, attempt to repeal Hamilton's system for the funding of the national and state debts, or try to dismantle the Bank of the United States. To be sure, he introduced some reforms. He reduced the size of the army and navy, repealed all internal taxes, established a program to pay off the national debt completely, and instituted policies to encourage settlement in the national domain. But it was all done within the framework of the Constitution. When extremists within the Republican party complained that these changes did not go far enough, Jefferson responded by observing, "What is practicable must often control pure theory." Jefferson's decision not to engage in root-and-branch reform when he assumed the presidency contributed in a very significant way to the much valued constitutional stability that has been a characteristic of American politics since 1789.

During his presidency, Jefferson had a particularly difficult time dealing with the national judiciary. This branch of the government had been totally dominated by the Federalists in the 1790s and had actively extended the powers of the federal government and vigorously enforced the detested Sedition Act. Since its members held their office for life tenure during good behavior, the judiciary was not subject to popular control, and it emerged from "the revolution of 1800" without a single Republican member. Even more infuriating to Republicans, after the election results were known, the Federalist-controlled lame-duck Congress had passed the Judiciary Act of 1801, further expanding the power of the national courts and increasing its personnel by creating a system of circuit courts. Moreover, before he relinquished his office to Jefferson, John Adams made sure that all the appointments under the new law went to Federalists. At the same time, he appointed John Marshall, whom Jefferson did not like, chief justice of the United States Supreme Court.

Jefferson and his followers were enraged by these "midnight appointments." They were convinced that the Federalists planned to use their control over the national judiciary to undermine Republican policies and to reduce further the rights of the states. The more extreme "Old Republican" members of the party proposed amending the Constitution to reduce the powers of the national judiciary. They also suggested impeaching a number of the more partisan Federalist judges. But Jefferson pursued a more moderate course. He simply brought about in 1802 a repeal of the Judiciary Act of 1801, returning the national court system, with minor modifications, to the way it had existed throughout the 1790s under the Judiciary Act of 1789.

The Federalists denounced these proceedings. They argued that the repeal of the Judiciary Act of 1801 was unconstitutional because federal judges could only be removed from office when found guilty of high crimes and misdemeanors. What the Republicans had done, they believed, was to dismiss the circuit-court judges without a trial. They took the matter to the United States Supreme Court, but that Federalist-dominated body, fearful of further provoking the Republicans, refused to declare the repeal of the Judiciary Act of 1801 unconstitutional. At the same time, another, and as it was to turn out, more significant case had come before the Supreme Court. William Marbury and a number of other "midnight" appointees had gone to the Supreme Court complaining that the Jefferson administration had failed to deliver the signed and sealed commissions for their positions as justices of the peace for the District of Columbia, thus preventing them from assuming their offices. As a remedy they requested the Court to issue a writ of mandamus ordering Secretary of State Madison to deliver the necessary papers.

Marshall and the other members of the Supreme Court approached *Marbury* v. *Madison* very cautiously. Although they sympathized with Marbury and the other complainants and believed they had a right to their commissions, they realized that if they ordered the commissions delivered and the administration refused to comply with the decision, it would only embarrass the Court. Marshall therefore decided to dismiss Marbury's suit on the grounds that the Supreme Court lacked jurisdiction. The case is significant, however, because it was the first time the Court held a portion of a law of Congress unconstitutional: it declared Section 13 of the Judiciary Act of 1789, which empowered the Court with original jurisdiction in issuing a writ of mandamus, to be contrary to the Constitution and therefore void.

Jefferson's feelings about the decision were undoubtedly mixed. It contained a long lecture to the administration on why the commissions should have been delivered. Jefferson felt this portion of the decision was obiter dicta and thus unnecessary, and it annoyed him a great deal. The decision also implicitly supported, although it did not explicitly take a stand on, the Federalist claim that the Supreme Court should be the final arbiter on constitutional issues. Jefferson, as we have seen, did not agree with this theory. In the Kentucky Resolutions he had indicated that on federal-state questions, such decisions were better left in the hands of the states. As to the question that arose over relations between the different branches of the federal government (legislative, executive, and judicial), Jefferson had addressed this problem in the original draft of his first annual message to Congress. In it he observed that the three branches of the federal government were equal and independent and that in areas under their respective jurisdictions, Congress, the president, and the Supreme Court each "acts in the last resort and without appeal, to decide on the validity of an act according to its own judgment, and uncontrolled by the opinions of any other department." This was an explicit denial of the Federalist concept of judicial supremacy. Upon the advice of his advisers Jefferson dropped this passage from the final draft of the message sent to Congress in December 1801. He did so, however, because he was determined to avoid any kind of controversy over the Constitution, not because he abandoned the idea of three separate and equal departments, whose differences over how to interpret the Constitution, if fundamental enough to impair the functioning of the government, would have to be resolved by amendment.

Jefferson chose in 1803 not to make an issue over the Supreme Court's decision in *Marbury* v. *Madison,* because he wanted to pursue his policy of moderation and conciliation. He could adopt this course because in at least one important way the decision was a victory for him: it rejected Marbury's request for a writ of mandamus and did not order the administration to deliver the commissions. The decision was palatable to the new president also in that it did not try to take away any powers being used by the president or Congress but did reject an attempt by Congress to increase the powers of the Supreme Court by giving it original jurisdiction in cases involving writs of mandamus. Finally, while the Supreme Court claimed for itself the right to oversee the Constitution, it did not explicitly declare that its power to do so was either exclusive or final. *Marbury* v. *Madison* was later, long after Jefferson had died, to take on enormous significance as the first example of the Supreme Court's declaring a congressional act unconstitutional, but at the time it was handed down it was considered by many as a defeat for the more belligerent members of the Federalist party and as a conciliatory gesture on the part of the Supreme Court toward Jefferson's administration.

There was some hope on Jefferson's part that the controversy with the national judiciary would now abate. But it was not to be, for the president soon received word about the activities of a Federalist district-court judge in New Hampshire named John Pickering, who was engaging in bizarre and partisan activities on the bench. Closer examination revealed that Pickering was both insane and alcoholic. At first, Jefferson tried to persuade prominent New Hampshire Federalists to pressure Pickering into resigning. But they refused to do this unless Jefferson guaranteed that he would be replaced by someone of their own choosing. Reluctantly, therefore, he decided to ask for Pickering's impeachment. The trial that followed was a mess. Impeachment required a conviction for "high crimes and misdemeanors," but if evidence indicating Pickering's insanity were admitted, it would not be possible to find the demented judge guilty on these grounds. As required by the Constitution, the case was tried before the United States Senate with the vice-president as presiding officer; and members loyal to the administration, with Jefferson's support, conspired to prevent any discussion of the judge's mental condition. Although Pickering was convicted, it was a very unpleasant and partisan business, and a number of moderate Republican senators absented themselves from the final balloting. The outcome of the case, however, was a clear victory for the more extreme Old Republican

wing of the party, as the impeachment clause of the Constitution had been successfully used to remove a federal judge from office.

What this meant became clear just a few days later when the Old Republicans, led by John Randolph, moved to impeach Samuel Chase, a justice of the United States Supreme Court. An overbearing and difficult man and a strong Federalist partisan, he had vigorously enforced the Sedition Act against Republican editors and had continued to use the bench, even after the election of 1800, to attack Jeffersonian policies. At first, Jefferson seemed to sympathize with the move against Chase, but it soon became clear that Randolph and his allies intended to redefine the impeachment process so that it would be a way of removing political opponents from office as opposed to a means of removing public officials who had engaged in criminal activities. The attempted impeachment was a direct assault on the independence of the judiciary as provided for in the Constitution, for had Chase been convicted, it is highly likely that other members of the national judiciary would have been removed from office. Jefferson opted not to go along with this effort and quietly withdrew his support from the impeachment proceedings against Chase. Randolph botched the ensuing trial, and this, along with Jefferson's refusal to enforce party regularity in the final vote, as he had done in the Pickering trial, led to Chase's acquittal.

Having successfully defended the Constitution against major alteration, Jefferson generally followed a strict constructionist and states'-rights policy on domestic matters throughout his first administration, and he sharply cut governmental spending. In his second administration he began to talk about a nationally financed system of internal improvements that would include the building of roads, canals, and various educational, scientific, and literary institutions. By these operations, he asserted in his Sixth Annual Message, "new channels of communication will be opened between the States; the lines of separation will disappear, their interests will be identified, and their union cemented by new and indissoluble ties." Such a program, clearly, had strong nationalist implications. Some precedents existed. The Ohio Enabling Act of 1802, under which that state entered the Union in 1803, provided that 5 percent of the proceeds from the sale of its public lands be used to build roads to connect it with the East. A national road also was started, stretching from Maryland into Pennsylvania and through western Virginia into the Old Northwest. But neither was on such a scale or as systematic as what was now proposed, and although Jefferson strongly favored a federal system of internal improvements on policy grounds, he recognized that it raised constitutional problems. How were the various sites and routes to be chosen? Who would control or maintain them—the states or the federal government? Should the states have a veto power over the decisions of the federal government that affected their lands and citizens?

Jefferson denied that the "general welfare" clause of the Constitution, as some argued, gave the federal government the authority to act without consulting the states in these matters. He therefore requested an amendment to the Constitution to clarify the issues involved. As it turned out, the difficulties in foreign affairs and the economic hard times that dominated the end of Jefferson's second administration forced the matter to be postponed. It was not taken up again until after the War of 1812, by which time he had retired from politics. But Jefferson's successors James Madison and James Monroe both followed Jefferson's admonition and insisted upon a constitutional amendment. When Congress refused to go along with this and tried to establish a federally controlled system of internal improvements, they vetoed the measures. As a consequence, the building of schools and universities, libraries and scientific centers, and roads and canals had to be undertaken by the state governments and private enterprise.

On the other hand, in the general area of foreign policy, where political exigencies often dominated and where Jefferson believed the country had to act decisively and with one voice in order to obtain respect on the international scene, he often had to take a much more flexible attitude toward constitutional interpretation. This was particularly true in regard to the Louisiana Purchase. Given his long-standing interest in the development of the West and his belief that it was America's destiny to settle and control the North American continent, Jefferson was very upset when he learned that Napoleon was planning to establish a French colonial empire in the Mississippi Valley. He immediately instructed the American minister to France to begin negotiations to find out more about what France intended and a way to guarantee protection for American commerce on the Mississippi. To his surprise he learned that Napoleon had changed his mind, had abandoned his scheme for a colonial empire in the New World, and now wanted to sell not only New Orleans but more than 800,000 square miles of land lying between the Mississippi River and the Rocky Mountains. Such an acquisition would literally double the size of the United States.

Jefferson was eager to take advantage of this spectacular opportunity, but he was troubled because the Constitution contained no provision for purchase and incorporation into the United States of foreign territory. Unsure how to proceed, he suggested to his advisers that a constitutional amendment be adopted. He even drafted a proposal for such an amendment. But it was pointed out that this could be a risky and very time-consuming process, and because it was feared that the ever mercurial Napoleon might change his mind and withdraw the offer, Jefferson proceeded to go ahead with the purchase despite his doubts about its constitutionality.

In effect, on this particular matter, Jefferson was found to have adopted Hamilton's "implied powers" in interpretation of the Constitution, and it bothered him a great deal. Not only did he agonize over the decision, but he embarked on it with the expectation, as he put it in a letter of 9 August 1803 to John Dickinson, that he would have to "rely on the nation to sanction an act done for its great good, without its previous authority." In other words, the treaty could be rejected by Congress or the people could express their disapproval at the next election. As it turned out, the treaty was quickly ratified and proved to be very popular; the only real opposition came from a rapidly dwindling minority of Federalists. In fact, the Louisiana Purchase is probably the single greatest achievement of Jefferson's presidency. Nonetheless, he continued to have doubts about its constitutionality. In a letter of 7 September 1803 to Wilson C. Nicholas, a fellow Republican who believed the purchase could be justified under the treaty-making power of the Constitution, he responded,

When an instrument admits two constructions, the one safe, the other dangerous, the one precise, the other indefinite, I prefer that which is safe and precise. I had rather ask an enlargement of power from the nation, where it is found necessary, than to assume by a construction which would make our powers boundless. Our peculiar security is in the possession of a written Constitution. Let us not make it a blank paper by construction. I say the same as to the opinion of those who consider the grant of the treaty making power as boundless. If it is, then we have no Constitution. If it has bounds, they can be no others than the definitions of the powers which that instrument gives. It specifies and delineates the operations permitted to the federal government, and gives all the powers necessary to

carry these into execution. . . . Nothing is more likely than that [this] . . . enumeration of powers is defective. . . . Let us go then perfecting it, by adding by way of the Constitution, those powers which time and trial show are still wanting. . . . I confess, then, I think it important, in the present case, to set an example against broad construction by appealing for new power to the people.

Probably no other president in American history has expressed greater doubt about the constitutionality of his own actions. His caution testifies to the seriousness with which Jefferson treated constitutional issues.

The last year of Jefferson's second administration was dominated by the problem of maintaining American neutrality in the face of the revived war between Great Britain and France. Both countries interfered with American commerce, the former through its orders-in-council and the latter through its Continental System. In addition, England had impressed numerous seamen who were United States citizens and in June 1807 assaulted the American naval frigate *Chesapeake* off the coast of Norfolk, Virginia. In response, Jefferson adopted a policy of "peaceable coercion" by which he hoped to rely upon economic pressure to bring the belligerent countries to terms. He recommended, and Congress speedily adopted, an embargo. It prohibited United States ships from sailing for foreign ports and required vessels engaged in the coastal trade to post substantial bonds to guarantee that they would go to American ports. Opposition to the measure was widespread in New England and in many parts of the Middle Atlantic states. The constitutionality of the measure was attacked, but it was upheld by a Massachusetts district court, from which no appeal was ever taken to the Supreme Court.

Other means were found to evade the embargo. Merchants engaged in widespread smuggling, and a substantial clandestine trade developed along the border with Canada. At first Jefferson did not fully comprehend either the unpopularity of the measure or the economic distress it was causing. Preoccupied with America's foreign-policy problems, he called for even harsher measures to ensure the vigorous enforcement of his embargo policy. The discretionary power of customs officials to engage in search and seizure was increased as numerous ships and warehouses were inspected without benefit of search warrants, and the military was increasingly used to enforce the laws. Despite these measures the suppression of the various kinds of illegal activity that had developed proved to be an impossible task in a country the size of the United States. At no point was Jefferson ever able to rally public opinion effectively to his side. The federal courts also handed down a number of decisions unfavorable to the government's enforcement procedures.

Increasingly, the opposition accused Jefferson of being an arbitrary tyrant. This was a particularly painful charge for someone who, as a member of America's revolutionary generation, had stressed throughout his life the importance of individual liberty and governmental restraint. It made him a truly miserable man. When Jefferson finally fully comprehended the disastrous internal consequences of his embargo policy for America, he abandoned it and actually signed the law for its repeal during his last days in office. Although the enforcement of the embargo does not reflect favorably on Jefferson, it is worth noting that in the end, however reluctantly, he acceded to the will of the people.

Jefferson left the presidency a very unhappy man, yet by no means a broken one. Although he never again held elective office or strayed very far from Monticello, he was very active in his retirement. In addition to pursuing his interests in botany, agricul-

tural reform, architecture, music, paleontology, and education, he kept abreast of current affairs and maintained a special interest in constitutional issues. Free from the restraints of power, his opinions could be fairly radical. He once again pushed hard, but without notable success, for a reform of the Virginia Constitution. He expressed concern about the many nationalist tendencies that emerged after the end of the War of 1812 and was especially critical of the activities of Marshall and the Supreme Court. And he renewed his friendship with John Adams; the two men engaged in an extensive correspondence that examined, among other things, the origin and meaning of the American Revolution and explored many of the key assumptions behind the American tradition of constitutionalism.

Jefferson had a long and full life. He was a major public figure for over fifty years, a period during which the United States underwent enormous changes. Since Jefferson never wrote a systematic treatise summarizing his political and constitutional values, it is often difficult to explain with precision what motivated him on a number of key issues. The problem is further complicated by the fact that he had a playful and philosophical mind that often embraced ideas that he abandoned upon greater deliberation. Consequently, he often sounded more radical than he was in reality. In fact, when he had real power, during his two terms as president, he tended to be pragmatic, nonideological, and, if anything, overly cautious. He never tried to take advantage of his enormous popularity, although he definitely misjudged popular sentiment on the problems that arose out of his embargo policy. Nonetheless, certain conclusions about Jefferson are inescapable: he was fundamentally committed to the idea of a limited government through a written constitution; he believed that the federal government's main sphere of activity should be in foreign affairs and that domestic matters, unless specifically provided for in the Constitution, should be left to the states; and he was critical of all forms of judicial activism. Jefferson was by no means a perfect man, but he was definitely a great one and a figure of monumental importance in the development of the American constitutional tradition.

The Classical World

MEYER REINHOLD

"For classical learning I have ever been a zealous advocate," the septuagenarian Jefferson wrote to the distinguished polymath, educator-scientist Thomas Cooper. "The classic pages" occupied pride of place among the "supreme delights" in his pursuit of knowledge, and throughout his life he enjoyed with undiminished zest what he called "this rich source of delight."

EARLY CLASSICAL YEARS IN VIRGINIA

Such dedication to the classics was remarkable for an early American born and bred on the raw frontier. Many self-educated Virginians like Patrick Henry, Edmund Pendleton, and William Wirt climbed to the highest offices without classical learning. Jefferson had the advantage of receiving a traditional liberal education, with its classical curriculum, between the ages of nine and sixteen. Even if this training was not as fashionable as the schooling of John Adams and other New Englanders, it gave Jefferson a fair start

in Latin and Greek. His five years at the grammar school of the Reverend William Douglas in nearby St. James were not memorable, for Douglas was, as Jefferson recalled, "but a superficial Latinist, less instructed in Greek." An orphan at fourteen, after the sudden death of his beloved father, young Jefferson was sent to board for two years at the school of Parson James Maury, a graduate of William and Mary College, an Anglican clergyman of Whig persuasion who was for Jefferson "a correct classical scholar," and the owner of a superb library. Parson Maury, who had other distinguished Virginia youths as his students, among them perhaps James Madison, was himself skeptical about the suitability of the dead languages for the sons of the plantation gentry; in 1762 he proposed a more practical education for them, declaring that he could not name a single son of parents of large fortune who had entered the learned professions.

But in fact the Virginia aristocracy was not so unlearned and anti-intellectual. Many of them, aspiring to live like English country gentlemen, associated gentility with classical learning. This provided them with an elitist cachet, bestowing on them a veneer of classical vocabulary and ideas together with a store of timeless wisdom, a wide range of historical and political knowledge, and authoritative models of taste in writing, oratory, and ethics. Though it was not an especially bookish society, many leading Virginians possessed extensive libraries. To escape from the prison of provincialism, they sought through reading and travel to enter the mainstream of European culture, and in the eighteenth century some, like Jefferson, were deeply influenced by Enlightenment thought.

The few Virginians who went to William and Mary stayed no more than a year or two, as compared with the four-year program at Harvard. Jefferson, fired by his intellectual gifts and patrimony, aspired to more than a grammar-school education. At the age of seventeen he asked for and obtained permission from his guardian to enroll in William and Mary in order to pursue his studies in Greek, Latin, and mathematics. He received the A.B. degree in 1762, shortly after his nineteenth birthday, hardly a finished scholar but fortunate in his intellectual associations there.

In Williamsburg began one of the great passions of his life—collecting books for his own library. In his old age he reminisced that as a young man "the destinies of my life" were fixed by two men: William Small, professor of mathematics, from whom he acquired an interest in the natural sciences, and George Wythe, distinguished lawyer in Williamsburg. It was Jefferson's good fortune to become a protégé of Wythe, who was later to be the first professor of law at William and Mary and chancellor of the judicial system of Virginia, as well as signer of the Declaration of Independence. Though largely self-educated, Wythe had a lifelong enthusiasm for the Greek and Latin classics. Under Wythe's tutelage, Jefferson studied law (including Roman law) for five years and

diligently read Greek and Roman authors as "extracurricular" study, an activity Wythe continued to indulge in with many other law students whom he took under his wing. Jefferson remembered him as "the best Latin and Greek scholar in the state," later calling him "my second father."

Through Small and Wythe, Jefferson had entrée to the residence of the royal governor of Virginia, the remarkable Francis Fauquier, Fellow of the Royal Society, distinguished humanist, and possessor of an extensive library and art collection. What an odd foursome they made, Jefferson with men who were two and three times his age. Those conversations at Fauquier's residence Jefferson recalled as "truly Attic societies." At an impressionable age he was immersed in an atmosphere that throbbed with intellectual adventure, humanist interests, Enlightenment thought, deism, and love of books and art.

Though it was to Small, Wythe, and Fauquier that Jefferson was indebted for the foundations of his intellectual life, it was to his father that he frequently expressed his indebtedness for his beloved classical learning. In 1800, over forty years after his father's death, he wrote to Joseph Priestley, "I thank on my knees him who directed my early education for having put into my possession this rich source of delight; and I would not exchange it for any thing." His great-granddaughter Sarah Randolph recalled from her personal experience, "In after years he used to say, that had he to decide between the pleasure derived from the classical education which his father had given him and the estate he had left him, he would decide in favor of the former."

From Wythe, Jefferson acquired an admiration for and some expertise in Roman law (or civil law, as it was then called). This interest in Roman law in the colonies had its origins in efforts to develop a native American jurisprudence separate from the English common law, which had superseded feudal law. Americans like Wythe and Jefferson turned to Roman law as a sort of "higher law" that embodied "natural law" and universal rational principles of justice.

Early in his legal practice in Virginia, Jefferson argued a case for the plaintiff on the basis of a principle found in classical sources of the "law of nature," that "all men are born free." The case (*Howell* v. *Netherland*) involved a mulatto woman who was the grandchild of a white woman and a black man. By enactments of Virginia, children of such a union were slaves, bound to servitude until age thirty-one. Jefferson argued on the basis of "natural law" that the legislation did not apply to grandchildren. "It remains," he declared in court, "for some future legislature, if any shall be found wicked enough to extend it to grandchildren and other issue more remote, to *nati natorum et qui nascitur ab illis*" (children of children and those born of these). Jefferson, a slave owner, lost the case on clear statutory grounds; the lawyer for the defense was Wythe, who was opposed to the institution of slavery.

Later, when Jefferson was president, he personally prepared a lengthy and learned brief ("The Batture at New Orleans") in which he argued for governmental property rights in New Orleans on the beach of the Mississippi River, liberally citing Roman legal principles and discussions (from such Roman legal sources as the *Digest* and Justinian's *Institutes*) and incorporating a long treatment of the linguistics and meaning of the word *ager* in the Roman law codes. In the course of the brief, he praised Roman law in general as "the legal system of a nation highly civilized, a system carried to a degree of conformity with natural reason attained by no other." And on 24 August 1819, in his famous letter to John Brazier concerning the value of classical learning for the United States, he stated that Roman law was "the system of civil law most conformable with the principles of justice of any which has ever yet been established among men, and

from which much has been incorporated into our own." Despite the efforts of Wythe, Jefferson, and others, Roman law found no secure place in American jurisprudence. It ceased to be a living force in the legal system and courts of the country by 1850. After that it survived as an esoteric subject in some universities.

From this period of his life—a time that Jefferson was to call "my classical days," when he was in his twenties and a student of George Wythe in Williamsburg—it is possible to gain insights into the wide range and focus of his reading. From those years, two of Jefferson's commonplace books have survived, which reveal what and how he read. What Jefferson was doing in these notebooks was commonplacing, jotting down passages from his reading that he thought worthy of preserving for future reference—moral statements, flashes of wisdom, or bits of valuable information. In one of his commonplace books Jefferson copied excerpts from his readings in law, ancient history, and political institutions, passages that he liberally annotated with quotations from classical authors. In the second—the one that Gilbert Chinard extravagantly called his "Literary Bible"—there are 150 quotations from thirteen classical authors, most notably Euripides, Homer, Cicero, Horace, Virgil, Terence, and Ovid. Curiously, Euripides is represented in almost half of these passages, with brief excerpts from five plays: *Hecuba, Orestes, Phoenissae, Medea,* and *Hippolytus.* These plays were not special favorites of Jefferson; they just happen to be the first five plays customarily printed in standard editions of Euripides' plays since the Middle Ages. All the excerpts chosen for commonplacing by Jefferson reveal the character of his interest in classical writings at this time: he considered them as moral teachings from which he might draw lessons. He was not concerned with dramaturgy, aesthetic beauty, or Euripides' social, religious, or political views. His excerpts from Horace—

ever a gold mine of pithy phrases—include a large part of his Epode 2, beginning "*Beatus ille qui procul negotiis*" (Happy the man who far from business), though Jefferson omitted what was not appropriate to Virginia or to his own needs on his estate. Later Jefferson recalled the poem and thought that he might use it in his plans for Monticello.

Some of these plans we can find in his Account Book for 1771—for example, his plan for a landscape garden. This, one of the earliest American English-style landscape gardens, was characteristically eclectic in design, combining classical and romantic elements. The complex was to include a burial area, in which he hoped to include the simple Latin verse epitaph for his beloved sister Jane that he had composed after she died in 1765. At this time, he deemed the tombstones of his relatives deserving of the lapidary dignity of Latin or Greek. For Jane's inscription he wrote:

> *Ah! Joanna, puellarum optima,*
> *Ah! aevi virentis flore praerepta,*
> *Sit tibi terra levis;*
> *Longe, longeque valeto.*

(Ah! Jane, best of girls, / Ah! snatched away in the flower and bloom of life, / May the earth rest lightly on you; / Forever and forever farewell!)

In the garden there would be a temple, the roof of which would be in Chinese or Greek style. Nearby would be the statue of a sleeping nymph on a marble slab with the following inscription:

> *Huius nympha loci, sacri custodia fontis,*
> *Dormio dum blandae sentio murmur aquae,*
> *Parce meum, quisque tangis cava marmora,*
> *somnum*
> *Rumpere. Sive bibas, sive lavere tace.*

Alternatively, he would have the following English version, by Alexander Pope:

> Nymph of the grot, these sacred springs I
> keep
> And to the murmur of these waters sleep;
> Ah, spare my slumbers, gently trod the cave!
> And drink in silence, or in silence lave!

The Latin inscription is a pseudoclassical text composed in the fifteenth century, one that appeared in many epigraphical collections until weeded out as a modern counterfeit in the standard corpus of ancient Latin inscriptions. The scene of Jefferson's nymph and the inscription had both been used long before—for example, by Albrecht Dürer for his painting "Sleeping Nymph," as well as by Cranach. In 1725, Pope assembled similar elements for his country estate at Twickenham. Jefferson also proposed adding an inscription on stone or a metal plate containing lines in Latin from Horace's Epode 2 that he had recently copied into his literary commonplace book and that translate as follows:

> Happy the man who far from business, as the early race of mankind, works his paternal fields with his own oxen, entirely free from payment of interest. . . . He shuns the forum and the proud mansions of the more powerful citizens. . . . He delights in lying now under an ancient oak, now on the luxuriant grass. Meanwhile, the waters glide by in the deep streams, the birds warble in the forests, and the leaves rustle as the waters plash, inviting gentle sleep.

By the time he was twenty-eight, Jefferson had fantasied Monticello as a sort of Roman villa. He was to endure and enjoy city life many times in his career, in Williamsburg, Philadelphia, Paris, and Washington. But urban living was to him fraught with tensions—intrigue, politics, corruption, luxury, factions, a mix of the economically dependent poor and the overweening, degenerate rich. From Roman authors he had internalized the view that it was not possible for free men to be truly free except on their own land. For Jefferson, as for many English country gentlemen, Horace's "Sabine Farm" was the ideal model.

But in fact Jefferson's agrarianism and life-style were romanticized country living—half rustic and half urban, patterned on the English marriage of *rus* and *urbs* in the eighteenth century and on the villa ambience of such cultured Romans as Cicero, Varro, Horace, and Pliny the Younger. For Jefferson, as for his Roman models, villa life afforded the leisure provided by his slave family, the pleasure of books and works of art, and a busy intellectual life shared by occasional visitors. Moreover, Jefferson's conception of the indispensability of an agrarian base for a free and stable republic had its origins in classical thought—especially in Aristotle and a host of Roman sources. Freehold farmers, Jefferson believed, possess the rustic virtues that underpin the freedom of the republic. In the dominant view of the eighteenth century, this was presumed to be the case with the Romans at the height of their republic.

To Jefferson, Roman and Greek agriculture was also superior to modern knowledge and practice. In March 1817, when asked for a comprehensive bibliography for an agricultural library, he wrote to George Jeffreys: "I speak as a Southern man. The agriculture of France and Italy is good, but has been better than at this time . . . , the latter in the time of Cato, Varro &c. Lessons useful to us may also be derived from Greece and Asia Minor, in the times of their eminence in science and population." Jefferson esteemed ancient agriculture, but his life at Monticello was neither that of the working small farmer nor that of an American Cincinnatus on a few acres—though he would have been pleased with that role model, already preempted for other Founding Fathers, especially George Washington. The Marquis de Chastellux, who described in detail his visit to Monticello in April 1782, concluded perceptively, "It seems indeed as though

ever since his youth, he had placed his mind, like his house, on a lofty height, whence he might contemplate the whole universe."

In 1771 Jefferson thought of filling his "Roman villa" at Monticello with books and works of art. This was a time in American cultural history when immediate practical needs had the highest priority. As late as 1819, John Adams was unappreciative in his response to a letter from the French sculptor Jean Binon informing him that he had made a portrait bust of Adams: "The age of painting and sculpture has not yet arrived in this country, and I hope it will not arrive very soon. . . . I would not give sixpence for a picture of Raphael or a statue of Phidias."

But Jefferson "panted after the fine arts," wrote Edmund Randolph in his posthumous appreciation of his fellow Virginian. And Benjamin H. Latrobe, the great architect of the Capitol in Washington, said of Jefferson in 1807, "You have planted the arts in your country . . . [through] your love and protection of the fine arts."

Architecture was the art par excellence for Jefferson because it produced visible, public, useful works. He was also passionately fond of sculpture, but only for personal enjoyment and not as public art. He once spoke of "the ineffable majesty of expression in ancient sculpture." He began to build Monticello in 1769. In 1771, on a leaf of his Construction Book under the heading "Statues and Paintings, etc.," he outlined a plan to acquire copies of thirteen sculptures, as well as portrait busts of famous historical figures, and a number of paintings. Most of these works were on classical themes, known to him secondhand from books and engravings in his library. The sculptures were all well-known statues that had been popular for centuries on the Continent. He chose the paintings not for their aesthetic charm but for their moralizing themes. Eventually Monticello became a veritable art museum containing numerous works of sculpture, many portrait busts, and 120 paintings, many on classical subjects.

Americans began to immortalize the Founding Fathers in sculpture, and the issue of classical or modern costume for their portraits was discussed. On 14 August 1787, Jefferson wrote to George Washington from Paris that American artists in London believed that "a modern in an antique dress [is] as *just* an object of ridicule as an Hercules or Marius with periwig and chapeau bras." Yet, in truth, Roman grandeur appealed powerfully to him as he strove to distance himself and the nation from provincial tastes. Indeed, the earliest portrait of Jefferson that was done in America was a colossal marble bust in Roman style by Giuseppe Ceracchi, which was for display at Monticello. Jefferson wrote to Nathaniel Macon on 22 January 1816 about the statue of Washington to be made for the capitol building in North Carolina by the sculptor Canova: "As to style or costume, I am sure the artist, and every person of taste in Europe, would be for the Roman, the effect of which is undoubtedly of a different order. Our boots and regimentals have a very puny effect."

Before he went abroad as minister to France, he often indulged his love of classical things in his private life—he named one of farms near Monticello Pantops (that is, "All Seeing") and gave classical names to some of his slaves and horses. In 1784, when the organization of the new western territories was being discussed, Jefferson could not resist the temptation to propose the following names for western lands: Sylvania, Cherronesus, Metropotamia, and Polypotamia.

When his wife, Martha, died in 1782, he chose for her monument a quotation in Greek—two lines from Achilles' lament for his dead friend Patroclus in the *Iliad:* "Even if in Hades the dead forget the dead, yet even there should I remember my dead comrade." Some thought this an ostentatious display of learning, but it was actually a delicate personal statement that allowed Jefferson to hide his feelings, since few people would have been familiar with the lines in Greek. Contemplating his own death, he left a memorandum for his own tombstone inscription on the back of an old letter. This musing contained the following skeptical comment: "Could the dead feel any interest in Monuments or other remembrances of them, when, as Anacreon says [he quotes two lines in Greek that translate 'we lie a bit of dust after our bones have been loosed']."

Jefferson also called upon his knowledge of the classical heritage for the symbolism of the infant nation. For example, in 1774 he suggested for the emblem of the United States a theme from one of Aesop's fables: a father presenting a bundle of rods to his sons, with the motto *Insuperabiles si Inseparabiles* (Invincible if Inseparable). It took several years and three committees of Congress before the great seal of the United States was authorized in 1782. Essentially the creation of Charles Thomson, secretary of Congress, whom Ashbel Green, president of Princeton, eulogized as "one of the best classical scholars our country has ever produced," the seal was designed in a manner that Jefferson approved. It is best seen today on the American one-dollar bill, with its Roman-style eagle and three Virgilian tags, *annuit coeptis, novus ordo seclorum, e pluribus unum.*

At this time, Jefferson, who was a large slaveholder, felt the need to explain himself regarding the institution of slavery. A few years after the flaming words of the Declaration of Independence—self-evident truths, the laws of nature, inalienable rights, the equality of all men—he confronted the problem of slavery in his *Notes on the State of Virginia.* It was not the institution of chattel slavery itself that concerned him, but the racial characteristics of blacks. From his own experience and the evidence of ancient slavery, he concluded that blacks were innately inferior to whites, not as the result of restrictive conditions but because of genetic determinism. He supported this conclusion by analogy from the history and institutions of his beloved Romans, whose slaves, however, were white. Though conditions were more deplorable for the slaves of Rome than for the black slaves in America, many Roman slaves and freedmen achieved eminence in literature, philosophy, and the arts. Blacks, in Jefferson's personal experience, were incapable of competence in the intellectual fields in which he excelled—mathematics, science, and literature. Hence, the distinction between whites and blacks was the product of nature, not environment. He considered intermarriage objectionable, and if slaves became free he thought it best to expatriate them from the United States.

It is surprising that Jefferson did not cite Aristotle's dictum in the *Politics* that slaves are by nature inferior to free men, a doctrine that had enormous influence in Virginia in the early nineteenth century. Jefferson's views on slavery in the *Notes* were often cited by southerners in the decades before the Civil War. To the end of his life, Jefferson did not substantially deviate from these views about blacks. He knew that he had a "wolf by the ears," but he was always ambivalent about the matter, for he shared the interests and prejudices of the plantation owners. He held to his views despite troubling doubts, mounting antislavery sentiment in the country, his own growing skepticism about the adequacies of Greek and Roman culture, and the contrary views of such friends as Wythe, Fauquier, Benjamin Rush, and David Ramsay, distinguished South Carolinian patriot, scientist, and physician. Ramsay took issue directly with Jefferson's views in the *Notes,* writing to him on 3 May 1786, "I believe all mankind to be originally the same and only diversified by accidental circumstances. . . . The state of society has an influence not less than climate."

ON CLASSICAL GROUND: ROMAN REVIVAL ARCHITECTURE

In the years when he committed himself to "the boisterous ocean of political passion," he had little time for his beloved classics. But in 1785–1789, when he served as minister to France, he was finally enabled to fulfill a lifelong dream to visit "the classic ground" and to experience with his own eyes the visible remains of antiquity in their "purest form," rather than through books. In the eighteenth century the vogue of the Grand Tour was at its height, with its standard itinerary of visits to Rome, the classical sites near Naples, and, for the intrepid, the malaria-ridden Paestum (Italy) with its Greek temples. But despite Jefferson's yearnings he did not reach the promised lands. On 25 November 1785, writing to Thomas Elder, he advised that two young Virginians should study in Rome, where they would find "new delight from every page of the Latin poets and historians." But, as for himself, he wrote Wythe on 16 September 1787, "I scarcely got into classical ground," and to his friend Maria Cosway, "I took a peep only into Elysium." He was especially eager to see Rome and to experience its "classical enjoyments," but he could not spare the time. In all his years abroad he managed only a brief tour through southern France and northern Italy. On 12 December 1816, when he was in his seventies and his young friend George Ticknor was abroad as a student, Jefferson wrote to Ticknor's father, "I believe were I twenty years younger, instead of writing, I should meet [George Ticknor] there and take with him his classical voyage to Rome, Naples and Athens."

In March 1787 he settled for the Roman remains in southern France, where for him the most radiant moment was the sight of the small Roman temple at Nîmes, the so-called Maison Carrée (built in the time of Augustus), which he had seen and loved in the drawings by Andrea Palladio. For twenty years his knowledge and adaptations of Roman architecture to Monticello had come from his extensive library of architectural works, including drawings and engravings of classical buildings and Giacomo Leoni's 1742 London edition of Palladio's *Four Books of Architecture.* Palladio served, he said, as his architectural Bible. In 1787 he finally experienced an "original" work of classical art. In high excitement he wrote to his friend the Comtesse de Tessé from Nîmes in a celebrated letter of 20 March 1787:

Here I am, Madam, gazing whole hours at the Maison quarrée, like a lover at his mistress. . . . From Lyons to Nismes I have been nourished with the remains of Roman grandeur . . . [including] the Pont du Gard, a sublime antiquity, and [well] preserved. But most of all here . . . Roman taste, genius, and magnificence excite ideas. . . . I am immersed [in antiquities from morning to night]. For me the city of Rome is actually [existing in all the splendor of its] empire.

He was ecstatic, for he had seen his beloved Maison Carrée with his own eyes, and he called it "the most perfect remains of antiquity which exist on earth," writing from Paris to Thomas Shippen in September 1788.

For Jefferson the premier art was architecture, because it was visible to the public and functional rather than merely ornamental. Whereas his reading and pleasure in works of literature remained a private luxury, in architecture his aim was to lift the national taste, to help transcend provincialism by introducing into American buildings what he called "a chaste style," characterized by simplicity and purity, a universal style that "had the seal of ages behind it," but that was in reality an eclectic classicism. By going to the source for authoritative precedents, he desired to make "architectural quotations," derived directly from ancient buildings, with

Roman structures serving as the supreme models. To Jefferson the art of building had reached its ultimate forms in the buildings of the end of the Roman Republic and the early Roman Empire. In transplanting the models of the Old World, Jefferson conceived the revolutionary idea of using the ancient Roman temple form (despite its pagan associations) as a model for American secular buildings. Thus Jefferson combined Roman classicism, French neoclassicism, and American functional utility to launch the classical revival in American architecture.

In Paris, in September 1785, he commissioned a classical architectural plan and a small-scale model for the new capitol of the state of Virginia, to be erected in Richmond. It was to be based on the Maison Carrée, a building he knew at that time only from books. He wrote to James Madison: "It has obtained the approbation of fifteen or sixteen centuries, and is therefore preferable to any design which might be newly contrived. . . . It will be superior in beauty to any thing in America, and not inferior to any thing in the world. It is very simple." Soon after, he wrote to Madison about the Maison Carrée:

[It is] one of the most beautiful, if not the most beautiful and precious morsel of architecture left us by antiquity. . . . It is very simple, but it is noble beyond expression, and would have done honour to our country as presenting to travellers a morsel of taste in our infancy promising much for our maturer age. . . . But how is a taste in this beautiful art to be formed in our countrymen, unless we avail ourselves of every occasion when public buildings are to be erected of presenting to them models for their study and imitation? . . . You see I am an enthusiast on the subject of the arts. But it is an enthusiasm of which I am not ashamed, as it's object is to improve the taste of my countrymen, to increase their reputation.

Despite opposition in Richmond, he fought for the plan and won. Thus there arose on

American soil the earliest instance of the classical revival in a monumental building, a proclamation of America's coming of age by joining the mainstream of world culture in architecture.

In 1791, after returning from France to become secretary of state, he advised the first architect involved in planning the new city of Washington, Major Pierre Charles L'Enfant. He wrote to L'Enfant, "Whenever it is proposed to prepare plans for the Capitol, I should prefer the adoption of some one of the models of antiquity which have had the approbation of thousands of years." When Jefferson was president he corresponded with the architect Benjamin Latrobe, who sought to tilt plans toward Greek models and also warned against slavish imitation of ancient models as inappropriate to the functional purposes of American public buildings. But Jefferson insisted that the Capitol follow Roman models, and predicted in a letter of 10 October 1809 that "when finished [it] will be a durable and honorable monument of our infant republic, and will bear favorable comparison with the remains of the same kind of the antient republics of Greece & Rome." And on 12 July 1812 Jefferson exulted to Latrobe that the new Capitol, with its combination style of a Roman temple with a Pantheon-like dome, was "the first temple dedicated to the sovereignty of the people, embellishing with Athenian taste the course of a nation looking far beyond the range of Athenian destinies." It was a gallant tribute to Latrobe's contributions to the embellishments of the Capitol, which followed his taste for Greek architecture.

In rejecting "the range of Athenian destinies" Jefferson was enlisting Roman grandeur in his effort to overlay the rawness of America with universal patterns of acknowledged beauty in public buildings. But, as early as 1810, neoclassical Roman revival architecture was already being assailed as unsuitable for America; it was considered too lavish, ornamental, and ponderous in its magnificence. Artistic manifestos were issued calling for replacement of the Roman Pantheon with the Greek Parthenon, and this view prevailed, for the demand was for greater simplicity and economy. It was in part Latrobe who launched the Hellenic revival architecture in America to counter Jefferson's Romanism. Soon the "Greek temple style" was born, and it swiftly replaced Jefferson's Roman grandeur, becoming the first truly national style of architecture.

This did not deter Jefferson from his Roman-style plans for the new University of Virginia, the construction of which he personally supervised. In 1822, a visitor to Charlottesville saw the seventy-nine-year-old Jefferson at the building site take a chisel from the hand of an Italian stonecutter and show him how to model the volute of an Ionic capital.

RETIREMENT YEARS: RETURN TO THE CLASSICS

For decades, administrative and political obligations and architectural interests diverted Jefferson from regular communion with the classical authors. But he actively directed the classical education of his daughters, grandsons, and granddaughters. To Jefferson, however, the study of the classical languages was a male preserve, inappropriate for women. Most men of the time considered any involvement of women with classical learning to be useless, if not sheer pedantry. In 1804 Gertrude Meredith wrote in her *Port Folio* that men would "titter . . . at her expense, if a woman made a Latin quotation, or spoke with enthusiasm of classical learning." Yet there were women in the early national period who acquired a high competence in Latin and Greek and received a "masculine education" largely through tutors—for example, Lucinda Foote, Theodosia Burr (Aaron Burr's brilliant daughter), Judith Sargent Stevens Murray, and Margaret Fuller.

Unlike his friend Benjamin Rush, Jefferson was not interested in the education of women as a matter of public policy. In his active direction of the education of the girls of his family, he provided for a liberal education, but without the classical languages. He required that they read the classical authors in translation, together with works in ancient history, especially Livy, Thucydides, Tacitus, Plutarch, Gibbon's *Decline and Fall of the Roman Empire,* Middleton's *Life of Cicero,* and the Abbé Barthélemy's *Life of Anacharsis.* Fifteen-year-old Martha Jefferson, in school in Paris, tried to live up to her father's expectations:

> *Titus Livius* [in Italian translation] puts me out of my wits. I can not read a word by myself, and I read of it very seldom with my master; however, I hope I shall soon be able to take it up again. . . . I go on pretty well with my Thucydides, and hope I shall very soon finish it. . . . As for *Tite Live* I have begun it three or four times, and go on so slowly with it that I believe I shall never finish it. (From letters of 25 March and 27 May 1787.)

Under his guidance, his granddaughter Ellen Wayles Randolph was reading Goldsmith's *Ancient History,* Plutarch's *Lives* in French, Diodorus Siculus in English, and Pope's *Iliad* of Homer when she was twelve years old.

Thus, directing the education of the women in his family was Jefferson's contribution to overcoming what Rush called "the present immense disparity" in the education of the sexes in America. This he would have agreed with, but not with Rush's proposal that by discontinuing the study of Greek and Latin for American men, equality in the education of men and women would be achieved.

As for his own study of the classics, it was not until his retirement to Monticello after his presidency that Jefferson could return to it with complete absorption and enthusiasm. In search of tranquillity, he turned from practical politics, and even newspapers, to "Tacitus and Horace, and so much other agreeable reading," including Thucydides, Newton, and Euclid, striving "to beguile the wearisomness of declining life . . . by the delights of classical learning and of mathematical truths." As time went on he felt more and more content with his pursuit of classical learning. He wrote to Nathaniel Macon on 12 January 1819:

> I feel a much greater interest in knowing what has passed two or three thousand years ago, than in what is now passing. I read nothing, therefore, but of the heroes of Troy, of the wars of Lacedaemon and Athens, of Pompey and Caesar, and of Augustus too, the Bonaparte and parricide of that day. . . . I slumber without fear, and review in my dreams the visions of antiquity.

One of his granddaughters recalled that "he derived more pleasure from his acquaintance with Greek and Latin than from any other resource of literature. . . . I saw him more frequently with a volume of the classics in his hand than with any other book."

Except for architecture and his plans for education in Virginia, Jefferson's lifelong communion with the classics was a private pursuit, a separate sphere of his inner life. He would, acknowledging its privacy, call it "an innocent pleasure" that gave him great personal delight. This preoccupation of his was not at variance with the Enlightenment conception of the utility of knowledge, for the classics enlarged his own understanding of moral philosophy, politics, and history— at the same time, he drew from the ancient authors understanding and the humanistic heritage of the centuries. He would sometimes share thoughts on and enthusiasm for the classics with friends and acquaintances in conversations and letters. His state papers, on the other hand, are almost devoid of classical allusions and quotations, which in this sphere he would have condemned as pedantry. He would surely have approved of the advice given by William Wirt, on 29 August 1815, to his nephew the very scholarly young Francis Walker Gilmer, a protégé of Jefferson, when Gilmer was about to begin law practice in Virginia: "Keep your Latin and Greek, and science [that is, knowledge] to yourself, and to that very small circle which they may suit. The mean and envious world will never forgive you your knowledge, if you make it too public."

In his own enthusiasm for the classics, Jefferson found in John Adams a kindred spirit and enthusiastic correspondent. After a long estrangement, their mutual friend Benjamin Rush succeeded in reconciling them, and the two former presidents began a famous exchange of letters between Monticello and Quincy that lasted without interruption from 1812 to 1826, a correspondence that Ezra Pound once called "a landmark of American culture . . . a shrine and a monument." Jefferson was delighted. "But why," he wrote to Adams on 5 July 1814, "am I dosing you with these Antediluvian topics? Because I am glad to have some one to whom they are familiar, and who will not recieve them as if dropped from the moon."

This exchange took place at a time when classical learning was in great disfavor in America, and vigorous assaults (especially by Rush himself) were being made on all fronts to remove the classics from American education entirely. Equipped with superb minds and libraries, the two scholar-statesmen shared the fruits of their wide reading of the classics, with frequent quotations in Greek and Latin. Most often it was Jefferson who took the lead in initiating a discussion on some particular classical topic that interested him. The range of interests and the intellectual sophistication of this correspondence has never been equaled by American

political leaders, particularly regarding a knowledge of antiquity and classical literature.

"I cannot live without books," wrote Jefferson in 1815 to a like-minded Adams. Ever since his William and Mary days, books were a "necessity of life" for Jefferson. From the 1760s to his very last days, he was a tireless book collector, assembling three libraries of his own over a period of sixty-five years. Though his interests were encyclopedic, in belles lettres and history his books were predominantly Latin and Greek texts and modern works in the field of ancient history. Jefferson sold his second library, an epitome of eighteenth-century Enlightenment thought, to the Library of Congress to replace the books burned in the British capture of Washington in 1812. Out of this huge collection he kept 152 titles for himself, mostly classical authors and mathematical works. No sooner did this library leave his hands than he began to collect a third one, "for amusement, not use," he said. His new purchases, together with the library of Wythe, which he inherited, made a total of several thousand volumes at the time of his death. Unfortunately, these had to be sold at auction to pay Jefferson's debts. In the last years of his life, Jefferson also organized the library of the University of Virginia, and of the purchases about 25 percent of the books were in the classics.

Jefferson's knowledge of books was so sophisticated, even from his youth, that he was often called upon to recommend book collections for others. On 5 February 1769 he wrote Thomas Turpin: "The only help a youth wants is to be directed what books to read, and in what order to read them. . . . One difficulty only occurs, that is, the want of books." In 1771, Robert Skipwith, who was married to Jefferson's wife's half-sister, asked Jefferson to recommend a list of books for a library suited to "a common reader who understands but little of the classicks and has not leisure for any intricate or tedious study." Jefferson sent him a list of 140 titles, of which only sixteen had any connection with the classics—they were translations of classical authors and works on ancient history. Jefferson even included some works of fiction, fully aware of the predictable reaction of traditional classicists. He wrote on 3 August 1771: "But wherein is it's utility, asks the reverend sage, big with the notion that nothing can be useful but the learned lumber of Greek and Roman reading with which his head is stored? I answer, every thing is useful which contributes to fix us in the principles and practice of virtue."

When he was abroad, he extended himself to buy books for friends. Later, when it was his good fortune to have Ticknor as his book purchaser abroad, Jefferson put great stock in German editions of classical authors because he valued their superior scholarship. He preferred editions with both translations and notes. An insight into the character of his own scholarship is revealed in a letter he wrote to Ticknor regarding editions of the classics: "I value explanatory notes, but verbal criticism and various readings, not much. I am attracted to Scholia of the Greek classics because they give us the language of another age; and with the Greek classics prefer translations as convenient aids to the understanding of the author." Francis Gray, who visited Monticello in 1814, noticed that Jefferson's texts of Greek and Latin authors were interlined with English translations.

But, in fact, Jefferson took special pleasure in reading the classics in Greek and Latin rather than in translation. On 27 January 1800 he wrote to Priestley that "to read the Latin and Greek authors in the original, is a sublime luxury. . . . I enjoy Homer in his own language infinitely beyond Pope's translation of him." When, in 1785, he outlined a course of reading in ancient history as an extracurricular subject for his nephew Peter Carr, he advised reading the Greek and Roman historians "in the original and not in translations." For the study of ancient

history at the University of Virginia, he recommended reading in the "original authors." He had come to recognize that reading the ancient historians in translation might be necessary, but he objected to the use of modern surveys of ancient history.

This is not to say that Jefferson ever harbored a pedantic interest with respect to the study of the classical languages and Greek and Roman authors. For him the study of the classics was a practical preparation for life, and to this end the languages were to be acquired as tools for the attainment of knowledge and not as ends in themselves. He sought to explain his enjoyment of the classics, on 16 August 1813, to John Waldo, who had sent him a copy of his new English grammar. His interests, Jefferson explained, have been "devoted to more attractive studies, that of grammar having never been a favorite with me." To Thomas Cooper he wrote, on 7 October 1814, that he did not have "a hypercritical knowledge of the Latin and Greek languages. I have believed it sufficient to possess a substantial understanding of their authors."

FAVORITE CLASSICS

Though Jefferson's libraries contained an imposing array of the whole range of classical authors, his favorites among them were relatively few. Like most Americans of the time, Jefferson read classical poetry not as an aesthetic experience but for moral and political edification. In time, whatever inclination he may have had in his youth for the appreciation of poetry was dissipated by the pressures of a long political life. Early in his presidency, on 21 June 1801, he sadly explained to John D. Burke: "In earlier life I was fond of [poetry], and easily pleased. . . . So much has my relish for poetry deserted me that at present I cannot read even Virgil with pleasure." But Homer abided. About 1789, when he was secretary of state, he wrote in a letter to the Marquis de Chastellux that when one is young, any bit of poetry can please, "but as we advance in life these things fall off one by one, and I suspect we are left at last with only Homer and Virgil, perhaps with Homer alone." He so admired Homer's perfection as a poet that he wrote that even if a passage from Homer should be printed in the manner of prose, "it would still immortalize its author were every other syllable of his compositions lost." He once boasted, with mock national pride, that Americans "are the only farmers who can read Homer." He was thinking not of peasant yeomen but of planters like himself.

With respect to the Greeks, he had a particular penchant for the great Athenian tragedians throughout his life, even though he warned his grandson Francis Wayles Eppes on 21 September 1820 that Aeschylus is "incomprehensible in his flights among the clouds. His text has come to us so mutilated and defective and has been so much plaistered with amendments by his commentators that it can scarcely be called his." Though he had texts of many other Greek authors, Jefferson paid little attention to the didactic poet Hesiod, the Greek lyric poets such as Sappho, Alcaeus, and Pindar, the orator Isocrates (who was carefully studied in American colleges as a model of pure style), the historians Herodotus and Thucydides, the favorite classical author par excellence in the eighteenth and early nineteenth centuries, Plutarch (who was extolled by Cotton Mather as the "incomparable Plutarch" and by Emerson as "the elixir of Greece and Rome").

But Jefferson did not neglect Plato. In 1787, Adams had plundered Book VIII of Plato's *Republic,* approvingly excerpting extensive passages to document his *Defence of the Constitutions of Government of the United States of America.* As for Jefferson, Plato was the classical author he disliked most of all, and, in their correspondence in 1814,

Adams vigorously concurred with Jefferson's contempt for him. Jefferson's antipathy to Plato flowed from his own empiricism, his aversion to metaphysics, abstract theories, closed systems, and utopianism, and his rejection of any form of determinism in history, human behavior, or education, all unacceptable to the ethos of America. In 1814 he began to read the *Republic* methodically for the first time in his life. His aim was not political enlightenment but guidance in planning the projected University of Virginia. It was a time in American culture when classical models in general, especially classical political theory, were being jettisoned, and in this widespread retreat from the disenchantment with antiquity, classical analogies, parallels, and precedents were being abandoned. When Jefferson began to study the *Republic,* he and Adams had both experienced the practical rigors of the presidency and were fully aware of the extraordinary innovations begotten by the dynamism of American society. They and many other Americans had, in effect, repudiated Lord Bolingbroke's famous dictum "History is philosophy teaching by examples." Jefferson and Adams had already turned from "the lamp of experience," derived from ancient models, to practical experience, American pluralism, and freedom of individual conscience.

Jefferson wrote to Adams on 5 July 1814 that reading Plato was "the heaviest taskwork I ever went through. I had occasionally before taken up some of his other works, but scarcely ever had the patience to go through a whole dialogue." The *Republic,* Jefferson fumed, was full of "whimsies," "puerilities," and "unintelligible jargon." And he concluded, "I laid it down often to ask myself how it could have been that the world should have so long consented to give reputation to such nonsense as this?" He ridiculed Plato's "sophisms, futilities and incomprehensibilities," the "foggy mind" of a "genuine Sophist," and concluded that "his dialogues are libels on Socrates." He revived his tirades against Plato in letters to William Short, as he did on 4 August 1820, writing:

> When, therefore, Plato puts into [Socrates'] mouth such paralogisms, such quibbles on words, and sophisms as a schoolboy would be ashamed of, we conclude they were the whimsies of Plato's own foggy brain. . . . Speaking of Plato, I will add that no writer, ancient or modern, has bewildered the world with more *ignis fatui,* than this renowned philosopher, in Ethics, in Politics, and Physics. . . . But Plato . . . is . . . all but adopted as a Christian saint. It is surely time for men to think for themselves, and to throw off the authority of names so artificially magnified.

Yet in 1813–1814, before the exchanges between Jefferson and Adams on the *Republic,* they had already convinced themselves that Plato's views were quite unoriginal, having been derived from the works of two minor Greek authors, Ocellus of Lucania and Timaeus of Locri. Learned contemporaries knew nothing of these philosophical writers and their short works "On the Nature of the Universe" and "On the Nature of the Universe and the Soul," both of which have survived. They contain resemblances to some of Plato's thought, and Jefferson and Adams were misled in assuming that they were authoritative Pythagorean predecessors of Plato. In fact both were post-Platonic pseudonymous tracts by unoriginal philosophical dilettantes who sought to authenticate the Pythagorean priority of Plato's doctrines.

But Jefferson's greatest favorites were the Latin authors—Virgil and Horace among the poets, and Sallust, Livy, and Tacitus among the historians. Jefferson gave little attention to Cicero, none to the Roman dramatists Plautus, Terence, and Seneca, none to the lyric poets Catullus, Propertius, and Tibullus, and none to Lucan, Lucretius, or even the enormously popular Ovid.

Besides Homer and Virgil, the Roman historians were to Jefferson the most attractive group among the classical authors. In 1788 he wrote excitedly to Madison about a rumor that a complete translation of Livy in Arabic had been discovered. On 15 January 1825, when he was eighty-one years old, he wrote to Joseph Coolidge, Jr., that he had received a communication from the American Consul at Leghorn:

> I have been informed that there has been lately discovered at Athens, in a subterranean vault, a collection of 2,000 volumes or rolls of papyrus of Grecian authors, in a great state of perfection, with several statues of the highest order of sculpture. If true, we may recover what has been lost of Diodorus Siculus, Polybius, and Dion Cassius. I would rather, however, it should have been of Livy, Tacitus and Cicero.

On 8 December 1808 he wrote to his granddaughter Anne Cary Bankhead about his favorite ancient historian: "Tacitus I consider as the first writer in the world without a single exception. His book is a compound of history and morality of which we have no other example."

Jefferson's interest in ancient history was not academic but pragmatic, a corrective for blind optimism concerning innovations based solely on reason. It provided what Patrick Henry called "the lamp of experience." One of his granddaughters wrote, "Of history he was very fond, and this he studied in all languages, though always, I think, preferring the ancients."

In Jefferson's lifetime the ancient historians provided political and moral enlightenment, long serving as "a school of private and public virtue," in Lord Bolingbroke's words. The study of history was not an autonomous discipline in the curriculum of American colleges. Ancient history was acquired not by reading modern textbooks but through study of the ancient historians. Jefferson wrote to Thomas Mann Randolph, Jr., on 27 August 1786: "It would be a waste of time to attend a professor of [history]. It is to be acquired from books. . . . The histories of Greece and Rome are worthy a good degree of attention; they should be read in the original authors." Not that the ancient historians were to be read naively without a critical attitude. Thus he wrote to Peter Carr on 10 August 1787 and to William Short on 4 August 1820 that Livy, his beloved Tacitus, and Diodorus Siculus should be read critically, rejecting matter not in accordance with "the ordinary course of nature" as "fables not belonging to history," and he expressed impatience with "a multitude of false subtleties and refinements" in the study of history or literature." Clearly, in this critical approach to the ancient historians Jefferson sought to shift the study of history from the area of belles lettres closer to the field of the social sciences.

Throughout his life, the value of the study of ancient history was taken for granted. In his *Notes on the State of Virginia* he wrote: "History by apprising [students] of the past will enable them to judge of the future; it will avail them of the experience of other times and other nations; it will qualify them as judges of the actions and designs of men." Enlightenment thought provided Jefferson and many of the Revolutionary generation with a uniformitarian view of history and human nature. Hence, the ancient world offered models of republican states and pluralistic societies, vibrant cultures before the domination of feudal and ecclesiastical institutions, as guidance for the statesmen of Jefferson's time. Though an eager student of ancient history, Jefferson was profoundly future-minded. Hence his ambivalence about the past: the lessons of antiquity were useful not as an antiquarian study but for their relevance to problems of the present and future. The ancient world had been idealized by the Founding Fathers, plundered by them selectively and purpose-

fully for lessons and legitimation, as universal authoritative standards by which to judge their unprecedented innovations in government and society. Yet Jefferson wrote to Priestley on 27 January 1800 that "to look backwards instead of forwards for the improvement of the human mind, and to recur to the annals of our ancestors for what is most perfect in government, in religion and in learning, is worthy of those bigots in religion and government. . . . But it is not an idea which this country will endure."

Yet, like many of the Founding Fathers, Jefferson was trained as a lawyer and was thus prone to value precedents. Hence his frequent reaching back to antiquity for republican models as precedents. For example, General Arnold's march to Quebec reminded him of Xenophon's march in the *Anabasis;* King George, of the King of Persia; Aaron Burr, of Catiline; Washington, of Cincinnatus; Wythe, of Cato; Franklin, of Solon; England, of a modern Athens or Carthage. This eighteenth-century search for parallels from antiquity was, however, in conflict with his own deeply held belief in the individuality of specific events. He could write ahistorically about contemporary political parties, as he did to Adams on 27 June 1813: "The same political parties which now agitate the United States, have existed through all time. Whether the power of the people or that of the *aristoi* should prevail, were questions which kept the States of Greece and Rome in eternal convulsions." Similarly, regarding problems with England, he wrote to Francis C. Gray on 4 March 1815: "But if they go on checking, irritating, injuring and hostilizing us, they will force on us the motto *'Carthago delenda est'* [Carthage must be destroyed]. And some Scipio Americanus will leave to posterity the problem of conjecturing where stood once the ancient and splendid city London." About the "Missouri Compromise" on slavery he wrote to Adams on 22 January 1821: "Are we then to see again Athenian and Lacedemonian confederacies? To wage another Peloponnesian war?''

In retirement he read extensively in Tacitus, Sallust, Livy, and Thucydides, reviewing, as he said, "in my dreams the visions of antiquity." Although in his youth, and in the ardor of the Revolutionary period, he had admired the ancient republics, in time he became more and more aware of their serious defects and believed that they were in the graveyard of history. The experience of practical politics in the turbulent evolution of the new nation, and a better understanding of the American character shook Jefferson's faith in the ancient republics as rational models for the United States.

Despite his lifelong love affair with classical learning, Jefferson was often critical of darker aspects of those "civilized and learned nations," as he called the Greeks and Romans. He deplored the frequency of wars in antiquity, the pagan religious practices, the everlasting convulsions and class antagonisms in the small Greek cities, the limitations of ethical systems like Epicureanism and Stoicism (which were concerned only with the individual and not society as a whole), and the severity of the Roman *patria potestas* ("father's power") that gave legal sanction to infanticide and the sale of children into slavery. On the latter he wrote to John Wayles Eppes on 18 September 1813: "But we, this age, and in this country especially, are advanced beyond those notions of natural law. We acknowledge that our children are born free; and that freedom is the gift of nature." Interestingly, Jefferson did not criticize the generally low status of women in antiquity, the paucity of civil rights for aliens among the Greeks and Romans, or the bloody sports such as gladiatorial combats.

Jefferson's increasingly critical views of antiquity and loss of reverence for classical political theory and practice became more frequent after his presidency, leading to a profound revisionism in his thinking. For example, on 26 August 1816 he wrote to Isaac Tiffany:

> But so different was the style of society then, and with those people, from what it is now and with us, that I think little edification can be obtained from their writings on the subject of government. . . . The introduction of this new principle of representative democracy has rendered useless almost everything written before on the structure of government; and, in a great measure, relieves our regret, if the political writings of Aristotle, or of any other ancient, have been lost, or are unfaithfully rendered or explained to us.

Having already disposed of Plato, and now Aristotle, he next turned to Cicero and the Roman Republic. On 10 December 1819, he wrote Adams at length about his doubts:

> I have been amusing myself latterly with reading the voluminous letters of Cicero. They certainly breathe the purest effusions of an exalted patriot, while the parricide Caesar is lost in odious contrast. When the enthusiasm . . . subsides into cool reflection, I ask myself, what was that government which the virtues of Cicero were so zealous to restore, and the ambition of Caesar to subvert? . . . They never had [good government] from the rape of the Sabines to the ravages of the Caesars. . . . But steeped in corruption, vice and venality, as the whole nation was . . . what could even Cicero, Cato, Brutus have done, had it been referred to them to establish a good government for their country?

Jefferson's ambivalences regarding antiquity can be discerned in his hopes for and understanding of modern Greece. When he was in Paris in 1785 and learned of plans to liberate the Greeks from Turkish rule, his principal interest was in the revival of the ancient Greek language. To Ezra Stiles and John Page he wrote, "I am persuaded the modern Greek would easily get back to it's classical models. . . . We might still hope to see the language of Homer and Demosthenes flow with purity from the lips of a free and ingenious people." But about forty years later, when the Greeks had won their independence and the Greek scholar A. Koraïs sent him new editions of several classical Greek authors edited by him, Jefferson commended his efforts to elevate the Greeks culturally. "Nothing is more likely to forward [self-government] than a study of the fine models of science left by their ancestors, to whom *we* also are all indebted for the lights which originally led ourselves out of Gothic darkness." But he warned that the ancient forms of government were completely outmoded, cautioning:

> The circumstances of the world are too much changed for that. The government of Athens, for example, was that of the people of one city making laws for the whole country subjected to them. That of Lacedemon was the rule of military monks over the laboring classes of people, reduced to abject slavery. These are not the doctrines of the present age.

Jefferson then set forth a long summary of American government and the American educational system, adding:

> Should they furnish a single idea which may be useful to them, I shall fancy it a tribute rendered to the manes of your Homer, your Demosthenes, and the splendid constellation of sages and heroes, whose blood is still flowing in your veins, and whose merits are still resting, as a heavy debt, on the shoulders of the living, and the future races of men. . . . We offer to heaven the warmest supplication for the restoration of your countrymen to the freedom and science of their ancestors.

That same year Gilmer sent from Richmond one of the first copies to arrive in America of the newly discovered *Republic* of Cicero, with the words, "to so distinguished a champion of freedom in the New World, this brilliant exposition of the principles of popular Liberty, by the greatest statesman of antiquity." Jefferson graciously acknowledged the gift but took no further notice of Cicero's famed *Republic.*

Surely he was weary, but he had come to learn that, with all his love of the classics, retrospection into the ancient world was a brake on change for the new nation, which was dynamically and turbulently racing into the future. He had already confessed to Adams on 1 August 1816 that "I like the dreams of the future better than the history of the past." Jefferson in his old age might have agreed with the perceptive words of the Marquis de Chastellux in 1782:

> It has seemed to me that America abounds in *demi-philosophes* of two different sorts: the older men, in matters political, look only to the Greeks and the Romans, and the young men are satisfied with ready-made opinions they have found in Locke and Montesquieu. Now I believe that reading of the ancients and the moderns is no more capable of suggesting the plan of a good government than Horace's Art of Poetry is of bringing forth a good poem.

Jefferson's advocacy of the classics, guarded as it was, was not shared by many Americans in decision-making positions. In the first four decades of the national period, a massive and spirited campaign raged to eliminate the classics from American education and intellectual life; they were considered elitist, ornamental, impractical, and even detrimental to republicanism. Some of the Revolutionary generation, such as Franklin and Rush, joined the fray as public opponents of classical learning. In 1803, Samuel Miller regretted that the classics had "come to be regarded by a large part of the literary world, as among the most useless objects of pursuit."

Jefferson, on the other hand, characteristically defended the classics in private, not speaking publicly about an issue that brought forth combatants on both sides. In a memorable letter to John Brazier on 24

August 1819, he responded to what he called "this litigated question." He presented nine reasons for considering classical learning valuable: the classics provide models of pure taste in writing; reading of Greek and Roman authors in the original gives pleasure; they are a solace for old age; the classics contain a treasure house of knowledge in many fields; they are valuable for moral edification; Greek is essential for ministers' understanding of the New Testament; lawyers find a system of rational civil law in the ancient sources; statesmen find much political wisdom in the classics; and the sciences are indebted to the classical languages for technical terminology. Jefferson conceded, however, that the classics were not suitable for all. For merchants, farmers, and mechanics the classical languages were not necessary. It is true, he concluded, that there have been many eminent men without classical education. "But," he mused, "who can say what these men would not have been, had they started in the science on the shoulders of a Demosthenes or a Cicero, of a Locke or a Newton?" In conclusion he wrote, "To sum the whole, . . . it may truly be said that the classical languages are a solid basis for most, and an ornament to all the sciences."

For models of prose style and oratory, Jefferson knew no greater works than the classics. On 27 January 1800 he wrote to Priestley, "I know of no composition of any other ancient people, which merits the least regard as a model for its matter or style." The finest models for what Jefferson considered the best style—pithy language with no unnecessary words—were Sallust and Tacitus, "which on that account are worthy of constant study."

He considered oratory of prime importance in a republic, and the finest models were found among the Greeks and Romans. As a young lawyer, he recommended careful study of the speeches of Demosthenes and Cicero. Later, for models of Congressional oratory he recommended to John Wayles Eppes the speeches to be found in the Roman historians Livy, Tacitus, and Sallust —"and most assuredly not in Cicero. I doubt if there is a man in the world who can now read one of his orations through but as a piece of task-work." It was the brevity and compact style in the historians that he admired, though he still thought highly of Demosthenes for senatorial eloquence and Cicero for the law courts. To David Harding, president of the Jefferson Debating Society of Hingham, Massachusetts, he wrote on 20 April 1824:

In this line antiquity has left us the finest models for imitation; and he who studies and imitates them most nearly, will nearest approach the perfection of the art. Among these I should consider the speeches of Livy, Sallust and Tacitus, as pre-eminent specimens of logic, taste, and that sententious brevity which, using not a word to spare, leaves not a moment for inattention to the hearer. Amplification is the vice of modern oratory.

An important end achieved through reading of the classics was knowledge of the principles of morality. A disciple of the Enlightenment, Jefferson rejected a moral code based on faith and revelation, and sought a secular alternative arrived at through reason. He sought to reconcile the pursuit of personal happiness with the greater good of society. In general, he thought the ancient philosophers "really great" in moral philosophy because they sought to inculcate peace of mind. For long his solution was an eclectic blend of the teachings of Epicurus and the principles of Stoic philosophy.

It was Epicurus' teaching, which he learned not directly from the remains of Epicurus' works but from the *Syntagma* of Pierre Gassendi, that attracted him most. The genuine doctrines of Epicurus had stressed the quest for quietism and individual peace of mind through rational and scientific understanding of the cosmos and moderate living with friends in a rural setting, without commitment to marriage, family, state, religion, or belief in an afterlife. On 31 October 1819 he declared to William Short his admiration for "our master Epicurus. I too am an Epicurian. I consider the genuine (not the imputed) doctrines of Epicurus as containing every thing rational in moral philosophy which Greece and Rome have left us." On 27 June 1813 he had written to Adams, "The *summum bonum* with me is now truly epicurian, ease of body and tranquillity of mind; and to these I wish to consign my remaining days." On 9 January 1816 he wrote to Charles Thomson concerning "the doctrines of Epicurus, which, notwithstanding the calumnies of the Stoics and the caricatures of Cicero, is the most rational system of the philosophy of the ancients." Jefferson sent to Short with the letter above a syllabus of the physical and moral doctrines of Epicurus, which he had prepared about twenty years before.

Like many other Americans, Jefferson was also strongly attracted to "the sound and practical morality" of the Stoic writers because of their excellent and sententiously given moral rules, their fostering of virtue, civic duty, and natural law, their opposition to tyranny, and their doctrine of "the brotherhood of man." Like Epicureanism, Stoicism was a guide to individual peace of mind.

Jefferson, however, in his retirement became critical of the narrowness of ancient moral philosophy that appealed only to individual happiness without concern for social needs and the gentler virtues. To Short he wrote on 31 October 1819, "I have sometimes thought of translating [the Stoic philosopher] Epictetus . . . by adding the genuine doctrines of Epicurus . . . and an abstract from the Evangelists of whatever has the stamp of the eloquence and fine imagination of Jesus." With regard to the ancient philosophers, he said, "I give them their just

due, and yet maintaining that the morality of Jesus, as taught by himself, and freed from the corruption of later times, was far superior." And again to Short he wrote, "Epictetus and Epicurus give laws for governing ourselves, Jesus a supplement of the duties and charities we owe to others."

EDUCATION AND THE CLASSICS

In one area, Jefferson gave public expression to the importance of Latin and Greek: in American education. He considered foreign languages important and Greek and Latin indispensable. Moreover, he proposed higher standards of education than prevailed at the time. His Bill for the More General Diffusion of Knowledge, proposed in 1778 to the Virginia House of Burgesses, provided for the teaching of Latin and Greek in grammar schools. He considered children under fifteen or sixteen years old best suited for foreign language study. He deemed the classical languages excellent exercises in discipline and memory, as well as sources for models of moral wisdom and literary and oratorical style, and guides for future reading for the acquisition of knowledge. After six years in grammar school, ten youths would annually be awarded scholarships to William and Mary. The bill did not pass due to the unwillingness of the Virginians to support free higher education.

About forty years later, as "Father of the University of Virginia," Jefferson devised for the new university an innovative structure, combining traditional subjects with a variety of specialized schools and the radical innovation of the elective system. He took it for granted that the easier Latin and Greek authors would be mastered first in the district schools (or colleges). "This," he stated, "would be useful and sufficient for many not intended for a university education." Admission to the proposed School of Ancient Languages had a stringent requirement:

proficiency in reading the "higher" Latin and Greek classics. The principle of free electives in the curriculum was, however, surprisingly qualified before Jefferson's death by a decision of the board of visitors in October 1824 (Jefferson was its leading member). The "Minutes of the Board of Visitors of the University of Virginia" read:

But no diploma shall be given to any one who has not passed an examination in the Latin language as shall have proved him able to read the highest classics in that language with ease, thorough understanding and just quantity; and if he be also a proficient in the Greek, let that too be stated in his diploma. The intention being that the reputation of the University shall not be committed but to those who, to an eminence in one or more of the sciences taught in it, add a proficiency in those languages which constitute the basis of a good education, and are indispensable to fill up the character of a "well-educated man".

In the early national period, when the traditional role of the classics in education was being vigorously challenged, Jefferson was intent not only on holding the line at the University of Virginia—he also insisted on high standards. In 1827 German-trained George Bancroft, with a Ph.D. from the University of Göttingen, acknowledged the great opposition to the classics in America, and asked "whether it is worth our while to study Greek in this country." And in 1828, the scholarly South Carolinian Hugh Swinton Legaré spoke a valedictory to classical learning as it had flourished in America during the revolutionary age: "There is something melancholy in the reflection that the race of such men is passing away, and that our youth are now taught to form themselves on other models." Mounting pressure by advocates of "modern" subjects and practical and vocational programs erupted in a resolution placed before the Yale Corporation to omit the dead languages from Yale's entrance requirements. But a comprehensive investigation led to the definitive Yale Report of 1828, which affirmed for the next few generations the traditional classical curriculum as the best possible for liberal education in America.

Jefferson took pride in the facilities for a liberal education that existed in the United States. Whatever may be the case elsewhere, he wrote in *Notes on the State of Virginia*, our aspirations are different: "The learning of Greek and Latin, I am told, is going into disuse in Europe. I know not what their manners and occupations may call for, but it would be very ill-judged to follow their example." Even in 1785 he saw no need for American youths to go to Europe for education. On 15 October 1785 he wrote John Banister, Jr., that in America the subjects of a useful education start with classical knowledge. Yet, despite his own enthusiasm for Greek, of all desirable foreign languages taught in America "I think Greek the least useful," he wrote John Eppes in 1787.

However great his own enthusiasm for the Greek and Latin languages, Jefferson deplored their influence in imposing formalism in English, and he criticized what he called "scrupulous purism" of style and vocabulary, and "rigorisms of grammar." While setting high value on "the beautiful engraftments we have borrowed from Greece and Rome," he frowned upon "linguistic purists" and encouraged "a judicious neology," favoring copiousness and flexibility of language to keep pace with inevitable changes in circumstances and ideas. He sought analogy in Tacitus, citing to Edward Everett on 24 February 1823 the vigor of the Roman historian's style: "It is by boldly neglecting the rigorisms of grammar that Tacitus has made himself the strongest writer in the world." On 16 August 1813 he wrote to John Waldo praising the literary splendor of the Greeks because of their great variety in language and style that "made the Grecian Homer the first of poets, as he must remain, until a language equally ductile and copious shall again be spoken."

Though Jefferson disclaimed pedantry and hypercriticism, he nevertheless kept abreast of a number of scholarly problems in classical learning that had long interested him. This was especially the case with what he called "the long agitated question of what was the original pronunciation of the Greek and Latin languages." As a young student at William and Mary he had learned the Italianate pronunciation of Latin from the Italian teacher Mazzei, and to the last he remained convinced that "we must go to Italy . . . for the most probably correct pronunciation of the language of the Romans," and for that reason he spoke scornfully of "Connecticut Latin." It was his conviction for about fifty years, from "very early in my classical days," that the authentic sounds of the classical languages were preserved and handed down by tradition in Greece and Italy, rather than as pronounced in any other countries.

In 1818–1819, in the fervor of rising Philhellenism in America, Jefferson received two American studies on the pronunciation of classical Greek, by John Pickering and by Nathaniel F. Moore. He recalled that in Paris he had learned the modern Greek pronunciation from some learned Greeks and in general "trusted its orthodoxy." It is, therefore, a tribute to his objectivity that, at the age of seventy-six, after studying the treatises of Pickering and Moore, he confessed a more skeptical view of his pronunciation of the ancient Greek. He surmised that the more authentic "Erasmian" pronunciation could still be obtained in Italy, and he was now ready to concede that the matter could not be positively determined and that there was "little hope indeed of the recovery of the ancient pronunciation of that finest of human languages." Despite the uncertainties, he was glad, he wrote to Moore, "to see the question stirred here; because it may excite among our young countrymen a spirit of

inquiry and criticism, and lead them to more attention to this most beautiful of all languages." As for Latin, he remained committed to the Italianate pronunciation.

In the 1820s, Jefferson was not unaware of new trends in classical learning in America. A rebirth of interest in Greek and Hellenism and a desire for higher levels of critical scholarship were sparked by such young Harvard men as Everett, Ticknor, George Bancroft, and Joseph Green Cogswell. In letters to Everett, when Jefferson was already eighty, he pursued another of his long-held views on the Greek language: that, despite the denial of grammarians, Greek did have an ablative case (the form being the same as the dative case). Eventually, he bowed to the merit of Everett's scholarly explanations, conceding his limitations in this area of learning. "I acknowledge myself . . . not an adept in the metaphysical speculations of Grammar. By analyzing too minutely, we often reduce our subject to atoms of which the mind loses its hold."

Although he loved the classics, Jefferson deplored "too exclusive a prejudice in favor of the Greek and Latin languages" as absolute standards of perfection in language. This is especially evident in his justification of the introduction of Anglo-Saxon as a regular academic subject in the curriculum of the University of Virginia. To establish Anglo-Saxon on a sound basis he insisted that it be taught as a different type of language, not as a learned tongue, and not with the "structure of the Greek and Latin languages" and their "cumbrous scaffolding."

JEFFERSON THE HUMANIST

During the Revolutionary generation, the Golden Age of classical learning in America, before the emergence of professional American scholars, Jefferson was the most learned and dedicated classicist, with John Adams a close second. Living in the afterglow of the Renaissance and the radiance of the Enlightenment, he was America's greatest humanist. His reverence for antiquity was clearly tilted toward the Roman grandeur, talent for order, and creativity in literature and the arts; he came too late to be touched by German neohumanism and its Grecomania. From the vast treasures of antiquity he selected what suited him, transforming it purposefully with broad strokes to fashion his own image of the classical world. Judged by the standards of modern scholarship, Jefferson's classical knowledge thins out in a sort of reductive simplicity. With Enlightenment perspectives, he drew parallels from antiquity that were used as universal authoritative standards, as ideals for comparison and imitation, to impose a rational order upon the rawness of an infant society. In architecture, literature, and political theory, with a uniformitarian view of human nature and history, he forged a conception of the past in a contemporary context, with utility as the test of its value to the present. But he was also a future-minded pragmatist as well as a scholar and a dreamer. Eventually, this ambivalence manifested itself in a critical attitude to the limitations and deficiencies of the Greek and Roman world, although to the end of his life he remained a lover of "the classic pages" and a "zealous advocate of classical learning."

Yet, in the spate of eulogies spoken after his death in 1826, few remarked on Jefferson's classical learning. Even Everett, who two years before had been professor of Greek literature at Harvard and was celebrated as the most distinguished Hellenist in America at the time, could say of both Jefferson and Adams only that "they were both familiar with the ancient languages, and the literatures they contain." More knowledgeable was the testimonial of Daniel Webster, who, speaking at Faneuil Hall in Boston, said of Jefferson, "To the physical sciences, especially, and to ancient classical literature, he is understood to have had a warm attachment, and never entirely to have lost sight of this in the midst of the busiest occupation." Often, Webster added, classical learning was superficial and pretentious pedantry: "This has exposed learning, and especially classical learning, to reproach. Men have seen that it might exist without mental superiority, without vigor, without good taste, and without utility. . . . Those whose memories we now honor were learned men; but their learning was kept in its proper place, and made subservient to the uses and objects of life." A fellow Virginian, Attorney General William Wirt, speaking in the Capitol in Washington before the House of Representatives, caught the essence of Jefferson's classicism best: "He read with a sort of poetic illusion, . . . enraptured with the brighter ages of republican Greece and Rome."

Jefferson's Library

DOUGLAS L. WILSON

WHEN news reached Thomas Jefferson in September 1814 that the invading British army had burned the Capitol building in Washington and destroyed the congressional library, he made a momentous decision. He sat down and wrote a letter offering Congress his own collection of books and manuscripts as a replacement, making one condition—that his library must be accepted in its entirety. If Congress were agreeable to this, he would accept whatever compensation its members thought fit to provide. The former president could not have foreseen all the implications of this fateful decision, but he was certainly aware of some of them. He knew that the congressional collection was much smaller and more narrowly based than his own, for he had materially contributed to its development during his term as president. He knew, therefore, that acceptance of his library would constitute a considerable upgrading of the congressional collection. And he knew enough about congressmen to expect that eyebrows would be raised at any "unnecessary" expenditures, such as those for books

not dealing with law and government. Anticipating this objection, he wrote of his library to Samuel H. Smith on 21 September 1814: "I do not know that it contains any branch of science which Congress would wish to exclude from their collection; there is, in fact, no subject to which a member of Congress may not have occasion to refer." He must also have had some idea that the library would ultimately reach a larger public than members of Congress and the government. What he may not have foreseen, but what would have given him the greatest satisfaction, was that his collection would become the foundation of a great national library, and that its acquisition and special character would prove the inspiration for a Library of Congress that would embrace the whole expanse of human knowledge and be open and free to all.

Jefferson's letter to Smith, a Washington newspaper publisher and close friend who was to be his agent in the negotiations that followed, included for the inspection of the joint library committee a handwritten catalog of his library, which he had made in

1812. In this letter he characterized his collection, described the care with which it had been chosen, and made the case for its fitness as a replacement for the lost congressional library. He pointed first to its richness in "works relating to America," many of which he had acquired while living in Europe:

> In that department particularly, such a collection was made as probably can never again be effected, because it is hardly probable that the same opportunities, the same time, industry, perseverance and expense, with some knowledge of the bibliography of the subject would again happen to be in concurrence. During the same period, and after my return to America, I was led to procure, also, whatever related to the duties of those in the high concerns of the nation. So that the collection, which I suppose is of between nine and ten thousand volumes, while it includes what is chiefly valuable in science and literature generally, extends more particularly to whatever belongs to the American statesman.

The congressional committee professed great interest but wanted to know how much the books were worth. Jefferson was unwilling to put a value on them himself and asked a Georgetown bookseller, Joseph Milligan, who was familiar with his library, to make an exact count from the catalog and suggest an average price per volume. Milligan's count was 6,487 volumes, far short of Jefferson's estimate, and less even than an earlier estimate Jefferson had made of "seven or eight thousand volumes." He had expressed to Smith the hope that Congress would allow him "to retain a few of the books, to amuse the time I have yet to pass," which would revert to Congress on his death. "Those I should like to retain would be chiefly classical and mathematical. Some few in other branches, and particularly one of the five encyclopedias in the catalogue. But this, if not acceptable, would not be urged." Unfor-

tunately for Jefferson, the question was never put, and, as reported in William Dawson Johnston's *History of the Library of Congress,* Milligan's formula—"for a folio ten dollars, for a quarto six dollars, for an octavo three dollars, for a duodecimo one dollar"—when approved by Jefferson, was translated into a total price of $23,950 and promptly written into the committee's resolution.

With the price thus fixed for the Monticello library and with no express provision for his retaining any books for his personal use, Jefferson began to fear that the number of books listed in the catalog but missing from the library might be large and the books themselves difficult to replace. "The compensation embracing the whole of the catalogue, I shall not retain a single one," he wrote to Smith on 27 February 1815, "the only modification to be made being a deduction from the compensation in proportion to the size and number of the books which on review shall appear to have been lost." Upon the return of the catalog in March 1815, Jefferson made his own count, carefully comparing the catalog to the volumes on his shelves, and, according to Library of Congress Manuscript 37212, arrived at a grand total of 6,707. Greatly relieved to discover that the volumes not entered exceeded those that were missing, he duly included them in the catalog and the library, remarking pointedly to the secretary of the treasury, Alexander J. Dallas, when he applied for payment on 18 April 1815: "I have not thought it right to withdraw these from the library, so that the whole delivered exceeds on the principles of the estimate, the sum appropriated."

Meanwhile the congressional deliberations, once they reached the floor of the House of Representatives, were far from disinterested and had become blatantly partisan. The political opponents of Jefferson and his party made the most of the fact that the country was at war and in debt and that many of the books in Jefferson's library seemed outside the purview of a congressional library. The most outspoken Federalist opponent, Cyrus King, argued that Jefferson's books would help disseminate his "infidel philosophy" and were "good, bad, and indifferent, old, new, and worthless, in languages which many can not read, and most ought not." In the end, as detailed in Johnston's history, the purchase was agreed to by a narrow margin along party lines, but the spirit of the opposition is captured in the grudging comment of the *Boston Gazette:* "The grand library of Mr. Jefferson will undoubtedly be purchased with all its finery and philosophical nonsense."

When these matters were decided, Jefferson began calculating the volume and weight of the books and determining the best method of packing and shipping them to Washington. That he took the trouble to find out how many wagons would be needed, what it would cost to hire them, and what would be the best route for the wagon train to take was characteristic of the man and his meticulous concern for detail. After the catalog had been carefully revised, labels were pasted on the spine of each book, giving the number of the section or "chapter" to which it belonged and its shelf order within the chapter. Like most libraries of his day, Jefferson's was shelved by format or size, with the duodecimos and petit-format volumes occupying the upper shelves, octavos and quartos the middle and somewhat deeper shelves, and the folios ranked at the bottom. In shipping his books Jefferson first protected them with waste paper and then nailed boards across the front of the presses, so that they functioned as shipping crates in transit and permanent bookcases when set up in Blodget's Hotel, the temporary Capitol. By the middle of April ten wagons were loaded and on their way to Washington, carrying in them the foundation of an alto-

gether new and revolutionary Library of Congress.

THE BEGINNINGS OF THE LIBRARY

Peter Jefferson, the father of the future president, was without formal education but according to his son's autobiography "read much and improved himself." By the time Thomas was sent to school at the age of five, he was said to have read all the books in his father's modest library. At nine he was placed in the Latin school of the Reverend William Douglas, where he encountered a more substantial library and where he seems to have begun a collection of his own, for his father's account book, now at the Huntington Library, records the expenditure of a sizable sum, £1/10/6 for "Books for my Son." At the death of Peter Jefferson in 1757, the fourteen-year-old Thomas inherited some forty-odd volumes, which must be regarded as the core of his first collection. This was a conventional planter's library, consisting mainly of practical and nondescript items, but it also contained Paul de Rapin's *History of England,* George Anson's *Voyages,* and such literary favorites as the works of Joseph Addison and *The Spectator.*

In 1758 he was sent to a more accomplished schoolmaster, the Reverend James Maury, to acquire a classical education in accordance with the dying wishes of his father. There he met with a library of at least two or three hundred volumes, as well as a learned and discriminating advisor, whom he described in his autobiography as "a correct classical scholar." Maury's advice to his son, which appears in the first volume of Dumas Malone's *Jefferson and His Time,* may have been urged on his other pupils as well, for its message was very much taken to heart by the young Jefferson:

159

I would recommend it to you to reflect, and remark on, and digest what you read; to enter into the spirit and design of your author; to observe every step he takes to accomplish his end; and to dwell on any remarkable beauties of diction, justness or sublimity of sentiment, or masterly strokes of true wit which may occur in the course of your reading.

Jefferson was by every account an unusually apt and studious pupil, and it was probably during his two years at Maury's school that he began to keep a commonplace book of his reading, the better to fix in his mind the beauties and retain the masterly strokes. In his commonplace book he began first with the classical writers—Horace, Cicero, Ovid, and Virgil—and then went on to make extracts from the great English poets—Pope, Milton, and Shakespeare. As Malone reports, during these years he was a "hard student," and years later he was recalled as being habitually seen with a book in his hand —a Greek grammar.

When he entered the College of William and Mary in 1760, Jefferson at last had access to an institutional library and found himself for the first time within reach of a shop where he could buy books. He lived in Williamsburg on a regular basis for two years as a college student and intermittently for five years thereafter as a student of the law under the tutelage of George Wythe. A sample of his Williamsburg book purchases survives in the daybooks of the *Virginia Gazette*, the leading bookstore in the colony. From these we learn that during the years 1764 and 1765, he bought thirty-two titles, amounting to fifty-six volumes. Predictably, the largest category (nine books) is law. Next largest (five books) is history; "when young, I was passionately fond of reading books of history," Jefferson reported in a letter of 29 August 1787 to the editor of the *Journal de Paris*. The *Virginia Gazette* books included Enrico Caterino Davila's history of the civil war in France, David Hume's *History*

of England, William Robertson's *History of Scotland*, and William Stith's *History of the First Discovery and Settlement of Virginia*. Three works in Italian, plus an Italian-English dictionary, testify that he was teaching himself in 1764 to read that language, which, along with French and Spanish, was one of three modern languages he eventually mastered. The other notable category is poetry, including the works of Milton, Edward Young, and William Shenstone, all of which he read and extracted in his commonplace and memorandum books. Classical literature, agriculture, medicine, and religion were also represented by one or two titles, affirming the fact that the remarkable breadth of interests he exhibited in later life was an early phenomenon. In light of their subsequent importance in Jefferson's development, the presence of two volumes should be noted: an influential work on landscape gardening, which he referred to as *James on Gardening*, and a volume designated *Bacon's Philosophy*. Landscape gardening became one of his most absorbing artistic interests, an art that he never failed to study in his travels and that he was to practice at Monticello all his life. Bacon he came to regard, with Locke and Newton, as one of the three greatest men who ever lived.

Invaluable as the daybooks are, they reveal nothing of the books that Jefferson must have been acquiring from abroad. The books imported for resale by the *Virginia Gazette* were very expensive, and the selection was limited. The literary and legal commonplace books that Jefferson was keeping during these years help to fill in the picture of his reading and, in all likelihood, his library. (The reader is directed to Gilbert Chinard's editions of these writings: *The Literary Bible of Thomas Jefferson: His Commonplace Book of Philosophers and Poets* and *The Commonplace Book of Thomas Jefferson: A Repertory of His Ideas on Government*.) He was fond of English poetry, and, in addition to the writers already mentioned, he read and commonplaced the

Scottish poet, James Thomson—whose glorification of rural life and landscape in the manner of Virgil's *Georgics* attracted him—and another eighteenth-century poet, Mark Akenside. We know that he liked to see plays, and the Literary Commonplace Book shows that he read them as well. He was also reading and commonplacing at great length two writers who had a profound affect on his developing sensibility and modes of thought: the English politician and philosopher, Lord Bolingbroke, and the Scottish jurist, Lord Kames. Passages copied from Bolingbroke's deistic arguments in his *Philosophical Works* fill more pages in the Literary Commonplace Book than any other work, just as Kames's *Principles of Equity* predominates in his Equity Commonplace Book. Jefferson's rationalistic deism and his deeply rooted belief in natural rights, both of which contributed significantly to the character of his thought, were indelibly marked by the reading of these two works in the mid-1760s. He seems to have read and been influenced by other books by Lord Kames during this period, most notably a key work on aesthetics, *Elements of Criticism,* and *Essays on the Principles of Morality and Natural Religion.* Kames, who was represented in Jefferson's mature collection by no fewer than ten titles, was himself a famous lawyer and legal scholar with universal interests and must be regarded as one of Jefferson's early role models.

One further glimpse of his first library comes by way of an invoice of books purchased from London, dated 2 October 1769. This was the year that Jefferson was first elected to public office, and the thirteen books listed all reflect an interest in legislation and government. Half of the books are on the history and workings of Parliament, a subject that Jefferson was to research with great care; but even more important for the momentous turn that his mind was about to take were a half-dozen works of political theory, including treatises by Montesquieu,

Burlamaqui, and Locke. The young lawyer, whose knowledge and range of interests had constantly been expanded through reading and study, now applied himself in the same way to the questions of politics, though he often complained in later life that the need to study politics had taken him away from intellectual pursuits that were more congenial to his scholarly temperament.

A MORE EXTENSIVE PLAN

On 1 February 1770, a fire destroyed the house at Shadwell, and most of Thomas Jefferson's library was lost. A family tradition has it that his first reaction on learning of the fire, which happened while he was away, was to inquire after the fate of his books. There is no doubt that he would have regarded his library as his most valuable possession, and not merely for the cash value it represented. On 20 February, he wrote to his college friend, John Page:

> My late loss may perhaps have reached you by this time, I mean the loss of my mother's house by fire, and in it, of every paper I had in the world, and almost every book. On a reasonable estimate I calculate the cost of the books burned to have been £200. sterling. Would to god it had been the money; then had it never cost me a sigh!

Jefferson had been a serious collector of books for about ten years, and during that time he was first a student, and then a practitioner of the law. "Nothing is more remarkable about his youth," Merrill D. Peterson asserts in the transcript of a symposium, *Thomas Jefferson and the World of Books,* held in September 1976, "than his love of books and learning." According to William S. Simpson, whose "Comparison of the Libraries of Seven Colonial Virginians, 1755–1789" appeared in the January 1974 volume of the *Journal of Library History,* the library at

Shadwell probably contained the standard works found in most Virginia collections of the time: *The Spectator, Paradise Lost,* the Bible, the *Book of Common Prayer,* Shakespeare's plays, Pope's works, *The Tatler,* Richard Allestree's *The Whole Duty of Man,* the laws of Virginia, Dryden's Virgil, and Butler's *Hudibras.* But Jefferson was not an ordinary reader nor did his library long remain conventional. It seems likely from their early bookmarks, for example, that two standard reference works on the ancient world were there: John Potter's *Antiquities of Greece* and Basil Kennett's *Antiquities of Rome.* In addition to legal works, which must have predominated, we may be sure that his library contained books on the subjects in which he had a demonstrated interest: history, classics, philosophy, English poetry, languages, architecture, mathematics, music, natural science, and, most recently, politics. The most tangible clue to its size is the £200 "reasonable estimate" Jefferson made of its value, but this is by no means a precise indicator. A comparison of the prices paid for the books purchased in Williamsburg from the *Virginia Gazette* with those he would cite a few years later suggests that prices for Williamsburg books were much higher than those for books imported directly from London, and that law books, of which he apparently had many, were more expensive than most others. Considering these factors, we may estimate the library lost in the Shadwell fire at three to four hundred volumes.

For his time and place, particularly for a young man of twenty-six, this was a huge library. Even for a rich man, which Jefferson was, it represented a tremendous financial investment; according to Cynthia and Gregory Stiverson's article in *Printing and Society in Early America* (edited by William L. Joyce et al.), it was worth as much as a day laborer might expect to earn in ten years, or the cost of a herd of nearly two hundred cows. But large and valuable as his first library un-

doubtedly was, Jefferson's ideas for a replacement were far more ambitious. To some extent, the Shadwell library had been a circumstantial accumulation, beginning with the inheritance of his father's books and gaining additions with each successive intellectual venture—studying law, learning Italian and Anglo-Saxon, designing Monticello, serving in the legislature. Now he was free to indulge his wide-ranging intellectual interests and his passion for books in a grand plan for a library that would embrace virtually all of human knowledge. He may well have had such a plan in mind earlier, but the Shadwell fire forced the issue and offered a rare opportunity to give his plan the name of action.

Jefferson's grand plan for his library almost certainly had a model. While he had only made one foray outside of Virginia and had had little opportunity to observe large collections, he had undoubtedly seen the great library of William Byrd II of Westover, which was one of the marvels of the American colonies. Byrd (who died a year after Jefferson's birth) had been a wealthy Virginia landowner, educated in England and a member of the Royal Society at age twenty-two. He had assembled a collection of books on his Virginia plantation that was so large as to be awesome by contemporary standards. Arranged, cataloged, and cared for by a resident librarian, it numbered an unprecedented thirty-five hundred volumes. But perhaps of more importance for the omnivorous young Jefferson was its unusually broad range. The Greek and Roman classics formed one of the most imposing parts of the library, while substantial sections were given over to typical categories such as law, divinity, and medicine. But quite untypically, one of the largest sections was classified as "Entertainment, Poetry, Translations, &c." where, according to Louis B. Wright in *The First Gentlemen of Virginia: Intellectual Qualities of the Early Colonial Ruling Class,* "the works of the Elizabethan and

Restoration dramatists were more completely represented than in any other American library." It contained

a large number of books of architecture, including the works of Vitruvius, Palladio, and more recent writers on that subject; a sizable collection of books on drawing and painting; collections of music, including examples of Italian and English operas; many books of philosophy, classical and modern—among them the works of Hobbes, Descartes, Boyle, Shaftesbury, Locke, and other relatively recent writers; twenty or more works on gardening and agriculture; an ample assortment of other utilitarian books, such as treatises on distilling, cookery, and related subjects; a scattering of textbooks on language, rhetoric, mathematics, and logic. . . . [Moreover, it represented] a carefully balanced collection of the best literature and learning of the day [that] had no equal in America.

Whether Jefferson was closely familiar with the Westover library or knew it mostly by reputation, its grand scale and universal scope must have made a lasting impression on the young man, who was already gaining a reputation as one of the most learned men in the colony. Three years after the fire he seems to have visited Westover to consider the possibility of buying the great library for himself, for he listed in his 1773 Memorandum Book, under the heading "Westover library," the numbers of volumes by format (that is, folio, quarto, octavo, and so on) and price, calculating the size of the library at 3,486 volumes and the total price at £1,219/18. On the next page he seems to have calculated what he could realize from the sale of books in his own library that presumably could be spared, but he could only come up with 669 volumes with a total value of £218. Though his marriage the year before had doubled his considerable fortune, the difference of £1,000 was an astronomical sum and must have far exceeded his means. Eventually, the great library of William Byrd

would find a buyer in Isaac Zane, who in 1778 purchased the entire collection and carried it to Philadelphia for resale. In the years that followed, having missed a unique opportunity to accomplish a major portion of his grand plan at a single stroke, Jefferson nonetheless acquired a good many Westover volumes for his own library. (Edwin Wolf II) has written about the dispersal of Byrd's library in the April 1958 issue of the *Proceedings* of the American Antiquarian Society.)

An important indication of Jefferson's grand plan for his library is contained in a remarkable letter he wrote on 3 August 1771 to Robert Skipwith, who had requested a list of books "suited to the capacity of a common reader who understands but little of the classicks and who has not leisure for any intricate or tedious study," costing £25 or £30. Jefferson's reply and the accompanying list of 148 titles are revealing documents, but due notice must be taken of Skipwith's phrasing, which is pointedly intended to underscore the difference between his own conventional interests and those of his scholarly advisor. While there is no doubt that the list, which mentions prices and the address of a London bookseller, is an outgrowth of Jefferson's energetic efforts to rebuild his library after the 1770 fire and that it contains many books that were personal favorites and influential in his development, it is not modeled after his own library. This is most evident in its range and proportions. For example, nearly half of the items on the list are the works of English literary writers, a fair number of which—such as the novels of Henry Fielding, Samuel Richardson, and Tobias Smollett—Jefferson seems never to have acquired himself, while only a small handful of books appear on subjects such as politics, natural science, and law, which bulked so large in Jefferson's own interests and in the collection he sold to Congress. Clearly he was attempting to heed Skipwith's admonitions and recommend something like a gentleman's library, but what he found himself unable to heed, significantly, was the limitation on cost, recommending finally a collection priced at more than £100. The letter to Skipwith contains a defense of fiction that is often quoted, but as Jefferson himself was little attracted to novels and seems to have ready very few, Julian P. Boyd is probably right in saying that this defense is "less noteworthy (since it represents the views of English critics from Sir Philip Sidney to Addison and Johnson) than the up-to-the-minute character of the list," some of whose titles had been very recently published. Perhaps the most indicative thing in the letter in terms of his own library is his remark that Skipwith is welcome to come to Monticello, "from which you may reach your hand to a library formed on a more extensive plan."

BUILDING THE COLLECTION

The fire of 1770 gave new impetus both to the development of Jefferson's library and to his plans and efforts to build his own private residence, which he was then calling the Hermitage. The plan for the library seems to have been integral to the ambitious design of the whole. "It is clear," W. H. Adams writes in *Jefferson's Monticello*, "from the earliest notes on Monticello that Jefferson intended its basic program to encompass the functions of a museum of art and of natural history as well as to house a comprehensive library." As he pushed his efforts to complete a livable portion of his new house, he moved just as vigorously to rebuild and expand his library. On 4 August 1773, according to his Memorandum Book, he counted the astonishing total of 1,256 volumes at Monticello, and these, he noted, did not include "vols. of Music; nor my books in Williamsburgh." Thus, in three and a half years—during which he was managing a large estate, laboring under a heavy case load as a lawyer, courting and marrying a young widow, and building a new residence—he had managed to acquire a library collection three or four times as large as the one he had lost, averaging about one new book per day.

While he must have succeeded in importing a substantial number of books from abroad, we know that he bought a great many books in America during these and succeeding years. The Westover library of Byrd eluded him, but he was more fortunate a few years later in acquiring what were probably two of the best libraries in Virginia, those of the illustrious Peyton Randolph and the learned Richard Bland. Randolph had inherited a valuable library from his father, Sir John Randolph, and, according to E. Millicent Sowerby's *Catalogue of the Library of Thomas Jefferson,* Jefferson bought the entire collection, "book-cases and all as they stood." As reported by Hugh Blair Grigsby in *The Virginia Convention of 1776,* Bland enjoyed a reputation as a "fine classical scholar" and a man whose "great learning lay in the field of British history in its largest sense, and especially that of Virginia." Both of these libraries contained manuscript records of early Virginia history, which Jefferson prized and carefully preserved, fully aware of their uniqueness and their historical importance.

Years later, when the frontier had receded, Jefferson remarked in a letter to John Taylor on 28 May 1816 "the difficulties of getting new works in our situation, inland and without a single bookstore." During the 1770s those difficulties were many times greater, for the problems of geography were compounded by the disruptions of war, domestic turmoil, and a wildly inflated currency. Still he succeeded by characteristic diligence in steadily adding to his book collection. When his law practice took him to Williamsburg, he bought books at the office of the *Virginia Gazette,* which in 1775 listed some three hundred titles available for sale. Books came to him at the death of his father-in-law, John Wayles, and that of his brother-in-law and closest friend, Dabney Carr. He purchased books from the estate of the Reverend James Horrocks, the president of the College of William and Mary, and from the collections of at least two members of the faculty, Samuel Henley and Thomas Gwatkin, who returned to England after the outbreak of hostilities in 1775. From Henley's varied collection he acquired an impressive array of books, including some standard authors—Dante, Milton, and Tasso—and some titles that were especially important to him, such as Thomas Whately's *Observations on Gardening* and the botanical works of Linnaeus (*Papers*, 8). From the library of the fleeing Royal Governor of Virginia, Lord Dunmore, some books found their way into Jefferson's library, and from the estate of one Parson Wiley he acquired a run of early Virginia newspapers that he believed to be unique.

Being a member of the Continental Congress in 1775 and 1776 meant having access to the bookstores of Philadelphia, the commercial and cultural heart of the colonies, and his memorandum books attest that Jefferson made the most of his opportunity. With the ready availability of books, he recorded more purchases in his Memorandum Book for 1776 than in any previous year. His correspondence reveals that during the memorable session in which he produced the Declaration of Independence, his thoughts were often on his library. When word reached him of the availability of Gwatkin's books, he wrote at once for a catalog and asked his friend John Page in a letter of 17 May 1776 to purchase immediately "two of them which I recollect he had and have long wished to get." He was greatly concerned about the fate of the books he had left in Williamsburg, which was in danger of becoming enemy territory, and sent directions for their removal. Later, as governor of Virginia, he was to do the same for his Monticello books when the British threatened Charlottesville in 1781.

When he decided to accept the appointment as minister plenipotentiary in 1782,

one of the attractions of Europe was the opportunity to further enhance his library. Waiting to take ship in Philadelphia, he roomed with his friend James Madison, who was preparing a list of books to be included in a library that he hoped to persuade the Congress to establish, and the two men apparently exchanged bibliographies and desiderata lists. Jefferson had with him a catalog of the books he owned and was including in it books he intended to purchase abroad. It was presumably the books he owned that he counted and recorded in the front of the catalog on 6 March 1783: 2,640 volumes. If any further proof were needed that Jefferson had in mind a grand plan for his library, we have it here. Having painstakingly, over a period of thirteen years, built a library that was one of the largest and finest in America, adding two hundred volumes annually in the face of enormous difficulties, he embarked for Europe determined to make very substantial additions.

In the letter to Samuel H. Smith offering his library to Congress in 1814, Jefferson described his Paris book collecting in some detail:

> While residing in Paris, I devoted every afternoon I was disengaged, for a summer or two, in examining all the principal bookstores, turning over every book with my own hand, and putting by everything which related to America, and indeed whatever was rare and valuable in every science. Besides this, I had standing orders during the whole time I was in Europe, on it's principal book-marts, particularly Amsterdam, Frankfort, Madrid and London, for such works relating to America as could not be found in Paris.

According to William H. Peden—whose Ph.D. dissertation at the University of Virginia, *Thomas Jefferson: Book-Collector*, is the most detailed study of the subject—Jefferson had not exaggerated, for the five years that he spent in Paris, 1784–1789, were "probably the most important ones during his entire career as a book collector." He regarded books as one of the few areas in which Europe had the advantage over his own country and therefore as her most valuable commodity for Americans. "In science, the mass of the people [of France] is two centuries behind ours," he wrote to Charles Bellini on 30 September 1785; "their literati, half a dozen years before us. Books, really good, acquire just reputation in that time, and so become known to us, and communicate to us all their advances in knowledge." In addition to frequenting the shops in Paris, where the offices of the honest bookseller Froullé were particularly valued, Jefferson ordered heavily from the catalogs of London booksellers such as Lackington and John Stockdale, the man entrusted with the publication of *Notes on the State of Virginia.* Not content with these efforts, he used his friends and fellow diplomats as agents where he could not go in person, though the book-hunting chores he tirelessly performed for his friends back home far outnumbered his own requests for help. The books that he took particular pains to select for Madison played an important role in the latter's studious preparation for the constitutional convention. The amount of money that Jefferson spent for books while he was in Paris and throughout his life was prodigious, even for a wealthy Virginia planter. He was aware that his indulgence in books amounted to extravagance and sought to moderate it by buying cheaper and smaller format editions wherever possible and driving a hard bargain when offered an expensive book. To one of his agents in London he wrote on 1 June 1789: "Sensible that I labour grievously under the malady of Bibliomanie, I submit to the rule of buying only at reasonable prices, as to a regimen necessary in that disease."

Before he returned to America late in 1789, Jefferson compiled a separate catalog of the books he had purchased abroad. The majority of the books, not surprisingly, were in French, and the largest categories were Politics and Geography, with marked emphasis on books relating to America. Another notable concentration was in languages; grammars, dictionaries, and lexicons in both ancient and modern languages clearly had a high priority in his foreign purchases. Written in the tiny handwriting that he occasionally employed, and arranged according to his own classification scheme, this undated catalog in the Massachusetts Historical Society seems to contain books acquired for others as well as for himself, and the entries are such that an accurate title or volume count is difficult to arrive at. But it is safe to conclude that during his five years in Paris Jefferson managed to add at least two thousand volumes to his library. This represents an increase of 75 percent over the 2,640 volumes he counted in March 1783 and probably does not include the books he acquired in Philadelphia, Annapolis, and elsewhere between that time and his departure for Europe in July 1784. Jefferson thus returned to America in the fall of 1789 the possessor of a magnificent library of approximately five thousand volumes.

Drawn almost immediately into Washington's cabinet upon his return and burdened for the next four years by the heavy demands of his office and political affairs, he seems not to have added greatly to his library. He had the Paris books with him during much of this period, and he used them to good advantage in his work as secretary of state, as shown by his well-known statement on relations with France, drawn up at the request of President Washington, in which he cites works he had acquired in Paris by Grotius, Wolf, Pufendorf, and Vattel. Before resigning his office at the end of 1793, he echoed sentiments he had uttered upon leaving his governorship in 1781 and would invoke again on leaving the presidency, on the pleasures of returning to his family, his farms, and his books. These were versions of a famous passage of Latin verse that had attracted his attention as a schoolboy when he found it in Horace and copied it into his Literary Commonplace Book: "O rural home: when shall I behold you! When shall I be able, now with books of the ancients, now with sleep and idle hours, to quaff sweet forgetfulness of life's cares." His library, from an early period, formed an essential part of his vision of the good life.

Jefferson's retirement ended in 1797, when he took up his duties as vice-president, and for the next twelve years, while serving in Philadelphia and Washington, he resumed the building up of his book collection with renewed vigor. Although he told a Paris bookseller in 1803 that "my collection of books is now so extensive, & myself so far advanced in life that I have little occasion to add to it," Peden has shown that he continued buying books from a host of booksellers. His many purchases during this period reflect a continued interest not only in reading but in the creation of a truly distinctive library, and it is clear that his grand plan by now included creating a collection that was intended to have a utility well beyond what was required for his personal use. After assuming the presidency, he lent his considerable knowledge of bibliography and the book market to the task of assembling a congressional library, now rendered essential by the government's move from Philadelphia to the marshy shores of the Potomac. By this time, he was receiving regularly and in large numbers presentation copies of books from their authors, and in 1806 he was left the extensive library of his close friend and mentor, George Wythe, who, as reported by Peden, allowed in his will that while his books were "perhaps not deserving a place in [Jefferson's] Museum," they were "the most valuable to him of any thing which I have power to bestow." There is little doubt that Wythe knew whereof he willed.

While holding public office in New York, Philadelphia, and Washington, Jefferson assembled a reading library of standard authors and favorite books in smaller formats, many of which he had bought in Paris. Hampered since 1786 by a dislocated wrist, Jefferson found larger formats, such as folios and quartos, awkward to handle and came to prefer octavos and duodecimos, which had the added advantages of taking less space and being cheaper. On his retirement, he installed this select collection, which he called his "petit format library," at Poplar Forest, his plantation near Lynchburg, where he spent several weeks each year. According to an unpublished catalog compiled in 1873 by Jefferson's grandson Francis Eppes, prominent in the petit-format library, which in the end exceeded 650 volumes, were an edition of the English poets in 109 volumes and an edition of Shakespeare in thirty-eight, both published in London by John Bell. Henry S. Randall, in his *Life of Thomas Jefferson,* noted that the petit-format library at Poplar Forest contained "a considerable collection of Italian and French, and a few favorite Greek and Latin poets, and a larger number of prose writers of the same languages—all, it is unnecessary to say, in the original."

AN ABUNDANCE OF BOOKS

The library in the first Monticello was a large room on the second floor directly above the parlor. When the house was rebuilt, this space was occupied by the dome room so much admired by Margaret Bayard Smith, and the books were moved to the suite of rooms at the south end of the first floor, which included his "cabinet," where he did much of his reading and writing. When Mrs. Smith visited Monticello in 1809, she was impressed by the strictness with which Jefferson's privacy in this suite was observed and called it his "sanctum sanctorum." Isaac Jefferson, a slave who spent much of his long life at Monticello, vividly recalled his master in his library:

Old Master had abundance of books; sometimes would have twenty of 'em down on the floor at once—read fust one, then tother. Isaac has often wondered how Old Master came to have such a mighty head; read so many of them books; and when they go to him to ax him anything, he go right straight to the book and tell you all about it.

Isaac's recollections afford us a rare glimpse of Jefferson's characteristic way of using his library. That he liked to lay many books out on the floor so as to be able to consult and compare differing accounts underscores the utility, as opposed to the mere mania, of possessing a full range of books on subjects of interest. Moreover, Isaac's picture of his master going straight to a book when he was asked a question reinforces our sense, so apparent in other places, that Jefferson's prodigious and wide-ranging knowledge was largely drawn from his reading. "His library expressed much more than the instinct of a collector," Peterson has written. "Jefferson was dependent on books, tended to take his knowledge from them rather than from direct experience, and approached the world with studied eyes."

One of the important aims of Jefferson's grand plan for his library was clearly to provide for the fullest possible access to information and ideas. The need to know seemed to come as naturally to him as the need to breathe. He spoke often of his belief that nature had formed him for study, and he exercised his remarkable powers of discipline to find time for reading even in the busiest and most hectic times of his life. His earliest interests were literary and philosophical, as his commonplace books attest, but the study of the law fed his interest in history, which in turn shaped his understanding of religious and political institutions. He acquired from his teacher at William and Mary, Dr. William Small, a taste for mathematics, to which he returned in later life with relish. In his autobiography he paid high tribute to Small, whose friendship and interest in his intellectual development, he declared, "probably fixed the destinies of my life." From Small he got his "first views of the expansion of science & of the system of things in which we are placed." His intense interest in this "system of things" never waned, and his library is a testament to his lifelong effort to come to terms with it.

Jefferson also developed and used his library as a potential source of new knowledge, the sphere of research. As a young lawyer, perhaps inspired by the example of Lord Kames, he began collecting legal documents and court records. Kames had first made his mark as a legal scholar by assembling and publishing the important decisions and precedents of Scottish law, which had been neglected by the English reporters. Jefferson began in the early years of his legal career to perform the same task for Virginia and managed to salvage and preserve many documents that would otherwise have been lost. He assiduously collected information on the American Indians, particularly on their languages, in the belief that a sufficient mass of material and proper analysis would eventually provide answers to such questions as whether their ancestors had migrated from Asia. Unfortunately, his years of effort went for naught when this collection was stolen while being shipped back to Monticello from Washington.

Besides being a collector of valuable research materials, Jefferson had preeminently the temperament and qualities of mind requisite for research, and he was doubtful that one could become learned by studying "mere compilers" rather than primary sources. For this reason, he lamented the preemptive use of Blackstone's *Commentaries* by law students and required those who studied with him to begin with more basic works, such as *Coke on Littleton.* "Now men are born scholars, lawyers, doctors," he commented wryly to John Tyler on 26 May

1810; "in our day this was confined to poets." He believed and tried by his practice to demonstrate that answers to important questions—philosophical, historical, political, or scientific—could very often be found or formed by determination and effort. A classic example of what resourcefulness and diligent research are capable of producing is his only book, *Notes on the State of Virginia* (1785), a carefully documented compilation of facts and interpretation. In it he strove to assemble a coherent and accurate account of his "country" from bits and pieces of information sought out by direct inquiry or found in widely scattered and often problematical sources. "A patient pursuit of facts, and cautious combination and comparison of them," he wrote in a footnote to Query VI, "is the drudgery to which man is subjected by his Maker, if he wishes to attain sure knowledge."

Thomas Jefferson's library was not only a locus for intellectual endeavor and research; it was also an active tool in the varied enterprises of its creator. Though its beginnings were shaped by the accidents of his father's death and his schooling, its first definite shape and character was that of a library to support the study and practice of law. When it was destroyed by fire in 1770, Jefferson complained to his friend Page in a letter dated 21 February of that year: "To make the loss more sensible it fell principally on my books of common law, of which I have but one left, at that time lent out." The letter makes clear that he believed he could not practice law without books, though others, like his friend Patrick Henry, performed successfully at the bar with little or no recourse to them. As Edmund Randolph famously put it, "Mr. Jefferson drew copiously from the depths of the law, Mr. Henry from the recesses of the human heart."

As the troubles between the colonies and Great Britain deepened in the early 1770s, Jefferson's readings in history and politics increased. By the time the law courts were closed in 1774, his political activities and researches had practically become a full-time occupation. In addition to his well-known role as a political leader and spokesman, his notebooks show that he seized upon the dispute with the mother country as the occasion for intense research into the history of Virginia, the prerogatives of Crown and Parliament, the nature of the English Constitution, the origin and development of the common law, the original basis of land tenure in Saxon England, and the makeup of various confederations of states. He went thoroughly into the literature of parliamentary procedure, an effort of scholarship that paid important dividends later, when he used his findings to compile the *Manual of Parliamentary Practice* adopted by the United States Senate. And when, during the Revolution, the government of Virginia was being reconstituted, he was a principal contributor to the revisal of its laws, a task for which his talents as a legal scholar and researcher were ideally suited and his library was indispensable.

Even farming, to which he was born and bred, was something that Jefferson sought to master through books. To be sure, the age in which he lived had begun to take agriculture very seriously, and there were countless books produced on what were proclaimed modern and scientific methods. While he maintained his admiration for the writings of the ancients on the subject, he owned most of the agricultural books of his own time that were recognized as significant, and his letters show that he read them and weighed their merits. "I am much indebted to you," he wrote an English correspondent, William Strickland, on 23 March 1798, "for Mr Kirwan's charming treatise on manures. Science never appears so beautiful as when applied to the uses of human life, nor any use of it so engaging as those of agriculture & domestic economy." Of a man who used the words "beautiful" and "charming" sparingly, it is utterly indicative that he should employ them to describe science and a pamphlet on fertilizer.

For a variety of reasons, none of which seems attributable to his characteristically studious approach to agriculture, Jefferson did not enjoy much success as a farmer. But he did succeed in spectacular fashion in another art he learned from books—architecture. Completely self-taught, Jefferson studied architecture to grasp and assimilate its principles and to enable himself to build in exemplary fashion. "It is not at all surprising," writes Malone, "that he turned to books. . . . His distinction lay in the fact that he referred to more books than others did, that he went beyond British works to more remote sources, that he attained results which accorded with his own superior tastes and special needs." The evidence that he consulted many books is found not only in his library, which has an extensive section devoted to the subject, but also in his architectural drawings themselves, where he has written references to the books containing his models and sources. His great master was the sixteenth-century Italian, Andrea Palladio, whose classic work, *The Four Books of Architecture,* set forth principles and practice based on an intensive study of Roman architecture and the exact proportions that they exhibited. Palladio was undoubtedly, like Lord Kames, another role model for the young Jefferson, and the opening of the preface to his *Four Books* sounded a note that the student was often to echo: "It seemed to me a thing worthy of a man, who ought not to be born for himself only, but also for the utility of others, to publish the designs of those edifices, (in collecting which, I have employed so much time, and exposed myself to so many dangers)."

Jefferson's library was constantly changing; what was true of his collection in 1815 may not have been true earlier. Nevertheless, the sixty-seven hundred volumes he sold to Congress represent the library in its most fully developed form. Perhaps the most striking thing about it is its amazing breadth. The major categories of knowledge are, as one would expect, abundantly represented, but the number and range of minor categories Jefferson included is extraordinary. Nowhere is this more readily apparent than in the section labeled Technical Arts. Here are subsections, to cite only a few, on Cooking, Brewing, Printing, Watchmaking, Writing, Dying, a substantial selection of works on Tactics, and two on Aerostation, or flying. True to his claim, the library proves upon examination to be particularly well suited for "the American statesman." The section on Politics is immense, far and away the largest in the library and constituting more than a quarter of the entire collection. Its range extends from the great theoretical treatises of Aristotle, Plato, Machiavelli, Montesquieu, and Locke to the nameless hackwork of the ephemeral tract. To preserve the discourse of an age that carried on political disputation by exchanging printed salvos, Jefferson carefully organized and gathered into bound volumes hundreds of pamphlets. Quite unobtrusively, in a surviving volume entered in the catalog as "Great Britain & America. tracts. 1765–1781. 10. v. 8vo," appears *A Summary View of the Rights of British America,* a pamphlet written by Jefferson himself and published by his friends in 1774. The section on Politics is complemented by the next largest sections, Law and History. In both there is impressive historical range and depth, but the major preoccupation is with the legal and historical tradition to which Virginia and America belong. And in the sizable Geography section, the subject of America is predominant. More even than its size and remarkable range of subject matter, this extraordinary concentration of American material, as Peden has pointed out, is what is most distinctive about Jefferson's library. Congress may have lost a serviceable reference library to the British invaders, but it gained as a consequence an unparalleled collection of materials on its own country.

CLASSIFICATION

Sometime before 1783, when he was preparing the list of books he wished to acquire in Europe, Jefferson began a classified catalog of his library. He had previously arranged books by categories in recommended reading lists, such as the Skipwith list of 1771. The books he recommended to Skipwith were grouped under nine headings:

Fine Arts
Criticism on the Fine Arts
Politicks, Trade
Religion
Law
History. Antient
History. Modern
Natural Philosophy, Natural History &c
Miscellaneous

In some of the numerous lists he compiled for law students, which were usually not confined to works on the law, he arranged the recommended categories of books by the time of the day at which they should be read, explaining to Bernard Moore: "A great inequality is observable in the vigor of the mind at different periods of the day. It's powers at these periods should therefore be attended to in marshalling the business of the day" (Paul Ford, ed., *Works of Thomas Jefferson*, 11). Accordingly, he recommended the following reading schedule:

Before eight:	Physical Studies, Ethics, Religion, Natural Law
Eight to twelve:	Law
Twelve to one:	Politics
In the afternoon:	History
From dark to bedtime:	Belles-lettres, Criticism, Rhetoric, Oratory

But when he came to catalog his library he chose a much more ambitious classification scheme that aimed at encompassing all knowledge and was based on the faculties of the mind, a scheme set forward by Francis Bacon and promulgated in the eighteenth century by Jean Le Rond d'Alembert in the first volume of the monumental *Encyclopédie*. Jefferson's versions were his own adaptations, but he followed Bacon and d'Alembert in embracing a correspondence between the faculties of Memory, Reason, and Imagination and the three principal categories of human knowledge, History, Philosophy, and Fine Arts. His basic classification scheme, more orderly and less vague than those of his models, reveals much about his own predispositions, as well the makeup of his library. As Arthur E. Bestor has written in *Three Presidents and Their Books*, Jefferson's classification scheme is "in some sense, a blueprint of his mind," but it also represents a practical accommodation to the kinds of books he had selected for himself. Jefferson speaks directly to this point in a letter of 7 May 1815 to the Librarian of Congress, George Watterston:

Thus the law having been my profession, and politics the occupation to which the circumstances of the times in which I have lived called my particular attention, my provision of books in these lines, and in those most nearly connected with them was more copious, and required in particular instances subdivisions into sections and paragraphs, while other subjects of which general views only were contemplated are thrown into masses. A physician or theologist would have modified differently, the chapters, sections, and paragraphs of a library adapted to their particular pursuits.

The 1783 manuscript catalog of his library shows evidence that the classification scheme employed there had undergone some evolution over the years, but the table he affixed to the front of the catalog (now in the Coolidge Collection of the Massachusetts Historical Society) displays the scheme in its most representative form (see pages 172–173).

CLASSIFICATION TABLE OF THE 1783 CATALOG

Books may be classed from the Faculties of the mind, which being

I. Memory *II. Reason* *III. Imagination*

are applied respectively to

I. History *II. Philosophy* *III. Fine Arts*

					Chapter
			Antient. . . .	Antient hist	1
		Civil Proper		Foreign	2
	Civil		Modern	British	3
				American	4
		Ecclesiastical		Ecclesiastical	5
				Nat^l.Philos^y.	6
				Agriculture	7
I. History		Physics		Chemistry	8
				Surgery	9
				Medicine	10
			Animals	Anatomy	11
	Natural	Nat^l.hist^y.prop^r.		Zoology	12
			Vegetables	Botany	13
			Minerals	Mineralogy	14
		Occupations of Man.		Technical arts	15

		Ethics		*Moral Philos^y. Law Nature & Nations	16
			Religious	Religion	17
	Moral			Equity	18
				Common Law	19
			Domestic	L. Merchant	20
		Jurisprudence		L. Maritime	21
			Municipal	L. Ecclesiast^l.	22
			Foreign	Foreign Law	23
II. Philosophy				Politics	24
		Oeconomical		Commerce	25
				Arithmetic	26
		Pure		Geometry	27
	Mathematical			Mechanics Statics Dynamics	
		Physico-Mathematical		Pneumatics Phonics Optics	28
				Astronomy	29
				Geography	30

*in classing a small library one may throw under this head books which attempt what may be called the Natural history of the mind or an Analysis of it's operations. the term and division of Metaphysics is rejected as meaning nothing or something beyond our reach, or what should be called by some other name

CLASSIFICATION TABLE OF THE 1783 CATALOG (Continued)

	Gardening.		Gardening	31
	Architecture.		Architecture	32
	Sculpture		Sculpture	33
	Painting		Painting	34
	Music	Theoretical	Music Theory	35
			Music Vocal	36
		Practical	Music Instrument	37
		Narrative.	Epic	38
			Romance	39
III. Fine Arts			Tragedy	40
			Comedy	41
	Poetry	Dramatic.	Pastorals / Odes / Elegies / Dialogues	42
		Didactic	Satire / Epigram / Epistles	43
	Oratory		Logic / Rhetoric / Oration	44
	Criticism.		Criticism	45
	Authors who have written in Various branches		Polygraphical	46

Jefferson begins with the three basic divisions that he borrowed from Bacon and d'Alembert and then subdivides these as many as four times until he arrives at classes that he calls "chapters." The serious thought given to the ways in which different aspects of human knowledge interrelate is evident, but his principal aim is to arrive at meaningful classes for his books. Leo E. LaMontagne, a student of Jefferson's various classification schemes, has noted in *American Library Classification* that some of them, such as that found in his 1779 bill for the reorganization of the College of William and Mary or his 1818 plan for the University of Virginia, are so different from that of his library catalog "that they might well have been the products of different minds." One of the reasons for this is that Jefferson embarked upon the scheme with his own books and intellectual interests in mind. An obvi-

ous example is the classing under Civil History, which subdivides into Antient and Modern, with Modern being further broken down into Foreign, British, and American. Thus he begins with all of non-Ecclesiastical History and arrives at four classes or chapters perfectly adapted to his own interests. More idiosyncratic is his category for Foreign Law, which not only includes books on the law of foreign countries but on the law of the other American states as well. Books on the laws of Great Britain and Virginia appear in the chapter on Common Law, but those on Massachusetts, for example, are classed as foreign, apparently because of Jefferson's belief, cited in Sowerby's scholarship, that the basis of law in the Eastern states was a "compound," put together from various sources, with "an abundance of notions of their own."

The most conspicuous departure that Jefferson made from the schemes of his predecessors, as well as the most eye-catching innovation, was in his treatment of religion. Whereas Bacon and D'Alembert gave prominent places in their schemes to theology and the sacred, Jefferson's treating religion as a branch of jurisprudence strikes some observers as strange and even capricious. LaMontagne reports that Judge A. B. Woodward, who corresponded with Jefferson and produced a serious treatise on classification, found much to praise in his friend's scheme but was dismayed that religion "comes out to be nothing more than *a part of jurisprudence,* and is the commencement of that branch, while commerce is the termination of it." He wondered if, "in strict language," either religion or commerce could be "parts of jurisprudence," particularly in a country that has taken the unprecedented step, led by Jefferson himself, of "disclaiming the right of interfering with religious sentiment." The judge's points are well taken, but Jefferson's unusual designation of religion as belonging to jurisprudence shows that he approached religion less as theology, for which he provided no category, and more as a sphere of institutionalized moral suasion. This is clarified somewhat in the modified scheme he created for his much smaller retirement library, where the Ethical branch of Philosophy is subdivided into Morality, Moral Supplements, and Social Organisation, and Moral Supplements breaks down into two chapters, Religion and Law. Another innovation pointed out by Judge Woodward is Jefferson's treatment of Gardening, following Lord Kames's *Elements of Criticism,* as belonging to Fine Arts rather than Agriculture.

As a practical instrument for everyday use, Jefferson's fully elaborated scheme was too cumbersome. In conferring upon James Ogilvie, his schoolmaster neighbor, the privilege of using the Monticello library while he was in Washington, Jefferson described in a letter dated 31 January 1806 his working arrangement: "1. Antient history. 2. Modern do. 3. Physics. 4. Nat. Hist. proper. 5. Technical arts. 6. Ethics. 7. Jurisprudence. 8. Mathematics. 9. Gardening, architecture, sculpture, painting, music, poetry. 10. Oratory 11. Criticism. 12. Polygraphical. You will find this on a paper nailed up somewhere in the library." The more usual arrangement of large libraries in Jefferson's day was alphabetical, but, as he explained to Watterston on 7 May 1815, he found this "very unsatisfactory, because of the medley it presents to the mind, the difficulty sometimes of recalling an author's name, and the greater difficulty, where the name is not given, of selecting the word in the title, which shall determine its alphabetical place. The arrangement according to subject is far preferable." The subject arrangement described to Ogilvie, with its emphasis on basic categories, would suffice for finding one's way around the library. The purpose of the catalog, on the other hand, was to function less as a finding aid than as a detailed map showing where the contents of the books lay on the landscape of knowledge.

By 1812, his manuscript catalog had become so congested with original entries, later additions, erasures, marginal insertions, and interlineations that Jefferson made a fair copy, in which he combined and reordered certain chapters, reducing their number from forty-six to forty-four. Thus Politics and Commerce are combined into a single chapter, as are Gardening, Painting, and Sculpture. Some books he moved to a different chapter altogether, so that Ossian, pronounced by Jefferson in a letter of 25 February 1773 to be "the greatest Poet that has ever existed," is demoted from Epic to Romance. But the most important difference lay in the ordering of the books within the chapters. Far more deliberately than he had been able to do in the 1783 catalog, and with the entire collection before him, he gave each chapter a meaningful catalog order that he described to Librarian of Congress Watterston, as "sometimes analytical, sometimes chronological, & sometimes a combination of both." This is the order that Watterston replaced, much to Jefferson's chagrin, with an alphabetical rendering in the catalog printed by Congress in 1815 and that Sowerby in her modern edition of the catalog sought to restore by recurrence to the order of the 1783 manuscript catalog, which, unlike the fair copy, still survives. But Jefferson substantially reorganized his catalog in the 1812 fair copy, as is demonstrated conclusively by the recent reappearance of a manuscript (now in the Rare Book Division of the Library of Congress) in the hand of Jefferson's grandson-in-law, Nicholas P. Trist, that proves to be a copy of the catalog of the library sold to Congress with the entries in Jefferson's order and corrected in his own hand. Here we see Jefferson's orderly and original mind at work, as he lays out his books on a variable grid that is "sometimes chronological," progressing from ancient to modern, "sometimes analytical," from general to particular, and "sometimes a combination of both," from theoretical to practical.

"One of the most systematic of men," Malone has written, "he was in character as a cataloguer." Jefferson's efforts to arrange and bring order to his library present the man in a representative action. Nothing that he would do would more perfectly capture his scholarly and exacting cast of mind, his distinctive intellectual combination of order and pragmatism. His strong sense of history is always present in the chronological aspect of the arrangement, which, even when it is not the overarching principle, is nonetheless a part of the pattern. Thus his chapter on architecture begins not with the treatises of his master Palladio, or even Palladio's model, Vitruvius, but with books on the ancient ruins. After a series of subtle transitions, in which the focus shifts from the ancient world to the modern and from period

to place, he introduces the works of individual architects, the central arena of artistic theory and practice, and concludes his chapter with books needed by the practitioner, such as *Langley's Practical Geometry* and *The Builder's Dictionary*. This deliberate ordering of historical, theoretical, and practical elements, which Jefferson characterized as "chronological" and "analytical," is more than an arrangement of disparate parts; it is, in fact, a carefully articulated whole.

THE RETIREMENT LIBRARY

In April 1815, the wagons that left Monticello for Washington carried the library that Thomas Jefferson had labored forty-five years to create and which he believed to be, in a phrase that might sum up the grand plan, "the choicest collection of books in the United States" (Malone, 6). The rooms at the southern end of the first floor that had recently been filled to overflowing with six thousand and seven hundred volumes were now quite empty, but Jefferson seems to have been neither sad nor regretful. In the first place, he was in serious financial straits and needed the $23,950 he received to meet pressing obligations. Nor was he entirely bereft of books, for he still had several hundred volumes of his favorite works in his petit-format library at Poplar Forest. But the greatest consolation must have been the knowledge that his fondest wish for his library had been realized—that it would remain intact, just as he had built it, and be accessible to the public as a permanent possession of the nation.

"I cannot live without books," Jefferson wrote to John Adams on 10 June 1815, shortly after the wagons departed, "but fewer will suffice where amusement, and not use, is the only future object." In fact, he had already taken steps to acquire a good many replacements by this time, and Adams was to render valuable assistance by introducing him to George Ticknor, a precocious graduate of Dartmouth who was on his way to Europe. Jefferson was greatly impressed with Ticknor's learning and knowledge of books and quickly engaged him as a book-buying agent abroad. "Mr. Ticknor," he told Adams, "is particularly the best bibliograph I have met with, and very kindly and opportunely offered me the means of reprocuring some part of the literary treasures which I have ceded to Congress to replace the devastations of British Vandalism at Washington." It was through Ticknor that Jefferson first learned of and acquired, to his great delight, the superior editions of the classics produced by the notable German scholars of the period.

On hearing that Jefferson's library was to go to Congress, Adams had written to his friend, "I envy you that immortal honour." These two former presidents, who had begun as political allies but whose friendship had been bitterly broken off, were happily reunited through the intercession of their mutual friend, Dr. Benjamin Rush. Their revived correspondence, which continued from 1812 until a few months before their deaths, is one of the ornaments of American letters. It began, appropriately enough, with an exchange of books. Adams sent Jefferson a copy of *Lectures on Rhetoric and Oratory* (1810) by his son, John Quincy Adams, and Jefferson responded with a copy of his own printed brief in the Batture case, *The Proceedings of the Government of the United States, in maintaining the Public Right to the Beach of the Missisipi, adjacent to New-Orleans, against the Intrusion of Edward Livingston* (1812). Both men were intensely bookish, and their letters abound in references to their reading. Even when they are cautiously feeling each other out in the initial stages of the correspondence, the touchstone is their reading. "I have given up newspapers," Jefferson writes somewhat disingenuously on 21 January 1812, "in exchange for Tacitus and Thucydides, for Newton and Euclid;

and I find myself much the happier." Adams replies on 3 February with a pose of his own: "I have read Thucidides and Tacitus, so often, and at such distant Periods of my Life, that elegant, profound and enchanting as is their Style, I am weary of them. When I read them I seem to be only reading the History of my own Times and my own Life." As the correspondence progresses, the authors and titles of books fill their pages, as they discuss the Bible, Theocritus, translations of the Psalms, Endfield's *History of Philosophy*, Plato, Thomas Morton's *New English Canaan*, Theognis, and Joseph Priestley, to name only a few from the early letters. Their sparring over, they unburden themselves with a candor that is sometimes quite remarkable, as with Jefferson's unguarded dismissal on 7 July 1814 of Plato's *Republic:* "While wading thro' the whimsies, the puerilities, and unintelligible jargon of this work, I laid it down often to ask myself how it could have been that the world should have so long consented to give reputation to such nonsense as this?"

The libraries and reading tastes of the two old friends make for an interesting comparison. Adams' collection was not so large as Jefferson's, but his passion for books was at least as great. Argumentative by nature, Adams disputed with the authors in the margins of his books, where he was just as excitable and impatient as he was elsewhere. Jefferson, by contrast, rarely wrote anything in his books besides his special bookmark and an occasional cross-reference or correction. An exception is this wry annotation in a religious pamphlet, recorded by Sowerby: "doctrines not true prove the miracles not true. the miracles prove the doctrines & the doctrines prove the miracles, circularly." Adams' interests were also somewhat narrower than Jefferson's; he had comparatively little in his library by way of belles lettres and far less in science and mathematics.

In the eleven years that passed between the sale of his library and his death, Jefferson continued to acquire books at an astonishing rate, amassing a sizable collection that would have had few peers. When the indebtedness of his estate required that his second Monticello library be put up for auction in 1829, the Washington bookseller, Nathaniel Poor, issued a catalog based on Jefferson's own, listing 931 titles and some 1,600 volumes. His retirement library would be for "amusement and not use," Jefferson had told Adams, meaning that he could dispense with much that had been necessary to support his public and private occupations and concentrate on books and subjects that engaged his deepest interests. The implied narrowing of scope is reflected in the catalog, which focuses on fewer writers and topics. Old favorites—such as the essays of Montaigne and Hume, and Shaftesbury's *Characteristics*—are represented, and *Don Quixote,* said to be the only novel Jefferson ever reread, is present in two editions. A surprising amount of poetry is listed, though almost all of it from classical writers; Milton is there, but otherwise only a smattering of English poetry is included. The largest category, Jefferson's protests notwithstanding, is still Politics, though much of it relates to recent American history and probably reflects not so much his intellectual interests as his obsession with the political events of his own time, which were often being called into dispute. In Philosophy, as in other categories, the writers that drew his attention tend to be marked by the presence of several editions, so that nearly half of the thirty-eight items listed under Ethics–Antient are devoted to only three writers: Epictetus, Cicero, and, surprisingly, Plato. Jefferson probably paid so much attention to this philosopher he so little admired (there were six entries relating to Plato) because of his impact on Christian theology, a subject to which Jefferson often referred. Christianity was arguably the topic that engaged his interest more than any other in his presidential and retirement years. Nearly one-third of the sixty-one catalog entries under Religion are editions of or commentaries on the Bible, particularly the New Testament, and his letters to certain trusted correspondents show that he was deeply read in the development of Christianity from its founding to his own time.

The most informative account of his retirement reading, recorded in Randall's biography, comes from his favorite granddaughter, Ellen Randolph Coolidge, who was her grandfather's secretary, companion, and student during these years:

> Books were at all times his chosen companions, and his acquaintance with many languages gave him great power of selection. He read Homer, Virgil, Dante, Corneille, Cervantes, as he read Shakespeare and Milton. In his youth he had loved poetry, but by the time I was old enough to observe, he had lost his taste for it, except for Homer and the great Athenian tragics, which he continued to the last to enjoy. He went over the works of Eschylus, Sophocles and Euripides, not very long before I left him [1825]. Of history he was very fond, and this he studied in all languages, though always, I think, preferring the ancients. In fact, he derived more pleasure from his acquaintance with Greek and Latin than from any other resource of literature, and I have often heard him express his gratitude to his father for causing him to receive a classical education. I saw him more frequently with a volume of the classics in his hand than with any other book.

Though he sold his great library to Congress, Jefferson never lacked for books, and his frequent protests about the lack of time for reading need to be understood in the context of his wishes rather than in absolute terms, for the amount of reading he succeeded in doing was prodigious by any standard. Plagued as he was in his retirement by a multitude of unwelcome distractions, as well as financial and family difficulties, he responded by indulging what he himself described to Adams on 17 May 1818 as "a canine appetite for reading."

THE LIBRARY AND THE LEGACY

Thomas Jefferson was a man for whom books were "a necessary of life." They were the indispensable tools of his work, whether the law, government, or farming, and they were his favorite recreation. The case of Patrick Henry, who had little use for books and reading, mystified him, and he wondered where Henry's golden eloquence could have come from. His own talents and abilities had been carefully cultivated from his earliest days, and he spared no effort of research to extend or enhance his knowledge. The Marquis de Chastellux, when he visited Monticello in April 1782, remarked in his *Travels in North America* on his host's impressive "mind and attainments" and described him for his European readers as "an American, who, *without ever having quitted his own country*, is Musician, Draftsman, Surveyor, Astronomer, Natural Philosopher, Jurist, and Statesman." (Italics added.) The attainments that so impressed the sophisticated Frenchman, in a man who lived in the middle of nowhere and had never traveled abroad, were mostly earned or prepared for in his library.

Being recognized as an extraordinarily learned man was part of Jefferson's public character from the outset of his career. Before they were well acquainted, John Adams was attracted to him because he had been described by a friend as "the greatest rubber off of dust" he had ever known. Jefferson was constantly being consulted on matters relating to books and education and conscientiously made out dozens of reading lists at the requests of his friends. Not surprisingly, this reputation had its negative side as well. One of the things always said about him by his critics and political enemies was that he was an impractical theorist, the captive of mere book learning. Even those who

conceded his greatness could not resist this means of neutralizing his opinions, as in the case of Mathew Carey, who genuinely admired him but whose zealous promotion of native manufacturing seemed to require a denunciation of Jefferson's agrarianism, outlined so memorably in the *Notes on Virginia*. "His Arcadia," Carey wrote in *The New Olive Branch*, "must have been sought, not in Virginia or Maryland, but in Virgil's or Pope's pastorals, or Thomson's seasons." Unfair as this is to Jefferson's much-altered views on manufacturing subsequent to the *Notes*, there is a measure of truth in the charge that his vision of a society made up of "those who labor in the earth" owed much to his reading. Great learning has its vulnerabilities, and Jefferson was apparently content to accept them. "Emerson's idea that the reading of books warped or suffocated the scholar," Peterson says, "would have been incomprehensible to Jefferson."

Eventually, reading and study came to represent more than an occupational means and a recreational end. He had long believed that the state should provide public schools and libraries to insure an enlightened citizenry and preserve democracy. As he grew older and became more engrossed in the struggle for mutual toleration and rational self-government, he began to speak of learning as a political and even a moral responsibility. "Enlighten the people generally," he advised in a letter of 24 April 1816 to his friend P.-S. Du Pont de Nemours, "and tyranny and oppressions of body and mind will vanish like evil spirits at the dawn of day." This remark bears not only on the benefits that will accrue to the people but on the responsibilities of the learned. Near the end of his life, on 8 March 1824, he wrote that "The cultivation of science [that is, knowledge] is an act of religious duty to the Author of our being." By a similar progression, his early plan for a comprehensive library came eventually to have, as with so many Jeffersonian endeavors, an important public dimension, and at some point he determined that his collection should not remain "private property."

The need for a replacement for the congressional library in 1814 was thus a timely opportunity for Thomas Jefferson to place his splendid collection at the disposal of the public. The second Monticello library, as we have seen, was sold at auction three years after his death. These books are now in public and private libraries, including the Library of Congress, which purchased some items at the dispersal sale and has added others since. The Poplar Forest library, containing the petit-format collection, remained the property of Jefferson's grandson, Francis Eppes, until 1873, when it was advertised to be sold at auction. A substantial number of these volumes have found their way to another library originally chosen by Thomas Jefferson, that of the University of Virginia, which has, for example, his set of Bell's petit-format edition of the English poets.

The six thousand and seven hundred books that went to Washington in 1815 became the Library of Congress, and as such were subjected to the rigors of regular use. Some were lent out and lost, while others were repaired or rebound in such a way as to obliterate their provenance. But most devastating was a fire in the Capitol on Christmas Eve 1851 that destroyed nearly two-thirds of the original Jefferson volumes. Not until the twentieth century were the surviving books assembled and set apart as a special collection within the library. When E. Millicent Sowerby was retained in the 1940s to compile a catalog of the books Jefferson had sold to Congress, she was able to identify some additional books still in the stacks as having been part of the original purchase. Her *Catalogue of the Library of Thomas Jefferson,* an invaluable work in five large volumes, contains bibliographical information on the works known or believed to be in Jefferson's library when it came to Congress, as well as extracts on books and authors from his letters and other writings. An unfortunate limitation of this catalog is that, in being restricted to the great library, it does not include the multitude of volumes in the retirement library—either the second Monticello library or the Poplar Forest collection—nor does it take into account the many other books known to have been in his possession.

Of all the treasures in the Library of Congress, perhaps none is more highly prized than the 2,465 surviving volumes from the library of Thomas Jefferson. They are kept together under controlled atmospheric conditions in the Rare Book and Special Collections Division, where they are frequently called for and examined by scholars. Many have been rebound and bear the marks of prolonged use, though others are still in their original bindings and are in excellent condition. A few sections have survived in surprising completeness, such as the chapters on religion and law, while others, such as the chapters on literature, are almost entirely absent. Some volumes still display the bookplate or signature of distinguished previous owners: William Byrd II, Peyton Randolph, Richard Bland, and George Wythe. A few have "Ex Libris Thomæ Jefferson" inscribed in his hand on the title page, which seems to represent an early practice, but most carry merely the tiny, unobtrusive initials that Jefferson settled on as his private book mark.

In one sense, it might be said that Jefferson's library is now only a cherished remnant, a priceless portion of a once-great collection. But it seems truer to say that during the nearly two centuries it has belonged to the nation, Jefferson's library has grown prodigiously in size and in stature until it has become a great national library, one of the finest and most accessible in the world. Just as its richly ornamented main building on Capitol Hill now bears his name, so the Library of Congress, in collecting and preserving materials on every subject from every part of the world for the use and benefit of all, faithfully perpetuates the spirit and ideals of Thomas Jefferson.

Man of Letters

ROBERT DAWIDOFF

THE American colonies at the time of the Revolution were a little like a bright but unlettered prince, an Alexander, perhaps, who needed tutors to help him realize his prospects. The colonies were lucky in their tutors. Among them Thomas Jefferson, more than anyone, gave us our national words, translated into sentences the sentiments we have chosen to be guided by. It is of interest, therefore, to think about Jefferson in terms of his preferred medium, the written word. What kind of writer was he? How may we consider him as a man of letters?

We would do well to begin at Monticello. Few men ever get to make their immediate worlds over as much to their liking as Jefferson did in Albemarle. If he had a tremendous effect on the big world of America, the smaller stage of Monticello concentrated his notions in actualities small enough to compass.

Two scenes in particular at Monticello concern Jefferson's writing. The spare obelisk rising plainly down the road from the house in the family burying ground memori-alizes the "Author of the Declaration of American Independance / of the Statute of Virginia for religious freedom / & Father of the University of Virginia." It is as an author that Jefferson chose to be remembered. The modesty of his statement that the Declaration was an expression of the American mind was also his ambitious claim on an audience of the American future. Jefferson figured that Americans would be reading some of what he wrote always. The suspicion arises that he wanted them, while they were at it, to read the Statute for Religious Freedom, which specifies more controversially what the Declaration advances in general terms on the wave of a people's angry fervor. He also commended to the care of his audience his university, which might just institutionalize the impulses, perpetuate the ideals, and train the sorts of public men Jefferson valued. Knowing how connected his future glory and his authorship would be, Jefferson enjoined American posterity to a canon of his writings on his memorial stone.

Certainly few writers have ever achieved what Jefferson enjoyed—a permanent national audience. If Jefferson fancied himself a sometime-recorder of American sentiments, what writer would not envy him that post since, in recording it, Jefferson suffered no alienation from the American mind. He expressed in the highest terms the eighteenth-century Enlightened version of the wisdom of the ages, sentiments sealed in blood and a constitution, words acted upon as writers only dream of. In a country where the best writers have tended to be alienated, unappreciated, ambivalent, at odds with the national audience or sentimentalized to the point of eclipse, there is something lasting and potent in the thought of an American author who has had Jefferson's originating rapport with the nation.

The second setting at Monticello that frames Jefferson as a man of letters is his study. In a house of elegant and convenient arrangement—where the social and individual requirements and amenities, the soft and keen edges of our natures are so attended to —no room is more attentively outfitted with comfort and contrivance than Jefferson's own, his study, writing area, library, the open heart of his private world. The instruments of his reflection—books, telescope, measuring devices, the light-giving windows out from which he might look, even his bed of rest—all center on his chair, candles in the arms, couch under his long legs, desk drawn up over, with his writing materials and his own copying machine as the focus of his labors. As his study reminds us, there was something Jefferson wrote for almost everything he did.

His writing was so much an aspect of his doing that the two did not really form separate activities at all. It is extraordinary how much of what we know about Jefferson we know from his own hand, his records, his books, his letters, and his notes. He was writing all the time; the scratch and dip of his quill punctuated his life as surely as his breathing or the natural changes he so deliberately noted. He started writing early and stopped only a few days before he died;

when he broke his right wrist, he wrote with his left hand.

In Monticello Jefferson wrote, near the Blue Ridge and ringed by the countryside he loved, surrounded by neighbors, the focus of a literate, liberty-loving world, a university founded near to hand, his plantations, his orchards, his family, his slaves, his busy and useful life, at its center, in the core of his private rooms, where he observed, read, slept, reflected. Somewhere between the famous, powerful words Jefferson wrote and the ceaseless work of writing things down that consumed so much of his time—he seems to have been one of those men for whom writing is the act of thinking—lies Jefferson's career as a writer. The public face and the private activity bound a life devoted to what are properly called *letters.*

The nineteenth century had a phrase, *man of letters,* for which we have two words, *writer* and *intellectual.* The man of letters was called to his vocation in a dignified way; it was a potentially heroic life in writing. Emerson was a man of letters in this sense, and Jefferson was not. The man of letters did his work in the world self-consciously in his writings. Jefferson acknowledged the world of literature, even writing a technical work on English prosody, but the notion of a career in that line would never have occurred to him. Unlike Franklin, he never thought of himself as a literary artisan. More to the point, however much Jefferson cared for literature, he did not take the nineteenth-century view of its heroic possibilities.

Jefferson admitted of an alternative to the gentleman's civic obligations to the state, one that might raise the tone of life and advance the cause of humanity. This vocation was philosophic, by which Jefferson meant what we call *scientific.* He wrote to David Rittenhouse on 19 July 1778 stipulating "an order of geniusses" above the obligation of public service "& therefore exempted from it. No body can conceive that nature ever intended to throw away a Newton upon the occupations of a crown." Accepting his own responsibility for public service, Jefferson exempted the scientific genius as those in the nineteenth century might the literary genius from some of the rules of ordinary life. However much Jefferson valued the literary genius, it never occupied the central position for him that it did for the nineteenth-century man of letters. He did not see genius in this sphere as connected to its own higher calling and fashioned no role for such. He believed in the sufficiency of politics guided by reason and natural philosophy to lead public life. He stuck to the available understanding that provided for belles lettres within the cultivated life of the civilized, an essentially private role.

A twentieth-century view of the writer would suit Jefferson even less. The ideal of the engaged intellectual as a willing and venturesome participant in public life might in some ways be said to resemble Jeffersonian views of the public responsibility of the educated. But the self-consciousness and ideological cast of the modern intellectual writer, his sense of alienation, his frank ideological task, his adversarial relation to the culture, would have distressed Jefferson. The human type is closer to the sort of newspaperman Jefferson was known to use but hardly to be like. Jefferson did not think of writing as the focus of a career.

Writing was part of the seamless web of concentration and communication, with self, Creator, Nature, the particular worlds that defined life, extending principally to the worlds of family and friends, the enlightened republic of science the world over and in the service of the *patria*. Although Jefferson launched communications in many ways and to various audiences, his only book, *Notes on the State of Virginia*, was composed initially in response to a philosophe's questions as an act of scientific collegiality. The text some scholars would have us read as his autobiography is specifically addressed, as is his long essay on prosody. Jefferson could even address posterity as if directly without the intermediary of a writer's role. Much

that Jefferson did in writing we have parceled out to the spheres of separate activity with which people now tend to concern themselves.

Thomas Jefferson believed that knowledge was power. Echoing through almost every sentence he wrote is the validating confidence that this notion brings to communication of almost every sort. How hard it is to find a Jeffersonian text that does not get down to this truth. His writings are characteristically about knowledge; whether of books, crops, architecture, conversations, weather, discoveries, or explorations, the yield is knowledge. Nor did Jefferson let things be. He actively reduced life to knowledge, considered according to the Enlightened rules of reason.

The Puritans had believed that the signifying Fall of Adam branded the human brain incomplete. Knowledge required faith and grace. Human reason could not fathom the workings of creation unaided. For the likes of Jonathan Edwards, logic and natural philosophy were tools that spanned the awkward, tragic chasm between man's capacity and God's omniscience. Jefferson did not believe this. However much, as a wise and experienced man for whom life did not always go well, Jefferson understood that the human condition required character and endurance, he did not seem to have doubted the capacity of the human mind, using reason, to understand the order of the world. However much he resorted to the ancient creeds of endurance, he never substituted something else for the knowledge a man might gain.

JEFFERSON'S LITERARY VIEWS

Jefferson's tastes in literature reflected the conventional wisdom of his class and time. There are writer-readers for whom poetry, novels, and drama are the preferred stuff of life. It could not be said that Jefferson was one of these. No philistine, he was an enthusiastic and happy instance of the conventional literary taste of his day, possessing a regard for the classical authors, an inclination for the traditional and popular English writers, and a certain delight in the poses of sentimental literature. He held rationalist views of literature that stopped considerably short of the poetic notion that it might be its own means to its own end. For Jefferson, *sweet and useful* and limited were the uses of literature.

At twenty-eight, Jefferson designed for Robert Skipwith a gentleman's library—a task he was often called upon to perform. Although written with a certitude and at times copy-book attitudinizing that betrays the youthful Jefferson, it tells much that would remain characteristic of his literary tastes. The 1771 list includes Pope, Milton, Steele, Richardson, Chaucer, and Rousseau. The accompanying letter anticipates a demurral at the deal of fiction present: "A little attention however to the nature of the human mind evinces that the entertainments of fiction are useful as well as pleasant." The pleasure, Jefferson expects, is in the things being well written. The use? "I answer, everything is useful which contributes to fix us in the principles and practices of virtue."

Jefferson then propounds a version of the familiar moralistic criticism of the day:

> When any signal act of charity or of gratitude, for instance, is presented either to our sight or imagination, we are deeply impressed with its beauty and feel a strong desire in ourselves of doing charitable and grateful acts also. On the contrary when we see or read of any atrocious deed, we are disgusted with it's deformity, and conceive an abhorrence of vice.

Jefferson says that fiction appears like truth to the mind under the sway of its style and is to be preferred to history "as a moral exercise." History may be philosophy teaching by examples, but it is less likely to afford the sympathetic instances of virtue that fiction can.

In time, early attitudinizing relaxed into comfortable cultivation. Jefferson became an immensely well-read and belletristically cultivated man whose own elegant, graceful writing bore the happy stamp of his reading. *Knowledge is power, dulce et utile,* mottoes of his life, urged Jefferson to take a moralist's view of literature.

On 25 February 1773, Jefferson wrote to Charles McPherson, whose acquaintance he had made in Virginia, about his relation James Macpherson, the collector or perpetrator of the verse of Ossian:

> These pieces have been, and will I think during my life continue to be to me, the source of daily and exalted pleasures. The tender, and the sublime emotions of the mind were never before so finely wrought up by human hand. I am not ashamed to own that I think this rude bard of the North the greatest Poet that has ever existed.

He goes on to profess his desire to learn the Celt language in which Ossian was purported to have sung and to request an original copy of the poems, printed or copied out: "I should not regard expence in doing this." He wants the books necessary to study the language and advances an opinion or two. Jefferson continued to love Ossian, chanting him aloud over punch with the Marquis de Chastellux, during that fellow enthusiast's visit at Monticello in April 1782, and in 1785 describing the gloom of Paris after the departure of Adams as fitting "the dark and narrow house of Ossian." Ossian's rough and gloomy moods suited Jefferson's own occasional and robust glooms. Something in the Celtic bard appealed to Jefferson. He shared a conventional literary enthusiasm; the fraud deceived almost everyone. His taste for Ossian expressed certain of his moods and feelings, bound certain intimacies of shared tastes, and called to mind descriptive phrases. Calling Ossian "sublime" and admitting him into one's life in this way was reacting to him on cue.

The second aspect of Jefferson's reading of Ossian was equally characteristic. If his taste was perhaps subsumed by that of his age, his intense investigations were not. Jefferson, loving Ossian, must have the originals, must learn the language, must acquire the knowledge, the use of it. Here stands Jefferson's true aesthetic: the sublime emotion must be banked with knowledge; *knowledge is power.* Ossian's appeal to Jefferson, for whom, as for many Anglo-Americans of his sort, the Saxon past had considerable resonance in their disputes with Mother "modern" England, was also political and cultural assertion. The myth of the ancient Saxons formed a part of the foundation for the Rights of Englishmen that preceded the Rights of Man in colonial thinking. Jefferson's interest in Anglo-Saxon persisted, and his philological prescriptions found a home in his university. His passion for Ossian and for the ancient English languages expressed his provincial attachment to English culture, which was to prove harder to transform than the political attachment because, unlike the constitution, about which there were binding, empowered authorities, it might remain in the eye of the beholder and, unlike the imperial system, it seemed to serve his purposes quite well enough.

In 1786, Jefferson addressed himself to literature in his informal treatise, *Thoughts on Prosody,* which he addressed to Chastellux. It arose out of a dispute with the Frenchman over whether English verse "depended, like Greek and Latin verse, on long and short syllables arranged in regular feet," which Chastellux denied. Jefferson concluded in time that his friend was right.

To the student of Jefferson's political writings of the time, the *Thoughts* sound an echo. Jefferson here takes the authoritative view of true English culture that had become impos-sible in the constitutional struggle of the previous decade. The legalism of poetic feet, the units of the poetic line, is like the proper construction of constitutional legalism.

We may perhaps discern here the often forgotten price that the colonists paid for their independence. As provincials, they had an exaggerated interest, an unrelaxed correctness about English things. Politics forced Jefferson to transcend this and he, like his colleagues, rose immortally to that challenge. Culturally, for all the founders, the Englishness that had been their standard was harder to forgo. The Americans yet remained an English literary people. English prosody remained Jefferson's as certainly as the English constitution no longer did.

Certainly Jefferson was intellectually English. Francis Bacon, Sir Isaac Newton, and John Locke formed his trinity. His relation to English literature was crucial to his status as a man of letters because he never professed a knowledge of French literature as he did French philosophy and some French tastes. English stayed his language, and English literature, having educated him, nurtured him yet awhile. The *Thoughts* suggest that he reclaimed the literary heritage for Americans in something of the way *A Summary View of the Rights of British America* tried to reclaim English constitutionalism.

Considered from this point of view, then, the *Thoughts* is a somewhat more interesting work than has been previously believed. It essentially proposes a revision of Dr. Johnson's prosody, substituting accent for Johnson's quantity, altering somewhat the reliance on what Jefferson calls "the doubtfulness, if not the error" on which Johnson's system was founded, namely its relation to classical poetry. Jefferson characteristically proposes improvements in prosody that in effect make it possible for an American gentleman to claim equal authority with respect to the English literary tradition.

Jefferson, the autodidact, approaches the

technical questions with the same methodological confidence (perhaps overconfidence) that distinguishes his interest in every field. It is an impressive but unedifying display because for all his ancient and English learning, his exposition of the subject is not gripping. His *Thoughts* cannot rival Johnson because they do not connect to anything in poetry that goes beyond conventional and external aspects of form.

At the end, Jefferson gives a clue to his own taste and views, in preferring blank verse to rhymed:

> If we continue to read rhymed verse at a later period of life it is such only where the poet has had force enough to bring great beauties of thought and diction into this form. . . . But as we advance in life these things fall off one by one, and I suspect we are left at last with only Homer and Virgil, perhaps with Homer alone.

Jefferson's concluding anthology of examples of mixed length of line in English verse gives an extended view of some of the poetic sentiments he prized. From Gray, Shenstone, and Collins he calls the beautiful, clean statements of sensibility and the sublime that show how familiar he was with the moralizing poetical stance toward ultimate questions of the English poetry of that age.

Sentiment added to sound made sense to Jefferson. So far it was the conventional English taste of the Age of Sensibility, a good taste no doubt. It prized sentiment, tender and plaintive; sensibility; a susceptibility to the claims and beauties of Nature; and the independence of the gentleman of high purpose from the "clamors fierce and loud" of "the angry crowd." These tastes show Jefferson as a more conventional, characteristic man of his class and breeding than do his philosophical or political ones. Poetry, for reading people of his sort, was meant to provide an acceptable language of feeling, to describe how a person might be feeling about certain experiences; it was formal and intimate, public and private, all at the same time. Thus its morality was central to its purposes. Quoting poetry, Jefferson would be drawing on its expressions either to authenticate philosophical and moral views already held or to help him respond in situations for which no private or other public language of feeling existed.

The English poetry Jefferson liked suited the salad days of his fervency. In time, his precocious expectation of confining himself to Homer came essentially true. His espousal of a Greek philosophy of the personal life, his Epicurean conviction, seems to have suited him more than the poetry of his youth. He did not lose his taste for it as much as his sense of the use of it, a fatal loss to Jefferson, *dulce* without *utile*.

THE NOTES ON VIRGINIA

Jefferson's only book, *Notes on the State of Virginia,* presents his character as a man of letters directly. It was written in response to the inquiries of François de Barbé-Marbois, secretary of the French legation for information, and presented itself as an act of high diplomatic and Enlightened communication. Written to inform, the *Notes* got published in a hesitating, awkward, but deliberate way. Whatever the intention that attended its composition, it bears the Jeffersonian trademark: all his writings were composed situationally.

The *Notes* themselves make an intriguing book. It is sometimes argued, sometimes plausibly, that they make a concerted argument, and perhaps they do. They do make sense on the level on which they present themselves—as scientific responses to the queries of "a Foreigner of Distinction, then residing among us." The questions bind the *Notes* and appear to give direction to a story that is really the drama of the author's own investigations of Virginia. Jefferson is the person to whom the queries about Virginia happened to be addressed. His answering them authenticates him as a Virginian, a patriot, a gentleman, a scientist, a traveler, and a man of the world. Jefferson reveals who he is by casting his delicate shadow on what he knows.

Query VI shows Jefferson's method in the *Notes.* "A notice of the mines and other subterranean riches; its trees, plants, fruits, etc." may appear dry, but it recapitulates the history of Virginia in fact and in fancy as a kind of *el dorado* or hell. Virginia was an early archetype of the New World, a focus for that vaunted European ambivalence about its own expansion. Virginia was a land of riches, a country of desolation, the scene of human growth, a habitat where the species degenerated, the home of freedom and the home of slavery. Jefferson in Query VI establishes the natural riches of Virginia with an eye to the lavish tradition of description that had prevailed, and his descriptions are moderate in tone, full of specifics, scientific dispute as if to establish Virginia as a country for fact, a subject at last freed for serious discussion and estimation; he concludes the query with his famous defense of American nature against the aspersions cast by Count Buffon, ending in a spirited brief in behalf of American civilization.

The way Jefferson writes his natural history is curious. Discussions of copper and iron mines, the discovery of an emerald, the species and riches of nature that he notes give way to spirited treatments of Voltaire on the evidence for shell remains of the Great Flood ("Ignorance is preferable to error; and he is less remote from the truth who believes nothing, than he who believes what is wrong"), to intense argument with Buffon, to classification, to patriotic paean. The modern reader is struck with the differences among these subjects. Jefferson's even tone and consistent attitude throughout the turns of his argument show that he was not.

Essentially three things seal Jefferson's argument. His true subject, Virginia, binds information, discovery, advocacy, defense, and celebration all together. Virginia is related to all kinds of information. Second, the republic of science, whose scattered membership constitutes one of Jefferson's principal audiences, requires that Jefferson take up a certain attitude as well as collect data. What we may consider straying is, in this context, not straying at all. Jefferson regards all his information with an Enlightened scientific eye and need not, by the canons he accepts, distinguish, even where we might. Third and most important, he uses himself as the eye through which all is seen and argued. Abundant information, the degree to which Jefferson's interests and information and the very world coincide, and the relative uninsistence of his personal presence may blind us, but if you look at how he establishes credibility, you will find Jefferson himself.

Query VI not only presents an objective answer to a question, but it is also Jeffersonian rumination, an occasion for Jefferson to collect information, sift hearsay, judge theories, visit mines, question authorities, redraw maps, classify species, and examine seashells. Considered as a performance, it is extraordinarily confident and versatile. He commences, "I knew a single instance of gold found in this State" and recounts his own observations, and the reader feels reported to, answered, addressed, and informed. Here and there, Jefferson employs the second person to enforce this effect. But Virginia's plentitude is no fairy tale—the Virginian who tells it to us speaks our language. Franklin played the noble savage, rube *savant.* Jefferson assumes the guise of the philosophe representing his native country at the court of the republic of science.

At stake in Jefferson's works, are visions of real things, a university, a natural aristocracy in the disinterested service of a people, a rational system of weights and measures. The Jeffersonian imagination envisioned, made up the possible, the desirable, the hopeful, set in a pervasive future that might invade the present and that surely colored the past. Reading Jefferson one is reading stories about the way life in America should be, stories in which the vast learning and wide reading and experience expressed in the advanced scientific language of the day seem to furnish such a future. His information grounds and releases a vision of the possible, infuriatingly frustrating to his interlocutors in practical measures but everlastingly liberating to his readers. The *Notes* abound in this special sort of Jeffersonian vision, his way of reading the scientific tea leaves and picturing the future. In the book Virginia becomes a scientifically delineated and republican paradise, the right setting for the free government Jefferson has in mind.

Jefferson's account of agrarian virtue in the query on manufactures in the *Notes* remains a quintessential Jeffersonian expression, plausible, fantastic, not exactly arguable, irresistible to Americans in one form or another down the years:

> Those who labour in the earth are the chosen people of God, if ever he had a chosen people, whose breasts he has made his peculiar deposit for substantial and genuine virtue. It is the focus in which he keeps alive that sacred fire, which otherwise might escape from the face of the earth. Corruption of morals in the mass of cultivators is a phenomenon of which no age nor nation has furnished an example. It is the mark set on those, who not looking up to heaven, to their own soil and industry, as does the husbandman, for their subsistance, depend for it on casualties and caprice of customers. Dependance begets subservience and venality, suffocates the germ of virtue, and prepares fit tools for the designs of ambition.

It is generally the case that when Jefferson brings God or the Creator into things that he is about to soar above the plane of natural philosophy as scientifically demonstrated and means to venture into a discussion of the self-evident.

This attractive setting, the Jeffersonian version of the middle landscape—English in its celebration of a kind of order and independence, American in setting and in its political hopes—resembles something of what makes people still partial to the idea of the family farm, the still-hallowed connection between the health of the American regime and the grounding of it in the independent cultivators of the soil. Here he develops a view of the people whom God would have chosen but whom the republic chooses instead.

The vision is a pastoral, an idealized farmer-citizen in an idealized landscape-republic. Everything you can possibly know about Virginia leads you to this man, Jefferson claims. Unlike his cofounders, he sensed the requirement for views that might guide a future hopefully. That husbandman of Jefferson's is probably not a particularly accurate version of the Virginian poor farmer of the late-eighteenth century, who probably depended on a deferential hierarchical order to stay in check and who was more likely to be the chosen person of the Christian God than the Lockean one. Still, at a crucial moment of his argument, Jefferson imagined such a fellow in an old-new fashion, a traditional sturdy yeoman, English and classical, native to Virginia and to the republic.

Jefferson's attractive pastoralizing of the farmers was not decorative. In his book and as a practical matter it was a didactic fantasy, meant to instill in that necessary class the kinds of virtues and habits and self-image that such citizens must have if the republic is to survive. As almost always in the Jeffersonian fiction, there is a tough-minded core, the realization that the desired goal may require a transformation of present conditions. Jeffersonian writing characteristically attempts that transformation.

The true enemy of the agrarian republic

was slavery; the reality of Jefferson's countryside was the slave society with its aristocrats, its perversions of community, and its proliferating dance of dependency. Jefferson's sections on slavery in the *Notes* tend to concentrate on the damage the institution does to those habits of independence and virtue that a republic must cultivate in her citizens. The slavery section also presents very clearly a natural aristocracy that would replace the habituated ruling class; and we see, as perhaps John Adams could not, how necessary to Jefferson was his hope of a meritocracy. Adams saw in New England, enfranchised about him, a respectable if imperfect oligarchy and citizenry. Jefferson loathed the privileged in his own class, as they affronted with their exercise of privilege his belief that power must be the reward for the modern, the virtuous, the hard working, the best.

Slavery, like so many other situations in Virginia, made Jefferson a visionary. The best country in the world seemed to him in the grip of a backward, superstitious, and detrimental social system that might well prove its undoing. Jefferson was not much in advance of his class or country in racial views. He opposed slavery and tried to give the Afro-American his due, but he did not envision a multiracial paradise. Instead, he imagined a terrible retributive revolution. The slave rebellion is a negative variety of the healthy letting of the blood of tyrants. It poses the peculiarly Jeffersonian problem that leads to the equally peculiar Jeffersonian fiction. On the one hand, Jefferson opposed slavery and tyranny, believing firmly in the right of the oppressed to rebel, stating that it was a healthy social process. On the other, seeing the imminence of such a war of black slaves against white masters, his own people, he recoiled in horror, a horror that had its fair share of straightforward slavemaster feelings too. Jefferson could not bring himself beyond the point of pious hope that slavery would be ended, that

slaves would be colonized. He wanted slaves and blacks out of Virginia, as in his picture of the idealized agrarian republic.

Having failed to figure out this toughest issue and having failed to transcend his personal stake in the institution and its attitudes (as did almost everyone else fail, it must be said), Jefferson did two things. He propounded an interesting series of arguments against slavery, hoping to tie the future of the republic to its extinction, most famously in the Declaration but in the *Notes* also. The equality and freedom of all mankind is a principle worth keeping as a standard even if one does not quite know how to implement it at any given time. He also glimpsed horror, revolution, and race war, and his memorable images for the slavery situation —holding a wolf by the ears, the fire bell in the night—catch his true sense of things.

In the *Notes,* he "trembles" when he remembers that God is just. Now Jefferson did not often have occasion to recall this just and wrathful God; men were just and life was susceptible of improvement. Slavery, however, created a political and moral problem for Jefferson that only this grim reaper of a God could address and then only on the familiar Jeffersonian plane of imagination— one of the few appearances of this old deity in Jefferson's work, a memorable one. The contradiction Jefferson resolved in a rather extreme and intense imagining—the avenging God, the images of trouble and bloodshed, and a rending civil conflict—came true. If Jefferson was unable to think and act his way clearly through the thicket of slavery, he also uniquely provided the metaphors for the ultimate solutions to his conundrums. It is a hard mystery of Jefferson's, but it is a clue to his literary interest in that his images predicted what his thinking could not resolve.

There is a moment in the *Notes* when we see Jefferson in the similar grip of an attitudinal pull, one that touches as directly on his literary and perhaps his personal feelings as do his confusions about slavery generate his political imagination. If there was a consistent passion in Jefferson's life, it was Nature. Every day Jefferson noted weather, growth, and species, reassuring himself that life on earth was of a connection, if not of a piece.

The *Notes* reflect his characteristic preoccupation with natural phenomena and his fortunate possession of a faith in the advanced scientific and poetic language of the time to describe what he saw. For in his observations of nature Jefferson's different discourses coincided. The natural setting was at once something to be measured, described precisely, and placed and wondered at in the language of sensibility and the sublime. This was more than a pose—this was the two-pronged possibility of understanding offered to Jefferson by the rational language of the time, for the sublime was the rational language of feeling, a way of expressing without faith what scenes of nature did to the observer's insides, what they made him feel, and it was learned from poetry.

And so it is immensely interesting to discover in the *Notes* a passage where this conjunction seems to fall short of resolution. The scene is the Natural Bridge, a natural wonder in Virginia especially dear to Jefferson, not only as an example of the sublime works of Nature but also because it was on his own land. The passage occurs in Query V on Virginian cascades and caverns:

> The *Natural bridge,* the most sublime of Nature's works, though not comprehended under the present head, must not be pretermitted. It is on the ascent of a hill, which seems to have been cloven through its length by some great convulsion. The fissure, just at the bridge, is, by some admeasurements, 270 feet deep, by others only 205. It is about 45 feet wide at the bottom, and 90 feet at the top; this of course determines the length of the bridge, and its height from the water. Its breadth in the middle, is about 60 feet, but more at the ends, and the thickness of the mass at the summit of the arch, about 40 feet. A part of this thickness is constituted by a coat of earth, which gives growth to many large trees. The residue, with the hill on both sides, is one solid rock of lime-stone. The arch approaches the Semi-elliptical form; but the larger axis of the ellipsis, which would be the cord of the arch, is many times longer than the transverse. Though the sides of this bridge are provided in some parts with a parapet of fixed rocks, yet few men have resolution to walk to them and look over into the abyss. You involuntarily fall on your hands and feet, creep to the parapet and peep over it. Looking down from this height about a minute, gave me a violent head ach. If the view from the top be painful and intolerable, that from below is delightful in an equal extreme. It is impossible for the emotions arising from the sublime, to be felt beyond what they are here: so beautiful an arch, so elevated, so light, and springing as it were up to heaven, the rapture of the spectator is really indescribable! The fissure continuing narrow, deep, and streight for a considerable distance above and below the bridge, opens a short but very pleasing view of the North mountain on one side, and Blue ridge on the other, at the distance each of them of about five miles. This bridge is in the county of Rock bridge, to which it has given name, and affords a public and commodious passage over a valley, which cannot be crossed elsewhere for a considerable distance. The stream passing under it is called Cedar creek. It is a water of James river, and sufficient in the driest seasons to turn a grist-mill, though its fountain is not more than two miles above.

We accompany Jefferson on his walk at the bridge, his muted presence authenticating our visit and his precise language of surveying the scientific sublime describing it for us. This is how Jefferson meant to learn from Lewis and Clark, indeed, how he collected much of the information for the *Notes,* the very point of his own painstaking recording of his observations. The universal language of measurement, the shared assumptions of natural philosophy, and the collegiality of the cosmopolitan Enlightenment are combined in his method.

Jefferson approaches the bridge, and his language shifts abruptly to describe not the natural wonder but the human experience of it, easing, with a sudden use of the second person, into an easily rendered, conventional statement of the sublime, employing the language of poetic emotion to express human feelings in the way that measurement expresses human knowledge. Jefferson handles each well. He resumes the language of measurement as he returns from the bridge to its setting, as it recedes into the countryside, across a commodious public road. The passage is a satisfying example of two linked kinds of descriptive writing merging to create a vivid impression of a distant wonder.

And yet there is something amiss. In between the scientific and poetic, there comes another tone. Jefferson is on top of the bridge and looks over into the abyss and has an episode of dizziness, agoraphobia, passion, falling "involuntarily" to his knees, feeling in a "violent" headache the unsettling power of the natural. The "painful and intolerable" view is what for the nineteenth century (and perhaps earlier) engendered the sublime. The terror of the world has more to do with it than the airy grace of a natural arch. The sublime was meant to express with awe and terror a human understanding of the world beyond the resource of ordinary language. It was not just another way of being precise about something. It challenged the descriptive power of language with experiences that seemed to transcend comprehension even as they tyrannized conscious feeling.

The picturesque might be a more domesticated emotion. Jefferson has his indescribable rapture with his feet firmly planted on the ground. Struck down—dizzied by the simple physical force of the natural world, his headache the image of his experience—conventional language did not serve. He has to hold on too fast for dear life to attitudi-

nize or record. This is the experience of the natural that prompted the nineteenth century, as exemplified by the Romantics and Emerson, to doubt the finality of that scientific-literary grasp of the world that Jefferson stuck by. They made changes in language to express the doubt, expanding the range of the literary first person from Jefferson's careful observer to include and emphasize the rapturous self of his headache. The tension between the rational and the emotional that this passage shows became the basis for the age to follow. As the issue of slavery also suggests, the Jeffersonian literary stance, powerful though it was in its own terms, could not go beyond its conventions, even when his own experiences seemed to impel it and despite the fact that his writing reveals clearly the images of his distress.

THE HEAD AND THE HEART

On 12 October 1786, Jefferson wrote a letter to Maria Cosway, who with her husband had just left Paris and Jefferson's company. Whatever the exact nature of their relationship, it was of a sentimental, passionate, and intense sort, and Jefferson felt her departure very keenly. In his letter, Jefferson presents to Mrs. Cosway a "dialogue" between "my Head & my Heart" as he confronts his feelings about her, "seated by my fireside, solitary and sad." The letter has been prized for its own sake and for its presumed rare insight into Jefferson's private emotions. It is an engaging instance of Jeffersonian authorship, and although it does not catch him *in flagrante*, it does catch him in the act of writing literature.

Jefferson casts his letter in the form of a conceit, the dialogue of the head and the heart being a familiar convention founded on contemporary moral psychology, an accepted metaphor for the contrary pull of human passion and human reason. The conceit pays Mrs. Cosway the compliment of

Jefferson's desolation after losing the company of husband and wife following their recent spate of high times; it also conveys a deeper emotion of Jefferson's about Mrs. Cosway and safely explores his own feelings for her delectation. All of this is carried off in the high convention of the conceit, presumably extending the mood of gallantry and deliberate charade that must have masked some of their feelings during their frequent personal encounters.

The first mood of the dialogue is playful and ironic, a light rendering of the stance of sensibility's formulae of wretchedness. Jefferson's Heart is inclined to be sad but initially expresses itself in the conventional language of sensibility, drawn out by Jefferson with some irony. Thus, in answer to the Head's gruff observation that "you seem to be in a pretty trim," the Heart rends his claim: "I am indeed the most wretched of all earthly beings. Overwhelmed with grief, every fibre of my frame distended beyond its natural powers to bear, I would willingly meet whatever catastrophe should leave me no more to feel or to fear."

The Heart rants and in exaggerated grief flatters the absent Maria Cosway, laying these emotions safely at her door. The Head in turn provokes the Heart in a send-up of prudence and philosophical coolness toward passion. Together they tell the history of the affair. Jefferson had been busy with his country's business and his own, busy with friendship and philosophy, chastened by his own life to avoid the forming of new attachments that would be dangerous to his hard-won tranquillity. Jefferson describes himself as happy enough and no stranger to loss, properly self-protective. The Head blames the Heart for once again exposing them both to the havoc of feeling, the tribulations of loss. The Head and Heart, in playing philosophical charades, speaking a double language of flirtation, also express Jefferson's feelings about his attachment after it has already upset his peace of mind. The Head

tends to look at things from Jefferson's point of view before meeting Mrs. Cosway; the Heart speaks of what life is like since Jefferson came to know her.

Jefferson's feelings run characteristically on American subjects. The Head quickly reminds the Heart that the Cosways belong to Europe; "perhaps you flatter yourself they may come to America?" The dialogue plunges into a discussion of America, its tone changing perceptibly from the elegant to the earnest. The Heart rhapsodizes about the subjects an artist would find to paint in Virginia. The familiar setting of the *Notes* becomes the scene of a romantic friendship. In his book Jefferson was solitary; now he is joined by Mrs. Cosway amid the picturesque glories of Virginia.

Jefferson shows how his feelings have indeed caught the mood of his literary tastes. He creates for himself and Mrs. Cosway a Virginian pastoral to which she repairs after a grief he is peculiarly placed to understand —he who has lost all. Jefferson's chief loss was that of his wife, who died in 1782. He disowns his desire, forbears a proposal, and utters a pious hope that no grief should come to the Cosways, which means in context that there is no reason for Mrs. Cosway to join him in Virginia. The Head forces the Heart to create a romantic fiction, which in essence obviates a liaison.

Although presented as adversaries, Jefferson's Head and Heart understand and complement one another pretty well. The Head commences a discussion of the false light in which America is seen from Europe as a way of saying that the Cosways will not visit unpersuaded. The Heart responds with a proud patriotic defense of American progress only to bring the Head back to the earlier case at hand, the pain of separation from the Cosways as it reflects on the Heart's conduct of life. The Head advances a view that the "art of life is the art of avoiding pain." It draws the lesson that to retire into self and duty is the prudent course; intellectual pleasures are presented as safe and a kind of sublimity is broached:

> Those, which depend on ourselves, are the only pleasures a wise man will count on: for nothing is ours which another may deprive us of. Hence the inestimable value of intellectual pleasures. Ever in our power, always leading us to something new, never cloying, we ride, serene & sublime, above the concerns of this mortal world, contemplating truth & nature, matter & motion, the laws which bind up their existence, and that eternal being who made & bound them up by these laws.

At the core of this letter, beneath the charming skein of its conceit—whatever Jefferson's real relations with Mrs. Cosway—we see that there is no serious way in which even his excited Heart can compete for Jefferson's attention with his Head.

The Jeffersonian view of literature is one that does not grant it centrality. Here we see literary sensibility at play, doing the work in a letter that such a sensibility was supposed to do in life. It is entrancing and sincere by turns, a charming letter and the makings of a most affecting and interesting little romance. Nothing in Jefferson is so intimate as his discrete, idyllic picture of himself with Maria Cosway in the Virginia of the *Notes.* But however much he was under the sway of his feelings and however powerful a moment he gave to his Heart, Jefferson once again showed the limits of his capacity to take literature seriously. Its fictions have not the interest and its poses are insufficiently expressive of what he valued in public and private life. This is not to denigrate his emotions but to suggest that the properly literary is not the key to Jefferson's ultimate interest as a man of letters, although it is refreshing to see his ease with the literary conceits and sensibility of the age. But the Head's statement about the pleasures that depend on ourselves does describe the life that Jefferson chose and that seemed to him sweet and useful, however inattentive it caused him to be to the promptings of his secret heart.

JEFFERSON THE WRITER

Jefferson wrote thousands of letters in a long lifetime of correspondence, and these letters constitute his chief literary remains. His varied work in the world, knowledge about it, and his interests in it shine through his somewhat formal, ever graceful, and fluid style of writing. Jefferson's voice changed and grew during his lifetime, and although it is as hard to describe as any American voice, it remains distinctly familiar.

The Jeffersonian voice is reticent and clear, elegant and graceful, easeful but not easy, generous of spirit, clear in expression, and enthusiastic, but it is governed always by the disciplines that founded his life. Jefferson was not a teacher, but he was didactic to the bone. It is rare to find a Jefferson letter that does not transmit some piece of news, but news is the news of Enlightenment, not the gossip of the Rialto. Jefferson assimilated himself into several worlds, and his correspondence with the citizens of those worlds transacts their business—the business of science, exploration, diplomacy, revolution, friendship, politics. In Jefferson's letters the presence of that world within which Jefferson and his correspondent are participants is always felt.

More than what they evoke, a kind of audience is sensed. It is a commonplace that Jefferson's generation performed, as it were, in the presence of posterity. Jefferson assimilated many such audiences in his life and letters. It is as if they kept him company. At Monticello he seems to have summoned up with ease the several worlds of his activity in letters. The rules of scientific discovery, the machinations and subtleties of politics, the duties of friendship and family life, and the delights of flirtation—all seem to take place within his remarkable sentences. Jefferson wrote well, sometimes with memorable felicity, but the most powerful impression of reading his letters is how meet to his purposes his sentences were.

Jefferson wrote an eighteenth-century prose—formal, balanced, reserved in expression, polite, aristocratic. It is not that he did not say what he meant, it is that what he meant seldom boiled down to the plainest speech. The eighteenth-century sentence had a purpose largely lost to the modern reader. It was meant not to cut through, but to include an ethos of enlightened communication; the hallmark of elegant style was not necessarily to find the shortest route to meaning. Each sentence Jefferson wrote was meant to span a variety of discourses and make it possible to speak of all subjects in the same language; specialization was meant to occur within the sentence, not in different kinds of sentences. The English sentence Jefferson wrote was an act of comprehension, launched for truth more than pleasure, although the latter was supposed to be founded in the former. For Jefferson, writing was not the subject itself of reflection, it was an instrument. Just as a house could not be beautiful unless it stood and fit certain architectural theories, so a sentence must do its duty and such beauty or elegance as it had must be founded in its use. *Dulce et utile* was the motto for his writing as for everything else.

The sweet and the useful conjoin in Jefferson's writing. Writing is the work, the act of man's highest attribute, his rational mind. The basic strengths of Jefferson's sentences, like his design, are their stability, clarity, elegance, and capacity to serve equally the shifting purposes of his letters. His several styles have different characteristics—he does not, as was said of Calhoun, begin a love poem with "whereas"—but they all depend on the same sentence, roomy enough to house all his interests, expressive enough

to suggest his many moods but withal a recognizably restrained, disciplined instrument of his ideas and the ideas of his century.

It has been said that Jefferson's use of the passive is a significant and troublesome characteristic of his writing. It is true that Jefferson's writing was not aggressive in the way that Franklin's or Adams' was. His writing was a fluid in which Jefferson floated notions. Grievance and philosophical hope both float in the tides of the Declaration. Expressing the American mind, as he said, it must not be too idiosyncratic. But although recognizable, Jefferson's prose is distinguished for what it permitted him to say; content is almost impossible to separate from style in his case.

The voice was not loud. Jefferson was not the character in his writing that Franklin was in his nor the person that Adams was in his diaries. Jefferson's sentences constructed an arena for rational philosophic action. They were a superb medium for Jefferson to present his ideas, his investigations, and they do not betray him more than occasionally as a subjective presence. Jefferson acted in his sentences, but his action was notoriously undirected. As we see Jefferson's intellectual vocabulary growing, we see him taking shape. We can see him getting used to new words and new ideas, getting used to the things he will have to communicate—measurements, events, experiments, places, people of all sorts, the jottings of the universal mind—getting used, that is, to his job in the world.

Jefferson's sentences had to be able to convey the most detailed scientific information, the moral home truths of a father instructing his family, the thoughts of a revolutionary, of a leader in and out of party and power, of a statesman and a friend. And Jefferson was never satisfied. There was always some new thing to categorize, some new notion to assimilate, some new audience to address and be aware of, some new sentiment to express, some new depth to sound. This is the key to Jefferson as a man of letters, his commitment on the practical level of his prose and his ability to express with equal clarity to the stunning variety of his correspondents the several aspects of what he remained convinced was a world comprehensible by human reason. His genius as a writer was that he fashioned an instrument of such flexibility that was also felicitous. Jefferson's prose also served humbler and stringent purposes; he could turn a homely phrase and concentrate into vivid metaphors complicated situations. Slavery prompted some of his most powerful metaphors, "holding a wolf by the ears," for instance. His prose welcomed all the bits and pieces that made up his intellectual breadth, the Greek phrases, the calculations and measurements, the descriptions, quotations, allusions, lists. Like the walls at Monticello, his prose set off with impassive hospitality the elegant and the practical, the fresco and the tusk.

Jefferson's style was like his mansion, and he shambled through its many rooms, host to the advanced, the civilized, the curious, and the morally circumspect. Jefferson's letters extend a kind of hospitality to the republic of Enlightened letters. He addressed the general principle in a letter written on 19 February 1809 to John Hollis, on the eve of his retirement from the presidency; the subject was the commerce among the scientific communities of nations:

> I mention these things, to show the nature of the correspondence which is carried on between societies instituted for the benevolent purpose of communicating to all parts of the world whatever useful is discovered in any one of them. These societies are always in peace, however their nations may be at war. Like the republic of letters, they form a great fraternity spreading over the whole earth, and their correspondence is never interrupted by any civilized nation.

It is characteristic that Jefferson would place a request for seeds in this context of universal cooperation. His prose was meant to erect in his writing the republic of America, the republic of friendship, the republic of letters, the republic of science. He writes as a citizen of the several republics, and the prose is fashioned as a means by which he can carry on his business.

The Jeffersonian voice carried conviction that human relations reach their highest expression through rational exchange. His reserve was probably founded in character, but it was also the reserve and even caution of a man who had more faith in the exchange of information according to natural philosophic rules—in the commerce of political sympathy, in the tendency toward the same ends, the reading of the same books—than in the direct encounter of personalities. He shied from the sort of fight that Adams loved and seldom wrote with the self-conscious comic flare that marked Franklin. It has been said that Jefferson had little sense of humor, but there is a lightness and sometimes an irony and a wit that refreshes Jefferson's writing. It must be admitted, however, that he was agreeable, even amiable rather than funny, and that the airiness and elegance of the lovelier moments in his writing are earnest and serious and have little of the special grace the sense of humor prefers to gracefulness.

Fortified by some acquaintance with Jefferson's life and times, one can read his writings with an enormous sense of discovery and delight. They offer pleasures intensely political and intellectual and only mildly personal. There are also frustrations. His mind seems to change, and the consistency of his particular views is hard to track. There clings to him yet a quality of elusiveness. It is always chastening to feel how little of his private self Jefferson felt a man need advance in order to advance the causes of freedom and enlightenment. There is also that annoying Jeffersonian utilitarianism; everything turns to account, all of life has lessons, duties, mottoes, and uses. The moral and the useful and the virtuous and the energetic and the studious and the wise sometimes spoil the fun. There are times when the reader longs for a sense of the romantic emotionalism of the nineteenth century or merely wonders whether the only proper reaction to the Old World is to resist its corruptions in the name of the New. Jefferson's prose sometimes seems to flow too freely, his facility to cause him to escape too effortlessly the confines that bedevil others.

It is possible reading Jefferson to share the frustration of those masters of the concrete and the consistent, Hamilton and Adams. Jefferson was so damnably blithe and sure. It is not difficult to imagine how irritating it must have been for Madison, so serious and so alert to argument and to the tug of the real and practical in thought and ideal, to hear even Jefferson's softened critique of his Constitution. One feels it all the time—Jefferson is too versatile, gifted with too optimistic a philosophic temper. Look at all he missed. And yet Madison could not resist him and neither can we. Jefferson flew higher than most of his peers. If he lacked the extraordinary grip on the political past of an Adams, on the political present of a Hamilton, on the political future of a Madison, who understood better than he what they were doing, from the writing of the Declaration on? It was Jefferson who gave voice in writing to the terms of American nationality. As Merrill D. Peterson has shown, one can read American history in the way Americans have read Jefferson.

Reading Jefferson should be preliminary to reading the American writers who came after him. To go from Edwards to Emerson does not make sense. The literary descent from Mather to Franklin to Jefferson to Emerson makes as much sense as the line from Mather to Edwards to Emerson. Newton inspired Franklin *and* Edwards *and* Jefferson. American letters should tell about what Americans made of the wisdom of the ages and the wisdom of their time. Jefferson made the most complete republican American synthesis and mastered democracy first as well, amazingly at the same time. The very inconclusiveness of much of his work has made it possible for him to inspire the American generations. Jefferson was so sure about method and the fundamental order of the world reflected in the order of his prose that he could afford to say all sorts of things about all sorts of subjects to all sorts of people.

It is not yet clear what role we should assign to Jefferson as a man of letters in the tradition of American literature. It is worth remembering that Hawthorne, who learned from the same eighteenth-century sentimental literature as did Jefferson about the quarrel of the head and heart, wrote about problems that might not be encountered by a Jeffersonian worldview. Jeffersonian fictions take place in Virginia, the Virginia of his imagination, which is compounded of fact and theory. Jeffersonian optimism and ideals, at least as much as Emersonian, function as the high-minded ground in American literature. Jefferson's importance as a man of letters has something to do with the way in which American writers have seen in the Jeffersonian legacy of individual liberty the very dilemmas of American lives.

Jefferson's letters are rewarding to read in part because there is simply so much in them. There is the always fascinating instance of Jefferson the provincial cosmopolite, whether ordering wines and books, discussing the latest ideas, describing his country pleasures and his experiments or attitudinizing, as he does in a wonderful letter of 6 February 1795 to Monsieur D'Ivernois concerning the possible relocation of the Geneva Academy to Virginia:

It is now more than a year that I have withdrawn myself from public affairs, which I never liked in my life, but was drawn into by emergencies which threatened our country with slavery, but ended in establishing it free. I have returned, with infinite appetite, to the enjoyment of my farm, my family & my books, and had determined to meddle in nothing beyond their limits. Your proposition, however, for transplanting the college of Geneva to my own country, was too analogous to all my attachments to science, & freedom, the first-born daughter of science, not to excite a lively interest in my mind, and the essays which were necessary to try it's practicability.

Good old Jefferson—earnest, unembarrassed—writes a preamble to his letter with the same felicity of borrowed expression that makes it his own as in the Declaration. The decent opinion of mankind requires an explanation for his retirement from public affairs, which he never liked, although he cared deeply for public objects. It is not cynical to note in this characteristic Jeffersonian moment his little drama of self-presentation and to smile at its breathy grace—"the first-born daughter of science" indeed!

The Jeffersonian has to explain himself this way, that fiction of self is the putting into effect of notions of virtue and self-control and republican and enlightened citizenship on which the fate of free civilization depends. We may smile, and should, at some of its intrusions into the little things, but it is the pervasiveness of Jefferson's thinking about such questions, his ultimate connecting of Enlightenment to America, and his recognition that writing was action because knowledge was power, that defined him as a man of letters.

Jefferson's continuing discovery and declaration of American cultural independence from England is an important element in his position as an American man of letters and his advocacy of the classics. This was the sublime with which he rested, a more private and less tumultuous sublime than he had earlier sought but one that comported better with his view of what counted. Jefferson does define a standard of utility and endurance that ill suits the rantings of the American self and must be seen as the partial view of what American letters should do. This aspect of Jefferson has made him a difficult founder for the students of American literature and letters who have dominated the twentieth century's views of such matters. His sense of the limits of the human imagination suggested to him that human reason be consoled for its limits with the classics and their spirit of calming resignation and that keen sense of public duty that connects the individual to society. This was not the conclusion to which Emerson was drawn. It is worth restoring to the history of American letters, however, Jefferson's constant model and his descendants. Emerson and Jefferson may be the originating parties to our national literary dispute. Surely the Jeffersonian vision of that life deserves revival.

Jefferson's real rival is not Emerson, it is not even Hamilton. It is Madison, whose standing as the favorite founder among the intellectual classes has deservedly grown. Madison and Jefferson understood each other as allies and their partnership will survive other people's partisanship of them. But there is a sense that the Madisonian grasp of what is difficult and unyielding in the world and his tough-minded arrangements for a republican future please us now more than that Jeffersonian vagueness in the middle distance. Selfishness makes a lot more sense than happiness. One reason that Jefferson must be considered as a man of letters is so that we can restore to our vocabulary of the American past that peculiarly Jeffersonian fiction, the vision of the American future, the pastoral of the American democratic republic. He supplied the imaginative grounds of faith in the republic that Madison understood would ease a future about which he was worried. The Jeffersonian political imagination generated notions of freedom of expression, notions that Jefferson himself did not always keep pace with. He emphasized the value of the practical, the connection between philosophy and the common life, the responsibilities of the highest human types to the activities and purposes of the republic and its ordinary citizens. The care with which Jefferson invested both the ordinary and the superior person with a role in a free and enlightened future is his companion piece to Madison's harder-headed political thinking. They should not be separated. The Jeffersonian man of letters applies himself to the connections between the highest human qualities—those the analysis in *The Federalist,* number 10, leaves out—and the republic that will need more than the metabolic luck of a system of dispersed human self-interest.

In his last letter, written on 24 June 1826 to Roger C. Weightman, Jefferson apotheosized his authorship. His subject was the approaching celebration of the fiftieth anniversary of the signing of the Declaration of Independence:

> May it be to the world, what I believe it will be, (to some parts sooner, to others later, but finally to all,) the signal of arousing men to burst the chains under which monkish igno-

rance and superstition had persuaded them to bind themselves, and to assume the blessings and security of self-government. That form we have substituted, restores the free right to the unbounded exercise of reason and freedom of opinion. All eyes are opened, or opening, to the rights of man. The general spread of the light of science has already laid open to every view the palpable truth, that the mass of mankind has not been born with saddles on their backs, nor a favored few booted and spurred, ready to ride them legitimately, by the Grace of God. These are the grounds of hope for others. For ourselves, let the annual return of this day forever refresh our recollections of these rights, and an undiminished devotion to them.

Like any author, Jefferson reworked his important themes into his essential statements. Like no other author, Jefferson tells us how to celebrate the Fourth of July. As an American man of American letters, Jefferson created a masterwork of the imagination in his successive expressions of the terms on which life in the United States might be enjoyed.

The Fine Arts

WILLIAM HOWARD ADAMS

THE geography of Jefferson's imaginative life, as revealed in the "maps" he has left us, is an amazing topography. His explorations through books, travel, correspondence, architectural experiments, the study of the arts and sciences, and the designing of governments and gadgets reveal a lifelong preoccupation and sympathy with all of man's creative efforts. In the Virginian's ranging curiosity, he was in tune with Denis Diderot's ambitious goal for his *Encyclopédie, ou Dictionnaire raisonné des sciences, des arts et des métiers* (1751–1765), which was to demonstrate the sequence and interplay of man's attainments and to describe the essential details of every art and science. Jefferson had a thirty-six-volume set of the *Encyclopédie* at Monticello, where it was integral to his small, select collection of books on the fine arts, now accepted as probably the best to be found anywhere in America at the time. The systematic, rational organization of man's knowledge into a neat, comprehensive package deeply appealed to Jefferson as a man of the Enlightenment, and it was through the printed page that he would first discover the arts, along with law, natural history, science, architecture, and the other branches of learning that engaged his supple, inquiring mind. It is one of the glories of the human mind that it demands a myth out of a need to codify its thoughts. For Jefferson the myth was ready-made in his library.

His love of books came naturally, but it was stimulated from the earliest years of his education. Like other educated men of his age, he was heir to the Renaissance humanist traditions. He learned Latin and Greek and began a dialogue with the ancient world through its literature, in the original languages. "It is no overstatement to say that, at the end of his life, the Sage of Monticello had read more of ancient literature, both poetry and prose, than any other man of his time, apart from a group of professional classicists," Karl Lehmann-Hartleben wrote in *Thomas Jefferson, American Humanist.* But if his literary imagination was fed with the texts of ancient authors, the classics provided little stimulus for the development of his interests in painting and sculpture.

The book dominated learning and aesthetic cultivation in colonial America, and if Jefferson's knowledge and taste in sculpture and painting does not seem to have reached much beyond that of any cultivated eighteenth-century gentleman, it is due to that fact. It was the book that gave eighteenth-century culture its cohesion and cosmopolitan quality, thereby allowing the middle-aged Jefferson to move easily into the cultivated circles of Europe without provincial embarrassment. Even though his artistic interests, except in the field of architecture, did not exceed that of a cultured amateur, the extraordinary range and intensity of his intellectual curiosity reached further than that of any of his fellow Virginians, giving him a reputation as an aesthete that set him apart. His kinsman Peyton Randolph said that he "panted after the fine arts," suggesting an uncommon enthusiasm and one not considered entirely proper for a Virginia gentleman. If his enthusiasm occasionally made him metaphorically short of breath, it was because he had to exert himself in a society with few resources.

The American colonial gentry was not necessarily philistine in its artistic values; an indigenous appreciation of painting and sculpture simply did not exist. During Jefferson's youth, significant artistic production and art collecting had not yet appeared in Williamsburg. Conditions were not appreciably different in the larger colonial centers of Boston, New York, Philadelphia, and Charleston. Outside of a few pictures by reputed old masters in the private houses of some of these cities, the colonies possessed almost no examples of European painting. Family pride stimulated a certain amount of portraiture, but most artisan talent went into furniture making and other domestic crafts. The eighteenth-century grandees of Virginia did have a well-established reputation for fitting out their plantation houses with good English silver, furniture, porcelain, and other imported luxuries befitting their station. "The chief magnificence of the Virginians," the Marquis de Chastellux wrote in his travel journal, "consists in furniture, linen, and silver plate; in which they resemble our own forefathers who had no private apartments in their castles, but only a well-stored wine cellar and handsome sideboards." On the eve of the Revolution an anonymous British observer thought that the great Virginia planters made "a greater show" and lived more luxuriously "than a country gentleman in England on an estate of three or four thousand pounds a year." (It is interesting to note that the average English manor house of the time displayed few paintings or art works.) Works of art beyond an occasional portrait or engraving were nonexistent even in the larger Virginia establishments. Jefferson's father, mother, and wife were not painted during their lifetimes, and his own likeness was not done until he went to London in 1786.

The history and appreciation of art as academic subjects did not exist in American colleges, nor was there even the suggestion of a collegiate art collection at Harvard College, King's College (later Columbia University), or the College of William and Mary, let alone at the lesser and newer educational institutions. The potential menace that "luxury," which included painting and sculpture, held for the new society was viewed as a palpable threat by many concerned Americans long before the Revolution. It was not to be tolerated even in seats of learning, where its dread threat of corruption would infect innocent students. Josiah Quincy proudly told a fellow American traveler in Europe in the 1770s that the Harvard College library had recently acquired a set of prints depicting the ruins at Herculaneum. Quincy thought that the information would meet the approbation of any classically enlightened compatriot, but to his surprise, his companion expressed the hope that Harvard would keep them safely locked up: "They will infuse a taste for building and sculpture, and when a people get a taste for the fine arts, they are ruined.''

The middle colonies (Virginia in particular) demonstrated, at least overtly, little of New England's deeply ingrained Puritan antipathy to the arts. According to William Short, it was an old cabinetmaker operating near the gate of William and Mary who sold the young Jefferson his first art book, a work on architecture. The library of the college had a sizable working collection of about three thousand volumes, mostly classical and theological works. Some were illustrated with engravings, and as meager as these examples of art appear in retrospect, they were the only resource available for educating the visual sense when Jefferson was a student in Williamsburg in the 1760s.

Even though Williamsburg was in no sense an artistic center either during Jefferson's student days or after, there were occasional exhibitions by painters seeking portrait commissions from the local gentry. In March 1773 Matthew Pratt held such a show and advertised for sale "a small but very neat Collection of paintings, which are now exhibiting at Mrs. Vobe's, near the Capitol; among which are, first, a very good Copy of Correggio's *St. Jerome,* esteemed to be one of the best pictures in Italy.'' Jefferson, a practicing lawyer, was in Williamsburg at the time to meet with the Burgesses and probably visited Pratt's exhibition.

Until he was twenty-three, Jefferson did not travel outside Virginia. His physical world was confined to trips between his family's up-country plantation at Shadwell and the colony's capital at Williamsburg. In the spring and early summer of 1766, his aesthetic and geographical horizons were enlarged by a trip to New York that took him through Annapolis and Philadelphia. The latter was the largest city in the colonies and among its leaders were several individuals who had begun to assemble small art collections in their town houses and country estates. Many of these affluent, sophisticated

citizens had, like the physician John Morgan, traveled abroad, acquiring through the grand tour at least a passing introduction to European art and architecture as presented in the ubiquitous guidebooks of the period.

Jefferson, who made the trip to Philadelphia to be innoculated against smallpox, carried a letter of introduction to Morgan. The young provincial was very likely impressed by Morgan's travels to Rome, Naples, and Venice. More important was the doctor's collection of architectural books and artworks, including copies of paintings of the old masters, engravings and drawings by Nicolas Poussin, Titian, Domenichino, and Charles Le Brun that Morgan had brought back from his travels. This visit was one of Jefferson's first introductions to the cultivated company of a traveled and worldly connoisseur with ambitions as a collector, and it no doubt made a lasting impression on the young lawyer. Two years later when Jefferson began to plan his country villa, Monticello, Morgan's example confirmed his intention to create a design that would place his library and art collection at the center of his life.

In 1771, Robert Skipwith sought Jefferson's advice on the selection of a list of basic books for a gentleman's library. Included in Jefferson's response were Daniel Webb's essays on painting, William Hogarth's *Analysis of Beauty,* and Lord Kames's *Elements of Criticism,* all books Jefferson had owned before the fire that destroyed his first library at Shadwell in February 1770. Jefferson's major complaint about the fire was the loss of his library and a prized violin. Other nonarchitectural art books that Jefferson had owned at an early date included Jonathan Richardson's tripartite *Essay on the Theory of Painting* (1715), *Two Discourses: I. An Essay on the Whole Art of Criticism as It Relates to Painting . . .* and *II. An Argument in Behalf of the Science of a Connoisseur . . .* (1719). Prints and engravings would eventually make up a large part of the art collection at Monticello and, as a guide to methods of engraving and printmaking, Jefferson owned William Gilpin's *An Essay on Prints* (1768). Giorgio Vasari's *Delle vite de' piu eccellenti pittori, scultori et architetti* (1548–1563) and a "Da Vinci on Painting" were both on the shelves of Jefferson's first library.

For Jefferson, as for Morgan, books were the foundation for an acquaintance with the arts. His library divided books according to three mental faculties, memory, reason, and imagination, and their respective applications, history, philosophy, and the fine arts. The fine arts were further subdivided into the categories of architecture, gardening, painting, sculpture, music, poetry, oratory, and criticism.

In order to have a comprehensive view of Jefferson's large fine-arts library, one must consult the five-volume *Catalogue of the Library of Thomas Jefferson* compiled by E. Millicent Sowerby, who focuses on books actually owned by Jefferson. The art books with which Jefferson was familiar and which he included in his list of recommendations for the library of the University of Virginia have been assembled in William B. O'Neal's *Jefferson's Fine Arts Library.* As O'Neal points out, Jefferson considered architecture integral to music, painting, sculpture, and gardening, so that in addition to the substantial section on architecture, the other disciplines were generously represented. Notable among the titles recommended for the university are Johann Joachim Winckelmann's *Storia delle arti del disegno presso gli antichi,* 3 vols. (1783–1786), Matthew Pilkington's *Gentleman's and Conoisseur's Dictionary of Painters* (1810), William Hogarth's *Analysis of Beauty* (1791), and Pierre François Hughes d'Hancarville's *Recherches sur l'origine, l'esprit et les progres des arts de la Grèce,* 3 vols. (1785).

Jefferson was by turns a classicist and a romantic, as A. Hyatt Mayor has noted in his perceptive essay "Jefferson's Enjoyment of the Arts," published in the *Metropolitan Museum of Art Bulletin* of December, 1943. It appears that he was in a romantic mood during the days in 1771 when he jotted down plans to surround his new mountain retreat with gushing springs, grottoes, a miniature pantheon, a Chinese garden house, a Gothic chapel, and an assemblage of copies of Roman statues. The selection of sculpture listed in his building notebook was based on the best aesthetic judgments available in contemporary books and guides; it would be more than ten years before he would see original artworks in European collections. Collecting copies or casts of masterpieces was fashionable in the eighteenth century and was no doubt especially appealing to Americans, like Morgan and Jefferson, who probably never dreamed of collecting original sculpture from antiquity or paintings by old masters.

It was Jefferson the classicist rather than the art connoisseur who compiled the list, beginning with "Venus of Medici," the celebrated image of the goddess of love and female beauty. By the late eighteenth century, copies of that famous sculpture had become a favorite of antiquarian collectors. She could be found standing in chilly galleries or hallways of stately houses throughout the British Isles. As far as we know, she had not yet crossed the Atlantic.

The thirteen works were probably intended for the house and grounds of Monticello, since the list was recorded in Jefferson's building notebook. Although no directions for placement have been discovered, it is possible that Venus and Apollo were intended for the two niches flanking the entry into the drawing room. The list reads as follows:

Venus of Medici, Florence
Hercules of Farnese, Rome
Apollo of Belvedere, Rome
Antinous, Florence
Dancing Faunus
Messenger pulling out a thorn
Roman slave whetting his knife

The Gladiator of Montalto
Myrmillo expiring, Rome
The Gladiator reposing himself after the
    engagement (companion to the
    former)
Hercules and Antaeus
The two wrestlers
The Rape of the Sabines (3 figures)

In his essay "Jefferson and the Arts," published in 1943 in the *Proceedings of the American Philosophical Society,* Fiske Kimball has identified the sources for the desiderata list in the descriptions of ancient statuary compiled by Richardson, Joseph Spence, and François Perrier and in Joseph Addison's *Remarks on Several Parts of Italy* (1705). None of these works was acquired by Jefferson, although he did accept the gift of a marble copy of the Sleeping Ariadne in the Vatican museum. If the listed pieces were intended for garden decoration, it may have been Jefferson's growing commitment to the sweeping, natural English-park landscape that cooled his interest in sculptural accents. The list of sculpture replicas was followed by a shorter group of six subjects to be copied from paintings of the old masters. Later this list was revised and enlarged to include eleven items illustrating classical and religious themes, among them "St. Paul preaching at Athens; St. Ignatius at prayer; Jephtha meeting his daughter; Sacrifice of Iphigenia; History of Seleucus giving his beloved wife Stratonice to his only son Seleucus who languished for her, Florence; Diana Venetrix (see Spence's Polymetis)." The subject matters, heavy with moral messages, would have been considered limited and conventional by European standards. In prerevolutionary America, an interest in such subjects was most unusual.

Most Americans before and after the Revolution harbored a basic distrust of luxurious display that signaled a decline or loss of virtue, if the ancient poets and historians were correct. Corroboration was forthcoming from contemporary thinkers. Jean Jacques Rousseau in *The Social Contract* had linked art and luxury to the fall of Rome, and John Adams agreed. "Are we not in too great a hurry in our zeal for the fine arts?" Adams asked Benjamin Waterhouse. Benjamin Rush stated that the arts could be "highly pernicious" in new, immature societies. "The character . . . of popular government depends on the character of the people," Richard Price wrote to Jefferson on 21 March 1785. "If the people deviate from Simplicity of manners into luxury, the love of Shew, and extravagance, the governments must become corrupt and tyrannical." As late as 1834, John S. Barbour, Jefferson's neighbor and friend, declared in a speech before Congress that "those periods of the world when painting and sculpture were at their highest point of perfection were not the periods of its highest character."

Jefferson himself advised young Americans traveling in Europe not to waste too much time on art. Under "painting, statuary" in his letter to John Rutledge, Jr., dated 19 June 1788, he noted that they were "too expensive for the state of wealth among us. It would be useless therefore and preposterous for us to endeavor to make ourselves connoisseurs in those arts. They are worth seeing, but not studying." Against such a backdrop of cultural attitudes, Jefferson's youthful plan to extensively decorate his new house with sculpture and painting would have been a daring step. Not only might such a house be viewed as a superfluous display of luxury and wealth, but the association of art collections with Old World aristocracies posed serious questions of appropriateness for a republic.

In conflict with these misgivings was the belief, especially prevalent among Europeans, that identified national greatness with artistic maturity. Allied with this issue was the skeptical charge advanced by European biologists, led by the Comte de Buffon and the Abbé Raynal, that men and beasts in the New World were diminished in size, vigor, and intelligence. Beyond the discomfort that many Americans felt in answering this accusation because of deep-seated moral reservations, the suggestion that the arts could not flourish in the New World was frustrating for men of Jefferson's cultivation and sensitivity. It was difficult to counter the charges because concrete evidence of artistic progress was difficult to identify. In a country that was still clearing wilderness and fighting Indians, it was preposterous to consider art among the nation's first priorities. This, at least, was the defense in the face of the few examples of homegrown American art that could stand comparison with European models.

Consistent with his sense of priorities for a new country and his rationalization of the art he loved the most, Jefferson did urge Americans abroad to study architecture. In the letter to Rutledge, he wrote,

> As we double our numbers every 20 years we must double our houses. Besides we build of such perishable materials that one half of our houses must be rebuilt in every space of 20 years. So that in that term, houses are to be built for three fourths of our inhabitants. It is then among the most important arts: and it is desireable to introduce taste into an art which shews so much.

For Jefferson the architect, America's buildings placed its very civilization on trial, since they were readily available for study by foreigners and would be evaluated by future historians, as he had done in his analysis of the monuments of Rome through the study of Vitruvius, Sebastiano Serlio, and Andrea Palladio. The capitol of Virginia, which he had based on the Roman Maison Carrée, would do "honour to our country as presenting to travellers a morsel of taste in our infancy promising much for our maturer age," as he declared from Paris in a letter to James Madison of 20 September 1785 when he forwarded the plans to Richmond. In the same letter Jefferson declared his love of the arts without apology: "You see I am an enthusiast on the subject of the arts." It was specifically to architecture, however, that he referred when he made this famous declaration: "But it is an enthusiasm of which I am not ashamed, as it's object is to improve the taste of my countrymen, to increase their reputation, to reconcile to them the respect of the world and procure them it's praise."

When it came to matters of taste in art and architecture, Jefferson was no egalitarian, and in his eagerness to promote his design for the Capitol, he revealed to Madison his fear that extravagant bad design might appeal to an uneducated public susceptible to corruption. Jefferson assumed that in the new Republic the style that would first dominate the visual arts, particularly public architecture, would be difficult to dislodge; he thus determined to set a course based on classic sources. Fiske Kimball has called the Virginia capitol "the first monument of the classical revival in America."

In spite of the limited resources of his native Virginia and the distractions of the Revolution, Jefferson's interest in the arts had continued to develop. The journal of the Marquis de Chastellux's visit to Monticello a few months after the British surrender at Yorktown would have us believe that the two men spoke of almost nothing else. When Jefferson arrived in Paris in August 1784, he found himself for the first time congenially surrounded by a society of classicist artists, architects, connoisseurs, and collectors, a society "saturated with antique motives and forms" in the words of Lehmann-Hartleben. For the next five years, "the vaunted scene of Europe," as Jefferson called it, with its rich texture of art, architecture, and antiquity, was to absorb the critical eye and finely tuned curiosity of the American diplomat.

For the first time, he met major artists with international reputations, such as Jean-

Antoine Houdon and Jacques-Louis David, and visited their studios regularly. Precisely when he first encountered the works of Houdon is not clear, but in January 1785, only a few months after his arrival in Paris, he had no problem deciding who should be given the commission for the sculpture of George Washington authorized by the state of Virginia. "There could be no question raised as to the Sculptor who should be employed, the reputation of Monsr. Houdon of this city being unrivalled in Europe," he replied in January 1785 to Gov. Benjamin Harrison, who had written asking for his advice. In December 1784 he had reassured Washington that Houdon's was "the first statuary in the world. . . . [He] is so enthusiastically fond of being the executor of this work that he offers to go himself to America for the purpose of forming your bust from the life. . . . A bust of Voltaire executed by him is said to be one of the first in the world."

In 1778, Benjamin Franklin had sat for the sculptor and the result has become an integral part of the iconography of revolutionary America. John Paul Jones had been recorded by Houdon when the naval hero visited Paris in 1780. The sculptor's bust of Jefferson, first exhibited in the Salon of 1789, added one more piece to his gallery of American revolutionary figures. For Jefferson and other admirers of the sculptor, Houdon's ability to produce a moving and faithful portrait and at the same time to endow it with an antique, legendary quality constituted a rare combining of artistic and public aims—an inspired equilibrium of international proportions. When the Virginian returned home from Paris in 1789, seven plaster portrait busts by Houdon, including his own, came with him and were eventually installed at Monticello. Their style and quality could not have been more in tune with the architect's idealized aspirations and the classical setting that he had created.

In the concentrated intellectual and artistic atmosphere of Paris, the ideal world of the ancients, which Jefferson had studied and thought about for so long, seemed to merge with the heady atmosphere of contemporary experience and personalities. The euphoria created by such a congenial setting and the company of so many sympathetic men and women who shared the same ideals enabled him to move with confidence into areas of learning in which he admitted he had little or no experience. His intuitive response to Houdon's work was of a piece with his almost spontaneous and original inspiration to base the Richmond capitol on the drawings and research of Charles-Louis Clérisseau, the eminent architect and teacher who had published superb measured drawings of the Maison Carrée. Just as he had turned to Houdon without second thought, Jefferson sought out Clérisseau and later his model maker to assist him in translating for the Virginia commissioners his ideas of directly adapting the Roman temple as a serviceable headquarters for a modern state.

On the personal, domestic level, his new house in Paris, a splendid *hôtel particulier* on the Champs Elysées designed by Jean-François Chalgrin, required furnishings suitable to his official and social position. As a result, and on an unprecedented scale for him, he purchased household fittings and acquired objets d'art. The mounting entries in his household accounts recording the acquisition of these decorations and artworks suggest the enthusiasm and abandon of an amateur collector: "Two pictures of heads, 7 Livres; d° half lengths, viz. an ecce homo and another, 18 livres; two small laughing busts, 21 livres; a Hercules in plaister; five paintings (heads)."

Throughout his stay in Paris he bought copies after established artists that followed the desiderata list in his building notebook of 1771. His confidence and discrimination seem to have grown when in February 1785 he selected five canvases from more than three hundred offered at the sale of a collection formed in the early part of the century by M. Dupille de Saint Severin. "L'envoie d'Amerique" is recorded as purchasing *St. Peter Weeping for His Offense,* by Guido Reni; *Magdalene Penitent,* by Joseph de Ribera, called Spagnolet; *Democritus and Heraclitus, Called the Laughing and Weeping Philosophers; Herodiade Bearing the Head of St. John on a Platter,* by Simon Vouet; and *The Prodigal Son,* by an "unknown master." Among his new acquisitions were no works by the contemporary artists he admired, such as David and Elisabeth Vigée-Lebrun. Surprisingly, considering Jefferson's enthusiasm for portraitures, there were none, although he would later acquire in Paris a good likeness of Franklin.

In the years immediately following the Revolution, when most of the major figures of that heroic enterprise were still on the scene, American portrait painters like Gilbert Stuart and Charles Willson Peale found their sitters to embody the ideals of the new nation. Adams, Washington, Jefferson, and Franklin were men whose lives and apotheoses in art expressed glories like those of the noble subjects of antique legend. As their portraits became icons, artists set up painting factories to turn out images of the new saints.

Alfred Bush in *The Life Portraits of Thomas Jefferson* has recorded twenty-five paintings and sculptures by twenty-two artists executed between 1786 and 1825. The first was painted in the London studio of Mather Brown on Cavendish Square sometime during Jefferson's visit with John and Abigail Adams. Brown, an American artist working in London, was only twenty-four at the time; Jefferson may have given him the commission as a gesture of encouragement. The United States minister to France had also met in London another young artist, Connecticut-born John Trumbull, who had "pined for the arts" so much that he had turned down his family's offer to set him up in business or the law and instead had

moved to Europe to pursue the uncertain profession of painter. Trumbull had caught the eye of Benjamin West, later president of the Royal Academy, and was studying in West's·London studio when he first met Jefferson. The artist's idealism and dedication appealed to Jefferson, who "highly approved" of his determination to prepare himself for "the accomplishment of a national work" as an artist-patriot and invited Trumbull to visit him in Paris, where the artist would enjoy Jefferson's intimate and cosmopolitan circle of artists and intellectuals. "I now availed myself of this invitation," Trumbull later wrote in his *Autobiography,* "and went to his house, . . . where I was most kindly received by him. My two paintings, the first fruits of my national enterprise, met his warm approbation, and during my visit, I began the composition of the Declaration of Independence, with the assistance of his information and advice." The two paintings Trumbull had brought with him were his *Battle of Bunker's Hill* and *Death of Montgomery,* which he planned to have engraved during his stay. He told his host that he intended to commemorate "the great events of our country's revolution" and to pay for the project by publishing a series of engravings for subscribers. Since *The Declaration of Independence* was not originally included in Trumbull's list of historical subjects, Jefferson may have suggested it. His host was able to provide a firsthand account of the event and a rough floor plan of the room in the Pennsylvania State House, where the document had been signed. Jefferson's architectural recollection of the room was inaccurate in both the placement of doors and the number of windows.

Jefferson was immediately sympathetic to the young artist's ambitions and gave him 12 francs toward a subscription. Jefferson offered further encouragement by telling Trumbull that he undervalued his own talents but recognized that America "is not yet rich enough to encourage you as you desire." With this advice, Jefferson again expressed his misgivings about the future of the arts in a new country. Since recording the glorious events and main participants of the Revolution served the didactic purposes Americans required of their art, Jefferson's support of Trumbull's plan was in the mainstream. As the artist wrote to the American minister,

> The greatest motive I had or have for engaging in, or for continuing my pursuit of painting, has been the wish of commemorating the great events of our country's revolution. I am fully sensible that the profession, as it is generally practiced, is frivolous, little useful to society, and unworthy of a man who has talents for more serious pursuits. But, to preserve and diffuse the memory of the noblest series of actions which have ever presented themselves in the history of man . . . were objects which gave a dignity to the profession, peculiar to my situation.

The Revolution had been a godsend to American art, at least in theory. "It made private events public events," Neil Harris has written, in *The Artist in American Society,* "and private figures public men; it shed an air of importance on a thousand actions. . . . It brought to the life of the larger community a sense of purpose and provided a pattern for the minutiae of daily existence" (p. 16).

Trumbull became an important figure in the minister's circle. When the artist arrived in Paris in the winter of 1787–1788, he stayed at the Hôtel de Langeac as Jefferson's guest and painted from life the drafter's portrait for *The Declaration of Independence.* For this work, no idealized portraits were to be introduced "lest it being known that some that were found in the painting, a doubt of the truth of others should be excited in the minds of posterity." On his return to the United States, Trumbull continued his research, traveling up and down the eastern

seaboard collecting portraits to join the principal figures of Adams, Franklin, Jefferson, Roger Sherman, and Robert Livingston. Jefferson found Trumbull's methods impressive and pronounced the artist "superior to any historical painter of the time except David." As a personal response to the Virginian's encouragement, Trumbull later gave him an oil sketch of his *Surrender of Lord Cornwallis at Yorktown,* which Jefferson proudly hung at Monticello, where it remained until his death.

Trumbull knew David, calling him "a warm and affectionate friend." Jefferson had seen David's *Oath of the Horatii* when he had attended the Salon of 1785, before Trumbull saw the famous work during his visit to David's studio in 1787. David returned the compliment by paying a visit to see the beginnings of the American's historical series at Jefferson's residence.

After Jefferson attended the Salon of 1787, he wrote Trumbull on 30 August, "The best thing is the Death of Socrates by David, and a superb one it is." It so happened that Sir Joshua Reynolds, the leading contemporary English painter and writer on aesthetics, had also singled it out for special praise, comparing it to the Sistine Chapel and declaring it "perfect in every way." So the untutored Virginian who disclaimed any critical judgment of painting had his opinion confirmed by one of the reigning experts of the day. In March 1789, Jefferson wrote to Madame de Bréhan, "I do not feel an interest in any pencil but that of David." He then added a self-depreciating note: "But I must not hasard details on a subject wherein I am so ignorant, and you such a Connoisseur." David had inaugurated the neoclassical movement, and the new concept of art it embodied was perfectly calculated to appeal to a man of Jefferson's temperament and classical education. For him, David's paintings were self-evident documents, political statements that required no more special training or knowledge than was needed to understand the clear logic of the Declaration of Independence. Since the Renaissance, theories of art had maintained that the ideal human form in noble action was the most beautiful, and of all images of the human form, the Greco-Roman were the most ideal. If classical mythology provided the most noble examples, paintings should follow the Roman model in as precise and authentic detail as possible. David in his French logic accomplished this but insisted that paintings must go even further to instruct mankind. It was here that Jefferson found the artist so congenial, for the message, in uncompromising clarity and uncompromising form, consisted of the virtues of republican self-government and the vices of absolute monarchy. If in France the message was a subversive protest, in Jefferson's America the ideal had become reality.

Jefferson's intense response to the neoclassical spirit in painting is perhaps best expressed in a letter to Madame de Tott dated 28 February 1787, after he had seen *Marius Imprisoned at Minturnae,* the work of David's student, the young Jean-Germain Drouais:

> Have you been, Madam, to see the superb picture now exhibiting in the rue Ste. Nicaise, No. 9. chez Mde. Drouay? It is that of Marius in the moment when the souldier enters to assassinate him. It is made by her son, a student at Rome under the care of David, and is much in David's manner. All Paris is running to see it, and really it appears to me to have extraordinary merit. It fixed me like a statute a quarter of an hour, or half an hour, I do not know which, for I lost all ideas of time, "even the consciousness of my existence."

Drouais had at the age of twenty-three painted his masterpiece at the French Academy in Rome, where it was an immediate sensation. Critics compared it to David's *Oath of the Horatii,* which earlier had been shown in Rome to great acclaim. A near-

contemporary writer, Chaussard, recalled, "The young Drouais taking an even more daring step created a painting of Marius alone and without advice, which he timidly exhibited to the Roman public. This work had the greatest possible success there and was equally praised by artists and connoisseurs. All of Paris rushed to see this painting."

Although Jefferson never visited Rome, he was attuned to the stimulating atmosphere that young neoclassical artists like Drouais found so exhilarating. On 15 October 1785 he wrote to John Banister, Jr., in reply to his inquiry regarding "the best seminary for the education of youth in Europe" with more advice on European travel. Rome, he told his fellow Virginian, was the preeminent place to acquire "a just taste in the fine arts, more particularly those of painting, sculpture, architecture, and music." While he felt "the balance in favor of Rome" for a cultural sojourn, the lasting value of a European education for Americans was by no means certain. To the question of why one should send an American youth to Europe for education, he responded that the study of modern languages, mathematics, and natural philosophy were the only disciplines that were better pursued on the Continent than in America. Europe's monopoly of the fine arts in collections and connoisseurship did not even enter into the debate as far as Jefferson was concerned, for the simple reason that they were not worth studying. Given Jefferson's interest in architecture and his belief in its importance to the new Republic, it is surprising that he does not mention it among the advantages of a European education, as he had done earlier in his letter to John Rutledge, Jr. It may well be that he thought the necessary documents for the study of building could be found in books, a process he had followed in his own architectural studies.

It is clear that Jefferson was again expressing the traditional fears of the temptations of aristocratic Europe. Works of art, like other luxuries, were expensive, and in the end they served no real purpose. To encourage a private interest in art was to encourage class divisions that would undermine the principles of American democracy. If the student "acquires a fondness for European luxury and dissipation and a contempt for the simplicity of his own country," he will forget "the lovely equality which the poor enjoys with the rich in his own country." Here again was the besetting dilemma of the role of the arts for Americans, a dilemma involving the many ties between luxury, art, and money that posed a threat to virtue and personal restraint.

As far as his countrymen were concerned, Jefferson's level of connoisseurship was more than adequate to carry out official art commissions; they conveniently overlooked the inconsistencies in Jefferson's personal predilections for the arts and artists and in his private collections of objects and fine furniture. American visitors to his house in Paris and to Monticello did not dwell on the moral issues implied in the collection or in Jefferson's ambivalence toward the arts. During the later part of his stay in Paris, Jefferson was asked to supervise the completion of a series of medals voted by Congress for award to officers of the Revolution "who distinguished themselves on particular occasions." The first of ten had been ordered by Washington in 1776; the execution of the other nine was delayed until 1787 when Jefferson was asked to have them completed. It was, for Jefferson, another opportunity to make an official gesture in celebration of patriotic, republican virtue. To complete the commission, he requested the artisans Nicolas-Marie Gatteaux, Augustin Dupré, and Pierre-Simon-Benjamin Duvivier to provide dies for the medals. When Jefferson left France in 1789, he took with him a set of proofs in tin, which he later hung in the parlor at Monticello.

For all his declarations on the dangers of developing a taste for extravagant display, Jefferson not only collected paintings and sculpture during his years in France but also indulged his taste in the decorative arts and small objets d'art. He confessed to Charles Bellini in a letter of 30 September 1785, "Were I to proceed to tell you how much I enjoy their architecture, sculpture, painting, music, I should want words. It is in these arts they shine." He had an intuitive eye for the smallest details in silver, marble, porcelain, and even textiles. This refinement can be seen time and again in his commissions for objects, such as the elegant black marble, brass, and ormolu clock made by Chantrot in Paris. He cautioned his secretary, William Short, to be sure there is "no gilt head . . . on the obelisk," an embellishment that must be avoided. Years later at Monticello he ordered the upholsterer to fashion the bolster for his bed with republican simplicity, even though the red damask brocade that he had selected might have inspired a more elegant execution.

Abigail Adams relied implicitly on Jefferson's taste. In September 1785 he wrote to her regarding her request for "three plateaux de dessert with a silvered ballustrade round them, and four figures of Biscuit." Abigail had apparently been specific about the iconography of the figures; she requested Minerva, Diana, Apollo, and one unidentified deity. Jefferson, who was busy furnishing his elegant new quarters at the Hôtel de Langeac, could not locate the last god Mrs. Adams had requested for her London dining room. He wrote to her,

I was obliged to add a fourth, unguided by your choice. They offered me a fine Venus; but I thought it out of taste to have two at table at the same time. Paris and Helen were presented. I conceived it would be cruel to remove them from their peculiar shrine. . . . At length a fine Mars was offered, calm, bold, his faulchion not drawn, but ready to be drawn.

This will do, thinks I, for the table of the American Minister in London, where those whom it may concern may look and learn that though Wisdom is our guide, and the Song and Chase our supreme delight, yet we offer adoration to that tutelar god also who rocked the cradle of our birth, who has accepted our infant offerings, and has shewn himself the patron of our rights and avenger of our wrongs. The groupe then was closed, and your party formed.

In this felicitous passage of antique gallantry, Jefferson demonstrated that even in small domestic matters he was a true descendant of the humanist tradition. He was always "civilized and learned" even in so minor an assignment as decorating the table of the first American minister to Great Britain.

The minister himself, John Adams, insisted again and again that luxuries, including the fine arts, were a potentially lethal poison that threatened national virtue. The arts could even be enlisted in the cause of tyranny. In his opinion the arts had from "the dawn of history . . . been prostituted to the service of superstition and despotism." In his old age Adams was still troubled by the specter of corruption and in 1816 wrote Jefferson, whom he admired for his personal artistic taste, asking the Virginian how art was to be accommodated without debasing the simple virtues of the Republic. The fine arts, "which you love so well and taste so exquisitely," he wrote Jefferson, "have been subservient to Priests and Kings, Nobles and Commons, Monarchies and Republicks." All of the arts had served despots at one time or another. These sentiments were not so remote from the sermon Jefferson had himself preached to John Banister about the perils of European society and, by extension, about personal aesthetic indulgence. Even though Jefferson found his years in Paris among the most satisfying of his life, he apparently felt no hypocrisy when he wrote Banister that "an American coming to Europe for education loses in his knowledge, in his morals, in his health, in his habits, and in his happiness."

Yet, Jefferson's ambivalent attitude about the arts allowed him to frequent the brilliant circles of Parisian society, including the famous salons of the late eighteenth century, celebrated for their wit, knowledge, and sophistication. At these fashionable gatherings, people of congenial tastes and interests exchanged information and opinions on all manner of subjects, and the state of the arts figured prominently, for Paris was the artistic and cultural capital of Europe.

In the famous letter he wrote to the painter Maria Cosway in October 1786, in which a "dialogue took place between my Head and my Heart," the Heart expressed the deep sentiments Jefferson felt for art and architecture. Jefferson, Mrs. Cosway, young Trumbull, and a few other friends had formed a "charming coterie," and in this romantic, sympathetic atmosphere, Jefferson's natural interest in the arts seems to have been heightened. Trumbull later recalled how they "went with M. and Madame Houdon to the *salon* on the Boulevards, to see his little Diana in marble a very beautiful figure . . . a dignity worthy of chastity and virtues of the goddess." On subsequent tours the group visited the studio of the sculptor Augustin Pajou and the gallery of the French Academy to see works by Vigée-Lebrun, David, and Jean-Baptiste Regnault. At the Palais Royal they saw paintings by Poussin, Peter Paul Rubens, Annibale Carracci, and Charles Le Brun. In the private cabinet of the Count D'Orsay they admired a fine collection that included works by Rubens, Rembrandt, Vandyck, Teniers, Wouvermans, Frans van Mieris, and Gabriel Metzu. Trumbull also records in his journal a visit to the Salle des Antiques in the Louvre. Whether or not Jefferson was with him on this occasion, it was a place that Jefferson surely enjoyed at other times, with its storeroom of "statues, casts, bas reliefs, etc., belonging to the academy." Jefferson's pursuit of the arts in Paris was quite personal, haphazard, and no different from the usual pattern of viewing and visiting that other cultivated and well-connected visitors followed. His infatuation with the beautiful Mrs. Cosway only encouraged him to devote more time to the arts, for his pleasure and appreciation of them often depended on personal association with congenial people whose critical judgment he respected.

Jefferson's attention to the three official Salon exhibitions of 1785, 1787, and 1789 was an important aspect of his artistic education. These exhibitions, which had been held biennially in the Louvre since 1737, were important to artists, connoisseurs, and collectors because they were the only regularly scheduled survey of contemporary work in France. A Salon exhibition was, as Pierre Rosenberg has written, "the only real opportunity that the artist had to make himself known, to compare his most recent creations with those of his colleagues, and to make an attentive critic appreciate the progress made from one exhibition to the next." Jefferson did not consider himself either a serious collector (except for sculpture and prints, he bought no contemporary works) or a connoisseur but rather a well-informed, enthusiastic member of the public. While he enjoyed talking about the latest work with Trumbull, Mrs. Cosway, Baron Grimm, and Madame de Tott, he declared in a letter to William Wirt of 12 November 1816 that he "dispised the artificial canons of criticism. When I have read a work in prose or poetry, or seen a painting, a statue, etc., I have only asked myself whether it gives me pleasure, whether it is animating, interesting, attaching? If it is, it is good for these reasons." This does not mean that he was indifferent to contemporary trends and fashions, for as in his admiration of the works of Houdon, David, and Drouais, he was susceptible to the latest artistic currents. Even after he had retired from the presidency, his reputation

prompted people to ask for his advice. He did not hesitate, for example, to recommend the Italian sculptor Canova to carry out a commission of a statue of Washington for the state of North Carolina even though it is unlikely that he ever saw an example of Canova's work.

He left us no annotated livret of the Salon exhibitions or other record of his impressions. There are a few lines in a letter to Trumbull urging the artist to return to Paris from London, using the Salon of 1787 and its catalog, which he enclosed with the letter, as a lure. "I inclose you a list of it's treasures," he wrote. After praising David's *Death of Socrates,* he mentions a crucifixion by Roland, which

> in imitation of Relief is as perfect as it can be. Five pieces of antiquities by Robert are also among the foremost. Many portraits of Madme. Le Brun are exhibited and much approved. There are abundance of things in the stile of mediocrity. Upon the whole it is well worth your coming to see. You have only to get into the Diligence and in 4. days you are here. . . . And as it happens but once in two years, you should not miss it.

The Salon of 1787 displayed several hundred works of art, drawings and engravings crowded in with paintings and sculpture. While there were many other artists he might have singled out, he had in the works of David identified the greatest painter of the century. Hubert Robert's paintings of Roman antiquities in Provence also appealed to Jefferson, whose imagination was stimulated by any pictorial reference to the classical past.

Seven months before the Salon opened, Jefferson had set out on his long-contemplated journey to the south of France and Italy, where he made a pilgrimage to all of the monuments recorded by Robert. In March 1787 he reached Nîmes, where he saw the Maison Carrée, the building that he had selected as the model for the capitol in Richmond. Jefferson addressed his famous "love letter to a Roman temple," as Marie Kimball called the letter of 20 March 1787, to his friend Madame de Tessé:

> Here I am, Madam, gazing whole hours at the Maison quarrée, like a lover at his mistress. . . . From Lyons to Nismes I have been nourished with the remains of Roman grandeur. . . . At Vienne I thought of you. But I am glad you were not there; for you would have seen me more angry than, I hope, you will ever see me. The Pretorian palace, as it is called, comparable for it's fine proportions to the Maison quarrée, defaced by the barbarians who have converted it to its present purpose; its beautiful fluted Corinthian columns cut out, in part, to make space for Gothic windows, and hewed down, in the residue, to the plane of the building, was enough, you must admit, to disturb my composure. . . . I thought of you again, and I was then in great good humour, at the Pont du Gard, a sublime antiquity and well preserved. . . . I am immersed in antiquities from morning to night. For me, the City of Rome is actually existing in all the splendor of its empire.

Classical history was central to Jefferson's intellectual and aesthetic life as a foundation of faith and a source of identity for the New World. A continuous tradition extended from the original Roman Shrine at Nîmes, through the measured drawings later made by Charles-Louis Clérriseau and used by Jefferson for the capitol plans, and on to the new temple building on the hillside above the James River in Richmond. Hubert Robert's painting had been yet one more concrete method of documenting the past for the use and inspiration of the modern world. Art was above all an important source of factual information, and it was with this view, more than with any other critical, aesthetic, or philosophical consideration, that he assembled at Monticello his collection of portraits, copies of old masters, and engrav-

ings. The fine arts might be postponed in a new country with little history worth recording beyond the Revolution, a subject Trumbull and others were already addressing.

Jefferson's intellectual life was threaded with strands of Italian culture. He was steeped in classical studies and admired the architecture of the Italian Renaissance, especially the work of Palladio. His interest in Italian culture, is further manifest in his study of the language; in his friendship with Philip Mazzei, the Tuscan intellectual who became his Virginia neighbor; and in his taste in music, particularly that of Pergolesi, Boccherini, Vivaldi, and Clementi. Even before the first version of Monticello was finished, the visiting Marquis de Chastellux noted the "name which bespeaks the owner's attachment to the language of Italy and above all to the Fine Arts, of which Italy was the cradle and is still the resort." It was about the time of the French aristocrat's visit that Jefferson had completed the list of paintings and sculptures that he wished to have copied. All the paintings save one were of Italian origin, and all the pieces of classical sculpture were in Italian collections.

Given Jefferson's strong tie to Mediterranean culture, and Italy in particular, one expects to find a rich record of his continuing education in the fine arts during his visit in 1787. But the letters and account books are disappointing. George Green Shackelford has made a thorough study of the brief visit, giving the most complete analysis in his essay "A Peep into Elysium" (reprinted in *Jefferson and the Arts,* edited by William Howard Adams). Even with the finest sifting, the evidence suggests that the arts had little priority during Jefferson's stay. The primary purpose of the excursion into northern Italy was to learn about the cultivation and milling of rice in order to pass on to American growers information that would improve production and quality. He never deviated from this goal during his two-week stay. While he had been familiar with Italian guidebooks long before he came to Europe and was in regular communication with well-traveled friends in Paris (including Mrs. Cosway, who had been born in Italy and who had been elected a member of the academy in Florence as a young painter), nothing took him off his intended path.

It is easier to name the places and treasures that he did not see: Venice, Vicenza (where he could have studied the work of Palladio firsthand), Florence, Naples, Rome. Again, the utilitarian nature of his visit seems to be in keeping with his deep-seated notions and expressed ideas on what America, consistent with its infant development, needed essentially from Europe. In his letter to Rutledge of June 1788, Jefferson included "Objects of Attention for an American"; he placed at the head of the list the improvement of agriculture: "Every thing belonging to this art, and whatever has a near relation to it. Useful or agreeable animals which might be transported to America. New species of plants for the farm or garden, according to the climate of the different states."

But paintings and sculpture aside, it is hard to explain Jefferson's neglect of architecture while in Italy. Architecture was his deepest and oldest love among the visual arts, and in his careful rationalization he had given it a special importance for Americans. In his travel hints, his scale of values is clear. Architecture followed closely behind agriculture, the mechanical arts, manufactory, and gardens. During his brief stay in Milan, Jefferson did single out three houses—the Casa Candiani, the Casa Roma, and the Casa Belgioioso—that he thought deserving of study. The Duomo, however, according to the letter to Rutledge, was "a worthy object of philosophical contemplation," not for its aesthetic merits but in order that it "be placed among the rarest instances of the misuse of money. On viewing the churches of Italy," the author of the Virginia Statute for Religious Freedom concluded, "it is evident without calculation that the same expense would have sufficed to throw the Appennines into the Adriatic and thereby render it terra firma from Leghorn to Constantinople."

Eighty-six packing cases of household belongings followed Jefferson back to America in 1789. He took a house on Market Street in Philadelphia after the government, in which he was to serve as the first secretary of state, was moved there in 1790. William Short, his chargé d'affaires in Paris, was left with the shipping arrangements, and Jefferson asked him to secure a portrait of his friend the Marquis de Lafayette. "My pictures of American worthies will be absolutely incomplete till I get the M. de la fayette's." Joseph Boze, *peintre du roi,* was given the commission. A number of Jefferson's Paris acquisitions were hung temporarily in the Philadelphia house, where some of the elegant furniture he had acquired for the Hôtel de Langeac also was used.

In the winter of 1809, after finishing two terms as president, Jefferson returned to Monticello, where he would remain to the end of his life. The house had been extensively remodeled and enlarged and now awaited its curator of collections. The compact, airy library on the second floor of the original house had been destroyed, but its sacrifice was offset by the large entry hall, where art, artifacts, and specimens from Jefferson's natural-science collections were intermingled. While much additional space was gained by remodeling to house the large assortment of acquisitions he had brought back, there were a number of losses in convenience and simplicity. But to Jefferson's mind, the analogies between the new Republic in America and the ancient Republic of Rome demanded examples of an architecture that proclaimed the modern succession to Rome's destiny. America must succeed to Rome's prominence in architecture, both publicly and privately, at least in the design of the houses of its leading citizens. Monticello therefore had to be transformed into an appropriate architectural symbol, with dome and portico to remind the beholder of the Roman virtues that had animated its designer, who also happened to have helped create the new republican state.

With the addition of bedrooms, halls for circulation, and staircases, the remodeled pavilion lost something of its original, urbane charm as a private art gallery, library, and museum, although it continued to serve these needs for the larger public who made pilgrimages there in growing numbers throughout Jefferson's retirement. Aside from the conventional copies of the accepted masters, Jefferson's collecting at Monticello concentrated on assembling representations of distinguished individuals who had played a part in gaining American independence. Contemporary paintings celebrating the great events of the Revolution, however, were not part of Monticello's collections, although Jefferson did eventually acquire prints from Trumbull's series and the preparatory sketch for the *Surrender at Yorktown.* The collection, according to the tax record of 1815, totaled 120 pictures. No sculpture was listed in the assessment, although there were in fact a number of pieces. The walls of the public rooms "hung thick with the finest reproduction of the pencil," as William Wirt observed. Like Diderot's *Encyclopédie,* the scope and variety of objects displayed illustrated "essential details of every art and science" rather than a connoisseur's carefully selected and critically measured accumulations of a lifetime.

Everything fit into an historical scheme. Portraits of Bacon, Newton, and Locke represented Jefferson's household gods of the intellect. His revolutionary contemporaries and friends were there both in paintings and in the seven splendid examples of Houdon's sculpture. In situ, the artworks were aesthetically and emotionally undemanding, blending in without comment as background to the tastefully furnished rooms dominated by bold Roman moldings, entablatures, and pediments.

It was in the spirit of Diderot and the eighteenth-century Enlightenment that the objects of art, science, and even archaeology —the entry hall originally displayed the *os frontis* of a mammoth from Big Bone Lick on the Ohio and a map of an Indian battle painted on a buffalo hide—were grouped in a comfortable, domestic melange befitting the learned curiosity of the age.

In its cosmopolitan atmosphere, Monticello posited a universal equality of creative potential conveying to the visitor the Enlightenment's faith that "no nation has a proud monopoly of genius," as George Clymer put it at the opening of the Pennsylvania Academy of Fine Arts in 1807. If Jefferson believed that the country's economic and cultural immaturity precluded an early flowering of the fine arts, the house and collections of one of its foremost citizens declared that the arts and sciences nevertheless were cultivated and ultimately would flourish as an expression of American independence.

Architecture

FREDERICK D. NICHOLS

"ARCHITECTURE is my delight, and putting up and pulling down, one of my favorite amusements." This statement by Jefferson suggests that he was a mere dilettante with a lighthearted manner, when actually he was entirely serious in his architectural endeavors.

Jefferson's friend and one-time secretary, William Short, said that Jefferson was a student in Williamsburg at William and Mary College when he bought his first architectural book from an old cabinetmaker near the college gate. The book was either James Gibbs's *Rules for Drawing the Several Parts of Architecture* or Leoni's edition of Andrea Palladio's *Four Books of Architecture.* From then on, architecture was to become one of the passions of Jefferson's life. At his death in 1826 he left over eight hundred architectural drawings. He was without question the most important native-born American architect of his time.

There were few architects in America before the Revolution. The brilliant but short-lived William Buckland, trained in England, was brought to Virginia as an indentured servant to complete Gunston Hall for George Mason. He did an excellent job, and Mason recommended him to several of his friends who needed an architect-contractor. His masterpiece is the Harwood-Hammond house in Annapolis, which caught the attention of Jefferson, who made a mass study of it in sketch form. A merchant architect of the time named Peter Harrison was responsible for the Brick Market, the Synagogue, and the Redwood Library in Newport, as well as the impressive King's Chapel in Boston. Aside from these two men, there were virtually no other architects in the colonial period. Housewrights produced beautiful houses with the guidance of the owners and the aid of pattern books, relying on the long tradition of English craftsmanship to cover the design faults in buildings, but the great day of the architect in America was not to begin until well after the American Revolution.

In 1767, when he was only twenty-four, Jefferson began studies of his new house in Albemarle County and decided on *Monticello* for its name, to be pronounced the Italian way. The design was based on the works of the sixteenth-century Venetian architect, Andrea Palladio, whose books Jefferson studied very carefully. He owned at least five different editions of Palladio and was careful to follow the rules of proportions for the interior as well as the exterior. Monticello had a two-story portico like those Palladio had built at the Villa Cornaro and the Villa Pisani at Montagnana. The center block with low wings of single rooms was a favorite device of Robert Morris, whose book *Select Architecture* was also in Jefferson's library. This large and important library was to be on the second floor, with only quarters for a bachelor below. These included a parlor, a dining room, and a master bedroom with two small bedrooms over the wings for guests.

In the autumn of 1769, work was begun on the southwest outbuilding, which, according to dimensions stated in Jefferson's Account Book of 1766, had probably been designed in the latter year. On 26 November 1770 the building was well enough advanced that Jefferson could move to Monticello. In one of the first dated letters (20 February 1771) from his new home, he described it to James Ogilvie: "I have lately removed to the mountain from whence this is dated. . . . I have here but one room, which, like the cobbler's serves me for parlour, for kitchen and hall. I may add, for bed chamber and study too. . . . I have hopes however of getting more elbow room this summer." It was to this single room that Jefferson brought his bride on a snowy day in January 1772.

Jefferson was devoted to his wife, Martha Wayles Skelton, who died ten years later following the birth of their sixth child. At their marriage, she brought to Jefferson a fortune equal to his own. Although Monticello was more or less finished in 1782, the year his wife died, Jefferson was eventually to double the size of his original design by adding a dome and a U-shaped arrangement of service buildings—like a Palladian courtyard but set into a hill, so as not to obscure the view, with ice house, laundry, kitchen, and stables opening out on the lower level. This was similar to various villas by Palladio in which great farms were designed around a courtyard, which contained all the farm's activities—the courtyard held washhouse, smokehouse, meat house, kitchens, stable, ice house, and coach house. The Palladian villa was set on a high basement where the winter kitchen, storage, and wine cellar were located. The living room and bedrooms were on the upper floor, and sometimes a small mezzanine of bedrooms was tucked under eaves like those at the Villas Malcontenta and Emo. Stairs were suppressed, for Palladio knew that Roman houses were usually of one story only but often had mezzanines reached by small hidden stairs, and he believed in reproducing what he thought was a true Roman house. Palladio also thought Roman houses had temple-form porticoes, which we know today was not the case. In the villas in the Veneto, near Venice, attics under the roofs were used to store hay. This was possible because the houses were of brick with brick vaults and could not burn. Thus an owner had a very functional farmhouse, and only upon close study did a visitor see that actually the imposing house was made up of the components of a farm.

At Monticello, Jefferson showed his admiration for the Romans by using a different order for the entablature of each room. This prompted the Marquis de Chastellux to comment, when he visited in 1782, that Jefferson was the first American to consult the fine arts to shelter himself. For example: the parlor entablature came from the Temple of Jupiter the Thunderer in Rome, and his bedroom was finished with that from the Temple of Fortuna Virilis near the Temple of Vesta, also in Rome. For architectural questions, Jefferson said one should always refer to the master—that is, to Palladio.

Jefferson's gift for architecture was not only a private pursuit but would also be em-

Above: General view of Monticello as completed in 1809. Reproduced by courtesy of Alderman Library, University of Virginia.

Below: Plan of Monticello showing the first house and service wings. Reproduced by courtesy of Alderman Library, University of Virginia.

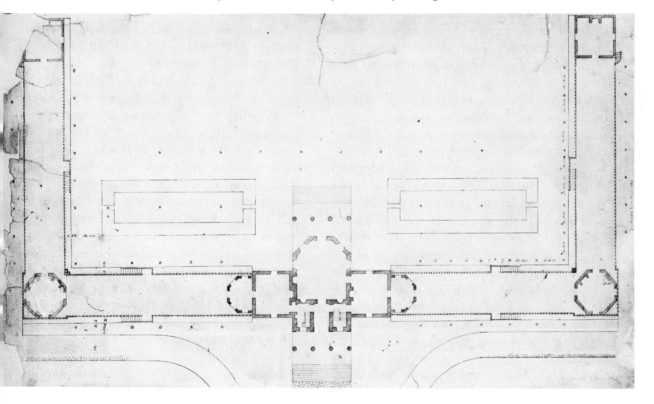

ployed for the public good. Between 1772 and 1774 he made a drawing for William and Mary College in which the U-shaped plan was enlarged into a closed court. Titled "Plan for an addition to the College of William and Mary, drawn at the request of Ld. Dunmore," who was then governor, it would have been the first collegiate quadrangle in America.

In 1780, Jefferson was appointed head of a committee to erect the public buildings in Richmond, and he drew a new plan for enlarging the town with some four hundred new lots located four to a block on an "egalitarian" gridiron. Later he was also to design Jeffersonville, Indiana, on a similar model. He described his plan to C.F.C. de Volney in a letter dated 8 February 1805 as "building our cities on a more open plan. Take, for instance, the chequer board for a plan. Let the black squares only be building squares, and the white ones be left open, in turf and trees. Every square of houses will be surrounded by four open squares, and every house will front an open square."

Between 1779 and 1781, he made plans to convert the Governor's Palace into a temple-form building by adding a pedimented portico at each end. If this had been built, it would have been the first temple-form public building of the modern world. Jefferson had become a devotee of romantic classicism even before he had been to France.

Although a deist, Jefferson designed churches. The first design was probably for Williamsburg. His notes for it read: "Design of a Chapel, the model of the temple of Vesta. Pallad. B. 4. Pl. 38. 39." The watermarks on the paper indicate a date of about 1770, and there is a design similar to it in *Selected Architecture,* Plate 31, where it is titled, "An octagonal Temple or Chapel, 60 feet in outer diameter and the internal 40 feet." Drawings exist for two other churches by Jefferson, which were never built. Christ Church, in Charlottesville, was by Jefferson, but no drawings for it survive.

In 1784, Jefferson was on diplomatic assignment in France, where he lived until 1789. He rented one of the most beautiful houses in Paris, L'Hotel de Langeac, on the Champs Elysées at the Rond Point, where the Rue Neuve de Berry crosses. Designed by Jean F.T. Chalgrin, who later designed the Arc de Triomphe, the house opened up a whole new world to the American. The exterior was "plain but elegant," though it did have lovely neoclassical bas reliefs over the windows. There was a garden large enough for Jefferson to begin turning it into a miniature landscape enclosure. On the interior, the large and well-lit public rooms were ovals and circles. The bedrooms *en suite* offered incredible luxury and a privacy unknown in America. The hotel had a sitting room, a dressing room, and a private stair for each bedroom. The hotel also had a flush toilet that had been invented by the English. In Paris it was called, not without a touch of malice, "lieu à l'anglaise." Chalgrin, who built L'Hotel de Langeac in the latest fashion of Louis XV, was also the architect of nearby St. Philippe du Roule, which Jefferson admired and used as the basis for Christ Church in Charlottesville.

Paris was a revelation to Jefferson. He wrote home saying that he was enchanted with French music, painting, and sculpture, but above all he was devoted to French architecture. He believed that a new republic in an undeveloped country could not afford the luxuries of painting and sculpture, but that architecture was a necessary and practical art and should be studied assiduously. Jefferson set out to become truly proficient in the art so that he could render yet another service to his countrymen. Through his own efforts and his good luck in being in Paris at a time when all the arts were flourishing, Jefferson had the opportunity to get an excellent architectural education.

Since he was a man of the Enlightenment, it is not surprising that Jefferson should have found so congenial the ideas of the

French visionary architects. When he was in Paris, he lost no opportunity to meet and discuss the latest ideas with them and on occasion with artists such as Jean-Antoine Houdon, Jacques-Louis David, Hubert Robert, and the architect Charles-Louis Clérisseau. He would invite the younger, avant-garde architects—and on occasion Baron de Grimm, the leading art critic of the day—to his beautiful embassy on the Champs Elysées. Over a delicious dinner provided by his servant, Petit, with a good claret, he would lead the conversations, which ranged from new building materials to style. Jefferson found most impressive the Parisians' ideas on the social importance of buildings and readily accepted their beliefs that good buildings made good people, that cruel ghettos made vicious people. Jefferson interested himself in the latest ideas behind the design of prisons, universities, great libraries, and hospitals. All were meant to improve the common good of his countrymen.

The importance of nature and of close contact with nature was another tenet among the intellectuals of Paris. Mathematics and geometry were natural sciences in the sense that two plus two is always four. Buildings based on mathematics and geometry would always be viable, because they are based on natural laws. This idea is most clearly shown in the design of the Rotunda at the University of Virginia where a sphere is inscribed in a cylinder, the top of the sphere being the dome of the building. The idea is also expressed in the six oval rooms inscribed around the free-form central entrance hall. The resulting Rotunda remains one of the most remarkable and original plans in all American architecture.

Jefferson only had to look out his window onto the Champs Elysées to see one of the beautiful *barrières* that the gifted architect, Claude-Nicolas Ledoux, had built at the gateways of Paris. Jefferson also knew Jacques Molinos and Jacques Guillaume Legrand, who were building the Halle aux Bleds and experimenting with a lightweight wooden dome made up of short pieces of compressed wood. This method was based on the one used for the Château d'Anet, a masterpiece of Renaissance art built by Philibert Delorme, whose splendid book on architecture Jefferson owned.

Jefferson tells us that the residences in Paris he most admired were elegant, one-story houses that had minimal stairs. He thought stairs were expensive and dangerous, and they took up valuable interior space. He also liked the expedience of putting mezzanine rooms in the upper floor, allowing some first-floor rooms to be two stories in height. Because he could not live without light and air, he liked the octagon-shaped room with windows on all outside walls, which were protected by porticoes. The protection of the porticoes prevented the high hot sun of summer from penetrating the rooms and allowed the sun's low winter rays to warm them. This arrangement was to be a favorite of his and was used in many of his houses. This combination of the practical and the classical again reflected Jefferson's wish for buildings and details that would be "plain but elegant."

At the Château Marly-le-Roi, where Jefferson picnicked with his intimate friend Maria Cosway, he saw a rotunda, inscribed in a rectangle on axis, that served as the king's quarters, with six pavilions on each side connected by arches of trellis. Set on falling terraces, the great courtyard, open on one end toward the view, suggests the Villa Trissino at Meledo di Savego. Undoubtedly because of his thorough reading and understanding of Palladio, Jefferson selected the most Palladian of the buildings in the French capital for close study. Another of the great *barrières* by Ledoux that he admired was Villette, a cylinder set on a square basement. There are four porticoes on the ground floor, one on each side, reminiscent of Palladio's Villa Rotunda but with square columns. The main floor has an arcade running around the entire building—another example of Jefferson's admiration of the portico plus arcade that Palladio so often used.

While in Paris, Jefferson was called upon for a design for the new Virginia state capitol in Richmond. Jefferson disapproved strongly of buildings of the previous generation. He found Williamsburg filled with buildings that were "little better than brick kilns." When he began thinking of a design for the new capitol, it was to be a revolutionary classical building with separate quarters provided for the various branches of the new government. In a letter from Europe to James Madison of 20 September 1785, he stated what his ideas and hopes were: "Much time was requisite, after the external form was agreed on, to make the internal distribution convenient for the three branches of government." Combining the three branches in one building was a unique idea, as it made the building larger and more monumental:

The plan however was settled. The gentlemen had sent me one which they had thought of. The one agreed on here, is more convenient, more beautiful, gives more room, and will not cost more than two thirds of what that would. We took for our model what is called the Maison quarrée of Nismes, one of the most beautiful, if not the most beautiful and precious morsel of architecture left us by antiquity. It was built by Caius and Lucius Caesar, and repaired by Louis XIV., and has the suffrage of all the judges of architecture, who have seen it, as yielding to no one of the beautiful monuments of Greece, Rome, Palmyra, and Balbec, which late travellers have communicated to us. It is very simple, but it is noble beyond expression, and would have done honor to our country, as presenting to travellers a specimen of taste in our infancy, promising much for our maturer age. I have been much mortified with information, which I received two days ago from Virginia, that the first brick of the capitol would be laid within a few days. . . . But how is a taste in this beautiful art to be formed in our coun-

trymen, unless we avail ourselves of every occasion when public buildings are to be erected, of presenting to them models for their study and imitation? . . . You see I am an enthusiast on the subject of the arts. But it is an enthusiasm of which I am not ashamed, as its object is to improve the taste of my countrymen, to increase their reputation, to reconcile to them the respect of the world, and procure them its praise.

Jefferson describes the changes made in the final design, and it seems that Charles-Louis Clérisseau, the pensioner of the French Academy in Rome, who was the architect mentioned in the letter, was mainly an advisor, and most of the ideas were Jefferson's. The following account is from Jefferson's *Autobiography*:

I applied to M. Clerissault, who had published drawings of the Antiquities of Nismes, to have me a model of the building made in stucco, only changing the order from Corinthian to Ionic, on account of the difficulty of the Corinthian capitals. I yielded with reluctance to the taste of Clerissault, in his preference of the modern capital of Scamozzi to the more noble capital of antiquity. This was executed by the artist whom Choiseul Gouffier had carried with him to Constantinople, and employed while Ambassador there, in making those beautiful models of the remains of Grecian architecture, which are to be seen at Paris. To adapt the exterior to our use, I drew a plan for the interior, with the apartments necessary for legislative, executive and judiciary purposes.

At the same time, Jefferson was asked for a plan for a prison. With his humanitarian views, it is not surprising that Jefferson was fascinated by the latest ideas in prison reform. He recalled in his *Autobiography*:

I had heard of a benevolent society in England which had been indulged by the government in an experiment of the effect of labor in *solitary confinement* on some of their criminals, which experiment had succeeded beyond expectation. The same idea had been suggested in France, and an Architect [P. G. Bugniet] of Lyons had proposed a plan of a well contrived edifice on the principle of solitary confinement. I procured a copy, and as it was too large for our purposes, I drew one on a scale, less extensive, but susceptible of additions as they should be wanting. This I sent to the Directors instead of a plan of a common prison, in the hope that it would suggest the idea of labor in solitary confinement instead of that on the public works. . . . It's principle accordingly, but not it's exact form, was adopted by Latrobe in carrying the plan into execution, by the erection of what is now called the Penitentiary.

Jefferson not only studied the architecture of France, which he loved, but also that of England, which he did not. Jefferson very much wanted to study the *jardins aux Anglais,* which were all the fashion in Europe. So in 1787, Jefferson and John Adams, two future presidents, set out on a garden tour of England. They took Thomas Whately's book on English gardens with them, and each wrote his comments on the designs of the sixteen grounds they visited. Oxford, Stowe, Syon, Chiswick, the Leasowes, Wotton, Kew, and Claremont were among the places they saw that inspired Jefferson to write in *Hints on Travel* that the landscape gardens of England were the best in the world; he did not care much for the formal gardens of the French. He went on to advise travelers and prospective landscapers that these gardens were "peculiarly worth the attention of an American, because it is the country of all others where the noblest gardens may be made without expense. We have only to cut out the superabundant plants."

So it happened that when Jefferson came home from Paris in 1789, his architectural abilities were truly professional, and he was no longer merely a gentleman amateur. This was due to his love of architecture, his belief that it was the only art for a new republic, and his interest in improving the taste of his countrymen.

Upon his return, Jefferson was immediately called to New York as secretary of state, and with a brief interruption he was to remain in service to the government until after his presidency in 1809. He was to have a profound influence on the new city of Washington. Due to his skills as a negotiator, he was able to resolve the conflict between the northern and southern states over the site for the new national capital city by placing it on the Potomac River between Alexandria and Georgetown. Jefferson promoted as the designer for the new capital Pierre Charles L'Enfant, an engineer and surveyer who had come to America as a major in the French army fighting for American independence. Jefferson loaned L'Enfant some two dozen of his engraved maps of the most famous cities of Europe to serve as models. But L'Enfant's stubbornness eventually forced President Washington to fire him, and it was up to Jefferson to fill the gap. It was Jefferson who laid out the Capitol on Jenkins Hill, who planned the Mall and the White House in their final locations. But it was L'Enfant who designed the diagonals and the circles after the plan of Versailles, where he had grown up as the son of a palace employee.

We must credit Jefferson with the establishment of the city of Washington and its general design, because he constantly pushed the work and lent support to the surveyors in laying out the city. Although he did not approve of the immorality and corruption of cities and preferred country life, he realized that the country needed a new capital, and he was determined to see it through. One of the greatest advocates of American rural life became one of the builders of a great American city.

Before Major L'Enfant was discharged, Jefferson wrote to him from Philadelphia on 10 April 1791, telling him how he wanted the new capital city to look:

Whenever it is proposed to prepare plans for the Capitol, I should prefer the adoption of some one of the models of antiquity, which have had the approbation of thousands of years; and for the President's house, I should prefer the celebrated fronts of modern buildings, which have already received the approbation of all good judges. Such are the Galerie du Louvre, the Gardes meubles [on the Place de la Concorde], and two fronts of the Hotel de Salm.

During Washington's administration, Jefferson not only planned the location for the White House, then called the Executive Mansion, but also established designs for it. Jefferson entered the competition under the pseudonym of A.Z. and submitted a design based on the Villa Rotunda by Palladio. The Villa Rotunda was one of the most famous houses in the world and was one of the highlights of the eighteenth-century European grand tour. Lord Burlington used its design as the basis for his Chiswick near London in 1729. Mereworth Castle and two other rotundas, Foot's Cray and Nuthall Priory, also followed the design of the Villa Rotunda. The last two have disappeared. It is just as well that James Hoban won the competition, since the four porticoes, one on each side, would have precluded any wings or additions. Jefferson would have used Palladio's dome with a large finial instead of the series of circular shed roofs of tile that Scamozzi used, after the death of Palladio, to complete the design of the Villa Rotunda.

Even though Jefferson did not win the competition for the White House, he had great influence on it. He added the hyphens connecting to the wings on either side, and he was responsible for the two porticoes. He was not responsible for the Oval Office and the opposite building on the north end, which were built in the twentieth century.

Jefferson's most important building achievement in Washington was the Capitol; he steadfastly pushed for its completion during his presidency. He strongly believed that as long as the Capitol remained unfinished, it would be a monument to an uncertain young republic that was unsure of its unity. From 1801 to 1809, he did everything in his power to aid and assist the architect Benjamin H. Latrobe in his efforts to complete it, not that Jefferson always agreed with him. Latrobe, who came to America from England where he had received his architectural education, was appointed by Jefferson to complete the Capitol. Jefferson sometimes questioned Latrobe's designs, particularly the dome, in which Jefferson wanted panels of glass to light the interior like the Halle aux Bleds in Paris. But Latrobe resisted, saying it would be impossible to make it watertight. They worked out other portions of the design together. When designing the American order, as they called it, Latrobe sent the tobacco-leaf version to Jefferson at Monticello for his approval. The capital, which had ears of corn carved on it, derived its basic form from the little Temple of the Winds at the foot of the Acropolis in Athens. When the design was agreed upon, it was used in the two small rotundas on either side of the central one at the Capitol.

All the years Jefferson spent in Washington did not keep him from adding to the design and the building of Monticello, which was a lifelong passion for him. Indeed, in the last year of his life, when the marble capitals for the University of Virginia arrived from Italy, he had arranged for marble facings for the fireplaces at Monticello to be shipped along with them. He also found time for the design of other private houses. In 1794 he had complained to George Wythe, his teacher, that "We are now living in a brick kiln, for my house, in its present state, is nothing better." Two years later he described what he was doing: "My house, which had never been more than half finished, had, during the war of eight years, gone into almost total decay. I am now engaged in repairing, altering, and finishing it." He was also engaged at the time in the design of the "sky room" on top of the house.

The design and details of the first house were mainly Palladian. But for the new enlarged house, Jefferson used the design books of Charles Errard and Roland Fréart de Chambray, and of Antoine Desgodetz. Recently, in an amazing stroke of luck, an Errard and de Chambray volume was found in the Library of Congress titled *Parallele de l'architecture antique avec la moderne* (Paris, 1766). It had survived the fire of the 1850s when the library burned. In the book, in pencil and ink, are Jefferson's notations for the orders he wanted in the new Monticello. He would use the Doric of the Theater of Marcellus (page 26) for the "porches of windows of Dining Room and Chamber." From the Baths of Diocletian (page 27) he would complete the cornice of the "North Piazza." From the Temple at Albano near Rome (page 28) he would finish the cornice of the "North Bow." Palladio's Doric (page 30) was to be used for the "dining room," and on page 49 was the Temple of Fortuna Virilis that he desired for the cornice and fireplace of his "chamber." At the bottom of the page he had written in ink for the purposes of comparison, "see the same Palladio L. 4. Pl. 34. 5. 6. 7.," "also Pa. 66 post, and Desgodetz pal. 41 [or 47]."

For the "Hall," Jefferson planned to use (page 53) the Ionic order of Palladio, which had only a front and back volute; he selected it over the Ionic of Scamozzi, which had four faces for a volute on all four sides. Jefferson used all of these orders, from the same book, for the University of Virginia buildings. But at Pavilion IX, he also used the Ionic of Scamozzi with four sides, possibly due to the influence of an old-fashioned carpenter, for the four-sided Ionic capital was a favorite of the Georgian period. For the parlor Jefferson planned to use the Corinthian of Palladio (page 82); for the bedrooms, he wanted the Tuscan of Palladio (page 105).

Always alert to the latest developments in architecture, Jefferson was also very interested in methods of heating. He owned a book on Rumford fireplaces by Benjamin Thompson, later Count Rumford, an extraordinary American with a brilliant mind who was the inventor of central heating. Thompson remained a loyalist during the Revolution, after which he went to England and became a noted physicist and intellectual leader. The general principle of the Rumford fireplaces was like that of ancient Roman, Russian, and Chinese heating arrangements, in which brick flues provide additional heat in winter. Rumford made a wider brick fireplace that stayed warm all night.

Other examples of Jefferson's heating methods are to be found on the upper floors of Monticello and in the pavilions at the University of Virginia. He used Franklin stoves at Monticello because they used less fuel and burned with less ash than the stoves for the university that he obtained from Philadelphia, where they were called Rittenhouse stoves. Both stoves were made of cast iron and were set in fireplace openings. At Monticello, the traditional brick fireplaces were lined with cast-iron panels on the back and sides to radiate heat.

When coal came into general use for heating, in the latter part of the nineteenth century, coal grates were often miscalled Franklin stoves. But to Jefferson, both names were used to describe a demountable stove that came apart into six pieces, including the hearth panel, which often had legs to keep it off the floor. These were connected and held by means of a tongue that locked into an opening in the adjoining panel; the whole thing could be taken apart for convenience in shipping. The top portion, which had a fascia of some eight inches, was embellished with molded designs. Of the two that have survived, one is embellished with a medallion design with a ship in the center, the other with a garland of flowers in a sway design that admirably suits the frieze in the upper drawing room in Pavilion II.

Jefferson was always ready to improve on an invention, for as he said, he liked ideas in building that were "plain but elegant," and function for him was a kind of elegance. In the dining room at Monticello, he used the deep flanks of the fireplace to provide two dumbwaiters at either side. These had holders for wine bottles, so an empty one could be returned to the wine cellar and a full bottle sent up with a single pulley action.

In Philadelphia, the second largest city in the British Empire in the eighteenth century, Jefferson found workmen and its *Book of Prices* among the best available. The *Book of Prices,* written for the use of architects and workmen, gave costs of various building materials and labor. Because the work on Monticello was proceeding slowly, in 1798 Jefferson brought James Dinsmore, an experienced housewright, to work on it. Three years later he brought another skilled workman, James Oldham, and in 1804, another Philadelphian, James Neilson, to assist on the project. All these men were to assist Jefferson later on the University of Virginia.

By 1805, when work was well along on the house, Jefferson decided to design a landscape garden, possibly the first of its kind in the United States. Although the garden was never completed as planned, lawns and groves were to enrich the top of Monticello mountain, and there were to be framed vistas of the mountains and surroundings from the roundabouts or paths that circled the hill. On one side, there was to be a *ferme ornée* and dells, and glens were to be designed to enhance the landscape. But, Jefferson said, nature in Virginia had been so bountiful that one needed only to use judicious pruning and cutting to compose a landscape garden. Garden temples were also planned, but none was ever built.

In 1803, before Jefferson left the presidency, he had taken Robert Mills, one of the first native-born professional architects in the United States, to Monticello, where Mills had the use of the great architectural library and where Jefferson taught him to draw. The final elevation on the garden side of Monticello is by Mills, and he drew plans for a villa rotunda, probably a design for the Governor's House in Richmond. The plan still bears the pedigree of a Virginia plantation house, as it has an outside kitchen and offices connected to the rotunda by a colonnade.

Jefferson experimented with four versions of a rotunda house: the Governor's House in Williamsburg (1772–1781), which was to have two porticoes and a pedimented roof; the Governor's House in Richmond (about 1780); the President's House in Washington (1792); and Barboursville (1817). Built by James Barbour, governor of Virginia between 1812 and 1814, Barboursville contains some of Jefferson's favorite architectural ideas. Like Monticello, the plan was T-shaped, with two porticoes, an octagonal parlor, and two-story rooms facing the garden, as well as triple-hung windows and mezzanine rooms at the front. The parlor was to have been crowned with a dome, which was never built. None of Jefferson's clients would or could build domes, and Monticello is the only house by Jefferson with a dome.

Before Monticello was essentially complete in 1809, Jefferson started work on the last and finest of his house designs, his retreat at Poplar Forest. Three years later he was able to stay in the house. Painting was begun in 1817, and ornaments were ordered in 1822. It is one of the most imaginative houses in America, for the octagon is the theme that is carried out completely, even to the privies. It is also a brilliant plan: all the rooms are semioctagons or true octagons, except for the contrasting square dining room at the center of the house, lighted with a skylight. A fireplace on the diagonal in the dining room, the one variant in the harmonious series of octagons, adds the final touch of contrast to the sophisticated plan of geometrical shapes. The terraces around the house were also octagonal in character, and the two privies were hidden from the house by two mounds planted with trees.

If Poplar Forest is Jefferson's most original house plan, Bremo is the finest and final version of the type he had experimented with at Monticello. It is not too much to say that he was the architect, even though Gen. John Hartwell Cocke, the owner and a friend of Jefferson, put the name of the housewright, John Neilson, in the cornerstone. Bremo has been called the finest Jefferson house not by Jefferson. Actually, it is a design that would be very much at home in the Veneto, because of its function as a farm, as was the case with almost all of Palladio's sixteenth-century villas. Writing about Bremo's design before it was built, Jefferson recommended that whenever any questions regarding architectural design should come up, "Palladio is the Bible."

Bremo is one of the grandest houses in America and the only one with a stone barn that has a four-columned portico at the entrance and a cupola with a bell (given by Lafayette in 1824). The house exhibits the details so beloved by Jefferson: four porticoes; a setting on a hillside so that the house would be of one story at the front entrance and two stories on the garden side; a plan with a T-shaped center hall for interior circulation on three sides; a splendid series of jalousies to prevent glare on the south; small stairs at each end of the cross hall; a grand entry with a high ceiling; two monumental bedrooms that are almost cubes in proportion; and mezzanine bedrooms on the front. On the ground floor there is a large original pantry, a dining room with a Monticello-type revolving serving door fitted with shelves, a library with tambour covers, and a black-and-white marble floor. The design is all Jefferson's, even if John Neilson built the house. The drawings for it may have been done by Jefferson's granddaughter, Cornelia Jefferson Randolph.

Although Bremo was Jefferson's finest house, his greatest achievement of his architectural career came in his old age. Architects and artists often mature late; Frank Lloyd Wright was working at the time of his death at the age of ninety-one, and Jefferson began his masterpiece, the University of Virginia, in 1817, at the age of seventy-four.

As early as 1804–1805, Jefferson had been considering the idea of a new university for Virginia. The new university was to be in the form of an "academical village" rather than center around one large building. By 1810, his ideas had formed a complex with "a small and separate lodge for each separate professorship, with only a hall below for his class, and two chambers above for himself; joining the lodges by barracks for a certain portion of students, opening into a covered way to give a dry communication between all the schools. The whole of these arranged around an open square of grass and trees."

Jefferson wrote to Latrobe and to Dr. William Thornton, another leading architect of the time. Thornton suggested placing pavilions at the corners of the lawn to emphasize the change of direction. Latrobe suggested that there should be a building on axis, preferably a rotunda to give a focal point, an idea that was similar to that for Marly-le-Roi, which had been the favorite château of Louis XIV, near Versailles.

The cornerstone of the university was laid on 6 October 1817. Jefferson not only designed all the buildings but also fought off attempts to make changes in the original design, saying that it had been approved by the Rockfish Gap Commission and that no alterations could be made. He never allowed a single deviation from his original design, nor did he ever say that he would have changed the design in any aspect if he had had more money. The architectural nucleus of the university today is as Jefferson left it. In a letter to George Ticknor of 24 December 1819, he summarized the intended design:

> [We] have completed all the buildings proposed . . . ten distinct houses or pavilions containing each a lecturing room with generally four other apartments and the accommodation of a professor and his family, and with a garden, and the requisite family offices; six hotels for dieting the students, with a single room in each for a refectory, and two rooms, a garden and offices for the tenant, and a hundred and nine dormitories, sufficient each for the accommodation of two students, arranged in four distinct rows between the pavilions and hotels, and united with them by covered ways; which buildings are all in readiness for occupation, except . . . the garden grounds and garden walls to be completed, and some columns awaiting their capitals not yet received from Italy. . . . The remaining building (the Rotunda) . . . was to contain rooms for religious worship, for public examinations, for a Library and other associated uses.

Because of the difficulty of finding appropriate marble and practiced workmen, Jefferson finally gave up trying to have capitals carved in Charlottesville and ordered the Ionic and Corinthian capitals from the famous quarries of Carrara, near Florence, Italy.

Along with the design and the drawings, Jefferson had to supervise all the construction, so that his design would not be altered. He had to raise the money from a parsimonious legislature, select all the faculty, choose all the books for the library, lay out the curriculum, and act as the first rector, or chairman, of the faculty. The University of Virginia was truly the work of one man.

These contributions were not the only innovations that Jefferson brought to the university. Attendance at chapel was not required, and there was no regular schedule of religious services. Any group could ask for a room in the Rotunda when it wished to have a service, making this university the first to have no religious affiliation. The other universities had been founded for the training of clergymen: Princeton was Presbyterian, Harvard was Congregational, and Columbia was Episcopalian. A student could stay as long as he wanted, he could take whatever courses he fancied, and he was free to leave at any time, when he thought he had an education. There were no degrees and no diplomas: a student received a certificate stating that he had completed so many courses, and that was all. In every sense it was a free university, except that the students paid their expenses and a fee for each course.

The plan of the University of Virginia is very like that of Marly-le-Roi. The two sites were similar, and each complex commanded a distant view. Both had rotundas on axis (the university's was freestanding; Marly's was set in a parallelogram). Both had pavilions placed to form a courtyard open on one side to the distant mountains. In both cases, the pavilions were connected by arcades and colonnades. The university provides other evidences of Jefferson's French design experience; Pavilion IX is patterned after Ledoux's pavilion at Louveciennes, built for Madame du Barry. Pavilions IX and X, the two that terminate the lawn, are both framed by small porticoes. The colossal portico of Pavilion X is framed by two projecting diminutive porticoes, and the opposite pavilion, IX, is framed by two receding porticoes. In a letter to Latrobe of 12 June 1817, Jefferson described what he had in mind in the detail of these pavilions: he wished them to be "models of taste and good architecture, and a variety of appearances, no two alike, so as to serve as specimens for the Architectural lecturer."

Jefferson took full advantage of his imposing site, composing his buildings to frame the view that he carefully orchestrated. The

The University of Virginia, as designed by Thomas Jefferson: Henry Howe's engraving of the Lawn in 1845. Reproduced by courtesy of Alderman Library, University of Virginia.

The University of Virginia: View of the Lawn looking toward the Rotunda (Library). Reproduced by courtesy of Alderman Library, University of Virginia.

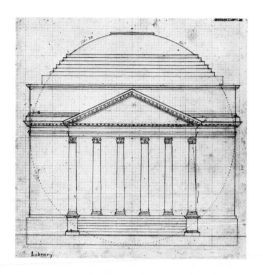

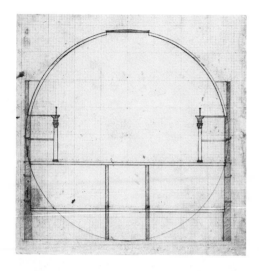

The Rotunda (Library) at the University of Virginia, as drawn by Jefferson. The dotted circle indicates that the design is based upon a sphere. Reproduced by courtesy of Alderman Library, University of Virginia.

Jefferson's drawing of the section of the Rotunda (Library), University of Virginia. Jefferson designed the Dome Room to be exactly half the size of the Pantheon in Rome. Reproduced by courtesy of Alderman Library, University of Virginia.

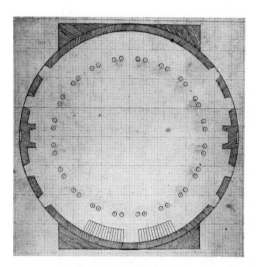

Plan of the Dome Room showing the double columns (University of Virginia). Reproduced by courtesy of the Alderman Library, University of Virginia.

View of the Rotunda (Library) from Pavilion I, University of Virginia. Reproduced by courtesy of Alderman Library, University of Virginia.

Rotunda is not only emphasized by terraces that surround it but also by the pavilions, which get farther apart as they are placed away from the Rotunda, giving the lawn the illusion of a longer perspective. The French did not use this subtle design element at Marly; it is one of Jefferson's most original ideas.

The focal building, the Rotunda, was to be the most influential of all the university buildings in forming the taste of the new republic. Jefferson planned to have the Rotunda built at half the scale of the Pantheon in Rome; both the facade and the dome room followed the rule of half scale. As the Pantheon had been admired for two thousand years, Jefferson felt it was a worthy model for his country.

As Jefferson's section and elevation drawings indicate, the building is a perfect sphere with a dome as the upper portion of the sphere; the base of the sphere is on the ground level. In turn, the sphere is set inscribed in the three sides of the Rotunda. The south front enters into an hourglass-shaped hall, the first free-form room in American architecture. This brilliant solution is a perfect expression of the theories the French visionary architects were experimenting with at the time Jefferson was in Paris.

This wonderful building is far more than just a smaller version of the Pantheon, for by taking full advantage of the site, Jefferson was able to fit three useful floors into the building, whereas the prototype in Rome has only one. For the basement floor, he planned laboratories; for the main floor of

View of serpentine walls showing necessary house, West Lawn (University of Virginia). Reproduced by courtesy of Alderman Library, University of Virginia.

Garden behind Pavilion VIII, University of Virginia. Reproduced by courtesy of Alderman Library, University of Virginia.

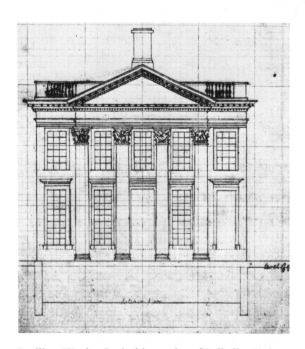

Pavilion III: the Corinthian order of Palladio (University of Virginia). Reproduced by courtesy of Alderman Library, University of Virginia.

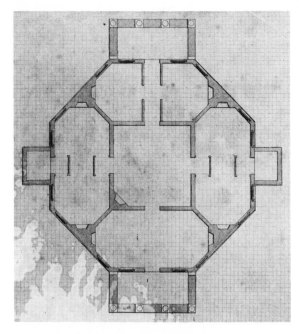

Poplar Forest, designed by Jefferson with a drawing probably by his granddaughter Cornelia Jefferson Randolph. Reproduced by courtesy of Alderman Library, University of Virginia.

the portico, he wanted classrooms and a natural history museum. He would fill the gracefully proportioned room at the top, the Dome Room, with the books that he had chosen for the library.

The cornices of the Rotunda were carefully selected to suit the rooms and their uses: the large east oval room was to be enriched with the cornice from the Pantheon; the opposite on the west was finished with the Doric entablature from the temple of Fortuna Virilis. The entrance hall was finished with the Tuscan order. The most elaborate of all—the Composite order of Palladio—was saved for the Dome Room, the most important room in the university, which housed the library.

The forms and relationships of the interiors compose this great building and give it its great distinction. It is entirely original, and along with the grounds, it echoes the teachings of the French architects. The Rotunda would be quite at home in Paris. It is certainly the greatest example of French visionary architecture in North America and one of the few extant.

Jefferson was careful not to let the university open until he had in hand the $55,000 for building the Rotunda, because he was afraid that the legislators might not appropriate the money to finish the whole design. Because there was nothing but woods and farmland to the north, he did not build the north portico, although he did design the return for it, in the corners of which he placed two of the four circular fire escapes. In the two thousand documents relating to the building, there is no evidence that he wanted or asked for more money. For Jefferson, the design of the Rotunda was complete at its original conception. Begun in 1823, it was finished in 1826 along with the rest of the university, except for Anatomy Hall.

When several members of the board of visitors wanted to open the university before the Rotunda was completed, Jefferson, answered:

The great object of our aim from the beginning, has been to make the establishment the most eminent in the United States. . . . We have proposed, therefore, to call to it characters of the first order of science from Europe, as well as our own country; and, not only by the salaries and the comforts of their situation, but by the distinguished scale of its structure and preparation, and the promise of future eminence which these would hold up, to induce them to commit their reputation to its future fortunes. . . . To stop where we are, is to abandon our high hopes, and become suitors to Yale and Harvard for their secondary characters.

By making his version of the Pantheon, the greatest of all circular temples, the focal point of the lawn, Jefferson built a hierarchy in which the pavilions, interspersed with students' rooms, lead up a series of terraces to the great building with its dazzling white dome. The real stroke of genius is that the library, or Dome Room, is the capstone of the architectural composition, at the top of the focal building. This spatial form symbolized for Jefferson the importance of education and its indispensable tool—books. The grandest urban architectural composition in North America features a library as the capstone on the north and, on the south, a vista suggesting the endless possibilities of the educated human mind.

Jefferson's genius for public office and statesmanship has overshadowed his abilities as an architect; however, it is not too much to say that he would have been remembered for his architectural genius if he had not excelled in so many other fields. His only rival, Latrobe, was born and trained in England, and did not come to the United States until 1796. And Latrobe's masterpiece (the Basilica of the Assumption of the Blessed Virgin Mary, in Baltimore) was only a single building, whereas Jefferson's was the capstone of a university with its attending buildings.

Jefferson's wish that his buildings might

influence the taste of his countrymen was more widely realized than he could have hoped. Of fifty-two capitols, at least forty-eight are a variation of the Rotunda. Many universities were built during the Colonial Revival period (1880–1910); the rotunda at the University of Louisville shows a strong Jeffersonian influence. During the years of World War I, work was completed on the Federal Triangle in Washington, D.C. (the three sides are Pennsylvania Avenue, Constitution Avenue, and 15th Street, N.W.), culminating in the great building for the National Gallery of Art, which has a splendid marble rotunda. If John Russell Pope had had his way, the rotunda at the National Gallery would have had four porticoes, echoing Jefferson's favorite building by Palladio, the Villa Rotunda.

In 1976, the American Institute of Architects chose Jefferson's buildings at the University of Virginia as the finest complex erected in the United States since 1776. At the time, the *New York Times* carried the headline, "Jefferson is still winning awards." With good reason.

Education

JOSEPH F. KETT

JEFFERSON counted an educational institution, the University of Virginia, as one of the three accomplishments for which he wished to be remembered. In retrospect, his paternity of a university, however distinctive its design, seems less important than the other two achievements engraved on his tombstone, his authorship of the Declaration of Independence and the Virginia Statute for Religious Freedom. The Declaration of Independence proclaimed the secession of the United States from the British Empire. The Statute for Religious Freedom expressed the exhilarating doctrine that churches had no right to dictate truth. Both were, in a sense, negative accomplishments, acts that smashed the barriers to progress but that, in themselves, could never guarantee the advance of mankind in wisdom, virtue, or happiness. Education, in contrast, was the true agent of change. Finding men in barbarism and ignorance, it would carry them to civilization and wisdom.

Jefferson was by no means the only philosopher of the eighteenth century to believe this. The Enlightenment provided the basic assumptions and postulates that guided his educational activities. He was in the company of Enlightenment thinkers when he asserted that man must have untrammeled freedom to pursue knowledge, that knowledge was an ever-expanding rather than a fixed body, that philosophy was a method of inquiry rather than a set of doctrines, that the purpose of this inquiry was to discover the natural order of things, and that this natural order lay beneath all branches of learning. Everything worth knowing was part of a science with a body of immutable laws. There were laws governing the workings of the mind (John Locke), the economy (Adam Smith), and the cosmos (Isaac Newton). Knowledge not only was desirable for its essential harmony (Jefferson often said that nothing in nature could be disharmonious), but it was the indispensable tool of progress. Progress, in turn, meant the diffusion of inventions and conveniences that would make life healthier and happier as well as the diffusion of republican principles of government that would enable all men to pursue happiness. Just as knowledge was the fount of progress, ignorance was the root of evil, superstition, poverty, monarchy, papacy, despotism, and all other forms of political and ecclesiastical tyranny.

These ideas formed the common property of Enlightenment philosophers in England, Scotland, and France during the eighteenth century, but in America the cause of education acquired a peculiar intensity because of the role it played in the ideology of Whig supporters of the Revolution. Viewing history as the story of the suppression of liberty by tyranny, American Whigs applauded the declaration of the Massachusetts Constitution of 1780 that "wisdom and knowledge, as well as virtue," had to be diffused among the people "for the preservation of their rights and liberties," and that it was a duty of government to spread "the opportunities and advantages of education in the various parts of the country, and among the different orders of the people." American Whigs of the revolutionary era saw everywhere a struggle between rulers and the ruled in which the former could call upon standing armies, patronage, and other engines of corruption while the latter were armed only with their own virtue. In republican thought, virtue connoted a willingness to sacrifice one's individual or private interest for the common weal, a willingness that itself depended on an ability to identify the public interest. Those incapable of reading newspapers or following arguments were incapable of the vigilance needed to protect liberty by detecting the early incursions of tyranny. Men not naturally virtuous had to be educated into virtue. As Benjamin Rush put it, the goal of education was "to convert men into republican machines."

Jefferson subscribed to these views and remained wedded to them during the 1780s and 1790s, a time when other Whigs like John Adams were transferring their trust from education and virtue as the basis of republican liberty to the construction of foolproof constitutions. Jefferson's faith in the transforming power of education survived the political conflagrations of the 1790s and his two terms as president. He wrote one of his most eloquent testimonials to education in 1818, when he was seventy-five. In that year he drafted the report of the commissioners appointed by the Virginia legislature to draw up plans for the University of Virginia. In this document, known as the Rockfish Gap Report, he wrote:

> Education, in like manner, engrafts a new man on the native stock, and improves what in his nature was vicious and perverse into qualities of virtue and social worth. And it cannot be but that each generation succeeding to the knowledge acquired by all those who preceded it, adding to it their own acquisitions and discoveries, and handing the mass down for successive and constant accumulation, must advance the knowledge and well-being of mankind, not infinitely, as some have said, but indefinitely, and to a term which no one can fix and foresee.

Jefferson combined this durable faith in education with political influence. When he drew up plans for education, he addressed them to legislative bodies rather than to conventions of philosophers. His position as a statesman forced him into compromises, but it also stimulated his inventiveness, for it fell to him to draw up education blueprints that were complete to the last detail and to wrestle throughout his life with concrete issues that a less influential man would neither have addressed nor even considered. Starting with assertions that can hardly be called original, Jefferson produced educational plans that were always distinctive and often unique.

One stimulus to his inventiveness was the fact that at the start of his public life he found the field of education relatively unploughed. His native Virginia had but a single college (William and Mary), some private academies taught by ministers, and a scattering of "old field" schools that were kept on unused land belonging to the Angli-can Church. It lacked anything like the thriving system of grammar schools that dotted the landscape in Massachusetts, and its leading men were convivial squires more interested in the hunt than in the book. Confronting a wealthy state with impoverished educational institutions, Jefferson conceived a drastic change, which was embodied in his draft in 1778 of a Bill for the More General Diffusion of Knowledge.

This bill was one of the two landmarks in Jefferson's career as an educational statesman. The other, nearly forty years later, was his plan to establish the University of Virginia. Unlike the latter, formulated in the relative tranquillity of his retirement from public life, his Bill for the More General Diffusion of Knowledge was the offshoot of an often anxious period in his public life. After drafting the Declaration of Independence, Jefferson's thoughts increasingly turned to his native Virginia. There the problem was less the Tories, who were in full retreat, than the conservatism of the rebels, many of whom seemed to think that their work was finished when the separation from Britain was complete. While Jefferson was in Philadelphia, a legislative body that succeeded the colonial House of Burgesses had drafted a constitution for Virginia that was little to his liking. Failing to change it, Jefferson plunged into the work of statutory reform, and over the next few years he drafted bills to improve the system of criminal justice in Virginia, to establish religious freedom, to abolish the institutions of primogeniture and entail, and to create a system of general education. The last-mentioned objective was embodied in the Bill for the More General Diffusion of Knowledge, presented to the legislature in June 1779, a few days before Jefferson's election as governor.

The key element in Jefferson's bill was his proposal to divide the state into wards, or "hundreds," each with an elementary school established and maintained at public expense. In these ward schools, each child was to receive three years of free instruction in reading, writing, and arithmetic. Although Jefferson did not attempt the impossibly difficult task of legislating boundaries, he made it clear that each ward school was to be within daily walking distance for every child. He outlined in considerable detail the administrative apparatus for establishing and supervising the schools. He stipulated, for example, that there was to be one overseer for every ten schools and that his job was to appoint and supervise teachers.

In Jefferson's plan the ward schools were to form the base of a pyramid of schools. In addition to the establishment of an elementary school in each ward, he proposed the division of the state into twenty great districts, each of which was to contain a grammar school for instruction in Latin, Greek, English grammar, geography, and advanced arithmetic. He envisioned these as boarding schools, each containing twenty to twenty-five scholars. The grammar schools would consist of a mixture of tuition-paying scholars and "public foundationers." The latter were to be the survivors of a rigorous system of selection. Each overseer of ward schools could appoint annually the best male scholar in the ward schools under his supervision to a grammar school, where he was to be maintained at public expense if his parents were too poor to pay for his schooling. In each year the one-third of these public foundationers who showed the least ability were to be discontinued. After two years of grammar school, all of the remaining public foundationers were also to be cut off from public support, with the exception of the most promising scholar. The latter was to continue in grammar school for four more years at public expense. Then, in odd-numbered years overseers of districts south and west of the James River and in even-numbered years overseers north and east of it were to select from their districts the grammar-school senior of greatest promise to attend the College of William and Mary at public expense.

Although William and Mary stood at the top of the structure that Jefferson envisioned, it was scarcely a crown jewel in his eyes. He had attended William and Mary in his own youth and developed a lasting regard for one of its professors, the Scottish-born William Small, but Jefferson thought that the old college needed drastic changes. In a companion to the Bill for the More General Diffusion of Knowledge, a Bill for Amending the Constitution of the College of William and Mary, he proposed various changes in the governance of the college. These were designed to reduce the influence of the Anglican church and to augment that of the legislature over its affairs. The Bill for Amending the Constitution of the College of William and Mary advocated changes in the college's curriculum, specifically the addition of professorships of history, ancient languages, modern languages, and law, and the dropping of the existing professorships of Hebrew and scripture and that of theology and apologetics. The legislature never enacted this bill, but when Jefferson became governor in 1779 he was able to use his influence as ex-officio visitor of William and Mary to eliminate the two professorships of divinity and to substitute professorships of law, medicine, anatomy, chemistry, and modern languages.

The Virginia legislature periodically took up Jefferson's Bill for the More General Diffusion of Knowledge, but never enacted its substance. Not until 1796 did any part of the bill become law. In that year the legislature passed the bill's provisions relating to elementary schools but then left to county courts the decision to put the schools into operation. Jefferson thought nothing of this partial success, and indeed only one county appears to have actually launched public elementary schools. Some of the hostility to the substance of the bill resulted from a combination of hostility to direct taxes to support education and resentment from western parts of the state over the inequality in the size of proposed grammar-school districts east and west of the Blue Ridge.

In addition, religious factors contributed to the frustration of Jefferson's plan. For want of an alternative, he had placed the College of William and Mary at the apex of his pyramid of schools. Anglicans had long viewed William and Mary as belonging to them rather than to the state. Throughout the colonial period the governing board of the college was Anglican, its president was the deputy of the Bishop of London in Virginia and effectively the head of the Anglican church in Virginia, and its professors were expected to sign the Thirty-nine Articles. Jefferson's plan to increase state influence on the college's board guaranteed Anglican (and later Episcopalian) hostility to his plan. Ironically, dissenters like the Presbyterians opposed the plan because it did not appear to go far enough in destroying Anglican influence at the college. In trying to reform education, a field in which religious groups had a keen interest, Jefferson found himself without any notable religious allies.

Although Jefferson's bills had little practical impact, they provide considerable insight into his ideals. Believing that popular ignorance was the root of all evil and that the only secure basis for republican government lay in a "diffusion," or popularization, of knowledge, he affirmed that education had to reach the mass of free men and women. He candidly referred to his "quixotism for the diffusion of knowledge." The only dependable agency of popular education, according to Jefferson, was the school. Jefferson, it is true, was an enthusiastic believer in what we call continuing education. Because knowledge was ever expanding, men had an obligation continually to educate and re-educate themselves. In his correspondence he advised young men on programs of self-education. He also esteemed newspapers as agencies of popular education. Yet when all of this is said, it remains true that in speaking of education, Jefferson referred primarily to schools rather than to self-education. The latter left too much to chance in a society where random circumstances could not be presumed to favor intellectual development. Much of Virginia was little more than a rowdy frontier. Accordingly, education had to be planned and controlled.

Throughout his life he planned schools in extraordinary detail. The Bill for the More General Diffusion of Knowledge runs to over ten pages of modern print and fixed such minute matters as the time and place for the meetings of county aldermen who were to decide the boundaries of each ward. The idea of wards was itself a bold attempt to legislate into existence something like the New England townships that Jefferson admired. Without communities there could be no schools. Since the character of agriculture in Virginia seemed to discourage communities, Jefferson thought that the legislature would have to create them.

Yet Jefferson did not think that legislatures could create a desire for schools. That had to come from the people themselves, and Jefferson was sure that it would. Just as the common people did not desire to live under monarchy, they did not prefer ignorance. Confident of the existence of a popular desire for knowledge, he urged that the financing of elementary schools be left to the residents of each ward, who would pay taxes to support the education of the children of the poor and tuition to support all others. There was an alternative to this approach to financing education, an alternative embodied in the Literary Fund, which the legislature created in 1810 out of funds accruing to the state from forfeitures, escheats, and similar sources. Jefferson did not oppose creation of the Literary Fund, but he continued to believe that support for public education had to rest on the taxes and tuition paid by the residents of the wards: "It

is surely better, then, to place each school under the care of those most interested in its conduct." He argued that if the ward schools, numbering from 1,200 to 1,500, were placed under a single central administration, the result would be such a fragmentation of attention that no single school would be well supported.

Just as Jefferson's ideals contained a combination of centralized initiative and decentralized administration and support, they also revealed a mixture of meritocracy and democracy. The democratic features of his educational thought are clearly reflected in his belief that the rudiments of education had to be extended to all free persons. One problem with the Literary Fund, in his eyes, was that such central financing would fail to provide mass education.

Jefferson's egalitarianism was reflected not only in his desire for mass education but also in his belief that children of the rich and poor should be educated under the same roof. His elaborate plans for identifying and educating the talented children of the poor as public foundationers never envisioned a separate system of charity schools. In the 1770s Virginia had a few charity schools and an assortment of private academies. Jefferson had direct experience of the latter, for after the death of his father in 1757 he had been sent to the school run by the Reverend James Maury, "a correct classical scholar," in the vicinity of Shadwell. Yet he had no plans to incorporate these private academies into his system of education; indeed he later referred contemptuously to them as "petty academies." The limited curricula of these schools may have been one source of his disdain for them, but the grammar schools that he proposed in the Bill for the More General Diffusion of Knowledge had curricula that were no less restricted. It is hard to escape the conclusion that the real problem he saw in existing charity schools and academies was that they educated the poor and rich on separate tracks.

That the rich and poor should be educated in common was an important objective for Jefferson because of the distinctive emphasis that he attached to the competitive features of education. At each step he provided for winnowing the weak scholars and harvesting the strong ones. Each level of schooling was charged not only with educating the many but with selecting the few. Once a public foundationer had reached grammar school, the winnowing became annual. In each grammar school one third of the public foundationers were to be cut off from public support after one year, all but one after the second year. "By this means," Jefferson wrote, "twenty of the best geniuses will be raked from the rubbish annually." The ideal that animated these proposals was Jefferson's vision of a "natural aristocracy" of talent and virtue that was to replace the "artificial aristocracy" of wealth and birth. He never doubted either the need for leaders or the importance of educating them apart from the multitude, but he insisted that the class of leaders be open to all free men. He sought "to avail the state of those talents which Nature has sown as liberally among the poor as the rich, but which perish without use if not sought for and cultivated." In Jefferson's eyes the prerequisite for the formation of a natural aristocracy was the matching of each youth against every other youth in academic competition. This matching demanded that the children of all classes break out of the same starting gate.

Like most of his contemporaries, Jefferson believed that higher education was for the few. These few constituted the "learned class"; they were either men of independent wealth or those who aspired to public life or those destined for the learned professions. Everyone else belonged to the "laboring class," which included farmers, tradesmen, and artisans, as well as day laborers. Although he built three tiers of education into his plans, the real division came after the elementary school, not after the grammar school. As he wrote to Peter Carr in 1814, "At the discharging of the pupils from the elementary schools, the two classes separate." All of this was consistent with widely held assumptions. Most writers on education during the eighteenth century believed that even in republics the few would govern and indeed dominate economic and social as well as political life.

Yet these conventional features of Jefferson's thought should not obscure the novelty of his idea that schools should be so arranged as to maximize academic competition. Today this idea is a pedagogical commonplace. Its roots are usually traced to nineteenth-century school reformers, who had a passion for age-graded schools with standardized textbooks, written examinations, and other prerequisites and agencies of academic competition; but in the eighteenth century such competition was the exception even in the colleges, where the emphasis was more on virtuoso exhibitions by students in the form of orations and declamations than on the pitting of each student against all others in an academic free-for-all. There was no real contradiction between Jefferson's desire to educate all free persons in the rudiments of knowledge and his hope that keen academic competition would guarantee the survival of the few truly fit scholars. His plan contained some features that were democratic, others that were elitist, but none that was simultaneously democratic and elitist.

In retrospect, the weakness of his plan probably lay in his belief that supervision could be left to parents and overseers within each ward. He probably exaggerated the local demand for education and certainly exaggerated the demand for the sort of pyramidical system of schools that he proposed. Virginia did not develop a true system of public schools until after 1900, and then the impetus came primarily from the top rather than the bottom of society. During the twentieth century, school reformers in Virginia quickly found that their hopes for the establishment of academically rigorous and carefully supervised schools depended on a far-reaching augmentation of state and county control and a corresponding diminution of local influence. This was, of course, the very opposite of what Jefferson advocated. He thought, not unreasonably, that the counties were run by wealthy men who would be indifferent to the education of the poor and that the state was too remote to supervise education.

PLANNING A UNIVERSITY

Jefferson was on public duty away from Virginia almost continuously during the 1780s and 1790s—as minister to France, as secretary of state under George Washington, and as vice-president under John Adams. Yet his interest in education did not diminish during these years. While in France he studied the universities of Switzerland, Italy, and Scotland, and by 1791 he could confidently describe the University of Edinburgh as "the best in the world." Because France, Scotland, and the United States were all rife with schemes for national education during the last two decades of the eighteenth century, it is impossible to identify any single source of influence on his educational thought. He acknowledged his indebtedness to the ideas of Antoine Destutt de Tracy and to the American theorist Samuel Knox, and he was familiar with La Chalotais' *Essai d'éducation nationale* and with Condorcet's 1792 report on the need for public education for the masses in France. Yet Jefferson's Bill for the More General Diffusion of Knowledge contained many features of these later plans. On balance, the 1780s and 1790s are less important for the treatises on education that he read than for the way in which he responded during these decades to the projects of others.

The first of these projects was a plan to establish an academy of arts and sciences, modeled on the French Academy, in Richmond. This project was the brainchild of Quesnay de Beaurepaire, a grandson of the personal physician of Louis XV, who had come to America to fight against the British during the Revolutionary War. Quesnay's idea was to bring French scholars to America to investigate the natural resources of the new nation and to form branches of the proposed Richmond academy in which Americans could be taught a host of subjects, from medicine to architecture and painting. Jefferson's response to this scheme was lukewarm, in notable contrast to his enthusiastic response during the early 1790s to the plan of Francis D'Ivernois to transport the entire faculty of the University of Geneva to America. Jefferson had no doubt that Virginia was the ideal place for this faculty, but the Virginia legislature showed no interest.

Jefferson then turned to George Washington, who had an interest in establishing a national university in America and who intended to donate to a worthy educational cause some canal shares that had been given to him by Governor Patrick Henry and the Virginia legislature. But just as Jefferson had rebuffed Quesnay, Washington now rebuffed Jefferson, partly because he viewed the Geneva professors as insufficiently familiar with English to instruct Americans, partly because Jefferson's desire to locate the Geneva faculty in Virginia conflicted with his own belief that a national university should be situated in the national capital, and perhaps also because the whole scheme smacked of elitism at a time when attacks on "aristocracy" were becoming a political battle cry.

Jefferson continued to toy with the idea of a national university and instigated a number of proposals for one. He lured Samuel Du Pont de Nemours, a friend from his days in Paris, to Monticello and encouraged him to complete his treatise *Sur l'education na-*

tionale dans les États-Unis, which proposed the founding of a national university (in the District of Columbia) composed of separate schools or "grandes écoles" of medicine, mineralogy, social science and legislation, and higher mathematics. Similarly, with Jefferson's encouragement, Joel Barlow drafted a *Prospectus of a National Institution to Be Established in the United States* in 1806. Like Du Pont de Nemours, Barlow called for a national university based in Washington and composed of separate schools based on academic subjects. Inspired by Barlow, Senator George Logan introduced a bill that contemplated the establishment of a combined university and national scientific academy. Jefferson seems to have been of two minds about these proposals. He encouraged their drafting, but, in contrast to the astounding energy that he was to throw into the establishment of the University of Virginia after his retirement from public life in 1809, he did not use the weight of the presidency to advance them.

Several factors explain his inactivity as president. Support for a national university would undoubtedly have renewed the long-standing charge of "philosophism" that his political opponents threw at him. A national university was of doubtful constitutionality, and most Republicans were, at best, lukewarm to the idea. Further, while Jefferson was drawn to the idea of a cosmopolitan university that drew students from all parts of the nation, he wanted the institution to be located in Virginia, not in the District of Columbia. In part, his preference for Virginia reflected regional and indeed local pride, for the final location of the university was not merely in Virginia but within a few miles of his home. In addition, he had political reasons for establishing a superior university in Virginia. He recognized that the absence of such a university propelled the youth of Virginia to northern colleges where "opinions and sentiments inimical to the interest and happiness of their parent coun-

try" [Virginia] were instilled "into their young, open, and unsuspecting minds." Although Jefferson was to warn after the Missouri Compromise against the "anti-Missourianism" prevailing at northern colleges, his primary fear was that the "poison" of Federalist doctrines would corrupt the youth of Virginia. The very fount of Republicanism, Virginia would reap benefits from a university founded on the broad principles of Republicanism. Whenever he had sought to remove a Federalist officeholder and substitute a Republican during his first term as president, Jefferson had had to confront the reality that the ranks of educated men were far thinner on the Republican than on the Federalist side. A university in his native state would go far toward balancing the scale.

Perhaps the most important effect of Jefferson's exposure to higher education in Europe and to the various schemes for a national university that were advanced between 1790 and 1810 was the sharpening in his mind of the distinction between a college and a university. In Europe a university was a degree-granting institution that consisted of faculties of law, medicine, and theology, as well as a faculty of arts. Although eighteenth-century Americans at times used the terms "college" and "university" interchangeably, no eighteenth-century American institution fitted this definition of a university. No American college had a school of law or theology before 1800. It is true that Tapping Reeve conducted a law school in Connecticut between the 1780s and the 1830s, but Reeve's school was not attached to a college. Nor was the faculty of the Andover Theological Seminary, established in 1807. Medical faculties had appeared at the College of Philadelphia and at King's College in New York City during the 1760s, and each of these institutions had taken the title of university by 1800 (the University of Pennsylvania and Columbia University), but it can scarcely be said that Jefferson had plausible domestic models for his conception of a university. Nor can it be said that he simply took over European conceptions of a university. He admired several European universities, notably Edinburgh, Geneva, and some Italian universities, but he had no intention of emulating Europe to the point of introducing faculties of theology in American colleges. More importantly, he increasingly portrayed colleges as mere preparatory schools without any integral connection to universities. In the plans that he had put forth during the Revolution, he had been content to portray an improved College of William and Mary as the appropriate apex of Virginia's educational pyramid and the grammar schools below the college as little more than glorified elementary schools.

Jefferson's thought developed after 1800; he assigned higher subjects like the classical languages to the intermediate schools (which he now called colleges), and increasingly described the ideal university as an institution "where every branch of science, useful at this day, may be taught in its highest degree." Colleges and universities might teach many of the same subjects, in other words, but where the former did so to a "competent" extent, the latter offered the most advanced instruction possible. Jefferson may have derived this distinction from Samuel Knox, whose *Essay on the Best System of Liberal Education, Adapted to the Genius of the Government of the United States* (1799) proposed the creation of a national university distinct from all existing or projected "colleges" and charged with the objective of accommodating "such as wished to indulge their literary genius to the greatest possible extent." Or, as is more likely, Knox may have merely reinforced Jefferson's conviction that something more than the traditional American college had to be brought into existence if young men were to glimpse the ever-expanding boundaries of knowledge.

Jefferson's conception of higher education clearly envisioned something more than the establishment of just another college, even a "national" college. In a letter of 18 January 1800 he described to Joseph Priestley his wishes to establish "in the upper and healthier country [of Virginia], and more centrally for the State, an University on a plan so broad and liberal and *modern,* as to be worth patronizing with the public support, and be a temptation to the youth of other states to come and drink the cup of knowledge and fraternize with us." In 1805 he wrote a four-page prospectus for such a university, which was mainly notable for its declaration of the progressive nature of knowledge. Any attempt to freeze knowledge by devising an unalterable curriculum was bound to fail. "What was useful two centuries ago is now become useless; e.g., one half of the professorships of William and Mary."

The events that led up to the chartering of the University of Virginia in 1819 began in 1814 with Jefferson's appointment to the board of the newly revived Albemarle Academy in Charlottesville. This was the sort of petty academy that Jefferson held in disdain. "They commit their pupils to the theatre of the world," he told John Adams in a letter of 5 July 1814, "with just enough taste for learning to be alienated from industrious pursuits, and not enough to do any service in the ranks of science." Jefferson and his friends on the board (including his nephew Peter Carr) immediately set out to escalate the academy into a college and then the college into a university. Jefferson drafted a bill, passed by the legislature in 1816, to convert Albemarle Academy into Central College. The latter's charter gave the governor of Virginia power to appoint members of its board of visitors, on which Jefferson was soon joined by James Madison and James Monroe.

Although Central College still lacked a faculty, students, and buildings, the presence of so many luminaries on its board divested it of its local character. Yet the name of the new college was intended to remind legislators of the geographical centrality of Charlottesville and its suitability as the seat of a state university. To achieve his grand objective, Jefferson relied on faithful lieutenants in the legislature, most notably Joseph Carrington Cabell. Thirty-five years younger than Jefferson, Cabell became his "main pillar" in the legislature and was later to serve the University of Virginia both as a member of its board and as its rector.

Cabell and Jefferson faced opposition from many sources. Some opposed any state funding for higher education on grounds that a university would serve only the few. But this view had probably been stronger in 1800 than it was by 1816. Support for a state university was building during the second decade of the nineteenth century. The real danger was that Jefferson would lose control of the project to advocates of establishing the state university west of the Blue Ridge. For a while, Washington College in Lexington, which had been endowed by George Washington and by the Society of Cincinnati, seemed a likelier candidate than Central College to become the University of Virginia. In the intense legislative scrimmaging during the session of 1816–1817, Jefferson's main rival was Charles Fenton Mercer, a Federalist delegate from Loudoun County and chairman of the House of Delegates' committee on schools and colleges. In February 1817, Mercer drew up an education bill to provide for primary schools, academies, colleges, and a state university. The scope of this bill reveals the extent to which the issue of establishing a state university was still intertwined with broader concerns of public education. Everyone professed to be in favor of public support for education at all levels, yet no one seriously believed that the state would provide adequate funding for primary schools, academies, colleges, and a university. The time had come

when the achievement of some goals demanded the jettisoning of others.

Mercer's bill contained several features unacceptable to Jefferson and his supporters. It proposed to finance education out of the Literary Fund, which was to be supplemented by the creation of a network of twenty-three state Literary Fund banks capitalized from the fund and from the sale of bank stock to private individuals. Jefferson's supporters opposed this not only on the grounds that it mandated state rather than local support for education but also because it linked the noble cause of education to "usurious gambling institutions," and they asked rhetorically whether it might not be better to establish gambling houses or bawdy houses to support the Literary Fund. In addition, the Mercer bill contained a clear preference for primary rather than higher education. No monies from the Literary Fund were to be allotted to academies, colleges, or the university until all of the needs of primary schools had been met. Finally, the Mercer bill proposed to establish the state university west of the Blue Ridge rather than in Jefferson's Albemarle.

Geographical realities doomed the Mercer bill in the state Senate. Ironically, Jefferson's plan for a futuristic university was saved by an anachronistic holdover from colonial times, for in contrast to the House of Delegates (where Mercer's bill passed) the Senate (where it failed) was malapportioned; twenty of the twenty-four districts represented in the Senate were located east of the Blue Ridge. Jefferson responded to the failure of the Mercer bill by renewing his efforts to establish the state university in Charlottesville. He had already engineered the changes that brought James Madison and James Monroe to the board of visitors of Central College and thus contributed to the removal of any local taint from that institution.

More importantly, in October 1817 he forwarded to the legislature a single Bill for

Establishing a System of Public Education. This bill carried some of the proposals for elementary schools that Jefferson had initially advanced in the 1779 Bill for the More General Diffusion of Knowledge, but just as Mercer's bill paid lip service to higher education while advancing the cause of elementary education, Jefferson now slanted his proposal in favor of higher education while suggesting ways to save money on elementary education. Jefferson now spoke of using log cabins as elementary schools and employing the sick, crippled, and aged as teachers. He had not abandoned his interest in primary education, but primary and higher education were no longer conjunctive ideals in his mind. Rather, they were competing alternatives, and in the competition his preference was clearly for higher education. Although there was no real chance that the legislature would authorize support for primary schools from local taxes (as Jefferson had long favored), Jefferson continued to oppose the use of the Literary Fund for primary schools out of a fear that they would exhaust the fund and leave nothing for a university. The act that finally passed both houses in February 1818 (once again it was the Senate rather than the House that saved Jefferson) provided for appropriations from the Literary Fund for the education of the poor only in "charity schools" and, thanks to a last-minute rider attached in the Senate by Cabell, a $15,000 annuity from the Literary Fund for the support of a state university.

THE CREATION OF THE UNIVERSITY OF VIRGINIA

Jefferson described himself as the father of the University of Virginia, but it is more accurate to describe him as its creator. No other American college or university has so fully exhibited the influence of a single man as has the University of Virginia. Jefferson designed its buildings, wrote its curriculum, and recruited its faculty. The visual image that guided his plans was that of an "academical village." Consulted in 1810 about a new college in Tennessee, he had advised against erecting a single central building and in favor of a small building for each professor, with a hall below for his classes and chambers above for residence. The architectural plan of the University of Virginia built on this conception. The university was laid out as a rectangle, open at one end. The long sides of the rectangle contained a series of two-story pavilions separated by flat-roofed dormitories. A covered colonnade in front of the pavilions and dormitories provided a visual unity. Benjamin Latrobe suggested placing a large building at one end of the rectangle; in Jefferson's plans this became a scale model of the Roman Pantheon. Known as the Rotunda, it served as the university's first library. For the facades of the pavilions, Jefferson relied on classical models. He derived these from various sources, notably Giacomo Leoni's 1742 London edition of Andrea Palladio's *Four Books of Architecture* and Inigo Jones's 1742 London edition of *The Architecture of A. Palladio.*

While imitative in details, Jefferson's academical village was astonishingly original. As Merrill Peterson notes, "No prototype has ever been discovered for it." Jefferson was certainly familiar with Samuel Knox's *Essay on the Best System of Liberal Education* (1799), which had proposed the grouping of buildings around a square, but the differences between Knox's conception and that of Jefferson are striking and not at all to Knox's advantage. Jefferson obviously drew on classical models, but they were not models for a university, and it is unlikely that anyone of lesser genius than Jefferson could have achieved such a marvelous integration of form and function. He hoped that, at the very least, the beauty of the university would attract a distinguished faculty. George Ticknor, the Harvard professor whom Jefferson tried to recruit for the professorship of modern languages, exclaimed on first seeing the university in 1824 that it was "more beautiful than anything architectural in New England and more appropriate to a university than is to be found, perhaps, in the world." The beauty of the university would also elevate the taste of the students, Jefferson hoped, while the assignment of each professor to a separate pavilion and the grouping of small bodies of students in adjoining dormitories would foster more intimate relations between faculty and students while checking the student combinations and riots that were common at many American colleges.

Jefferson's plans for the curriculum of the university were, if less original than his architectural design, nevertheless distinctive. His starting point was based on doctrines widely held by philosophers of the Enlightenment but first articulated by Francis Bacon. Jefferson's admiration for Bacon was unrestrained. He counted Bacon, John Locke, and Sir Isaac Newton as the "three greatest men the world had ever produced." From Bacon, Jefferson derived a general orientation toward knowledge and specifically the superiority of induction over deduction, the futility of speculation not grounded on fact, and the refusal to accept as true that which was merely old. In addition, Bacon bequeathed to Jefferson phrases like "advancement of learning," "diffusion of knowledge," and "useful knowledge," which became virtual battle hymns for educational philosophers during the Age of Reason.

Of these slogans none was dearer to Jefferson than "useful knowledge." He wrote that universities should "comprehend all the sciences useful to us, and none others." In the course of American history an immense number of often conflicting meanings have been assigned to the phrase "useful knowledge." During the twentieth century, for example, educational utilitarians have usually construed the goal of education as vocational advancement. Bacon himself wrote of knowledge as an aid "in business," but he also described knowledge that was useful for "pleasure in meditation" and knowledge that served as an "ornament in speaking." Jefferson inherited this broad conception of utility. As long as knowledge was valued not in itself but as a means to some end, it could be useful. Indeed, so far from narrowing the meaning of useful knowledge, Jefferson added another form that useful knowledge could take. In the Bill for the More General Diffusion of Knowledge, he declared the objective of knowledge was to render the young "useful instruments for the public," by which he and others meant the use of knowledge to instill republican attitudes such as political responsibility, love of liberty, and hatred of tyranny.

In celebrating induction from facts rather than deduction from preconceived ideas, and in warning that the infestation of the human mind with error was traceable to its fascination with words rather than with things, Bacon had suggested still another meaning for useful knowledge. Knowledge had to be practical in the sense of being based on things or facts. Since no single fact spoke for itself, the method of philosophy demanded the assemblage and assimilation of many facts out of which scientific laws were to be constructed and scientific advancement made possible. A corollary of this view, widely accepted during the eighteenth century, was that a suitable test for the value or use of any scientific law was whether it could be reduced to practice. Any general idea that could not be so reduced was suspect. The preface to the *Transactions* (1771) of the American Philosophical Society, the oldest and most prestigious learned society in North America, had proclaimed that

knowledge is of little use, when confined to mere speculation. But when speculative truths are reduced to practice, when theories, grounded upon experiments, are applied to the common purposes of life; and when, by these, agriculture is improved, trade enlarged, the arts of living made more easy and comfortable, and, of course, the increase and happiness of mankind promoted; knowledge then becomes really useful.

This doctrine was common among eighteenth-century philosophers, but taken in itself it did not dictate any specific form to the academic curriculum. At one point Jefferson entertained the idea of building the curriculum around professions and occupations rather than around academic subjects. In a letter to his nephew Peter Carr on 7 September 1814 he suggested that his ideal university would have schools of law, medicine, surgery, military and naval "architecture and projectiles," and agriculture to serve the respective interests of lawyers, physicians, surgeons, army and navy officers, and farmers. To these he added a school of fine arts, designed for gentlemen and pleasure gardeners, and a school of "technical philosophy," to which mariners, carpenters, pump makers, opticians, soap makers, tanners, and wrights of every sort would come to learn the scientific principles that underlay their crafts. In sum, the university that Jefferson envisioned in 1814 sounded like a foreshadowing of the Morrill Act of 1862 or of Andrew Dickson White's conception of Cornell University as a place where anyone could learn anything.

Jefferson's belief that universities should teach only useful sciences was as sincere as his admiration for Bacon was genuine, but he made selective use of the criterion of useful knowledge as a principle of exclusion. He used it to rule out a professorship of divinity but he found ways to reconcile it with his inclusion of the classics in the school of ancient languages. Jefferson himself was an avid classicist who could describe to Joseph Priestley how much more he enjoyed read-

ing Homer in the original Greek than in the translation by even Alexander Pope, and he took pride in the continued popularity of the classics in America. He also esteemed the study of Italian for its beauty. Yet, however much he valued languages for their beauty, he included them in the curriculum for their utility. He had no difficulty finding "utilities" in the study of Latin and Greek; they would provide "models of pure taste in writing" and were "stores of real science deposited and transmitted to us." Neither a model of pure taste nor a store of real science, Anglo-Saxon posed a greater challenge to the principle of useful knowledge, but Jefferson also included it in the curriculum on the grounds that to study the development of the English language was to comprehend the orderly and ultimately scientific quality of language itself. One is left with the suspicion that, if Jefferson felt an attraction to a language (and he was attracted to many), he would find a way to pronounce it useful.

While his letter to Peter Carr expressed fully the high value that he attached to useful knowledge, the curriculum that he actually fashioned for the university rested on the more traditional organizing principle of academic subjects. He continued to believe, for example, that the university should teach agriculture, but he now placed that subject within the broader "school" of natural history. Similarly, "military and naval architecture," which dealt with fortifications, fieldworks, redoubts, trajectories of "bombs, balls, and other projectiles," and the construction of warships, was now incorporated into the school of mathematics. Yet these changes amounted merely to a shift in tactics rather than strategy: as long as scientific principles could be reduced to practical applications that men valued, they qualified for entry into the curriculum. By the same token, subjects like metaphysics and divinity, which lacked practical applications and (at least in the case of divinity) were open to other objections, were excluded.

In general, the natural sciences had the easiest time meeting the criterion of useful knowledge, and it is hardly surprising that Jefferson assigned them a larger place in the curriculum of the University of Virginia than they occupied in the curriculum of any other contemporary American university. Within the school of natural philosophy, for example, Jefferson encompassed instruction in mechanics, hydraulics, acoustics, pneumatics, optics, and astronomy. The school of natural history embraced chemistry, mineralogy, botany, zoology, geology, and agriculture. This was a large number of subjects for two professors, but Jefferson advised that some subjects could be sacrificed to others. Because of its potential to increase human happiness, Jefferson urged that more lectures be devoted to chemistry than to other sciences. In contrast, geology—a subject that Jefferson viewed as relatively useless ("What difference does it make whether the world is six hundred or six thousand years old?")—was accorded only a quarter of the number of lectures that were to be devoted to chemistry.

More innovative than the subjects that he proposed for the curriculum was his idea to divide the university into distinct "schools," a term that he sometimes used interchangeably with "departments." In the Rockfish Gap Report he contemplated ten such schools, but when the visitors organized the university in 1824 limited resources permitted the establishment of only eight schools: ancient languages, modern languages, natural history, mathematics, natural philosophy, anatomy and medicine, moral philosophy, and law. At first these schools corresponded to professorships, with eight of each, but Jefferson envisioned the schools as distinct entities, each of which might employ several professors. Further, he believed that students should be free to enter any school they chose and to move from one to another. There were neither required courses nor the lockstep movement of four classes (freshmen, sophomores, juniors, and seniors). All students were on an equal footing and free to follow their inclinations.

Jefferson's conception was far more radical than that of the elective systems that gradually infiltrated American colleges during the nineteenth century. The latter allowed a growth of elective branches off a trunk of required courses. In contrast, Jefferson made no provision for required courses of any sort. Nor were there to be general degrees such as bachelor of arts and master of arts. With the exception of the degree of doctor of medicine, the university did not offer degrees. A student who had demonstrated proficiency by passing the written examinations of one or more schools of the university received no more than a certificate of graduation from that school or schools. Since there were no classes (in the sense of freshman, sophomore, etc.), students could take written examinations for certificates whenever they thought themselves ready. For a man who devoted so much energy to planning the details of a university, Jefferson was remarkably insouciant about what students did once admitted.

The fact that Jefferson did not make the elective system part of his plan for the university until 1820 might lead one to suppose that the elective system bore only a tangential relationship to the main body of his educational philosophy. In reality, however, it reflected his deepest convictions about the discipline appropriate to youth and about the nature of a university. The immediate occasion of the elective system was his dissatisfaction with the regimented curriculum imposed upon his grandson Francis Eppes at Columbia College, in South Carolina. Yet the impulse behind the system was evident as early as 1760, when, in a letter to John Harvie, the seventeen-year-old Jefferson described his decision to attend William and Mary with disarming casualness: "I shall get a more universal Acquaintance, which may hereafter be serviceable to me; and I suppose I can pursue my Studies in the Greek and Latin as well there as here, and likewise learn something of the Mathematics." Jefferson attributed to all students the same intellectual curiosity and maturity that he had carried with him to William and Mary. Never having been an unruly youth in need of restraint and constant monitoring, he was reluctant to impose restraint on others. His fondest recollections of his student days at William and Mary were those of his close relationship to Professor William Small. Jefferson and Small, the apprentice and the master, had walked together in the garden of learning.

Jefferson's preference for the elective system also reflected his awareness that the traditional system of collegiate discipline, with its emphasis on close surveillance and the segregation of students into large dormitories, was breaking down during the early 1800s. Between 1800 and 1820, Harvard, Yale, Princeton, and other colleges were kept in an uproar by student riots. Anyone with an interest in higher education recognized the problem and, while Jefferson did not specifically describe the elective system as a means of discipline, the system harmonized with his stated preferences on the subject of discipline. His plan for an academical village in which small groups of students lived in proximity to professors rather than in a single large dormitory sought to promote an identification of students with professors rather than with other students. Similarly, the elective system encouraged an intellectual identification of students with professors by placing relationships between students and teachers on a voluntary basis. In each case the assumption was the same: students who were treated maturely would act maturely.

The same conception of a university lay behind Jefferson's preference for instruction by lectures rather than by the recitation system that prevailed at most American colleges. Lectures gave professors the opportunity to convey the depth and complexity of a subject, making them more than schoolmasters who forced daily recitations by students as the academic equivalent of parade-ground drill. His conception of a university also helps to explain his preference for written examinations rather than daily oral quizzes as tests of a student's grasp of a complex body of knowledge. For much of the nineteenth century the University of Virginia was to be distinguished by the stress it placed on both lectures and periodic written examinations.

Gripped by so ambitious a vision, Jefferson naturally devoted a great deal of attention to the selection of the faculty. He sought out scholars wherever he could find them. Most of the university's first faculty came from Europe, but Jefferson had no reflexive preference for Europeans. He tried to recruit George Ticknor, Harvard's first professor of modern romance languages, and Nathaniel Bowditch, a self-taught New Englander whom Jefferson viewed as the nation's premier mathematician, but both declined. Even before the university was chartered, he had offered a professorship to Thomas Cooper, an ardent political supporter of Jefferson and a friend of Priestley. Cooper's well-known attachment to Unitarianism guaranteed a hostile reception from the clergy in Virginia, particularly the Presbyterians. Jefferson believed little more of Christianity than did Cooper, but the latter was neither a Virginian nor a venerated elder statesman and hence was an easy target. Privately, Jefferson vented his disdain for the Presbyterians, but publicly he accepted Cooper's proffer of his resignation from the faculty.

The Cooper affair was profoundly troubling to Jefferson. In all of his plans for higher education he included only one provision for teaching theology. In his letter to Peter Carr in 1814 he had made a passing reference to a school of theology and ecclesiastical history, but the public record showed only that he had used his influence as a visitor of William and Mary in 1779 to eliminate its professorships of divinity and that his plans for the University of Virginia contained no provision for theology. Over the years he had gained support from the Baptists, who shared his desire to disestablish the Anglican church if not his reasons for doing so, but his most cherished intellectual companions were skeptical of orthodox Christianity and often, like Priestley and Cooper, were victims of religious persecution. In the wake of the Cooper episode, Jefferson invited the various denominations to establish theological schools "on the confines" of the university and independent of it, but none of them took up the offer and all of them continued to view the university with suspicion. For his part, Jefferson continued to affirm the independence of the university from sectarian influence. "This institution," he wrote William Roscoe in December 1820, "will be based on the illimitable freedom of the human mind. For here we are not afraid to follow truth wherever it may lead, nor to tolerate any error so long as reason is left free to combat it." Indeed his plan for theological schools "on the confines" was less a device to give religious denominations a modicum of influence on the university than a way to expose theological students to the secular instruction of the university and thereby to "soften their asperities, liberalize and neutralize their prejudices, and make the genral religion a religion of peace, reason and morality."

However much he resented sectarian influence and extolled the illimitable freedom of the human mind, Jefferson was not above imposing restrictions. The professorships of moral philosophy and law were reserved for Americans; George Tucker accepted the former in 1825, John Tayloe Lomax the latter in 1826. Jefferson insisted that the law professor be politically sound, free of John Marshall's "toryism." He even prescribed some of the books that the law professor was to teach, in order to keep out "heresies" and check the diffusion of "poison." This restriction obviously conflicted with his more resounding declarations of the value of intellectual freedom, but it was understandable if not entirely defensible. The law professorship was particularly sensitive because the study of government was one of the subdivisions of the school of law. Jefferson had spent his life studying law and government (not to mention engaging in the practice of each). He concluded that, along with other members of the Board of Visitors like James Madison, James Monroe, and Cabell, he knew more about these subjects than anyone he was likely to hire to teach them.

All of the other professors were Europeans. Jefferson sent a young protégé, Francis Walker Gilmer, on a recruiting mission. Gilmer had more trouble finding suitable professors than Jefferson had expected, mainly because the income of many of the British professors contacted by Gilmer was more than Jefferson could match. Yet Gilmer was able to attract several highly competent professors to come to Virginia. George Blaetterman, a German recommended by Ticknor, assumed the professorship of modern languages. From Britain came Thomas Hewett Key (mathematics), Charles Bonnycastle (natural philosophy), Robley Dunglison (anatomy and medicine), and George Long (classics). Immediately after returning to America, Gilmer arranged for the services of John Patten Emmet, an Irishman, to teach natural history.

As remarkable as was Jefferson's conception of a university, the realities of southern education and society frustrated many of his hopes. Contrary to his expectations, a sizable proportion (probably over half) of the antebellum students who attended the University of Virginia had no previous collegiate training, and many had weak preparatory educations of any sort. The university attracted more sixteen- and seventeen-year-olds than he expected and fewer of the mature young men of nineteen or twenty than he had hoped for. Despite his desire to create a university that would draw students from all regions, most of the students came from the South and brought with them their section's code of honor. The result was a series of sharp clashes between students and professors, particularly the European professors. Professors who reproved students with sarcastic barbs found themselves attacked by the latter for calculated affronts to their honor. Violent attacks by students on professors (including the murder of a professor by a student in 1840) and fights and duels among students quickly gave the university a reputation for disorder, while the university's absence of academic requirements gave it a parallel reputation as an institution well-suited to the indolent. In response the university's faculty instituted a stricter system of discipline, and in 1831 it voted to award the M.A. degree to students who had obtained certificates from the schools of ancient languages, mathematics, natural philosophy, natural history, and moral philosophy. These were the subjects that were composing the required curriculum at many American colleges during the second quarter of the nineteenth century. While not destroying the elective system, the degree program provided an alternative to it.

Some of Jefferson's contemporaries, who were antagonistic to his political and religious views, interpreted the turbulence that marked the university's early history and the modification of aspects of Jefferson's plan after his death as proof that he was an impractical visionary. In reality, however, the essential features of Jefferson's plan were practical. Indeed the impractical visionaries of the nineteenth century were those who believed that colleges could go on forever emphasizing fixed curricula and instruction by recitation. With the establishment of over five hundred new colleges between the Rev-olution and the Civil War, competition for students intensified. The successful colleges were those that could attract students, and by this measure the University of Virginia was highly successful. In 1860 it was one of the largest American universities and was considered the leading southern university. Virtually all of Jefferson's innovations contributed to this success. The presence of schools or departments of law and medicine alongside those of natural history and natural philosophy acted as a magnet for students. Even with the creation of a degree program, the university continued to offer students an unprecedented degree of freedom through its elective system. The lecture system proved to be extremely practical, for it made possible the instruction of students in far larger numbers than did the recitation system. The departmentalization of the university made it possible to augment the size of the faculty in response to student demand.

JEFFERSON'S LEGACY

Many of Jefferson's ideas about higher education, such as the elective system, the emphasis on science and useful knowledge, and the conception of a university as distinct from a college, were to become components of educational orthodoxy by 1900. Yet his direct influence on higher education is easily exaggerated. Jefferson undoubtedly helped to inspire Ticknor's efforts to reform the Harvard curriculum during the 1820s, but Jefferson's influence on higher education waned after his death. There is not a single idea in the preamble of the Morrill Act of 1862 (which provided federal support for the land-grant universities) that was not foreshadowed by Jefferson, but the framers of the Morrill Act paid far more attention to northern institutions devoted to useful knowledge, such as the Rensselaer Polytechnic Institute and the Illinois Industrial University (later the University of Illinois), than to either Jefferson or the University of Virginia.

When President Charles W. Eliot of Harvard outlined the distinctive features of the "new education" (scientific and technical) in two articles that he contributed to the *Atlantic Monthly* in 1869, he mentioned neither Jefferson nor the University of Virginia. Eliot's elective system is often traced to Jefferson, but similarities do not amount to influence. Eliot's elective system was essentially an amplification and ratification of developments that had been taking place at many American colleges and universities during the second and third quarters of the nineteenth century, and these developments were themselves reflections of local pressures, especially the need to attract students, rather than a conscious emulation of the University of Virginia. The first president of Johns Hopkins University, Daniel Coit Gilman, saw a resemblance between his early plans for Hopkins and the University of Virginia, "an institution already favorably considered in Baltimore," but Johns Hopkins owed more to German models than to that of Virginia.

Several factors limited Jefferson's influence on American education. He may have had the right ideas, but they were in the wrong place and at the wrong time. For example, it is hardly surprising that, in the wake of the Civil War, Eliot refused to acknowledge the ideas of a southern slaveholder. Further, Jefferson's conception of a university as a place where every useful science could be taught in its highest degree differed in subtle ways from the modern conception of scientific research that American scholars brought back from Germany after the Civil War. However advanced for its day, the University of Virginia was fundamentally a teaching rather than a research institution. The decision to award the M.A. rather than B.A. degree was a nice gesture toward Jefferson's vision of the university as

a graduate institution, but most of the students were really undergraduates. The burden of teaching undergraduates was a major factor in the decision of the university's two most luminous faculty members of the nineteenth century to leave for other institutions, William Barton Rogers to found and head the Massachusetts Institute of Technology and Basil Lanneau Gildersleeve to become the first professor of Greek at Johns Hopkins University.

Although it is easy to exaggerate Jefferson's direct influence on education, it is fair to speak of his legacy in the sense that an image of Jefferson has often inspired and propelled educational reformers. In assessing his legacy, the fact that this image of Jefferson has often distorted the real Jefferson is of little importance, for men and women have been impelled by the image regardless of its historical accuracy. For example, leaders of the southern "education revival" during the 1890s canonized Jefferson as the source of all that was durable and good in American education: the idea that the state had a duty to educate its citizens, the principle that states should have unified systems of public education extending from the primary and grammar schools through the university, and the notion that to harmonize with American institutions education had to be secular and practical. The prominent figures of the education revival, a mixture of northern philanthropists and southerners like Edwin A. Alderman (who became president of the University of Virginia in 1904), sought to modernize southern education by introducing the kind of state systems of primary and secondary education that had developed in the North between the 1830s and 1890. For ideological and political purposes it was important for leaders of the education revival to find southern sources of these ideas. Jefferson became their patron saint, and southerners repeatedly invoked his memory. In reality, the objectives of the education revival demanded a much greater enhancement of state and county supervision of education than Jefferson had sanctioned. The South was scarcely bereft of schools in 1900; rather, it had thousands of small school districts, each a law unto itself. The reformers consciously challenged the kind of local control that Jefferson had extolled and sought to substitute professional administrators employed by the state or county for district officials. They forgot that Jefferson was more interested in higher than in primary or secondary education, and that he advocated free public education only for the few. Yet these examples of selective amnesia scarcely mattered. However much reformers distorted Jefferson, they made him their prophet. Jefferson the historical personage had been transmuted into Jeffersonianism, an ideology that impelled men and women long after Jefferson's influence on education had evaporated.

Man of Science

SILVIO A. BEDINI

THOMAS Jefferson is often called a scientist but could more accurately be described as "a man of science," inasmuch as he was not professionally trained in the sciences and did not derive an income from them. There were very few who deserved the name *scientist* in America in his time. He was, however, involved with virtually every science as a "zealous amateur," sincerely devoted to science but making no claim to be a specialist. His greatest contribution to the sciences proved to be as their promoter and popularizer, roles in which he had no peer throughout a period when such involvement while in public life brought ridicule and criticism. He lost no opportunity to utilize his position to advance the application of science for national improvement and to benefit mankind. He was adamant in the conviction that Americans must and should profit from scientific accomplishments, whether originated at home or abroad, in order to produce a true democracy. Furthermore, he visualized science as the common ground for engendering fraternal relations with other peoples and nations.

More than any other individual of his time, Jefferson epitomized the "Renaissance man." Categorized by his biographer Dumas Malone as "statesman, diplomat, author, scientist, architect, apostle of freedom and enlightenment," he was particularly fitted for a career in science by training as well as by inclination. In a letter to Harry Innes dated 7 March 1791, he called science "my passion" and politics "my duty," thus summarizing a remarkable career that spanned more than a half century in public service and even longer in scientific pursuits.

EDUCATION

Born and raised at the edge of the Virginia frontier as the son of a successful land developer and surveyor, Jefferson was inspired from his boyhood by the surrounding world of nature and the unknown that lay beyond. His early environment taught him the importance of the practical sciences for the development of the American colonies into an independent nation. From his earliest childhood he experienced the limitations of frontier life, learned about the beauties and hazards of the wilderness, and developed an interest in flora and fauna. Jefferson's awareness of the natural world was kindled by his father, who also first taught him to write, introduced him to the magic of mathematics, and instructed him in the elements of surveying, a science he would pursue as an avocation for most of his life. As he listened to his father and his companions describe their experiences in the wilderness, the young boy's curiosity was aroused. Curiosity would become a basic characteristic of his adult life.

Jefferson's attraction to the sciences was influenced not only by his father but also by several of his teachers. At the Reverend James Maury's school he was introduced to fossils, geological specimens, and other natural curiosities, and he may have been at liberty to read in the schoolmaster's ex-

Engraving of the *Jeffersonia diphylla*. It was named *Jeffersonia binata* by Benjamin Smith Barton in 1792 and renamed by Persoon. Reproduced from Curtis's *Botanical Magazine.*

tensive library. During his studies he drew inspiration from the works of Homer, Epicurus, Epictetus, Cicero, Shakespeare, and the Bible, and particularly from the writings of Francis Bacon, Sir Isaac Newton, and John Locke. Later in life, he wrote on 16 January 1811 to Dr. Benjamin Rush, "Bacon, Newton and Locke . . . were my trinity of the three greatest men the world has ever produced."

Undoubtedly the strongest influence directing him to scientific pursuits came from William Small, the professor of natural and moral philosophy with whom he studied at the College of William and Mary and whose privileged associate he became during their leisure hours. Important, too, were friendships he developed with Gov. Francis Fauquier and the lawyer George Wythe. Both were interested in natural phenomena and, with Small, formed an intellectual circle to which Jefferson was admitted. Men of wide interests, they met in the Governor's Palace to participate in musical concerts and lively discussions on questions of natural philosophy. Fauquier's account of an unusual hailstorm was reported to the Royal Society, and his weather diary, maintained from 1760 to 1762, was subsequently published. Jefferson's lifelong system of weather observation may have been inspired by Fauquier's example.

An idiosyncrasy that Jefferson developed as a student and that was closely associated with his scientific interests was a compulsion to collect and record in pocket memorandum books random bits of information, which he would apply eventually to practical purposes as opportunity offered. These consisted of the most unlikely combination of data, some useful and some trivial. In general, they related to measurement in one form or another. His notations ranged from the weight of a dwarf at birth to how many cotton seeds were required to fill a bushel, to how much land that bushel would plant if the seeds were placed four to a hill and the hills spaced two feet apart. In the same manner, he recorded meteorological data, noting daily temperatures, amounts of rainfall and snowfall, wind directions, and the first appearances of certain plants and birds in the spring. He justified his preoccupation with the statement in Query VI of his *Notes on the State of Virginia* that "a patient pursuit of facts, and cautious combination and comparison of them, is the drudgery to which man is subjected by his Maker, if he wishes to attain sure knowledge."

Following two years at the College of William and Mary, Jefferson undertook the study of law with Wythe. From this training he learned the discipline and methods of research required by the principles of scientific inquiry, which he later strongly promulgated. During the following decade he became one of the most distinguished politicians, diplomats, and statesmen of his time. Each year he found himself increasingly involved with the historic events that finally culminated in a call to arms.

"Nature intended me for the tranquil pursuits of science," he was to write to Pierre-Samuel Du Pont de Nemours on 2 March 1809, "by rendering them my supreme delight. But the enormities of the times in which I have lived, have forced me to take a part in resisting them, and to commit myself on the boisterous ocean of political passions." With these words, he summarized the new direction his life had taken, leaving little time for scientific activities. Nonetheless, he continued to maintain his Garden Book, begun in 1766, and his Farm Book, initiated in 1774, as well as his weather observations.

NOTES ON THE STATE OF VIRGINIA

During his tenure as governor of Virginia, Jefferson undertook the compilation of the work that was to become the *Notes,* one of his major scientific achievements. The French government had expressed a desire to know more about the country that it had assisted during the American Revolution. The request was transmitted to the French legate to the United States, Chevalier de la Luzerne, and so the legation secretary, Marquis François de Barbé-Marbois, prepared twenty-two questions to be submitted to each of the states. The questionnaire for Virginia was referred to Jefferson as the individual believed to be most knowledgeable not only about Virginia's political structure but also about its geography and flora and fauna.

Shortly after Jefferson's retirement from the governorship came the death of his wife and then a fall from a horse, which forced him to retire to his summer residence at Poplar Forest. There he reviewed his notes and compiled answers to the questionnaire. As he stated later in his *Autobiography,*

> I had always made it a practice whenever an opportunity occurred, of obtaining any information of our country, which might be of use to me in any station, public or private, to commit it to writing. These memoranda were on loose papers, bundled up without order. . . . I thought this a good occasion to embody their substance, which I did in the order of Mr. Marbois' queries, so as to answer his wish, and to arrange them for my own use.

Although most of the data was collected by Jefferson at first hand, he also relied on others for information on subjects on which he was not well versed. He sent the manuscript to several friends and associates for comments and suggestions, and as it underwent revisions, the *Notes* developed into much more than a response to the questions of Barbé-Marbois. In a letter to Jefferson of 6 March 1785, Charles Thomson wrote that it was "a most excellent natural history not merely of Virginia but of North America and possibly equal if not superior to that of any

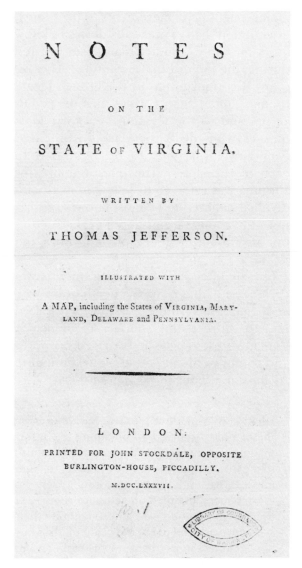

NOTES

ON THE

STATE OF VIRGINIA.

WRITTEN BY

THOMAS JEFFERSON.

ILLUSTRATED WITH

A MAP, including the States of VIRGINIA, MARY-
LAND, DELAWARE and PENNSYLVANIA.

LONDON:

PRINTED FOR JOHN STOCKDALE, OPPOSITE
BURLINGTON-HOUSE, PICCADILLY.

M.DCC.LXXXVII.

Title page of the first commercial edition in English of the *Notes on the State of Virginia,* published in London in 1787. Reproduced courtesy of the Library of Congress.

country yet published." Structured on the format of the questionnaire, Jefferson's compilation included a description of Virginia's geography, including its topographical features, waterways, climate, natural resources, minerals, boundaries, and flora and fauna. Jefferson described Virginia's population, commercial development, military forces, and social and political life.

In the *Notes,* Jefferson vigorously refuted assumptions made and published by the distinguished French naturalist Georges Louis Leclerc, Comte de Buffon, concerning the American Indians and flora and fauna. Buffon had concluded that animals common to both the Old World and the New were of smaller scale in the latter. He claimed that animals domesticated in America had degenerated and that in general the New World had fewer species than were to be found in the Old. Ever jealous of the prestige of the new republic of which he had been an architect, Jefferson marshaled facts and arguments to refute Buffon's contentions. He also argued against the proposal made by one of Buffon's associates, Louis Daubenton, that the remains of the "mammoth" found on the North American continent were of two different species and that they belonged to either the rhinoceros or the elephant.

He particularly took issue with Buffon's detrimental estimate of the American Indian and emphasized his virtues. The Indians, wrote Jefferson, were "led to duty and to enterprize by personal influence and persuasion. Hence eloquence in council, bravery and address in war, become the foundations of all consequence with them." While compiling the *Notes* Jefferson undertook the excavation of an Indian burial mound near his home. It was not an endeavor to collect artifacts but a serious attempt to resolve conjectures concerning the purpose and structure of these aboriginal burial places. Without a precedent to guide him, Jefferson proceeded with his excavation methodically, carefully recording every detail of evidence that appeared as well as the stratigraphy. As reported in the *Notes,* the excavation was executed in the most professional manner, anticipating by almost a century the techniques of modern archeology.

The *Notes* provides ample evidence of Jefferson's vast erudition. He cited eighteen foreign authorities, quoting and translating from four foreign languages. The work, intended for distribution only to friends and colleagues, was privately printed in 1785. Subsequently reprinted in England, France, and the United States in numerous editions, it was the first comprehensive study made of any part of the United States and is now considered to be the most important scientific work published in America in the eighteenth century.

SCIENCE IN EUROPE

Summarizing his impressions of Europeans after his first year in France, he noted in a letter to Charles Bellini of 30 September 1785, "In science, the mass of people are two centuries behind ours; their literati, half a dozen years before us. Books, really good, acquire just reputation in that time, and so become known to us and communicate to us all their advances in knowledge." As major political changes took place on both sides of the Atlantic in the second half of the eighteenth century, great philosophical upheavals occurred, derived in some part from these events. Jefferson found himself intimately involved and influenced by the scientific materialism of such friends as Joseph Priestley and Thomas Paine. He noted in a letter to John Adams dated 28 October 1813,

> Even in Europe a change has sensibly taken place in the mind of Man. Science had liberated the ideas of those who read and reflect, and the American example had kindled feelings of right in the people. An insurrection has consequently begun, of science, talents and courage against rank and birth, which have fallen into contempt. . . . Science is progressive, and talents and enterprize on the alert.

In France, Jefferson dedicated himself to the task of bringing to the attention of his countrymen every scientific achievement of practical use to them that the rest of the world had to offer. He lost no time in reporting to his homeland new processes, inventions, and devices—even ones of long standing if they appeared to be labor-saving and could be usefully applied to American needs. He particularly sought out new achievements in agriculture, manufacturing, and other gainful pursuits. At the same time, he maintained an awareness of the progress being made in Europe and England relative to that in the United States. His efforts were directed to the encouragement of fellow Americans to make practical application of scientific and technological innovations that would improve their environment, develop their natural resources, and conserve energy and time. Science must be made useful, he was convinced, and the young republic would be advanced by means of the useful sciences and arts. "Science is more important in a republican than in any other government," he stated in a letter to an unidentified correspondent dated 18 September 1821. "And in an infant country like ours, we must much depend for improvement on the science of other countries, longer established, possessing better means, and more advanced than we are. To prohibit us from the benefit of foreign light, is to consign us to long darkness."

While in France, Jefferson constituted himself a one-man information center for the purpose of keeping Americans informed of scientific activities at home and abroad. He voluntarily became correspondent on scientific matters to the presidents of three colleges—Harvard, Yale, and William and Mary—as well as to the Congress. So successful was he in his endeavor, in fact, that Rev. James Madison of William and Mary commented to him in a letter, "It is certainly of great importance for us to know what is done in the philosophical World—but our Means of Information are confined almost entirely to you." Jefferson sent back descrip-

Engraved portrait of Thomas Jefferson, with scientific instruments, Cornelius Tiebout, 1801. Reproduced courtesy of the Thomas Jefferson Memorial Foundation.

tions of the new "phosphoretic matches," useful equally for lighting a bedside candle, softening sealing wax, and replacing flint and steel in the woods; the Argand lamp, which intrigued him because it used oil economically, gave maximum quality lighting, and dispensed with snuffing; and other inventions he found abroad.

Late in 1785, Jefferson reported his observation of a steam engine used for raising water for the fire protection of Paris, and later he wrote to Charles Thomson about the applicability of steam power for operating gristmills that he had seen in London. He forwarded to American associates the first news to reach the United States of James Watt's steam engine, which, using no more than one and one-half pecks of coal, could perform the equivalent of a full day's work by a horse. It was his conclusion, however, that in the United States steam power would lead neither to an industrial revolution nor to a proliferation of factories that would encourage the growth of cities and diminish the importance of agriculture. Steam would become a supplementary source of power, he believed, which would be applicable primarily to navigation, milling, small-scale manufacturing, and the performance of everyday chores, with the purpose of liberating men to follow agricultural pursuits. He contemplated various applications of steam to such chores and tried to interest others in them.

In 1787, Jefferson toured France and northern Italy and, in 1788, the Low Countries, everywhere finding things that delighted and thrilled him and technological innovations that intrigued him. He noted, for example, the "diamond-wise" placement of joists in house construction to provide greater strength to arches between. He observed windows made to admit air while keeping out rain, and in Germany he discovered a bridge over the Rhine supported by thirty-nine boats. As he traveled he noted climate, soils, crops, farming im-

plements, and breeds of cattle, all for the purpose of reporting useful information to his countrymen. In the Po Valley he studied Italian mills for cleaning rice and obtained samples of unhusked rice, which he sent back to the United States for planting in South Carolina, an experiment that proved successful.

During this sojourn he noted the type of plow used by French peasants near Nancy and eventually devised a more useful form. He designed a moldboard based on mathematical principles, which made it possible to duplicate it readily. After his return to Monticello he had it constructed and used it successfully. He submitted his design to David Rittenhouse and Charles Willson Peale, among others, and received their favorable responses. In 1799 his moldboard was described by him in the *Transactions* of the American Philosophical Society; it was subsequently described in the *Edinburgh Encyclopedia*. It also attracted attention in France, where Jefferson's paper was translated and published in 1802 in the *Annales du Musée National d'Histoire Naturelle*. In 1805 the Société d'Agriculture du Département de la Seine awarded him a gold medal for his invention, the first American to be so honored. Despite the successful design of the moldboard, it was soon to be eclipsed by the advent of the cast-iron plow.

Jefferson's preoccupation with agriculture in all its aspects was a dominant concern. He not only considered agriculture to be one of the sciences but also believed that it is "the first in utility, and ought to be the first in respect." It was his desire, as he put it in a letter to David Williams dated 14 November 1803, to restore agriculture "to its primary dignity in the eyes of men. It is a science of the very first order. It counts among its handmaids the most respectable sciences, such as Chemistry, Natural Philosophy, Mechanics, Mathematics generally, Natural History, Botany." Jefferson exchanged plants and seeds with numerous corre-

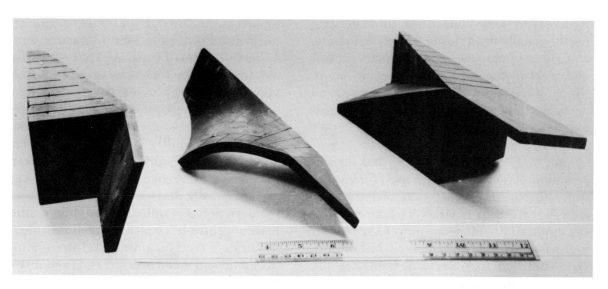

Above: Parts of a model showing the mathematical derivation of Jefferson's design for the moldboard plow. Reproduced courtesy of the National Museum of American History, Smithsonian Institution.

Below: Model of the moldboard plow. Reproduced courtesy of the National Museum of American History, Smithsonian Institution.

spondents at home and abroad and introduced many plants to the United States. He considered to be among his major achievements his importation of rice from northern Italy, dry rice from northern Africa, olive trees from Marseilles, and Merino sheep from Spain.

THE AMERICAN PHILOSOPHICAL SOCIETY

In his efforts to popularize the sciences, Jefferson found one of the greatest obstacles to be the lack of adequate means to inform the general public, despite the efforts of the nation's two scientific societies, the American Philosophical Society and the American Academy of Arts and Sciences, both of which attempted to combine research and productivity in the theoretical as well as the practical sciences. Believing that the high cost of import duties inhibited distribution of books produced in England and Europe on these subjects and thus prevented Americans from having unrestrained access to European learning, Jefferson opposed import duties on publications.

Jefferson was convinced that the most successful channels for bringing science to the public were the scientific societies, although they did not have the capability to inform society at all levels. "These societies are always in peace, however their nations may be at war," he commented to John Hollis in a letter of 19 February 1809. "Like the republic of letters, they form a great fraternity spreading over the whole earth, and their correspondence is never interrupted by any civilized nation." He was elected to membership in the American Philosophical Society in 1780, appointed a councillor in 1781 and again in 1783, chosen one of its vice-presidents in 1791, and in 1797 elected its president to succeed the deceased David Rittenhouse. After the seat of the federal government was moved from Philadelphia to Washington, Jefferson was no longer able to attend meetings, although he was re-elected to its presidency each year until 1815. At his death, he had been a member for almost forty-six years. His participation in the Society's activities also did much to promote the sciences in public service.

Soon after he became vice-president of the Society, Jefferson served on a committee to collect information about the destructive Hessian fly, a study sponsored by President Washington and to all intents and purposes the first entomological survey with American government sponsorship. He made numerous gifts to the Society's collections, ranging from Roman bronze coins to a wide range of geological and paleontological specimens and models of inventions. Several accounts of his scientific endeavors were published in the Society's *Transactions*, beginning with meteorological observations that he had maintained in conjunction with Reverend Madison and that the latter submitted in 1779; then a letter on methods for calculating the altitude of mountains of the Blue Ridge; his description of the moldboard; and his account of a paleontological find he named the *Megalonyx*.

Notable among Jefferson's contributions to the advancement of American science was his promotion of the study of animal species and fossil remains. He first became interested in the subject in about 1780 while preparing the manuscript of the *Notes*. Among the animals he listed as common to both the Old World and the New he included the "mammoth" (later identified as the American mastodon), and he suggested it might still roam the American wilderness. "Such is the œconomy of nature," he noted, "that no instance can be produced of her having permitted any one race of her animals to become extinct; of her having formed any link in her great work so weak as to be broken."

EXPLORATION AND COLLECTION

Jefferson became increasingly intrigued with the subject, and in December 1781 he commissioned the explorer George Rogers Clark to acquire for him "some teeth of the great animal whose remains are found on the Ohio," the first of several such commissions he gave to Clark and his brother William. He informed himself of the work of English and French naturalists and kept abreast of American finds of fossil remains through correspondence.

Jefferson questioned claims by French

naturalists that tusks and skeletons recovered from the great fossil repository at Big Bone Lick in Kentucky were skeletons of elephants and that molars found at the same site were from a hippopotamus. As Jefferson recorded in the *Notes:*

> Wherever these grinders are found, there also we find the tusks and skeleton. . . . It will not be said that the hippopotamus and elephant came always to the same spot, the former to deposit his grinders, and the latter his tusks and skeleton. . . . We must agree then that these remains belong to each other, that they are of one and the same animal.

Inasmuch as no species of the elephant was known to have lived north of the tropics, he concluded that these remains were of a quadruped resembling the elephant, but not of any species then known, noting "I find it easier to believe that an animal may have existed, resembling the elephant in his tusks, and general anatomy, while his nature was in other respects extremely different."

Jefferson continued to pursue each new fossil find primarily for the purpose of building the collections of the American Philosophical Society. In the interim between his retirement as secretary of state and his installation as vice-president of the United States, he acquired some bones of "a Tremendous animal of the clawed kind late found by saltpetre manufacturers" in a cave in Greenbrier County, Virginia. He brought the remains with him to Philadelphia on his trip to assume the vice-presidency of both the nation and the American Philosophical Society. Donating the bones to the Society, he prepared a paper for publication in which he named the extinct animal "the Great Claw," or *Megalonyx*, and classified it as a predator belonging to the cat family. Quite by chance he found an article in a British periodical in which the French naturalist Georges Cuvier described the recovery in Paraguay of a great clawed animal named the *Megatherium*. Realizing the similarities between his *Megalonyx* and the *Megatherium*, Jefferson quickly revised his paper, which was subsequently published in the Society's *Transactions*. Cuvier later credited Jefferson as the discoverer of the *Megalonyx*, and in 1822 another French naturalist, Anselme Desmarest, named it *Megalonyx jeffersoni* in Jefferson's honor.

Often called "the father of American vertebrate paleontology," Jefferson's contributions to the subject were many. His tenacious pursuit of vertebrate fossils at considerable personal expenditure and his encouragement of collection and study by others promoted serious interest in the subject before it was recognized as a science. His position as one of the nation's most notable citizens created a social and political ambience within which these studies could prosper. He was primarily responsible for the preservation of many important specimens that otherwise would have been dispersed and lost. Relying on his own instincts and Indian traditions, however, he refused to accept the basic premise, promulgated by the naturalists of his time, that species might become extinct. As the paleontologist George Gaylord Simpson wrote, Jefferson "made two contributions such as no other man of the time could or did make: he helped to make paleontology a respectable and honored pursuit, and he was largely instrumental in bringing together the materials necessary for its advancement."

An obvious center for natural history studies and public information was the museum, and it is not surprising that Jefferson provided eager support for the first successful American museum enterprise, founded in June 1784 by Charles Willson Peale at Philadelphia. He enjoyed a long and fruitful friendship with Peale and provided his project with numerous specimens. Peale's museum was unique as a consequence of its success, for in the eighteenth century, museum projects intended for the edification and instruction of the public were generally short-lived, for several reasons. Men of science for the most part were reluctant to help promote the unusual and were distrustful of museums in general. The public was not yet oriented to museums and consequently did not support them adequately. The favorable response enjoyed by Peale's enterprise was due chiefly to his great talent as an entrepreneur and his unflagging efforts to provide novel and attention-getting dimensions to his displays. Nonetheless, he failed to engender sufficient support in scientific circles, and he could not later convince the federal government to convert the museum into a national institution.

Despite Jefferson's personal preoccupation with making collections, he failed to support the establishment of a national museum when it was proposed, for he was convinced the public would not support it. In a letter of 24 May 1807 to G. C. de la Coste, a French naturalist, he summarized the status of museums in this period:

> In the particular enterprises for museums, we have seen the populous and wealthy cities of Boston and New York unable to found or maintain such an institution. The feeble condition of that in each of these places sufficiently proves this. In Philadelphia alone, has this attempt succeeded to a good degree. It has been owing there to a measure of zeal and perseverance in an individual rarely equalled; to a population, crowded, wealthy, and more than usually addicted to the pursuit of knowledge.

From boyhood, Jefferson was a habitual and avid collector of oddities, natural and man-made, particularly of the anomalies of nature. He kept a variety of such curiosities at hand for his own amusement and study and for display to interested visitors. At Monticello he used his entrance hall for the purpose and had its walls hung with portraits of notable individuals ranging from

Unguals, phalanges, and metacarpals of the *Magalonyx jeffersoni* found in West Virginia and presented by Jefferson to the American Philosophical Society. Reproduced courtesy of the Academy of Natural Sciences of Philadelphia.

Christopher Columbus and Sir Walter Raleigh to the Marquis de Lafayette and George Washington. Also to be found there were portraits of Bacon, Newton, and Locke, in addition to paintings of classical subjects.

The upper part of the walls were hung with mounted heads and horns of a variety of American wild animals, with aboriginal art and artifacts layered over the whole, ranging from Indian peace pipes, costumes, war clubs, bows, quivers of arrows, wampum, and shields, some hung from the horns and antlers of the mounted heads. Featured were a great buffalo hide painted with the scene of a battle between two Indian tribes, and another hide with an Indian map of the southern basin of the Missouri River. Groupings of minerals and crystals, petrefactions, fossil shells and bones (including the upper and lower jawbones of the American mastodon), all shared space in the entrance hall. In accordance with Jefferson's wishes, the collection was donated to the University of Virginia, but in the course of time it was dispersed and lost its identity, except for a few pieces now displayed at Monticello. All that is known of it derives from his correspondence and the writings of visitors to Monticello during his lifetime.

When Jefferson moved into the President's House in Washington as the third president, he set aside one of the unfinished rooms, now the East Room, to use as his "cabinet." It became the repository of his gardening and carpentry tools, and his collection of artifacts. As Margaret Bayard Smith described it in *The First Forty Years of Washington Society,*

> Around the walls were maps, globes, charts, books, &c. In the window recesses were stands for the flowers and plants which it was his delight to attend and among his roses and geraniums was suspended the cage of his favorite mocking-bird, which he cherished with peculiar fondness, not only for its melodious powers, but for its uncommon intelligence and affectionate disposition. (p. 385)

It was in this room that he spread out the three hundred or more fossil remains collected for him by William Clark in 1807 from Big Bone Lick. With the assistance of the anatomist Dr. Caspar Wistar, whom he had invited to Washington to help him, the president divided the bones into three groups. The most important he donated to the American Philosophical Society, a few he kept for himself, and the remainder, consisting chiefly of duplicates, he donated to the Institute of France for its natural history collection.

INVENTION

During his lifetime Jefferson acquired a reputation as an inventor, derived chiefly from his inclination to modify and improve existing utilitarian objects and devices to respond to his own requirements. Everywhere that he traveled, he observed and noted such devices and furniture as might in some manner improve the quality of living. He sometimes acquired examples for his own use or as gifts to friends, and frequently had duplicates made from his sketches and specifications modified to fulfill particular functions. "One new idea leads to another," he wrote to Dr. Benjamin Waterhouse on 3 March 1818, "that to a third, and so on through a course of time until some one, with whom no one of these ideas was original, combines all together, and produces what is justly called a new invention."

Many of his "inventions" or modifications were designed for his comfort and convenience at Monticello. Among them are a dumbwaiter, which provided wines to the dining room from the wine cellar; a great hall clock that indicated the days of the week by the fall of its weights; an ingenious folding ladder for winding the clock; mechanized doors, both of which moved when one was opened; a weathervane over the East Pavilion designed to give wind directions on an indicator inside the building; and a revolving chair and a combination of revolving chair and chaise longue for his comfort and convenience while writing.

His lifelong concern for the preservation of records and the requirements of his large correspondence are reflected in his inventions of a portable writing desk, on which he drafted the Declaration of Independence; a portable version of James Watt's copying press; and numerous modifications of the multiple writing machine called the polygraph, which he used extensively during the last two decades of his life. When he learned that American secret diplomatic correspondence was being read by foreign powers while he was secretary of state, Jefferson invented a wheel ci-

Buffalo robe of the Mandan tribe, painted with the scene of a battle fought by the Sioux and Arikaras against the Mandans, Minitaris, and Ah-wah-har-ways. It was presented to President Jefferson by Lewis and Clark in 1805, and he displayed it in the President's House. Reproduced courtesy of the Peabody Museum, Harvard University.

Above: Jefferson's study of Monticello, showing his combination of furniture for his convenience in writing. Reproduced courtesy of the Thomas Jefferson Memorial Foundation.

Below: The polygraph, a multiple-pen writing device used by Jefferson for his correspondence between 1804 and his death. Reproduced courtesy of the Thomas Jefferson Memorial Foundation.

pher device to provide much greater security than other cryptographic methods then in use. It was never issued, however, and was forgotten until 1922 when it was independently reinvented by the United States Army Signal Corps and adopted for military use. It continued to be widely used even during World War II.

WEATHER RECORDING

"Of all the departments of science," Jefferson noted in a letter to George F. Hopkins dated 5 September 1822, "no one seems to have been less advanced for the last hundred years than that of meteorology." From his student days at Williamsburg on, he maintained detailed weather records. He shared his enthusiasm with others, particularly Reverend Madison, and the two developed what constituted a weather service for a period of many years, with records maintained in the mountains at Monticello and the lowlands of Williamsburg approximately 120 miles away. Jefferson read his thermometer and noted readings each morning at either sunrise or nine o'clock and again at four o'clock or sunset. At the same time, he recorded wind directions, snowfall, and other climatic events. He advised the Italian scientist Giovanni Fabbroni that "Fahrenheit's thermometer is the only one in use with us." His records of observations were maintained during his absence from Monticello by a family member. After Colonel Tarleton's raid on Monticello, Jefferson's greatest annoyance with the British troops seemed to be not that they destroyed his stock and crops but that they broke his barometer, which was almost irreplaceable (another would have to be imported from England).

Jefferson's network of observation with Madison was interrupted for a period because, as the latter reported, "the British robbed me of my Thermometer and Barometer. We have sent to England and expect a Return by this Spring." Others who cooperated with Jefferson's weather observations were the future president James Madison; the Philadelphia ironmaster Isaac Zane, Jr.; and Benjamin Vaughan in London. He also enticed William Dunbar in Natchez, Mississippi, and Hugh Williamson in Quebec to make observations.

Jefferson kept abreast of other phenomena, including the meteoric fall over Connecticut in 1807 and the comparative study of climate, as deduced from the flowering time of trees, made in 1818 in several states. He employed hygrometers to measure the moisture in the air, an interest first aroused by Buffon's inquiry about the comparative moisture of the French and American climates, and its probable effect on animal life. He arranged to have several hygrometers made for him, one for his own use in Paris and another to be sent to the United States so that a comparative record could be made. The instruments did not arrive before his return to the United States in 1789, and the project did not materialize. Nonetheless, his preoccupation with weather observation continued in many directions and involved numerous correspondents. As he explained to Constantine François de Chasseboeuf, Comte de Volney, he had once envisioned the formation of a huge network of observers in every county of Virginia who would make observations simultaneously; by proving its merits, the Virginia network might persuade the American Philosophical Society to establish a similar one in every state to maintain records over a period of years. The American Revolution had interfered with this ambitious project, and other activities kept Jefferson from returning to it. He never totally discarded the weather-recording idea and as late as 1824 discussed such a plan on a national scale with the object of discovering meteorological laws, noting that he had completed another series of observations maintained over a period of seven years.

STANDARDS OF MEASURE

Jefferson's preoccupation with statistics of measurement, discussed again and again in his correspondence, included measurement of distances traveled, whether on foot, by carriage, or by boat. Over a period of many years he acquired and tested a great variety of odometers. (He sought a triangular odometer from instrument makers in London as well as a new type utilizing a pendulum but was unable to obtain either.) In 1791, just prior to his departure from Philadelphia to return to Monticello, he installed a new odometer in his carriage. During his journey he kept careful records of the time required for travel from one town to the next. Upon arriving at Monticello, he discovered that his compilation was in error; the odometer was based on the assumption that his phaeton's wheel made 360 revolutions per mile and he discovered that in actuality it made only 354.95 revolutions, so that he had to add 1 mile for every 71 miles recorded to correct his record.

He experimented with odometers again during his second term as president, having learned that a new type of the instrument—it rang a bell inside the carriage to mark each mile traveled—had been invented by James Clarke of Powhatan County. Jefferson successfully used the one he obtained. A decade later Clarke patented his odometer and, with Jefferson's encouragement, went on to produce "a machine that could lay down the platt of a road by traveling the carriage over it." Clarke made one that Jefferson used on his carriage to survey a triangle of road about twenty miles in circumference. Another form of the odometer that Clarke produced for Jefferson was based on the latter's table for measurement of distances:

10 points = 1 line
10 lines = 1 inch
10 inches = 1 foot
10 feet = 1 decad

10 decads = 1 rood
10 roods = 1 furlong
10 furlongs = 1 mile

Jefferson submitted the table to Congress as the basis for a new national system of measure, but it was not adopted.

Jefferson used the example of the odometer to explain his proposal for a new system of currency. As he reported to Thomas Cooper in a letter of 27 October 1808, he had lately obtained proof of the ease with which people understood his proposed system of currency divided into dimes, cents, and mills. "I have an odometer fixed to my carriage," he wrote, "which gives the distances in miles, dimes, and cents. The people on the road inquire with curiosity what exact distance I have found from such a place to such a place; I answer, so many miles, so many cents. I find they universally and at once form a perfect idea of the relation of the cent to the mile as an unit."

To Jefferson, the establishment of a national system of uniform coinage and of weights and measures was among the foremost of the new nation's priorities. He had positive ideas on these subjects for many years, and while in France, he kept himself fully informed of discussions taking place in the United States. In 1776 he had compiled a report for Robert Morris on the comparative values of the various coins being used in the American colonies. The report was ignored, but when the subject was again raised in Congress, he once more submitted notes on his proposal. He suggested that the Spanish silver dollar serve as the base, to be subdivided into tenths and hundredths, each subdivision to coincide as closely as possible to a familiar existing coin. Congress eventually accepted the decimal system as well as most of his suggestions concerning other coins. Jefferson was closely associated with the establishment of the United States Mint while serving as secretary of state. He objected to having American coinage struck in Europe, as was the practice of the time, and at his insistence the mint was established at Philadelphia in 1792.

Jefferson then directed his attention to a system of weights and measures. He had undertaken considerable research on the subject, collecting data from a wide range of sources. He made careful studies of systems in use overseas, such as one submitted to the French National Assembly by the bishop of Autun and another developed by Sir John Riggs Miller that was under consideration by the British Parliament.

In a "Plan for Establishing Uniformity in the Coinage, Weights, and Measures of the United States," sent to the House of Representatives on 13 July 1790, Jefferson proposed to decimalize weights and measures in a manner similar to his earlier scheme for a decimal system of coinage, and to combine avoirdupois and troy weights, based on the ounce as the weight of the thousandth part of the weight of a cubic foot of rain water. He planned to establish the standard rod as 58.723 inches in length, divided into 587-1/5 parts, each designated as a line, ten of which formed an inch. Ten inches constituted a foot. Measures of capacity were to be rectangular in form rather than cylindrical, with the cubic foot as the unit. For the unit of measure of length that would be invariable, he selected the seconds pendulum, based on measurement of the motion of the earth on its axis, which could be measured in days and reduced in time to seconds. The seconds pendulum, adjusted to vibrate in seconds, was to be in the form of a cylindrical iron rod maintained at uniform temperature at sea level in the latitude of forty-five degrees, halfway between the equator and the poles. The system was ingenious and brought Jefferson much acclaim, but Congress repeatedly deferred action on his proposals, and none was taken while he was in office.

Another of Jefferson's concerns was provision for a system of granting patents that would protect the rights of inventors while making the inventions useful for the common good and that would encourage invention in general. When the law authorizing the issuance of patents was passed in 1790, it brought a considerable response from the public, who submitted applications in great numbers. As secretary of state, Jefferson was a member of the three-man panel reviewing applications, with the secretary of war and the attorney general. During the first year of the Patent Office, Jefferson also served as ex-officio keeper of the records of the patents. Largely as a result of his critical perusal of applications, only three patents were granted in the first year, thirty-three in 1791, eleven in 1792, and twenty in 1793. By this time Jefferson's rigid interpretation of the law brought considerable protest, and the rapid development of the manufacturing industries helped bring about a revision of the law. Congress did not pass a new bill that Jefferson drafted in 1791, by means of which he would retain only minimal involvement in the examination of patents. A new patent law enacted 21 February 1793 achieved the purpose.

SURVEYING AND ASTRONOMY

Closely related to Jefferson's concern for measurement of distance traveled was his involvement with surveying. He surveyed his own lands as well as properties of friends and neighbors. In 1773 he had been appointed surveyor of Albemarle County, the chief requirement of the position being the review of all surveys made in the county. Many of his survey sketches made between 1776 and 1778, as well as his survey notes for a period of twenty-two years, have survived. Jefferson maintained a great interest in the subject and continued to make surveys. In the final decade of his life he laid out the grounds and buildings for the University of Virginia. He evolved his own method of plotting a course that demonstrated his skill and experience as a surveyor as well as originality in the application of mathematics. He provided a simple description of it in 1814 to Louis Hue Girardin, a professor at the College of William and Mary.

Jefferson had inherited his father's surveying instruments and purchased others during his life. In addition to "a common theodolite or graphometer," a "pocket graphometer," a "perambulator," "Marshall's meridian instrument," and an "English camp theodolite," he also owned a theodolite made by Jesse Ramsden of London, considered to be one of the finest instruments available.

Jefferson's knowledge of astronomy was as advanced as that of anyone of his time excepting David Rittenhouse and Andrew Ellicott. He had pursued it as a hobby since his student days and owned an impressive array of astronomical instruments, some of which he modified to his own purposes. Among them was a universal equatorial instrument made by Ramsden that formerly had been owned by the Georgia surveyor William Gerard de Brahm. It was the only example of this sophisticated instrument in the United States, and he was inordinately proud of it. He also owned and used other astronomical instruments, including a Borda reflecting circle used for finding longitude by observing lunar distances, two pedestal achromatic telescopes made by the London instrument maker Peter Dollond, with which he observed the sky of the southern hemisphere from his study, and several hand telescopes, or "spyglasses."

When opportunity offered, he endeavored to bring to the attention of others innovations in instruments, such as a new type of object-lens for telescopes invented in 1777 by the French scientist the Abbé Alexis-Marie de Rochon. It was an achromatic objective made from double-refracting rock crystal, which Jefferson referred to as "Ire-land chrystal" and which was introduced by Ramsden. The invention was highly acclaimed in Europe, and Jefferson described it in letters to Rev. Ezra Stiles, David Rittenhouse, Rev. James Madison, and Robert Patterson.

He enjoyed watching the stars from the plateau above Monticello and from time to time made observations of special phenomena from the site, on the mountain he called Montalto. He purchased the land in 1777 with the intention of building an astronomical observatory for his own use. In the early years of the Revolution, he prepared drawings for an observatory building on Montalto, but it was never constructed. He later designed a layout for the astronomical instruments in his study at Monticello, from which he could observe the southern hemisphere. When planning it, he wrote on 29 December 1811 to Reverend Madison that he had "no telescope equal to the observation of the eclipses of Jupiter's satellites, but as soon as I can fit up a room to fix my instruments in, I propose to amuse myself with further essays of multiplied repetitions and less laborious calculations." In June 1783 he observed a solar eclipse, and in reporting it, he regretted his lack of an accurate timekeeper for astronomical purposes. He commissioned Rittenhouse to make one for him, and when the latter failed to do so, he ordered one from the Philadelphia clockmaker Thomas Voight.

He reported his observations of another eclipse of the sun in September 1811 to William Lambert, Reverend Madison, and Nathaniel Bowditch, and they were later published by Bowditch. He corresponded with numerous others about their observations; his letters reveal that his interest was far greater than that of a mere hobbyist, he had a professional understanding of their projects and problems, and his suggestions were substantive.

In 1791, while serving as secretary of state, he undertook an investigation of

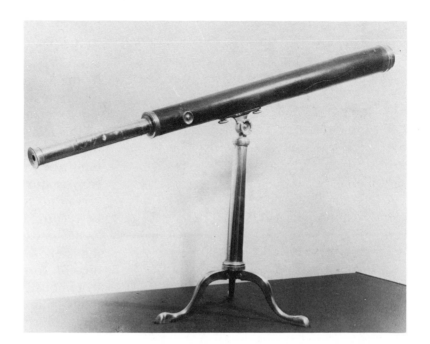

Pedestal telescope, made by Peter Dollond of London and used by Jefferson in his study. Reproduced courtesy of the Thomas Jefferson Memorial Foundation.

methods for obtaining fresh water from salt water at the request of the House of Representatives. In the same year the House published the report, the first scientific publication of the federal government.

The end of the American Revolution and the achievement of independence brought with them an urgent need for national expansion. As new industries and commerce developed, the communities along the eastern seaboard became crowded while a great segment of the continent remained unexplored and unsettled. An early priority of the new republic was western expansion, and even before formulating a federal constitution, Congress turned its attention to resolving the problems of the new territories. A congressional committee chaired by Jefferson developed a plan for the settlement of the western lands that resulted in the Ordinance of 1784. Its purpose was to provide for preliminary division of the Northwest Territory into states and to enable its settlers to form temporary governments.

"A great deal is yet wanting to ascertain the true geography of our country," Jeffer-

son wrote to Andrew Ellicott on 24 June 1812, "more indeed as to its longitudes than latitudes. Towards this we have done too little for ourselves and depended too long on the ancient and inaccurate observations of other nations." These concerns formed the basis of what became undoubtedly the greatest achievement of Jefferson's administration—the Louisiana Purchase of 1803. This acquisition added a little more than a million square miles of territory and provided an outlet for the Mississippi River to the sea. It provided a natural national boundary on the Gulf of Mexico and nearly doubled the size of the nation. The Louisiana Purchase also provided Jefferson with an excuse to plan, under government auspices, a series of exploring and mapping expeditions that resulted in some of the greatest national achievements of the period. In the detailed planning and preparations for these expeditions, Jefferson applied his considerable knowledge of surveying and astronomy, as well as his familiarity with other sciences, which contributed in large part to their success.

Jefferson had been interested in the un-

Two-faced clock in the entrance hall of Monticello, designed by Jefferson and made for him by Peter Spurck in 1793. It operates by the fall of weights resembling cannonballs. Reproduced courtesy of the Thomas Jefferson Memorial Foundation.

cal Society, and when the French botanist André Michaux approached the Society in late 1792 with a proposal for an expedition to the Pacific, Jefferson undertook a subscription to finance it. Jefferson also provided detailed instructions for the conduct of the expedition. Michaux was to ascend the Missouri River, cross the Stony Mountains (the Rockies), and descend the nearest river to the Pacific Ocean. He specified observations to be made and scientific data to be recorded and collected. When Edmond Genêt arrived in the United States as French minister, however, he changed Michaux's mission from exploration of the Northwest to a filibustering expedition to serve French interests in Spanish territory. Michaux and his exploring party descended the Ohio River, and when they reached Kentucky, they learned that the international climate had altered and that Genêt's scheme could go no further. Michaux returned to Philadelphia by the end of 1793.

The Louisiana Purchase enabled Jefferson to fulfill his long-held dream of western exploration. In 1803, even before negotiations for the purchase had been completed, he obtained the approval of Congress to send an expedition under his former secretary Meriwether Lewis to trace the course of the Missouri River to its source, cross the highlands, and follow natural waterways to the Pacific Ocean. (An ulterior motive for the venture was to modify trading arrangements with the Indians.) Nowhere else during his public career was Jefferson's command of the sciences more clearly demonstrated than in the preparations for this enterprise. His technical competence in surveying and astronomy provided the basis for the selection of the mathematical instruments and scientific procedures required to explore and map the region.

For determining longitude in the field, Jefferson concluded that the most practical method was by observation of lunar distances. Aware of the potential accidents and

known regions of the continent for most of his life. In France he had met John Ledyard, an American from Connecticut, and encouraged him to extend a planned expedition to include exploration of the western regions of the North American continent by continuing from Russia to Kamchatka, sailing to Nootka Sound, and then proceeding by land. Ledyard's expedition was terminated when he was arrested by the Russian police and taken back to Poland.

The increasing interest in the Pacific Northwest of British fur traders and exploring expeditions aroused concern among Americans for the future control of the region. An overland expedition was tentatively contemplated by the American Philosophi-

hazards that might be encountered, he proposed that the use of a timepiece be avoided by utilizing a universal equatorial instrument such as he owned. However, Ellicott and Patterson recommended instead the use of an octant and sextant with a chronometer. Jefferson provided the leaders of the expedition with detailed instructions of scientific observations to be made, records to be maintained, and artifacts to be collected. Lewis set out in July 1803, and the expedition remained in the field until the summer of 1806. The safe return of the exploring party caused considerable excitement throughout the country. The results not only justified Jefferson's foresight but proved to be most rewarding, from a scientific point of view, with the return of large numbers of botanical, zoological, geological, and other specimens. In other aspects it was not as successful, however, for although the expedition had been conducted in accordance with Jefferson's specified requirements, it did not fulfill all his hopes. The hostility of some of the Indian nations for the white man and for each other had not been resolved, and the explorers reported unanticipated topographical obstacles to future westward expansion, such as the considerable extent of mountain ranges. The difficulties encountered in the return of a Mandan Indian brought east by Lewis and Clark resulted in a large expenditure of unauthorized government funds. Lewis failed to produce the written account of the expedition he had promised, with the consequence that many of his personal observations and conclusions not recorded in the journals were lost to history. The journals themselves were not to be published until a century later; this was the greatest failure of the expedition: that its valuable findings were not available at the time they were most desired.

The completion of the Lewis and Clark expedition made possible government sponsorship of other expeditions during Jefferson's administration. In 1805–1806, a party under the command of Zebulon M. Pike was sent to explore the sources of the Mississippi, Arkansas, and Red rivers, and the western part of the Louisiana Territory as far west as what was named Pikes Peak. Other geographical and geological expeditions followed in fairly rapid succession, leading ultimately to the formation of the United States Geological Survey in 1879.

Not long after Lewis and Clark returned, Jefferson began to plan the establishment of a survey of American coasts. Several prominent figures have been credited with originally proposing a survey, including Albert Gallatin, Robert Patterson, and Ferdinand Rudolph Hassler. Whether or not the original concept can be claimed for Jefferson, he was nonetheless one of its most avid supporters. In 1806 he recommended the survey's establishment to Congress, and the proposal was favorably received. On 10 February 1807, Congress authorized a survey that was to include such physical features as islands, shoals, and harbors. Hassler was appointed the first superintendent of the newly formed United States Coast Survey.

The Coast Survey was not just another scientific project, for Jefferson was aware that within the next few years war with Great Britain was not only possible but probable. The only charts of American coastal waters available to American navigators had been published during the American Revolution and were thus considerably outdated. Consequently it was imperative to undertake as quickly as possible a comprehensive survey employing the most sophisticated instruments and methods. The Coast Survey was the last of the major scientific projects to be undertaken during Jefferson's administration, although it was not until long after his retirement that the first fruits of the survey were to be realized.

Not the least of Jefferson's endeavors during his presidency was his role in promoting vaccination as a preventive of smallpox. As part of a tour made in the summer of 1766, he had traveled to Philadelphia to have himself inoculated and later had the vaccine administered to his family and staff at Monticello. When Dr. Waterhouse of Harvard College was vainly seeking support of a nationwide inoculation program, he sought and received President Jefferson's cooperation. Jefferson personally served as the means for distributing the vaccine to physicians in Philadelphia, Washington, and parts of Virginia. He was also responsible for initiating vaccination among the Indians. In 1801 when an embassy of Indians under chief Little Turtle visited Jefferson at the White House, Jefferson took the opportunity to have the chieftain and his braves vaccinated by Dr. Edward Gantt, chaplain of the Congress. Later he provided Lewis and Clark with vaccine to distribute among the Indians they would encounter on their expedition.

SCIENCE EDUCATION

In a letter written not long before his death, Jefferson wrote, "I revolt against metaphysical reading. . . . The business of life is with matter that gives us tangible results. Handling that, we arrive at the knowledge of the axe, the plough, the steam-boat, and every thing useful in life. But, from metaphysical speculations, I have never seen one useful result." Thus did Jefferson express his lifelong impatience with pursuits that were not materially productive. This statement also reflects his concern for improvement of the American educational system at all levels to provide more practical training. He was thoroughly convinced that the national resources could best be developed and exploited by providing the people with an education in the practical sciences, which in his definition included chemistry, agriculture, and what is now encompassed under the rubric *technology.* He anticipated that given optimum conditions this could be achieved at three levels—the elementary school, the college, and the university. As early as 1779, while a member of the Virginia legislature, he had drafted a bill proposing the establishment of these three levels of education, and he remained convinced of this objective for the rest of his life. He sought to establish the principle of vocational education for "the limited wants of the artificer or practical man—the pump-maker, clock maker, machinist, optician." Jefferson believed that a course in the basic sciences provided a most desirable basis for careers in law and politics as well as the sciences. He later suggested such a course of action to his future son-in-law Thomas Mann Randolph, Jr., who was enrolled at his suggestion at the University of Edinburgh.

From time to time Jefferson voiced the desirability of establishing a government-supported university, a concept echoed in later years by others. His first involvement with such a project was with the proposed Academy of Science and Fine Arts, suggested in 1778 by his college friend John Page and planned by Chevalier Quesnay de Beaurepaire. Although the project at first moved forward with promised support from France as well as Virginia, the French Revolution effectively terminated it. A related enterprise conceived by Jefferson was to bring the University of Geneva, which was undergoing serious financial difficulties, to a site near the city of Washington, where it would become the nucleus for a national university. The project did not materialize, but Jefferson did not easily surrender his dream and referred to it again years later.

Jefferson's concern for education with emphasis on science is reflected in the substantial role he played in fulfilling George Washington's proposal for a military academy, which was established at West Point after the American Revolution. Jefferson successfully sought to incorporate in the curriculum of the United States Military

Academy the French method in mathematics, which was considerably more progressive than that taught in English schools.

Following his retirement from public service, Jefferson undertook the project of establishing a university at Charlottesville, a project to which he devoted considerable energy to his final days. He was responsible in large part not only for the creation of the University of Virginia but also for the design of its grounds and buildings as well as its curriculum of studies. When the university was opened to students in March 1825, it fulfilled his hopes in every way. Jefferson included the following passage in a letter to Waterhouse dated 3 March 1818:

> When I contemplate the immense advances in science and discoveries in the arts which have been made within the period of my life, I look forward with confidence to equal advances by the present generation, and have no doubt they will consequently be as much wiser than we have been as we than our fathers were, and they than the burners of witches.

Because of the pride that he took in every American achievement, each of which he exerted every effort to publicize, Jefferson was extremely sensitive to any implied slur from European and English writers. He rose instantly, and occasionally somewhat recklessly, to refute the charges. Abbé Guillaume Raynal had commented in his writings that America had not yet produced a poet, a mathematician, or indeed a man of genius in any single art or science. Jefferson made the following reply in Query VI of the *Notes on Virginia:*

> When we shall have existed as a people as long as the Greeks did before they produced a Homer, the Romans a Virgil, the French a Racine and Voltaire, the English a Shakespeare and Milton, should this reproach be still true, we will enquire from what unfriendly causes it has proceeded, that the

other countries of Europe and quarters of the earth shall not have inscribed any name in the roll of poets.

He went on to note that in war we had produced a Washington; in physics, a Franklin; and in astronomy, a Rittenhouse, who was second to no astronomer in genius because he was self-taught. On a comparison of population, since America had three million inhabitants, France, twenty million, and the British Isles, ten million, he reasoned that France should have half a dozen geniuses to every American one, and the British at least half that number.

Although Jefferson read widely, he was unable to keep abreast of all worldwide scientific and technological accomplishments or to give them the attention of a specialist. Occasionally he made erroneous evaluations of the work of others, particularly when his nationalistic bias caused him to react without adequate reflection. He ventured the opinion, for example, that Sir William Herschel's merit was "that of a good optician only," and he was critical of the value of Jan Ingenhousz' work on plant life and his assertion that light promoted vegetation.

At the same time, as his ever alert and inquisitive mind searched for truth in every dimension and direction, his imagination occasionally led him to reach conclusions too quickly. From time to time his momentary enthusiasms caused him to forget his basic precept that the only legitimate conclusions were those based upon careful observation and experiment. His dedication to another of his precepts—that the success of a new nation lay in its application of science and technology—sometimes caused him to become entrapped by naiveté and consequently fail to give sufficient consideration to the numerous proposals offered to him, particularly as examiner of patents.

Because of the pressures of his public career, Jefferson was unable to make lasting contributions to any of the sciences except vertebrate paleontology and agriculture. He was, nonetheless, eminently successful in the two directions to which his inclinations and opportunities led him, that is, as a mathematical practitioner and as a statesman of science, or promoter of such endeavors.

Jefferson's espousal of the sciences brought him little praise but rather fierce opposition and even derision from his political opponents, who sought to disparage him as a successful statesman and as a philosopher. In Europe, however, he received numerous honors, including membership in the Société Linnaenne of Paris and the Académie Royale des Inscriptions et Belles-Lettres of the Institut de France, and acknowledgment from the Royal Institute of the Sciences, Literature, and Fine Arts of Amsterdam; the Agronomic Society of Bavaria; and the Imperiale e Reale Accademia Economico-Agraria of Florence. He was also recognized with honorary degrees by four American colleges—the College of William and Mary, Yale College, Harvard College, and Princeton.

The last seventeen years of Jefferson's life, spent in retirement at Monticello, encompassed a period during which his financial problems increased and marred what otherwise might have been a much deserved, peaceful, and productive sunset to an incredibly active career. Nonetheless, he continued to have confidence in the future of a nation in which science by his definition had taken its place. In a letter dated 10 February 1814, he expressed to Dr. Thomas Cooper an evaluation of his endeavors in the sciences, which might have fittingly been added to his epitaph: "I was bold in the pursuit of knowledge, never fearing to follow truth and reason to whatever results they led, and bearding every authority which stood in their way."

Religion

E. S. GAUSTAD

WHEN Jefferson was born, the Anglican domination of Virginia was about to receive its first serious challenge. The Great Awakening of the 1740s led to a Presbyterian penetration of the colony by the end of the decade, notably in the preaching of Samuel Davies. Methodists, though still only a movement within the Anglican communion rather than a separate denomination, created enough stir in the Virginia of Jefferson's childhood to arouse the bishop of London to take action against "the spreading of that sect." And soon after, the Baptists aggravated the anxieties of Anglican authorities both in Virginia and back home.

Despite these new winds of doctrine blowing about the Piedmont, Jefferson lived his early years in the secure shelter of the Church of England, Virginia's officially established religious institution since 1619. He participated in its liturgy, learned from its clergy, received its communion, and shared in its political and social prestige. He would later attend its college, serve on its vestries, contribute to its edifices, and in his old age ride down from his hilltop home to join in its services of worship. But "Jefferson as loyal Anglican" is not a phrase readily applied to either his life or his thought. Neither his friends nor his enemies would so describe him, nor did he ever so describe himself. The Anglican ambience was a powerful shelter in mid-eighteenth-century Virginia, but Thomas Jefferson soon struck out for distant shores.

His formal intellectual development began at least as early as 1758, when he attended the small school in Albemarle County presided over by James Maury, Anglican rector of Huguenot lineage. From Maury, Jefferson acquired not only the skills of Greek and Latin but also, far more significantly, a familiarity with, and an affection for, the literary masterpieces of classical civilization. He would continue throughout his life to read, in their original tongues, the Greek historians and the Roman orators. He learned of Stoicism and Epicureanism from the writings of their greatest exponents rather than from the caricatures or apologetic dismissals of a Christianized era. And in his maturity he never found it easy to forgive those learned men who rejected the ancients without ever bothering to understand them. In religion no less than in politics, one could learn from Epictetus and Cicero, from Pythagoras and Seneca. Whatever reputation Jefferson would later achieve as inventor, innovator, and revolutionary, he did not seek this at the expense of the ancients. They were worthy instructors, not cheap foils.

When he was seventeen years of age, Jefferson left the hill country for the tidewater and the College of William and Mary. Though the college was embroiled in disputes between the local lay authorities and distant ecclesiastical superiors, Jefferson seems to have concentrated on his proper intellectual duty: namely, acquiring an education and developing further his openness to learning—all learning. All of his mentors were Anglican clergymen, with one exception. This one teacher, William Small, opened up to his young pupil the world of science and mathematics, and the philosophy of the Scottish realists. Major scientific figures such as Francis Bacon and Sir Isaac Newton had opened a new world of science to the entire Western world. Not only did such thinkers give to all scientific learning a new zest and adventuresome spirit, but by their examples they also encouraged the habits of careful observation, accurate measurement, and the bold construction of fresh hypotheses for testing and evaluation. Jefferson remained a Baconian all of his life. George Wythe, professor of law, led Jefferson into his profession as lawyer and intensified his curiosity regarding the world around him. In sharing with Jefferson his instruments for studying natural philosophy, Wythe developed with his pupil a friendship that lasted for decades. And from the royal governor in Williamsburg, Francis Fauquier, Jefferson learned more informally of that European world of culture, grace, enlightenment, and rationality into which he would soon enter. A fellow of the Royal Society, Fauquier demonstrated no mean interest in those phenomena that seemed to demand fresh eyes and fresh questions, promising in return original and exciting answers.

Though at the college for only a little more than two years, Jefferson carried away with him what any college would be proud to bestow upon its students: a love of learning that never diminished. A book lover and book gatherer, Jefferson, while still in his twenties, acquired a reputation for expertise in this area that led others to seek his advice in constructing an ideal, if modest, library in the American wilderness. To Thomas Turpin, whose son was headed for a career in law, Jefferson wrote on 5 February 1769 that the best course of action was expending the sum of £100 for books, "for a lawyer without books would be like a workman without tools." When a year later his home burned, Jefferson bemoaned particularly the loss of his library, which he valued at £200 sterling. "Would to God it had been the money," Jefferson to his young friend John Page on 21 February 1770, "*then* had it never cost me a sigh!" And a year after that, when his brother-in-law asked for help in amassing a gentleman's library of about £30, Jefferson, unable to lower his sights to that level, suggested books that would amount to many times £30 but could be acquired over a period of several years.

Examining this library as well as Jefferson's own leads quickly to the discovery that this grand new age of experimentation and reason required many "tools"—that is, books. Jefferson's tastes were catholic, his reading habits voracious: in law and politics, history and science, the arts and agriculture. In religion, Jefferson was early influenced by such English deists as Bolingbroke and Shaftesbury. The young Jefferson copied both men in his commonplace books, Bolingbroke most extensively. Bolingbroke, applying his own form of methodological doubt to religion, provided Jefferson with ample precedent for questioning most of the basic doctrines of Christian theology and most of the basic assumptions about Christian history. Jefferson found such intellectual exercise to be so invigorating and therapeutic that in 1787 he recommended it in a letter of 10 August to his young nephew Peter Carr: "Fix reason firmly in her seat, and call to her tribunal every fact, every opinion. Question with boldness even the existence of God, because if there be one, he must more approve the homage of reason than that of blindfolded fear." Throughout most of his twenties, thirties, and forties, Jefferson found answers more in politics than in religion. In the latter field, his posture was mainly that of questioning "with boldness," even as he read without ceasing Locke, Hume, Voltaire, Montesquieu, Kames, Tindal, Chubb, Hobbes, Mandeville, and more. He knew enough about religion to know what he did not believe and what he did not like, but the more positive construction of anything like a religious system had to await the personal assistance of such as Richard Price, a pro-American Unitarian minister in London, and Joseph Priestley, the English scientist-clergyman, who emigrated to America in 1794. With their help and his own sustained investigations, Jefferson ultimately arrived at more positive assertions of his private religion.

FREEDOM FROM AND
FOR RELIGION

It was what he did not like in religion that gave impetus to Jefferson's activity in that troublesome and often bloody arena. He did not like dogmatism, obscurantism, blind obedience, or any interference with the free exercise of the mind. Moreover, he did not like the tendency of religion to confuse truth with power, special insight with special privilege, and the duty to maintain with the right

to persecute the dissenter. Ecclesiastical despotism was as reprehensible as despotism of the political sort, even when it justified itself, as it so often did, in the name of doing good. This had been sufficiently evident in his native Virginia to give Jefferson every stimulus he needed to see that independence must be carried over into the realm of religion. The Church of England could be as imperious as the nation of England; to restrain the latter, it had been necessary to go to war, and to restrain the former, it would be necessary to go to legislature, to court, or to an entirely new structure of government.

The constitution that Jefferson proposed in 1776 for his own state included this statement: "All persons shall have full and free liberty of religious opinion; nor shall any be compelled to frequent or maintain any religious institution." Because Virginians were already far along in their deliberations before Jefferson's draft arrived and because George Mason had already provided a declaration of rights, this Jeffersonian language did not become part of the new state's constitution. Mason's language, which provided that "Christian forbearance, love, and charity" be manifest toward all, also declared that religion "can be directed only by reason and conviction." Moreover, by the end of 1776 the Virginia legislature had suspended fixed salaries for ministers, exempted dissenters from the burden of being taxed for the support of the Anglican Church, and nullified those actions of the British Parliament favoring the Church of England that had been built into Virginia law. From Jefferson's point of view, all of this was good. But from Jefferson's point of view, all of this was not enough. In 1779, therefore, Jefferson wrote a bill that would in his opinion establish religious freedom on firm and enduring ground. First introduced into the legislature after he became governor later that year, this Bill for Establishing Religious Freedom suffered neglect, abuse, and incredible delay. Its fascinating legislative history, a story that cannot be detailed here, ended with its final victory (in revised form) in January 1786.

From its language, Jefferson's opinions about religion at this stage of his life can be readily deduced. He was thirty-six years of age when the bill was first written, forty-two when it became law. Religion, it was clear from history, had been propped up and propagated more by force than by reason. The sad result, wrote Jefferson, had been to inculcate the "habits of hypocrisy and meanness" in mankind. The sad fact, moreover, is that though Almighty God always had the power to coerce belief, He has chosen not to do so, preferring rather to extend religion's influence on the basis of "reason alone." If this is the path chosen by Omnipotence and Infallibility, what sense can there possibly be in "fallible and uninspired men . . . setting up their own opinions and modes of thinking as the only true and infallible"? No sense at all, argued Jefferson, who found compulsion in religion to be irrational, impious, and tyrannical. If such compulsion is bad for the vulnerable citizen, its consequences are no more wholesome for the church: "It tends also to corrupt the principles of that very religion it is meant to encourage, by bribing, with a monopoly of worldly honours and emoluments, those who will externally profess and conform to it." When Jefferson looked at religion in history or at religion in the world around him, this is what he saw: hypocrisy among the worshippers, corruption within the houses of worship. But beyond all that, the eternal and unchanging reality is that "Almighty God hath created the mind free." God had faith enough to make human kind free; we must have faith enough to believe "that truth is great and will prevail if left to herself; that she is the proper and sufficient antagonist to error, and has nothing to fear from the conflict unless . . . disarmed of . . . free argument and debate; errors ceasing to be dangerous when it is permitted freely to contradict them." Five years earlier, writing in *A Summary View* in a wholly political context, Jefferson had declared that "the God who gave us life gave us liberty at the same time: the hand of force may destroy, but cannot disjoin them." Now he declared that the God who gave us a capacity for truth determined at the same time the only proper path to such truth: the freedom of the human mind. Religious truth is no exception to this rule; the tragedy of human history is that over and over again it was religion that had been made the chief exception to the rule.

So at last, in 1786, Virginia's assembly was ready to adopt Jefferson's language in order to declare

> that no man shall be compelled to frequent or support any religious worship, place, or ministry whatsoever, nor shall be enforced, restrained, molested, or burthened in his body or goods, nor shall otherwise suffer, on account of his religious opinions or belief; but that all men shall be free to profess, and by argument to maintain, their opinions in matters of religion, and that the same shall in no wise diminish, enlarge, or affect their civil capacities.

Jefferson, who in general believed that legislative or judicial actions of one generation should not bind those of the next, was willing to make an exception for this bill, for all it did was acknowledge a natural right, a God-given right, an inalienable right that no future legislature, no future court had the authority under heaven to deny. The assembly, while accepting Jefferson's conclusions, eliminated some of his more explicit deistic premises; nonetheless, in passing the bill it gave to Jefferson one of his most cherished victories and to the state one of its most needed remedies for anxiety, bitterness, a flood of legislative petitions, and the great reluctance to leave a Constantinian world for a Jeffersonian one.

When Jefferson offered to the public his first approved English edition of *Notes on the State of Virginia* in 1787, he proudly included the Bill for Establishing Religious Freedom in the Appendix. Subsequent editions continued to carry this writing, which Jefferson rated so highly to the very end of his life. But the book itself made some of the same points as the bill, occasionally in language that religious partisans found offensive. After reviewing portions of Virginia's religious history, especially of its "statutory oppressions" therein, Jefferson argued that conscience is subject only to God, not to government: "The legitimate powers of government extend to such acts only as are injurious to others. But it does me no injury for my neighbor to say that there are twenty gods, or no God. It neither picks my pocket nor breaks my leg." Most Christian clerics in America were not prepared to agree that society or government could view with utter indifference the convictions of atheist, polytheist, and monotheist alike. And Jefferson's words came back to haunt him in the presidential campaign of 1800. In the later years of his life, he came to see the public role of religion in somewhat different terms. At this early stage, however, his mind was mainly on the inviolable nature of the religious conscience. What I believe is my business, my business alone, not yours, not your neighbor's, and surely not the government's. This is not to be antireligious, for "it is error alone which needs the support of government. Truth can stand by itself." The effects of coercion, moreover, have been only to "make one half the world fools, and the other half hypocrites." Give the experiment in religious freedom time to work, Jefferson pleaded in the *Notes;* he would find it necessary to make that plea over and over.

When the United States Constitution was drafted in Philadelphia in 1787 and presented to the people for their ratification, Jefferson—far away in Paris—expressed his great disappointment that it included no explicit guarantee of basic human rights. In his letter to James Madison of 20 December 1787, the first such right he listed was freedom of religion. Many arguments could be offered, and were, why the federal government did not need to be in the business of guaranteeing human rights. In the months of debate over ratification, however, it became clear that the Constitution was unlikely to be ratified, particularly in Virginia, if such a bill were not included. Jefferson had other deists on his side, but he also had many pietists on his side as well. Those dissenters in Virginia who had chafed under the privileges extended to Anglicanism often saw full religious freedom as the most sensible alternative. Some, such as the Baptist itinerant John Leland, even adopted Jeffersonian premises and Jeffersonian language in the call for such a guarantee. Others can talk about implications and inferences all they want to, Jefferson wrote, but this matter is too momentous to be left to interpretation and sophism. Over a generation later, in a letter to Charles Clay of 29 January 1815, Jefferson continued to warn against "this loathsome combination of church and state." So it was agreed that the Constitution, if ratified, would be swiftly amended to give to all Americans some assurance about those inalienable rights that must not be left to the whim of popular passion or the vagaries of federal fiat. In the first Congress assembled under the Constitution, that other libertarian from Virginia, James Madison, proposed such a bill of rights in 1789. By 1791 the first ten amendments had been adopted, and Jefferson was no doubt pleased to observe that the initial guarantee concerned religion: "Congress shall make no law respecting the establishment of religion, or prohibiting the free exercise thereof."

But how widely or how strictly was this now-constitutional protection of religious freedom to be understood? Jefferson understood its language in stricter terms than many of his contemporaries or most of his successors. When he became president in 1801, he awaited some opportunity to make his own understanding explicit, thereby perhaps setting the precedent that would direct future generations. Late that year, the opportunity came in the form of a letter from a group of Baptists meeting in Danbury, Connecticut. Expressing their approval of Jefferson and of his refusal "to assume the prerogatives of JEHOVAH," these dissenters (for such they still were in Connecticut, where Congregationalism remained the official church) requested their deist president to designate a day of fasting on behalf of the nation, which had come through so bitter an election. This request came from a group that, as described in William McLoughlin's *New England Dissent, 1630–1833,* not only was sympathetic to Jefferson's sentiments but even dared to hope that those sentiments "will shine and prevail thro' all those states and all the world, till Hierarchy and tyranny are destroyed from the earth." Jefferson saw his opportunity. This was the suitable occasion, he wrote, "which I have long wished to find, of saying why I do not proclaim fastings and thanksgivings, as my predecessors did." Recognizing that his stand would be controversial ("I know it will give great offence to the New England clergy"), the president asked advice from his attorney general, Levi Lincoln. Lincoln read the draft that Jefferson had prepared and advised him against sending it. But Jefferson felt too strongly about the matter to let the opportunity pass. On 1 January 1802, he sent his reply to the Danbury Baptists. It included this long and destined-to-be significant sentence:

Believing with you that religion is a matter which lies soley between man and his God, that he owes account to none other for his faith or his worship, that the legislative powers of government reach actions only, and not opinions, I contemplate with sovereign reverence that act of the whole American people which declared that their legislature should "make no law respecting an establishment of religion, or prohibiting the free exercise thereof," thus building a wall of separation between Church and State.

This powerful metaphor, once employed, became even more familiar to the American public than did the constitutional language itself.

Just before he left the White House, Jefferson took yet another opportunity to explain why he, unlike Washington and Adams, did not set aside days of fasting, feasting, or prayer. Such exercises are beyond question religious in nature, Jefferson argued in a letter of 23 January 1808 to Samuel Miller, a Presbyterian minister, and are therefore not the proper business of a civil government. Denominations and churches themselves have the full and exclusive authority of determining all religious exercises for their own adherents, "and this right can never be safer than in their own hands, where the Constitution has deposited it." Jefferson acknowledged that in setting this precedent he was going against the earlier precedent of Washington and Adams. But, he explained, their practice was simply an unreflective continuation of what had been done in the several states (including by Jefferson in Virginia—as a burgess, in June 1774 he had called for a patriotic prayer service in Albemarle); thus, they acted "without due examination." Even if this argument was not persuasive, and Jefferson seemed not too fond of it, "one must act according to the dictates of his own reason, and mine tells me that civil powers alone have been given to the President of the United States." What the Constitution said in words, Jefferson would italicize in practice.

A final example of Jefferson's separationism may be drawn from his founding of the University of Virginia in the last years of his life. Prepared to transform the College of

William and Mary into the principal university of the state, Jefferson would do so only if the college divested itself of all ties with sectarian religion—that is, with its old Anglicanism now represented by the Protestant Episcopal Church. The college declined to make that break with its past, and Jefferson proceeded with plans for his own university well to the west of Anglican-dominated tidewater Virginia. In Charlottesville this new school ("broad & liberal & *modern,*" as Jefferson envisioned it in a letter to Priestley of 18 January 1800) opened in 1825 with professorships in languages and law, natural and moral philosophy, history and mathematics, but not in divinity. In Jefferson's view, as reported in Robert Healey's *Jefferson on Religion in Public Education,* not only did Virginia's laws prohibit such favoritism (for divinity or theology was inevitably sectarian), but high-quality education was not well served by those who preferred mystery to morals and divisive dogma to the unities of science. Too great a devotion to doctrine can drive men mad; if it does not have that tragic effect, it at least guarantees that a man's education will be mediocre. What is really significant in religion, its moral content, would be taught at the University of Virginia, but in philosophy, not divinity. If Almighty God has made the mind free, one of the ways to keep it free is to protect young minds from the clouded convolutions of the theologians. Jefferson wanted education separated from religion because of his own conclusions concerning the nature of religion, its strengths and its weaknesses, its dark past and its possibly brighter future.

JEFFERSON'S RELIGION

In 1786, Thomas Jefferson met Richard Price in London. He had exchanged letters with this English Unitarian, philosopher, and reformer before this time and had, like many other American leaders, honored Price for his several tracts criticizing Britain for provoking an unjust and unnecessary war of revolution. The year before, Jefferson had written to Price, commending him for his attack on slavery and urging him to write at greater length on this "spectacle of justice in conflict with avarice and oppression." Price replied that, though flattered and honored, he was through with politics. "Divinity and morals will probably occupy me entirely during the remainder of a life now pretty far spent." Jefferson, though hardly finished with politics, was happy to maintain his contacts with Price for the remaining five years of the latter's life. Jefferson wanted help on questions of "divinity and morals." Never reluctant to order books, Jefferson needed only to be told what books he should order. In a letter to Price dated 12 July 1789, Jefferson asked for more help in defining the precise nature of the Christian deity. Perhaps Unitarianism could rescue Christianity from its tragic fall into abstract speculation and metaphysical meandering. In any event, would he please send some books or sermons, preferably those of Price himself, "levelled to a mind not habituated to abstract reasoning?" Price responded with some work of his own, but even more significantly, in that same year he introduced Jefferson to sermons by Priestley.

In 1793, Priestley published the second edition of his lengthy work entitled *An History of the Corruptions of Christianity,* an exposé of what early Christian theologians did to mystify, Hellenize, and corrupt the pure primitive gospel of Jesus Christ. When Jefferson read and reread this work in the 1790s, it opened wide the doors of understanding. He thought that he had rejected Christianity, but what he had rejected were only its corruptions. Those corruptions, unfortunately, now pervaded all of Christendom to such a degree that genuine Christianity needed desperately to be rescued. Otherwise, all thinking persons would feel obliged to conclude, as had he, that Christianity is inseparable from what the priests and Platonists, the necromancers and soothsayers, have declared it to be. The simple gospel "Fear god and love thy neighbor" is free of all that priestly absurdity; therefore, as he later wrote to Dr. George Logan, on 12 November 1816, the clergy would not abide it: "It gives no scope to make dupes; priests could not live by it." Was it possible that he, Jefferson, was on the verge of an incredible discovery—namely, that he was one of the few real Christians in America? Was it possible that Jefferson, rather than being the infidel, the atheist, the destroyer of social order and moral purpose, might be another mighty reformer, like those of the sixteenth century, of a truer, purer Christian religion? "It is only by banishing Hierophantic mysteries and Scholastic subtleties . . . and getting back to the plain and unsophisticated precepts of Christ, that we become *real* Christians," he wrote to Salma Hale on 26 July 1818.

In 1803, President Thomas Jefferson, while riding back to Washington from Monticello, read a pamphlet of Priestley's: *Socrates and Jesus Compared.* This was better yet, for it came from a scholar who really knew the classics, was prepared to acknowledge their merits, but could show why the message of Jesus was still essential to the welfare of humankind. Jefferson could hardly wait until he reached the White House so that he might write Priestley, on 9 April 1803, of "the pleasure I had in the perusal" of the brief treatise and of "the desire it excited to see you take up the subject on a more extended scale." Priestley's book also excited in Jefferson a desire to arrive at some more reflective, more satisfying statement of his own religion. He offered a swift outline of his ideas to Priestley: Jefferson would begin with the ancients, doing "justice to the branches of morality they have treated well"; then, to the Jews, showing in what respects they needed a reformation; then to the "master workman," Jesus, demonstrat-

ing "that his system of morality was the most benevolent and sublime probably that has been ever taught; and eminently more perfect than those of any of the antient philosophers." What a tragedy that this sublime system has been "disfigured and sophisticated" to such a degree as to cause those who do not understand "to throw off the whole system in disgust." This is the outline, Jefferson wrote, "but I have not the time, & still less the information which the subject needs." There was time only to reflect, not to write.

But when Jefferson reflected, he usually wrote. Ten days later, in a letter to Edward Dowse, he explained why the ancients needed the complementary teachings of Jesus. The moral philosophers of Greece and Rome were concerned chiefly with "the government of our passions . . . and the procuring our own tranquillity. In our duties to others they were short and deficient." Jesus, on the other hand, embraced "with charity and philanthropy, our neighbors, our countrymen, and the whole family of mankind." The earlier thinkers also confined their attention to external deeds, while Jesus did not rest with the moral or immoral act: "He pressed his scrutinies into the region of our thoughts, and called for purity at the fountain head." Then, two days after this communication, Jefferson wrote to his old Philadelphia friend and physician Benjamin Rush; he was now ready to fulfill in a modest way the promise he had once made to give Rush some clearer expression of his own views concerning the Christian religion. He did so willingly, but privately, for he was averse to the communication of his religious tenets to the public. If Jefferson responded to questions about his religion, soon the public might deem itself to have the right to question and receive answers. Public opinion itself could become an inquisition, thus making the constitutional prohibition against a religious test of no effect: "It behoves every man who values liberty of conscience for himself, to resist invasions of it in the case of others." But to Benjamin Rush as trusted friend, Jefferson unfolded his inner thoughts.

He was opposed not to Christianity, Jefferson explained, but only to its corruptions. With respect to the "genuine precepts of Jesus himself," he asserted, "I am a Christian . . . sincerely attached to his doctrines, in preference to all others." To illustrate what this meant, Jefferson set down a somewhat fuller outline, or "Syllabus . . . of the Doctrines of Jesus, compared with those of others." In an effort to be fair to both the ancient Greeks and the early Christians, Jefferson noted, we should perhaps ignore how the ignorant corrupted the former and the learned the latter. In private moral teachings, the classical philosophers were "really great"; in the realm of public morality, their vision and their charity were severely limited. The Jews of antiquity were deists, but the attributes associated with their deity "were degrading and injurious." As a result their ethics "were not only imperfect, but often irreconcilable with the sound dictates of reason." Their ethics, like those of Greece and Rome, needed reformation "in an eminent degree." So then appeared Jesus, his parentage obscure, his condition poor, his education null. Fortunately, his natural endowments were great and his eloquence sublime. Unfortunately, that eloquence was obscured, since we have nothing directly from his pen (so also Socrates), and what we do have was committed to "the most unlettered and ignorant men." His teachings reach us in a form that is "mutilated, misstated, and often unintelligible" because his "schismatizing followers" have engrafted upon what little he did leave behind "the mysticisms of a Grecian Sophist, frittering them into subtleties, and obscuring them with jargon." The question of his divinity or the degree of inspiration was, for Jefferson, beside the point; his concern was with "the intrinsic merits of his doctrines." Jesus returned to the Jewish idea of one God, but gave us "juster notions of his attributes and government." He corrected both ancient Jews and ancient Greeks in "gathering all into one family, under the bonds of love, charity, peace, common wants, and common aids." And he taught, "emphatically, the doctrine of a future state."

So here, in brief compass, Jefferson laid out a syllabus of his own view of history, morality, divinity, and high-flown philosophy. He sent a copy to Levi Lincoln and perhaps to other members of his cabinet as well. In his letter of 26 April 1803, he warned Lincoln to keep it private, saying the clergy would love to get their hands on it so that he could become "the butt of every set of disquisitions which every priest would undertake to write on every tenet it expresses." Even worse, if the Syllabus got out, it "would furnish matter for repeating in new forms all the volumes of divinity which are now mouldering on the shelves from which they should never more be taken." Jefferson shared this document with members of his own family and sent a copy to Priestley and, later, to John Adams. This outline was as far as he cared to go in giving systematic form to his religious opinions. When Charles Clay urged him to write a whole book on religion, Jefferson replied, in a letter on 29 January 1815, that he had never entertained such an idea: "I should as soon think of writing for the reformation of Bedlam, as of the world of religious sects. . . . I not only write nothing on religion, but rarely permit myself to speak on it, and never but in a reasonable society." So the Syllabus would have to bear a heavy weight.

Yet Jefferson recognized that if great weight were set upon it, a structural weakness would be revealed. So much rested on the pure teachings of Jesus, the "genuine precepts," the wheat separated from so much chaff, the "diamonds in a dunghill." But who could rescue that wheat and those diamonds, and who would? Jefferson rested his hopes initially on Priestley, who had, years earlier, published *A Harmony of the Evangelists* in Greek (1777) and in English (1780). Jefferson wrote to Priestley on 29 January 1804, thanking him for copies of "your Harmony, which I have gone through with great satisfaction." He urged Priestley to prepare a digest of the moral teachings of Jesus, leaving out all the extraneous history and comments about Jesus. Such a compendium "would be short and precious." But for his own satisfaction only, Jefferson indicated that he would attempt something along that line, ordering Bibles in Greek and in English, which would enable him "to cut out the morsels of morality, and paste them on the leaves of a book." Priestley would do it better, Jefferson wrote, but Priestley did not live to execute this task (he completed only Part I of the assignment). The burden of distilling the teachings of Jesus, therefore, ultimately fell to Jefferson. By the end of 1804 he had compiled, in English only, the "Philosophy of Jesus," no copy of which survives. (A careful reconstruction is made in Dickinson W. Adams, ed., *Jefferson's Extracts from the Gospels*.) A decade or so after retiring from the White House, Jefferson completed a more ambitious *Life and Morals of Jesus of Nazareth*, rescuing in Greek, Latin, French, and English the "genuine precepts" of the world's master workman.

LIFE AND MORALS OF JESUS OF NAZARETH

No biblical scholar, no trained exegete, no expert in ancient manuscripts or textual traditions, Jefferson determined that which was genuine by the "style and spirit" of the words. In compiling the "Philosophy of Jesus," he had no difficulty distinguishing the true from the false, he declared in a letter to Francis Adrian Van der Kemp of 25 April 1816, though it was done too hastily, "being the work of one or two evenings only, while I lived at Washington, over-whelmed with other business: and it is my intention to go over it again at more leisure." In a letter to William Short dated 13 April 1820, Jefferson indicated that the Gospels attribute to Jesus so many contradictory statements that they cannot have proceeded from the same individual. Among commentators, Paul was the first great corrupter, he being to Jesus as Plato was to Socrates. Fine imagination was found next to charlatanism, correct morality embedded in "so much absurdity." "These palpable interpolations and falsifications of his doctrines led me to try to sift them apart. I found the work obvious and easy."

Jefferson tells of Jesus' birth (following the account in Luke), but he leaves out the angels and all heavenly predictions concerning the supernatural significance of the event. He then includes the accounts of Jesus' baptism, his driving out the money changers from the temple, and his calling of the disciples to be with him. But Jefferson's consuming interest is in the teachings of Jesus: the Sermon on the Mount, and long teaching sections, mainly from Matthew and Luke (for example, Matt. 19–20, 22–25, and Luke 14–18). Jefferson stresses the parables and those teaching sections that emphasize obedience to the spirit, rather than the letter, of the law. He omits any claims by Jesus to divinity and all discussion by the disciples or others concerning who the Christ is. When Jesus performs a miracle in connection with some teaching, the teaching is there but the miracle is not. In the story of the man with dropsy being healed on the Sabbath (Luke 14:1–6), Jefferson's interest is concentrated entirely on the ethical issue of whether or not it is lawful or right to do good on the Sabbath—even if some labor be required. The whole story is there except for the few words "And he [Jesus] took him, and healed him, and let him go."

Similarly, any comments of Jesus concerning his relationship with God or his divine mission are omitted, even when everything else in the episode is there (for example, "I and my Father are one," John 10:30; "Lo, here is Christ," Matt. 24:23; "for the Son of Man is coming," Matt. 24:44b; "Now is the Son of Man glorified, and God is glorified in him," John 13:31). While Jefferson wished to magnify the teaching passages, some teachings clearly did not please him. The major portion of Mark 13, sometimes called the "Little Apocalypse," held little appeal for the deist. Indeed, Jefferson expressed himself strongly on that larger apocalypse, the Book of Revelation, in a letter to Alexander Smyth of 17 January 1825: it is "merely the ravings of a maniac, no more worthy, nor capable of explanation than the incoherences of our own nightly dreams." Apocalyptic writing deserved no commentary, for "what has no meaning admits no explanation"; therefore, apocalyptic prophecies associated with Jesus deserved and would receive no attention from Jefferson in his *Life and Morals of Jesus.*

Jefferson was interested, finally, in describing only the death of Jesus, not his resurrection. Jefferson was even careful in recounting the parable of the grain of wheat that falls to the ground, dies, and only then bears fruit (John 12:24) to omit the very next verse, which spoke of eternal life. Drawing from all four Gospel accounts, Jefferson offered much detail concerning the last days of Jesus: the trial, the bearing of the cross, the two thieves, the crucifixion, the burial. But there is no Easter morning. Jefferson's *Life* ends (conflating John 19:42 and Matt. 27:60) as follows: "There laid they Jesus, and rolled a great stone to the door of the sepulchre, and departed."

DEIST DOCTRINE

Jefferson's debt to Priestley was enlarged by his reliance upon the latter's *Harmony* in compiling his own summary of Jesus' ministry and message. He made that debt fully explicit in writing to John Adams on 22 August 1813: "I have read his Corruptions of Christianity, and Early opinions of Jesus, [1786] over and over again; and I rest on them, and on Middleton's writings, especially his letters from Rome, and to Waterland, as the basis of my own faith." Conyers Middleton, English deist but also Anglican clergyman, launched unrelenting attacks against those defenses of Christian orthodoxy that seemed most vulnerable. Shortly after his death, his writings were gathered into four volumes (1752), the *Miscellaneous Works* becoming part of the Jefferson library. Middleton assaulted Roman Catholicism for having preserved most of the elements of Greek and Roman idolatry in its own ritual and symbolism, many of the old gods and goddesses being merely renamed (hardly reclothed) as more modern Christian saints. A truly rational and humane religion must rigorously rid itself of all lingering traces and taints of idolatry, Middleton argued. Also the notion of the Bible as an accurate historical record could not bear up under critical examination. The Old Testament and the New Testament did not, contrary to orthodox defenders, stand in mutual support of one another. The God of one bears little resemblance to the God of the other, and neither resembles very closely that God known through nature. All history is of one piece, making it impossible to place the Bible in some privileged sanctuary called "sacred history" where it can be immune to all of the ordinary tests of historical truth. Finally, Middleton attacked with effectiveness and vigor (and in the same year as Hume) the whole notion of miracles. To repeat many of the stories of miraculous cures or of exceptions to the regularities of nature is to see at once their absurdity. These stories are told for profit and power on the part of those who officially guard the religion. The stories of miracles are not just instances of unbridled enthusiasm or a too-credulous faith: they are, rather, cases of deliberate fraud and reckless imposture. In the new and rational age into which we are moving, such nonsense will simply not be believed.

The spirit, if not the words, of Richard Price, Joseph Priestley, and Conyers Middleton can be found in the doctrinal and ecclesiastical views of Thomas Jefferson. Concerning the nature of God, for example, Jefferson shared with the deists a belief in Him as Creator; therefore, in looking at the world that He made (and not too long ago), we learn most reliably of His existence and attributes. We must trust what we see with our own eyes: "When once we quit the basis of sensation, all is in the wind." Materialism is no heresy, for it treats of reality. Immaterialism, on the other hand, is only "talk of *nothings.*" It is the immaterialists who are the atheists, not the materialists, who recognize that the senses, taken together with the faculty of reasoning, will not deceive us. In a letter of 15 August 1820 to John Adams, Jefferson wrote that the senses "evidence realities; and there are enough of these for all the purposes of life, without plunging into the fathomless abyss of dreams and phantasms." When we consult our senses in order to know whether there is a God, as he wrote to Adams on 11 April 1823, we approach nature rather than revelation to arrive at this irrefutable result: "a conviction of design, consummate skill, and indefinite power in every atom of its [the universe's] composition." Finding the cosmological argument as persuasive as did the English deists whom he was reading, Jefferson concluded that it is impossible "for the human mind not to believe that there is, in all this design, cause and effect . . . a fabricator of all things from matter and motion." This fabricator is also a regulator and preserver, even a regenerator "into new and other forms." These "evident proofs" make it irresistible to believe that God is; "infinite numbers of men" have so believed, making any contrary hypothesis highly improbable.

Jefferson wrote that we have no doubt as to God's being, but we have little information as to His nature. Jesus told us that God is a spirit, but he did not define spirit. Jesus also told us that God is "good and perfect" but did not proceed to offer an explicit definition: "I am, therefore, of his theology, believing that we have neither words nor ideas adequate to that definition" (letter to Ezra Stiles Ely, 25 June 1819). One attribute we can know with crystal clarity concerning the nature of God: He is one, not many; single, not plural; a unity, not a trinity. The notion of the Trinity is one of those nonsensical propositions that the rational mind can only reject: it is "mere Abracadabra," a totally unintelligible proposition, the most unhappy example of what happens when man gives up "morals for mysteries, and Jesus for Plato." The early church father Athanasius did more than anyone to foist this absurd doctrine on unsuspecting generations, "and I should as soon undertake to bring the crazy skulls of Bedlam to sound understanding, as to inculcate reason into that of an Athanasian" (letter to Benjamin Waterhouse, 19 July 1822).

For Jefferson, this caricature of what Jesus himself believed and taught is so patently absurd that it is impossible for "the incomprehensible jargon of Trinitarian arithmetic" to endure (letter to Timothy Pickering, 27 February 1821). It is therefore only a matter of time, perhaps no more than a single generation, before everyone comes to recognize and affirm the unity of God—as Jesus did: "The religion of Jesus is founded on the Unity of God, and this principle, chiefly, gave it triumph over the rabble of heathen gods then acknowledged. Thinking men of all nations rallied readily to the doctrine of one only God" (letter to Jared Sparks, 4 November 1820). And thinking men once again, Jefferson was convinced, would return to that rational, simple, ennobling affirmation: "I have little doubt that the whole of our country will soon be rallied to the unity of the Creator." Indeed, the whole world would never have abandoned that standard had not the "religion-builders . . . so distorted and deformed the doctrines of Jesus, so muffled them in mysticisms, fancies and falsehoods. . . . Had there never been a commentator, there never would have been an infidel" (letter to Timothy Pickering, 27 February 1821). Jefferson affirmed monotheism, not polytheism; rational religion, not "the hocus-pocus phantasm of a god like another Cerberus, with one body and three heads"; the employment of all one's mental faculties in religion, not the abandonment of them: "Gullibility . . . takes the helm from the hand of reason, and the mind becomes a wreck" (letter to James Smith, 8 December 1822).

What, then, of Christ? Jesus is the greatest of moral teachers and never, in Jefferson's view, claimed to be anything more. In one of his few disagreements with Priestley, Jefferson was unwilling to assert even that the mission of Jesus was a divine one. He was willing, Jefferson told Benjamin Rush, to ascribe every human excellence to Jesus, but human only. Priestley responded to this idea, as well as to Jefferson's Syllabus, by writing on 7 May 1803 as follows: "You will allow me to express some surprize . . . that you should be of the opinion, that Jesus never laid claim to a divine mission. It is an opinion that I do not remember ever to have heard before." Priestley proceeded to instruct his "pupil" that apart from some sense of divine authority, it is impossible to explain either the ministry of Jesus or the rise of Christianity. Years later, Jefferson was willing to acknowledge the "possibility" that Jesus thought of himself as inspired, but the whole question of inspiration bothered the ex-president very much. As he wrote in a letter to William Short on 4 August 1820, men, "perfectly sane on all other subjects," seem to lose their critical faculties and their restraint when it comes to "inspiration." Jefferson, like Middleton, was more interested in rescuing Jesus from charges of fraud and imposture, in purging Christianity of its accretions and corruptions. "And the day will come when the mystical generation

of Jesus, by the supreme being as his father in the womb of a virgin, will be classed with the fable of the generation of Minerva in the brain of Jupiter," he wrote to John Adams on 11 April 1823. "But we may hope that the dawn of reason and freedom of thought in these United States will do away [with] all this artificial scaffolding."

Deists, it is generally alleged, all believe in God, freedom, and immortality. Jefferson's assertions with respect to freedom in a political context are deservedly well known. In a theological context, those assertions principally took the form of attacks upon Calvinism and condemnations of slavish surrender to any prepackaged system of thought. John Adams, tongue in cheek, once wished Jefferson good health and long life until he became a Calvinist. A wish like that, Jefferson replied on 11 April 1823, "would make me immortal." Good humor generally aside, Jefferson flailed away at the Calvinist domination of people's minds and arrogant determination of their fate. "The truth is," he wrote to Salma Hale on 26 July 1818, "that Calvinism has introduced into the Christian religion more new absurdities than it's leader had purged it of old ones. Our saviour did not come into the world to save metaphysicians only." What was all so simple has been made all too subtle. What was freely available "to the simplest understanding" has now become privileged, secretive truth to be apprehended only by a chosen and predetermined few. Calvin's "insanities" make it impossible to reason with his disciples or bring them to any kind of rational understanding. If he were to establish a new sect, Jefferson wrote to Thomas B. Parker on 15 May 1819, "my fundamental principle would be the reverse of Calvin's, that we are to be saved by our good works which are within our power, and not by our faith which is not within our power." The Calvinists have not perpetuated Christianity, they have defeated it. "Their blasphemies have driven thinking men into infidelity." Had it not been for their "counter-religion," "the whole civilized world would now have been Christian." The only difference between Calvinism and paganism, Jefferson wrote to Jared Sparks on 4 November 1820, is that the latter is more intelligible.

On the doctrine of immortality, Jefferson tended toward restraint. As noted above, he regarded such a doctrine as part of the essential teaching of Jesus and as one of Jesus' major reforms of Judaism. The world beyond was, nonetheless, a subject to which he did not give much attention. True, he speculated about such things in his youth but soon concluded that reason cannot solve questions about life after death; the laws of nature "leave us in the dark as we were." In this whole realm of thought, therefore, as he put it in a letter to Isaac Story dated 5 December 1801, he was content "to trust for the future to Him who has been so good for the past." With a kind of Confucian practicality, Jefferson preferred to aim at those targets that he could see before him: love to neighbor and good to society. Yet the subject would return, even on a personal level. Jefferson would go so far as to say, in a letter to Francis Adrian Van der Kemp of 14 July 1816, that "it may be desirable, it may be made plausible" that man should be immortal; however, he could not offer a firm ground upon which to base his belief in "my continued existence, although I might long for it."

In this same letter, Jefferson indicated that the resurrection of Jesus can be a major argument for immortality, yet, as we have seen, he omitted all reference to that event in his personal biblical summation. A "dark veil" is drawn away if the resurrection of Jesus, who "was a man, in every respect," really occurred in the sense that he was revived "with his former consciousness," but our knowledge in this business is limited, partial and dark." As he put it in a letter to John Adams dated 14 March 1820, "Ignorance, in these cases, is truly the softest pillow on which I can lay my head." When William Canby wrote to express concern about the state of Jefferson's own soul and the prospects for his eternal salvation, Jefferson took no offense. Rather, he gently replied, on 18 September 1813, that "no subject has occupied more of my consideration than our relations with all the beings around us, our duties to them, and our future prospects." Jefferson added that he was certain he and his Quaker inquirer were agreed on all the essentials in religion, "and I am too old to go into inquiries and changes as to the unessential."

Like most deists Jefferson saw the doctrine of immortality as being, in some generalized and impersonal sense, a necessary guarantor of morality. Justice and goodness must ultimately prevail, else this is not a moral universe. Since in this life that they do prevail is not always conspicuously evident, then it must be the case that the moral demands of man's nature are met by some "future state of rewards and punishments." A moral sense is deeply engrained in humankind: "Nature hath implanted in our breasts a love of others, a sense of duty to them, a moral instinct, in short." Indeed, Jefferson wrote to Thomas Law on 13 June 1814, this instinct "is the brightest gem with which the human character is studded; and the want of it [is] more degrading than the most hideous of bodily deformities." Just as morality is built into our nature, so it is reasonable to assume that this same Creator who made it "so much a part of our constitution" would also make it part of the cosmos. And the doctrine of immortality is both an expression of that cosmic character and an enforcer of the better side of human character. Jefferson's Syllabus concluded with the assertion that Jesus taught, "emphatically, the doctrine of a future state . . . and wielded it with efficacy, as an important incentive, supplementary to the other motives to moral conduct." This, an important element of the "pure deism" of Jesus, marked a major improvement over ancient Judaism, which either "doubted or disbelieved" in immortality. If that first-century deist could efficaciously wield this doctrine on behalf of morality, the eighteenth-century deist would do no less.

DEIST DENUNCIATION AND RESTORATION

Moving well beyond the traditional deistic triad of God, freedom, and immortality, Jefferson revealed his strongest feelings and convictions with regard to the ecclesiastics. On two counts he found them critically deficient. In the realm of politics and power, they were tyrannical; in the realm of theology and truth, they were perverse. Jefferson's strongest language is reserved for those clergy who, as he said in a letter to Moses Robinson of 23 March 1801, "had got a smell of union between church and state" and would use their political power to impede the advance of liberty and science. Such clergy, whether in America or abroad, have so adulterated religion that it has in their hands become "a mere contrivance to filch wealth and power to themselves" and a means of grasping "impious heresies, in order to force them down [men's] throats" (letter to Samuel Kercheval, 19 January 1810). In his old age, Jefferson softened his invective not one whit: "The Presbyterian clergy are the loudest, the most intolerant of all sects, the most tyrannical and ambitious, ready at the word of the lawgiver, if such a word could be now obtained, to put the torch to the pile, and to rekindle in this virgin hemisphere, the flames in which their oracle Calvin consumed the poor Servetus, because he could not find in his Euclid the proposition which has demonstrated that three are one, and one is three." And if they cannot revive the holy inquisition of the Middle Ages, they will seek to mobilize the inquisition of public opinion, "that lord of the Universe" (letter to William Short, 13 April 1820). Jefferson, the enemy of all arbitrary and capricious power, found that which was clothed in the ceremonial garb of religion to be particularly despicable.

Even more disturbing to Jefferson was the priestly perversion of simple truths. If "in this virgin hemisphere" it was no longer possible to burn men's bodies, it was still possible to stunt their minds. In the "revolution of 1800" that saw Jefferson's election to the presidency, the candidate wrote to his good friend Rush that while his views on religion would please deists and rational Christians, they would never please that "irritable tribe of priests" who still hoped for government sanction and support. Nor would his election please them, "especially the Episcopalians and the Congregationalists." They fear that I will oppose their schemes of establishment. "And they believe rightly: for I have sworn upon the altar of God, eternal hostility against every form of tyranny over the mind of man" (23 September 1800).

It was this aspect of establishment that Jefferson most dreaded and most relentlessly opposed—not just the power, profit, and corruption that invariably accompanied state-sanctioned ecclesiasticism but the theological distortion and intellectual absurdity that passed for reason and good sense. We must not be held captive to "the Platonic mysticisms" or to the "gossamer fabrics of factitious religion." Nor must we ever again be required to confess that which mankind did not and could not comprehend, "for I suppose belief to be the assent of the mind to an intelligible proposition" (letter to John Adams, 22 August 1813). The propositions set forth by Jesus were so intelligible, so simple that the priesthood knew it would quickly be out of business if these were not somehow mystified, obscured, and turned into ambiguity. Therefore, the priesthood drew upon Platonism: "The doctrines which flowed from the lips of Jesus himself are within the comprehension of a child; but thousands of volumes have not yet explained the Platonisms engrafted on them." But that is the point: the purposes of the priesthood are served by "nonsense" that can never be explained (letter to John Adams, 5 July 1814). (Plato, Jefferson added, is appealed to as a strong believer in immortality, "yet I will venture to say that were there no better arguments than his in proof of it, not a man in the world would believe it.") The priests are the enemies of knowledge no less than they are of liberty, and progress in human understanding requires total emancipation from their control.

Toward the end of his life, Jefferson spoke more and more in terms of restoring "primitive Christianity." This was a major interest of Priestley's, but in early-nineteenth-century America it was likewise the interest of many pietists on the frontier. Such bold preachers as Alexander Campbell and Barton Stone also called for a return to the simplicities of Jesus and the apostolic age. In 1822, Jefferson used language that would have been most congenial to the frontier restorationists: "Happy in the prospect of a restoration of primitive Christianity, I must leave to younger athletes to encounter and lop off the false branches which have been engrafted into it by the mythologists of the middle and modern ages" (letter to Benjamin Waterhouse, 19 July 1822). But in writing to Unitarian James Smith on 8 December, Jefferson indicated once again that on the doctrine of the Trinity the deist and the pietist would part ways, despite their common concern for a "revival of primitive Christianity," for "no historical fact is better established than that the doctrine of one God, pure and uncompounded, was that of the early ages of Christianity."

Two years before his death, Jefferson asked for simplicity and purity in the religion that he was prepared to call his own, if only "Christianity" were truly the religion of Jesus himself rather than some monstrosity made up of "the metaphysical abstractions of Athanasius, and the maniac ravings of Calvin, tinctured plentifully with the foggy dreams of Plato" (letter to John Davis, 18 January 1824). Just as the exercise of reason and common sense has brought us political freedom, so by this same means shall we find intellectual freedom as well.

Though at times Jefferson expressed confidence that the whole country soon would be Unitarian, at other times he recognized the novelty, if not the idiosyncrasy, of his own religious ideas. "I am of a sect by myself, as far as I know," he wrote to Ezra Stiles Ely on 25 June 1819. While he entertained high hopes that his one-man sect would prove attractive to a new and groping nation, no evidence suggests that he would ever take any step to establish his own views through governmental sanction or support. Whatever the theological content of his credo, its political bedrock remained solid: government at all levels must hold itself aloof from the realm of religious opinions. If there is to be a "civil religion" of the Republic, it can come about only through the quiet, steady operation of reason coupled with the instrumentality of education and voluntary persuasion. However mighty his pen in treating of religion, Jefferson would never resort to sword nor countenance such activity by others.

For all the color and vigor of his attack upon dogmas, institutions, and clergy, Jefferson could not let the subject of religion rest. Unlike Madison, for example, Jefferson found the religious quest to be intellectually challenging and socially vital. While some of his remarks imply that religion is exclusively a private affair, nothing more than the relationship of the individual with the creator, at other times he speaks to and reflects upon the public dimension of religion. As president, he was unwilling to declare days of thanksgiving or of prayer, but in his First Inaugural Address, he—like his predecessors and successors—did not fail to invoke the blessing of "that Infinite Power which rules the destinies of the universe." In his Second Inaugural Address, he sought for himself, the nation, and all its citizens the "favor of that Being in whose hands we are, who led our forefathers, as Israel of old, from their native land, and planted them in a country flowing with all the necessaries and comforts of life; who has covered our infancy with his providence, and our riper years with his wisdom and power."

All of this could be seen as hollow presidential rhetoric, the mere manipulation of religious sentiments in order to further political ends. The intensity and earnestness of Jefferson's private spiritual wrestling argue otherwise. He sought resolution of fundamental theological and moral issues, but he sought such resolution not for himself alone. Despite repeated protestations to the contrary, Jefferson wished that his private understandings could somehow become public ones. A nation could not be built upon superstition and ignorance; neither, however, could it stand firm with a citizenry given over to self-indulgence and Promethean pride. Destinies, be they national or personal, truly were in the hands of an "Infinite Power." A moral sense, implanted in every human breast, truly was enlivened and instructed by the pure teachings of Jesus. For the nation that he had helped bring into being, Jefferson continued to seek, not the lowest common denominator in religion, but the highest standard that the faculty of reason and the moral instinct could possibly attain.

Political Parties

NOBLE E. CUNNINGHAM, JR.

NATIONAL political parties in the United States originated despite an atmosphere of hostility toward them. Most Americans equated parties with factional divisiveness or conspiracy against government. They saw parties as evils to be avoided or, failing in that, devices whose dangerous tendencies were to be checked. The framers of the Constitution shared this widespread feeling and believed that they had devised a system to discourage parties. James Madison argued in *The Federalist* that the Constitution would control "the violence of faction." Because the drafters of the Constitution did not anticipate political parties, they made no provision for their existence. Under the new government early signs of party formation were greeted with stern warnings about their dangers. In *A Definition of Parties* (1794), John Taylor of Caroline County, Virginia, warned: "The situation of the public good, in the hands of two parties nearly poised as to numbers, must be extremely perilous. Truth is a thing, not of divisibility into conflicting parts, but of unity." Taylor reflected the common outlook that did not recognize the concept of a legitimate political opposition. Those in control of the government regarded opposition as conspiracy against the government, while those seeking to change its administration saw themselves as trying to rescue the government from persons whom they saw as subverting it from within. Neither side thought in terms of a loyal opposition.

In his Farewell Address on 19 September 1796, President Washington dwelt at length on the evils of parties, declaring:

> There is an opinion that parties in free countries are useful checks upon the Administration of the Government and serve to keep alive the spirit of Liberty. This within certain limits is probably true, and in Governments of a Monarchical cast Patriotism may look with endulgence, if not with favour, upon the spirit of party. But in those of the popular character, in Governments purely elective, it is a spirit not to be encouraged.

While sharing a distrust of political parties, American opinions differed as to whether parties, on the one hand, could be avoided, suppressed, or abolished, or on the other hand, checked or limited but not eliminated. Alexander Hamilton held the former view. James Madison subscribed to the latter. But no American of major influence argued for the position that parties were both inevitable and necessary and also on balance good. Thomas Jefferson tended to the Madisonian view. He wrote to John Taylor on 4 June 1798:

> In every free and deliberating society there must, from the nature of man, be opposite parties and violent dissensions and discords; and one of these, for the most part, must prevail over the other for a longer or shorter time. Perhaps this party division is necessary to induce each to watch and delate to the people the proceedings of the other.

There is danger of reading into Jefferson's words a modern concept of the usefulness of political parties, but Jefferson's own actions as a party leader never indicated the acceptance of the concept of a continuing legitimate opposition.

As an opposition leader Jefferson justified his own participation in a political party in a letter to William B. Giles of 31 December 1795, saying that "where the principle of difference is as substantial and as strongly pronounced as between the republicans and the Monocrats of our country, I hold it as honorable to take a firm and decided part, and as immoral to pursue a middle line, as between the parties of Honest men, and Rogues, into which every country is divided." Thus Jefferson saw his partisan activities as being in the public interest, but he was unwilling to acknowledge the same motives in his political foes. When his party elevated him to the presidential office, he began by seeking to reconcile the two political parties, proclaiming in his inaugural address that "we are all republicans: we are all federalists." On 8 March 1801, a few days after taking office, he wrote privately, to Horatio Gates, "If we can hit on the true line of conduct which may conciliate the honest part of those who were called federalists, and do justice to those who have so long been excluded from [the government], I shall hope to be able to obliterate, or rather to unite the names of federalists and republicans." When Federalists rebuffed the overtures, Jefferson tolerated their opposition but never accepted them as constituting a legitimate political opposition.

THE FORMATION OF THE EARLY REPUBLICAN PARTY

Jefferson never set out to be a party leader. Nor did he ever seek credit as the founder of a political party. Yet no other American statesman of his time played so influential a role in the development of American political parties, and no American of his day was so successful as Jefferson in leading a national political party. Jefferson alone did not create a political party; in the early years of party formation, Madison was more active in an organizational sense than Jefferson. But more than anyone, Jefferson symbolized the party that came to recognize him as its leader. Jefferson always referred to the party that he headed as the Republican party, and so did most of his supporters, although their opponents often called them Antifederalists, Jacobins, and disorganizers. Republicans reciprocated by calling their Federalist rivals Antirepublicans, Tories, Monarchists, and similar opprobrious names. In a few states Republicans adopted the label Democratic-Republican, but Republican remained the name employed most commonly nationwide in self-designation. With the rise of the Democratic party in the Jacksonian era, Democratic leaders claimed descent from the Jeffersonian Republican party, and Jefferson and Jackson became the patron saints of the party that still celebrates that heritage two centuries later at Jefferson–Jackson dinners throughout the nation.

At the time Jefferson joined President Washington's first cabinet early in 1790, as secretary of state in the new government under the Constitution, there were no national political parties in the United States. Washington had been elected president by a unanimous electoral vote. The Federalist and Antifederalist competitors who had contested the ratification of the Constitution had not carried their divisions forward into the new government either in the executive branch or in the legislature. In the First Congress (1789–1791), alignments revealed in recorded roll calls reflected sectional interests more than anything else. No partisan voting blocs are recognizable in any of its three sessions. The same circumstances did not prevail in the Second Congress (1791–1793), where two opposing voting blocs are discernible in the House of Representatives. One group followed the lead of Madison in opposing the financial programs of Secretary of the Treasury Alexander Hamilton; the other constituted Hamilton's supporters in Congress. This division paralleled the growing split within Washington's administration between Jefferson and Hamilton and drew Jefferson and Madison, already close friends, into a political cooperation that provided the leadership for what contemporaries at first called the republican interest. This gradually developed into the Republican party.

In playing leading roles in organizing the Republican party neither Jefferson nor Madison was thinking in terms of a permanent system of political parties in the United States. They were seeking to organize opposition to Hamiltonian policies and to the general direction of the new government. They hoped to employ the mechanism of party to restore the government to what they saw as the true republican course.

A series of events thrust Jefferson into a position of party leadership that he at first only reluctantly accepted. Hamilton's proposal for a national bank prompted Jefferson in 1791 to write a number of private letters expressing his concern about the direction that the treasury head's programs were giving to the new government. When Congress passed the bill to charter the Bank of the United States, he argued vigorously within the administration that it was unconstitutional. He complained to Lafayette, in a letter of 16 June 1792, that "too many of our legislature have become stock jobbers," and told the president, in a letter of 23 May 1792, that too many members of Congress "have manifested their dispositions to get rid of the limitations imposed by the constitution on the general legislature." Jefferson thus early became the advocate of strict construction of the Constitution, and he insisted that it was "the republican party, who wish to preserve the government in it's present form."

As Jefferson's alarm over Hamiltonian policies mounted, it was less the carefully reasoned arguments that he prepared for the president than the incautious sentiments that he expressed in private letters that projected him to the forefront in the public mind as the bold champion of republicanism. The most sensational of his private remarks to reach the public in the early 1790s resulted from an inadvertent act on his part. In the spring of 1791 the first American printing of Thomas Paine's *Rights of Man* appeared in Philadelphia with an extract from a letter of endorsement by Jefferson published without authorization as a foreword. Jefferson had written the note in politeness to the printer, to whom he was returning a borrowed copy of the pamphlet prior to its American printing. His private remarks created a popular sensation when they appeared in print. The secretary of state had written that he was pleased that Paine's pamphlet was to be reprinted in the United States and that "something is at length to be publicly said against the political heresies which have sprung up among us. I have no doubt our citizens will rally a second time round the standard of Common Sense." The publication brought cries of protest from Hamilton, who proclaimed that Jefferson had put himself in opposition to the government. Vice President John Adams also took great offense. Privately Jefferson confessed that he had indeed had Adams' *Discourses on Davila* in mind when he wrote the sentiments. "I tell the writer freely that he is a heretic," Jefferson confided to Madison, "but certainly never meant to step into a public newspaper with that in my mouth." Because he had written the words of endorsement and fully approved of the content of Paine's pamphlet, Jefferson remained silent about the publication, though he resented the unauthorized use of his letter. No previous occasion had directed so much public attention to his opposition to Hamilton or so displayed the widening cleavage with Adams. In Jefferson the public saw a friend and defender of republicanism.

The attention elicited by this incident brought closer scrutiny to Jefferson's actions. When he and Madison made a trip to New York and New England in May 1791, many observers were quick to see political purposes in the journey. A New Yorker reported "every appearance of a passionate courtship" between the Virginians and Aaron Burr and Robert R. Livingston when the travelers passed through New York, and some historians have seen this as the beginning of the New York–Virginia alliance that was the foundation of the Republican party. While contacts made on this trip may well have been politically useful in future years, the main purpose of Jefferson's and Madison's journey was not to lay the base for a political party, but to see the land, observe the flora and fauna, and enjoy a respite from the politics of the capital city.

Neither Jefferson nor Madison drew up a plan to create a political party, restrained as they both were by the prevailing view that parties were divisive and disruptive. But they saw the need to get a wider public hearing for the political positions they were taking within the administration and in Congress, and this led them to encourage Philip Freneau to move to Philadelphia to establish the *National Gazette.* Jefferson regarded Philadelphia's leading *Gazette of the United States,* edited by John Fenno and enjoying the considerable patronage of the Treasury Department, as "a paper of pure Toryism, disseminating the doctrines of monarchy, aristocracy, and the exclusion of the influence of the people." He thought republicanism needed a voice and that Freneau, "a good whig," would provide one. Madison, writing on 13 September 1792 to Edmund Randolph, expressed their common aim when he said that he expected Freneau, a man of "republican principles, and a friend to the Constitution, would be some antidote to the doctrines and discourses circulated in favour of Monarchy and Aristocracy and . . . an acceptable vehicle of public information in many places not sufficiently supplied with it." Thus Madison conducted negotiations with Freneau; Jefferson promised him a part-time job as a translating clerk in the State Department, and they ultimately persuaded him to move from New York to Philadelphia.

Jefferson later said, in a letter to Washington of 9 September 1792, that his expectations for Freneau "looked only to the chastisement of the aristocratical and monarchical writers, and not to any criticisms on the proceedings of government." But Freneau was not so cautious. He was soon attacking Hamilton with such vigor that the secretary of the treasury responded by charging the secretary of state with providing a salary to an editor to vilify public officials, oppose the measures of government, and disturb the public peace. Hamilton wrote to Edward Carrington on 26 May 1792 that in Congress, "Mr. Madison, co-operating with Mr. Jefferson, is at the head of a faction decidedly hostile to me and my administration, and actuated by views, in my judgment, subversive of the principles of good government and dangerous to the Union, peace and happiness of the country." The newspaper war between editors Freneau and Fenno brought the differences between Jefferson and Hamilton before the public more starkly than ever before, opened up to public view the divisions within Washington's official family, and provoked the president himself to call upon his department heads to reduce the internal dissensions, pleading in this case with Jefferson in a letter of 23 August 1792 "that instead of wounding suspicions, and irritable charges, there may be liberal allowances, mutual forbearances, and temporising yieldings on *all sides.*"

Jefferson replied to the president in a letter of 9 September in which he expressed his concern at being a part of the internal dissensions within the administration but insisted that he had not schemed against Hamilton in Congress nor attacked him in the press. "That I have utterly, in my private conversations, disapproved of the system of the Secretary of the Treasury, I acknowledge and avow," he confessed, describing Hamilton's system as flowing from "principles adverse to liberty" and "calculated to undermine and demolish the republic." But "if it has been supposed that I have ever intrigued among the members of the legislatures to defeat the plans of the Secretary of the Treasury, it is contrary to all truth." While Jefferson blamed Hamilton for the divisions that Washington saw as tearing his government apart, Hamilton insisted that Jefferson bore the major responsibility. "I *know,*" he wrote, "that I have been an object of uniform opposition from Mr. Jefferson. . . . I *know,* from the most authentic sources, that I have been the frequent subject of the most unkind whispers and insinuating from the same quarter. I have long seen a formed party in the Legislature, under his auspices,

bent upon my subversion." The president's admonition did nothing to halt the growth of political parties.

The unsettled state of politics led both Jefferson and Hamilton, along with other leaders on the national scene, to urge Washington to stand for reelection in 1792. Although the president already had asked Madison to prepare a draft of an address announcing his retirement, he reluctantly agreed to continue. There was no opposition from any quarter to his reelection. Not so in regard to the vice presidency. The rising Republican opposition made a determined effort to deny John Adams a second term and to replace him with a man of more republican sentiments. This maneuver, though unsuccessful, was engineered by Republican leaders from Virginia, New York, and Pennsylvania who pushed the election of New York's Governor George Clinton. Jefferson was not directly involved, but Madison and Monroe were, as was the very active political manager John Beckley, the clerk of the House of Representatives. The interstate cooperation among Republican leaders that this party strategy required marked the beginning of the New York–Virginia alliance, so important to later party success. The fact that this effort produced fifty electoral votes for Clinton, against seventy-seven for Adams, demonstrated both the value of party organization and the potential for the future of the emerging Republican party.

By the time of Washington's second inauguration in 1793, Jefferson and Hamilton stood as spokesmen on opposite sides of most of the key issues before the new nation. Jefferson sought to keep the national government limited and argued for a strict interpretation of the Constitution. Hamilton, seeing the future greatness of the United States in a powerful national government, sought a loose construction of that instrument and a liberal view of the implied powers of government. Jefferson saw the future of the nation as that of an agrarian republic of independent farmers. "Those who labour in the earth," he said, "are the chosen people of God, if ever he had a chosen people." His devotion to agriculture did not rule out commerce, for Jefferson did not envision a nation of subsistence farmers. As minister to France prior to becoming secretary of state, Jefferson had sought to open European markets to American produce, and he recognized the necessity of commerce as the handmaiden to agriculture. But Jefferson did not share Hamilton's goal of transforming the United States into a manufacturing nation through protective tariffs, awards for inventions, and subsidies for new manufactories. Just as Congress divided over Hamilton's proposal for a national bank, legislators disagreed over his plans to promote manufacturing. Although the Bank of the United States was established, most of Hamilton's proposals to promote manufacturing were rejected; but both issues continued to be debated as party issues for years to come.

As policy differences divided the members of Washington's administration, Congress, and the country, one issue more than any other influenced the climate of opinion that moved Americans to separate into Federalist and Republican ranks: the foreign policy of the new nation. The commercial policy of Great Britain, the unsettled issues of the peace of 1783, and the increasingly tumultuous events of the French Revolution posed for the new republic challenges of such magnitude that differences as to how the nation should respond were to be expected. After war in Europe broke out between England and France in 1793, Jefferson noted that it had "kindled and brought forward the two parties with an ardour which our own interests merely, could never excite."

Jefferson differed with Hamilton over whether to recognize the new French Republic and receive its new minister, Edmond Charles Genêt, and over the status of the treaty of 1778 with France. Fearful of the French Revolution, Hamilton wanted to suspend the treaty and refuse to recognize the new French Republic. Jefferson saw the French Revolution as advancing liberty and equality in the world and saw no reason to suspend the treaty or deny recognition to the new government. The secretary of state's recognition policy was accepted by Washington, and both Jefferson and Hamilton supported the policy of neutrality proclaimed by the president. Though the pro-French Jefferson and the pro-British Hamilton remained in Washington's cabinet, the French issue became a heated subject in American politics. Widespread enthusiasm for the French Republic stimulated the organization of "Democratic" and "Republican" societies in many states. These popular societies supported Republican positions and Republican candidates, but they never performed the functions of nominating candidates or managing election campaigns. The only role they shared with the Republican party was that of publicizing issues and candidates. The leadership of the Republican party remained in the hands of members of Congress, where Madison was the principal leader, and under the direction of other national political figures, of which Jefferson was the most widely respected.

As long as he remained in Washington's cabinet, Jefferson continued to provide direction for the growing Republican party through the things he championed and his contacts with Republicans in Congress. When Republicans in the House of Representatives opened an inquiry into the Treasury Department early in 1793 that seemed designed to drive Hamilton from his post, Jefferson was in touch with their actions. While there is no evidence that he was responsible for the move, a draft in Jefferson's handwriting of a series of resolutions introduced by William Branch Giles censuring the conduct of the secretary of the treasury suggests that he was a party to the business and not so aloof from the affairs of Congress as he professed.

One of the best examples of Jefferson's early party leadership can be found in his role in regard to the increasingly difficult problem of the conduct of Genêt. The French minister openly defied the neutrality of the United States by fitting out privateers in American ports and recruiting Americans for an attack on Spanish territory. In August 1793 the cabinet voted unanimously to demand Genêt's recall, and Jefferson privately warned that Genêt would "sink the republican interest if they do not abandon him." In a long letter of 11 August 1793, written to Madison, he also detailed the policy that he believed Republicans should adopt, concluding by saying:

> So in Congress I believe that it will be true wisdom in the Republican party to approve unequivocally of a state of neutrality, to avoid little cavils about who should declare it, to abandon G[enêt] entirely, with expressions of strong friendship and adherence to his nation and confidence that he has acted against their sense. In this way we shall keep the people on our side by keeping ourselves in the right.

This important letter not only reveals Jefferson's role in planning party strategy but also demonstrates his commitment to the principle that a political party must be responsive to the popular will.

Jefferson had intended to resign as secretary of state at the end of Washington's first term, but he stayed on because he was under attack by Hamilton in the press and did not wish to appear to have been driven from office. When the year 1793 turned out to be a very critical time in foreign affairs, he did not feel free to give up his post until the end of December. After that trying year, he finally was "liberated from the hated occupations of politics," as he expressed it, and turned his attention to his family, his farm, and his books. He said that he never ex-

pected to return to public life and vowed that he would never leave Monticello again.

With Jefferson in retirement, the leadership of the Republican party fell to Madison, who remained in Congress, where his work in organizing Republicans in the legislature had already created a national center of leadership for the party. Within three years that party would recall Jefferson to public office.

In retirement Jefferson did not, from behind the scenes, pull the strings of Republican puppets in the capital at Philadelphia as some contemporaries suspected. He did receive visitors at Monticello and continued some political correspondence, but as he wrote to John Adams on 25 April 1794, "Instead of writing 10 or 12 letters a day, which I have been in the habit of doing as a thing of course, I put off answering my letters now, farmer-like, till a rainy day, and then find it sometimes postponed by other necessary occupations." Devoting his attention to expanding and remodeling Monticello, improving his exhausted farm lands, and developing his extensive gardens, he professed "a total retirement from all intermeddling with public affairs and public bodies." Despite his disclaimers, Jefferson never lost interest in politics and national affairs. Still, when his friends began to talk about who might succeed Washington as president, he said, in a letter to Madison of 27 April 1795, that his retirement "meant from all office high or low, without exception."

Madison ignored Jefferson's protestations and joined with other Republican leaders in putting him forward as the Republican candidate to oppose Federalist John Adams for the presidency in 1796. Although this was done without Jefferson's authorization, he did not withdraw his name after it became clear from the newspapers that he was the Republican candidate. At the same time, he did nothing to promote his election and avowed that he would be happier to come in second, which under the constitutional provisions then in force would make him the vice-president.

Although neither Jefferson nor Adams campaigned for the presidency, the election of 1796 was the first party contest for that office. As long as Washington, who stood above parties, remained in office, party development had been inhibited. The publication of Washington's Farewell Address, one contemporary commentator observed, was "a signal, like dropping a hat, for the party racers to start." For the first time in a presidential election there were two party candidates. Jefferson's supporters tried to make the election appear to be a contest between an ardent defender of republicanism and an admirer of aristocracy and monarchy. Republican campaign literature described Jefferson as a "firm Republican," a "steadfast friend to the Rights of the People," and "the uniform advocate of equal rights among citizens." Adams was depicted as "the champion of rank, titles, and hereditary distinctions," a "royalist," and "an avowed monarchist." One Republican campaign handbill reminded voters that *"Thomas Jefferson* first drew the declaration of American independence—he first framed the sacred political sentence that all men are *born* equal." Then the writer continued: *"John Adams* says this is all a farce and a falsehood; that some men should be born Kings, and some should be born Nobles." He followed by pointing out that Jefferson, like Washington, had no son, while Adams had sons who might aim to succeed their father.

The election of 1796 was highly partisan, warmly contested, and extremely close. When all the electoral votes were counted, Adams claimed the presidency with three more electoral votes than Jefferson, who accepted the vice presidency with good grace. Some had feared that Jefferson might decline the second office, but he both assumed the lesser station and indicated a willingness to work with Adams. Privately he suggested that it might be for the public good to reach some understanding with Adams regarding future elections as the best barrier against Hamilton's ambition. Adams likewise was at first receptive to the idea of working with Jefferson. Both men, however, had been too much isolated from the campaign to appreciate the extent of the firming of party lines that the election had produced. Never before had there been so much party organizing, campaign management, publicity activities, and efforts to get out the voters. In all of these efforts the Republicans were the most active and the most innovative in the campaign techniques employed. Many parts of the country were still unaffected by new practices of organizing party committees and directly soliciting voter support, but Republicans were taking the lead in transforming American national politics into an open contest for determining who would manage the government of the republic.

If Jefferson had ever expected that he could work with Adams in a nonpartisan way, he was disabused of the notion soon after taking the oath of office as vice-president. Within days Adams made it clear that he would not share executive matters with him. Soon afterward Jefferson resumed the leadership of the Republican party. One of the first things that the new vice-president did was to write a warm letter, on 17 June 1797, to Aaron Burr of New York asking his help in "the penetration of truth" into New England. "If the people there, who are unquestionably republicans, could discover that they have been duped into the support of measures calculated to sap the very foundations of republicanism, we might still hope for salvation," he wrote, while wondering if the middle, southern, and western states could hold on until the eastern states awakened. If Burr could offer any suggestions, Jefferson said he would welcome them. Burr responded promptly to the vice-president's confiding letter, but the cautious New Yorker suggested that he could not satisfactorily reply in a letter and promised to meet with Jefferson in Philadelphia on the following Sunday.

No better example of Jefferson's assumption of active leadership of the Republican party can be found than in his overture to Burr and their conference that followed in the capital. During Burr's visit to Philadelphia, Jefferson also brought Burr together with Albert Gallatin, the Republican leader of the House of Representatives, who had succeeded the recently retired Madison in that role, and with James Monroe, who had been recalled as minister to France and had just arrived home. Any knowledgeable observer who saw Jefferson, Burr, and Gallatin board Monroe's ship in the harbor to greet the returned diplomat could not have failed to see that Jefferson had returned to partisan politics.

As vice-president, Jefferson presided over the Senate, but having no role in Adams' Federalist-controlled administration, he was free to provide direction to the opposition party. With Federalist majorities in both houses of Congress, the nation had its first party government, which excluded Republicans from offices and patronage. And for the first time the nation had an uninhibited opposition party. With Madison in retirement in Virginia, the burden of party leadership fell heavily on Jefferson. The respect that his character as a committed republican commanded made him a center of unity for the party, and he augmented that position by maintaining contact with Republican leaders in Congress and by carrying on an extensive correspondence with party leaders throughout the country.

Jefferson also took an active, though often hidden, role in opposing unpopular Federalist measures. The leading example was his secret drafting of the Kentucky Resolutions of 1798 protesting against the Alien and Sedition Acts as violations of civil liberties and as unconstitutional. With Jefferson's encouragement, Madison prepared a similar protest adopted by the Virginia Assembly.

The Alien and Sedition Acts, ostensibly aimed at threats to internal security during the war crisis with France in 1798, were employed against Republican political opposition, especially against Republican newspapers. Moved by this threat to freedom of speech and press, Jefferson set down in the resolutions passed by the Kentucky legislature a systematic statement of states' rights grounded on the same concept of a limited government and strict construction of the Constitution found in the opinion he had earlier written denying the constitutionality of a national bank. Most Republicans were not prepared to push states' rights to the extreme to which Jefferson seemed prepared to go, but emphasis on the rights of states and opposition to a loose construction of the Constitution became major planks in the platform that Republicans were building to challenge President Adams' expected bid for reelection in 1800. Indeed, as attacks on the unpopular Alien and Sedition Acts, the Kentucky and Virginia Resolutions were the opening guns in the presidential election of 1800.

THE PRESIDENTIAL ELECTION OF 1800

In contrast to 1796, Jefferson in 1800 showed no reluctance to being the Republican candidate for president. The Republican consensus in favor of Jefferson's candidacy was so broad that no formal nomination was necessary, but the Republican members of Congress met in a nominating caucus to choose Aaron Burr of New York as his vice-presidential running mate. That caucus, which was to establish the mechanism for nominating presidential and vice-presidential candidates for the next quarter of a century, did not assemble until May 1800, after the campaign was well under way. Meanwhile Jefferson had begun making preparations for the election early in 1799.

In letters to correspondents throughout the country he spelled out the political principles that the Republican party stood for and formulated the platform for the next election. As he expected, the ideas in his letters circulated beyond the correspondents to whom they were addressed, and the basic themes that he emphasized began appearing in newspapers and political pamphlets throughout the country.

On 5 February 1799, Jefferson wrote to Madison from Philadelphia that the coming summer was "the season for systematic energies and sacrifices. The engine is the press. Every man must lay his purse and his pen under contribution." He appealed to Madison to set aside a portion of every post day to write something for the newspapers. "Send it to me while here," he instructed, "and when I go away I will let you know to whom you may send, so that your name shall be sacredly secret." Jefferson also encouraged other Republican friends to take up their political pens, though he adhered to his own rule not to write anonymously for publication.

Jefferson also was active in the circulation of political tracts. He sent bundles of pamphlets to friends in Virginia for distribution among their neighbors. In sending Monroe a dozen such pamphlets on 11 February 1799, he instructed: "I wish you to give these to the most influential characters among our countrymen, who are only misled, are candid enough to be open to conviction, and who may have most effect on their neighbors. It would be useless to give them to persons already sound. Do not let my name be connected in the business." Here is evidence of the practical political side of the philosopher-statesman who drafted the Declaration of Independence. On 7 April 1800 he sent eight dozen copies of a pamphlet to Philip Norborne Nicholas, chairman of the Virginia state Republican committee, asking him to send one copy to the chairman of each county committee, thus utilizing a statewide party network that was created for the first time during the election of 1800. Jefferson himself was not the architect of the new party machinery, but he recognized its usefulness. In sending political tracts to the Virginia Republican chairman for distribution, he said, "Tho' I know that this is not the immediate object of your institution, yet I consider it as a most valuable object, to which the institution may most usefully be applied." Political custom prevented presidential candidates from openly campaigning for office, but Jefferson employed all the avenues available to him to promote his own election—writing letters, encouraging his party supporters to prepare pieces for the newspapers, supporting Republican editors, circulating political pamphlets, and generally encouraging Republicans to be active. Above all he provided the symbol of Republicanism and more than anyone else defined the aims of the Republican party.

By 1800 the Republicans had formulated clear policy positions and a party program that offered the voters an alternative to the Federalist policies of Adams' administration. Jefferson's leading role in defining Republican principles and the party program can be seen in a letter to Elbridge Gerry of Massachusetts on 26 January 1799 in which he outlined many of the political principles and policies that he would later reiterate in his presidential inaugural address in 1801. He declared his commitment to preserving the Constitution "according to the true sense in which it was adopted by the States" and preventing the "monarchising" of its features. He continued:

> I am for preserving to the States the powers not yielded by them to the Union, and to the legislature of the Union it's constitutional share in the division of powers; and I am not for transferring all the powers of the States to the general government, and all those of that government to the Executive branch. I am for a government rigorously frugal and simple,

applying all the possible savings of the public revenue to the discharge of the national debt; and not for a multiplication of officers and salaries merely to make partisans, and for increasing, by every device, the public debt, on the principle of it's being a public blessing. I am for relying, for internal defence, on our militia solely, till actual invasion, and for such a naval force only as may protect our coasts and harbors from such depredations as we have experienced; and not for a standing army in time of peace, which may overawe the public sentiment; nor for a navy, which, by it's own expenses and the eternal wars in which it will implicate us, will grind us with public burthens, and sink us under them. I am for free commerce with all nations; political connection with none; and little or no diplomatic establishment. And I am not for linking ourselves by new treaties with the quarrels of Europe; entering that field of slaughter to preserve their balance, or joining in the confederacy of kings to war against the principles of liberty. I am for freedom of religion, and against all maneuvres to bring about a legal ascendancy of one sect over another: for freedom of the press, and against all violations of the constitution to silence by force and not by reason the complaints or criticisms, just or unjust, of our citizens against the conduct of their agents. And I am for encouraging the progress of science in all it's branches; and not for raising a hue and cry against the sacred name of philosophy. . . . These . . . are my principles; they are unquestionably the principles of the great body of our fellow citizens.

In no election in American history have the lines between political parties been more clearly drawn than in 1800, and Jefferson's statement marked out the party differences. It reflected his own basic political creed and at the same time responded to the controversial policies of Adams' administration. In reaction to the XYZ Affair the Federalists had expanded the army, created a navy, authorized an undeclared naval war against France, increased the public debt, raised taxes, passed the Alien and Sedition Acts, and curtailed dissent. Jefferson and the

Republican party made it clear that if elected they would reverse these policies, return to a more limited and frugal government, and chart a more republican course. The campaign was not waged solely on the high level of rational debate that Jefferson outlined, for both parties appealed to the interests, fears, and hopes of the voters in a campaign that saw Adams again charged with being a friend to monarchy and Jefferson painted as a man whose election would bring a collapse of public credit, the shattering of public morals, and the profaning of religion.

The election of 1800 was a close contest, and its outcome depended not only upon the principles and policies advocated by the opposing candidates and parties but also upon the activities of Republican party managers such as Aaron Burr in New York, John Beckley in Pennsylvania, Nicholas in Virginia, and Charles Pinckney in South Carolina. The party machinery and organization stimulated by the campaign left a permanent mark on American politics and political parties.

As it turned out, Republican party discipline was greater than party leaders expected it to be. This was demonstrated when all Republican presidential electors cast their electoral votes for Jefferson and Burr. Because the Constitution required that each elector vote for two candidates without distinguishing between presidential and vice-presidential choices, Jefferson and Burr tied with seventy-three electoral votes each; Adams received sixty-five electoral votes; and Charles Cotesworth Pinckney, sixty-four. The presidential election was so close that superior party organization by the Republicans may have made the difference, but in the congressional elections the Republican sweep was so wide that the new Republican majority in both houses of Congress showed that the Republican party had strong support in the country and that the election of 1800 was a decisive popular victory.

The election by the House of Representatives, which the Constitution mandated, to decide the tie between Jefferson and Burr proved a test of Republican party strength, unity, and determination. The choice had to be made not by the new Congress, which the Republicans would control but by the sitting Congress, in which the Federalists had a majority. Federalists did not, however, control a majority of state delegations. This was critical to the final result because the Constitution required that in such elections each state vote as a unit casting one vote. At the same time, the Republicans did not control a majority of state delegations either, some states being equally divided between Federalist and Republican members. The tie between Jefferson and Burr clearly demonstrated that the framers of the Constitution in devising the electoral college system had not anticipated political parties. The electoral outcome also showed that political parties had matured more rapidly than most people realized.

Before the deficiency in the Constitution could be corrected, the nation passed through a major constitutional crisis. The House of Representatives remained deadlocked over the election on thirty-five ballots between 11 February and 17 February. Jefferson had the votes of eight states, Burr, six states, and two states were divided. With the end of John Adams' term of office only two weeks away, the nation faced the critical test of whether the power of the national government could pass peacefully from one political party to another. That question was decided on the thirty-sixth ballot, on 17 February, when the Federalists, who had been supporting Burr, allowed Jefferson to be elected. Enough Federalists did not vote, or cast blank ballots, to give Jefferson the votes of ten states, and he was elected president. Burr, who retained four states on the final ballot, became vice-president. The constitutional crisis thus passed, and before the next presidential election in 1804 the Twelfth Amendment, providing for separate balloting for president and vice-president, was added to the Constitution, acknowledging the presence of political parties in American politics.

PRESIDENT JEFFERSON AS PARTY LEADER

President Washington always claimed to be above parties. President Adams was never able to take the leadership of the Federalist party from Alexander Hamilton. Jefferson became the first president to be both the head of a political party and the head of the nation. He clearly put the latter role first, and in his inaugural address he appealed for national unity. "Every difference of opinion is not a difference of principle," he said. "We have called by different names brethren of the same principle. We are all republicans—we are all federalists." Jefferson was sincere in hoping to reconcile the Federalists to his administration, though he seemed to be thinking primarily in terms of Federalists becoming Republicans. When Federalist opposition continued, he insisted that the mass of the people were Republican and renounced the Federalist leaders as irreconcilables. He never recognized the Federalist party as a legitimate opposition, yet he continued to accept the Republican party as legitimate because that party represented the majority of the nation. Jefferson may have preferred a government without parties, but as president he accepted his role as the leader of the Republican party.

Jefferson's presidency was a party administration. His cabinet, headed by Madison as secretary of state and Gallatin as secretary of the treasury, was composed entirely of men who had been active in the Republican party. He accepted the role of party in Congress, and both he and his department heads worked closely with Republican leaders in the House and Senate. He recognized the importance of party strength and unity, and without interfering in local party divisions, he served as the center and promoter of party unity throughout the country.

President Jefferson's patronage policy reveals his own inner struggle over the place of political parties in government. The initial declarations in his inaugural address seemed to indicate that party was not to be a consideration in his administration. His early failure to win support from the Federalists and the mounting pressures from Republicans who expected to see more changes in officeholders led him to modify his statements. The editors of the Republican New York *American Citizen,* reacting to Jefferson's cautious initial steps, declared on 5 June 1801 that "those who removed John Adams from office . . . naturally expect the removal of lesser culprits in office. If this should not be the case, for what, in the name of God, have we been contending?" And the Hartford *American Mercury* proclaimed on 30 July that "it was as well understood previous to the elections, that men who had advocated the baleful measures of several years past, who have been persecutors of the friends of republicanism, were to be removed and the offices filled by men of republican principles, if they succeeded in their candidates, as if it had been reduced to a written contract."

Jefferson wrestled with the issue. "That some ought to be removed from office, and that all ought not, all mankind will agree," he believed, "But where to draw the line, perhaps no two will agree." He began by limiting his removals to federal marshals, district attorneys, the "midnight appointments" made by Adams in his last weeks as president (and continuing through his last night in office), and all officials guilty of misconduct in office. Initially the new Republican president said he would not remove other officers for "a difference of political principle, practised on only as far as the right of a private citizen will justify." Mean-

while he would give jobs only to Republicans until they had obtained their proportionate share of offices. He would use vacancies rather than removals to effect changes. The pressures from his own party, however, together with the fading prospects of Federalist conciliation, caused him to alter his policies. In July 1801, four months after taking office, Jefferson issued a new statement emphasizing the right of Republicans to their proportionate share of public places. "If a due participation of office is a matter of right, how are vacancies to be obtained?" he asked. "Those by death are few; by resignation, none. Can any other mode than that of removal be proposed? This is a painful office; but it is made my duty, and I meet it as such."

In practice Jefferson's actions never became quite so sweeping as this statement suggested. In the matter of appointments he continued to appoint only Republicans to office, but he proceeded cautiously in regard to removals, not wanting to be guilty of the political intolerance with which he had charged President Adams. In 1803 Jefferson (who kept careful records of all his appointments) made a party analysis of the 316 offices subject to appointment and removal directly by the president. He listed 158 offices in Republican hands, 132 held by Federalists, and twenty-six as politically neutral. Thus, after two years of a Republican administration, Republicans held half of the more important federal offices, though Jefferson's figures did not include the federal courts, because judges were not removable by the president. Jefferson's policies in regard to appointments and removals were not partisan enough to satisfy many of his Republican supporters, who would have been content with nothing less than a clean sweep of all Federalist officeholders from their posts; but however the degree of Jefferson's partisanship or moderation is assessed, there can be no doubt that party was a prime consideration in his actions.

The best example of President Jefferson's role as party leader can be found in his leadership and relationship with Congress. Contrary to Federalist charges that Jefferson was more suited to be a philosopher than the chief executive of the nation, Jefferson was a strong president who was in command of his administration and exerted effective leadership of Congress. Most of the major legislation enacted during his two terms as president came from his recommendations and proposals, and he secretly drafted some bills in an era when presidents were expected to leave such matters to legislators. His department heads worked closely with Congress, providing information, drafting legislation, making recommendations for changes in bills during the legislative process, and maintaining informal contacts with legislators. Jefferson had an unusually stable cabinet, with the four major department heads holding their offices throughout his eight years as president, and he used the cabinet system effectively in his leadership of Congress. A major reason for Jefferson's success was the role of party in the relations between the president and congress. Jefferson took office with a strong party majority in both houses, the product of the partisan contest of 1800 that had produced the first party turnover in both the executive and legislative branches in the young republic's history. The new Republican majority was ready to work with the new Republican president, whose popularity with the voters was high.

The role of party in Congress was demonstrated in the election of the Speaker of the House of Representatives, in the Republican control of major committees in both houses, and in the partisan voting records of members. The partisanship of Congress was also reflected in the tendency of members to live together in boardinghouses with like-minded colleagues. The leading characteristic that separated members into different boardinghouses was their party identity. As the strength of the Republican majority increased during Jefferson's first term and party dissensions in various states erupted, Republicans were not always united. But every faction sought to retain its Republican identity, and the one person with whom nearly every Republican wanted to claim association was Jefferson. The president's vast popular support—he was reelected in 1804 with only fourteen electoral votes cast against him—gave him tremendous leverage with Congress, and he used his bargaining power effectively to advance the policies of his administration.

A systematic administrator who left little to chance, Jefferson sought to develop a working relationship with party leaders in Congress. Federalists accused him of exerting undue influence over Congress. Federalist Senator James Hillhouse of Connecticut charged, "Never was a set of men more blindly devoted to the will of a *prime Mover or Minister* than the Majority of both Houses to the will and wishes of the Chief Magistrate." And his Federalist colleague Timothy Pickering of Massachusetts agreed, saying that Jefferson *"behind the curtain,* directs the measures he wishes to have adopted; while in each house a majority of puppets move as he touches the wires." Jefferson never sought nor attained the degree of control that Federalists charged, but he did seek working relationships with Republican spokesmen in Congress and especially wanted to have a floor leader in the House to speak for the administration.

For a time Jefferson worked with John Randolph, the chairman of the House Ways and Means Committee, but Randolph was too independent and unpredictable to remain comfortable in the role. In searching for a replacement for Randolph, Jefferson explained to Congressman Barnabas Bidwell of Massachusetts what he had in mind in seeking an administration floor leader.

He did not mean, he said, that any member should relinquish his own judgment and implicitly support all measures of the administration, but that when he did not disapprove, "he should not suffer them to go off in sleep, but bring them to the attention of the house and give them a fair chance." He rejected the charges of "backstairs counsellors" that had been made against his administration. He wrote to Bidwell on 5 July 1806 that

> if the members [of Congress] are to know nothing but what is important enough to be put into a public message, and indifferent enough to be made known to all the world, if the Executive is to keep all other information to himself, and the house to plunge on in the dark, it becomes a government of chance and not of design.

Party provided the mechanism for a working relationship between the president and Congress. While John Randolph had come to his position of leadership in Congress as chairman of the Ways and Means Committee and did not owe his position to the president, once he broke with the administration, as he did in 1806, he lost his post as chairman of that powerful committee. Nathaniel Macon, the Speaker of the House of Representatives who had appointed his friend Randolph to the post, also lost the speakership, demonstrating that party loyalty to the president was essential to retaining a position of leadership in Congress.

Jefferson's success in isolating Randolph and his friends and preventing the schism from developing into a major party split demonstrated his skills as a party leader. As long as Jefferson remained in office, he was able to keep the Republican party sufficiently united to carry out his policies. Though the party was weakened by the divided public support for the Embargo Act of 1807, the Republican party in 1808 was able to elect Madison as Jefferson's successor by a substantial majority.

When Jefferson retired from the presidency in 1809, he ceased any active role in national politics or the affairs of the Republican party. He was from time to time consulted by his successors James Madison and James Monroe, both longtime friends and political associates, but he was careful not to interfere in their administrations. He shared with President Monroe a satisfaction that the party struggle that they had earlier engaged in had ended and that the country in the years following the War of 1812 seemed to be entering a period in which political parties were fading away.

In retirement, when Jefferson recalled the party battles in which he had engaged, he emphasized the ideological conflict. Looking back at the election of 1800, he saw that event as "as real a revolution in the principles of our government as that of 1776 was in its form." In 1818, when he wrote a preface for a group of memoranda and diary notes that he was collecting into what he called *The Anas,* he reflected that the party struggles of the 1790s were "contests of principle, between the advocates of republican, and those of kingly government." While this theme ran through Jefferson's thought as a participant, he also then saw the conflict in specific terms of party principles and programs, as the letters that he wrote at the time show. He recognized that to be successful the Republicans had to define what they stood for and how they proposed to govern more precisely than in terms of republicanism versus monarchy. Though the term "party platform" was not in use in 1800, Jefferson recognized the need for such a platform and provided specific planks to explain the differences between the Republican and Federalist parties. Moreover, Jefferson did not depend on the superior intellectual claims of republicanism to achieve the triumph of republican ideology over monarchy. He employed the mechanisms of a political party to bring success to republicanism.

Jefferson might never have become president without the assistance of a political party, and he probably would not have been as successful a president without the support of a majority party in Congress. Yet in the final analysis Jefferson was a successful political leader because he was in tune with the wishes of the American people and sought to implement the goals of the majority. At the base of his own political philosophy was an overriding faith in the people. He eloquently expressed this belief in his "Response to the Citizens of Albemarle" in 1790, on the eve of joining Washington's first administration:

It rests now with ourselves alone to enjoy in peace and concord the blessings of self-government, so long denied to mankind: to shew by example the sufficiency of human reason for the care of human affairs and that the will of the majority, the Natural law of every society, is the only sure guardian of the rights of man. Perhaps even this may sometimes err. But it's errors are honest, solitary and short-lived.—Let us then, my dear friends, for ever bow down to the general reason of the society.

This brief passage contains the essence of Jefferson's basic political creed. It was that faith that caused Jefferson's contribution to the formation of American political parties to have such lasting influence and significance.

Foreign Affairs

LAWRENCE S. KAPLAN

WHEN General Lord Charles Cornwallis had his military band play the old march "The World Turned Upside Down," at the surrender field in Yorktown on 19 October 1781, it symbolized European bewilderment over the events of his generation. The American Revolution had been the occasion for rude colonials to upset the world as it was in the eighteenth century. If this was true on the battlefield, it was equally true in the chanceries. The new nation seemed to possess ideas about the outside world that would overturn established international relations. Thomas Jefferson's career as diplomatist embodied this American outlook, and while he was not the first explicator of American foreign relations or the sole formulator of American diplomacy, his voice was the most pervasive in the first generation of the republic's history.

On at least three noteworthy issues Jefferson expressed America's position on foreign affairs as diametrically opposed to European tradition, and even logic. The first was an interpretation of history as expressed in his *Summary View of the Rights of British America*

and the Declaration of Independence, in which the history of British colonization was rendered in a form incomprehensible to the mother country. That any connection with the mother country was a voluntary contract for mutual benefit defied history as the British knew it.

The second interpretation resulted in a conception of natural law that provided an American law of nations not known to the Old World. Such was the reasoning behind Jefferson's confrontation with Spain in 1792 over navigation of the Mississippi. His interpretation would assure free navigation to the sea to inhabitants of the upper reaches of the river.

A third new view, and the most enduring of his new ideas, arose in the context of validating the treaty of alliance with France in 1793 despite the violent change of government from monarchy to republic. The treaty, according to Jefferson in his letter to Gouverneur Morris of 12 March 1793, had been made not simply with a monarch, but with the nation: "We surely cannot deny to any nation that right whereon our own government is founded, that every one may . . . change these forms at its own will. The will of the nation is the only thing essential to be regarded."

Each of these positions violated European understandings of colonial and interstate relations that went back to the beginnings of the modern nation state. The idea of colonies asserting their geographic separation as grounds for autonomy was impossible for the mercantilist nations to accept in the eighteenth century. The claim of riparian rights under the rubric of natural law seemed to abuse not only the meanings of international law but also the practice of the time. The claim that treaties are made with the people and not the princes undercut the principles of legitimacy on which European dynasties had functioned for almost three hundred years.

The need for a new order of foreign relations and a new method of diplomacy to manage it seemed inherent in the nature of the American Revolution. That central event in Jefferson's life devolved on the assumption that a *novus ordo seclorum* had come into being that was fundamentally different from that of the Old World. Europe represented assorted evils that should have no part in American life. It was governed by kings and princes seeking their own dynastic interests rather than the interests of the people; its nations related to each other with hostility and suspicion, vying for political and military advantage, and restricting economic ties with each other. War was endemic to this society, and international law was subjected to power politics. Diplomacy itself was an elite concept, summoning images of royal servants moving from court to court as their masters intrigued secretly in shifting combinations of alliances. The fundamental virtue of America was that it could lie outside this dangerous system because of its geographical position.

From the beginning Jefferson conceived of an American government that would not only limit its functions among its citizens but would limit its connections with the outside world. Commercial relations would perhaps be necessary but they would have to be kept to a minimum; alliances would be shunned, for America, if left alone, would prosper through its own rich resources. Such commerce as might be necessary would travel along free seas, protected by maritime law from predatory internecine European wars. If foreign relations policy were thus limited to protection of American citizens abroad, then the diplomats involved would be different in spirit as well as function from the court figures identified with monarchical regimes. They would be few in number and have few obligations beyond those of service to Americans abroad. Among their duties, however, would be the witnessing and reporting of international events, thereby warning Americans of situations to be avoided.

But while the normal diplomatic profile of America would be low, this situation could not be achieved until the new nation had secured its borders, minimized dangers from imperial neighbors, and fully divested itself from the vestiges of British economic and political control. The problems that these challenges posed made foreign relations a vital issue for the United States in the first generation of its history, and a major preoccupation for Jefferson in his successive roles as author of the Declaration of Independence, minister to France in the 1780s, the first secretary of state in the 1790s, and president in the first decade of the nineteenth century. During this critical period the Old World was very much present in conflicts over boundaries, western expansion, and the rights of neutrals on the high seas. America also had a vested interest in the secular conflict between France and Britain in the French Revolutionary and Napoleonic Wars. The result was a foreign policy that mixed ideals of isolation with the imperatives of continuing crises. The development of an American "empire for liberty" and the promotion of liberal maritime law were practical as well as ideal goals; the adoption of a more attentive attitude toward France throughout this period was a means of achieving them.

Britain always evoked mixed emotions in Jefferson. He took pride in the heritage of law and liberty from the mother country. America, he had always recognized, owed its values and indeed its experience in self-government to British models, and he never failed to respect this debt. The common culture of the Enlightenment proved an inspiration and justification for American independence, and the British philosophers, such as Locke and Hume, were the most important influences on Jefferson.

Even as he welcomed the stirrings of change in France in the 1780s, Jefferson noted that Frenchmen should not aspire to more than British liberties, given their backward condition; in the dark years of the next two decades he looked to British friends for aid even as Britain itself seemed to be the oppressor; in his old age he welcomed a rapprochement with Britain and was willing even to recommend a joint Anglo-American approach to the putative dangers of France or Spain interfering in Latin America in 1823.

Yet it was the same Britain that was the major threat to American liberties through violation of its own standards of self-government, by its attempts to impose a repressive regime on protesting Americans after 1763, and by its continuing efforts, even after its failure to subdue the colonies, to maintain economic control over their destinies. Britain long continued to give Jefferson reason to fear that it might repossess the colonies and undo the Revolution: in 1793 when he watched revolutionary France struggling for survival, in 1798 when he became aware of a British plot with Anglophilic Federalists, and in 1807 when the British impudently boarded the *Chesapeake.*

Jefferson's *Summary View,* prepared as instructions for Virginia delegates to the First Continental Congress in 1774, suggested a point of view with respect to the mother country that would be given a definitive form in the Declaration of Independence. It both welcomed and rejected the British connection. On the one hand, its author accepted with gratitude a British heritage and identified America with the Crown, much as Scotland before 1707 had been part of the British system. But he rejected Parliament's usurpation, with royal approval, of American rights, as Parliament replicated in the eighteenth century the assaults of the Crown against British liberties in the seventeenth century. Britain would now have to accept the equality of American legislatures with Parliament; they were joined in an informal federal system through the allegiance to the king. It was left to the Declaration of Independence, less than two years later, to spell out the consequences of Britain's continued trampling over American liberties.

But if Jefferson's use of history was selective with respect to the British role in America, his appeal to natural law and natural rights was applied to all his interests. This appeal to natural rights drew inspiration from the leading philosophies of the Enlightenment. The Declaration of Independence was clearly justified based on the opinion that a rule of reason should secure natural rights. Where those rights were jeopardized by arbitrary actions of government, the Declaration proposed a more liberal model for change than the Lockean model, in which the people in exercising sovereignty reshaped their government. He would later say to Henry Lee in a letter of 8 May 1825 that the Declaration was aimed not at any "originality of principle or sentiment, nor [was] yet copied from any particular and previous writing," but "was intended to be an expression of the American mind," with its authority resting "on the harmonizing sentiments of the day, whether expressed in conversation, in letters, printed essays, or in the elementary books of public right, as Aristotle, Cicero, Locke, Sidney, etc."

If there was a sense of confidence in Jefferson's *Summary View,* where he warned the king not to let his name be "a blot in the page of history," or in the Declaration, where he wrote of the colonies "that as free and independent states, they have full power to levy war, conclude peace, contract alliances, establish commerce, and to do all other acts and things which independent states may of right do," it was in large measure because he could draw inspiration from such figures as Thomas Paine and John Adams. He accepted along with Paine the belief expressed in *Common Sense* that the "true interest of America [is] to steer clear of European contentions, which she never can do while, by her dependence on Britain, she is made the makeweight in the scale of British politics." But the way out was clear. Through careful management of foreign relations the new nation could create an advantage out of Europe's dependence on American resources. It could open up the continent to all European nations interested in profiting from American trade. Such an arrangement would free the United States from a connection with any one nation and would make it in the interest of all to keep America secure from British domination. As Paine put it, "As Europe is our market for trade, we ought to form no partial connection with any part of it."

In 1776 Congress adopted the Plan of Treaties developed by Jefferson's friend, colleague, and sometime rival John Adams, which was designed to win allies from Europe, particularly from France, without requiring entangling obligations in return for support. Adams expected that a treaty of commerce with France would be an ample compensation for acknowledging America's independence. The ultimate treaty of alliance with France deviated from these princi-

ples, but not to the extent that Americans lost faith in the power of their geographic position to secure for them an economic advantage. In 1797 when Jefferson worried about the possibility of French neighbors in Louisiana, he took comfort, in a letter to Thomas Pinckney of 29 May, in the knowledge that "war is not the best engine for us to resort to, nature has given us one *in our commerce,* which, if properly managed, will be a better instrument for obliging the interested nations of Europe to treat us with justice."

Another interpretation of Jefferson's outlook on the world might fit his ideas into a new order of international relations, informed by the spirit of the Enlightenment, in which the old balance of power would be replaced by peace and free trade among nations. Felix Gilbert, in *To the Farewell Address,* saw Jefferson as a philosophe who anticipated the time when foreign policy and diplomacy would become unnecessary, when the new world order would be one without diplomats. America certainly fit into this philosophic scheme as the prototype of the new conception of international relations. Americans were, in the words of Gilbert, "representatives of a new diplomacy," trying to break the mold that confined diplomacy to an aristocratic caste representing dynasts rather than the people. There was thus a link made between the European philosophes, especially the French devotees of the late eighteenth century, and the working American model that put into practice ideas of an international order that the Europeans could only sketch conceptually.

If any individual personified the ideal American diplomatist, Jefferson fitted the role when he arrived in France to act as minister plenipotentiary of the United States. He had been offered an opportunity to join the American diplomatic mission to France in 1776, in the summer of 1781, and again in 1782. He turned down the first invitation because of the press of domestic politics, and the second because of the terminal illness of his wife. In neither case was it a lack of interest in the Old World or in the stakes a diplomatic success or failure held for the new nation. Indeed, he was fully aware of France's contribution to America's victory over England and was equally concerned with the continuing enmity the British had for the United States. It would have been reasonable to anticipate that his popularity in France, his taste for French culture, and his ardent interest in the ideas of the French philosophes (and their admiration for the forms of government blossoming in the new nation) would all be expressed in his support for free trade and the agrarian society promoted by French physiocrats.

His endorsement of both ideals was genuine but it was also qualified. A new kind of diplomacy—fresh and open, in pursuit of the emancipation of commerce and the abolition of war—was certainly a desirable goal. But would America, in search of a revolutionary foreign policy under the guidance of contemporary French philosophy, embody this new diplomatic ideal? The answer depended on the degree of sophistication of the statecraft exhibited by Jefferson and other Founding Fathers. There is little evidence of a naive attempt to engage the evil outside world in the hope of offering Europe the benefits of America's values. Rather, the Plan of Treaties, as James Hutson has observed in *John Adams and the Diplomacy of the American Revolution,* accepted the European balance of power, and Jefferson as well as Paine intended to use it to the American advantage. The goal of the minister to France in the 1780s was not free trade but a reorientation of American trade to France. Jefferson had been gratified by the provisions of the treaty of amity and commerce that addressed removal of mercantile restrictions and advancement of liberal principles of maritime law. But his reasoning went beyond a gratitude to France or an appreciation of French culture; France would be the

instrument to counter the continuing economic power of Britain. If the French would open up their ports to American ships and their markets to American goods, and would develop manufactures to counter Britain, they could help America wean itself from the British credit system and from dependence on British manufactures.

The key to Jefferson's foreign policy was his perception of enduring British hostility and his search for means to counter it. France was the primary instrument for doing this, and his philosophic friends with their putative influence were the aides in this polity. If these friends wished to regard him as a fellow physiocrat, devoted to agrarian values, it was agreeable to him as long as their influence could be used to fight the tobacco monopoly that excluded imports from Virginia. They and Jefferson operated from different agendas. Jefferson sought free trade to break the power of Britain; they were more interested in the principles of free trade. While he continued to believe that alliances with European powers were unnecessary and potentially dangerous, he would postpone the fanciful possibility of total isolation from Europe, "precisely on the footing of China," until independence was genuinely secured.

Jefferson's statecraft invited criticism. His means occasionally distorted his ends and diminished the stature of the man who tolerated the distortions. His reliance on economic coercion and blandishments was excessive, not only in the Napoleonic Wars but also in his ministry to France when his expectations from French commerce went unrealized. In fact his support of France, carefully measured though it was, was exploited by France at critical moments in the course of his career. But until the end of his life he continued to harbor a deeply felt anti-British animus that influenced all his activities.

In certain respects his service in Paris was a microcosm of his foreign relations over the next two decades. It began with a renewed awareness of British malevolence, exhibited by such events as the order-in-council of 1783, which excluded American commerce from former imperial preferences. By following the advice of Lord Sheffield rather than the more liberal inclinations of Lord Shelburne, the British revealed their intention to maintain dominance over the American economy by forcing minimal reciprocity under their navigation system. British mercantilists assumed rightly that a weak Confederation could not retaliate by closing American ports to British shipping when American ships were denied entry into the British West Indies.

To cope with British power Jefferson would invoke French power; it was not an uncongenial task. He enjoyed cultivating friends who admired America and he hoped for liberal reforms in French government. Increasingly he recognized that only serious French commitment would be useful. The attempts to win treaties from other European powers on liberal terms similar to the French commercial treaty counted for little. Psychologically, Sweden's and Prussia's willingness to sign such treaties was a symbol of legitimacy for the new nation. In practical terms it meant very little. The volume of trade was minuscule. France, on the other hand, had the potential to stand up to Britain on America's behalf should the British attempt to undo the military defeats of the Revolution. More important, the French could initiate a massive trade with the United States in which French manufactures would replace British.

Jefferson's French friends worked as hard at court as Franklin's friends had done a decade before, and they helped to reduce restrictions on direct trade with the United States. Import duties on American whale oil were lifted, to the gratification of New England. The minister made a spectacular although temporary breakthrough when Virginia tobacco farmers were able to expand their exports to France in the face of a powerful financial syndicate, the Farmers-General, who controlled the French tobacco market and who had made an exclusive arrangement with Philadelphia financier Robert Morris.

Most of the gains proved to be ephemeral. Freer trade, the French observed, did not translate into greater purchases of French goods. Cynical managers of the antiquated mercantile system noted that American merchants used their profits to invest in British purchases rather than to reinvest in France. This was hardly the intention of Jeffersonian statecraft, although the result was not surprising. The French lacked the goods and credits to replace the British even if the minister, in collaboration with French Americanophiles, could have torn American merchants loose from their accustomed British connections. But the difficulties were less with American habits than with French customs. The antiquated politico-economic structure of French mercantilism could not see its own advantage in building up extensive American commerce. A discontented merchant class had been so long abused by the corrupt and inefficient regime that it did not know how to direct its anger into proper channels. Those who would have been the first to profit from a free exchange of American tobacco, whale oil, and rice for French products feared the effects of free trade as merely a means for Britain to inundate France with cheap manufactured goods. They could not distinguish between the doctrinaire spirit of the physiocrats and the enlightened imperialism of a Lafayette, who wanted commercial privileges for the United States as a weapon against the British, as well as a means of strengthening the American economy. If the French could have broken the grip of the Farmers-General monopolists and opened French West Indian ports to American ships, as Jefferson advocated, the result would have been greater French control over both the economy and the politics of the United States.

France's confusion in the last days of the ancien régime seeped into the foreign ministry, particularly after the death of the able Vergennes in 1787. While Jefferson and Lafayette urged support for the weak Confederation against the hostile behavior of Spain and Britain, France preferred a weak America, on the assumption that French influence would be greater in an uneasy republic than in a strong and confident ally. Thus American weakness—in the face of Spanish intrigue with Indians in the South, or with British troops in northwest posts, or with Barbary pirate depredations in the Mediterranean—stirred no countereffort from France. The weakest position in America's foreign relations concerned its shaky financial base and its unpaid debts to foreign creditors. It was in this area that Jefferson encountered his most difficult moments abroad. Along with John Adams, minister to Great Britain, he turned to the Dutch republic for assistance. Dutch banks, along with the French government, were the major creditors of the United States. Although Jefferson had little faith in or respect for the motives of the speculators who had advanced funds for the Revolution and the Confederation, he preferred to have Dutch bankers purchase American debts to France, even at the risk of their directing America's economic future, rather than default to France. As Jefferson put it in in a letter to John Jay of 26 September 1786, "If there be a danger that our payments may not be punctual, it might be better that the discontents which would thence arise should be transferred from a court of whose good will we have so much need to the breasts of a private company."

While these financial concerns suggest a painful subservience to French goodwill, it would be a mistake to conclude that Jefferson exhibited a craven deference to French judgments in every instance. His willingness to court the Dutch was rather a measure of his desire to protect what goodwill he could

find at the court of Versailles. The sense of American isolation in a hostile world was made all the more vivid by the collapse in the Netherlands of the pro–American patriot republicans in their struggle against the Anglophile House of Orange. Jefferson also saw French impotence in the face of this challenge, which concerned France even more than it did the United States. Anger and contempt characterized his attitude toward the French government for the most part, not only for its shortsighted refusal to open trade channels or for its dangerous complacency over American political weakness in the Confederation, but for the state of the alliance itself. Even as he sought French assistance Jefferson recognized the dangers of entanglement. France's failure to be supportive might have evoked stronger reactions than it did. Jefferson was never unaware that a French imperialism could be a threat to the United States, even if to a lesser degree than could its British counterpart. When he heard of a French scientific expedition to the South Seas in 1785, he asked John Paul Jones to find out if the expedition had any designs on the west coast of America.

Nonetheless, the character of Jefferson's service in France was not primarily negative. He was well aware that much of the opposition he encountered at court was neither ad hominem nor aimed at America. His brief visit to England in 1786 enabled him to experience firsthand what John Adams had to endure from a regime that was not only anti-American but personally vindictive toward the new nation's representatives. In France the problem was with the inability of the ancien régime to help itself, let alone help its ally. Jefferson probably comprehended the dimensions of France's plight more fully than any foreigner because of his intimacy with those reformers who hoped to effect changes in France based on an American model. Although he was skeptical of France's ability to establish even a limited monarchy on a British model, let alone re-create on untested soil the ingredients of American liberties, he was flattered by the attention he received from the intelligentsia and hoped for their ultimate success. If they accomplished only a portion of their objectives they would be in a position to change the direction of foreign policy to the advantage of the United States. To preserve the image of American superiority as a republic and worthiness as an economic partner, he worried both over French exaggerations of American virtues and over signs of disorder at home—such as Shays' Rebellion—that would diminish the United States in the eyes of the French reformers. Considerations such as the need for a stronger central authority able to command funds for domestic and foreign creditors helped to reduce his sympathy for the farmers' complaints in Massachusetts and assuage his misgivings over the potentially repressive aspects of the new Constitution.

When he left France in 1789 the French Revolution had begun; the Bastille had fallen; moderate royalists such as Lafayette and moderate republicans such as Antoine Barnave appeared to be on the verge of realizing the hopes they had voiced at meetings in Jefferson's home. To a degree Jefferson was carried along by the escalating expectations. In 1787 he had believed tax reforms and the establishment of provincial assemblies to be as much as the French could assimilate. He was ready a year later to see a French parliament in the revival of the Estates-General, and in 1789 to welcome a Declaration of the Rights of Man as the expression of a new order. Yet he retained sufficient perspective to note in a letter to James Madison in August 1789 that the American system

> has been professedly their model, in which such changes are made as a difference of circumstance rendered necessary and some others neither necessary nor advantageous, but

into which men will ever run when versed in theory and new in the practice of government, when acquainted with man only as they see him in their books and not in the world.

Whatever reservations Jefferson may have had about French ability to achieve a liberal regime, the prognosis in 1789 was positive. France was still a monarchy, only mildly limited in powers and supported by a legislature that owed its place to the more substantial members of the bourgeois electorate. By contrast Great Britain remained for Jefferson what it always had been: powerful, malevolent, and unrelenting in its unwillingness to accept the integrity of the United States, no matter what form its government would take. Upon arriving in Norfolk, Virginia, in the fall of 1789 on a leave of absence from his duties in Paris, he found himself appointed secretary of state under a newly created office established by the Constitution—the presidency. He now would have to confront more directly the British menace that had touched him only indirectly in the past. President George Washington's choice seemed inevitable. Since John Adams was vice-president, there was no more distinguished American, and certainly no one better equipped to deal with foreign relations, than the minister to France.

Yet Jefferson was reluctant to accept the honor. His temperament was better suited to the Paris post, and he knew it. In retrospect his reluctance seems all the stronger and more understandable in light of the conflict that met him almost immediately and that ultimately consumed his position, causing him to resign at the end of 1793. For the British menace now took on a new and even more threatening dimension. After years of enjoying adulation as the exemplar of a society French liberals wished for themselves, he encountered in New York an aristocratic ruling class indulging in an Anglophilia that seemed to make a mockery of the new nation's values. At the center of this circle was the powerful young secretary of the treasury, Alexander Hamilton, who seemed to personify for Jefferson what he most abhorred in government: concentration of power in a central government, the ostentatious cultivation of urban, mercantile, and financial elites, and the promotion of a foreign economic policy that valued a British connection more than one with France. Perhaps the most discomfiting factor was the special favor this less distinguished rival enjoyed with President Washington.

Much of the early history of American foreign relations has been interpreted over the years in the form of a dichotomous relationship between Hamiltonianism and Jeffersonianism. The former is identified with the Federal party and Great Britain, the latter with the Republican party and France—the advantage falling to the Jeffersonians partly because of the sympathy of the passive president and partly because of Hamilton's manipulation of events in the 1790s. A personal rivalry has been equated with ideological differences. If the dichotomy was not quite one of republicanism versus monarchism, it was certainly a case of agrarianism and limited government versus mercantile-industrial society and a strong federal executive.

Historians have been caught up in continual replays of the original partisan quarrels, and indeed have contributed to the polarity. Many nineteenth-century historians were frankly reflecting their own political biases in dealing with the Federalist decade, but even more detached scholars of later eras were caught up in the divisions. The temptation to categorize is almost irresistible. Many modern scholars were caught up in the "realist-idealist" debate of the 1950s, when George Kennan and Hans Morgenthau tried to free American foreign policy from what they regarded as a dangerous idealist bias. Difficulty arose over who was the realist. Paul Varg, in *Foreign Policies of the Founding Fathers*, determined that Hamilton was "above all a realist who fatalistically ac-

cepted the existing framework." Albert Bowman, writing in *Political Science Quarterly,* found realism on the Jeffersonian side: both men "recognized the value of neutrality, but Hamilton would have surrendered it on Britain's demand . . . while Jefferson would have used it as a diplomatic weapon against all Europe."

Bowman was referring to the Nootka Sound crisis, but the charges from both sides may be applied to any of the issues of the 1790s. Not that historians, including the above-mentioned, have failed to recognize nuances. The most distinguished of Jefferson's biographers, Dumas Malone, in an article in *Theory and Practice in American Politics* (edited by William Nelson), scoffed at the idea that Hamilton and Jefferson broke their links upon Jefferson's return to America. Hamilton biographer John C. Miller, in *The Federalist Era, 1789–1801,* raised the alternative possibility that it was not only Jefferson and Hamilton who determined the foreign policy of this time when he noted that Washington was a prime mover in foreign policy and not just a befuddled conservative manipulated by his secretary of the treasury. Still, the differences between the two leading Cabinet members dominate historiography of the critical first federal decade of American foreign relations.

What the responsibilities of a secretary of state were to be was unclear, as the new Constitution did not spell out the duties of a foreign secretary. This was essentially within the purview of the chief executive; the "executive departments" were identified only parenthetically in Article II. It was the president who would make treaties and dominate and appoint ambassadors and consuls with the advice and consent of the Senate. Secretary Jefferson accepted an office that coupled home and foreign affairs under a title that made no reference to foreign relations. His predecessors under the Confederation, Robert R. Livingston and John Jay, were designated specifically as secretaries for foreign relations. The all-purpose title "secretary of state" suggested a diminution of the functions of foreign relations, reflecting the growing isolationism of the new nation.

The precise jurisdictions of all the departments were hazy. The intrusion of Hamilton into foreign affairs was legitimized, or at least rationalized, because of the commercial functions of the consuls. Many of the actions of the activist secretary of the treasury came about because of the uncertain jurisdictions of the executive departments. Hamilton's advantage in his contest with Jefferson, beyond the personal affections of the president, came about from Washington's ignorance of and discomfort with financial matters. Jefferson displayed much the same distaste for business affairs, as reflected in his recent depressing encounters with Dutch financiers and the French finance ministers.

Whatever the personal and professional issues dividing the two cabinet members, there were wide areas of agreement that made for consensus rather than conflict in 1790. The need for a constitution was one of them. Although each in his way objected to elements in the new basic law, the two secretaries agreed on the importance of a stronger instrument of government. Jefferson's experiences in Paris offered no reasonable alternative. His reports from France throughout his service as minister revealed clearly how unstable a support the French government, or any European government, would be to America's interests abroad. All his small triumphs were ephemeral; Jefferson had failed in what Merrill Peterson has called "nothing less than a diplomatic mission to convert all Europe to the commercial principles of the American Revolution." France along with Prussia, Sweden, and Holland disappointed Jefferson by its inability to amend mercantilism to the degree that would permit the United States to break the stranglehold of British commerce. Such was

hardly Hamilton's aim, but both men shared the faith in a stronger instrument to command the respect of Europe. A new Congress could arrange a most-favored-nation treatment of nations that responded to the American importunities, and it could punish British transgressions against American commerce through navigation laws. In principle Hamilton did not oppose this aspect of Jefferson's thinking. With all his admiration for the British ways of commerce he looked forward to the day when an American self-sufficient industrial system would prevail over the British. Similarly, Jefferson's warmth toward France in 1790 did not preclude an expectation of exploiting the new liberal monarchy for American advantage.

It is worth considering why Jefferson welcomed the principle of a strong executive power; his objections to the Constitution did not apply to foreign relations. As he wrote to Joseph Jones on 14 August 1787, "I wish to see our states made one as to all foreign, and several as to all domestic matters." He was as ready as Hamilton to defend the presidency's independence in foreign affairs. Shortly after taking up his duties, on 24 April 1790 he wrote a memorandum on the limited powers of the Senate over diplomatic appointments, "*except* as to such portions of it as are specially submitted to the Senate. *Exceptions* are to be construed strictly." In answer to Washington's question about the propriety of consulting with the Senate on which countries should be approached for diplomatic exchanges, the secretary of state asserted that there was no constitutional requirement for soliciting such advice, and that it would be impolitic to set a precedent. The Senate's powers extended no further than the approval of the presidential nominee. In displaying this conception of presidential prerogative, Jefferson put himself in a position indistinguishable from that of John Jay and Alexander Hamilton.

Jefferson's view of foreign relations went

beyond a presidency largely free from congressional restraints; it included other elements usually associated with Hamilton: repayment of obligations to foreign creditors through the federal government's assumption of state debts and the promotion of American shipping through an effective navigation system. Granted that he could not accept the domestic implications of funding and the unwillingness of Federalists to apply an American navigation system against the British, there was a consensus among Washington's first cabinet that permitted even Hamilton's jurisdiction over consular affairs to go unchallenged. His colleagues, despite monarchic and Anglophilic tendencies, were nonetheless "good men and bold men, and sensible men."

Part of Jefferson's tolerance for Hamilton's role in 1790 developed from his frustrations and annoyance with France. Notwithstanding new liberal regimes filled with his old friends, little had changed with respect to French mercantilism. Distressed as he was with British refusal to make a commercial treaty with the United States, he was even more distressed to find France after its revolution almost as unresponsive—and with far less cause. It was a shock to realize that the new bourgeois rulers of France were no more prepared than the ancien régime had been to let American goods into French markets. British hostility was taken for granted, but French opposition, particularly under the National Assembly, was less tolerable. The frustration of his hopes for a French counterweight to British power seemed even more important for a time than the systematic undermining of a navigation law against British shipping and the successful manipulation of foreign policy on the part of Hamilton.

Particularly galling was France's apparent position that any serious attempts to sever America from its British ties were impossible; thus France ignored Jefferson's clear invitation, through his illuminating reports on the whale-oil and codfish industries, to have the French replace those who had built "their navigation on the ruin of ours." Instead of responding to Jefferson's bids they revoked the concessions he had painfully extracted during his ministry to France. New duties were placed on American tobacco imports. The Consular Convention of 1788 that he had achieved with such difficulty was challenged by France's rejection of American consuls appointed to the West Indies. The most he could win in 1791 was permission for the consuls to remain in the French colonies, provided that they held no official title.

Yet Jefferson never lost sight of his objectives—the freeing of the United States from British economic domination and from future threats against its territorial integrity. Hamilton's increasing domination of the cabinet, his successful imposition of Federalist economic policies, and his disregard for state rights all evoked reaction; collusion with Madison in Congress and George Clinton in New York, establishment of a journalistic voice in Philip Freneau's *National Gazette,* and the shaping of a political party all reflected Jefferson's concerns. But the Anglophilic aspect of Hamilton's program was of less concern; Jefferson had no knowledge of the secretary of the treasury's personal ties with British agents. If the Hamilton bloc stopped a navigation law imposing duties on British shipping, the French government's behavior gave little reason to encourage it. And whatever Hamilton may have done to inhibit the British minister George Hammond from pressing for a commercial treaty, Jefferson had few expectations in this area.

Not even the Nootka Sound crisis of 1790 produced an open break on foreign affairs. As war threatened between Spain and Britain in the Pacific Northwest, the British would want passage through American territory for their troops, and conceivably France might be involved through the Bourbon family pact, strained as it was by the events of the Revolution. Both Jefferson and Hamilton saw in this growing crisis an opportunity to advance American objectives. Hamilton through private connections with British agent Major George Beckwith saw a commercial treaty with Britain as the prize for granting British passage. Jefferson on the other hand wanted to offer neutrality to the British in return for a commercial treaty —and more. By warning the Spanish of the possibility of an Anglo-American alliance he might secure American rights to navigate the Mississippi River, which he had been vainly seeking through specious appeals to international law before and after the Nootka Sound crisis.

Had Jefferson known that his rival was secretly informing the British (inaccurately) that the United States would not support Spain's position in the Pacific Northwest, he might have understood the source of Hamilton's actions even as he would have denounced his dealings with the British. In advising Washington to give passage to British forces, the secretary of the treasury was acting on the assumption that failure to do so might result in Britain seizing Louisiana and the Floridas without consultation with the United States. Such a consequence would increase British influence along American borders to a dangerous degree, as well as damage future Anglo-American commercial relations. Fear of Britain, not friendship, motivated Hamilton at this time. Out of the same fear Jefferson himself would have given in to Britain's demands. He would have postponed the moment, however, until Britain had made reciprocal concessions.

This community of interests does not contradict the mutual suspicions and antagonisms characterizing the emerging party system. But it was not just the intellectual incapacity of President Washington that made him fail to perceive irreconcilable differences in the cabinet in his first administration. In the realm of foreign affairs there

was as much to connect as to separate its members.

It was the new radical turn in the French Revolution in 1793 that brought friction to a head between the two men and that identified clearly a Hamiltonian and a Jeffersonian foreign policy. It contributed an emotional dimension to an ideological difference. Hamilton saw in the surging armies of the French Revolution the destruction of a civilization as surely as the death of a king. Only Great Britain was the bulwark to prevent anarchy from engulfing the United States. By the same token, the French Revolution in its republican guise appeared to Jefferson as a guarantor of the survival of the American republic; France's war with Britain seemed to him a struggle in the common interest of the two nations.

As the crisis deepened in the 1790s it was almost inevitable that the Jeffersonian Francophiles would be seen as agents of a dangerous French Revolution; conversely the Federalist Anglophiles would appear as surrogates of British domination. Jefferson was deeply affected by the war. Even though some of his own friends perished as aristocratic enemies of the Revolution, he endured these losses stoically, as if they were soldiers fallen in the battle for universal liberty. "My own affections have been deeply wounded by some of the martyrs to this cause," he wrote William Short on 3 January 1793, "but rather than it should have failed, I would have seen half the earth desolated."

In this emotional state, just a month before France declared war on Britain, Jefferson had to confront an opponent who found in the Continental struggle an occasion to strike a blow for Britain and against France. This assumed two forms: an attempt to invalidate the largely comatose alliance with France that Jefferson himself had no urge to invigorate; and, when this attempt failed, to proclaim American neutrality in that conflict, a neutrality that would not serve British maritime superiority. Jefferson appeared to win the first ploy and lose the second, and in the course of coping with these challenges, he set principles of American foreign policy that were to carry into the twentieth century.

The president set the scene for this contest by asking his secretaries if the new Girondist minister, Edmond Charles Genêt, should be received by the United States, and then how to maintain American neutrality in the face of the obligations of the alliance of 1778. Hamilton's response to queries he himself had prepared for Washington was to call the treaty with France void on the grounds that it had been made with a king and monarchy whose person and form of government had been destroyed by the French Republic.

Actually, the issue of legitimacy of treaties had been raised when the monarchy was overturned in the fall of 1792 and was presumably settled to Jefferson's satisfaction. "The will of the nation substantially declared" was the only criterion as long as its government discharged its international obligations. It is likely that Hamilton had no real expectation of revoking this judgment; the real issue was the alliance and the extent of American responsibilities. Jefferson seemed to have won his point, and president and cabinet accepted the important precedent for recognition of foreign governments: de facto control by the government in power.

Yet there lingers a temptation to wonder if Jefferson would have come to the same conclusion if a republican France had been overthrown by a pro-British monarchy. Would his revulsion at such a prospect have allowed him to grant legitimacy in this instance? With considerable feeling he asked, in response to Hamilton's mischievous attempts to deny to France the right to change its government from monarchy to republic, "Who is the American who can say with truth that he would not have allied himself to France if she had been a republic?" Certainly Jefferson carried emotional baggage

at this moment as great as Woodrow Wilson's when he deviated from the Jeffersonian tradition to deny recognition to Mexico in 1914 or to Bolshevik Russia in 1917.

Jefferson had greater problems with neutrality than he had with the legitimacy of treaties. He wanted to maintain the alliance with the nation that was fighting America's cause abroad, and at the same time he had no wish to see the United States as a belligerent alongside France. So a neutrality was preferable as long as it was a "fair neutrality," in which American vessels could carry goods from the West Indies to French ports, with produce for France and profit for America. He deluded himself in believing that the United States could have both neutrality and alliance. Could the claims of the alliance have permitted the kind of pro-French neutrality that Jefferson preferred?

There can be no answer to these queries, but there is sufficient evidence from 1793 to suggest that the secretary of state was subjected to such pressure over the next few years that his judgment was affected. He saw the nation on the brink of destruction. He left his office at the end of the year convinced that the government was in the hands of antirepublican Anglophiles determined to return the United States to the British Empire. He welcomed the arrival of the French minister Genêt in 1793 and sought to use his popularity in America to promote an American neutrality that would serve French interests. When Genêt angered the American public by an arrogant attack on President Washington, Jefferson had to accept the president's proclamation, which did not use the term *neutrality*, but violated, or appeared to, the moral if not the legal obligations of the alliance of 1778.

Jefferson objected to a neutrality proclamation on constitutional grounds. An executive proclamation without the approval of Congress would infringe upon the constitutional powers of the legislative branch to declare war. Against this construction of the

Constitution Hamilton in his anonymous *Pacificus Papers* replied that the president could make such a proclamation by virtue of his role as commander-in-chief when Congress was not in session. Under the pen name of Helvidius, Madison followed Jefferson's advice and condemned the neutrality proclamation as a betrayal of America's debt to France and as a dangerous accretion of executive authority.

What made matters worse was the impudence of Great Britain in refusing to reward these Hamiltonian gestures. Instead, British domination of the seas permitted a policy of restricting the neutral carriers, limiting maritime rights, impressing American sailors, continuing to occupy posts in the Northwest territories, and denying the United States access to British West Indian ports. From his retreat in Virginia, Jefferson witnessed these humiliations as well as the efforts of his Republican allies as they futilely attempted to close American ports to British ships and goods in retaliation for the behavior of the former mother country.

With public opinion aroused against Britain, the mission to London of special emissary John Jay in 1794 produced a treaty that insulted American sovereignty. Britain continued to deny effective entry to the West Indies and maintained its stance on maritime rights, although it did evacuate the Northwest military posts. These defeats at the hands of Britain took place while relations with the French ally suffered. Jay's Treaty gave to Britain the same privileges France enjoyed through its alliance. It is hardly surprising then that, when Jefferson agreed reluctantly to stand for president in 1796, he represented a Francophile position in support of the French Revolution's struggle with British-led coalitions. There is a loss of composure, to say the least, reflected in a letter of 27 April 1795 to William Branch Giles, to whom he wrote about his delight in the success of French armies occupying Holland and about the happy prospect of their liberating all of Europe, including Great Britain. He was so pleased about the new turn of France's fortunes that he was tempted to leave his "clover for a while," to dine with General Pichegru in London, where he could help his French friends "hail the dawn of liberty and republicanism in that island."

In this heated atmosphere Jefferson invited charges of being a passionate devotee of the French Revolution and the French military cause. These were strengthened by France's own efforts to intervene in the presidential election of 1796 on Jefferson's behalf. Presumably, its wrath over Jay's Treaty would be soothed and it would resume an exchange of ministers if its friend were elected president in place of the Federalist John Adams. Yet, Adams, not Jefferson, won that election, and the French minister Pierre Adet, who worked to influence the results, was moved to comment that "Jefferson, I say, is an American and, by that title cannot be sincerely our friend. An American is the born enemy of all European peoples."

If this statement could be made at the height of Jefferson's absorption with the crisis in Europe and its repercussions at home, it would be even more applicable at other times in his career. While Adet's language was hyperbolic, it was not really far from the mark at any time. Jefferson had certainly been intrigued with Genêt and hoped that his popularity would serve to cut down Hamiltonian power and British influence. But he never had any intention of furthering Genêt's plans for entangling the United States in the European conflict. Jefferson as much as Hamilton wished to maintain a neutral position, but a "fair neutrality" in which American vessels would carry goods to France from the West Indies, in accordance with the liberal understandings of neutral rights embodied in the Franco-American Treaty of Amity and Commerce of 1778. He would not accept Genêt's demands to have French privateers armed in American ports or even open encouragement of insurrection in Spanish territories from American soil, although Genêt later accused him of reneging on his promises of support.

But even if Genêt had not made himself personally obnoxious to the American government, there was little chance that the Jeffersonians could have achieved their "fair neutrality," that is, abstention from the conflict while still maintaining the French alliance. The British government had no intention of permitting what it called contraband goods to move from French colonial ports in American ships. As for the French, the Girondist government would have permitted the United States to remain technically out of the war, despite treaty obligations, only because it recognized other services that the alliance could extract through the transfer of supplies in American ships, the arming of privateers in American ports, and the staging of invasions from American territory. While none of these functions would have been acceptable to Jefferson, the issue of arming French vessels did come within the purview at least of Article XXIV of the Treaty of Amity and Commerce. The Treaty denied such a privilege to enemies of both countries, but the question was whether it granted it by implication to the ally. France's construction was not unreasonable. But if compliance meant war with Britain, Jefferson and his friends preferred embarrassment with France.

Jay's Treaty seemed to be more clear-cut. While its terms stipulated that nothing in the document would affect obligations already binding on the signatory powers, its contents made a mockery of the Franco-American treaties. Not only did it specifically forbid French privateers from arming in American ports but it also gave to Britain precisely the privileges France had enjoyed since 1778: namely, bringing prizes captured from the enemy to American ports. Considering its failure to challenge Britain's interpretations of neutral rights it was

hardly surprising that France read betrayal of the alliance into Jay's Treaty.

All of these tensions fitted Hamilton's pro-British designs. When the French exacted retribution through mistreatment of the American ally in French ports, and ultimately through an undeclared war against what the French now regarded as an undeclared ally of Britain, Jeffersonians were not unsympathetic. Unhappy though they were with France's descent to the level of British depredations against American commerce, they felt France to be the injured party provoked by Federalists anxious to serve the cause of monarchism. Washington's Farewell Address in September 1796 was in this light simply a Hamiltonian ploy to divert America from the real entangling connection, that with England.

Yet visceral support for the French cause against Britain and its surrogates in America did not signify that Jefferson had succumbed to the dictates of French military needs or to the spell of the French Revolution. His distress over Jay's Treaty was based on the dangers of war, whether initiated by the Federalists or by France. The alliance was the key. He feared France's denunciation of the alliance because it humiliated Adams in his efforts to restore relations in 1797, and he also opposed the Federalists' unilateral abrogation of the alliance in response to the treatment of the American commissioner in Paris. As a powerless vice-president he foresaw that Hamilton, now in private life in Philadelphia, would exploit the undeclared maritime conflict with France as an excuse to join Britain in a war against the French that followed from France's brutal rejection of a new American diplomatic mission (the XYZ Affair). But he was also worried about the ambitions of the French Directory in America; France's treatment of its satellite nations in Europe did not go unnoticed among Jeffersonians. The vice-president gloomily predicted to Thomas Pinckney in a letter of 29 May 1797 that there will be "new neighbors in Louisiana (probably the present French armies when disbanded)," which he equated with "combinations of enemies on that side where we are most vulnerable." The alliance in these circumstances was a symbol of the status quo, not of American loyalty or even of gratitude toward France.

It was the Federalist party dominated by Hamiltonians that openly voided the treaties with France in 1798 and exacerbated the prospect of war. That this frightening prospect was not realized was the consequence less of Jeffersonian protest (Jefferson himself was formally mute in his office of vice-president) than President Adams' movement toward rapprochement and the consequent break between him and the Hamiltonian Federalists. Adams persevered and won the Convention of Mortfontaine in September 1800, an agreement that formally ended the alliance as well as mutual claims of the two former allies against each other. While he won a peace he lost an election to Jefferson, in large measure because of his peacemaking activities.

In 1800 President-elect Jefferson called Mortfontaine a "bungling" treaty because it failed to gain compensation for damages done to American shipping and because it might be regarded with hostility by the British. In blaming Adams he made two points that are significant for understanding his sense of the national interest during his presidential years. The first was a new sensitivity toward the attitude of the British enemy. President Jefferson was not much impressed with the praise of his American friends in Paris, Joel Barlow and Thomas Paine, for a new maritime convention that Bonaparte was supporting in favor of the liberal maritime rights; they had not worked against Britain before, and French activity on their behalf was suspect. That Bonapartism affected his judgment of France is unquestionable. Jefferson ruminated about men on horseback and made a connection between Bonaparte and Hamilton.

But Jefferson's estrangement from France in 1800 was deeper than a reaction to the rise of the First Consul. Suspicion of French intentions in Louisiana, doubts about French reliability in commercial relations, and fear of American entanglement in French imperial projects had characterized his attitudes toward France from time to time ever since the beginnings of the alliance. Once the French Revolution passed its early phase, the American policy toward France was largely a function of domestic disarray and consequent fears of British designs on the United States. While British malevolence was to remain more dangerous to the United States than that of France (at least until the end of the War of 1812), Jefferson's old dream of France replacing England as an economic partner had died by 1800, never to revive. In its place was a vision of autarchy that would render America independent of all the outside world.

As early as 1799 Jefferson had written to Elbridge Gerry: "I am for free commerce with all nations; political connection with none; & little or no diplomatic establishment. And I am not for linking ourselves by new treaties with the quarrels of Europe." This was the sentiment of Washington's Farewell Address in 1796. It was also the theme of Jefferson's Inaugural Address of 1801, and as such represented much more than the healing of Federalist wounds. President Jefferson had no wish to restore the French alliance or to join any European league of neutrals, even when they pursued laudable goals of freeing the seas for neutral trade.

Jefferson's foreign policy reflected his sense of America's need for independence from both European superpowers. He was unable to achieve this goal in either of his two terms in office. In his first administration he was able at least to play one against another to the enormous benefit of the nation; the acquisition of Louisiana was a byproduct of his policy. But in the second administration he in turn was the victim of European belligerency as Britain and France exploited the inherent weakness of a small maritime power still tied to the Old World through economic need; the embargo of 1807–1808 was evidence of Jefferson's, and the nation's, disadvantage in coping with Britain and France. The president expressed an ideal position in a letter of 4 October 1803 to Benjamin Rush:

Tremendous times in Europe! How mighty this battle of lions and tigers! With what sensations should the common herd of cattle look on it? With no partialities, certainly. If they can so far worry one another as to destroy their power of tyrannizing, the one over the earth, the other the waters, the world may perhaps enjoy peace, till they recruit again.

Nevertheless, he still expected that the United States not only would survive the strife but would "fatten on the follies of the old [world] by winning new territories and new concessions from their wars."

The Louisiana crisis began with rumors that Spain had retroceded New Orleans to France, an event that indeed had occurred in secret one day after Bonaparte had signed the Convention of Mortfontaine. Rightly, the First Consul recognized that the United States would not welcome France in place of Spain as a neighbor along the Mississippi. It underscored fears for American access to the mouth of the river upon which American western commerce depended and which had been conceded by a weak Spain in the Pinckney Treaty of 1795. Pressured as he was by western farmers anxious for their future prosperity and by eastern Federalists wishing to embarrass the arguably Francophilic president, Jefferson did respond. But he needed no prodding to comprehend the nation's plight. He feared an aggressive France as much as any Federalist. His only problem was finding a method of dealing with the new situation.

His answer was not a declaration of war but a shrewd use of diplomacy, as Byzantine as that of any European statesman. On one level he raised the prospect of a British card. On 18 April 1802 he wrote to the U.S. Minister to France, Robert R. Livingston: "The day that France takes possession of N. Orleans . . . seals the union of two nations, who in conjunction, can maintain exclusive possession of the ocean. From that moment we must marry ourselves to the British fleet and nation." This letter would be delivered by a French friend and philosopher, Pierre-Samuel Du Pont de Nemours, who presumably would communicate its contents to Napoleon, after he delivered it to Livingston. Jefferson was consciously using "private friendships instrumental to the public good by inspiring a confidence which is denied to public, and official communications," as he wrote to Monroe on 8 January 1804.

On another level he employed a technique used earlier in the republic's short history: he sent a special emissary with blandishments. Monroe was empowered to offer, as minister extraordinary, $2 million for New Orleans and the Floridas. When Bonaparte sold not only New Orleans but Louisiana for $15 million, the transaction seemed to vindicate his statecraft. Not only had he managed to keep the United States free from ties to either superpower but he had cleared the West for further American expansion. The price he paid was enhancement of executive power and an implicit acceptance of loose construction of the Constitution in the acquisition of Louisiana.

There were other prices as well. Jefferson was emboldened by his triumph to seek the removal of the Spanish from the Floridas and to gain rights for neutrals out of the renewed Napoleonic Wars. Henry Adams' masterly nine-volume *History of the United States of America During the Administrations of Jefferson and Madison* presented Jefferson's new ambitions as a Greek tragedy in which the president's hubris resulted in near disaster for America. Jefferson never understood the reasoning behind Napoleon's cession of Louisiana. The renewal of war meant that the French could not hold the territory even if they could have occupied it before 1803; hence the sale to the United States was a temporary maneuver that would be reversed when Napoleon finally defeated the British. That the United States was a pawn rather than a master of European power politics did not occur to the president in his first administration.

Jefferson's foreign relations in his second administration were a shambles. Instead of using the uncertain terms of the Louisiana Purchase to claim all the Floridas, he found himself manipulated by both the British and the French. When in rapid succession in 1805 the British destroyed the combined fleets of France, Spain, and the Netherlands at Trafalgar and Napoleon destroyed the Austrian armies at Austerlitz, the two great belligerents turned to economic warfare. Without armies to fight on land, the British navy used its seapower to deny foreign trade to the French, and without ships to keep sea lanes open or to invade Britain, Napoleon countered Britain's blockade with the Continental System, in which British goods would be kept out of European ports. In this war of attrition, the United States as the principal, and ultimately the only, significant neutral carrier was the object of assault from both sides.

Napoleon with his grandiose decrees was the major offender in certain important respects. France, the traditional supporter of liberal maritime rights, seized American ships that had come from British ports or had subjected themselves to search by British frigates. Without ships to bolster his claim Napoleon justified his actions by declaring Britain to be in a state of blockade. At the same time he kept open the possibility of using French influence with the Spanish to secure the Floridas for the United States.

Britain, however, was far more visible as the primary enemy of the United States. Its withdrawal of de facto privileges to American ships carrying goods from the West Indies to France was done primarily not to keep contraband from France, but to enlarge British trade at American expense. Only if an American vessel would submit to visit and search and payment of duty would it be permitted to sail on to France. These indignities were exacerbated by the resumption of the practice of impressment whereby British naval ships removed former British sailors from American merchantmen.

While Britain and France issued orders-in-council and decrees respectively in 1805–1807, Jefferson pondered his plight. He tried diplomacy with another Monroe mission, this time to Britain with William Pinkney, only to find the British unwilling to give up impressment even if the United States would formally surrender the principle of "free ships make free goods," as it had done in Jay's Treaty. British arrogance reached its zenith in the summer of 1807 through the *Chesapeake* affair, in which a British frigate fired at and forced into submission an American frigate, removing four alleged deserters outside Norfolk harbor.

The consequence could have been war with Britain, the culmination of Jefferson's fears since the Revolution. Such a war might have won popular support at the time. Instead, Jefferson chose an embargo as his means of retaliation. Louis Martin Sears, in his classic *Jefferson and Embargo*, identified this choice as a form of Jefferson's pacifism. Henry Adams saw it as an example of Jefferson's unrealistic judgment on American powers of coercion. In *Neither Peace Nor War*, Clifford L. Egan found that Jefferson's greatest error as president was his failure to declare war after the *Chesapeake* incident. In the most authoritative of the new works on the subject, *Jefferson's English Crisis*, Burton Spivak suggests that the embargo was a departure from the economic coercion embodied in earlier nonimportation acts; the embargo initially was a desperate attempt to save American ships from seizure from either belligerent. Only after it was enacted did Jefferson make it a retaliatory weapon, which did not accomplish its purpose. No matter how debatable Jefferson's intentions, there is no doubt about two elements of the embargo: it was a substitute for war, and it intentionally favored Napoleon's Continental System.

Even as Jefferson was pushed into a corner by European tactics and domestic responses, he still hoped to extract benefits from foreign war. Since Britain would suffer more than France from stoppage of trade, a grateful Napoleon might help win Florida for the United States, while a desperate Britain would come to respect American sensibilities. As for the inevitable charge that Jefferson had fallen under Napoleonic influence, he provided his own answer. He was never under any illusion about Napoleon's deceit and even malevolence. He confessed to John Taylor, in a letter of 1 August 1807, that it was "mortifying that we should be forced to wish success to Bonaparte, and to look to his victories as our salvation." But obnoxious and even dangerous as Napoleon was, he could serve American interests.

The results were a personal disaster for Jefferson and general malaise and confusion for the nation. The slide into war with Britain in 1812 was accelerated by the failure of the embargo to change the behavior of either superpower. Once again France disappointed Jefferson with its inability or unwillingness to take advantage of the limited partnership that the United States offered as a counterweight to British domination. Rather than accept with appreciation Jefferson's blow against Britain, Napoleon not only demanded a complete break with Britain but also rebuffed efforts to secure Florida and seized American vessels in European ports. While Britain was hurt by the embargo, American hostility to Jefferson's policies, particularly in New England,

encouraged the government to hold fast. Three days before Jefferson retired from the White House, the Embargo Act of 1807 was repealed.

Henry Adams was correct; Jefferson had overreached himself and overestimated the ability of a small nation to manipulate larger powers. Yet this error was hardly fatal. The Napoleonic Wars helped develop an American economy less dependent on the Old World for its prosperity; and when war did come, the Old World once again proved unable to conquer the New. Before he died, sixteen years after leaving the presidency, Jefferson could witness the success of most of his aspirations. Isolation from the grip of European imperial competition had become a reality; removal of Europe from the American West was followed by a continental expansion that had already reached the Pacific; and a flawed but relatively stable American economy flourished. These successes overshadowed the strains of his administration and underscored the soundness of his basic policies. Even his unhappy entanglement in Napoleonic schemes had its redeeming feature. He was proven correct. Detestable and dangerous as the imperialism of Napoleon was, he was a single tyrant whose regime would fall with his destruction, whereas the British Parliament was a permanent entity commanding a naval strength that immediately threatened America. He could not, "with the Anglomen, prefer a present evil to a future hypothetical one." Even if he did not trust sufficiently in the "chapter of accidents" to take care of both Bonaparte and Parliament, he was correct in his judgment. And once the storms had passed he could even welcome a community of cultural and even ideological interests with the Britain that he had feared so deeply during his public life.

Jefferson's diplomacy, like that of Adams or Hamilton or Madison, was not revolutionary. If anything, the American diplomatists of the founding generation had demonstrated a mastery of Old World politics. What was revolutionary were the goals they had established and had largely won—independence and isolation from Europe. And with all the expansion of executive power accompanying the struggle to cope with the Old World, they managed to do so without leaving behind a foreign office very much larger than had been intended in 1789. While the accomplishments of the first generation were not the product of a single individual, no statesman gave longer and, on balance, more useful service than Thomas Jefferson.

Civil Liberties

LEONARD W. LEVY

ALTHOUGH history can be quoted to support any cause, just as scripture can be quoted by the devil, no wrenching of the past can alter this transcending fact about Thomas Jefferson: he believed in the right and capacity of the ordinary man to live responsibly in freedom. Abraham Lincoln testified for the ages that Jefferson's principles were "the definitions and axioms of free society." If not Lincoln himself, it is Jefferson who is the central figure in the history of American democracy. He fervently believed that the will and welfare of the people were the only prop and purpose of government. Others pitted liberty and equality against each other as if a tension, even a contradiction, existed between them. To Jefferson liberty and equality were complementary qualities of the condition to which man had a moral right. He suffused the Declaration of Independence with an ethical philosophy—not merely a political or legal one—that permanently nourished the American spirit.

THE JEFFERSON IMAGE

Jefferson's principles sprang from the deepest aspirations of the people. A communion of sentiment tied him to them, despite his tendency to shrink from too close a personal contact. He expressed himself in literary utterance that was a model of clarity and beauty—understandable, appealing, and almost unfailingly humane. With crisp eloquence he memorably voiced the noblest hopes for human fortune on earth. In so doing, he somehow illuminated the lives of his compatriots—their needs, their best values, their ambitions. His deepest sympathies belonged to the disadvantaged and downtrodden; his deepest trust was in the power of his fellow men to do justice and to fulfill themselves on their own terms, self-reliant and self-governing, so long as they had the opportunity to make informed, unfettered choices; his deepest faith was in the emancipating effect of education and freedom on the human personality. His confidence in popular government, bounded only by respect for minority rights, was anchored in a belief that counting heads was a much better way to rule than breaking them. It secured sounder policies, more beneficial to the general welfare, than those determined by the privileged few.

Jefferson "still survives," to quote the famous deathbed words of John Adams, because a free people still cherishes the spirit of liberty and the man who was its foremost exponent among the founders of the Republic. Jefferson hated tyranny and war, poverty and privilege, bigotry and ignorance; he hated whatever crippled man's spirit or body. He zealously devoted himself to securing the conditions of freedom that would make possible the "pursuit of happiness" by all. He championed free public education and attacked the aristocratic system of entail and primogeniture. He condemned slavery and recommended its gradual abolition. He saved untold thousands from bondage by championing the end of the foreign slave trade. He reformed the criminal code of his state, and he tightened the constitutional definition of treason to prevent the use of the criminal law as an instrument of political oppression. He advocated freedom of the press and resisted the noxious Alien and Sedition Acts. He insisted on subordination of the military to the civil authority. He converted James Madison to the cause of adding the Bill of Rights to the new federal Constitution. He supported a broadening of the base of popular government by public-land grants that would enable every citizen to meet the property qualification on the right to vote. Almost always Jefferson's impulses were generous and liberating. And on some matters, like religious liberty, he displayed a principled consistency.

When religious persecution still menaced Virginia, thanks to the legal establishment of the Church of England, Jefferson, in a magnificent collaboration with Madison, led a ten-year battle—the severest, said Jefferson, in which he had ever engaged—culminating in a victory for the free exercise of religion and separation of church and state. He agreed with Roger Williams that "compulsion stinks in God's nostrils." Toleration, a mere concession from the state, was only less repugnant; at its best it implied no enforced tithes or civil disabilities. Jefferson believed that religion was a private duty that free men owed their Creator. The manner of discharging that duty was none of the state's business. It was, rather, an unquestionable and illimitable natural right to be exercised freely according to the dictates of conscience.

Although the Virginia Declaration of Rights of 1776 recognized the principle of religious liberty rather than toleration, Jefferson lost on the main issue of the relation of church to state. The legislature reserved for future decision the question of whether religion ought to be supported on a non-preferential basis by a new establishment in which all denominations would proportionally share tax proceeds. When Patrick Henry, with the backing of George Washington, Edmund Randolph, and Richard Henry Lee, introduced a "general assessment" bill to create a multiple establishment benefitting all churches, Jefferson countered with his Bill for Establishing Religious Freedom. It was a classic expression of the American creed on intellectual as well as religious liberty, although Jefferson never applied its "overt acts" test to the expression of political opinion. The test, which insured the widest possible latitude for the expression of religious opinion, was that the government should not prosecute unless a statement breaks out "into overt acts against peace and good order." The bill provided also that no man should be compelled to frequent or support any worship whatever, nor be restrained in any way on account of his religious opinions. The bill became law in 1786. Jefferson's pride of authorship was so great that he ranked the bill with the Declaration of Independence as the contributions for which he most wanted to be remembered.

He faithfully adhered to the principles of his bill throughout his life. As president he departed from the precedents of Washington and Adams by refusing to recommend or designate any day for national prayer, fasting, or thanksgiving. For the president to recommend exercises of a religious character would, in his opinion, constitute an establishment of religion in violation of the First Amendment. Only a totally principled commitment to the privacy and voluntary nature of religious belief explained so exquisite a constitutional conscience.

Jefferson's consistency in applying the principle of the separation of church and state was also evident in the field of education. The complete secularist, he opposed the use of public funds for the teaching of religion in schools. His various proposals for establishing a system of public education in Virginia omitted religious instruction at a time when it was a prominent feature in schools everywhere else. He was instrumental in the abolition of the school of divinity at the College of William and Mary, and when he founded the University of Virginia, neither the professorships nor the curriculum related to religion. In colleges and universities in the rest of the country, ministers were commonly presidents and members of the boards, daily chapel attendance was compulsory, courses in religion were required, and professors of divinity held prominent positions on the faculties.

Jefferson cared deeply about religious liberty. Diligent study and thought had given him a systematic theory, the most advanced of his age, and he put it into practice. His position was clearly defined, publicly stated, and vigorously defended. Although it exposed him to abusive criticism he carried on his fight for separation of church and state, and for the free exercise of religion, throughout his long public career without significant contradictions. In sum, his thought on religious liberty was profoundly libertarian, and his actions suited his thought.

THE DARKER SIDE

However, Jefferson's ideas on many other issues were not always libertarian; and when they were, his practice did not always match his professions. Between his words and deeds on religious liberty there was an almost perfect congruence, but it was not one that was characteristic of Jefferson as a civil libertarian. Historians and biographers have fixed a libertarian halo around his brow as if he were a plaster saint or a demigod in the pantheon of freedom. He has been depicted as a noble figure caught in a mythic stance: swearing eternal hostility to every form of tyranny over the mind of man. But Jefferson had his darker side; it should be recognized and understood.

His baffling complexity on all matters other than religious liberty has been the subject of critical analysis from his own time to the present. Historians have been fascinated with him as a figure of contradictions and ambiguities. The incandescent advocate of natural rights was a slaveholder; the strict constructionist of constitutional powers purchased Louisiana and adopted an embargo; the philosopher wrote the *Manual of Parliamentary Practice;* the aristocrat championed democracy; and the democrat never introduced a proposal for universal manhood suffrage. A chiaroscuro of Jefferson would fill a huge canvas. But in spite of this, one image has remained relatively pure and undisputed, if not indisputable: Jefferson as the apostle of liberty. Inconsistencies between his actions and libertarian values have been regarded as momentary aberrations, the exceptions that proved the rule. Even unsympathetic historians have endorsed the traditional image that lays claim to our devotion and admiration, without ever suggesting more than the possibility that the democratic idol had even one toe of clay. Sympathetic historians have written of Jefferson as wholly committed to the rights of man.

Freedom's apostle was not its apostate, yet Jefferson's thoughts and actions on a variety of occasions and issues over an extended period followed a pattern that does not easily square with the conventional image. The familiar Jefferson is the one who in his *Notes on the State of Virginia* condemned temporary dictatorships even in time of war and impending invasion. The unfamiliar Jefferson, who requires our attention, is the one who, on 27 October 1808, wrote the following letter to James Brown shortly after the acquittal of Aaron Burr and his fellow conspirators:

> I did wish to see these people get what they deserved; and under the maxim of the law itself, that *inter arma silent leges,* that in an encampment expecting daily attack from a powerful enemy, self-preservation is paramount to all law, I expected that instead of invoking the forms of the law to cover traitors, all good citizens would have concurred in securing them. Should we have ever gained our Revolution, if we had bound our hands by manacles of the law, not only in the beginning, but in any part of the revolutionary conflict? There are extreme cases where the laws become inadequate even to their own preservation, and where the universal resource is a dictator, or martial law.

The unfamiliar Jefferson at one time or another supported loyalty oaths; countenanced internment camps for political suspects; drafted a bill of attainder; urged prosecutions for seditious libel; trampled on the Fourth Amendment's protection against unreasonable searches and seizures; condoned military despotism; used the army to enforce laws in time of peace; censored reading; chose professors for their political opinions; and endorsed the doctrine that the

means, however odious, were justified by the ends.

The conventional image of Jefferson has been partially fashioned from a national impulse to have a libertarian hero larger than life. When the American people honor Jefferson as freedom's foremost exponent, they reflect their own ideals and aspirations more, perhaps, than they reflect history. The darker side of both Jefferson and of the American experience is not venerated, but its existence is undeniable. American history yields more than one tradition. Abridgments of civil liberty are as old a story as the nation itself; Jefferson embodied and reflected both traditions.

From the standpoint of civil liberties Jefferson's conduct during the Revolutionary War conformed with the maxim that the laws are silent in time of war. The benefits of another maxim, more congenial to the spirit of liberty—"let justice be done though the heavens fall"—were denied to citizens suspected of Tory thoughts and sympathies. The imperatives of victory and political survival superseded the moral and legal values that normally claimed the respect of humane, libertarian leaders. Jefferson, like the others, believed that there could be no toleration of serious differences of opinion on the issue of independence, no acceptable alternative to complete submission to the patriot cause. Everywhere there was unlimited liberty to praise it, none to oppose it. Jefferson, as a member of Congress, a leader of the Virginia legislature, and a wartime governor, declared himself to be an enemy to traitorous views. In 1776 he and John Adams drafted the first American Articles of War, punishing "traitorous or disrespectful words" against the United States. In 1806 President Jefferson signed into law the bill that altered this provision by punishing any "contemptuous or disrespectful words" against the president or Congress. This clause, adopted in time of peace and under a Constitution protecting freedom of speech

—and passed after the Sedition Act of 1798, which it resembled—showed a Jeffersonian insensitivity to the First Amendment.

During the Revolution, Virginia's civilian counterpart of the military code against traitorous opinions consisted of a vicious loyalty oath and an act against crimes that were injurious to independence but less than treason. Jefferson supported both and had a hand in writing the loose prohibition against any "word" or attempt to "persuade" in behalf of British authority. This act bridged the abyss between defensible war measures—such as the punishment of incitement to seditious conduct—and the repression of opinion, such as punishment of a toast to the king's health. The same statute, which was broadened when Jefferson was governor, served as a dragnet against persons suspected of treason or disaffection but against whom proof was lacking.

The loyalty oath, which in Jefferson's phrase was aimed at "traitors in thought, but not in deed," stripped nonjurors of their civil rights. They could not vote, sue, or sell property; Jefferson himself wrote the amendment subjecting them to triple taxation. He also helped write the act retroactively legalizing the internment of political suspects in time of danger, and Governor Jefferson supported a similar bill authorizing him to jail or intern in places of security persons suspected of political disaffection. Many who were jailed languished without a hearing and without even learning of the charges against them.

The most striking departure from standards of due process of law was undoubtedly the Bill of Attainder and Outlawry, drafted by Jefferson in 1778, against the Tory officer Josiah Philips and unnamed members of his gang of reputed traitors and murderers. An attainder is a legislative declaration of guilt and punishment, devoid of judicial and procedural safeguards. Outlawry, which had been a suspect criminal classification since the Magna Carta, was controlled in England by an elaborate common-law process; Jefferson's bill declared an open hunting season on Philips and the unnamed men whose guilt was legislatively assumed. Anyone might be killed with impunity on the mere suspicion that he was an associate of Philips. Although Edmund Randolph and others connected with the attainder-and-outlawry bill subsequently regretted it and expressed their horror at what had been done, Jefferson continued long after to defend his attainder and to insist that an outlaw had no right to the privileges of citizenship or to ordinary legal process. He also sought to exclude opinions to the contrary from a historical account of the case. On 12 May 1815, when musing on the bill of 1778, he wrote to William Wirt: "I was then thoroughly persuaded of the correctness of the proceeding, and am more and more convinced by reflection. If I am in error, it is an error of principle." The libertarian standard was the one proposed by Jefferson himself in 1783 when he prepared a new draft constitution for Virginia, explicitly denying to the legislature any power "to pass any bill of attainder (or other law declaring any person guilty) of treason or felony."

Jefferson's reputation as a libertarian derived in part from his habitual repetition of inspired reveries about freedom, expressed in memorable aphorisms. On countless occasions, for example, he testified to his belief in liberty of the press; his maxims on the subject earned him a place with John Milton and John Stuart Mill. However, there were significant inconsistencies between his deeds and his words. In the long run his pen was mightier than his practice, for his rhetoric helped to create an American creed and to shape the standards by which even he must be measured. There was, for example, an imperishable remark in his First Inaugural Address in which he said, "If there be any among us who would wish to dissolve this Union or to change its republican form, let them stand undisturbed as monuments of the safety with which error of opinion may be tolerated where reason is left free to combat it." Yet his views on the scope of permissible freedom of political opinion were very narrow and did not change even after Madison, Albert Gallatin, and others in his camp had developed a very broad theory of free speech and press.

In 1776 Jefferson proposed a constitution for Virginia without a clause on freedom of either speech or the press. He also, incidentally, omitted guarantees against exclusive privileges, excessive bail, general search warrants, compulsory self-incrimination, and most of the positive rights of the criminally accused that the Virginia Declaration of Rights included. The restrictiveness of his thinking on political expression is suggested by a draft clause on religious liberty: "This [the liberty of religious opinions] shall not be held to justify any seditious preaching or conversation against the authority of the civil government." He was groping for a formula to ensure the unfettered right to propagate religious opinions without relinquishing the power of the state to curb dangerous political opinions. He finally settled on the "overt acts" test for religious opinions, but, significantly, he never applied that test to political opinions and never questioned the conventional doctrine that the government can be criminally assaulted by seditious words. The declaration "that religious faith shall go unpunished," Jefferson wrote to Madison on 31 July 1788, "does not give impunity to criminal acts dictated by religious error." In a draft constitution for Virginia in 1783 and again in a letter to Madison in 1788, he proposed that the presses be subject to prosecution for falsity, especially for false facts affecting the peace of the country. This was a particularly dangerous standard or test, because in political matters, one man's falsity is another's truth. Had Jefferson's test prevailed and been taken seriously, its suppressive possibilities can well be imagined in the midst of a for-

eign-policy controversy like the ones provoked by Jay's Treaty, the Louisiana Purchase, or the embargo. Noteworthy, too, is the fact that Jefferson did not propose that in trials for seditious libel the jury, rather than the judge, should be empowered to return a verdict on the alleged criminality of the defendant's words.

Jefferson's celebrated opposition to the Sedition Act of 1798, which he did not publicly attack, was primarily based on a states' rights doctrine. His concept of federalism, rather than a theory of free speech, dominated his thinking. Far from assaulting the concept of seditious libel, he contended that the Sedition Act was unconstitutional because the First Amendment intended that the states alone might wield the power of abridging the freedom of the press. In half a dozen instances when he was president, in both his correspondence and his public statements, he continued to endorse the exclusive power of the states to prosecute criminal libels against the government. On one occasion he urged a specific state prosecution and hoped that it would be emulated in other states. On another occasion, which his Federalist enemies exaggerated as Jefferson's "reign of terror," he permitted common-law prosecutions of his critics in a federal court during his presidency.

IN POWER

Jefferson was a thin-skinned, fierce political partisan. He once remarked that whether his neighbor said that there were twenty gods or none "neither picks my pocket nor breaks my leg." But political opinions could do both. His threshold of tolerance for hateful political ideas was less than generous. Eloquently and felicitously he declared himself in favor of freedom of speech and press, but invariably in favor either of the liberty of his own political allies or merely in abstract propositions. Under concrete circumstances he found it easy to make exceptions when the freedom of his opponents was at stake. To Madison the test of free speech or press was whether a man could with impunity express himself openly even in times of stress on matters that counted deeply. Freedom for the other fellow was the test; freedom not for the friendly opponent, but for the one with the detested, scurrilous, and outrageous views who challenged on fundamentals and whose criticism cut to the bone. Jefferson simply did not concern himself about such freedom. He cared deeply for the intellectual liberty of religious, scientific, or philosophical heretics, but not for the freedom of political heretics—unless political heresies of his own adherence were involved.

During the Burr case he betrayed an insensibility to standards of criminal justice and behaved as if he were prosecutor, judge, and jury. He wanted convictions on the treason charge and was not particularly scrupulous as to how he got them. After Burr had been freed by a federal grand jury in the West, the president mobilized public opinion against him by declaring him to be guilty beyond question, although there were at the time nothing but rumors and suspicions on which to base this judgment—and in any case it was the business of a jury, not of the president, to declare Burr guilty. To secure a conviction, Jefferson accepted the word of a real traitor, General James Wilkinson, and praised him as a loyal and honorable patriot. Jefferson also found it necessary to betray a witness by violating a pledge not to reveal or use against him his self-incriminatory statements. And Jefferson was prepared to sign a bill that would have suspended the writ of habeas corpus in order to keep in military custody Wilkinson's illegally held prisoners. Jefferson assaulted the integrity and loyalty of the federal courts that ensured due process in Burr's case, and he accused them of protecting traitors. He supported a constitutional amendment that would have made the judges removable from office by vote of Congress. He favored committing a prisoner for trial on probable suspicion rather than on prima facie evidence of guilt. He yearned for a packed jury in Burr's case. He flirted with doctrines of constructive treason when citing as proof of Burr's guilt his flight from arrest. Yet Jefferson admitted that he did not know what overt acts of treason would be proved by the government three months after he had publicly declared Burr guilty and three weeks after indictment. He suspected critics of the government's case as being associates of Burr's treason.

Jefferson also condoned Wilkinson's despotic acts in New Orleans. The general defied both the civil authorities and judicial writs of habeas corpus; he arrested men without warrants—including a judge and an editor; he transported his prisoners in chains out of the territory, denying them trial by jury of the vicinage. He rifled the mails in an illegal search for evidence, generally terrified the city, and subordinated the civil to the military, acting as if he were ruling by martial law. In response to all this, Jefferson applauded and merely cautioned Wilkinson against arresting on suspicion only for fear that the general might lose public support. The president judged his general not by legal or moral standards, but by the extent to which his actions would be supported by public opinion. An officer must risk going beyond the law when the public preservation requires, wrote Jefferson. On 3 February 1807 he informed Governor William Claiborne that the political opposition "will try to make something of the infringement of liberty by the military arrest and deportation of citizens, but if it does not go beyond such offenders as Swartwout, Bollman, Burr, Blennerhassett, Tyler, etc., they will be supported by the public approbation." As in the Philips attainder case, Jefferson's position was that bad men do not deserve the benefit of the usual forms of the law. His position was reprehensible on both constitutional and libertarian grounds. His final view on Wilkinson's actions (expressed in a letter of 20 September 1810 to J. B. Colvin)—that there were only two opinions: one held by "the guilty" and the other "by all honest men"—betrayed an impulse to stamp all opposition and criticism as illegitimate.

That same impulse, so dangerous to democratic procedure, was revealed abundantly during the embargo era, when a national policy of passive resistance was enforced at home by bayonets. Jefferson cannot be faulted for the embargo itself as an experiment in the avoidance of war, but for the manner of its adoption, its execution, and its abridgments of public and private liberty, as well as its failure, he bears the greatest responsibility. The failure was the failure of responsible democratic leadership. The task of the president was to enlist bipartisan support by educating the nation on the need for complying with laws that required a free people to suffer loss of some liberty and acute economic privation for the sake of a national goal. But Jefferson never explained, never gave the facts, and never sought understanding, and he treated Congress as he did the nation, expecting blind, dutiful obedience. His sphinxlike silence during fifteen months of agonizing national trial contributed to the subversion of principles of self-government.

The first four embargo acts—the last of which was a severe-force act—were rammed through Congress almost without debate. Jefferson showed no concern whatever about constitutional questions, not even in regard to the force act that carried the administration to the precipice of unlimited and arbitrary powers as measured by any known American standards. There was an unprecedented concentration of powers in the executive: he could detain vessels on his authority, employ the navy for enforcement purposes, and search and seize on mere suspicion without warrant in disregard of the Fourth Amendment. The president was un-

able, however, to get from Congress the power that he wanted: to search and seize without court process any goods, any time, any place. He wanted a power far more despotic than the writs of assistance that the patriot party condemned in the years before the Revolution.

As civil disobedience spread, Jefferson was increasingly tempted to more severe measures to force compliance. The embargo, begun as a means of coercing European powers into respect for American rights, became an instrument of coercion against American citizens, abridging their rights. Albert Gallatin, Jefferson's secretary of the treasury, apprised Jefferson on 29 July 1808 that the embargo was failing and probably could not be enforced under any circumstances, but that if the attempt were made, "arbitrary powers" that were "equally dangerous and odious" would have to be employed, including enforcement by the regular army. Jefferson, who two months later expressed the opinion that in extreme cases "the universal resource is a dictator, or martial law," replied decisively: "Congress," he instructed Gallatin on 11 August 1808, "must legalize all *means* which may be necessary to obtain its *end.*" The standing peacetime army, formerly the bête noire of republicanism, had already been tripled; now it was used (on a prolonged and systematic basis) to enforce the embargo at home, without lawful authority in numerous instances. In accord with the dangerous theory that the ends justify the means, Jefferson also permitted his attorney general to experiment with a treason prosecution as another means of enforcement, and he deliberately and lawlessly ordered his collectors of the customs to ignore a federal court ruling that stated that he had exercised his detention power illegally. However, he resisted his temptation to adopt the guilt-by-association principle by attainting and blockading entire towns whose citizens showed "a great spirit of resistance." Still, he recommended a new and terrible enforcement measure, the Fifth Embargo Act.

In the detention case, it was Justice William Johnson, a Republican of Jefferson's own choice for the Supreme Court, who declared that even the president was subject to legal restraints and should not attempt an unsanctioned encroachment upon individual liberty. Jefferson, defying Johnson's ruling, issued orders that it be ignored—a subversion of the concept of the independent judiciary which Jefferson had once valued as a bulwark against zealous rulers. In the treason case, growing out of a violation of the embargo, Justice Brockholst Livingston, another Republican appointee of the president, thwarted him by delivering a scorching attack on the theory of the prosecution. Pointing out that the crime at hand was merely a riot and trespass, Livingston declared that the court would not permit the establishment of so dangerous a precedent that would destroy the constitutional protection against constructive treason.

The Fifth Embargo Act, which like its predecessors was framed by Jefferson and Gallatin, disclosed an ugly spirit. It contained unbelievable violations of many provisions of the Bill of Rights, including the right to be free from compulsory self-incrimination, from unreasonable searches and seizures, and from unfair trial. The statute also authorized the regular army, at the president's discretion and without procedural safeguards, to enforce the embargo laws. The Federalists were not so wrong in denouncing the act as a step toward military despotism.

In retirement, during his declining years, the fires of Jefferson's faith in his fellow men flickered as if damped by the ashes of disillusion. Although he still claimed that men would choose wisely if given the facts, his doubts revealed themselves even in the area of intellectual liberty and academic freedom. Afflicted with that occupational vanity of intellectuals, the notion that reading can profoundly influence a man's ideas, he began to worry about dangerous books. Although he wanted citizens to think freely, he wanted them to think republican thoughts. William Blackstone and David Hume, he believed, stood in the way; particularly Hume, whose widely read *History of England* was filled with pernicious political heresies. Reading Hume, Jefferson thought, made Americans Tories. For years, therefore, he tried to secure publication of a "republicanized" version of Hume edited by an English radical, John Baxter. What attracted Jefferson to Baxter's edition was its intellectual deception. Baxter had hit upon the "only remedy" for reading Hume, which Jefferson expressed in a letter to Mathew Carey on 22 November 1818: he "gives you the text of Hume, purely and verbally, till he comes to some misrepresentation or omission . . . then he alters the text silently, makes it what truth and candor say it should be, and resumes the original text again, as soon as it becomes innocent, without having warned you of your rescue from misguidance." For years Jefferson tried to switch American readers from Hume to Baxter, apparently in the belief that truth could not best error in a fair encounter. Eager to influence young minds, future political leaders, Jefferson did not want them exposed to wrong opinions.

His career as a censor continued as founder and rector of the University of Virginia. By that time Jefferson had become a narrow localist, a strict contructionist, a southern advocate. "In the selection of our law professor," he wrote to Madison on 17 February 1826, "we must be rigorously attentive to his political principles." And on 3 February 1825, denouncing northern principles of "consolidation," he proclaimed it a duty to "guard against such principles being disseminated among our youth, and the diffusion of that poison, by a previous prescription of texts to be followed in their courses." The law school, which taught the principles of government, became a training ground for the propagation of the Virginia creed of 1798 as expressed in the Virginia and Kentucky Resolutions of that year.

The evidence taken as a whole discloses an antilibertarian pattern in Jefferson's thought and action extending throughout his long career. This tendency requires some explanation.

AN EXPLANATION

A few years after Jefferson's death, John Quincy Adams, upon reading Jefferson's *Autobiography,* yielded to his censorious and cantankerous nature. Jefferson, confided Adams to his diary, told nothing that was not creditable to him, as if he had always been right. Yet he had a "pliability of principle," a "treacherous" memory, a "double-dealing character," and was so filled with "deep duplicity" and "insincerity" that in deceiving others, "he seems to have begun by deceiving himself." The curious thing about this massive indictment, which was founded on just enough shreds of truth not to be utterly ridiculous, was that Adams spiced it with a dash of credit and a pinch of praise. Even from his jaundiced view, Jefferson was a great patriot with an "ardent passion for liberty and the rights of man." Thus the image of Jefferson as the apostle of freedom had formed even in his own time.

Unlike the Liberty Bell, that image never tarnished or cracked in any serious way. After all, nations live by symbols and have a need for vital illusions. Thomas Jefferson was by no means ill-suited for the symbolic role in which he has been cast by American history. It was a role that he had cast for himself when he left instructions for the epitaph bearing testimony to the three achievements by which he wished most to be remembered. The words chosen for inscription on the Jefferson Memorial, swearing "eternal hostility against every form of tyranny over the mind of man," reflect his enduring spirit and will speak to mankind as long as liberty is cherished on earth. At the dedication of the shrine built by a grateful nation, President Franklin D. Roosevelt in 1943 quite naturally discoursed on "Thomas Jefferson, Apostle of Freedom." "We judge him," declared Roosevelt, "by the application of his philosophy to the circumstances of his life. But in such applying we come to understand that his life was given for those deeper values that persist throughout all time." The sentiment was a noble one, poetically true. But it was not the whole historical truth.

When judged by his application of "his philosophy to the circumstances of his life," a fair enough test, the saintly vapors that veil the real Jefferson clear away. He himself hated hagiolatry. Posterity, about which he cared so much, had a greater need for a realistic understanding of their heritage than for historical fictions paraded as "images." Jefferson was not larger than life; he was human and held great power. His mistaken judgments were many, his failings plentiful. Much of Jefferson that once passed for wisdom has passed out of date. He was, to be sure, a libertarian, and American civil liberties are deeply in his debt. But he was scarcely the constantly faithful libertarian and rarely, if ever, the courageous one.

The finest moments of American liberty occurred when men defied popular prejudices and defended right and justice at the risk of destroying their own careers. Thus John Adams, at a peak of passionate opposition to the British, defended the hated redcoats against a charge of murder that grew out of the Boston Massacre. By contrast Thomas Jefferson never once risked career or reputation to champion free speech, fair trial, or any other libertarian value. On many occasions he was on the wrong side. On others he trimmed his sails and remained silent.

As secretary of state Jefferson signed the

proclamation against the Whiskey Rebels; as vice-president and presiding officer of the Senate, he signed the warrant of arrest for the journalist William Duane for a seditious contempt of that august body. Jefferson chose the easy path of lawful performance of his duties instead of conscientious opposition on the ground that liberty and justice were being victimized. In neither case did he speak out *publicly*. He signed in silence and characteristically complained in his private correspondence about the government's abridgments of freedom. His opposition to the Alien and Sedition Acts is famous: what is not so well known is that he never publicly declared his opposition during the period of hysteria. He kept his participation in the Kentucky Resolutions of 1798–1799 a secret. In the winter of liberty's danger, there was the greatest need for the heated and undisguised voice of dissent to be heard in the land, but Jefferson kept his silence.

Any depiction of Jefferson as the nearly faultless civil libertarian, the oracle of freedom's encyclicals and model of its virtues, should provoke a critical reader who is reasonably aware of human frailties—from which political figures are not notably exempt—to react with skepticism. Jefferson was no demigod. That he was a party to many abridgments of personal and public liberty should neither shock nor surprise. It would have been surprising had he not on occasion during his long career taken his hatchet in hand and cut down a few libertarian cherry trees. He said himself that he had been bent like a long bow by irresistible circumstances, his public life being a war against his natural feelings and desires. The compulsions of politics, the exigencies of office, and the responsibilities of leadership sometimes conspired to anesthetize his sensitivity to libertarian values. Nor did his own drives have an opposite effect. He yearned for the contemplative intellectual life but he could not resist the temptations of power.

He had as great a need for the means of carrying out policies in the national interest, as he understood it, as he did for the quiet life of scholarship.

He was capable of ruthlessness in the exercise of power. As president he acted as if he had disciplined himself to serve in office with energy and decisiveness, at whatever cost. A hard resolution to lead and triumph certainly characterized his presidency. Often the master politician, he was not averse to the most devious and harsh tactics to achieve his ends. Usually gentle and amiable in his personal relationships, he possessed a streak of wilfulness that sometimes expressed itself in flaring temper, violence, and toughness. His grandson portrayed him as a "bold and fearless" horseman who loved to ride booted, with whip in hand. "The only impatience of temper he ever exhibited," recalled his grandson Thomas Jefferson Randolph, "was with his horse, which he subdued to his will by a fearless application of the whip, on the slightest manifestation of restiveness." He rode the nation in the same way, booted and spurred during the embargo days, notwithstanding the fact that one of his most memorable utterances announced his belief that mankind had not been born with saddles on their backs to be ridden booted and spurred by those in power over them.

It is revealing that Jefferson arrogated to himself the power to decide personally how much bread, and with what degree of whiteness, the American people could eat during the Embargo. He regulated the nation down to its table fare, despite an aversion to centralized government and a dedication to the belief that domestic concerns were a matter of personal or local government. The eye of President Jefferson was so prying, his enemies bitterly joked, that a baby could not be born without clearance from a government customs house.

Practices once reprehended by Jefferson

as shocking betrayals of natural and constitutional rights suddenly seemed innocent, even necessary and salutary, when the government was in his hands. His accession to power seemed to stimulate fresh recognition of the existence of public dangers requiring forceful measures that often did not result in a union of principle and practice. When, for example, Republican party members were victims of the Sedition Act, unchecked tyranny was abroad in the land with frightening consequences for the future of liberty. On the other hand, when Jefferson was in power the uncontrolled licentiousness and malice of the opposition press took on the hideous features of sedition, deserving of a few exemplary prosecutions to protect the public. Jefferson's presidency—particularly the second term, which witnessed the federal sedition prosecutions in Connecticut, the Wilkinson-Burr imbroglio and trials, and the five embargo acts—was an obbligato on the arts of political manipulation and severity.

Some of his antilibertarianism can be explained by the ironic fact that he was, in the words of Dixon Wecter, a clear-eyed admirer, a "terrifying idealist, tinged with fanaticism." Only such a man would impersonally applaud a little bloodletting now and then to fertilize the tree of liberty. Jefferson held his convictions with a fierceness that admitted little room for compromise—if he was in a position to deny it—and no room for self-doubt. He was also unduly sensitive to criticisms by others.

Jefferson had the mentality and passion of a true believer certain that he was absolutely right, a marked contrast to the skepticism of modern libertarians such as Justice Oliver Wendell Holmes or Judge Learned Hand. Holmes believed that the first mark of a civilized man was the capacity to doubt his own first principles, while Hand remarked that the spirit of liberty was the spirit which was not too sure that it was right. Jefferson was a product of the eighteenth century, which regarded truths as immutable and self-evident. Yet philosophic truths concerning the nature of man or the first principles of government were not on a footing with practical legislation or executive policies. Jefferson had read John Locke and the British empiricists as well as the deists, scientists, and French philosophes. He might reasonably have been somewhat more skeptical of the rightness of his own favorite theories that he translated into national policy; he might have been less cocksure, less ready to subscribe to the proposition that certitude was the test of certainty.

In politics, particularly, where the art of the possible is often the highest value, making compromise a necessity, the capacity to doubt one's own convictions is indispensable. The poorest compromise is almost invariably better than the best dictation that leaves little if any scope of freedom to the losing side and corrupts the spirit of those in power. In his old age, writing to Edward Livingston on 4 April 1824, Jefferson observed wisely:

> A government held together by the bands of reason only, requires much compromise of opinion; that things even salutary should not be crammed down the throats of dissenting brethren, especially when they may be put into a form to be willingly swallowed, and that a good deal of indulgence is necessary to strengthen habits of harmony and fraternity.

The observation was not an abstract one. Jefferson was arguing at the time in behalf of a constitutional amendment that would authorize the national government (which by then he was denominating the "foreign" department) to build roads and canals. Although he had recommended such an amendment when he was president, his constitutional conscience seemed more finely honed when he was not in power.

Jefferson's only constitutional qualms during his presidency concerned what he believed to be his questionable authority to purchase Louisiana. He never doubted for a moment the rightness of his behavior during the Burr and embargo episodes. The intensity of his convictions and his incapacity for self-criticism propelled him onward, more resolute than ever in the face of outside criticism. The certainty that he was right, combined with his terrifying idealism, led him to risk the fate of the nation on the chance that an experiment in commercial sanctions might prove a substitute for war. Opposition only goaded him to redouble his efforts to prove himself right. He behaved as if a prisoner of his ideas, or, to put the thought less charitably, as a doctrinaire "tinged with fanaticism."

The self-skeptic, the practical politician, and the democrat conduct themselves otherwise. Any one of them in a position of power tends to operate with an understanding of the necessity of compromise and the obnoxiousness, not to mention the immorality or political stupidity, of cramming legislation "down the throats of dissenting brethren." Legislation, as William James once observed about democracy generally, is a business in which something is done, followed by a pause to see who hollers; then the hollering is relieved as best it can be until someone else hollers. Jefferson, however, was faintly doctrinaire. Exhilarated by the experience of putting an idea in motion and backing it by force, he could not back down or admit that he had been wrong. What counted most was the attainment of his objective, the validation of his conviction, not its impact on those who, failing to appreciate his idealism or personal stake, hollered long and loud. He reacted not by relieving their hollering but by a stretch of the rack that increased their protests and his own power to override them.

Jefferson tended to stretch his political power as he stretched his mind in intellectual matters, leaving his conscience behind —and sometimes his good sense. His volu-minous correspondence showed no hint that he suffered from uncertainty or was tormented by his conscience when he so readily used the army to enforce the embargo and recklessly disregarded the injunctions of the Fourth Amendment. Lincoln, in the greatest of all crises in American history, had a supreme moral objective as well as a political one to sustain him; but he was often racked by self-doubt. The exercise of power, not always constitutionally justifiable, exacted of him a price that included melancholy and an agonized soul. In moments of despair he could doubt that Providence was with him and even that his position was indeed the morally superior one.

The contrast with Jefferson is towering. Thwarted by the courts in Burr's case, Jefferson doubted not himself but the loyalty of the judges. Evasions of the embargo filled him with astonishment not that his policy could have such a result but that the people could be so rankly fraudulent and corrupt. Rumors of resistance were matched by his impulse to crush it by force. There was no inner struggle in Jefferson; the tragedy of his antilibertarianism lacked poignancy. He was oblivious of the tragedy itself, symbolized by that moment of enormity when he approved of the use of any means, even if odious and arbitrary, to achieve his end.

Vanity, the enemy of self-doubt, also played its role in fashioning his darker side. His amour propre prevented him from checking an illiberal act once begun or from admitting his error after the event. Evidence of this was his conduct of the Burr prosecutions and the way in which he was driven to defend Wilkinson. His persistent defense of his role in the attainder case of Josiah Philips bears testimony to the same trait. When caught in a flagrancy, as when it was revealed that he had hired the journalistic prostitute James T. Callender to poison the reputation of political opponents, or when he was accused of permitting sedition prosecutions in a federal court, he denied the truth. In deceiving others, as John Quincy Adams said, he deceived himself. In deceiving himself he denied himself insight into his abridgments of liberty, though he was acutely perceptive of abridgments by others.

Perhaps the chief explanation of his darker side was his conviction that the great American experiment in self-government and liberty was in nearly constant danger. He completely identified with that experiment, to the point that an attack on him or on the wisdom of his policies quickly became transmuted in his mind into a threat to the security of the tender democratic plant.

During the Revolution, coercive loyalty oaths and proscription of Tory opinions seemed a cheap price to pay when independence was the goal and the outcome was in doubt. The Alien and Sedition Acts, following the enactment of Hamilton's economic policies, forever convinced Jefferson that his political opponents were unalterably committed to the destruction of public liberty in America. In the flush of victory, at that splendid moment of the First Inaugural, he admitted the Federalists into the camp of loyal Americans, but not for long. If the scurrilousness of the Federalist press did not convince him that his magnanimous judgment had been mistaken, opposition to the purchase of Louisiana, coupled with threats of secession, proved his belief that popular government in America was imperiled. Burr's conspiracy brought the ugly menace to a head, justifying drastic countermeasures.

Open defiance of the Embargo once again threw the Union's future into grave doubt. That defiance seemed to sabotage majority rule and the only hope of avoiding a war that might end the democratic experiment. In time of such acute crisis, when insurrection existed on a widespread basis and treason itself again loomed, the methods of Draco were tempting. The behavior of the Essex Junto during the War of 1812 reconfirmed Jefferson's worst fears. In the postwar period, from his hilltop at Monticello, he imagined that a monarchistic, clerical cabal had re-formed under a new party guise, employing doctrines of nationalistic consolidation to destroy public liberty.

Over the years he constantly sensed a conspiracy against republicanism. He had a feeling of being besieged by the enemies of freedom who would use freedom to subvert it. The face of the enemy changed: now that of a Troy; later that of a monarchist, a political priest, an Essex Junto man, a Quid, or a Burrite; still later that of a judicial sapper-and-miner, an American-system consolidationist, or a Richmond lawyer. The face of the enemy or his name might change, but not his Tory principles or his subversive goal.

To the experiment of democracy in America, as Jefferson called it, he was committed heart, mind, and soul. Believing that experiment to be in great jeopardy throughout most of his public life, he was capable of ruthlessness in defeating its enemies. His own goal was free men in a free society, but he did not always use freedom's instruments to attain that goal. He sometimes confused it with self-vindication or the triumph of his party. On other occasions instability and a lack of faith were revealed by his doubts of the opposition's loyalty. They were prone, he believed, to betray the principles of the Revolution expressed in the Declaration of Independence. On still other occasions his eagerness to make America safe for democracy made him forgetful of Benjamin Franklin's wise aphorism that they who seek safety at the expense of liberty deserve neither liberty nor safety.

The terrible complexities of any major issue, such as Burr's conspiracy or the embargo, particularly as seen from the White House, also help to explain Jefferson's conduct. The strain and responsibilities of the highest office did not stimulate the taking of bold risks on the side of liberty when it seemed to be pitted against national security. Moreover, problems had a way of presenting themselves in a form that mixed conflicting political considerations and obscured clearcut decisions on libertarian merits. To a mind that was keenly alerted against the conspiracies of Federalist bogeymen and sensed a union between self, party, and nation, the virtue of an independent judiciary became the vice of judicial interference with majority rule; fair trial and a strict interpretation of treason became obstacles to the preservation of the Union; academic freedom became a guise for the dissemination of pernicious doctrines.

Jefferson's darker side derived in part, too, from the fact that he had no systematic and consistent philosophy of freedom. He was neither a seminal nor a profound thinker. Part of his genius consisted of his ability to give imperishable expression to old principles and to the deepest yearnings of his fellow citizens. Style, as much as substance, accounted for his staying power. He once defended himself against the accusation that there was not a single fresh idea in the Declaration of Independence by replying that the objective was not to find new principles or arguments never before thought of. It was, rather, as he put it in a letter to Henry Lee of 8 May 1825,

> to place before mankind the common sense of the subject, in terms so plain and firm as to command their assent. . . . Neither aiming at originality of principle or sentiment, nor yet copied from any particular and previous writing, it was intended to be an expression of the American mind, and to give to that expression the proper tone and spirit called for by the occasion. All its authority rests then on the harmonizing sentiments of the day.

As a distinguished admirer, Felix Frankfurter, has written in *Of Law and Men:* "Jefferson's seminal achievement was to institutionalize familiar eighteenth-century ideas. He made abstract notions about freedom a dominating faith and thereby the dynamic element in the strivings of men." Moreover he had the superlative political talent to organize a party that might realize his ideals by infusing the new nation with a sense of its special democratic destiny. But his failure to develop a theory of liberty more than likely influenced his antilibertarian thought and action.

In the thousands of pages of his published works there is a notable scarcity of extended treatments on a single subject. Insatiably curious, he knew a little about nearly everything under the sun and a great deal more about law and politics than any man of his time. But in all his writings, over a period of fifty years of high productivity, there is not a single sustained analysis of liberty. He was pithy, felicitous, repetitive, and ever absorbed by the subject, but he never wrote a book or even a tract on the meaning of liberty, its dimensions, limitations, and history.

That he made no contribution of this kind is not per se a criticism, for the brief preambles to the Declaration of Independence and the Virginia Statute for Religious Freedom are worth all the books that have been written on liberty. He had not, however, thought through the tough and perplexing problems posed by liberty: the conditions for its survival and promotion; the types of liberty and conflicts between them; the validity of various legal tests for measuring the scope of liberty or its permissible area of operation; and the competing claims of other values.

Jefferson contented himself with a dedication to the general principle, apparently without realizing that general principles do not satisfactorily decide hard, concrete cases. Only in the area of religious liberty did he have a well-developed philosophy, replete with a usable and rationalized test for application to specific cases. There his contribution was preeminent, even if it derived from English sources. It is significant, however, that he did not apply the "overt acts" test outside the realm of the free exercise of religion. It is even more significant that his literary remains show no evidence that he ever tried to work out a usable test for cases of verbal political crimes.

A philosopher of freedom without a philosophy of freedom, Jefferson was ill-equipped, with only his ritualistic affirmation of nebulous and transcendental truths, to confront the problem posed by General Wilkinson's conduct in New Orleans, the circulation of Hume's *History of England* in the colleges, or the savage distortions of the opposition press. He reacted expedientially on an ad hoc basis and too often hastily. Then his amour propre prevented his candid acknowledgment of a mistaken judgment, which demeaned the libertarian values he symbolized to the nation.

Regret and remorse are conspicuously absent from Jefferson's writings, as is reflective reconsideration of a problem. Something in his makeup, more than likely a stupendous ego, inhibited second thoughts. Whether he would deny the plain facts or stubbornly reiterate his original position, he failed to work out fresh guidelines for future conduct. Restatement, not reevaluation, marked his thinking, and beneath an eloquently turned phrase there lurked a weary, problem-begging cliché. That it was commonplace rarely deprived it of its profundity as a libertarian principle. The "self-evident truths" of the Declaration of Independence will continue to survive all scorn of being glittering generalities. They tend, however, to overarch real cases.

Jefferson, for example, might declare in his First Inaugural Address that enemies of the Republic should be free to express themselves, but the principle was so broad that it failed to have pertinence for him when he learned that a few "political Priests" and "Federal printers," who had been confident that no federal court would take cognizance of their seditious calumnies, were being criminally prosecuted for their libels against him and his administration. His awareness of the general distinction between preparation and attempt, or between conspiracy to commit treason and overt acts of treason, escaped application in the case of the Burrites, though not in the case of the Whiskey Rebels. A commitment to the large principle of intellectual liberty had no carryover when the possibility arose that some "Richmond lawyer" might be appointed professor of law at the University of Virginia.

Maxims of liberty were frail props for a sound, realistic libertarianism. A mind filled with maxims will falter when put to the test of experience. A mind filled with maxims contents itself with the resonant quality of a noble utterance. Such a mind, although libertarian, cannot produce a libertarian analysis such as Madison's *Report* of 1799–1800 on the Alien and Sedition Acts, or Tunis Wortman's *Treatise Concerning Political Enquiry.* Jefferson's only tracts and books were *A Summary View of the Rights of British America,* which was a protest against British encroachments on colonial freedom on the eve of the Revolution; *Notes on the State of Virginia,* a guidebook and utilitarian history; the *Manual of Parliamentary Practice;* his *Autobiography* and the *Anas,* which comprise his memoirs; *The Life and Morals of Jesus of Nazareth;* and the philological work *Essay on Anglo-Saxon.* Despite his interest in freedom, its meaning did not interest him as a subject for even an essay.

A plausible but not convincing explanation of Jefferson's darker side may be found in the argument that he lived at a time when the understanding of civil liberties was quite different from that of our own. Libertarian standards were quite new and inchoate then, making modern yardsticks of judgment anachronistic as well as unfair and lacking in understanding. The first bills of rights did not come into existence until 1776; the national Bill of Rights not until 1791. The meanings of their provisions were not always clear; their restraints in that formative era constituted an experiment in government. Deviations, inconsistencies, and even gross abridgments were to be expected when experience provided few guides. It was a time of testing, of groping and growth, of trial and error, out of which issued the improved wisdom of subsequent generations. In any case, counsels of perfection and hindsight come rather cheap when aimed by those not on the firing line or of a later time.

This explanation is certainly a plausible one. Yet the theory is spoiled by the facts. During the Revolutionary War, only Tory voices—and they were not necessarily wrong—could be found in opposition to loyalty tests, bills of attainder, and suppression of "traitorous" speech. Thereafter there were always respectable, instructive voices, even if heard only in dissent, to sound the alarm against abridgments of liberty. Jefferson needed only to hear or read in order to know that a particular measure could be seriously construed as a threat to the Bill of Rights, undermining a libertarian value. For every example of his darker side that has been mentioned here, a congressional speech, a popular tract, a letter, a newspaper editorial, a judicial opinion, or, more likely than not, a pronouncement by Jefferson himself can be adduced to show a judgment of his own time placing his action in an antilibertarian light. By 1800 or thereabouts the standards of his own time did not noticeably differ from those of ours on the kind of civil-liberties questions that he confronted.

Though he contributed little to any breakthrough in libertarian thought, except in the important realm of freedom of religion, Jefferson more than any other man of his era was responsible for the public sensitivity to libertarian considerations. If the quality of the new nation was measured by the ideals and aspirations that animated it, Jefferson had erred only slightly in confusing his own reputation with that of the democratic experiment. Notwithstanding the reciprocal scurrilities and suspicions of the opposed parties, or more importantly their conflicting interests, Americans were indeed all Federalists, all Republicans. They were equally attached to the "experiment in freedom" and the "empire of liberty." Anyone who depreciates the national commitment to libertarian values, which were based on an extraordinary legal and political sophistication, deprives himself of an understanding of the times—and of the impact of Thomas Jefferson upon it.

That Jefferson's libertarianism was considerably less than perfect or that his practice flagged behind his faith does not one whit diminish the achievements by which he is and should be best remembered. That he did not always adhere to his libertarian principles does not erode their enduring rightness. It proves only that Jefferson often set the highest standard of freedom for himself and posterity to be measured against. His legacy was the idea that as an indispensable condition for the development of free men in a free society, the state must be bitted and bridled by a bill of rights that should be construed in the most generous terms, its protections not to be the playthings of momentary majorities or of those in power.

The Presidency

ROBERT M. JOHNSTONE, JR.

THE coming to power of the Democratic-Republican party in the election of 1800 marked for many what amounted to a "second American Revolution." Throughout Jeffersonian America relief and gratitude were voiced for the emergence of the people from a long night of monarchism, militarism, commercialism, corruption, and the violation of civil liberties. Their victorious leader spoke for many when, shortly after his inauguration, he wrote to Joseph Priestley that the victory marked a "new establishment of republicanism" and a "recovery from delusion" that augured well for the future of the young Republic.

This "revolution of 1800" was thought to be redemptive in character. The first peaceful transfer of power from one political party to another presaged a restoration of the basic principles and the better nature of the original Revolution after their temporary betrayal by the Hamiltonian system. To the Jeffersonians, the Federalists had threatened, with their "ministerial" government, to destroy the balanced institutional arrangements of the Whig Revolution and to usher in a decadence of speculation in wealth and corruption in officeholding. As Dumas Malone wrote in *Jefferson the President: First Term,* "Nothing was more characteristic of the Patriots at the birth of the Republic than the conviction that the American people were unique in their character, their opportunity, and their mission, and that their experiment in self-government was destined to set an example for the world. To that faith and that vision Jefferson purposed that the country should return."

How did the Jeffersonians propose to effect this return to first principles? What was the Republican program for reform? Jefferson outlined his political testament nearly two years before his election to the presidency. As he put it in a letter to Elbridge Gerry dated 26 January 1799, he would see effected

an inviolable preservation of our present federal constitution, according to the true sense in which it was adopted by the States . . . I am opposed to the monarchising it's features by the forms of it's administration with a view to conciliate a first transition to a President and Senate for life, and from that to a hereditary tenure of these offices, and thus to worm out the elective principle. I am for preserving to the States the powers not yielded by them to the Union, and to the legislature of the Union it's constitutional share in the division of powers; and I am not for transferring all the powers of the States to the general government, and all those of that government to the Executive branch. I am for a government rigorously frugal and simple. . . . I am for relying, for internal defence, on our militia solely, till actual invasion, and for such a naval force only as may protect our coasts and harbors. . . . I am for free commerce with all nations; political connections with none; and little or no diplomatic establishment.

Jefferson wished to promote the liberties of the people by reducing the size, scope, cost, and influence of the general government. As he expressed in his First Inaugural Address, to him the sum of good government was to be "wise and frugal," to "restrain men from injuring one another," and to "leave them otherwise free to regulate their own pursuits."

To achieve these aims, the Jeffersonians offered a range of domestic reforms. To pursue frugality, they proposed to cut public expenses, pay off or sharply reduce the public debt, and then to repeal internal taxes, relying for revenues primarily on the duties from imports. Reductions in expenditures would be achieved mostly by cutting the military and naval establishments.

To restore the protection of civil liberties, the new president underscored his repudiation of the hated Alien and Sedition Acts, by pardoning those convicted under them and remitting their fines. On a broader front, the Jeffersonians sought to curb the power and pretensions of the federal courts, to which, Jefferson believed, the discredited Federalists had retreated after being repudiated by the electorate.

Within the spectrum of Republican opin-

ion, Jefferson occupied a moderate position. His overriding faith in the people gave his views on policy a flexibility that avoided the doctrinaire and caused him to align more often with the moderate than the radical, or "Old Republican," perspective. He chose to retain the basic constitutional and institutional arrangements. He and his treasury secretary, Albert Gallatin, while reducing expenditures and cutting internal taxes, did not dismantle the Hamiltonian fiscal system or the bureaucratic machinery of the treasury. Support for agriculture would be balanced by a concern to protect, as well, the trading and commercial interests. In appointments and removals, Jefferson never wholeheartedly embraced the "spoils" system but rather sought a policy that would isolate Federalist leaders while appealing to their followers to give the new administration broad support. In foreign policy, Jefferson's balance-of-power approach avoided a radical turn from Federalist Anglophilia to a contrary love of the French.

Jefferson's need was to consolidate power and to use that power to unify the Republicans and the nation. His centrist position enhanced his appeal to all factions. His problem was to institute a program that would gain wide support for his broader political principles. This delicate balance was largely achieved with the policy successes of his first term. By the end of 1803 most of his party's political program had been accomplished: the public debt was on its way to extinction; most internal taxes had been abolished; the army had been reduced and the frigates laid up; the Judiciary Act of 1801 had been repealed and replaced by the Republicans' own measure; and, most dramatic of all, the problem of access to the port of New Orleans had been settled by the purchase of the vast Louisiana Territory. It was an impressive translation of party aims into policy achievements.

Unfortunately, difficulties foreign and domestic during his second term cast a shadow over these attainments and threatened to tarnish Jefferson's high reputation as president. Indeed, his presidential tenure can be divided appropriately into his two terms, the first highly successful and the second fraught with problems.

In part, the success of his first term lay in the popularity of his programs with the people. As Malone wrote in *Jefferson the President: Second Term,* "Laws based on a policy of peace, economy, and tax reduction lightened burdens and called for no sacrifice on the part of the public." In foreign affairs, Jefferson benefited from the fact that the warring European powers enjoyed a respite from fighting for the middle two years of his first term. The Louisiana Purchase, achieved without new taxation, was a happy accident, the result of Napoleon's recalculation of advantage rather than a triumph of subtle statecraft on Jefferson's part.

In the second term circumstances altered for the worse. Domestically Jefferson's policy leadership was severely tested. Internal factionalism and schism threatened the Republican party after its sweeping electoral victories of 1804 had reduced the Federalist threat. Furthermore, shortly after his second inauguration, Jefferson let it be known privately that he would not be a candidate for a third term. This decision significantly altered the president's relations with Congress, as political attention inevitably shifted from the lame-duck incumbent to the struggle for the succession.

The major cause of trouble in the second term was the course of foreign affairs. The growing intransigence of Britain and France revealed the difficulties in Jefferson's pursuit of a policy that would avoid dependence on either power. After 1805, "the days of tender treatment of neutral commerce, fidelity to international law, and decent bargaining with third parties were past," according to Ralph Ketcham in *James Madison: A Biography.* Total war to the finish in Europe frustrated Jefferson's ability to control events. Britain's determination to use the Royal Navy to control trade with the Continent led to growing interference with American commerce and the increased impressment of American seamen. Napoleon's counter to Britain's continental blockade was a paper one of his own that further restricted American neutral trade.

Some scholars, notably Forrest McDonald in *The Presidency of Thomas Jefferson,* have argued that the responsibility for Jefferson's second-term troubles lies less with the circumstances of British and French intransigence than with Jefferson and a Republican ideology that fatally undermined the ability of the president to cope with the altered conditions of the European struggle. Jefferson clearly underestimated the ruthless character that the European war was taking and the hardening disposition of both Britain and France to do whatever was necessary to win. Another dilemma arose from the difficulties of Jefferson's reliance upon a policy of peace, neutrality, and trade with all when he lacked the means of enforcing fair treatment. The refusal of either major power to accommodate American interests made particularly difficult the task of choosing which country to oppose if force became necessary. Finding an alternative to war led Jefferson and his secretary of state to champion an embargo on trade. This fateful decision, so dependent for its success on factors beyond American control, and in its operation and implementation so destructive of deeply held Republican values, was to darken the final months of Jefferson's presidency.

THE NATURE OF EXECUTIVE POWER

Jefferson's life spanned a period of fundamental change in the understanding of governance, from traditional notions based on an aristocratic politics of deference, to a conception derived from democratic ideas of consent and the competition of material interests. Jefferson's own vision of leadership reflected the tensions of this change. He determined, as Ketcham put it in a recent article, "The Transatlantic Background of Thomas Jefferson's Ideas of Executive Power," to "implant in the new United States the benefits of *both* the life of freedom espoused by Locke and the Radical Whigs *and* the ideal of a moral human community responsive to nonpartisan leadership." In so doing, Jefferson attempted to reconcile traditional notions of a government of talent and republican virtue directed to the common good with the newer conceptions of government tied to popular consent, "motivated by material and secular considerations," and responsive to the competition of private interests.

Jefferson's greatest contribution to the development of the presidency was his perception of the office as potentially a popular one. By using the presidency as a vehicle for the furtherance of majority rule, Jefferson grounded presidential authority firmly upon popular support. As he developed his understanding of the office during his tenure in it, he altered in significant ways the original conception of the framers of the Constitution—a conception shared by the first two occupants of the presidency—as essentially a nonrepublican institution inserted into the constitutional design to temper and control the effects of popular government.

Moreover, Jefferson developed far beyond his predecessors the policy-making role of the president. George Washington had never believed it proper for the president to influence congressional debates by mobilizing support for his own ideas. Rather, he understood his role in the legislative process to begin when an enacted bill was laid before him for approval or veto. The embrace of Bolingbroke's notion of the "patriot-king" who embodies a sense of nationhood and presides above partisan faction as a grand arbiter of the public interest proved inadequate as a model for democratic leadership. Under Washington it was his "ministers"—especially his "first" minister, Secretary of the Treasury Alexander Hamilton—who provided policy guidance to Congress and day-to-day direction of administration. Hamilton erected an informal scheme of ministerial government based upon the direct communication that Congress had established by statute between the head of the treasury and the House of Representatives.

While Jefferson in part endorsed the notion of the patriot leader who embodied a sense of nationhood, he rejected the method of rule implied by the concept. He was aware of a central flaw in the Hamiltonian scheme of ministerial government: its lack of a popular base of legitimacy, its lack of a direct relationship to the consent of the governed. Cabinet officers, as appointed "auxiliaries," were no substitute for a president who provided direct leadership firmly tied to his electoral responsibility to the people. Jefferson replaced ministerial government with presidential government. Through his use of the political party as a mechanism to bridge the separation of powers and energize the government for policy leadership, Jefferson "combined the constitutional powers of the presidency with a 'political' power grounded on popular support," as I observed in *Jefferson and the Presidency*. Jefferson put it well in a letter to John Garland Jefferson dated 25 January 1810: "It is the duty of the Chief Magistrate, in order to enable himself to do all the good which his station requires, to endeavor, by all honorable means, to unite in himself the confidence of the whole people. This alone . . . can produce a union of the powers of the whole, and point them in a single direction, as if all constituted but one body and one mind."

Jefferson was constrained in implementing his theory by certain constitutional and political realities. Policy leadership by the executive had to contend with the fragmentation of policy-making caused by the separateness of institutions and the sharing of power imposed by the Constitution. More specifically, the framers had intentionally limited the role of the president in the legislative process. With formal powers restricted to the initial recommendation of measures and the veto of Congress' product and without any institutional mode of access or influence, the president's task of mobilizing and moving a working congressional majority was a formidable one. This constraint was reinforced by elements of republican ideology that viewed power, especially executive prerogative power, with suspicion and that expressed an abiding faith in the rightness of legislatures.

The Jeffersonian solution was the development of a style of presidential government characterized by the cultivation of influence. Power rested on personal and situational, rather than constitutional or systemic, factors. Policy leadership was effected by means of the extraconstitutional use of informal tools of persuasion and bargaining. These included Jefferson's leadership of the party and the motivation of party loyalty in Congress as well as in the executive; his use of legislative lieutenants on the floor, of a party press, and of patronage and appointments; and his reliance upon his own sizable personal skills of persuasion.

The personal assets that Jefferson brought to his task were imposing; indeed, he was remarkably well qualified to be president. His career of public service had been long and distinguished. He had gained extensive legislative experience in Virginia and the Continental Congress and varied executive experience as governor of Virginia, minister to France, secretary of state, and vice-president. The reputation gained from this service as well as his symbolic identity with the deeper principles of republican America were significant factors in enhancing his authority as a popular leader.

His personal style contributed to his success. "No one can know Mr. Jefferson and be his personal enemy," observed a political adversary. He possessed an amiability that proceeded from a basic optimism toward his fellow human beings and a desire to promote harmony in both his public and his private life. His advice to others was "to take things always by the smooth handle." A keen intelligence, a penchant for conciliation, a ready deference to others, good humor, politeness, a talent for the pen, a skill at conversation, and personal honesty and integrity provided him a formidable array of persuasive gifts.

Jefferson possessed some weaknesses as a popular leader. He was a cultural aristocrat. He had little talent and less liking for the direct cultivation of popular approval. He was a poor public speaker with a distaste for large assemblages and a love of privacy. His dislike of controversy amounted at times to an active avoidance of difficult issues. He tended toward secretiveness in his political relations. Despite a height of six feet, two inches, he was physically unimposing, lanky and raw-boned rather than stately in bearing, and he often dressed with a simplicity bordering on carelessness.

Yet even these defects often became assets. Jefferson cultivated the image of a popular republican. Practices that not only suited his temperament but served his democratic statecraft included his decision to walk alone to his inauguration, to dress simply, to relax the protocol at diplomatic functions, to end the practice of personally delivering his annual messages to Congress because of monarchical associations, and to engage in a correspondence with citizens of every station.

Jefferson's theoretical conception of the presidency was tempered by a pragmatic spirit. He recognized more than many the need to adjust theory to practice. He was acutely aware of the maxim that politics is the art of the possible. As he put it in a letter to Walter Jones dated 31 March 1801, "No more good must be attempted than the nation can bear." As he later advised Pierre-Samuel Du Pont de Nemours in a letter dated 18 January 1802, "What is practicable must often control what is pure theory; and the habits of the governed determine in a great degree what is practicable."

ORGANIZATION OF THE EXECUTIVE

Notwithstanding the changes in policy, ideology, and methods noted above, Jefferson's conduct of the presidency followed in many respects the example established by Washington. Jefferson accepted, as had Washington, the rightness of a balanced constitutional system of divided powers. His respect for the separation of powers was keen. Nevertheless, as his adversary Hamilton had recognized, he favored "a large construction of the Executive authority" and would not hesitate to defend executive powers and prerogatives when they suffered attack. As secretary of state, he had argued against substantive involvement by the Senate in the appointing power. He defended the president's right to control outside access to privileged information. He protected his cabinet officers from investigative subpoenas. And he asserted the exclusive power of the executive to conduct the diplomatic relations of the nation.

Jefferson's administrative theory and behavior emerged from his understanding of the obligations of democratic leadership. As Merrill Peterson observed in *Thomas Jefferson and the New Nation*, Jefferson was "more concerned with the control than the organization of power, with responsibility than with energy, with administration as a simple tool rather than an awesome machine." While Jefferson never expressed a general theory of administration, scholars have isolated a number of underlying assumptions that informed his administrative practice.

The first was a need for administrative responsibility. Jefferson was generally opposed to the exercise of broad discretionary authority. He favored a narrow construction of powers. He required of his administrative subordinates strict accountability under a simple system of clearly articulated laws and procedural regulations.

A second assumption was the importance of frugality and simplicity in government. He made clear his hostility to vast bureaucracies, as in a letter to Albert Gallatin dated 1 April 1802, in which he denounced their "pomp, patronage, and irresponsibility." His hopes in this regard were sometimes frustrated, and on those occasions when they were fulfilled, the outcome often created new problems (austerity measures that skeletonized the fleet and sharply reduced American diplomatic representation abroad did not always serve an effective foreign policy). In either case, Jefferson retained a deep suspicion that elaborate structures and swollen civil lists provided a cover for waste, intrigue, and the reign of vested privilege.

Third, Jefferson believed in the decentralization of administration, not only to avoid the potential for power to become despotic but to cultivate the talents and habits of self-government among the people. Ironically, his attempts to enforce the embargo of 1807–1809 led to the greatest concentration of executive authority known to the government before the Civil War.

Within his own "official family," Jefferson sought to ensure unity of interest and purpose and to promote harmony of will. He brought to the presidency a well-defined view of the proper relationship between the president and the heads of the departments. Experience in Washington's executive council and observation of Adams' failure to control his cabinet confirmed his determination to be the undisputed authority in his own administration. He considered the department heads to be auxiliaries who served the president in carrying out his executive functions. He sought, therefore, to organize the executive in ways that combined the advantages of presidential authority with those of collective consultation.

To further his aims, Jefferson determined to involve himself more than had his predecessors in the daily conduct of public affairs. He required that all correspondence between department heads that concerned matters of substantive policy be sent to him for action or for information, thereby ensuring his centrality in the policy process. He explained his action in a circular to heads of executive departments dated 6 November 1801, saying that the president would thus be "in accurate possession of all facts and proceedings" so as to be able to "meet personally the duties" of his office.

Jefferson declined to establish regular weekly cabinet meetings, preferring for reasons of efficiency and flexibility to call meetings only as needed and to conduct other business with his cabinet advisers individually. He saw individual department heads frequently, often without appointment, to keep him abreast of events and alert to problems. He routinely consulted them individually in the preparation of his annual messages to Congress, state papers, and recommendations for legislation, as well as for political advice.

In meetings of the full cabinet, proceedings were informal. The president would state the matter for discussion and solicit opinions. He scrupulously consulted his cabinet on all issues of importance and in all moments of crisis, asking each member for his views. Often, especially on sensitive matters, he would seek their opinions in writing. Jefferson's readiness to solicit advice and his willingness to alter his own views when presented with a better argument aided in es-

tablishing the confidence and loyalty of his department heads.

Most of the time, decisions were reached by a process resembling consensus. If the issue were deemed of sufficient importance, a vote would be taken on which, as Jefferson wrote, "the president counts himself but one." He likened his cabinet to a "directory" but admitted that it was one "which certainly the President might control." It is a measure of his surety of control that he never was constrained to assert it to overrule his advisers. Unity on principles combined with collegiality in deliberation to preserve a remarkably consistent harmony within the administration.

That such harmony existed is attributable in part to Jefferson's careful selection of his cabinet officers. He determined to appoint only men whom he could trust and rely upon for sound advice. He was fortunate in the circumstances that surrounded his cabinet appointments. As undisputed head of the party with few obligations to pay off, he had a relatively free hand in selection. His criteria, when possible, included personal acquaintance, political loyalty, collegiality, administrative talent, political acumen, party factional representation, and geographical distribution.

James Madison, the only Virginian and indeed the only southerner in the cabinet, was the obvious choice for secretary of state. The founder (with Jefferson) of the party, Madison had gained a distinguished reputation as constitution maker and legislative leader. He was Jefferson's closest political colleague and an intimate personal friend. His cautious and analytical mind served as a steady counterpoint to the president's more imaginative and impulsive nature. Their collaboration in foreign policy was so close that it is often difficult to distinguish each man's particular contribution.

The treasury was by far the largest and most extensive of the executive departments. To run the financial operations, Jefferson chose Albert Gallatin of Pennsylvania, an important congressional leader who combined fiscal and administrative talents with shrewd political wisdom. Gallatin was the economic architect of the administration. He became an important counselor in matters beyond his portfolio as well, serving as the president's principal political liaison with Congress.

The other members of the cabinet, while not maintaining the close relationship with the president enjoyed by Madison and Gallatin, nevertheless had his confidence and served him well. General Henry Dearborn, from the Maine district of Massachusetts, was a Republican citizen-soldier of the Revolution. As secretary of war, he presided with competence over a tiny department that not only administered the army but conducted relations with the Indian tribes. With no military staff to assist him, Dearborn's load was heavy, but he managed to find time to provide political advice on party affairs in New England.

Republican ideology interfered with the maintenance of a satisfactory defense establishment, especially the navy. Expensive to build and maintain, the seagoing fleet bore the brunt of budget cuts in the Jeffersonian years. To head this backwater department, Jefferson, after rejections by his first three choices, settled on Robert Smith of Maryland, brother of the powerful Sen. Samuel Smith. Hampered as was Dearborn by the lack of a professional staff, Smith adequately ran the department, although he is generally regarded as one of Jefferson's weaker appointments. His frequent budgetary disputes with the frugal Gallatin put the severest strains on harmony.

The attorney general, while a member of the cabinet, headed no department and had no staff. Massachusetts Republican Levi Lincoln was nevertheless a busy man, giving legal counsel to the president, arguing the government's cases in federal court, and

serving in the cabinet councils. The postmaster general, while not in the cabinet, was then, as later, an important political figure, for Gideon Granger of Connecticut was the administration's patronage chief through his control over the appointment of postmasters. Jefferson's cabinet was remarkably stable in membership; there was only one resignation in eight years and only one office, that of the attorney general, had any change of leadership.

DOMESTIC POLICY

To achieve the success of his "second American Revolution," Jefferson had not only to assemble a harmonious and effective cabinet but to ensure that subordinate positions in the administration were occupied by men willing to accept the new directions implied by his election. He necessarily became concerned with questions of patronage. Owing to his Whig conception of public office as a public trust, Jefferson's use of patronage was tentative and equivocal. He was never a convinced spoilsman. Nevertheless, pressure to remove Federalists and appoint only tried and true Republicans was severe. Jefferson's responsibilities as party leader, furthermore, demanded that he not only reward the faithful with office but also provide an essential basis for coordination and execution of Republican policies. This inevitably meant, as he put it in a letter to Levi Lincoln dated 26 August 1801, that "the first republican President who should come into office after all the places in government had become exclusively occupied by federalists, would have a dreadful operation to perform. . . . On him . . . was to devolve the office of an executioner, that of lopping off."

Jefferson's appointments policy evolved under the force of experience and changing circumstances. At first he hoped to pursue a policy of conciliation, embracing those Federalists who were "detachable" while isolating their irreconcilable leaders. A policy of moderation seemed in order. But partisan Republicans would have none of it. They understandably clamored for their long overdue share of the spoils of power. Only wholesale removal of the hated Federalists and their replacement by loyal party stalwarts would suffice. More moderate Republicans, including Gallatin and Madison, cautioned against cultivating a spirit of persecution such as characterized their predecessors.

Unfortunately for moderation, it quickly became apparent that the Federalists, far from perceiving and appreciating Jefferson's forbearance, denounced each removal as a dagger aimed at the heart of the Republic. This reaction, coupled with the need above all to conciliate his supporters, caused Jefferson to adopt a more partisan policy, intended to achieve a Republican balance in office that reflected the party's strength in the country.

The president applied four basic criteria in making new appointments to vacancies: evidence of sound Republican sentiments; a record of military service, preferably in the Revolution; proper geographical distribution of offices; and a reputation for respectability and standing in the community. While he scrupulously avoided the widespread nepotism of the era, Jefferson did not go so far as to declare kinship with families of breeding and eminence a disqualification for office.

Recent scholarship reveals that Jefferson's reputation in some quarters as a spoilsman is exaggerated. In the summer of 1803, the president prepared a table that showed that of 316 offices subject to his direct appointment, only about half had changed party hands. Sidney Aronson, in *Status and Kinship in the Higher Civil Service*, calculates that of ninety-two "elite," or policy-making, appointments at Jefferson's disposal, thirteen were retained from the Adams administration. Indeed, a few notorious retentions in

office became a source of frustration and resentment among Republicans.

The question of patronage was to Jefferson the most persistently annoying and unrewarding problem of his presidency. In a letter to John Dickinson dated 13 January 1807, he complained, "Every office becoming vacant, every appointment made me donne un ingrat, et cent ennemis." Nevertheless, it was through the appointing power that he was able to remold an administrative machinery that extended Jeffersonian influences over a broad range of policies and over an extended sphere of territory.

To achieve the president's purposes required not only an executive bureaucracy attuned to his wishes but a Congress willing to join in a productive partnership to enact the party's program. One of Jefferson's major achievements as president was to pioneer a set of strategies to provide sustained leadership of the legislative process. It was not an easy task. Commenting on his relations with Congress as he neared the end of his presidency, Jefferson cautioned in a letter to Joel Barlow dated 10 December 1807, "There is a snail-paced gait for the advance of new ideas on the general mind, under which we must acquiesce. A forty years' experience of popular assemblies has taught me, that you must give them time for every step you take. If too hard pushed, they balk, and the machine retrogrades."

The natural tendencies of legislatures were aggravated for Jefferson by the jealousies and suspicions of executive power that were a leading element in Republican ideology. In the 1790s, congressional Republicans had sharply attacked Hamiltonian interferences in the legislative process. Republican doctrine demanded that the executive confine itself to the broad identification of problems and the recommendation of general subjects for congressional attention. In dealing with Congress, Jefferson displayed a keen understanding of the primacy of that body in the constitutional design and was sensitive to the institutional jealousies of its members. Executive influence had to proceed informally and with circumspection, with due attention to legislative prerogatives. Jefferson and his department heads maintained at all times a public posture of deference to Congress as the embodiment of the popular will. They took care in public messages to credit Congress with the success of policies. Jefferson's personal talents for persuasion helped him to mobilize his contentious Republican majorities for support of his programs.

Nevertheless, the president determined to provide not merely suggestions but guidance and direction to legislative affairs. He wrote, in a letter to Barnabas Bidwell dated 5 July 1806, "If the members are to know nothing but what is important enough to be put in a public message, and indifferent enough to be made known to all the world; if the executive is to keep all other information to himself, and the House to plunge on in the dark, it becomes a government of chance and not of design." During his administration most major legislative proposals originated in the executive, as Jefferson and his colleagues suggested ideas, offered legislative strategies, shared information, and even drafted legislation to be introduced by friendly members. The president normally preferred to suggest only general policy preferences, leaving room for compromises with congressional interests and for the legislators to take the public credit. He was careful to keep his own role confidential so as to avoid ruffling the feathers of congressional pride and so as not to provide political ammunition to the opposition.

For the most part the president relied upon his department heads to act as spokesmen for his views to Congress. While Jefferson took care to preserve the integrity of the separation of powers, his cabinet advisers were routinely engaged in activities with members of Congress, providing technical assistance and substantive advice. Gallatin, in particular, worked closely with Republican members of key committees, for Congress relied heavily on the executive departments for information as well as for routine staff work in the absence of staff assistance of its own.

The administration's success with Congress was enhanced by the fact that all of the cabinet, except for Secretary of the Navy Robert Smith, had served in Congress and understood the ways of legislative assemblies. In addition, they were personally acquainted with the characters and politics of individual members. All department heads entertained members of Congress. Gallatin, who lived on Capitol Hill, had almost daily contact with leading members of the Republican majority.

It was Jefferson himself who most used social occasions to lessen friction with members of Congress. While he sometimes communicated with legislative leaders by letter and more often met with them in private conference, his most telling informal contributions in influencing the members were his famous dinners. While shoptalk of any kind was scrupulously avoided at these gatherings, they nonetheless brilliantly served the president's political purposes. The dinners were a means of cultivating the personal acquaintance of members without violating the norms of distance and decorum expected between the two branches. Excellent food and wine (Jefferson spent lavishly on both), delightful conversation led by their gracious host, a carefully chosen guest list (mixing Republicans who lived in different boardinghouses, while inviting Federalists only on separate occasions) all contributed to provide Jefferson's legislative colleagues with memorable experiences. The seating arrangements, the precise selection of people, and an informality conducive to engaging social intercourse were designed to give the guests a more intimate understanding of the president's amiable character and seductive personality. The political effect of these dinners was not so much to coordinate legislative strategies or to lobby for votes as to strengthen the bonds of allegiance within the Republican ranks and, where the Federalists were concerned, to soften the personal, if not the political, animosity of the opposition.

To perform his role as party leader, Jefferson had to have legislative lieutenants who would not only set agendas and control the flow of business but would represent the president's views. As he put it in his letter to Bidwell of 5 July 1806, there was a constant need for someone "to take the lead . . . to consider the business of the nation as his own business, to take it up as if he were singly charged with it, and carry it through."

Jefferson was limited in his capacity to select his floor leaders. Members jealously guarded their prerogative to choose their own leaders. He had to accept and work with the material already at hand, although he did seek to influence talented individuals to assume leadership positions.

In the Seventh Congress (Jefferson's first), leadership in the House was shared by Speaker Nathaniel Macon of North Carolina and John Randolph of Roanoke, the majority leader. Randolph, a "pale, meagre, ghostly" little man from the Virginia southwest, quickly assumed the dominant position of party influence. The eccentric and tempestuous Randolph's relations with Jefferson were correct but never intimate. His temperament made cordial relations difficult at the best of times. A born oppositionist, he worked ill in harness to another's lead. But Jefferson needed his talents and attempted the task of cultivating him.

For nearly five years Randolph, as chairman of the powerful Ways and Means Committee, was the recognized leader. He reached the peak of his influence in 1803–1804, when he skillfully shepherded the Louisiana Purchase and the Louisiana government bills through the House. When he broke with the administration in 1806, he lost his Ways and Means post, a key illustration that party leadership in the Jeffersonian Congress was at least indirectly connected to the president as party leader. After Randolph's break, floor leadership devolved upon lesser though competent men whose power rested less upon independent bases than upon the fact that they recognizably had the confidence of the president.

Jefferson's influence over the Republicans in Congress was sufficient to be the subject of harsh criticism by the Federalists, many of whom complained of the "blind devotion" of the congressional party to the president's will. For their part, the Republicans learned to exploit in debate the asset of presidential support. Jefferson's moral authority and prestige were often sufficient, especially in his first term, to ensure at least a fair hearing and usually a good approximation of his wishes.

Congressional passage of the Louisiana Government Act in February 1804 nicely illustrates the hold that Jefferson maintained over Congress and the methods he employed to influence the process of legislation. After the acquisition of Louisiana in 1803, a government had to be established in the new territory. Conditions in Louisiana indicated to Jefferson the inappropriateness of extending the full range of republican principles in the formation of that government. The population was a polyglot mixture of races and types. Illiteracy, corruption, and ignorance of American law and custom were characteristic, as was an unfamiliarity with the practices of self-government and the tenets of political liberty. Jefferson determined that the people of Louisiana would have to experience a period of political tutelage and apprenticeship in the art of governance. His plan provided for presidential appointment of the governor and other major officials, with the governor in turn appointing the legislative assembly.

Jefferson sent a draft of a bill to Sen. John C. Breckinridge of Kentucky with an admonishment to keep its authorship secret. Breckinridge chaired the committee that would examine the issue, and he used the president's draft as if it were his own. Meanwhile, Jefferson privately surveyed members to gauge the bill's chances. Opposition came not only from Federalists but from some of the president's own party who balked at the violation of Republican principles that the bill seemed to endorse. Nevertheless, armed with the president's views, Breckinridge lined up proponents whose floor arguments closely reflected Jefferson's position on the territory's incapacity for self-government and the need for a period of probation. Jefferson helped his cause behind the scenes, communicating information and making a timely concession to the Senate on a few minor points. He quietly comforted those who feared despotism by letting it be known that his choice as territorial governor was his sound young Republican friend James Monroe. The bill that emerged, with minor alterations and a time limit of one year (from 1 October 1804), was largely Jefferson's bill. Despite its apparent inconsistency with Republican views, the strength of Jefferson's authority and the skill with which he brought Congress to support his view were clearly demonstrated.

He was not always so fortunate; he met with defeat from time to time on minor issues. Perhaps his most serious defeat was Congress' repeated refusal to approve his plans for reorganizing the militia under a uniform national system. Traditional congressional sensibilities favoring local control of the militia and Republican fears of anything that might lead to a standing army doomed every effort by the president, however sensible from a military or an administrative perspective, to achieve this reform. Such defeats were rare, and the accumulation of legislative successes served further to cement his reputation as a strong leader.

Jefferson's great popularity was demonstrated by the election of 1804. There was never any doubt that he would stand for re-election, the only question of interest being the identity of his running mate. Vice-President Burr's penchant for intrigue had damaged his standing in the party and with the president, and he was losing his base of support in New York to the faction headed by Gov. George Clinton and his nephew, DeWitt Clinton. In February 1804, the Republican congressional caucus unanimously renominated Jefferson and, by a near consensus, selected sixty-five-year-old Clinton for vice-president. The Federalists nominated a ticket composed of Charles Cotesworth Pinckney of South Carolina and Rufus King of New York. Both men had distinguished careers, with service as delegates to the federal constitutional convention and in sensitive diplomatic posts, Pinckney to France and King to Great Britain. So respectable was King, in fact, that Jefferson retained him at the Court of St. James until 1803. Their eminence gained them little with the voters, for their hopes were buried under one of the greatest electoral avalanches in American history. Jefferson and Clinton received 162 electoral votes to fourteen for the Federalist ticket, with only staunchly Federalist Connecticut and Delaware in the losers' column. Jefferson's was a party victory as well as a personal triumph, as Republicans were swept back to power by increased majorities, even in New England.

Perhaps ironically, the greatest threat to Jefferson's leadership arose from his party's success in destroying effective Federalist opposition. With little to fear from that corner, the Republicans lapsed into a complacency that contributed to internal party divisions. No one recognized the danger more than Jefferson. The disaffected could look to the two rallying points of the schismatics: Vice-President Clinton and John Randolph, with Randolph proving the greater problem.

The first serious internal strains arose during 1804–1805 in the Yazoo controversy. Land frauds by the Georgia legislature and numerous speculators led to an attempt by the Jefferson administration to seek a compromise that would at least mollify all the parties concerned. But they reckoned without Randolph. His bitter opposition to the settlement gave notice that the administration could no longer count on the undeviating support of its House floor leader.

The final break occurred in the next session of Congress when Randolph denounced the administration for its secret efforts to secure a two-million-dollar appropriation to purchase the Floridas from Spain. The danger of Randolph's schism was the potential disruption of the party in its traditional strongholds of the South and Southwest. Fortunately for Jefferson, a mere handful joined Randolph. The president moved quickly to heal the breach, pointedly advising susceptible colleagues to resist the allure of the schismatics. By the end of the session, the moderates had rallied to isolate and contain the dissidents.

Nevertheless things never quite returned to the status quo ante for the president and his party colleagues in Congress. Jefferson's hold over Congress had been weakened for the first time. While the party closed ranks again and continued to support the president on the major issues, the factionalism within had been publicly aired. Divisions continued to threaten party unity, especially as Jefferson's impending retirement became evident and the competition for the succession grew apace.

FOREIGN AND MILITARY POLICY

"The conduct of foreign affairs is executive altogether," Jefferson wrote while secretary of state. He accepted the constitutional qualifiers, including the prerogative of the Senate to advise and consent to treaties and the power of Congress to declare war. Nevertheless, in the conduct of negotiations, in intercourse with foreign envoys and governments, and even in the formulation of policy, Jefferson assumed that the preponderance of authority and responsibility was his.

Jefferson's extensive experience in world affairs naturally caused him to take a particular interest in foreign policy as president. He did not attempt to act as his own foreign minister, preferring to leave the conduct of day-to-day diplomatic business to Madison, but he did work closely with his secretary of state in the formulation of policy. The president did not limit his consultation to Madison; major foreign policy, even tactical questions of the moment, were usually discussed by the full cabinet. Nevertheless, Jefferson's was the controlling voice.

Where the actions of the executive threatened or implied the use of force, Jefferson was scrupulous (some would say overly so) in respecting the authority of Congress, not only out of deference to the constitutional powers of the legislative branch but from an awareness of the closeness of the members of Congress to popular sentiment.

Jefferson, as did many of his successors, struggled with the constitutional ambiguities of the problem of undeclared war. In repelling a hypothetical unprovoked enemy attack, he questioned his authority, in the absence of congressional approval, to go beyond the line of defense and take offensive countermeasures. He doubted as well his authority to call out the regular armed forces to quell domestic insurrection. When the occasion first arose to exercise such authority, in the Burr conspiracy, Jefferson, advised by Madison that he had no such power, asked Congress to give it to him. It did so in March 1807, too late to affect his actions in dealing with Burr. How he handled the Burr conspiracy reveals much about Jefferson's understanding of his obligation to keep the peace.

Separatist movements in New England and the West had long been a problem for the young nation. Burr's own machinations began in early 1804 when he approached Gen. James Wilkinson and a few others with a plan the nature of which varied with the particular audience of the moment: to separate the western states from the Union and establish a new sovereign state on the Gulf of Mexico; to invade Spain's Mexican possessions and seize them for the United States; or merely to raise a force to defend Louisiana against the Spanish. Soon rumors of a plot were circulating, first privately and then in the press. Wilkinson (who as a long-time paid agent of the Spanish government understood well the dynamics of conspiracy) began to have second thoughts and took steps, unknown to Burr, to protect himself should his coconspirator's efforts collapse.

Unsubstantiated reports of "Spanish intrigues" reached Jefferson's desk from Kentucky in February 1806, but the vagueness of the charges and the informant's Federalist sympathies caused Jefferson to discount them. In the autumn, however, more specific reports from more reputable sources spurred the president to take action. The uncertainty of the facts and the slowness of communications with the West urged caution, and the cabinet decided to dispatch an agent to shadow Burr and to alert western governors. Jefferson determined to guard against the rebellion's success without unduly alarming the country or Burr, whose vulnerability to a charge of treason depended upon the commitment of an overt act. The commander-in-chief also needed assurances of the loyalty of Wilkinson before attempting more drastic actions that might call for the use of the army. Since his authority to employ federal forces applied only in cases of conspiracy against foreign countries, the president issued a proclamation on 27 November ordering the suppression of an enterprise against Spanish territories, while saying nothing about Burr or a domestic conspiracy.

Through December, Jefferson waited for news while urging the state authorities to repel any threat to western security. By January, the danger of a serious problem had so abated that Jefferson, in a letter to Charles Clay dated 11 January 1807, could compare Burr's activities with the enterprises of "Don Quixote." Unaware that Burr had given himself up a few days earlier, on 22 January the president documented the conspiracy in a special message to Congress. In handling the matter, Jefferson took pleasure in avoiding the use of federal military force. He did not, as Hamilton had done in the Whiskey Rebellion, use it as a pretext for displaying the strength of federal arms. Rather, he praised the state governments and the people of the affected region for preserving their own and the Union's safety and for demonstrating the vigor of republican institutions.

The achievement of these aims goes some way to explain Jefferson's sometimes questionable conduct during the subsequent trial of Burr for treason. For the conspiracy to serve its constructive purpose of strengthening the Republic it was necessary to bring the conspirators to justice. Yet Jefferson suspected that the Federalist courts might release Burr. The conduct of Jefferson's political and personal enemy, Chief Justice John Marshall, who, in his capacity as circuit judge presided over the judicial proceedings against Burr, confirmed the president's suspicions. Through a series of rulings from the bench, Marshall crippled the efforts of the government to present a case of treason. Jefferson was convinced that the Chief Justice was in fact using the law both to cover treason and to embarrass the Jeffersonians. Legal, political, and personal antagonisms led to excesses on both sides. Jefferson, acting for a time as his own attorney general, took on some of the responsibilities for preparing the prosecution's case. He dispatched agents to retrace Burr's steps and gather evidence of his guilt. He interviewed witnesses and corresponded with the government attorneys in Richmond about trial strategy, all the while maintaining his indifference to the outcome. Anticipating acquittal, Jefferson looked to the achievement of a higher justice, to be meted out to the federal courts at the bar of public opinion. To this end, after Burr's final release in September, the president sent a full record of the proceedings to Congress, recommending that it limit the capacity of the courts to encourage this "highest order of crimes."

Although he chose to avoid military action in dealing with the Burr conspiracy, Jefferson was no pacifist. He understood the natural propensity of mankind to be "eternally and systematically engaged in the destruction of its own species," and in moments of pessimism, as when he wrote to Madison on 1 January 1797, he saw "civilization" as having "no other effect on him than to teach him to pursue the principle of bellum omnium in omnia on a larger scale." Furthermore, he recognized the utility of force in international affairs in certain circumstances, as illustrated by his readiness to pursue a naval war against the Tripolitan pirates.

Nevertheless, Jefferson, like many of his Republican countrymen, believed that the American experiment in self-government was also an experiment in finding alternatives to the seemingly eternal resort to war. His views also reflected Republican suspicions of large military and naval establishments as threats to civil liberties, drains on the nation's economic resources, and stimuli by their very existence to adventurism in foreign policy.

Jefferson was more concerned about military preparedness than either the general public or his Republican colleagues in Congress. Efforts by the president to reform the militia system, to create a military academy, and after 1807 to rebuild the army were ei-

ther rejected or curtailed by Congress. Under the pressure to economize, naval effectiveness was sharply reduced. Warships were laid up and new construction was canceled. In his second term, as serious difficulties developed with the European powers, Jefferson's concern to defend the nation began to outweigh his desire to realize economies. Even Gallatin saw the risk of injuries and insults that resulted from a weak navy. But Congress refused to vote the money for new frigates, preferring to rely upon the construction of inexpensive shallow-draft gunboats, an idea that Jefferson, in his innocence of naval matters, had championed. The result was that during his administration the state of the army and navy never approached what would be needed in time of war, nor did it satisfactorily constitute a deterrence to foreign governments. Austerity toward the military reduced diplomatic leverage and damaged the credibility of America's willingness to fight, if necessary, to protect its interests.

Jefferson's foreign policy rested on his conviction that the security and prosperity of the new nation depended upon the maintenance of peace. To a French friend, Comte Diodati, he wrote on 29 March 1807: "More blest is that nation whose silent course of happiness furnishes nothing for history to say." Such a view called for a policy of separation from the affairs of the Old World and a strict neutrality toward its political and military controversies. Only through the avoidance of involvement in major power politics could the young nation consolidate its gains and develop its independence.

Given these views it was perhaps unfortunate for Jefferson that, save for a few months of his first term, his presidency was conducted under the perpetual threat of international tensions. Jefferson's response to this situation was a balance-of-power strategy designed to avoid "entangling alliances" and to preserve his options by playing off each European power against the other. Unfortunately, American strength and importance were insufficient to affect the balance in ways that would have secured American interests.

Although the immediate aim of American foreign policy remained essentially the same as under the Federalists, Jefferson and Madison, in response to the sources of their political support, generated policies that tended to favor the interests of the South and Southwest. The Administration's Indian policy reflected such considerations. Jefferson was concerned both to promote economic prosperity in the region and to protect American borders. Both aims, in his judgment, required the removal of the Indians to the west of the Mississippi River and their transformation as far as was possible from nomadic hunters into farmers. In adopting the ways of civilization, as Malone observes in *Jefferson the President: First Term,* the Indians would require less land than they had needed for hunting; the remainder, ceded to the United States, would be used to establish a protective cordon of white settlement along the frontier borders. Jefferson's policy, while supportive of the interests of white settlers, reflected his conviction that the Indians' very survival depended upon their embrace of an established agricultural life. In his Second Inaugural Address, he denounced the counselors among the Indians who would have their people resist the march of progress, "to remain as their Creator made them, ignorance being safety, and knowledge full of danger" and to "maintain the ascendency of habit over the duty of improving our reason, and obeying its mandates." Jefferson had long maintained a scientific and humane, if paternal, interest in the Indians. His views toward them, while unsentimental, were benevolent. As president, he sought to live in peace and to engage in commercial relations with the tribes. He met often in Washington with visiting

delegations of tribal chiefs to hear their concerns. Through the expedition of Lewis and Clark, he sought scientific information about the trans-Mississippi tribes and he hoped to cultivate their friendship and win their trade.

Two other major issues were central to Jefferson's desire to serve the interests of the South and Southwest: the maintenance of American maritime commerce, especially the neutral carrying trade made so lucrative during the European war, and the settlement of lingering boundary disputes, notably the questions of free access to the mouth of the Mississippi River and the acquisition of the Floridas. While the former issue proved intractable, the latter problem seemed well in hand during Jefferson's first term when, through persistence and great good fortune, the Louisiana Purchase was achieved. No other event of Jefferson's presidency so altered the character of the nation. It serves to illustrate some of the assumptions that informed his conduct of the office.

Determined to defend the agricultural and commercial interests of the Southwest, Jefferson and Madison were alarmed in the spring of 1802 when they learned of the retrocession of Louisiana from a relatively feeble Spain to Napoleonic France. Jefferson was alive to the danger of "daily collisions" leading to possible war with France and so informed the French government. Robert Livingston, the minister to France, was instructed to negotiate for the cession of the port of New Orleans and, if possible, the Floridas. In the autumn, provoked by a sudden suspension of the right of deposit of goods at New Orleans, Jefferson sent James Monroe to Paris with full powers to purchase New Orleans. Word from Monroe of the purchase of all of Louisiana reached Jefferson on 3 July 1803, providing the nation with a happy birthday present. The president quickly seized the windfall, applauding his two envoys for exceeding the letter of their instructions. Popular reaction was overwhelmingly favorable. Jefferson's personal standing reached new heights.

For a time, the president's constitutional scruples, which held him to a narrow construction of his powers, threatened to mar the triumph. He was concerned about two related questions: the power to acquire new territory and the constitutionality of its incorporation into the Union. Cabinet discussions had temporarily resolved the first question in favor of an inherent right to acquire territory, derived from the fact of national sovereignty. Later Jefferson concluded that a constitutional amendment was needed to ratify the executive's action after the fact. Nevertheless, he was not so wedded to constitutional purity that he would risk the success of this magnificent "fugitive occurrence." Assured by his advisers and by key congressional colleagues that the constitutional sleeping dogs should be permitted to lie undisturbed lest Napoleon change his mind and revoke the agreement, Jefferson acquiesced "with satisfaction," confident that the good sense of the nation would never condone broad construction for evil purposes. In this instance, the strictures of Republican ideology, acknowledged by Jefferson to carry the force of logic, were nevertheless sensibly and properly made to yield to his conviction that the good public servant must risk himself and "accept great charges" on great occasions of high national interest.

Jefferson's good fortune in settling the issue of access to the Mississippi was not met by a corresponding success in acquiring the Floridas. The central problem was that the disputed territory belonged to Spain, then under French hegemony. As difficulties with France mounted after 1805, Spanish intransigence was encouraged quietly by the French. Attempts to negotiate a resolution of the problem failed utterly. American legal claims to Florida were dubious. Spain was in

no mood to surrender willingly a portion of its empire. Jefferson wanted the Floridas badly but was not ready to seize them and risk a war with Spain on such problematic grounds. He and Madison first tried to intimidate the Spanish and then sought to buy the territory with funds secretly appropriated by Congress. But backed by the French, Spain haughtily rejected all pressures, knowing that the United States was not prepared to back up its demands by force.

After 1805 the question of the Floridas was overshadowed by American struggles with Britain and France over the neutral carrying trade, an issue that put Jefferson's leadership to its severest test. British interference with American trade, highlighted by the problem of impressment, had been a source of strained relations since the Revolution. As a result of Britain's titanic struggle with Napoleon, tensions were raised to new heights. For the British, impressment and the interdiction of trade with their continental enemy were matters of necessity. But Jefferson saw things differently. The stopping of American vessels on the high seas for the forcible removal of seamen was a violation of human rights and an affront to the sovereignty of the United States. The president made a satisfactory resolution of the issue of impressment a *conditio sine qua non* in negotiations with Britain.

After a period of relative inaction, Britain resumed interdiction of American shipping in 1805. Impressment increased after Nelson's triumph at Trafalgar, coupled with the British Admiralty decision in the *Essex* case, which restored the "Rule of 1756," whereby a trade closed in time of peace (as was American trade with the French and Spanish West Indies) could not be opened in time of war. These events darkened relations with the British at a time when Napoleon, after his victory at Austerlitz, no longer needed to placate the Americans to fight his enemies.

The president's options seemed few. His was a policy of reaction, made necessary not only by the relative weakness of his resources but by the lack of timely information upon which to base proper initiatives. Sheer distance from the scene and the difficulty of communicating (reports from abroad and replies from Washington or Monticello could take from six to eight months to complete) often meant that decisions taken to meet one set of circumstances would be outmoded by altered cases long before they could be acted upon. For the most part, Jefferson sought to buy time and await events in the face of his difficulties.

Continuing British depradation of American ships and seamen reached a culmination on 22 June 1807, when the British frigate *Leopard* intercepted and boarded the American warship *Chesapeake* on the high seas, killing three seamen and impressing four others. Amid a storm of patriotic outrage, Jefferson believed that war with Britain was likely and fully justified, but by the winter, events had once more substantially altered cases. Napoleon's Berlin decree of 21 November, which ended French favoritism in the treatment of American neutral trade, turned public opinion sharply against the French, leaving the administration with the searing dilemma of which country to fight, Britain or France, or—horror of horrors—both at once. Jefferson and Madison sought to discover a policy that would avoid the undeniable costs of war while protecting America's vital trading interests from further humiliation. The result of this search, the embargo of 1807–1809, threatened to undo all of the achievements of the Jeffersonians and to destroy Jefferson's presidency.

The idea of economic coercion through embargo had long been considered an effective tool of policy by leading Republicans. Jefferson had urged nonimportation against the British before the Revolution. Even more than the president, Madison had been an advocate of its usefulness. Indeed, there is evidence that Madison was the policy's principal architect. Both believed that American commerce was so valuable to the warring powers that its curtailment or cessation would force their governments to moderate their policies.

On 18 December 1807, Jefferson sent a special message to Congress recommending a full embargo. In accompanying documents he informed the legislature of Napoleon's Berlin decree and of a report that the British were reviving impressment. Congressional action in approving the measure was swift, with little debate. Many members acted "largely on faith, in the belief that Jefferson and his advisers must have had good and sufficient reasons for advocating that particular policy at that particular time," as I noted in *Jefferson and the Presidency* (Johnstone, 268).

Jefferson originally understood the embargo as a temporary measure to protect American shipping, to play for time, and to prepare for war. Later, under Madison's influence, he saw it as a permanent policy of peaceful coercion, an alternative to war. Confusion over the purposes of the Embargo Act, indeed, led to serious difficulties in enforcing it.

No one foresaw the magnitude of the experiment so effortlessly begun in December 1807. Except for predictable grumbling from Federalist New England, the initial reaction to the embargo was favorable. Yet almost from the beginning, difficulties in enforcement loomed. Loopholes in the initial law permitted evasions of its intent. Gallatin obtained new legislation tightening the act and increasing penalties for its violation. As local pressures mounted nonetheless, violations increased, especially in regions bordering Canada and in the coastal waters of Georgia and the Carolinas. By the summer of 1808, Congress had enacted three supplementary embargo acts that extended executive enforcement powers beyond anything previously exercised by an American administration.

Jefferson sought to avoid direct involvement in the administration of the embargo, preferring to leave enforcement decisions to Gallatin and his custom officials. Nevertheless, as the weeks passed and violations grew, Jefferson seemed more and more obsessed by the need to prove that his experiment would succeed. His sporadic interventions were always on the side of stringent enforcement. All else seemed to take second place to the embargo; as he wrote to Gallatin on 27 May 1808: "I set down the exercise of commerce, merely for profit, as nothing when it carries with it the danger of defeating the objects of the embargo."

The success of the embargo depended upon the willingness of Britain and France to come to terms. Their refusal to do so doomed the policy to failure. No matter how diligent the enforcement at home, no American action could control decisions abroad. Nothing could be done but to wait patiently for the loss of trade to work its will. A patient policy proved impossible, however, given the growing impatience of Americans suffering under the domestic effects of the embargo. Jefferson overestimated the capacity of his countrymen to endure such economic hardship and political repression. He expected too much of human nature.

By November 1808, when Congress reconvened, it was evident that a reappraisal of the policy was necessary. The Republican party's fortunes had suffered in the recent elections, and more serious reverses were predicted. Returning members looked to the executive for guidance in determining a new policy, but Jefferson chose this time virtually to disclaim responsibility for leadership. Since the summer he had been less and less involved with the embargo. He was mentally and emotionally exhausted, weary of controversy and longing for retirement. With Madison's election as president, Jeffer-son determined to leave the major policy decisions to his successor. From the meeting of Congress in November until his retirement in March, Jefferson was *hors de combat.*

With the president's "abdication," Republican policy cohesion lessened dramatically. Madison and Gallatin tried to coordinate a new policy, but without the ultimate authority they could not act with effectiveness. The initiative shifted to Congress, where the mood was unpredictable and volatile. In a final humiliation of the president, Congress at last voted to repeal the embargo, to take effect on 4 March, the date of Madison's inauguration. Jefferson signed the bill into law three days before his retirement from public life.

JEFFERSON'S LEGACY

The failure of the embargo damaged the credibility of presidential leadership. It should not be surprising that a deep commitment to a policy whose failure was so momentous should discredit for a time the institution that conceived and carried it out. The embargo had been a presidential policy, proposed and administered by the executive. Its collapse served to undermine the prestige of executive policy-making and to hasten the shift of effective power to Congress.

In a larger sense, the embargo demonstrates the problematic nature of Jeffersonian policy. Forrest McDonald, a leading critic of Jefferson's presidency, has put it baldly: "Republican policy sorely impaired the nation's ability to determine its own destiny." Severe military and naval budget cuts reduced the president's leverage in defending the nation's interests. Jeffersonian taxing policies, especially the abolition of internal taxes and the reliance on customs duties, left the country's ability to pay for its defense painfully vulnerable to curtailment of foreign trade and tied American economic security to the control of Britain and its Royal Navy.

Difficulties in securing the independence of his very dependent country should not obscure the achievements of Jefferson as president, many of which were to have a lasting influence upon the shape and character of the office. Jefferson brought to the presidency the strongest personal leadership the office had yet experienced. He marshaled the force of his public prestige and the skills of his personality to the task of central policy leadership in his administration. As a president who enjoyed wide public support, he demonstrated in new and lasting ways the potential of the presidency as an institution of popular government.

As the first to combine the office of president with the role of party leader, Jefferson effectively bridged the separation of powers to provide masterful legislative leadership. He employed his considerable personal gifts for bargaining and conciliation to mobilize and direct his often uncongenial colleagues to achieve the party's program. He developed a host of informal resources of power —patronage, legislative lieutenants, his famous dinners, a party press—to develop a new conception of presidential government. He was the chief executive in fact as well as in name. He demonstrated effective use of cabinet advisers and administered the affairs of government with a concern for efficiency, service, and responsibility to the wishes of the majority of the people. It was, indeed, Jefferson's overriding purpose to make the institutions of public power truly reflective of the considered will of the majority. This may well be his most abiding legacy as president of the United States.

The West

DONALD JACKSON

THE Blue Ridge should have been a place of mystery and adventure, calling irresistibly to a young man like Thomas Jefferson as he rode across the fields of his beloved Albemarle County in Virginia. There were daily reminders of the fascinations that lay to the west. Jefferson's father, Peter, had surveyed deep into the wilds and collaborated on an important map. His neighbor Dr. Thomas Walker had traveled as far to the southwest as a place he called Cumberland Gap, pursuing the interests of the Loyal Land Company. Jefferson's teacher the Reverend James Maury hungered for knowledge of western geography and talked vaguely of sending men from the company as far as the Missouri River, "if that be the right name of it."

To all these stimuli Jefferson seemed immune. He did not care for land speculation and sold the western lands inherited from his father. He was not even tempted to ride across the ridge for the fun of it, although he made the forty-mile trip to Staunton on business as a new lawyer. Not until he was an old man in quest of healing waters for his aching body did he journey as far west as Warm Springs, a ride of only a few days. His physical presence beyond the Piedmont horizon was not important to him, yet events kept forcing him to consider, to deal with, and at last to adopt the West as part of his intellectual domain.

When as a young legislator he realized how vital the handling of western lands would be to the nation, he was forced to make this his problem. A central fact that he and all Americans had to face was that the original charters, granted to land companies by the British government, were so immense and indefinite—and thus conducive to conflict—that they hardly fit into a scheme whereby independent commonwealths might live together.

After 1745, the Crown had made many of these grants beyond the Alleghenies as a buffer against the French in the Ohio Valley. When the British victory in the French and Indian Wars dispelled the threat, the Crown no longer supported the land companies and indeed for a time set a complete ban on settlement beyond the mountains.

By the beginning of the Revolution, Jefferson was viewing Virginia's extensive land claims as the key to his vision for America as a nation of small farmers, with no "landless poor." He supported the successful move to make Kentucky a new Virginia county in 1776. The business of quieting Indian claims, the confusion over property titles, and the clamorous activities of speculators characterized the history of western lands during and immediately after the Revolution. Something resembling order in the trans-Allegheny region arrived when the Confederation proposed a plan requiring Virginia and other states to give up large holdings to Congress, which would then organize them into state governments. Virginia's holdings north of the Ohio would eventually become the property of the nation, a logical step toward the formation of western territories, in which Jefferson was to play a vital role.

His plan to bring the West under urgently needed control, as land-hungry settlers hurried along the watercourses of the Ohio Valley, lay in two ordinances that he had helped to advance as a member of the Continental Congress. A system of government for western lands became law in 1784. Although superseded by the Northwest Ordinance of 1787, it formed the basis of that piece of legislation, providing as it did that new states arising out of the western regions should come into the Union on the same basis as the original thirteen. Another ordinance that never became law but that bore the mark of Jefferson's ingenuity was a system for the orderly surveying and sale of lands, some aspects of which may still be seen on the plats and deeds of today's land documents.

DEVELOPING A NATIONAL VIEWPOINT

Jefferson's participation in the control of western land use was to sharpen his view of America as a national entity. An important step in his eventual "adoption" of the West was the writing of his *Notes on the State of Virginia,* his only book-length work. By the time he had studied and theorized about western geography as far as the Pacific and drawn together all that was known of the natural history of the continent, he had become a permanent and avid student of the West—collecting books in large numbers, assembling vocabulary lists from distant Indian tribes, and eventually sending exploring parties to answer in person the questions teeming in his mind about the Rocky Mountains, the Missouri River, and the Oregon country.

Jefferson had made a gesture, but hardly more, toward western exploration. In December 1783 he had written his longtime friend George Rogers Clark, hero of western victories during the Revolution, asking if the old soldier would consider leading such an expedition. During the Revolution, Jefferson had embraced the view of his fellow Virginian that Detroit and settlements along the Ohio were crucial for ensuring victory over the British. As governor, Jefferson had worked closely with Clark in planning and funding campaigns that were vital in securing the Old Northwest. Now he turned to Clark for an exploit in a more distant Northwest: "I am afraid they [the British] have thoughts of colonising into that quarter. Some of us have been talking here in a feeble way of making the attempt to search that country. . . . How would you like to lead such a party?" Jefferson probably made the inquiry not on behalf of the government, but as a member of the American Philosophical Society at Philadelphia. General Clark said he was so infirm and so beaten down by debt and adversity that he must decline.

Jefferson's appointment as minister plenipotentiary to the Court of France, which was to lead to a five-year stay abroad, might have diminished his interest in the western country. Instead, it offered him new ways to hone his enthusiasm. The bookstalls of Europe held treasures for him, volumes that he would later ship to Monticello in box upon box, works such as Louis Hennepin's *Description de la Louisiane* (1683), Daniel Coxe's *Description of the English Province of Carolana* (1741), and Pierre François Xavier de Charlevoix's *Histoire et description générale de la Nouvelle France* (1744). Eventually a printed catalog of his library would devote 197 pages to works on American geography and exploration.

In Paris he met a young Connecticut adventurer, John Ledyard, who had sailed with Captain James Cook and published a journal of his experiences. Ledyard was the first American known to have set foot in the Pacific Northwest and to report the riches to be harvested there in the form of sea-otter skins for the markets of Canton and London. Now he tempted Jefferson with a new notion. He would find a ship and return to Nootka Sound and other locations on the Pacific Coast to establish an American fur-trading business.

Although Jefferson and other Americans in Europe contributed money to Ledyard's proposal, the plan failed. It was followed by an even more visionary idea, which Jefferson thought this moon-gazing wanderer might bring to pass. Ledyard would travel through Europe to Russia, make his way across Siberia to the Kamchatka Peninsula, cross to the Pacific Coast of North America, and walk overland to the East Coast. It was a terrible idea, but Ledyard set forth and got as far as Siberia before he was expelled by Catherine, empress of Russia.

Jefferson now had another concern that involved the Pacific Northwest. France was about to launch an official voyage, meant to rival the successes of Captain Cook, and had chosen Admiral Jean François de Lapérouse to command a two-ship flotilla. One purpose of the expedition, carefully monitored by Louis XVI himself, was to search for the fabled Northwest Passage. Another motive, unverified but suspected by Jefferson, was to

seek a place for settlement in case France should enter the sea-otter trade. Jefferson's concern is shown in his comment to John Jay in his letter of 14 August 1785: "They give out that the object is merely for the improvement of our knowledge of the geography of that part of the globe. Their loading . . . and some other circumstances appear to me to indicate some other design; perhaps that of colonising on the West[n] coast of America, or perhaps to establish one or more factories there for the fur trade."

Lapérouse explored the Pacific Coast and selected a spot called Lituya Bay, in Alaska, as a possible fur-trading site. But his expedition failed when both his ships were unexplainably lost. Perhaps as an indication of Jefferson's total lack of interest when this threat of colonization was removed, he failed to purchase the journals of Lapérouse, published posthumously.

When he returned from France, and during the time he served as secretary of state and vice-president, Jefferson was involved in two more attempts to send American exploring parties westward, both sponsored by the American Philosophical Society. One can scarcely be called more than an inquiry made to botanist Moses Marshall about his possible interest in such an enterprise. The other, however, was the first thoroughly documented attempt to mount such an expedition.

French botanist André Michaux, who had been traveling and collecting botanical specimens in the United States for a decade, was naturally drawn for intellectual companionship to members of the society. He was received eagerly by its members and by the leaders of government. When Michaux visited Mount Vernon in 1786, George Washington offered to give him "any assistance in my power." Washington, Jefferson, and many notable Americans were quick to sign a subscription paper to raise money for Michaux's proposed travels to the West in 1793.

For Jefferson, this presented an opportunity to articulate his thoughts on what such an expedition should seek. Selected to draft the society's instructions to Michaux, he wrote a long letter dated 30 April 1793 that said in part, "You will, in the course of your journey, take notice of the country you pass through, its general face, soil, rivers, mountains, its production animal, vegetable, & mineral so far as they may be new to us." Of the Indians, he asked for "such particularities as you can learn of their history, connection with each other, languages, manners, state of society & of the arts & commerce among them." These were the thoughts of a man who still believed that the Blue Ridge Mountains of Virginia might be the highest on the continent and that the mammoth, the giant ground sloth, and other prehistoric creatures might still roam the West.

Michaux had gone no farther than Kentucky when the hidden political motive for his trip was discovered. Backed by elements of the French Republic, he had been instructed to raise a western force to attack Spanish settlements west of the Mississippi. The intrigue was uncovered when he approached such prominent western figures as George Rogers Clark for help, and he was recalled.

A common misconception is that when Jefferson became president in 1801 he began at once to plan an official expedition into the West. The facts do not support this version of history. It is commonly thought that Jefferson hired Meriwether Lewis as his private secretary or aide, soon after taking office, for the purpose of training him to lead such a venture. Apparently this was not so.

Jefferson had run for office on a platform that included a heavy reduction in the armed forces. By the end of his first year, the army of fifty-four hundred had been reduced by half. Knowing little of the military, the president eliminated the cavalry and reduced the number of engineers and artillerists. He nat-

urally relied upon various consultants, but he employed Captain Lewis expressly to advise him in this process.

In offering Lewis the position of private secretary (a kind of administrative assistant), Jefferson referred to "your knolege of the Western country, of the army and of all it's interests & relations." Historians have seized upon the term *Western country* as evidence that Jefferson planned a far-western expedition, forgetting that in common parlance the West meant the Ohio Valley, where young Lewis had served. Jefferson offered Lewis the appointment because he had known him since his boyhood, trusted his judgment, and needed his knowledge of the army to help in the reduction. Among Jefferson's papers in the Library of Congress is a document in Lewis' hand, rating the officers then in active service in terms of their military qualities and—most important to an administration that had just defeated the Federalists—their political leanings.

Jefferson took no action toward organizing an exploring team until he had read an important book. Late in 1801, Alexander Mackenzie's *Voyages . . . Through the Continent of North America, to the Frozen and Pacific Ocean* was published in London and was soon available in Philadelphia and New York. British trader Mackenzie had journeyed across Canada and reached the Pacific in 1793. At the end of his narrative he urged the British to act quickly in placing a trading house in the Pacific Northwest.

By the end of 1802 Jefferson had read the work and was taking steps to organize an American expedition to the region that had interested Mackenzie. It was not until then that Lewis the administrative assistant became Lewis the trainee for western exploration.

Lewis was replaced as Jefferson's aide but retained his captaincy. For the next year his assignment was to study in Jefferson's remarkable library; consult with various members of the American Philosophical Society on such subjects as zoology, botany, geology, and Indian ethnology; learn the rudiments of astronomical observation; and obtain advice from Dr. Benjamin Rush, the country's most notable medical expert, on health problems that he and his men might encounter.

With an amateur's interest in natural history, particularly botany, and the constitution of a man who had grown up in the rugged outdoors not far from Jefferson's own home, all that seemed lacking was a partner equally motivated and trained to lead men, who might in an emergency take over what until now had been known as "Mr. Lewis's tour." Lewis chose William Clark, younger brother of General Clark, a former Virginian and the equal of Lewis in woodsmanship, bravery, and the proven ability to lead—he had been captain of a company under Gen. Anthony Wayne in the Indian wars of the 1790s.

Jefferson himself would have made a splendid explorer if intellectual curiosity, a knowledge of natural history, and skills as a surveyor and astronomer were all that counted. Yet he might have failed wretchedly for two reasons: he was beset by real and imagined ills, with a lifetime history of migraine headaches, and he was psychologically unable to detach himself from his family. A breakdown in the mail between Monticello and Washington filled him with apprehension and pique.

So, with these shortcomings and his total lack of desire to explore in person, he became one of the finest armchair explorers of all time. His interest in detail as he and Lewis planned the expedition led him to seek formulas for finding the longitude without a timepiece; to write a letter of credit in case the explorers should meet with white traders on the Pacific Coast; to ponder with Lewis the correct amount of beads to carry as gifts and bartering goods for the Indians (they failed to include enough blue beads); and to arrange codes by which Lewis could secretly communicate with him along the way.

His written instructions to Lewis were reminiscent of those he had given to Michaux but were much more detailed. On 20 June 1803 he wrote:

The object of your mission is to explore the Missouri river, & such principal stream of it, as, by it's course & communication with the water of the Pacific Ocean, whether the Columbia, Oregon, Colorado or any other river may offer the most direct & practicable water communication across this continent, for the purposes of commerce.

Beginning at the mouth of the Missouri, you will take observations of latitude and longitude at all remarkable points on the river, & especially at the mouths of rivers, at rapids, at islands & other places. . . .

The interesting points of the portage between the heads of the Missouri & the water offering the best communication with the Pacific Ocean should be fixed by observation & the course of that water to the ocean, in the same manner as that of the Missouri.

Your observations are to be taken with great pains & accuracy, to be entered distinctly, & intelligibly for others as well as yourself, to comprehend all the elements necessary, with the aid of the usual tables to fix the latitude & longitude of the places at which they were taken. . . . Several copies of these as well as of your other notes, should be made at leisure times & put into the care of the most trustworthy of your attendants, to guard by multiplying them against the accidental losses to which they will be exposed. A further guard would be that one of these copies be written on the paper of the birch, as less liable to injury from damp than common paper. . . .

In all your intercourse with the natives treat them in the most friendly & conciliatory manner which their own conduct will admit; allay all jealousies as to the object of your journey, satisfy them of it's innocence, make them acquainted with the position, extent, character, peaceable & commercial dispositions of the U.S.

Even after Lewis had left Washington, had gone to Pittsburgh to build a fifty-five-foot keelboat, and was making his way down the Ohio to join Clark, Jefferson's letters followed him. Jefferson wrote to say that Lewis had left a pocketbook and a dirk, which would be sent after him, but that the bridle he left behind was too bulky to send by post. He passed on the last bit of geographical data he had obtained from a French savant. Only when Lewis and Clark had reached St. Louis and were headed up the Missouri would they pass beyond the guidance of Jefferson's pen.

EXPLORATION AND A CRUCIAL PURCHASE

In the beginning all these arrangements were being made to cross a part of the continent claimed by other countries. Some diplomacy was necessary. Jefferson obtained passports for the expedition from France, Spain, and Great Britain, stressing that the undertaking was entirely "literary," by which he meant it was in the interest of knowledge. At the same time, he tried to keep the matter secret from political enemies he thought might thwart it. He set the financial requirements at a ridiculously low $2,500 and allowed the belief to spread that the expedition was bound up the Mississippi, not the Missouri. In his message to Congress of 18 January 1803, Jefferson stressed the "extension of public commerce" and the desirability of bringing western Indian tribes into the factory or trade system through which the government now dealt commercially with tribes east of the Mississippi.

Lewis was at the point of leaving Washington in July 1803 when Jefferson received informally the word that Spain had ceded the whole of Louisiana Territory, the vastness of which could only be surmised. The Louisiana Territory had first been claimed by

France but was ceded to Spain in 1762, and was then retroceded to France by the Treaty of San Ildefonso in 1800. As the Spanish had never vacated the settled areas, the territory was in effect a French domain governed by Spanish officials.

Fearing that France might close the port of New Orleans and thus affect the commerce of the inland United States, Jefferson sent James Monroe as a special envoy to Paris to join with Robert Livingston, minister to France, in an effort to purchase an area at the mouth of the Mississippi that would forever protect the freedom of American shipping. Instead of offering New Orleans and East and West Florida for sale, Napoleon's foreign minister, Charles Maurice de Talleyrand, jarred Livingston—and eventually the American government—by offering to sell the entire territory. The effect on American growth was to be monumental, and an immediate result was the transformation of the Lewis and Clark Expedition from a low-profile, "literary" examination of another country's terrain to a public undertaking that a whole nation could watch and support.

When Aaron Burr turned to the West in 1805 and 1806, in a plan that suggested conspiracy if not actual treason, Jefferson was apprehensive that his schemes might separate a portion of the Old Southwest from the nation. While apparently willing to try extralegal means in suppressing Burr's activities, Jefferson seemed unsure about the role of James Wilkinson, federal governor of the Louisiana Territory. Whether Wilkinson was the mastermind behind Burr's intrigues is still a debatable subject. In a famous trial held in Richmond, Virginia, before Chief Justice John Marshall, Burr was acquitted of treason in 1807.

Lewis descended the Ohio in low water, several times hiring oxen or horses to pull his cumbersome keelboat out of the shallows. He met Clark either in Louisville or in Clarksville across the river and found that his old army colleague had recruited nine vigorous young men for the expedition. These, together with Lewis' own recruits and some soldiers from posts in the area, were to be the core of a band of men now famous in American history: John Colter, the discoverer of the wonders of Yellowstone; George Shannon, later to become a judge in Missouri; George Drouillard, hunter and interpreter; Patrick Gass, first to publish a book about the adventure; Charles Floyd, doomed to die of probable acute appendicitis before the expedition had passed the site of Sioux City.

By early December, Lewis and Clark had chosen a winter camp on the east side of the Mississippi where Dubois' River (now Wood River) enters. In a manner that was to become customary for them, the two leaders divided their work according to their skills. Clark stayed in camp and trained the men, assembled equipment, and drew a map. He was to reveal the greater ability as a cartographer, and all but a scrap or two of the incredible number of maps that were generated by the expedition came from Clark's hand. For the moment, Lewis played the diplomat and approached Spanish officials and prominent citizens across the river in St. Louis.

No official instructions about the transfer of the Territory had yet reached the city. Until they arrived, Governor Carlos Dehault Delassus denied Lewis and Clark the right to make a preliminary sortie up the Missouri. Everyone more or less settled down to await what promised to be an exciting spring, when the Spanish would turn a French domain over to the Americans, who were waiting to explore it.

By mid-May 1804, the transfer of Louisiana had been achieved. Lewis and Clark had forwarded as much information as they could to Jefferson and had even dispatched a delegation of Osage Indians to visit him in Washington. With twenty-seven men in their permanent party and about twenty others who were French boatmen or soldiers scheduled to return after the first winter, the expedition left its Dubois' River encampment and headed upstream on 14 May. Besides the keelboat, equipped with a sail, they moved in two smaller craft while hunters ranged the shores on horseback. Clark, whose spelling already had become one of the wonders of the adventure, began his all-important journal with the notation that they were proceeding "under a jentle brease."

By mid-October the expedition had made its way along the shores that later were to bear the names Missouri, Kansas, Iowa, Nebraska, South Dakota, and North Dakota. They had counseled with all the tribes along the way—the Oto, Missouri, Omaha, Ponca, Yankton Sioux, and Arikara—and had made a fine start toward collecting specimens of plants and animals unknown to the scientists of the American Philosophical Society. The two commanders decided to spend the winter among the Mandans above present Bismarck, North Dakota, gearing up for the long push across the mountains the following year.

The shipment that reached Jefferson that summer must have afforded him many a long evening's pleasure in his study at Monticello. The letters and maps have mainly survived and been made available for study. With those vital documents came a living magpie and prairie dog, survivors of a small menagerie that had been passed from hand to hand by way of New Orleans and up the coast by sea. There were magnificent Indian artifacts—robes, ornaments, and pottery. And there were not only descriptions but skins and skeletons of birds and animals that are commonplace today but were novelties then: the pronghorn, jackrabbit, coyote, grizzly bear, and black-tailed deer, and such common prairie plants as rabbit brush, pink cleome, and buffalo berry.

On 7 April 1805, when they were ready to proceed, Lewis wrote to Jefferson, "Our baggage is all embarked on board six small canoes and two perogues [dugouts]; we shall set out at the same moment that we dispatch the barge [keelboat]." They were sending the keelboat home with all their collections and surplus personnel. Continuing with them were two notable additions to the roster, interpreter Toussaint Charbonneau and his wife, Sacagawea.

"We do not calculate on completeing our voyage within the present year," Lewis wrote, "but expect to reach the Pacific Ocean, and return, as far as the head of the Missouri, or perhaps to this place before winter. You may therefore expect me to meet you at Montachello in September 1806." His estimate was not far off; they would be back in St. Louis by September 1806 and in Washington by the end of that year.

The expedition left the quarters they called Fort Mandan on 7 April 1805, entering waters that no white man had traveled. The party now contained thirty-two men and the young woman Sacagawea, who, being a Shoshoni captured in earlier days, was in familiar country.

A few days later Clark entered in his journal a line that seemed to foretell the discomfort, the hazards, and the sheer sweaty labor that lay ahead: "I saw a Musquetor to day." His journals were, as always, informative although misleadingly crude in spelling and grammar, containing such phrases as: "Saw great numbers of Gees feedin in the Praries. . . . The countrey to day as usial. . . . Formed a camp in a butifull elivated plain. . . . I saw the remains of two Indian incampmints with wide beeten tracks leading to them."

In two weeks they passed the mouth of the Yellowstone River, which they correctly believed would make an excellent site for a future military post. They made their way across what is now Montana, giving names to rivers and other topographic features: the Milk River, the Marias River, the Great Falls, and finally—where the Missouri divided into three separate streams—the Jefferson, Madison, and Gallatin. Their water travel was interrupted by a bitterly arduous crossing of the mountains, made possible by horses obtained from the friendly Shoshonis. They then made a descent of watercourses that led them to the great Columbia River and finally to the Pacific.

After wintering in quarters that they christened Fort Clatsop in honor of the local Indian tribe, enduring chill rain and scanty rations, they began their return in the spring of 1806. Clark traversed a part of the Yellowstone on the homeward trip; Lewis veered northward to scout the Marias, in case it was the northernmost arm of the Missouri watershed and thus vital in determining the boundaries of the Louisiana Purchase.

The adventure had been an unusually lucky one. Except for the death of Sergeant Floyd, who could not have been saved by any known medical procedure, and the killing of two Piegan Indians attempting to steal some of Lewis' horses on his Marias River trip, the mishaps had been worrisome but endurable: encounters with grizzlies; overturnings of canoes, with some loss of supplies; a face-off with a band of demanding Teton Sioux; hordes of mosquitoes; and a gunshot wound that Lewis received in the backside when a one-eyed French hunter with the expedition mistook him for an elk in the underbrush.

Perhaps the chief worrier was Jefferson himself, who had heard nothing authentic from the group since receiving the shipment of papers and specimens more than a year earlier. The strain shows in the letter he wrote to Lewis on 26 October 1806 upon learning of their safe arrival: "I received, my dear Sir, with unspeakable joy your letter of Sep. 23 announcing the return of yourself, Cap. Clarke & your party in good health to St. Louis. The unknown scenes in which you were engaged, & the length of time without hearing of you had begun to be felt awfully."

The Lewis and Clark Expedition was a remarkable odyssey, and the way the American people have remembered and celebrated it is equally remarkable. Jefferson spent years attempting to make sure that the journals, maps, and artifacts of the voyage were secure; most of them went to the American Philosophical Society. He appointed Lewis governor of Upper Louisiana and Clark superintendent of Indian Affairs for that region, both with headquarters in St. Louis. After Lewis' death—probably by suicide—in 1809, Jefferson and Clark worked together to see that a narrative of the expedition was prepared.

The original journals were published in 1904–1905 and are being reedited for publication today. The trail is followed annually by hardy admirers of the undertaking. Books are published in increasing numbers, telling and retelling the basic story, and an association of scholars and amateurs called the Lewis and Clark Trail Heritage Foundation meets every year in a place selected from those made notable by the expedition.

AN EXPANDING PLAN OF EXPLORATION

The Lewis and Clark Expedition had been a response to Alexander Mackenzie's challenge. Now that a territory of unimaginable and uncharted dimensions had been added to the United States, exploration was no longer a "literary" matter or tour de force. It became an essential object of national policy.

Far to the west, along the undefined boundary between Spain and the U.S., Spain protested the Louisiana Purchase, claiming France had no right to make the sale, objecting especially to the extent of the purchase. No one had—indeed, no one could have—delineated the boundaries, and the framers of the treaty had been content to say vaguely that the Louisiana Territory embraced the

same area that it had covered when France ceded it to Spain in 1762. The Lewis and Clark discoveries had answered some of the questions; others remained to be settled before westward expansion could proceed.

The need for further exploration was evident to Jefferson before Lewis and Clark had gone up the Missouri. He wrote of his plans to a correspondent near Natchez, Mississippi Territory, a man who was later to become a kind of western representative for Jefferson in matters of exploration. He was William Dunbar, a Scottish plantation owner whose interest in geography and the sciences was nearly as great as Jefferson's.

Writing to Dunbar on 13 March 1804, Jefferson said he planned to assign the task of exploring the Upper Mississippi to the surveyor-general, and that he expected Congress to provide funds for the exploration of the western rivers:

> In this case I should propose to send one party up the Panis river [Platte and North Platte], thence along the highlands to the source of the Padoucas river [South Platte], and down to it's mouth. Another party up the Arcansa[s] to it's source, thence along the highlands to the source of the Red river, & down that to it's mouth. . . . These surveys will enable us to prepare a map of La. which in it's contour and main waters will be perfectly correct.

Dunbar accepted the job of coordinating on the frontier the arrangements to explore the Red and Arkansas rivers. The Red River, which Jefferson called "in truth, next to the Missouri, the most interesting water of the Mississippi," originates in the Llano Estacado or staked plains region of eastern New Mexico and west Texas, in a confusion of small tributaries. It then meanders about 1,200 miles before joining the Mississippi in Louisiana. It was reported to be a rich stream, especially along its lower reaches, the shores thriving with new plant species and a variety of animal life; and it was thought to be navigable for a thousand miles. Dunbar wrote Jefferson that the Red flowed through "immense regions of the richest and most fertile lands," which would support a large population.

It was never intended that Dunbar should personally accompany any exploring party, but delays in getting a Red River expedition moving, due mostly to opposition from the Spanish, changed that policy. As a means of keeping the Red River personnel together while dealing with the objections, Jefferson authorized a minor exploration of the Ouachita River, which flows out of the Ouachita Mountains and joins the Red before entering the Mississippi below Natchez. Dunbar personally led this exploration, accompanied by Dr. George Hunter.

Spanish opposition to an expedition up the Red River appeared early. Jefferson began negotiations in mid-1805, asking the Spanish minister in New Orleans for a passport. Through William C. C. Claiborne, governor of the Territory of Orleans, he explained that the trip was to be purely geographic and that he was willing for two Spanish observers to accompany the party. In his letter of 26 May 1805 he wrote, "As we have to settle a boundary with Spain to the Westward, they cannot expect us to go blindfold into the business."

The Spanish official in New Orleans granted the passport, but it was canceled by Nemesio Salcedo, commandant-general in Chihuahua, who declared the enterprise hostile to Spanish interests. In a letter to the Marqués de Casa Calvo on 8 October he wrote, "The Governors of the Provinces adjacent to the United States are ordered to Suspend the operations of any and all expeditions which may present themselves, and therefore it is to be expected that [the expedition] of Mr. Dumbar will be so treated by them."

Despite Jefferson's usual sensitivity to Spanish obdurance, and indeed his chronic apprehension that some untoward action might set the two nations at war, he seems in this case to be the only person involved who thought the venture would succeed. He had plenty of warning. Claiborne wrote him on 26 March 1806 that Thomas Freeman, an engineer and surveyor appointed to lead the exploration, had arrived in New Orleans: "I very much fear he will be interrupted in his excursion by our jealous and ill-disposed Spanish neighbors."

Jefferson might have been expected to delay or cancel the expedition. Instead he ordered General James Wilkinson, commanding general of the U.S. Army, to leave his location in St. Louis and report to New Orleans. In ordering him to move, Secretary of War Henry Dearborn wrote on 6 May that "the hostile views of the Officers of his Catholic Majesty in that quarter, have become so evident, as to require the strictest precaution on the part of the United States."

Freeman and his assistant, a young doctor named Peter Custis who postponed receiving his M.D. degree from the University of Pennsylvania, left from Fort Adams a few miles below Natchez on 19 April 1806. They were guarded by a military detachment of about twenty men headed by Capt. Richard Sparks, and transported in two flat-bottomed barges and a pirogue. Later the detachment would be increased to forty men in seven vessels.

Freeman hoped to find the headwaters of the Red and then obtain horses from the Pawnees by which the party would continue to the Rockies. He was to return by the same route and prepare to ascend the Arkansas the following year.

By early June the expedition had reached a point about forty-five miles above Natchitoches, the most distant American outpost, and on the next day Freeman learned that a Spanish detachment was on the way to intercept him. Until the confrontation occurred he had no recourse but to follow orders and continue up the river. While advancing to meet the Spanish, the men achieved what was perhaps the ultimate in futility by getting their boats through the notorious Great

Raft, a giant mass of logs and brush nearly 100 miles long that the French perceptively called an *embarras.*

Freeman's nemesis was Don Francisco Viana, adjutant and inspector of the Internal Provinces of New Spain, who commanded the post at Nacogdoches in eastern Texas. With a detachment far outnumbering Freeman's little party, Viana halted the expedition on 29 July near where the states of Texas, Oklahoma, and Arkansas now meet. Freeman wrote in his journal, "In this conference the Spanish Commanding officer stated that his orders were not to suffer any body of armed troops to march through the territory of the Spanish Government; to stop the exploring party by force, and to fire on them if they persisted in ascending the river, before the limits of the territory were defined."

As hopeless as it seemed, Freeman went through the motions of terminating his voyage with some dignity. On that same day he wrote, "I stated that the object of my expedition was, to explore the river to its source, under the instructions of the President of the U.S. and I requested the Spanish commander to state in writing his objections to the progress of the party, and the authority upon which it was made." Viana refused to do so but pledged on his honor that he was acting under orders of his government.

By turning back after the parley, Freeman and his men avoided certain failure. The water was becoming too shoaly to keep the boats afloat, and not enough barter had been brought for the purchase of horses, even if the group could have made it to an area where Pawnee or Osage horses could be obtained.

That fall, General Wilkinson reached an agreement with the Spanish to withdraw beyond the Sabine River. He would keep his own forces east of the Arroyo Hondo, near Natchitoches, establishing an area of neutral ground between the two rivers.

In fairness to Jefferson, it must be observed that he was a victim of slow communication—he was forced to act without knowing what was occurring thousands of miles away. When he dispatched Freeman and Custis he did not know, for example, that the Spanish had tried three times to intercept Lewis and Clark, failing only because of poor timing and lack of knowledge about where the Missouri ran. Also, he did not know that they had succeeded in capturing Captain Zebulon Montgomery Pike and were not to release him until he had been taken under guard to Chihuahua, and that an exchange of acerbic diplomatic letters would follow.

Zebulon Montgomery Pike, a young army officer, must have seemed to Jefferson a man who was rising through the ranks with few qualifications except gall and luck. In the end it would be shown he possessed great courage, too, but it must have seemed to Jefferson that he was getting in the way of the master plan for exploring the West.

Pike's heart was with the military service. His friends called him Montgomery to distinguish him from old Major Zebulon Pike, his father, whose dull career as an officer young Montgomery did not intend to emulate. He was a potential protégé looking for a patron when in 1805 he came to the attention of General James Wilkinson. Until then, Pike's most prestigious assignment had been that of regimental paymaster for the First Regiment of Infantry. Perhaps he was the only officer available when Wilkinson decided to send an exploring party up the Mississippi. Or perhaps the dogged zeal with which he tackled every assignment had come to the general's attention. In any case, his career took on new luster when he was picked by Wilkinson for this special assignment, even though he had now dedicated himself to the service of one of the nation's truly knavish leaders.

To say that Wilkinson was a profoundly dishonest and self-serving man, ready to betray his country as quickly as he would betray a friend, is to reveal nothing new. He was a coconspirator with Aaron Burr in a plan to separate the western states from the Union and may have been the author of that plan, betraying Burr when failure seemed imminent. He received annual payments from Spain while serving as commanding general of the U. S. Army, a fact unproven during Jefferson's lifetime.

Jefferson was surprisingly easy on Wilkinson even when the facts, as brought out in courts of inquiry, seemed to indict the man. It must have been hard, however, for Jefferson to forgive him when he got in the way of the orderly exploration of the West. Jefferson had planned to put the surveyor-general in charge of exploring the Upper Mississippi, but Wilkinson beat him to it by dispatching Pike on that mission. Then Jefferson sent Freeman and Custis up the Red River, only to discover that Wilkinson had set Pike at the same task. For these reasons, Jefferson never fully accepted Pike as one of "his" explorers and never accorded him the respect he gave to Lewis and Clark.

Wilkinson had provided Pike a sextant and expected him to determine the "latitude with exactitude," but Pike's training with the instrument was scanty and the maps he brought back were of little value. Beyond the edges of civilization, he depended on a map belonging to Baron Alexander von Humboldt, the German explorer, who had never been in the region.

After escorting some Osages back to their villages and counseling with the Pawnee, Pike headed west along the Arkansas. At Great Bend, in Kansas, he detached a junior officer (Wilkinson's son James) according to orders and set out for the Rockies with a small party that included Dr. John Hamilton Robinson, interpreter Antoine F. Baronet Vásquez, and a dozen enlisted soldiers.

The ensuing fall and winter were a nightmare of cold, hunger, and navigational blunders. From a base camp at what is now Pueblo, Colorado, Pike, with Dr. Robinson and two privates, undertook a side trip to ascend the peak that now bears his name. Deceived by the apparent nearness of the mountain and faced with the difficult terrain and the harshness of the weather, he gave up the climb. During the next two months he left the Arkansas and traveled north into South Park, found the river again, and thought for a while that it was the Red. Later, across the Sangre de Cristo range, he built a small stockade on the west side of a river that he felt sure was the Red but that was actually the Rio Grande. He had erected a flagstaff and run up the American flag in Spanish territory.

The detachment of Spanish regulars and militiamen who picked him up and took him to Santa Fe seemed to know that he was coming. Dr. Robinson, who in later years would attempt to lead a filibustering expedition into Mexico, made overtures to the Spanish. The episode contained still unexplained aspects, typical of most Wilkinson projects, and since that time many historians have been convinced that Pike was somehow connected with the intrigues of Wilkinson and Burr. Despite these mysteries, there is every reason to believe that he was truly lost in an uncharted region, and that any interest he had in Santa Fe and the Spanish settlements was that of a loyal soldier keeping his eyes open on behalf of his government. After retrieving the stragglers he had left in the mountains, some ill and crippled by frostbite, he was taken to Chihuahua, escorted to the Texas-Louisiana boundary, and released in June 1807. Several of his men were detained longer, one for several years because he had killed a comrade while in a Chihuahua stockade.

Jefferson first learned of Pike's detention from a letter sent to Wilkinson by Salcedo on 8 April 1807. The commandant-general scolded the U.S. government for sending expeditions "into territories unquestionably belonging to his majesty" and insisted that "an offense of magnitude has been committed." Instead of considering Pike and his men prisoners, however, he said that in the interest of "harmony and good understanding" he was sending them home.

Realizing the importance of the official reply with respect to future boundary negotiations, Jefferson articulated for the War Department, in a letter to Dearborn on 22 June 1807, the gist of the reply he wanted Wilkinson to make:

On the transfer of Louisiana by France to the U.S. according to it's boundaries when possessed by France, the government of the U.S. considered itself entitled as far West as the Rio Norte [Rio Grande]: but understanding soon after that Spain on the contrary, claimed Eastwardly to the river Sabine, it has carefully abstained from doing any act in the intermediate country, which might disturb the existing state of things until these opposing claims should be explained and accomodated amicably. But that the Red river and all it's waters belonged to France, that she made several settlements on that river, and held them as a part of Louisiana until she delivered that country to Spain, & that Spain on the contrary had never made a single settlement on the river, are circumstances so well known, & so susceptible of proof, that it was not supposed that Spain would seriously contest the facts, or the right established by them. Hence our government took measures for exploring that river, as it did that of the Missouri, by sending Mr. Freeman to proceed from the mouth upwards, & Lieutenant [now Captain] Pike from the source downwards, merely to acquire the geography, and so far enlarge the boundaries of science. . . . I am persuaded that it must have been, as he himself declares, by missing his way, that he got on the waters of the Rio Norte, instead of those of the Red river.

Here Jefferson seems to include Pike's exploration as part of his master plan, after the fact. But that he did not recognize Pike's adventures on the Arkansas and elsewhere as anything but a kind of military survey is shown in his insistence that his own exploration of the Arkansas should proceed, even if Pike returned.

Convinced that his achievement was equal to that of Lewis and Clark, Pike expected similar acclaim. He waited in vain while friends on Capitol Hill lobbied for awards of land to him and his men, who obviously had suffered more than the members of the Lewis and Clark Expedition. The fact that they had not been volunteers, and that Pike was suspected by some of involvement in the Burr conspiracy, dampened the interest of Congress. Pike courted Jefferson's attention, bringing him a pair of grizzly cubs from Mexico and "a box and quiver of arrows which are the offensive weapons of the Appaches." Jefferson thanked Pike briefly and praised him in his next message to Congress. General Wilkinson continued to promote the hapless explorer's military career, and Pike rose quickly through the ranks. He was a brigadier general by 1813, when he was killed by the explosion of a powder magazine while commanding a force against the British.

Early in 1807, preparations were going forward for the second Freeman expedition. It was on Jefferson's mind on 14 February when he sent Dearborn a memorandum that he thought might aid "Freeman and our future explorers."

In Natchez, meanwhile, Freeman was proceeding in cooperation with the commander of his military detachment, Lieutenant James B. Wilkinson, Jr., who had come down the Arkansas the previous autumn. He had made few observations and lay ill in a small boat during most of the descent, but he was available and willing. William Dunbar was still in the picture, trying hard to find a naturalist since Peter Custis had returned to Philadelphia for his diploma and was now practicing medicine on the eastern shore of Virginia.

Because of the old problem of erratic communication, Dunbar and Freeman were still vigorously planning the Arkansas expedition six weeks after it was unaccountably canceled. By a letter of 30 March, Secretary Dearborn had written to Dunbar that Congress "by some mistake or inattention" had neglected to appropriate money for the expedition. Jefferson, he wrote, had directed him to suspend all plans "for the present season."

It may be as simple as Dearborn said it was. On the other hand, Jefferson may finally have grown tired of confronting the Spanish. A year later, when he received word from a resident of Vincennes, Indiana, of a silver mine on the Platte River, he wrote that he hoped to learn more about the Platte "after a settlement with Spain, as we wish to become acquainted with all the advantageous water connections across our continent."

RESPONDING AGAIN TO THE BRITISH

As one of the chores by which he earned his periodic honoraria from Spain, General Wilkinson had written in 1804 a report called "Reflections on Louisiana." He recommended that the Spanish intercept and arrest Lewis and Clark, which they made feeble efforts to do. And in looking ahead to future United States movements in the West, he predicted that within five years there would be an American post on the Pacific Coast. He was slightly off about the time but quite correct in his basic assumption. Meriwether Lewis himself, dining with scientist and legislator Samuel Latham Mitchill after returning from his expedition, said he thought its most valuable result was the promise it held for the setting up of a trading post on the Pacific.

Few individuals or combines had the resources to contemplate the logistics and financial risk of such an operation. John Jacob Astor, the poor German immigrant who was fast becoming the richest man in America by trading in furs, was such a person. In 1808, Jefferson received a letter from Astor, proposing such a venture. He needed "the countenance and good wishes" of the president if he was to succeed.

Jefferson did not know Astor, but after inquiring among his colleagues in government and receiving favorable reports, he replied on 13 April:

> I learn with great satisfaction the disposition of our merchants to form into companies for undertaking the Indian trade within our own territories. . . . You may be assured that in order to get the whole of this business passed into the hands of our own citizens & to oust foreign traders who so much abuse their privileges by endeavoring to excite the Indians to war on us, every reasonable patronage & facility in the power of the Executive will be afforded.

The message was vague, speaking of trade "within our own territories," and of course the Pacific Coast was not a part of the Louisiana Purchase. But Astor used it to good advantage and found further use for the support of Albert Gallatin, secretary of the treasury, who was his friend. By 1810, Astor had organized the Pacific Fur Company and had set his sights on the mouth of the Columbia. He sent the vessel *Tonquin* by sea and an overland party led from St. Louis by Wilson Price Hunt. They built a settlement called "Astoria" that had a short but important life in the history of the American West. The War of 1812 disrupted Astor's venture; his post fell into the hands of a British concern, the North West Company, and Astor did not regain possession until after the war.

When the war began, Jefferson had been out of office for three years and could do little but give advice. He pushed for an invasion of Canada and the addition of Cuba to United States possessions. He watched with apprehension as the war spread into the Mississippi Valley and threatened vital holdings there. Explorations were neglected and there was no significant advance in the gathering of information about Louisiana until after the Treaty of Ghent marked the end of the war.

Astor renewed his communication with Jefferson in 1812, expressing hope for reviving his Pacific Coast trade and also engaging in trade with the Russians. In his reply of 24 May, Jefferson seemed to recall that he had not only encouraged but actually suggested the Astoria venture. He spoke of a hope that seemed the key to his present and future thinking about the nature of the relationship between the old eastern states and the new western settlements. His ruminations included "the establishment of an independent nation on the Pacific Coast, bound to the United States by ties of blood, language and friendship."

The idea was still with him the following year, when on 9 November he wrote again to Astor, saying he viewed Astoria "as the germ of a great, free and independent empire on that side of our continent, and that liberty and self-government spreading from that as well as this side, will ensure their complete establishment over the whole."

During the War of 1812 and in the years following, Jefferson seemed rather lost, as George Washington had been after his presidency, turning to agriculture obsessively and struggling to clear himself of debts he had incurred during the years when he had been unable to attend more strictly to his farming.

The year 1814 saw the publication of the only Lewis and Clark material that Jefferson would ever see in book form. Written by Philadelphia litterateur Nicholas Biddle, after interviews with Clark and George Shannon, and with access to all the journals that had been recovered upon Lewis' death in 1809, the work was entitled *History of the Expedition Under the Command of Captains Lewis and Clark, to the Sources of the Missouri, Thence Across the Rocky Mountains and down the River Columbia to the Pacific Ocean.* Considering the difficulties Biddle faced in preparing the work, it was a masterful one. Biddle, however, would not allow his name to be used on the title page. He turned the manuscript over to journalist Paul Allen for final preparation, and Allen's name appears as author.

The publication did not satisfy Jefferson, who had hoped for a scientific presentation rather than a popular account. Dr. Benjamin Smith Barton, of the University of Pennsylvania, had not gotten around before his death to preparing the botanical and zoological material. Lewis' astronomical observations had been so erratic that mathematician Ferdinand Hassler, a teacher at West Point, had given up trying to clarify them. The part of the book that Jefferson might have approved of heartily was the map drawn by Clark, one of the monuments of western cartography, but the printer had cropped it severely at top and bottom, with the loss of valuable data. (The original, uncropped map, in four large sections, survives in the Yale University Library.)

At least Jefferson could do what seemed possible to ensure that every scrap of paper from the expedition was saved for future study and publication. He wrote Clark in 1816 that he was trying to gather the celestial observations, the many Indian vocabularies, and the natural-history materials. He would ask the War Department to republish the map with corrected longitudes, and the rest of the file would go to the American Philosophical Society, "who would have them properly edited."

A year of collecting and correspondence had not brought the results Jefferson had hoped for. He sent the society three manuscript journals that he had preserved and asked that organization to become a general depository for the papers—there being no national archival body at the time. As he wrote to Peter S. Duponceau, 7 November 1817:

And if it should be within the views of the historical committee to have the Indian vocabularies digested and published, I would add to them the remains of my collection. I had thro' the course of my life availed myself of every opportunity of procuring vocabularies of the languages of every tribe which either myself or my friends could have access to. They amounted to about 40 more or less perfect. But in their passage from Washington to this place, the trunk in which they were stolen was plundered, and some fragments only of the vocabularies were recovered. Still however they were such as would be worth incorporation with a larger work, and shall be at the service of the historical committee, if they can make any use of them.

A sheaf of Indian vocabularies painstakingly collected and placed in Dr. Barton's hands never came to light, but the bulk of the expedition papers finally went to the society.

DEFINING THE EMPIRE

The western developments that Jefferson was to see in the remaining years of his life were not sweeping. He was not to see Texas become a republic and then a state or California taken from Mexico. He was to see instead important boundary settlements, the beginnings of Indian removal, and the spread of his system for land survey. He was to see the techniques of exploration organized into a profession with the establishment of a corps of topographical engineers defined as a bureau under the secretary of war. It would produce such explorers as Stephen H. Long, who examined the Rockies in 1819–1820, and John Charles Frémont, whose explorations in the 1840s would become symbolic of the westering urge called manifest destiny.

Spain and the United States reached an agreement, however temporary, on boundary matters with the treaty negotiated by John Quincy Adams, secretary of state, and Luis de Onís, the Spanish minister in Washington. The treaty, ratified in 1821, gave the United States East Florida and recognized a border that ran along the Sabine, Red, and Arkansas rivers and then directly west to the Pacific along the forty-second parallel.

By the Convention of 1818, Britain and the United States agreed on a boundary along the forty-ninth parallel as far west as the Continental Divide, leaving the western line to the Pacific undetermined. A permanent line would be fixed at the forty-ninth parallel by treaty in 1846.

Although Jefferson served only as elder statesman in such negotiations, his influence was strong. Until his death in 1826 he advised leaders of government who were of like views: first Madison, then Monroe and John Quincy Adams. He fully supported the Monroe Doctrine, which was in part an evocation of his own views as expressed in a letter of 24 October 1820 to Correa de Serra: "Nothing is so important as that America shall separate herself from the systems of Europe, & establish one of her own. . . . Our circumstances, our pursuits, our interests are distinct. The principles of our policy should be also."

For a man whose life was half over before he began to shape events in the West, Jefferson wrought well. He was not always an innovator; more often he responded effectively to changing circumstances. For example, his early plan for the new Louisiana Purchase was that it should serve for years as a giant Indian preserve where displaced Native Americans could learn the arts of European civilization before moving back into the American mainstream. Manifest destiny changed all that. He did not visualize a United States from sea to shining sea, but rather a continent made up of men and women living free and independent, regardless of their affiliation with the Old Confederacy on the eastern shores.

"The future inhabitants of the Atlantic and Mississippi states will be our sons," he wrote on 12 August 1803 to John Breckenridge. "We think we see their happiness in their union, and we wish it. Events may prove it otherwise. . . . God bless them both, and keep them in union, if it be for their own good, but separate them, if it be better." His own and future generations would decide that union was better.

Agriculture

ROBERT E. SHALHOPE

"WHEN I first entered on the stage of public life (now twenty-four years ago) I came to a resolution never . . . to wear any other character than that of a farmer." This observation, offered while he served as George Washington's secretary of state, articulated Thomas Jefferson's lifelong commitment to agriculture as a way of life central to his own career and to the very nature of American society. For Jefferson, farming stood at the core of his hope for America and the world; for historians, farming stands as a key element of the complex character of Thomas Jefferson. To view Jefferson the farmer is to gain important insights into Jefferson the man.

Shortly after resigning from Washington's administration on 31 December 1793 and returning to Monticello, Jefferson declared himself the "most ardent farmer in the state" as he labored to improve property left too long in the hands of overseers or careless relatives. At this time Jefferson owned approximately eleven hundred acres of land divided primarily among estates in Albemarle and Bedford Counties. These in-

cluded Monticello, Tufton, Shadwell, and Lego in the former and Poplar Forest, Tomahawk, and Bear Creek in the latter. In addition, he owned the Natural Bridge property in Rockbridge County. While most of this land remained heavily forested, Jefferson intended to devote himself to returning the cultivated portions to their previous fertility. For him the restoration of the soil served as the essential starting point for all subsequent agricultural improvements. Focusing on his home estate of Monticello, Jefferson intended to apply the best scientific methods to land management in an effort to establish agriculture on a secure and productive footing.

Displaying a passion for order and design, Jefferson set out with mathematical precision to attack the problem of soil restoration. He devoted his initial efforts to discovering the right combination of crops as well as their proper rotation. This resulted first in an eight-shift system and then a seven-shift one that divided the tillable soil at Monticello into forty-acre fields. In each field Jefferson constructed a granary and to each field he assigned four men, four women, four horses, and four oxen, as well as a full complement of plows and other implements. In addition, his labor scheme called for teams of select laborers to man the plows. These men moved from field to field according to need. The rotation scheme itself allotted field one to wheat; field two to corn, peas, and potatoes; field three to winter wheat, which should be plowed under in the early spring to make room for peas and potatoes in areas of sufficient strength and fertility; field four to rye or wheat unless fields two, three, five, and six could provide subsistence for the farm, in which case clover should be planted in the spring; field five to clover; field six to clover, which should be turned under in the fall in order to substitute vetch; field seven to vetch and buckwheat in the spring, at which time the blossoming plants should be turned under in order to begin the cycle again by planting wheat in September. Within this plan Jefferson made careful calculations regarding the time of year to plow, plant, and to turn plants under, as well as precise notations regarding the spacing of plants and the manner in which separate species should be interspersed.

To accompany his rotation scheme Jefferson created detailed work calendars. Exemplifying Jefferson's desire to discover the most efficient use of a given number of laborers and animals on a given amount of land, these calendars outlined the manner in which laborers and draft animals should be employed each day of the year. For example, from 15 August through 28 August he allotted ten plowing days with horses. Four single-horse plows at four acres a day would put in forty acres of wheat. During this time the oxen teams were free and their laborers were to clear the fields for the horse plows. From 29 August to 15 September Jefferson assigned fourteen working days employing three double-horse and oxen plows and one harrow at three acres per day. Accordingly,

forty acres of clover would be plowed under and planted in wheat. During this same time the laborers from the fields being plowed were to gather peas. In this manner Jefferson accounted for each day in each of the fields that made up his seven-shift system.

At the end of the farming season in 1795 Jefferson planned, with mathematical exactitude, how the wheat harvest could be handled more efficiently the following year. He calculated the precise arrangement of the treading-floors as well as the placement of spare scythes. He even assigned Great George to move about with a portable grindstone in order to keep all necessary tools sharpened. The scheme called for eighteen cradlers (men), eighteen bundlers (women and abler boys), six gatherers (five small boys with one larger one as foreman), three loaders (Moses, Shepherd, and Joe), six stackers, two cooks, and four carters. Eight men would remain as plow teams to keep that operation going simultaneously with the wheat harvest. Having accounted for his entire work force, Jefferson calculated that in this manner "the whole machinery would move in exact equilibrio, no part of the force could be lessened without retarding the whole, nor increased without a waste of force." Thus, his "force would cut, bring in and shock 54 acres a day, and complete my harvest of 320 acres in 6 days." This was predicated on his initial eight-shift system.

As a mathematical calculation, there could be no doubt about the end result. Unfortunately, when put into practice the following year, the imponderabilia of farming and human development intervened and the machine failed to move in exact equilibrio. On 2 July Jefferson noted: "We stopped our ploughs, the pickers not keeping up with the cutters." Then, "though 18 mowers had been fixed on and furnished with 27 scythes, yet the wheat was so heavy for the most part that we had not more than 13 or 14 mowers cutting on the average." The final result:

"13 cutters × 12 days = 156, which gives near 2 acres a day for each cutter, supposing 300 acres." It should be noted that while the harvest took twice as long as calculated, it was also much heavier than the previous year.

The emphasis Jefferson placed on order and calculation in his harvesting scheme reflected a basic trait in his character: he had a passion for measuring, calculating, counting, and figuring. For example, with an efficiency engineer's penchant for work-time studies, Jefferson made the following observation:

Julius Shard fills the two-wheeled barrow in 3 minutes, and carries it 30 yards in 1½ minutes more. Now this is four loads of the common barrow with one wheel. So that suppose the 4 loads put in at the same time viz. 3 minutes, 4 trips will take 4 × 1½ minutes = 6, which added to 3 minutes filling = 9 minutes to fill and carry the same earth which was filled and carried in the two-wheeled barrow in 4½ minutes. From a trial I made with the same two-wheeled barrow, I found that a man could dig and carry to the distance of 50 yds, 5 cubical yds of earth in a day of 12 hours length. Ford's Phil did it; not overlooked and having to mount his loaded barrow up a bank 2 f. high and tolerably steep.

He filled his Garden Book with notations such as the weight of five hundred peas and the fact that it took about twenty-five hundred of them to fill a pint. In September 1791, while in the midst of his struggle with Alexander Hamilton over the direction of the new American government, he purchased an odometer, fixed it to his carriage, and made precise notations of mileage from place to place along his route from New York to Monticello. While president, Jefferson kept a log in which he noted the precise date each of thirty-seven varieties of vegetables arrived and left the market in Washington, D.C. Upon his retirement from the presidency, he kept a yearly calendar that

noted the variety of each vegetable planted, its exact location (every field in all of his estates had a name and each plant in the Monticello garden a Roman numeral), when planted, the date of its transplantation, and when it came to table. He kept a record of the first appearance of ticks, fireflies, and other insects, animals, and plants. He maintained a day-to-day record of weather observations as well as a daily record of his financial transactions. He constantly calculated costs. Even on his deathbed Jefferson noted that "a gallon of lamp oil, costing $1.25 has lighted my chamber 25 nights, for 6 hours a night which is 5 cents a night & 150 hours."

If agriculture were an endeavor such as architecture, where mathematical calculations and designs assumed primary importance, Jefferson would surely have been an outstanding farmer. Unfortunately, it was not. Jefferson was a realist, however, and so did not attempt to force his agricultural efforts to fit his mathematical calculations and plans. Instead, the latter served as blueprints for him to follow as he adjusted theory to practice. During a visit to Monticello in 1796 François de La Rochefoucauld-Liancourt summarized his host's approach to farming as well as anyone. Noting that Jefferson was "little accustomed to agricultural pursuits" and drew most of his principles from books and conversation, the duke observed, nonetheless, that "much good may be expected, if a contemplative mind like that of Mr. Jefferson, which takes the theory for its guide, watches its application with discernment, and rectifies it according to the peculiar circumstances and nature of the country, climate, and soil, and conformably to the experience which he daily acquires." Jefferson, it turned out, applied the same pragmatic approach to farming as he did to politics.

In response to conditions on his property, Jefferson gradually changed to what amounted to a three-shift, six-field system calling for two fields in wheat, one in corn, one in peas or oats, one in clover for cutting, and one in clover for pasture. He supplemented this with eight acres of pumpkins in an effort to help feed his livestock. In addition he planted as much timothy as his meadows could yield. Further, after reading John A. Binns's *Treatise on Practical Farming* (1803), which espoused the "Loudoun System" of clover, gypsum, and deep plowing, Jefferson began to apply massive amounts of plaster of paris as fertilizer. Ten years earlier he had written that it was cheaper to buy a new acre of land than to fertilize an old one. Clearly, his reading of Binns as well as his correspondence with Dr. George Logan of Pennsylvania convinced him otherwise. As time went by Jefferson collected over two hundred books and essays devoted to agriculture and corresponded widely regarding problems related to farming.

Jefferson's zeal for innovation and improvement made him receptive to every possible change in cultivation, marketing, and processing that promised to enhance the profitability of agriculture. This became manifest in his fascination with farm machinery. Nothing characterized the man more than his enthusiasm for laborsaving implements that would increase the efficiency of his farm. Believing "the plough is to the farmer what the wand is to the sorcerer," Jefferson worked continually to improve the implement itself as well as its practical applications. His own invention of a moldboard of least resistance revolutionized the design of plows and made them much more efficient. With his son-in-law, Thomas Mann Randolph, to whom Jefferson entrusted much of his land, he worked out a system of contour plowing that saved his hilly lands from erosion while conserving precious rainwater. In addition, he quickly adopted and widely recommended Randolph's ingenious hillside plow that always turned the furrow to the downhill side. He constantly experimented with seed drills, threshing machines, hominy beaters, cornshellers, apple mills, and presses to improve their capabilities. While Jefferson may never have fully comprehended machinery other than for its practical applications, he had an insatiable curiosity about gadgets and machinery of all kinds. Typically, he would obtain a sample of a piece of machinery, tinker with it in hopes of improving its design, and then correspond with others to compare results. As a consequence, he helped both to spread the use of agricultural machinery and to upgrade its performance.

In addition to his interest in machinery, Jefferson constantly worked in other ways to make Monticello as efficient and self-sufficient as possible. He placed a barn in each field rather than follow the standard practice of constructing a large centrally located structure. On his hilly property separate barns and granaries, combined with a portable thresher, made a great deal more sense. He built slave cabins close together so that older women could tend the young children more easily. He encircled his mountain with roads, or "roundabouts," linked by a series of oblique connecting lanes in order to facilitate movement of labor, animals, and machines. Going beyond his efforts to make the production of goods more efficient and prosperous, Jefferson spent a good deal of time, effort, and expense on improving the transportation and processing of his crops.

His concern with the Rivanna River, which flowed between the Monticello and Shadwell estates, was lifelong. From his youth when he took a canoe down the river to study obstacles to transportation, to the clearing, widening, and dredging necessary to make it navigable, to his installation of dams, locks, and canals, Jefferson worked to improve the river's capability to transport goods to market quickly and efficiently. In addition, Jefferson constructed a grist mill, a manufacturing mill, and a saw mill on the Shadwell side of the river. He spent over $20,000 constructing a canal for the manufacturing mill, which cost over $10,000 itself. He attempted to lease this facility but never realized a profit. By 1814 he had installed spinning and weaving machinery, which included four spinning jennies (three with twenty-four spindles and one with forty) and a loom with a flying shuttle. These facilities, with a machine-equipped nailery constructed earlier, helped to bring Monticello closer to Jefferson's goal of self-sufficiency. While he would never realize that dream, Jefferson could at least process the staples grown on his land, pack them in barrels made by his own coopers, and transport them on a river that he was largely responsible for making navigable.

The desire to achieve self-sufficiency affected Jefferson's choice of which crops to sow at Monticello, as well as the varieties of livestock raised on the estate. As in his other agricultural endeavors, Jefferson attempted to meld theory with practice. Here, though, practical necessities more often than not outweighed his theoretical reform efforts. Regarding corn and hogs, for example, he claimed "pork to be as destructive an article in a farm as Indian corn," and that "the first step toward the recovery of our lands is to find a substitute for corn and bacon." Yet, in order to feed his laborers, Jefferson continued to raise more hogs than any other animal, and he not only continued to raise corn but found it necessary to buy large quantities of it each year to feed his stock. While he did attempt to replace hogs with sheep (from 1809 to 1813 sheep raising and breeding became a major interest of his) he never succeeded. Instead, he remained locked in to planting corn to feed the hogs that fed his laborers.

Tobacco created quite a different set of problems. Here debts, not self-sufficiency, dictated Jefferson's choices. Regarding tobacco, Jefferson stated emphatically in his *Notes on the State of Virginia* that "it is a culture productive of infinite wretchedness. Those employed in it are in a continuous state of exertion beyond the power of nature to support. Little food of any kind is raised by them; so that the men and animals on these farms are badly fed, and the earth is rapidly

impoverished." In light of these observations, Jefferson attempted to raise wheat as the cash crop at Monticello and his other Albemarle lands. However, the high price of tobacco in 1798 caused him to abandon his previous system of crop rotation and land reclamation in order to plant his lands exclusively in that product. He lamented that tobacco's high price "has tempted me to go entirely into that culture, and in the meantime, my farming schemes are in abeyance." Large debts caused Jefferson to plant tobacco at the expense of his lands. His Bedford estates remained constantly mortgaged and planted in tobacco in an unsuccessful attempt to repay these obligations.

Debts plagued Jefferson for most of his adult life as a farmer. He inherited without encumbrance nearly five thousand acres of land (including the Monticello property) upon his father's death in 1757. In 1774 he added an additional eleven thousand acres of land upon the death of his father-in-law, John Wayles. This property, however, came with a huge debt. Jefferson's share amounted to about £4,300, which he attempted to pay off as soon as possible. To accomplish this, he sold nearly half of the inherited property, but received terribly depreciated Revolutionary currency in payment. This meant a loss of good land and still no lessening of the debt. Indeed, with the passage of time, the debt increased. In 1793 he sold the valuable Elk Hill farm in Goochland County, but a year later his debt remained at £7,500. In 1795 yet another judgment went against the Wayles estate and added an additional £1,000 to Jefferson's financial responsibility. By that time his land roles stood at 10,647 acres with 152 slaves. This represented a decrease in the number of slaves of about one-fourth over the previous decade. Clearly, he retained his lands more tenaciously than he did his slaves.

After the sale of Elk Hill, Jefferson's landholdings remained nearly constant until his death, despite the fact that his indebtedness continued to grow. When he left the presidency his debt stood at nearly $12,000. The panic of 1819 brought him to the verge of bankruptcy since he had recently endorsed notes to the amount of $21,200 for his friend Wilson C. Nicholas. When Nicholas defaulted, Jefferson's bank debts, contracted to combat the fall in agricultural prices, already stood at over $40,000. In the last year of his life Jefferson wrote his friend James Monroe: "To keep a Virginia estate together, requires in the owner both skill and attention. Skill I never had, and attention I could not have; and really, when I reflect on all circumstances, my wonder is that I should have been so long as sixty years in reaching the result to which I am now reduced."

Despite his chronic indebtedness, Jefferson never lost the will to pursue his visions and to work continually for the benefit of agriculture. His desire to improve the soil through crop rotation, fertilization, new varieties of plants, and better plowing methods established a solid foundation for others. All of Jefferson's experiments and plans, despite the disjointed empiricism of many and the seeming irrelevance of others, formed a unifying theme: to improve agriculture for the good of mankind. Although dependent upon agriculture for his own livelihood, Jefferson's desire to foster improvement emanated from interests larger than his own. Throughout his life he exhibited a "zeal to promote the general good of mankind by an exchange of useful things." This zeal found its greatest release in agriculture.

When he traveled in Europe in the 1780s Jefferson constantly kept a keen eye out for new varieties of plants that could benefit American farmers, as well as seeking out new markets for American crops. Once he stated that "the greatest service which can be rendered any country is to add an useful plant to its culture." Thus, while he was in Europe he smuggled out samples of Piedmont rice for planters in South Carolina and shipped a good many olive trees to America in the hope of starting such a culture in his native land. While riding in a carriage to Nancy he noticed the cumbersome nature of the moldboards on plows being used throughout the countryside. Although it would be years before this observation bore fruit, it typified Jefferson's ever alert eye, an eye trained particularly in favor of agriculture.

His intense interest in agriculture and agricultural machinery persisted upon his return home and did not abate even during the most trying political times. In the midst of the political turmoil of 1793 he took time to ask James Madison if he had "ever taken notice of Tull's horse-houghing plough." Then, at the height of the Genêt affair and with Philadelphia suffering from yellow fever, he informed Madison that a threshing machine had arrived and that "fortunately the workman who made it (a millwright) is come in the same vessel to settle in America. I have written him to persuade him to go on immediately to Richmond, offering him the use of my model to exhibit, and to give him letters to get him into immediate employ in making them." Shortly thereafter he wrote enthusiastically about a new seedbox that "reduces the expense of seeding from six shillings to two shillings and three pence the acre, and does the business better than is possible to be done by the human hand."

Throughout his life Jefferson corresponded tirelessly to promote the good of agriculture through improved methods and machinery. His exertion stemmed from a firmly held belief that farmers were "the first in utility, and ought to be first in respect." To help achieve this position for farmers, in 1811 Jefferson offered a proposal for the creation of a system of agriculture societies. He stressed above all else the importance of staple crops for the market; then he emphasized the need to provide subsidiary crops in order to make the farm self-sufficient. From these initial proposals sprang a number of others: good care of animals; crop rotation; innovative use of farm machinery; construction of buildings and roads in an efficient manner; proper use of fertilizers; keeping calendars of work; and providing succinct reports of both successful and unsuccessful farming practices to be shared with fellow members as well as other societies. This scheme represented Jefferson's mature thought on agriculture and typified his approach to farming: detailed observations, trial and error, and a constant exchange of information.

Jefferson's proposal, which culminated in the creation of the Albemarle Agricultural Society, captured an important characteristic of the man as farmer: continual concern for the benefit of other farmers. Upon perfecting the design for his moldboard of least resistance, Jefferson gave a correspondent perfect freedom to use his idea "as all the world is, having never thought of monopolizing by patent any useful idea which happens to offer itself to me. . . ." When Merino sheep seemed to be the great hope for Virginia farmers, Jefferson suggested to Madison that they help build up this strain in the state by giving a full-blooded ram to every county. His reason: "The few who can afford it should incur the risk and the expense of all new improvements, and give the benefit freely to the many of more restricted circumstances." The same held true regarding the shepherd dogs that Jefferson raised at Monticello. In order to sustain the breed, he gave them in pairs to whomever had a need.

Jefferson integrated his willingness to help others and his keen desire to foster agricultural improvements with another major goal: the creation of the University of Virginia. As early as 1800 he requested advice from friends regarding a totally new educational institution for his native state. Joseph Priestley's suggestion that courses in chemistry should incorporate the theories of agriculture reinforced Jefferson's own belief in the importance of agriculture within a uni-

versity. In 1803 he exclaimed that agriculture was "first in utility, and ought to be the first in respect. . . . It is a science of the very first order. . . . In every College and University, a professorship of agriculture, and the class of its students, might be honored as the first." Two years later, when he outlined his original plan for the University of Virginia, Jefferson included agriculture with botany and chemistry as major elements within the proposed curriculum. In his Report of the Commissioners for the University of Virginia to the state legislature in 1818, Jefferson clarified his position: "Chemistry is meant, with its other usual branches, to comprehend the theory of agriculture." In 1824 an enactment of the board of visitors provided that rural economy along with botany and chemistry would be taught in the school of natural history. Jefferson's desire to bring agricultural theory and methods into a university curriculum had become a reality. At the University of Virginia, students would receive a truly liberal education.

The suggestions for an agricultural society, his efforts on behalf of others, his improvements of his own property, and his efforts to create the University of Virginia capture Jefferson's strengths as an agriculturalist. He desired a successful commercial economy composed of prosperous, self-sufficient units. Yet Jefferson himself achieved neither prosperity nor self-sufficiency. Indeed, he displayed as many weaknesses as a farmer as he did strengths: these stemmed from inconsistencies or contradictions within the man himself.

The constant struggle with indebtedness exposed one of Jefferson's major weaknesses as a farmer. Although he kept meticulous financial records, just as he did for the weather, the garden, and the farm, Jefferson simply was not a good accountant. Itemizing everything, he had no understanding of debit and credit accounting. Instead, his records reveal incredible attention to minutia in the absence of any kind of system within which to provide order and meaning. He never rose above the level of petty detail. But, more importantly, Jefferson simply was not thrifty. While discrete in small expenditures, he engaged prodigally in large ones. He spent vast sums of money constructing, tearing apart, and rebuilding the mansion at Monticello, as well as its gardens and grounds. Then, to avoid the crush of guests at Monticello, he built a beautiful home at his Poplar Forest estate. His mills, locks, and canals on the Rivanna River involved huge outlays of money. Always the optimist, Jefferson constantly overestimated the ability of his land to pay his increasing debts.

More was involved than simple financial miscalculation. Jefferson's very character as a farmer presents a number of inconsistencies. The contradiction between theory and practice in persistently planting tobacco and corn or raising hogs may be attributed to the practical necessities of meeting debt payments and attempting to maintain self-sufficiency. Other contradictions are not so easily explained. They involved a deeper sort of paradox, a dialectic within his personality between scientific empiricism and a pastoralism emphasizing beauty and harmony. His careful calculations regarding the division of his land into equal fields of forty acres, for instance, called for supporting ninety head of cattle. These cows were to provide enough manure to fertilize each field in his proposed seven-year cycle. Yet his cattle, like his hogs, foraged freely. Jefferson lost the use of their manure because he delineated his fields with double rows of peach trees rather than fences. The aesthetic quality of these tree-lined boundaries enthralled Jefferson—especially in the springtime.

The same tension between the practical and the beautiful—with far more utilitarian results—emerged in Jefferson's description of contour plowing. Following a detailed, mathematical description of the method involved in laying out a field for contour plow-

ing, Jefferson waxed lyrical: "In point of beauty nothing can exceed that of waving lines & rows winding along the face of the hills & vallies." This doubleness of mind, balancing beauty and utility, appeared again in Jefferson's description of the Natural Bridge, which he acquired in 1774 and held throughout his lifetime of debt. In *Notes on the State of Virginia,* after describing the fissure below the bridge in mathematically precise terms, Jefferson exclaimed: "It is impossible for the emotions arising from the sublime, to be felt beyond what they are here: so beautiful an arch, so elevated, so light, and springing as it were up to heaven, the rapture of the spectator is really indescribable!"

Jefferson's devotion to both the practical and the ideal world formed a central part of his life. But his sense of the sublime seemed preeminent at Monticello. Many of Jefferson's practical problems as a farmer stemmed from the fact that he attempted to create a farm on a mountaintop. The aesthetic qualities of Monticello—its buildings and views and surrounding grounds—assumed predominance in his mind. John Taylor of Caroline, Jefferson's close friend, maintained Hazlewood in Caroline County, practiced agricultural reforms, lived practically, and made a good living from his farm. Taylor shared Jefferson's love of farming and the agricultural life, but he tended to resist the aesthetic and pursue the practical.

The very fact that Jefferson insisted upon referring to himself as a farmer, rather than a planter, was itself revealing. In common usage a Virginia farmer planted wheat and mixed grains, while a planter raised tobacco. Jefferson never managed to emulate George Washington or John Taylor by becoming entirely a farmer. Yet he always considered himself a farmer rather than a planter. His idealistic desire predominated over practical realities.

The paradoxes, inconsistencies, and eccentricities within Jefferson the Virginia farmer must be considered as integral parts of his very character, components of the great complexity and versatility of the man himself. This versatility, captured in James Parton's memorable description of the young Jefferson as one who "could calculate an eclipse, survey an estate, tie an artery, plan an edifice, try a cause, break a horse, dance a minuet, and play a violin," manifested itself in an overwhelming excitement about learning. His intellectual eagerness promoted a great interest in ideas, a fascination with the most recent discoveries of the sciences, and a devotion to the fostering of knowledge; but this was less from the perspective of technical expertise or systematic analysis than from the angle of amateur enthusiasm. A lover of learning, Jefferson threw himself—at times randomly or seemingly without clear purpose—into everything from epistemology to the mechanical arts.

Things factual and mechanical held the greatest attraction for him. An almost compulsive lover of counting, observing, and measuring, he exhibited a penchant for methodical industry, order, and classification. Fond of detail, his personal records, whether Farm Book, Garden Book, Weather Book, or Account Book, were all meticulous in order and detail. No matter what the undertaking, Jefferson never lacked facts; he felt far more at ease dealing with empirical data than with abstractions. The resultant emphasis upon clarity, precision, and proportion expressed an essentially mathematical mind given to utilitarian or practical applications rather than to grand speculations. Like fellow Enlightenment thinkers generally, Jefferson firmly believed ideas should act on the world, not merely reflect it. Nothing reveals this bent of mind more clearly than his observations, made while he was on the road to Nancy in April 1778, on the awkward nature of the plow's moldboard. He worked out, with what he considered "mathematical perfection," the design for a mold-

board and gave it to the world with no thought of personal gain. For him "the combination of a *theory* which may satisfy the learned, with a practice intelligible to the most unlettered laborers, will be acceptable to the two most useful classes of society." This may well be as succinct a summary of his methods as exists; thought for him became a tool to shape life, not merely to reflect it in some cosmic design. Along with this activist temperament, Jefferson exuded a hopeful vision of the nature of man and an optimistic outlook for America. He became a true spokesman for the Enlightenment: there could be a vindication of human nature against the past. An escape from the tyranny of the past became, in Jefferson's mind, the peculiar mission of America.

Jefferson's hope for a better future for mankind rested upon the creation of a virtuous republican government and society in America. Farming assumed a vital role in this hope because he perceived a dynamic link between agriculture and the maintenance of such a culture. The essential core of his thought lies in a frequently quoted passage from his *Notes on the State of Virginia*:

Those who labor in the earth are the chosen people of God, if ever he had a chosen people, whose breasts he has made his peculiar deposit for substantial and genuine virtue. It is the focus in which he keeps alive that sacred fire, which otherwise might escape from the face of the earth. Corruption of morals in the mass of cultivators is a phenomenon of which no age nor nation has furnished an example. It is the mark set on those, who not looking up to heaven, to their own soil and industry, as does the husbandman, for their subsistance, depend for it on casualties and caprice of customers. Dependance begets subservience and venality, suffocates the germ of virtue, and prepares fit tools for the designs of ambition. This, the natural progress and consequence of the arts, has sometimes perhaps been retarded by accidental circumstances; but, generally speaking, the proportion which the aggregate of the other classes of citizens bears in any state to that of its husbandmen, is the proportion of its unsound to its healthy parts, and is a good-enough barometer whereby to measure its degree of corruption. While we have land to labor then, let us never wish to see our citizens occupied at a work-bench, or twirling a distaff.

This eloquent statement captured Jefferson's ideal, a moral directive consonant with the American environment. He articulated his belief in a widely accepted tenet of Enlightenment thought: all cultures underwent a natural progression from the barbarous savagery of primitive society to the venality and corruption of extreme civilization. The dominant fact of the American environment, "an immensity of land courting the industry of the husbandman," saved Jefferson from pessimism about the future of his country. The abundance of land in America might stave off the natural progression experienced by Old World cultures. America could remain in the ideal "middle state" drawing upon the virtues of nature without suffering the vices of advanced civilization. He wrote from Paris to James Madison on 20 December 1787: "I think our governments will remain virtuous for many centuries; as long as they are chiefly agricultural; and this will be as long as there shall be vacant lands in any part of America. When they get piled upon one another in large cities, as in Europe, they will become corrupt as in Europe." By owning and tilling his own land, the American citizen-farmer could avoid subordination to superiors and cultivate the inner strength upon which republicanism itself depended. The virtue and judgment nurtured by such independent labor on the soil rendered Americans capable of being republican citizens and thereby rendered their society capable of supporting a republican government.

The idealization of farmers as God's chosen people implied a moral rather than an economic concern for agriculture: a belief that agriculture's value stemmed as much from its maintenance of human virtues and traits most congenial to self-government, as from any potential as a source of wealth. Farming had a sociological rather than an economic value. Such an attitude sprang from a love of the pastoral embedded deep in Jefferson's character. Yet, a subtle ambivalence permeated this pastoralism. In 1785, shortly after penning his observations regarding God's chosen people, Jefferson claimed: "Were I to indulge my own theory, I should wish them [Americans] to practice neither commerce nor navigation, but to stand with respect to Europe precisely on the footing of China. We should thus avoid wars, and all our citizens would be husbandmen." He admitted, however, that "this is theory only, and a theory which the servants of Americans are not at liberty to follow. Our people have a decided taste for navigation and commerce." Jefferson knew full well that a dynamic, individualistic economic system already had a strong foothold in America. A pastoral world inhabited by virtuous husbandmen was, unfortunately, a land of "theory only," not at all representative of the America Jefferson knew existed in reality.

Jefferson's passionate espousal of rural ideals and the practical tone he adopted in dismissing them mirrored similar polarities that characterized many aspects of his personal life. While praising the noble husbandman's virtuous lack of concern for worldly objects, Jefferson struggled arduously to attain and hold the nation's highest political office; extolling the simple life of a remote mountaintop, he surrounded himself with the fruits of high culture and gratified sophisticated tastes in architecture, music, literature, wines, and continental cuisine; attracted by the attributes of a bucolic world, he eagerly pursued advances in technology, science, and commerce; praising liberty and freedom, he held slaves. In other words, while cherishing the values of a pastoral culture, he firmly believed in the concept of progress, a concept that was inexorably destined to destroy the rural ideal.

Ambiguities of such depth—lodged in the very heart of his character—reflected a profound ambivalence, a complex reaction to the tension inherent in the conflicting demands of self and society. The tug-of-war between Jefferson's personal and public lives provides a striking example of the pattern of contradictions seen in his simultaneous idealization of and escape from the pastoral world. Throughout his life Jefferson claimed that all he really desired was to live peacefully at his rural retreat at Monticello. In 1775, at the age of thirty-two, he claimed to be contemplating a permanent retirement from active political life. In 1793, after serving as governor of Virginia, minister to France, and secretary of state, he continued to regard political life as a diversion, not his true calling. In 1795 he reveled in the fact that he had been away from public office, "which I never liked in my life, but was drawn into by emergencies which threatened our country with slavery. . . ." Instead, he had returned "with infinite appetite, to the enjoyment of my farm, my family and my books, and . . . determined to meddle in nothing beyond their limits." The next year Thomas Jefferson was a candidate for the presidency.

The pastoral idyll he had envisioned upon leaving Washington's administration had never materialized. Instead, retirement revealed its darker side: crop failures, difficulty with labor, dreary winters spent in isolation, frustrations with needed construction projects, and unrelenting debts. He had set out filled with optimistic plans to recoup the fortune he believed he had postponed through prolonged absence from the land, but after an experiment of several years devoted to those interests, he could take little satisfaction from the result. Instead he found himself ready for a "return to the world,"

though he could never actually consent to it or, once embarked upon it, resign himself to the "splendid torments" of public life. Calls to public duty followed by withdrawals to the country comprised the very rhythm of Jefferson's life.

Jefferson's ambivalence about the pastoral ideal is clearly analogous to his conflicting feelings regarding public and private life, as seen in the constant tension between withdrawal and return. When articulating a yearning for country peace and pleasure, Jefferson expressed himself in terms of sentimental pastoralism. And yet, his active political role rested upon a dispassionate estimate of social and economic forces present in American society. His pragmatic empiricism simply would not allow him to be blinded to the course of change and development in America. "What is practicable must often control what is pure theory, and the habits of the governed determine in a great degree what is practicable." Jefferson knew very well that Americans had commercial aspirations that could not be suppressed. In any event, by 1809 he observed that agriculture, commerce, and manufacturing "grow together, and [are] really handmaidens of each others." He envisioned an equilibrium between the three callings. In a brilliant letter to Benjamin Austin written on 9 January 1816 Jefferson reviewed the changes within the American states since 1785 and exclaimed that "we must now place the manufacturer by the side of the agriculturist." Clearly the central feature of Jefferson's social and political world did not rest on any fixed image of rural simplicity and virtue. Rather, the ideal of the "middle landscape" represented a dialectic that had to change with the times and adjust, however reluctantly, to altered circumstances.

Throughout the nineteenth century and beyond many Americans clung to a vision of pastoralism quite similar to Jefferson's vision of 1785. For some this view of the world assumed mythic proportions. But Jefferson's own ambivalence regarding his idealistic preferences and what he referred to as "circumstances"—the aggressive world of progress—was such that he himself could never fully accept the pastoral myth. The tension between "circumstances" and the bucolic ideal remained so intense that Jefferson virtually expressed each side in a different language. Sentimental, nearly poetic language expressed his feeling for the one, and cooly analytic, pragmatic, empirical language served the other. They existed in his mind simultaneously and often found expression in his writings within the same paragraph, even the same sentence—the mathematically precise descriptions of the preparation for contour plowing or the fissure below the Natural Bridge followed quickly by the lyric passages describing their beauty.

Thus, while Jefferson could never repudiate the pastoral myth, he realized that it failed to incorporate vital truths about the American experience. The aggressive, individualistic, and materialistic strivings of many of his countrymen could not be captured by a vision of domestic harmony based on subsistence farming. Jefferson did not retain a naive faith in the realization of the pastoral hope. Instead the ideal society of the middle landscape, like the theoretical calculations he made on his own farm, served as a guide or a model: a constant reminder of what was possible, rather than an accurate gauge of contemporary conditions or a stubborn guide to social policy. Jefferson's strengths as a political leader may well have emanated from his emotional engagement with the pastoral dream and his simultaneous ability to disengage himself from it. Rather than being a handicap, such ambivalence formed the basis of his political strength among his contemporaries. Further, his ability to articulate decisive contradictions within American culture as well as within individual Americans became a

source of scholars' continual fascination with Jefferson since his death.

The ambivalence he felt toward the pastoral ideal did not prevent Jefferson from working arduously throughout his life to advance agricultural interests. Here, he displayed still another facet of his complex character; for if he was a "pastoral" man idealizing virtue, frugality, moderation, and self-sufficiency, he was also an "agrarian" man. That is, his interest in agriculture was every bit as economic as it was sociological, and he intended to provide agriculture with a strong economic foundation in America. Unlike many democratic reformers, Jefferson realized that social hierarchies rested upon economic realities and an unthinking deference to tradition as well as upon formal privileges and social customs. Consequently, he worked to create a revolutionary theory of government integrating a program of economic development with a social policy for nation-building. Believing industrious, self-reliant farmers to be superior citizens, Jefferson made the commercial prosperity of ordinary farmers the economic base for a democratic, progressive America.

Agricultural prosperity would nurture the release of human potential long held in check by poverty and ignorance. This belief underlay his conception of a democratic republic: a fusion of economic freedom and political democracy. Jefferson's perception rested upon his faith in the innate capabilities of man, his optimistic hope for a new political and social order in America, and his dedication to the American husbandman. These elements provided the vital force of the political movement called Jeffersonian Republicanism.

While most political leaders realized the tremendous economic potential in America, the critical and divisive issue of the late eighteenth century became how and in support of which values this potential could best be realized. Federalists and Republicans both agreed on the need for an effective, unified national government, but they violently disagreed over whether that government should become highly centralized through the manipulation by a few citizens of public credit and public funds or should remain open and responsive to the individual needs of ordinary men.

For his part, Jefferson considered republicanism superior to all other forms of rule precisely because it prevented governments from restraining the free acquisition of wealth. In a republic all men should enjoy an equal opportunity to acquire a comfortable livelihood. This would be the case, however, only so long as government did not acquire significant powers to control or influence the economic behavior of its citizens. Here Jefferson voiced the classical libertarian's fear that increasing governmental power inevitably meant encroachments upon the realm of liberty. The more powerful the government, the stronger the exploiters and the weaker the producers. The best hope for a republic remained the constant free access of its citizens both to their government and to the means of getting a living. Consequently Jefferson firmly believed that republican government endured only so long as opportunities for the acquisition of property remained available to an ever-increasing population. By "property" Jefferson meant land. Widespread landholding and the predominance of farming in the economy remained essential to his republicanism; they created precisely the sort of individual industriousness that spawned the virtue upon which all republican states depended.

In many ways Jeffersonian Republicanism reflected the ambivalence of its namesake: it incorporated both his pastoral idealism as well as his advocation of the commercial exploitation of American agriculture by a nation of aggressive, independent farmers. In the abstract, Jeffersonianism represented a configuration of hopes, fears, and assumptions that formed a vision of expansion across space as a means of escaping the de-

velopment through time that was generally believed by Enlightenment philosophers to bring with it political corruption and social decay. The republican dream of prolonging the nation's social youth rested upon the hope that geographical expansion would continuously provide the ideal demographic basis for a republican social order.

This hope did not rest entirely upon abstract ideals. The golden age of grain growing that emerged in the early national period actually did provide a practical material base upon which to build the republican vision of America. Rising prices, resulting from an increasing world demand for staples, held out the promise of a flourishing trade in American foodstuffs that could easily be produced on family farms. Rather than stagnating in subsistence farming, the independent husbandman could partake in the spreading economic prosperity. Indeed, the prosperity of the ordinary farmer could now become the basis for a democratic, progressive America. Free land, free trade, and scientific advances in agricultural methods spelled progress and prosperity for Americans, progress and prosperity open to all rather than limited to a special few.

In order to support a nation of independent farmers engaged in the commercial exploitation of agriculture, America needed to combine landed and commercial expansion: open markets as well as open space became essential. American commerce, if linked to agricultural surpluses, could become the handmaiden of American agriculture and, as a consequence, be moderated by the nation's most virtuous class—its independent, economically secure farmers. To achieve such a political economy required wise political action. The Jeffersonian Republican party responded by making land in the national domain readily accessible to the individual farm owner and dramatically increasing the amount of such land available to future generations; employing diplomatic initiatives to open world markets for farm products; and committing public funds to internal improvements. At the same time, it vigorously opposed fiscal measures that bore unfairly upon ordinary taxpayers and that created special privilege and class distinctions. Thus the struggle between Federalists and Jeffersonians, involving two different kinds of property, did not stem from a conflict between patrons of subsistence agriculture and supporters of modern commerce. Instead it involved a struggle between differing conceptions of capitalistic development in the United States. Alexander Hamilton championed a highly centralized process involving a favored few at the center while Jefferson espoused the free competition of individual citizens in an open, competitive marketplace.

The emphasis Jefferson placed upon the individual in a competitive market economy reflected his optimistic view of human nature as well as his high expectations for progress, enthusiasm for economic growth, and lack of reverence toward the past. Throughout history, he believed, repressive environments had fostered vice and corruption, but the innate qualities of man offered great hope. A republican government in America presented mankind with a fresh start: a world shorn of formal hierarchy, which would liberate the natural forces so long suppressed by the Old World artifices of monarchy, nobility, and an established clergy. Free of such restraints, man's natural capacity for personal autonomy would flourish and nurture an unfolding of human potential long blocked by poverty and ignorance.

Consequently, Jefferson's emphasis upon agriculture stemmed as much from his faith in the vast potential for agricultural profits as from an attempt to protect a pastoral mode of life. His hope that ordinary men might free themselves from economic and political subservience to their social superiors rested upon the bright promise of commercial agriculture. Jefferson united the

husbandman and commercial prosperity to form a radical new moral theory of government and society. Dissolving society into its individual human components, he invested each with a fundamental economic character and a natural capacity for personal autonomy. The purpose of government in such a society was no longer to raise power to balance power but instead to foster an environment that liberated man's self-actualizing capabilities. Jefferson's political economy—democratic, commercial, capitalistic, agrarian—emphasized a government that fostered and protected the free individual's access to economic opportunities. He realized that John Locke's identity of interests among the propertied might be universalized in America. A new secular order could emerge in America.

When Jefferson exclaimed that America was a "chosen country with room enough for our descendents to the hundredth and thousandth generation," he gave voice to his unbounded optimism about the future of his country as well as his unlimited hopefulness about the nature of man. Indeed, his hope for an enduring republican society was "built much on the enlargement of the resources of life going hand in hand with the enlargement of territory, and the belief that men are disposed to live honestly, if the means of doing so are open to them." So long as American government did not fall into the hands of those who would manipulate its institutions in a repressive and self-serving manner, Jefferson believed that America could become an "empire for liberty," a compact with man's future, not his past mistakes. Henry Adams captured this faith when he wrote: "Jefferson aspired beyond the ambition of nationality and embraced in his view the whole future of man." For Thomas Jefferson, American agriculture constituted not only a virtuous way of life, but provided the essential basis for an economic and political system that held promise for free men everywhere.

American Indians

BERNARD W. SHEEHAN

FOR Jefferson, the Indian was at once a subject of unending philosophical speculation and a perplexing practical problem. Speculative philosophy as it was practiced by Jefferson and others of scholarly bent in the founding generation answered many questions about the native people, but it proved to be of little service in the formulation of policy. The problem was that the scholarly speculation of the time left virtually no room for the real Indian. It was not that much accurate information had not been gathered and published concerning the native way of life. It had, but little of this wealth of particular information allowed native society (or for that matter an individual Indian) to be taken on its own terms. The purpose of theoretical treatments of the Indian remained, until well into the nineteenth century, to conform the native people to the larger schemes of natural history. The position of the Indian in the Great Chain, the temporal origins of the tribes, and the progress of the natives in the unfolding process of civilization all involved questions of great moment in the white man's world but they were of slim meaning for the understanding of native culture. Indeed the question of social development, which attempted to estimate the character and velocity of change in native life leading toward the ideal of civilization, conceived of the Indian in a way largely hostile to the integrity of his culture. For Jefferson and most of his generation, the practical success of philosophy could be measured by the degree to which the Indian ceased to be an Indian. They were not interested in the slow process of acculturation, which would have taken place in any case, but in a program of change that would turn the Indian into a white farmer and cause his physical submergence in the white man's gene pool. In the end both philosophy and policy proved futile. The Indian changed, but he did not disappear, and he remained an Indian.

Throughout his life Jefferson evinced a deep interest in the native people, and his interest usually contained a strong quotient of sympathy. His sympathy declined sharply during those periods of conflict—the War of Independence, the hostilities in the Northwest in the 1790s, and later during the War of 1812—when he saw the tribes first as a threat to liberty in their support of the Crown and then as obstacles to the expansion of the new nation. But long before those periods of contention, he had enjoyed a number of youthful experiences with the Indians that no doubt made a deep impression on his memory. It may be that he found the native people all the more attractive because James Maury, his early tutor whom he came to despise, had expressed profound dislike for the Indians. As an adult and amateur scientist, he became an avid collector of native artifacts, an early and extraordinarily competent archeological investigator of a native tumulus on the Rivanna River, and a theorist of the nature and origins of native languages.

NOTES ON THE STATE OF VIRGINIA

Jefferson did his earliest serious writing on the native people in his *Notes on the State of Virginia,* written and published in the 1780s. The stimulus for this examination of the problem of the Indian had been the assault on the potency of the American continent by the Comte Georges-Louis de Buffon in his *Natural History.* As Jefferson expressed the argument, the French naturalist had maintained that animals common to the Old and the New World were invariably smaller in America; that those peculiar to the New World were constructed on a smaller scale; that those domesticated on both sides of the ocean degenerated in America; and that on the whole America exhibited fewer species. Buffon's theory held obvious consequences for the human inhabitants of the New World. Although Buffon himself had limited his accusations of inherent weakness to the native people, followers of the French naturalist, such as Guillaume Raynal and Cornelius de Pauw, extended the canard to all the people of the continent. Fresh from the

experience of the Revolution, Jefferson reacted sharply to this attack on the potentiality of America. Buffon claimed to detect an intrinsic deficiency in the very substance of the new continent that doomed indigenous life forms to limited growth and subjected alien species to a wasting degeneration.

Jefferson had no argument with the theoretical basis of the Buffon position. The Frenchman rested his contention on a materialist premise, a defect in the very matter of the continent. From this original deficiency, the processes of life conspired to create forms that were themselves lacking in essential vitality. If Buffon was right about the continent, he was surely right about the quality of the life found on it. In addition, by arguing that even imported animate beings would degenerate under the influence of America, Buffon affirmed environmentalist theory, a system of thought for which Jefferson held the greatest sympathy. Thus the case against Buffon had to be empirical. He could be refuted only by a demonstration that the American continent possessed the capacity to generate and nurture beings of superior capacity who equaled or even surpassed what Europe could exhibit.

In making his case in the *Notes on Virginia,* Jefferson examined the three categories of humanity that then made their home in America. Of these the blacks presented the most difficult problem, though the difficulty was more Jefferson's than Buffon's. The grave doubts that he held concerning the capacities and accomplishments of people of African descent made them of little use in countering Buffon's aspersions on the population of the continent. This was especially so because, in arguing that black inferiority rested on nature, not circumstances, Jefferson skirted close to believing in a separate creation for Africans. He also entertained the possibility in the *Notes* that blacks and orangutans occupied positions close enough on the scale of being to warrant sexual relations. Thus, they seemed immune even from the effects of a salutary environment. But Jefferson found it difficult to carry his position to its logical conclusion. He allowed, for example, for the deleterious consequences of slavery in explaining black inferiority. If so, it would follow that Africans were in some sense susceptible to environmental influence, though because of their putative inferiority they were hardly useful in countering Buffon.

Nor were the white immigrants to America of much help. Jefferson could note the accomplishments of George Washington, Benjamin Franklin, and David Rittenhouse against the Buffon-Raynal theory, but in the end he was reduced to citing the new nation's small population and its youth to explain its relatively modest contributions to art and science. That left the Indians to support the American position.

The native peoples were crucial to the Jeffersonian defense of America if only because Buffon had chosen to concentrate on the capacities of these indigenous inhabitants of the new continent. He portrayed the Indians as weak, animalistic creatures who had failed to master their environment. Nature in the New World had denied them the basic life-giving spirit and hence they lacked the inclination for self-perpetuation. Though they equaled Europeans in size, their organs of generation were "small and feeble." Hairless, sexless, timid, lacking in verve, the Indians maintained only tenuous family relations and no political order. They were naturally cruel and coldhearted, they reduced their women to servants and beasts of burden, and they showed no broad love of mankind.

For Jefferson this was a disturbing indictment, the more so because it came adorned with all the pretensions of science and rested on the environmentalist premise, the fundamental principle of natural history. There seems little doubt that, in leveling his criticism at the Indian, Buffon touched a

most sensitive spot in the American psyche. It was not only that Indians had long served as symbols of the American continent, and hence as the embodiment of the strength and virtue that Americans believed distinguished them from Europeans, but that the Indian was often envisioned by Americans and Europeans alike as the noble savage, an ideal of Western humanity. Jefferson was not much given to the sentimentality of noble savagism, but he did often rely on the savage conception in his discussions of native society. More significantly, Jefferson employed the image of the "middle landscape," a median position between paradise and wilderness, to describe America, a setting in which the native people, living a pastoral existence, represented the continent. Thus the Indian as an image or even an intellectual construct played an important role in the Jeffersonian perception of self. No wonder then that Jefferson reacted so vehemently to the Buffonian assault.

In the *Notes* he took up Buffon's indictment point by point. He found Indians no less ardent than Europeans. Their apparently lower birthrate he attributed to their peculiar habits. The women spent much time and energy accompanying the men on long hunting and war expeditions, suffered the consequences of annual periods of famine, and practiced abortion. Buffon's association of the native peoples' lack of sexual fervor with the absence of hair proved wrong on two counts. Indians were as hairy as Europeans, but preferred a glabrous body and hence plucked their hair. But the basic relationship between hair and sexual prowess was invalid, according to Jefferson, since blacks had less hair than whites and greater ardor. In addition Indians were brave, capable of enduring intense pain, affectionate, careful and indulgent with their children, and faithful in their friendships. It was true that the women were subjected to "unjust drudgery" but for that reason they were stronger than white women, whereas the men, who engaged in less arduous pursuits, were weaker than white men. "We shall probably find," Jefferson concluded, that Indians "are formed in mind as well as in body, on the same module with the 'Homo sapiens Europaeus.'"

Jefferson had more in mind in his defense of the native people than Buffon's faulty grasp of the facts. He wanted to demonstrate that Buffon had failed to consult the circumstances of native life despite his ostensible adherence to environmentalism. By attributing a basic defect to the continent, he had in fact conjured a native people who were themselves basically defective. Jefferson accounted for the character of the Indians by repeated reference to the way they lived. They were as ardent as whites "reduced to the same diet and exercise." The unfortunate condition of women was similar to the status of females among "every barbarous people." Moreover it was their excessive labor that made them stronger than white women. White traders testified that, removed from the native environment, Indian women were as fecund as Europeans. In an appendix added to the 1785 edition of the *Notes,* Charles Thomson, a member with Jefferson of the American Philosophical Society and Secretary of Congress, placed even greater stress, in refuting Buffon, on the customs and manners of the Indians. Jefferson drew on Thomson's knowledge of the tribes and obviously approved of his explanation of the native way of life. In the sense that he believed that native society was held together by manners and morals, the formations of historical experience, Jefferson had been led through his argument with Buffon to the beginnings of a realistic and even modern perception of native social order.

But the eighteenth century could not be evaded. Ultimately Jefferson used the common Enlightenment formulas for describing Indian society, although he did not see the origin of life quite in Lockean terms as a state of nature defined by the autonomous individual. He argued instead that the beginning of existence could be found in the family and that native society occupied a middle stage between the original condition and a later level that required submission to positive law. And yet his conception of native leadership sounded quite Lockean. Indian chieftains, for example, obtained their positions through the influence of personal character and were paid only voluntary allegiance by their adherents. Jefferson was also in the habit of employing the conceptual dichotomy that presented an excessively complex, rigid, and brutal European civilization in opposition to the simple, open, and virtuous arrangements of America. Given the choice between the state of "no law, as among the savage Americans, or too much law, as among the civilized Europeans," he opted for the savage Indians. As against the corrupted character of England and France, he told John Adams in 1812 that he wished his own country "to be ignorant, honest and estimable as our neighboring savages are." Indeed in a carefree though undoubtedly meaningful moment in which he described the differences between the Old and the New Worlds, he had referred to himself as "a savage of the Mountains of America." The Indians (and Jefferson himself) represented nature, whereas civilization, at least in its excessive form, stood for a measure of perversion. True to their natural affinities, the native people had "never submitted themselves to any laws, any coercive power, any shadow of government." The controlling forces in their society were manners (a moderate and quite realistic factor) and the moral sense of right and wrong. The problem was that Jefferson's view of the moral sense, derived from such Scottish common-sense popularizers as Lord Kames, identified that vital force with a static view of nature and not with the looser, developmental notion of manners. In this interpretation the moral sense was an innate part of the human makeup, akin to "the sense of tasting and feeling" that could be exercised and strengthened like a muscle but not improved in its content.

Thus Jefferson had a divided mind on the question of native American society. He did possess a certain insight into Indian culture, in the sense that he stressed the importance of customs and manners, the consequences of social learning, and the accretion of long years of experience. But at the same time he associated the native people with a conception of nature that raised the Indian as an ideal against which to measure the European world. As we shall see, on those occasions when the Indians menaced American interests or resisted Jeffersonian policy, that ideal faded in Jefferson's mind. The Indian would become an ignoble savage deserving extermination. Neither image afforded a realistic interpretation of native-American culture.

Perhaps the most revealing and extensive segment of the *Notes* concerned the Logan episode in Lord Dunmore's War. Jefferson included in his defense of the Indians against Buffon's views a speech delivered at the conclusion of that conflict by Chief Logan and printed soon after in a number of colonial newspapers. Jefferson's intention was to offer an example of native eloquence that would elevate the stature of the Indians, but he wanted also to explain the importance of public discourse for a native society devoid of the coercive rules that bound people with a European heritage. The controversy that ensued took two forms. The first involved Jefferson in an acrimonious argument with the partisans of Michael Cresap, whom Jefferson had accused of murdering Logan's relatives, but the second and far more pertinent dispute centered on the meaning of Logan's address for relations between whites and Indians. On the surface the significance of the event seemed simple enough. Logan, a respected native leader and a friend of the British, turned on the white settlers after his family had been slaughtered by vicious frontiersmen. Having "glutted" his vengeance against the settlers, at the conclusion of the war he delivered an eloquent epitaph for his life, the speech that Jefferson printed and that became famous in later generations. In Jefferson's view it illustrated the simple profundity of the unspoiled savage mind and refuted the Buffonian fiction that denied to the American continent the rhetorical brilliance characteristic of the Old World.

Perhaps the most interesting and revealing aspect of the speech was not so much Logan's eloquence but rather his choice of language. The piece as it was printed by Jefferson contained two obvious biblical references (meat for the hungry, clothing for the cold and naked), but more important the language possessed a rhythm and cadence reminiscent of the Scriptures according to the King James Version. In the entire address there appeared only one mildly allusive phrase ("beams of peace"), the form supposedly typical of the Indian mode of discourse. But it may be that the speech holds a deeper meaning. The principal themes can each be related to traits of native culture. Logan spoke of vengeance against his enemies and of peace once the revenge had been accomplished, of hospitality to his Indian and white neighbors, of ridicule by his native compatriots over his friendship for the British, and of condolence for the deaths of his family members. Although the style was European, the motifs buried in the oration may well have been Indian, though it might as easily be argued that each of these themes—vengeance, peace, hospitality, ridicule, and condolence—convey meanings of equal importance in the white man's world.

Jefferson believed that he had found an example of the pristine Indian uttering a last pathetic plaint for a dying world that deserved lamentation. In fact what he had discovered was evidence of the vast transformations that had overtaken native society since the European invasion. Far from being a pristine Indian, Logan was a Mingo, one of the Iroquoian people who had wandered from the main Iroquois groupings and lived on the borderland in close proximity to the white settlements. He may have been of mixed blood. At least he was closely identified with the whites, lived in a cabin, and drank heavily. He represented that median position in the transformation of native culture, disintegrated in part, acculturated in another part. And his famous speech reflected that very cultural mix. It rested on dimly perceived Indian themes, perhaps with equivocal meaning, and was transmitted in a language plainly European. In his discussion of the piece Jefferson missed entirely its relationship to the acculturative process that would be so important in his later dealings with the native peoples.

Although the sympathy Jefferson expressed for the Indian in his dispute with Buffon was genuine enough, it was in some sense tailored for the occasion. He could not combat Buffon and defend America without praising the Indian, and because of the nature of Buffon's argument, this meant praise for certain native customs. But he never lost sight of the major issues in his admiration of the native people. For Jefferson Indians were savages, which meant that they might be praised as an ideal that white men should emulate or condemned as the negation of civilized values. It also meant for Jefferson that the Indian lived at a rudimentary stage of life and could be expected to make improvements under the influence of civilization. Thus his praise for certain native ways was ultimately provisional, for he expected that soon those customs would be replaced by manners akin to the white man's.

THE REVOLUTIONARY WAR

Jefferson made his view of one aspect of native culture clear in the Declaration of Independence. The king, he wrote, had "endeavored to bring on the inhabitants of our frontiers, the merciless Indian savages, whose known rule of warfare is an undistinguished destruction of all ages, sexes and conditions." Early in the revolutionary conflict the British had made overtures to the tribes for support against the rebellious Americans, and the Americans feared that the British would gain the warriors as allies. Jefferson's attitude, and the attitudes of the vast majority of Americans, rested on his revolutionary principles and on his conviction that the savage state in this ignoble form defended a condition utterly antagonistic to civilization. The ideology of the Revolution as Jefferson expressed it in the Declaration established without cavil that the Americans were fighting not only for immediate but for what could only be described as universal human imperatives. They found it easy, therefore, to describe opposition as a basic assault on the human condition. Under the circumstances it seemed appropriate that the British, who for the previous dozen years had been engaged in a conspiracy to destroy American liberty, should have taken as their allies the savage Indians, who in one of their incarnations represented the very antithesis of humanity. American propaganda during the war made heavy use of this conspiratorial alliance between despotism and ignoble savagery. But the volume and intensity of the barrage leveled at the British make it evident that the Americans were engaged in more than propaganda. They saw the conflict as an affirmation of independence and a vindication of self, a process that could reach fruition only by a separation from Britain and the conquest of savagery.

Jefferson seized the opportunity to put his principles into practice in the case of Henry Hamilton. Hamilton, a captain in the British army, became lieutenant governor at Detroit early in the war and was responsible beginning in 1777 for dispatching bands of native warriors, officered by whites, against the Ohio and Kentucky frontiers. The carnage had been considerable and consequently Hamilton had achieved a singular reputation for infamy. Not only had he been instrumental in turning the warriors loose on the settlements, but he was accused of rewarding the returning tribesmen for white scalps. As a result he came to be known as the "Famous Hair-Buyer General." Whether he ever purchased scalps from the Indians remains an unsettled issue. It is clear, however, that he had been instrumental in mingling savage with civilized conflict. This, in Jefferson's eyes, was his major crime. The scalp-buying accusation, if it could have been sustained, merely added to Hamilton's iniquity.

Jefferson's opportunity to vindicate both the Revolution and civilization came in 1779 when George Rogers Clark in a brilliant maneuver surprised and captured Hamilton at Vincennes. Clark released most of Hamilton's men but he held the leaders captive on the ground that they had been deeply implicated in the Indian attacks on the frontier. With Hamilton they were sent east to Williamsburg where they would be administered justice by Jefferson, who had assumed the governorship of Virginia earlier in the year. Jefferson suspended the usual rules applying to prisoners and treated Hamilton and his officers as outlaws. They were shackled and thrown into the common jail. Hamilton remained fettered for two months. In time, when his gout flared, the regimen became less strict, but Jefferson continued to insist that the lieutenant governor deserved vigorous punishment. Prudent advice from Washington concerning the rules of war, the collapse of the "hair-buying" charge, and the threat of British retaliation led finally to an exchange of prisoners.

The Hamilton episode revealed Jefferson's tendency toward ideological reductionism. His case against the lieutenant governor rested on a stark differentiation between savagery and civilization and on his belief that it was in the very nature of the savage to menace the existence of civil

order. He was willing to sanction the use of Indians in the war against other Indians, but he was adamant that the native warriors should not be employed against whites. If the British allied themselves with the Indians, "let this reproach remain on them, but for ourselves we would not have our national character tarnished with such a practice" by exposing the British "to the inhumanities of a savage enemy." Hamilton had plainly broken a sacred rule. "Savages," Jefferson asserted, engage in "an indiscriminate butchery of men, women and children." Hamilton had made himself a "conductor" of this mode of war by sending out combined parties of Indians and whites, and sometimes Indians alone, to attack "not . . . our forts, or armies in the field, but the farming settlements on our frontiers. Governor Hamilton then is himself the butcher of Men, Women and Children." Jefferson interpreted the Indian threat in almost metaphysical terms, for the issue became for him not merely a question of excessive brutality or attacks on women and children but an effort "to extinguish human nature." Just as the British sought the creation of an unnatural despotism in the New World, the behavior of their allies, the savage Indians, represented nature denied. Large categories and absolute dichotomies led Jefferson, for a time at least, to abandon prudent policy for the futility of an abstract ideology.

The irony in this episode concerns the contrast between the behavior of George Rogers Clark, Jefferson's ally, and Hamilton. Clark was certainly no strict enforcer of the differentiation between savagery and civilization. He fought in frontier fashion, brutally and indiscriminately. But the revealing point had to do with his attitude toward the native warriors. Clark held opinions about savage war similar to Jefferson's, and when he captured Hamilton he threatened the suspension of the rules governing prisoners. But Clark was also an avid practitioner of the Indian mode of conflict. He and his men dressed in modified Indian style, used native weapons, danced and gave the war whoop in the native manner, took scalps, and generally disported themselves like tribesmen. Hamilton had done many of the same things in the course of performing his duties. Moreover, he showed a genuine interest in native culture as his journal and line drawings of native personalities demonstrate. He had indeed been responsible for directing the tribesmen in raids on the white settlements, but his views on the incompatibility of civilization and savagery were similar to Jefferson's and thus he was quite ambivalent in his role as "conductor" of frontier warfare. Jefferson ignored Clark's behavior, and he knew nothing of Hamilton's ambivalence. He was interested in vindicating the Revolution and hence the subtleties and ironies in the views of both his friends and his enemies eluded him.

THE WESTERN FRONTIER

Jefferson's attitude toward the native people may have been at base "philosophical," derived from his speculations on natural history, but his policies were not for that reason immune to the vicissitudes of circumstance. In his first administration he sent Lewis and Clark on a trek across the continent for the dual purpose of gaining knowledge of the natural history of the western lands and of expanding American influence into regions that Jefferson expected would someday be part of the empire of liberty. The explorers returned with much fascinating information about the lands they crossed and the native people they encountered, but they were frustrated in the practical ends they sought. Jefferson had intended that his "corps of discovery" should spread peace among the hostile tribal groupings of the West and establish a trading network that would attach the tribes to American interests. In this instance, as in so many others, philosophy did not go hand in hand with policy. Lewis and

Clark punctured a number of legends about the West, but their efforts to rearrange tribal relations and to bind those distant peoples to the rising power of the new nation proved futile.

Jefferson shifted policy to accommodate circumstances, but the basis of his attitude toward the native people remained consistent. When Indian warriors threatened the Revolution or attacked the frontier settlements, he stressed the distance between civil and savage ways and even recommended extermination. But once the warriors of the Northwest had been defeated in 1794 at Fallen Timbers and forced the next year to sign the Treaty of Greenville, Jefferson shifted his views toward the promotion of civilization among the tribes. In fact the two approaches rested on the same assumption: the incompatibility of civil and savage ways. Jefferson wished to promote the transition of native life from old habits to new precisely because he rejected the legitimacy of the old. When these outworn habits, violence and indiscriminate warfare, constituted a menace, he recommended decisive measures, extermination if necessary. But he much preferred a more pacific process of development by which the Indians abandoned the savage condition and became indistinguishable from the white farmers whose ancestors a millennium earlier had followed the same path.

Indeed Jefferson extended his vision beyond the expectation of progressive development. Not only would the native people follow the stages of progress that by the eighteenth century had become common parlance and enter the realm of civilization, but they could be expected to achieve biological amalgamation with the descendants of Europeans. At the same time that native culture disappeared in the progressive unfolding of the natural order, the very physical nature of the Indian would cease to be, submerged in the white man's gene pool. Jefferson's plan was in one sense a tribute to the Indian, for it burdened him with none of the natural liabilities that inhibited the rise of the blacks. In the Chain of Being, Europeans and Indians stood side by side. The transition, either in cultural or biological terms, seemed relatively minor. But this Jeffersonian vision engulfed the real Indian, whose existence was defined not by the categories of natural history but by a historically derived culture, in an overwhelming and supposedly inevitable process from which there was no escape.

After the close of the War of Independence, United States Indian policy evolved slowly. At the outset the new nation faced turmoil on the frontier. The Indians had supported the British in the Revolution but had been abandoned by their allies in the peace concluded in 1783 at Paris. They had not been defeated by the Americans and were not yet prepared to acquiesce in the hegemony of the new government. To compound the complexities, neither Britain nor Spain fully conceded American control of the western regions. The British continued to hold their western posts and maintained an interest in the fur trade south of the Great Lakes. The Spanish worked to retain their positions in Louisiana and Florida by fomenting discontent in the borderlands. But because neither government had formulated a long-range policy, local commanders acted as the moment demanded, thus contributing to the unrest. Despite these potential sources of embarrassment, the Americans emerged from the war convinced that the triumph of their Revolution established their sovereignty over the continent east of the Mississippi and over the Indians, whom they regarded as a conquered people.

By the late 1780s the situation had begun to clarify. The Confederation government in 1786 concluded that the policy of treating the Indians as a subjugated people had been impractical. The warriors had not in fact been vanquished. The Northwest Ordinance of the following year enunciated a new policy toward the tribes. It announced that:

The utmost good faith shall always be observed towards the Indians; their lands and property shall never be taken from them without their consent; and in their property, rights and liberty, they never shall be invaded or disturbed, unless in just and lawful wars authorised by Congress; but laws founded in justice and humanity shall from time to time be made, for preventing wrongs being done to them, and for preserving peace and friendship with them.

In one sense the ordinance was simply a concession to reality. The Indians were a formidable military presence that could not be excluded from their lands by the fiat of the Confederation authorities. But the ordinance as a whole made the white man's intentions very clear. The Americans intended to expand across the Northwest Territory, to settle the land and establish political authority. The plan left no room for the tribes. For the present the Indians would be appeased, but the future could not be in doubt. Yet, in another sense the ordinance signaled a new approach to the native people. Relations with the Indians would be a responsibility of the federal authorities. The government agreed, at least, to the possessory right of the tribes. They could not be excluded from their lands unless by purchase or conquest in a just war. Moreover, government policy henceforth would seek to maintain peace and provide the means to redress native grievances. Nothing here was designed to change the ends of national policy, though the new approach was calculated to significantly alter the process of Indian-white relations.

PRESIDENTIAL POLICY

With the establishment of the new government in 1789, Indian affairs fell under the jurisdiction of the War Department. Henry Knox, the new secretary, had thought seriously about the problem of the Indian and proved to be a quite sympathetic formulator of policy. Early in the new administration, in two significant memoranda to the president, he expressed his views on the Indian question. Washington accepted Knox's arguments, and in his third message to Congress he described the basis for a new Indian policy. Treatment of the native people, affirmed the president, should rest on an "impartial dispensation of justice." A regular procedure for the purchase of lands must be established that would at the same time avoid the imposition of unjust treaties on the tribes and minimize controversy over the purchases that were made. Equitable rules of commerce must be formulated for dealing with the native people, the president should be granted the authority to dispense gifts among the tribesmen, and provision must be made to punish those who violate Indian rights and thereby endanger the peace. Perhaps the most significant provision called for the formulation of "rational experiments" for imparting to the Indians the "blessings of civilization." Washington concluded by informing the Congress that he anticipated the establishment of "a system corresponding with the mild principles of Religion and Philanthropy towards an unenlightened race of Men, whose happiness materially depends on the conduct of the United States."

The application of these "mild principles of Religion and Philanthropy" awaited the success of Anthony Wayne in the Northwest and the Treaty of Greenville in 1795. But with that triumph the government began the process of separating the Indians from their land and gradually influencing them to adopt the white man's ways. The policy, enunciated by Knox early in the Washington administration, was maintained by Jefferson after he came to power in 1801 with perhaps greater emphasis on its "philanthropic" aspects. The Jefferson administration put into effect in 1802 a new trade and intercourse law that in great measure recapitulated the

laws of the 1790s but was intended as permanent legislation. It was not replaced until 1834. The new president also made a laudable though futile attempt to halt the liquor traffic. From the earliest initiation of a national Indian policy, government authorities saw no contradiction in a policy designed to acquire the Indians' lands and at the same time to seek the natives' welfare. As we shall see, Jefferson was most emphatic that the good of the native people required that they abandon their extensive real estate and in the process take on the characteristics of the white man's society. Philanthropy in this manner went hand in hand with the acquisitive instincts of a new and burgeoning nation, and though it required hard-fisted bargaining, frequent prevarication, and an increasing tendency to manipulate the Indians when they failed to equate their own interests with the white man's, on the government's part it was seen as the only hope for the survival of the tribes.

Judged by what actually occurred in his two administrations, Jefferson's policy emphasized the acquisition of Indian lands. The problem was that although Jefferson favored the eventual displacement of the native peoples and pursued a policy of purchasing Indian lands designed to promote an orderly advance of the frontier, the settlers themselves as often as not anticipated the government acquisition by squatting on the lands. As a result, Jeffersonian policy often seemed merely responsive and quite irregular. In more than one instance it moved in the other direction when government agents and military forces attempted to remove white farmers who had settled illegally on tribal lands. Yet there can be no doubt that in light of the white man's determination to obtain title to the land, the policy was spectacularly successful.

During Jefferson's years in power, Indian agents of considerable talent and influence—Benjamin Hawkins, Return J. Meigs, and Silas Dinsmoor among the southern tribes and William Henry Harrison in the North-west—constantly pressed the Indians for more transfers of territory. The policy was often indirect, resting on demands for land for military posts, tribal agencies, or trading factories, or for roads to connect distant white settlements and often as not to cover Indian debts to traders. But these minor grants were dwarfed by the major transfers of territory that occurred during Jefferson's presidency: one and a half million acres from the Choctaws in 1802, two million from the Creeks in 1804, five million from the Choctaws again in 1805, and some fifty million from the Sioux and Fox in 1804. And all of this for relatively little money. Expenditures on Indian affairs for the two administrations did not much exceed a half million dollars. The price of the land itself was half that amount in annuities during Jefferson's years in office, though many of the annuity payments extended into the post-Jefferson period. Altogether the Jefferson administrations extinguished Indian title to nearly a hundred million acres, a veritable real-estate bonanza.

Annuities granted to the tribes in return for lands were often delivered in goods and utensils designed to move native culture toward what the government considered a civilized mode. Furthermore, when missionaries applied for permission to establish churches and schools in the tribal areas, they were encouraged by the administration. In 1803 Henry Dearborn, the secretary of war, instructed the Cherokee agent to give Gideon Blackburn, a Presbyterian missionary, two or three hundred dollars to build a school. Government agents, army commanders, and the employees of the government trading factories all received instructions to further the plan to change the native way. Yet, despite frequent announcements by Jefferson and other members of the administration, very little in a concrete way was done to effect the plan. It was not until the following political generation, under the leadership of John C. Calhoun and Thomas L. McKenney, together with the major religious organizations of the nation, that a more impressive effort was made to transform the Indian. In the meantime, the government stressed the transferral of land.

The apparent failure of Jeffersonian philanthropy to result in a body of practical policy until after Jefferson's departure from power might readily be attributed to an excess of realpolitik or even hypocrisy. Certainly in his dealings with the native people Jefferson often made use of political realism, but there is little reason to believe that he was hypocritical in either the formulation or the implementation of policy. In the absence of other evidence, Jefferson must be taken at his word. To begin with, his view of the role of government in society militated against an extensive or vigorous intervention into human affairs. He stated policy, encouraged, and even exhorted, but he seldom felt the need to step in decisively. But most important, Jefferson viewed the incorporation of the Indians into the world of European culture as "the natural progress of things" that it was better to promote than retard, but that would occur in any case. It would occur, that is, so long as conservative Indians did not resist the future or the native people were not overwhelmed by the advancing frontier. Jefferson saw the process as part of a cosmic plan, a development of nature itself, but he never perceived it as beyond the influence of human action.

The key to the process could be found in the "coincidence of interests" that Jefferson discovered between whites and Indians. The native people, if they were to survive, must abandon hunting and gathering and take up farming and household manufactures. By making this transition they would require much less land than had been needed when their subsistence depended on hunting. In fact, the native people would be aided in their progress if they no longer had access to the great tracts of land that had been their birthright. Confined to narrower limits, they would see the wisdom of engaging in more productive means of subsistence. At the same time, the white inhabitants of America, whose numbers increased rapidly, required more land, which could be obtained only from the native people. As he explained in a letter to Benjamin Hawkins dated 18 February 1803, "the ultimate point of rest and happiness" for the Indians in this accultura-tive synchronization would be "to let our settlements and theirs meet and blend together, to intermix, and become one people." Thus Jefferson envisioned more than the transfer of property from one people to another, even though the transfer should benefit both. He had in mind a greater end, the obliteration of social divisions and cultural differences.

Jefferson's anthropology assumed a basic differentiation between the savage and the civil states, though progress could be expected from one to the other. (Indeed, retrogression might also occur.) The power of this encompassing conception induced a certain myopia in Jefferson's perception of native society and a naïveté in his anticipation of the future.

Invariably Jefferson associated the savage condition with an economy of hunting and gathering. The Indians were a people, he wrote, "who lived principally on the spontaneous productions of nature." In Appendix 1 to the *Notes,* Jefferson published the comments of Charles Thomson as follows: "All the nations of Indians in North America lived in the hunter state, and depended for subsistence on hunting, fishing, and the spontaneous fruits of the earth, and a kind of grain which was planted and gathered by the women, and is now known by the name of Indian corn." Over and over again he encouraged the Indians to become farmers. "We shall, with great pleasure," he told a delegation of tribesmen from the Northwest in 1802, "see your people become disposed to cultivate the earth, to raise herds of the useful animals, and to spin and weave, for their food and clothing. These resources are certain; they will never disappoint you: while those of hunting may fail, and expose your women and children to the miseries of hunger and cold." The theme so often repeated would appear to say much for Jefferson's good will but very little for his powers of observation. Ironically, the vast majority of the native people east of the Mississippi River derived significant portions of their subsistence from farming. They hunted, gathered, and fished to supplement their livelihoods. Toward the end of his presidency, Jefferson revealed that he knew something of the reality of native society, for in exhorting Captain Hendrick and the Delawares to become farmers he assured them that "nothing is so easy as to learn to cultivate the earth; all your women understand it." In part, the problem was that women farmers did not conform to Jefferson's vision of the proper organization of economic or social activity. Yeomen farmers were male and hence the constant entreaties to the native warriors to surrender the old ways. But more broadly Jefferson was held captive by his conception of the savage state, an early stage of human development that could be expected to give way to the pastoral and agricultural economy.

This progressivist ideology contributed to Jefferson's conviction that native society would be transformed with relative ease. Consequently, he did not share Knox's caution expressed in a letter dated 7 July 1789 to President Washington that the conversion of the native people would be "an operation of complicated difficulty." He did agree instead with the secretary that "to deny that, under a course of favorable circumstances, it could not be accomplished, is to suppose the human character under the influence of such stubborn habits as to be incapable of melioration or change—a supposition entirely contradicted by the progress of society, from the barbarous ages to its present degree of perfection." And he agreed also that it would be a pleasant sensation for the "philosophic mind" to reflect in later years that "instead of exterminating a part of the human race by our modes of population" the white man had saved the Indian by incorporating him into civil society. For Jefferson this process of conversion was not only necessary and desirable, but inevitable.

In time, the principal agents of this transformation would be missionaries, and the Jefferson administration did encourage and support a number of early religious efforts. But Jefferson's views in these matters were strongly secular. In keeping with his low opinion of organized religion, he preferred that the work of conversion be carried on by government representatives with instructions to promote practical changes in the native world. It may be that he condensed the Gospels to eliminate what he considered extraneous and superstitious materials for use by the Indians, but when he summarized the conversion process in a letter to James Jay dated 7 April 1809, he relegated religion to the last step.

> The following is what has been successful: 1st, to raise cattle, etc., and thereby acquire a knowledge of the value of property; 2d, arithmetic, to calculate that value; 3d, writing, to keep accounts, and here they begin to enclose farms, and the men to labor, the women to spin and weave; 4th, to read "Aesop's Fables" and "Robinson Crusoe" are their first delight.

What the Indians needed, he wrote James Pemberton on 16 November 1807, were "habits of industry, easy subsistence, [and] attachment to property," which will "prepare their minds for the first elements of science." Only then would they be ready for moral and religious instruction. To begin with, Jefferson argued, religion "has ever ended either in effecting nothing, or ingrafting bigotry on ignorance, and setting them

to tomahawking and burning old women and others as witches." Jefferson was confident that this practical method would yield great success.

Yet through Jefferson's statements of policy and exhortations to the Indians runs a note of apprehension, of haste lest disaster overtake them before they could be saved. In some parts of the continent the disaster had already occurred. Since 1669, Jefferson recorded in the *Notes*, the Virginia natives had been reduced to a third of their numbers. Loss of land, smallpox, and alcohol "had committed terrible havoc among them"; because of their low birthrate, they were unlikely to replenish the subsequent decline in population. Later when he assumed political authority and responsibility for the survival of the Indians, he often adopted the lugubrious locutions of the "vanishing Indian" theme. In 1808, he expressed his "sincere regret" to a delegation of tribesmen from the Northwest that their people were "wasting away" because of "frequent wars, and the destructive use of spirituous liquors, and scanty supplies of food." The native people, Jefferson believed, faced "the gloomy prospect" of their "total disappearance from the face of the earth."

Jefferson never doubted that his program of philanthropy would save the Indians from so sad a fate, but he became increasingly uncertain that the tribesmen would accept the plan or that the time allotted for the change would be adequate. As a consequence he showed a growing tendency to manipulate the native people. Often the manipulation was merely verbal, as, for example, in the language adopted by Jefferson in his Indian addresses. These were speeches delivered by Jefferson, mostly during his presidency, to delegations of Indians who visited the capital. The addresses were couched in a form white men believed appropriate for talking with Indians. The message was simple, repetitive, and spoken with what Jefferson thought of as primitive eloquence. In the early years, he referred to his native auditors as "friends" and "brothers" but in 1803–1804 the mode of address changed. The native leaders became "sons" and "children" in need of counsel rather than equals engaged in consultation. This new manner corresponded to important shifts in government policy: more pressing demands for land and the introduction of a removal policy. But Jefferson did not require new policies to transform his rhetoric. After all, the very nature of philanthropy could be infantilizing and manipulative. As Augustus John Foster, the British minister in Washington during the second administration, noted, the president was attached to Indians "from Philanthropy and because they were Savages as if they were his own children." Savage people were inherently infantile, children of nature who must be tutored into adulthood. And the philanthropist acted on the premise that he knew best what measures must be taken to achieve maturity.

Jefferson placed much stress on personal diplomacy. Until the practice became too expensive and inconvenient, he encouraged delegations of Indians to visit Washington, believing that such face-to-face meetings with native leaders would be an invaluable aid for transforming their society. They were feted in the capital with much dining and theatergoing and shown the variety and power of the white man's world. Typically a delegation would visit the gallery of the House of Representatives, be received by the president in the White House, and attend a reception in their honor. For a New Year's reception in 1806, Dorcas Dearborn, wife of the secretary of war, dressed the visiting women in plain, short dresses and petticoats of showy, large-figured chintz. The men wore blue coats and medals distributed by the president. As Jefferson's language showed, these were not the meetings of equals. He intended that the delegates

should become convinced of the advantages of civilization and that this message would accompany them to their home villages, but he also wanted the Indians to recognize the power of the new nation. In 1805 a delegation viewed naval maneuvers on the Potomac. Having been entertained in Washington, most of the delegations were then given a tour of the coastal cities in the hope that they would be impressed by the extent and numbers of American society. Lest they miss the point, Jefferson fell into the habit of reminding the delegates that the Americans were "as numerous as the Stars in the Heavens, and we are all gunmen." By this combination of hospitality and menace, he intended to convince the tribesmen that they had no choice but to become like white men.

Pressured by the need to obtain more Indian lands and by the fear that the philanthropic program would not work quickly enough, Jefferson, especially in his second administration, resorted to more blatant methods. He sanctioned bribery, or at least government agents were instructed to distribute largess to the more pliant native leaders. In addition, he determined to make more efficient use of the government trading factories. These frontier institutions had long been given the secondary purpose of encouraging the transition in native culture. Now Jefferson intended to use them directly in what he considered the necessary transfer of land. His plan was to encourage the tribesmen to contract debts at the factories that could be repaid only by a disposal of territory. Jefferson made the suggestion to Henry Dearborn in December 1802 and to William Henry Harrison two months later. The letter to Harrison was a private communication, though the instructions to Dearborn were official, from the president to his secretary of war. But Jefferson was free in making his views known to government agents. According to John W. Hooker, the Cherokee factor, the president asked him whether it might be possible to induce the Cherokees to run up debts of ten or twelve thousand dollars. Hooker said he thought fifty thousand a realistic figure, and reported that Jefferson responded: "That is the way I entend to get there cuntry, for to get them to run in dett to the public store and they will have to give there land for payment." Apparently some of the native leaders became aware of the president's scheme, though, true to his belief that philanthropy knew best, Jefferson preferred that for their tranquillity the Indians should have seen "only the present age of their history." He did not wish the native people to be fully aware of how far the government might be willing to go in arranging for their future.

REMOVAL

Jefferson first gave serious consideration to the removal of the eastern tribes to new lands west of the Mississippi River in connection with the Louisiana Purchase in 1803. At this stage the idea had not yet become a counsel of despair as it was to be later among many who had come to doubt the success of the philanthropic program. Had removal been possible at this early date, Jefferson may well have seized it as a happy expedient, but there can be no doubt that he continued to see incorporation as the long-term solution to the Indian problem. For Jefferson in these early years, removal served two purposes: it supplied an outlet for those tribesmen, especially the older generation, who resisted the adoption of the white man's ways, and it answered certain internal questions raised by the acquisition of Louisiana.

From the very beginning the achievements of philanthropy had been mixed. Certain aspects of the white man's world were immediately attractive to the native people. Guns, tools and utensils of various kinds, clothing, and housing were promptly incor-porated by the Indians into their culture. Other elements of European life, especially those retailed by missionaries and government agents, proved less attractive. Christianity spread among the Indians only very slowly. Private property and the legal arrangements to support it caught hold in some places, but it was a long time before it displaced the Indians' communal habits. But most important, the deeper relationships of familial and clan loyalty persisted among the native peoples. The indirect influences of the white man's culture and the more direct proselytizing efforts did, however, have their effect. Many Indians, particularly mixed-bloods, were profoundly affected and became to all outward appearance white men, but the great majority of the native people were only marginally touched by white culture. Perhaps the major consequence was the exacerbation of factionalism within the tribal groupings, the divisions sorting themselves out according to their degree of sympathy to the new manner of life.

Jefferson became aware of these divisions and was of two minds about them. On the one hand, he was unsympathetic to any faction among the Indians that failed to see the necessity of change. He equated such groups with recalcitrant Federalists in his own political world, antiphilosophers who refused to conform their lives to the imperatives of the new age. In his political discourse, he more than once mixed the controversies, making clear that he conceived the Federalists as the greater menace, though revealing at the same time his views of the Indians who resisted the wave of the future. Yet Jefferson was not a man devoid of sympathy for human foibles, even if these set a people against what he considered the natural course of events. This was especially so for the Indian because after 1803 he could conceive of a solution other than incorporation. Many Indians from the eastern regions, beset by the advancing white settlements, displaced by war and loss of land, and discontented over the factionalism in their villages, had already moved west and would do so in increasing numbers before formal removal in the 1830s. When factionalism among the Cherokees led a delegation from the upper and lower dissident towns to request in 1808–1809 an exchange of lands in the East for a grant in the West, Jefferson seized the opportunity. If the hunters would not become farmers, then it was better that they should go where game still abounded. With uncharacteristic complacency he told the Cherokees: "I do not blame those who, having been brought up from their infancy to the pursuit of game, desire still to follow it to distant countries. I know how difficult it is for men to change the habits in which they have been raised." It can be argued that by promoting removal Jefferson had admitted implicitly that incorporation would not occur. At most, for Jefferson removal was a concession that incorporation would not work for all Indians, but he certainly did not believe the two policies were in contradiction. He was more inclined to think them complementary. He remained convinced that some of the native people would be quickly incorporated into the white man's society and that eventually the great majority would be brought in, even many of the tribesmen who for the present had escaped civilization by following the game across the Mississippi. In the meantime removal served at least some of the Jeffersonian aims. It cleared new lands for white settlement; it left the native factions that favored civilization and remained in the East free to continue their progress; and it removed an uncivil obstacle to the cohesion of the new nation. Thus, for Jefferson, removal in 1803–1804 and again in 1808–1809 (the two periods during which his administration vocally favored the idea) was somewhat different from the policy as it came to be advocated in the 1820s and 1830s. In those decades leading to the final transferral of

native population west of the Mississippi, the idea of removal rested among philanthropists upon virtual despair that incorporation could take place and among many others upon decidedly unbenevolent thinking about Indians.

The acquisition of Louisiana no doubt concentrated Jefferson's mind on the possibilities of removal. In this sense the policy was fortuitous and his reaction to events opportunistic. But he quickly lent intellectual coherence to circumstances. Jefferson's conception of the native people had always been part of a wider philosophical vision that associated Indians and whites in the same human processes that required the expansion of civilization and the cultural and ultimately physical amalgamations of the two people. But Jefferson was apparently sensitive to the risks of expansion. He wished the process to be an orderly, stage-by-stage advance, rather in the way the eighteenth-century philosophers had come to conceive of the progress of mankind from savagery to civilization. If the native people retained their old ways, clung to savagery, and stayed in the East, they would remain a living obstacle to the advance of civilization and also an impediment to the creation of the orderly and cohesive society promised by the republicanism of the Revolution. By turning over the Louisiana land north of the thirty-first parallel to the native hunters in exchange for their eastern lands, the purchase would, he explained to John Breckenridge in a letter dated 12 August 1803, be a means "of filling up the Eastern side, instead of drawing off it's population. When we shall be full on this side, we may lay off a range of States on the Western bank from the head to the mouth, and so, range after range, advancing compactly as we multiply." In the end, there would be no ultimate refuge for the hunters. For Jefferson they too would be incorporated or they would be destroyed.

Jeffersonian philanthropy failed because it could not account for the persistence of the native way of life, even amidst the vast changes that did occur, and because its humanitarian expectations of incorporation were resisted by the great majority of white men. They wanted Indian land, not amalgamation with native society. And then there were unintended consequences that worked against the success of the Jeffersonian program. Proselytization or simply the indirect influence of the white man's culture sometimes turned Indians into white men, or partially so, but as often the consequences entailed the collapse of native society and the incapacity of the surviving Indians to make the transition. Even success yielded paradoxical results. As the southern Indians absorbed the lessons of two hundred years of relations with Europeans, the changes in their ways strengthened the tribal bond, thus making them in the early nineteenth century resistant to absorption into American society. Jeffersonian policy sought nothing less than an end to the Indians as a people. In a letter to Governor Harrison of 27 February 1803 he referred to incorporation as the "termination of their history." If they resisted by force, he threatened extermination, and if they failed to respond, he predicted their demise. The actual process turned out quite differently. The Indians both changed and remained the same, but above all they survived.

Slavery

JOHN C. MILLER

THROUGHOUT his life, Thomas Jefferson was inextricably involved with slavery. He grew up on a plantation surrounded by slaves; he inherited slaves from his father and more than doubled their number by his marriage; at the time he wrote the Declaration of Independence he owned almost two hundred slaves; in 1790 the dowry of his daughter Martha included twenty-seven "negroes little and big"; as president of the United States he bought and sold slaves surreptitiously; and of the more than two hundred slaves he owned at the time of his death, he manumitted only five by his will. Monticello, today a shrine of American liberty, was built largely by slave labor. The books in magnificent libraries he collected, one of which became the nucleus of the Library of Congress, were acquired with profits derived from the labor of men, women, and children who received no more than a bare subsistence.

This is hardly the record of a zealous opponent of slavery. Jefferson and many other Virginia planters managed to combine abhorrence of slavery with willingness to appropriate the fruit of the labor of slaves. As was said of the Empress Maria Theresa of Austria when she joined Prussia and Russia in the first partition of Poland in 1772, Jefferson and his friends wept—but they took.

As a student at the College of William and Mary, Jefferson acquired from his teachers and from his reading a conviction that slavery was a violation of the laws of God and nature. Early in his career as a member of the House of Burgesses and as a lawyer, he tested the antislavery waters in Virginia. He found them disconcertingly tepid and shallow. A large majority of the House of Burgesses rejected a bill, seconded by Jefferson, designed to give the government more control over the treatment of slaves. Jefferson also served as counsel for several mulattoes suing for their freedom; when he asserted that all men were born free, he lost the case. He blamed these reverses upon the "colonial state of mind" produced by British imperialism, but he later learned that the roots went deep in the American mind itself.

These rebuffs did not discourage Jefferson or impair his conviction that Virginia was destined to take the lead in the abolition of slavery. But, for the moment, he was wholly occupied in averting a different kind of slavery—the servitude that George III seemed bent upon inflicting upon Americans. "We have counted the cost of the contest," Jefferson said in 1775, "and find nothing so dreadful as voluntary slavery." The word *slavery,* in this context, was often used by Americans, but they usually avoided drawing a comparison between the servitude they feared from abroad and that which they themselves inflicted upon their fellow human beings.

In June 1776, when he was commissioned to write the Declaration of Independence, Jefferson was known to be an enemy of slavery. Even so, the members of the Continental Congress received in Jefferson's draft of the Declaration much more on the subject of slavery than they had bargained for.

In the preamble to the Declaration, Jefferson stated unequivocally that all men are created equal. No one objected to this generalization as long as it was confined to the white race. But did it apply to blacks? Few members of Congress would have agreed to that proposition if they thought for a moment that blacks, whether free or slave, were to be treated as equals of whites. Yet in Jefferson's draft they were not specifically excluded from the category of "all men" and therefore they presumably were entitled, as the equals of whites, to life, liberty, and the pursuit of happiness.

This matter had already been disposed of to the satisfaction of slave owners by the Virginia Declaration of Rights. That document, adopted in June 1776, was largely the work of George Mason, himself the owner of a hundred slaves. That circumstance did not prevent Mason from asserting that "all men are by nature equally free and independent, and have certain inherent rights. . . ." This was strong stuff for the slaveholders who composed the Virginia legislature, several of whom objected that it gave slaves the right

to freedom and equality. But a reassuring answer was immediately forthcoming from the proponents of the bill: slaves, not being constituent members of society, could not expect to reap any benefit from a declaration that applied solely to free white men. Thus, white Americans could proclaim the rights of man without in any way inconveniencing themselves as slave owners.

The Virginia Declaration of Rights provided the institution of slavery with an additional safeguard: it said that "all men" had an inalienable right of acquiring and possessing property and that they could not be deprived of that right or the property obtained under it by an arbitrary government. Since slaves were considered property— next to real estate they were the largest form of capital investment in the United States in 1776, far exceeding manufactures or shipping—and since slavery existed in every state in the Union, the institution seemed secure. The ownership of human beings was elevated into one of the inviolable rights of man.

By substituting "pursuit of happiness" for "property," thereby departing from the text of the Virginia Declaration of Rights, Jefferson deliberately, although only by implication, excluded property in slaves from the rights of man. Unlike James Madison, who regarded slaves as "a species of property," Jefferson denied that there could be property in human beings even though he in fact held them as property. By eliminating the word "property" from the Declaration, he strengthened the case for including blacks among "all men."

Jefferson intended that the climax of the Declaration should be an indictment of George III for his part in perpetuating the institution of slavery in the American colonies. In his draft, Jefferson accused the king of waging "cruel war against human nature itself" by carrying enslaved Africans across the Atlantic and forcing them upon innocent, freedom-loving Americans who wanted nothing so much as to stop this "execrable commerce." Jefferson left little doubt that once Americans were free of the malign control of the "Royal Brute," they would abolish the slave trade and set about abolishing slavery itself.

In the exuberance of pillorying George III, Jefferson omitted to mention that Georgia and South Carolina had never attempted to restrain the importation of slaves —their only complaint was that there were too few slaves on the market—and that northerners, especially New Englanders, had played an active part in the slave trade and had applauded the king's refusal to permit any interruption of it. Even in Virginia, the demand for restrictions on the importation of slaves stemmed largely from the fact that the Old Dominion had a surplus of slaves.

Taking these considerations into account, Congress struck out both paragraphs of the final draft dealing with George III and slavery. Jefferson lamented the "depredations" and "mutilations" inflicted upon his work, but, he clearly had been guilty of rhetorical overkill. The two deleted paragraphs did not come under the heading of "facts" presented to a candid world.

By expunging these references to slavery, Congress weakened the Declaration as an antislavery document. After Congress had finished its revision of Jefferson's handiwork, only the doctrine that all men are created equal and have certain inalienable rights gave hope of eventual emancipation. The War of Independence, it was made clear, was fought to prevent the enslavement of white men by Great Britain, not to free black slaves held by white men.

Shortly after the adoption of the Declaration of Independence, Jefferson returned to Virginia. For the duration of the war he ceased to be a national leader, confining his attention to his "country," as he often called his native state. There, in 1778, he supported a bill abolishing the foreign slave

trade. The adoption of this measure appeared to Jefferson to herald the early demise of slavery; henceforth, he said, it was merely a matter of "leaving to future efforts its final extinction." But even though the supply of African slaves was cut temporarily off, the institution of slavery stubbornly refused to die.

In 1784, soon after his election to Congress and his reemergence as a national leader, Jefferson was given a rare opportunity to strike a blow against slavery. He was called upon by Congress to formulate a scheme for the government of the western territories recently ceded to the Confederation, and for their eventual admission to the Union as states. Again, as in the Declaration, Jefferson gave Congress more than it had expected. He presented that body with an Ordinance that stipulated, among other things, that slavery should be excluded from the entire western part of the United States, south as well as north of the Ohio River, after the year 1800.

In the Ordinance of 1784, Jefferson acted upon the conviction that slavery must be placed in the course of eventual extinction and that there was no better place to begin than in the West. But his plans to create an "Empire of Liberty" encountered strenuous opposition in Congress; on this issue, the entire Virginia delegation parted company with Jefferson, and only one southern member voted in favor. Even so, thanks to the strong support of the northern states, the measure failed of adoption by only one vote, and it would have passed had not one of the New Jersey delegates been prevented by illness from casting his ballot. "Thus we see," Jefferson said long after the event, "the fate of millions unborn hanging on the tongue of one man, and heaven was silent in that awful moment."

It is possible that Heaven was silent because the juncture was less fateful than Jefferson supposed. By permitting slavery until 1800, Jefferson's plan would have opened the territories to slave owners and proponents of slavery who would have formed proslavery constitutions when the new states applied for admission to statehood—the course followed by Missouri in 1819. The only effective way to halt the advance of slavery was to stop it dead in its tracks. The Northwest Ordinance of 1787 declared slavery abolished in the region north of the Ohio River as of that date; even so, the creation of several slave states in that region was only narrowly averted.

Moreover, the confrontation between the North and South produced by Jefferson's proposal, had it been adopted, augured ill for the durability of the Union. The Northwest Ordinance, on the other hand, was unanimously adopted by Congress. This unanimity did not mean that the South had been converted to the idea that the national domain ought to be free soil: the Northwest Ordinance was part of a compromise by which the North accepted the three-fifths rule regarding representation of the slave population in Congress and in the electoral college, in exchange for making the Ohio River a line of demarcation against the intrusion of slavery. The opponents of slavery had to be content with half the loaf Jefferson proffered them in 1784.

Prior to the Ordinance of 1784, Jefferson had not revealed himself publicly as an uncompromising enemy of slavery. His views regarding that institution and what was to be done about it had been known only to a few like-minded friends. Even his efforts to prevent the expansion of slavery into the Western territories did not prove that he hoped to abolish slavery as it already existed. Proof that Jefferson intended to do away with the institution wherever it existed did not appear until 1785 with the publication of the *Notes on the State of Virginia*. Since this work was not intended for publication, Jefferson expressed his views with a candor that has confused and embarrassed his admirers even to the present day.

In 1781, writing, as he supposed, for a small audience of French savants, Jefferson delivered in the *Notes on Virginia* an indictment of slavery as caustic as any made by a latter-day abolitionist. He declared that the day-to-day intercourse between masters and slaves gave rise to "the most unremitting despotism on the one part, and degrading submissions on the other." His main concern was with the effect of this intercourse upon whites: in them, he found, it produced "the most boisterous passions," as well as self-indulgence, love of luxury, and aversion to labor.

Not content with excoriating slavery and lamenting its effects upon the human beings involved, Jefferson included in the *Notes on Virginia* the plan he had drawn up in 1778 for its gradual abolition—the most comprehensive, detailed, and, Jefferson would have said, feasible plan yet devised. He proposed that slave infants be taken from their parents and trained at public expense in "tillage, arts or sciences, according to their geniuses." At the age of eighteen for females and twenty-one for males, they were to be colonized in Africa. By "colonized," Jefferson meant that they were to be equipped with tools, arms, household implements, seeds, and domestic animals. Nor were they to be left unprotected: as a free and independent people, they would enjoy the alliance and protection of the United States until they had acquired sufficient strength to stand on their own. To replace the expatriated blacks, Jefferson wanted the state of Virginia to arrange for the importation of like numbers of indentured white European workers.

Had Jefferson's plan outlined in the *Notes on Virginia* been implemented, the descendants of slaves brought to America as "articles of merchandize" would have returned to Africa as free men. In their new homeland they could put to profit the skills they had learned in this country and apply the principles of free government that they had observed, purely as spectators, in the United

States. Thus, said Jefferson, they might regenerate the African continent by introducing "the arts of cultivated life and the blessings of civilization and science." Finally, it would be the righting of a great wrong done the black race—a long-deferred act of indemnification for the suffering and humiliation they had endured at the hands of whites.

By admitting that the slaves were entitled to redress, Jefferson raised a question that he explicitly asked in the *Notes on Virginia:* "Why not retain and incorporate the blacks into the state, and thus save the expence of supplying, by importation of white settlers, the vacancies they will leave?"

Jefferson had disposed of this question in his draft of the Declaration of Independence when he observed that blacks were "a distant people" who, he implied, would forever remain strangers in the land. Because of the color of his skin, an African, in Jefferson's opinion, always remained an African; he could never become even an Afro-American. He was an intruder in the American Elysium, a blessed region reserved by God and nature for white men and women and such aborigines as were willing to conform to the white man's ways. Blacks bore the indelible mark of servitude—a black skin—that they would transmit to their latest posterity. Even as free men they were identified as the descendants of slaves. The victims of a cruel, conscienceless diaspora, they were stateless persons whose salvation depended upon their early return to their place of origin.

Because of ineradicable prejudice against people of color in the United States, Jefferson believed that they were condemned as long as they remained in this country to discrimination, degradation, and exploitation. Surveying the condition of free blacks in the United States, he concluded that for them freedom had proved to be a curse: they, even more than slaves, were the victims of racial prejudice and social discrimination.

Slaves were at least regarded as part of the economic system that enriched their owners, whereas free blacks were generally pictured as lazy, shiftless, ignorant, parasitic unemployables given to vicious habits and crime and utterly beyond hope of redemption. A free black said that he and his fellows were looked upon "with an eye of contempt, considered rather as brutish and scarcely capable of mental endowments." By a foreign visitor to the United States they were compared with the Helots of Sparta or the pariahs of India. When a slave attained freedom, he or she merely exchanged one form of oppression for another hardly less intolerable and degrading.

Still, free blacks in Jefferson's scheme of things were not wholly bereft of the rights of free men. He did not envisage driving them out with whips and thongs: as he later said in private letters, such as one to Jared Sparks dated 4 February 1824, the exodus would be orderly, voluntary, and with good will on both sides. Blacks even would have the right to refuse to leave the United States and to take their chances with white supremacists—a course of action against which Jefferson strongly advised.

Whether as free men or as slaves, "God knows," Jefferson said, they had suffered enough in this hostile environment; they had experienced far more than their share of misery. In Jefferson's desire to see the blacks resettled in Africa there was an element of compassion. Abraham Lincoln, one of the most compassionate men to occupy the presidency, recognized that Jefferson really wished well to the blacks. He, too, believed that their long ordeal ought to be ended and that their removal from the United States was the only humanitarian solution to their plight.

In evaluating racial prejudice in the United States, Jefferson took into account black prejudice against whites. As injured parties, blacks could never forget the hurt and oppression they had suffered at the hands of whites: in the *Notes* he wrote of the "ten thousand recollections" of degradation and exploitation that ensured that racial tensions would never subside. New provocations would produce violence and counterviolence, and it would all end, he predicted, in a war of extermination between the blacks and their former masters. He persuaded himself that deportation was the only way of saving the freed blacks from genocide at the hands of whites fighting for their lives.

Whether free or slave, the black man represented to Jefferson a menace to the established order. He lived in dread of a servile uprising; when he said in 1787 that he liked "a little rebellion now and then. It is like a storm in the atmosphere," he certainly did not have a slave rebellion in mind. He believed that the blacks' love of liberty and their courage was as strong as that of white men. Jefferson did not suppose that the slaves had become psychologically adapted to their situation and converted into obsequious, fawning, happy-go-lucky "Sambos." Instead of a "Sambo," he saw in a black slave a potential Spartacus, the gladiator who in the first century B.C. led a slave uprising that shook the Roman state to its foundations. Unless slavery were abolished and the blacks deported, Jefferson prophesied that "our children, certainly, and possibly ourselves" would not escape the horrors of racial war.

Moreover, Jefferson acknowledged that black slaves, quite as much as white Americans, had the right to overthrow an oppressive government or, as in the slaves' case, the rule of an oppressive race. While he warned against rebellion for light and transient causes, he admitted that the blacks' grievances were neither light nor transient: they had suffered a "long train of abuses" that in the course of human events would produce and justify rebellion. In effect, he conceded that slaves had the right to act upon the maxim he inscribed upon his personal seal: "Rebellion to tyrants is Obedience to God."

If the slaves rose in rebellion, Jefferson thought that they would be as sure of the support of Divine Providence as were the Americans when they rebelled against British tyranny. The slaves, like the American patriots, had right and justice on their side, and Heaven seldom withheld its aid from a people fighting for freedom.

Despite Jefferson's forebodings, the South remained comparatively free of slave uprisings. The large-scale rebellion Jefferson feared occurred in Santo Domingo in 1791 when slaves took arms against their French masters and free mulattoes. But the violence did not spread to the United States, thanks, southerners believed, to their vigilance in nipping conspiracies in the bud. Both the Gabriel Conspiracy of 1800 and Nat Turner's rebellion of 1831 were localized and did not seriously threaten the system of slavery. It was white southerners, not the black slaves, who ultimately rose in a massive rebellion.

Jefferson believed that racial prejudice—on both sides of the color line—was a fixed and unalterable fact of life in America. He was able to appreciate the strength of racial prejudice because, as another part of the *Notes on Virginia* revealed, he felt it within himself.

Here Jefferson brought up a question that has not yet been wholly laid to rest: the intellectual capacity of the black race. On the strength of his experience, observation, and reading (his library contained nineteen volumes devoted to slavery, the slave trade, and the peoples of Africa) he concluded that for the most part blacks were earthbound Calibans so "dull, tasteless, and anomalous" in imagination that he could not remember ever having heard one speak eloquently, compose a line of music, paint a picture, or propound a philosophical truth. Not a single black, slave or freedman, to his knowledge, comprehended Euclid.

Of the work of black poets, writers, and intellectuals, Jefferson was an unsparing critic. He dismissed the religious poetry of Phillis Wheatley as "below the dignity of criticism" despite the fact that her poems had been praised in England and she had been feted by the nobility. He was equally curt in his appraisal of the letters of Ignatius Sancho, which had created a minor literary sensation in England. These letters, said Jefferson, indicated that Sancho was a man of feeling but of very little else; the intellectual content of his work was low, and, while he might rank high among members of his own race, he stood at the bottom when compared with whites. Nor could the intellectual and artistic work of American blacks stand comparison with the achievements of Roman slaves. Of course, the Roman slaves to whom Jefferson referred were household slaves, many of whom were educated Greeks who served their masters as secretaries, physicians, accountants, clerks, and business managers. In contrast, there was not a single black slave secretary in the entire South, and many of the states had laws forbidding slaves to read and write. Even so, Jefferson cited the discrepancy between Roman and American slaves as "proof" of blacks' inferiority to whites.

In this regard, Jefferson reflected the traditional attitude of a master class or race toward its slaves. Every slaveholding people, ancient and modern, considered its slaves, even if they were of the same skin color, as its inferiors. Slaves were inferior because they were slaves, and they were slaves because they were inferior.

By adducing in the *Notes on Virginia* "evidence" of the mental backwardness of blacks, Jefferson inevitably raised the question: was this condition owing to environment or to heredity? Jefferson declared in favor of a biologically determined rather than an environmentally induced inferiority. Rejecting the theological case for black inferiority—they were alleged to be the descendants of Ham, Noah's renegade son—Jefferson espoused the idea of a whole race

condemned by nature to irreversible intellectual sluggishness. In effect, he made skin color a determinant of intelligence: the "unfortunate difference of color" was accompanied by an equally unfortunate difference in mental acuity. The Ethiopian could change neither the color of his skin nor his intellectual capacity: both were determined by his genes.

Nothing in the Declaration of Independence had suggested that whole races were unequal in intellectual capacity and that such inequality was based upon an ordinance of God and nature. This concept was utterly foreign to the word and spirit of the Declaration but, like the exalted principles the Declaration enunciated, it expressed an aspect of the American mind.

Still, mental sluggishness was not, in Jefferson's opinion, the prime consideration in determining whether freed blacks should remain in the United States or emigrate to Africa. Even if blacks proved themselves to be the intellectual equals of whites, their skin color mandated their departure. They were an unassimilable minority, by reason of "that immoveable veil of black"; beside that cardinal fact, other differences were insignificant.

Nor did the alleged mental inertia of blacks—their inability to comprehend Euclid and to profit from the improving conversation of their masters—justify their enslavement. "Whatever their [the blacks'] degree of talent," Jefferson said, "it is no measure of their rights. Because Sir Isaac Newton was superior to others in understanding, he was not therefore lord of the person or property of others." On the other hand, the danger that this inferiority would be transmitted to the white race by miscegenation seemed to him to be a compelling reason for the removal of blacks from the United States.

In Jefferson's thinking about racial matters, miscegenation was always uppermost. He was haunted by the specter of racial amalgamation. To his mind, miscegenation spelled disaster to the experiment in self-government upon which the United States had embarked.

Because he believed that racial prejudice had been implanted by Providence to keep the races apart, Jefferson made no effort to combat it. In his view, the intermarriage of blacks and whites was contrary to the laws of God and nature. A salutary decree had gone forth from the Creator that blacks and whites were, if not separate species—a possibility that Jefferson did not wholly dismiss —so fundamentally different in skin color that intermarriage was prohibited. Seen in this light, racial prejudice was nature's way of preventing adulteration of the white race. Miscegenation thus became the supreme crime against racial purity; "it produces," Jefferson said, "a degradation to which no lover of excellence in the human character can innocently consent."

No passage in the *Notes on Virginia* more starkly illustrates Jefferson's fears of this eventuality than the two lines in which he compared the sexual drive of black males with that of orangutans—a comparison by which he sought to "prove" that blacks shared with anthropoids a primal urge to mix their genes with those of their superiors.

The orangutan, as it was known to eighteenth-century science, was a creature of fantasy, an improbable hybrid of the chimpanzee, the gorilla, and the orangutan itself. Reputedly, its habitat was in West Africa as well as Sumatra and Java. Travelers reported that this formidable animal—seven feet tall, with beetling brows and an ugly temper—carried off black women and girls, ravished them, and kept them as their slaves. One traveler reported that he had seen the offspring of such unnatural cohabitation. The natives considered this animal to be an underdeveloped human being, who could speak if he chose to do so. But the orangutan wisely remained silent, knowing that if he spoke he would certainly be put to work.

In abducting and raping black women, the orangutan, according to the conventional scientific wisdom of the eighteenth century, was obeying a primal urge to raise himself and his kind in the Great Chain of Being. In nature, an inferior always was drawn irresistibly to mate with the superior.

Everything Jefferson knew—or thought he knew—about the orangutan came from his reading of works of George-Louis Leclerc, Comte de Buffon; Henry Home, Lord Kames; Jean-Jacques Rousseau; and James Burnett, Lord Monboddo, the best-known anthropologists of the late eighteenth century. These philosopher-scientists debated whether the orangutan ought to be admitted to the human species or relegated to the company of anthropoids, and whether primitive man used language to communicate or, like the orangutan, was speechless or at least gave the appearance of being so.

To this debate, Jefferson made no contribution. His addition to the body of knowledge or pseudoscience of the period consisted in drawing a comparison between the upward-striving orangutan and the black male. Black men, said Jefferson, preferred white women "as uniformly as is the preference of the Oran-ootan for the black women over those of his own species." He attributed this preference to the superior attractiveness of white women, which black males, responding to a basic urge of their being to transcend their allotted place in nature, found irresistible.

The offspring of such unions proved that the blacks had succeeded in ascending in the Great Scale of Being. It was a "fact," Jefferson asserted, "observed by every one" that mulattoes were superior to blacks but still physically and mentally inferior to pure whites. Jefferson said nothing about poor whites—they were on the right side of the color line.

Actually, as Jefferson well knew, black females stood in far less danger from lascivious apes than from white males on southern plantations. Despite the laws of nature and of man forbidding such intercourse, the rapid growth of the mulatto population—white Americans seemed intent upon creating a new race altogether, a goal they have achieved to a remarkable degree—told Jefferson that all was not as it ought to be in the American Eden. He could only envy the Romans, who, being the masters of slaves of their own skin color, could free them "without staining the blood" of true-born Romans.

For these reasons, Jefferson joined emancipation indissolubly with colonization; until the black population had been removed beyond the "reach of mixture," he preferred the continuation of slavery. "Beyond the reach of mixture" meant to Jefferson an exodus of blacks from the North and possibly the South American continents. In 1801, he rejected the idea of colonizing freed blacks in a remote part of the North American continent: the United States, he observed, formed a "nest of freemen" from which a swarm of settlers would cover the entire continent with a network of allied republics. With this high destiny before them, Americans could suffer no "blot of mixture" to remain on the face of a land soon to be appropriated by white men and women. Since there was no telling where this process would stop, Jefferson was prepared to contemplate the removal of the blacks from both continents.

In writing the *Notes on Virginia,* Jefferson sought to justify, for the benefit of European intellectuals, a course of action that he believed the United States must adopt in order to attain the racial purity upon which the success of the republican experiment depended. He was aware that the ideas he advanced were anathema to many philosophes: the concept of the biological inferiority of the black race ran counter to the Enlightenment view that environment was all-important in explaining differences among humans. The

idea of a whole race condemned by nature to intellectual insignificance represented a regression to bigotry and superstition. Some of the philosophes regarded as the wisest of mankind the Chinese, to whom Caucasians ought to look for instruction in science and philosophy.

Addressing men of such liberal views, Jefferson realized that they required hard, factual, scientific proof of black inferiority. Moreover, Jefferson prided himself upon being a member of the scientific community, and he subscribed to the governing evidence of scientific canons. He was aware that the conclusions he had set down in the *Notes on Virginia* were hardly more than subjective surmises, based upon nothing more substantial than his personal experience and reading. And so, in his concluding remarks on blacks and slavery, he strenuously disclaimed any intention of degrading an entire race from "the rank in the scale of being which their Creator may perhaps have given them." What he had earlier cited as proof he now characterized as "suspicion only" and "conjecture" that he now advanced with the "utmost diffidence." Softening his initial position, he admitted that environment might have created many of the deficiencies in intellect that he had perhaps too summarily attributed to biology.

As though he were no longer wholly sure of his ground, Jefferson now said that he remained open to evidence that blacks were the intellectual equals of whites. He suggested that evidence might come in the form of scientifically controlled experiments. But Monticello never became the scene of such experiments: he made no attempt to educate his slaves with a view to determining their intelligence quotient. At Monticello, young slave boys were employed in making nails; they were never encouraged to learn to read and write. Perhaps he feared the results of such experiments; they might have shaken his comforting assumption that he was dealing with inferiors.

He reserved final judgment, however, pending further evidence of intellectual capacity. He laid the burden of proof upon blacks: it was up to them to prove him wrong. It would seem that he expected them to raise themselves by their own bootstraps. Jefferson made no effort to ameliorate the condition of free blacks in Virginia. On the contrary, when he codified the law of the Old Dominion in 1778, he added new restrictions upon their already rigidly limited freedom of action.

Manifestly, Jefferson found a measure of solace in the assumption of black intellectual inferiority and, for that reason, he tried to suppress his doubts and misgivings on that score. It was far easier for him to hold slaves —and he saw no alternative to that unhappy state as long as he remained a planter in his beloved Virginia—if he could feel certain in his own mind that they were of relatively low intelligence. Black inferiority was part of the defense mechanism that permitted him, a man of high moral principles and humanitarian instincts, to be in Dr. Samuel Johnson's caustic words, a "driver of Negroes." For Jefferson, it would have been intolerable to keep in servitude men and women he knew to be the intellectual equals of whites.

It was sufficient for his purposes to keep this view to himself or to confide it only to his like-minded friends. He felt no compulsion to assert publicly a theory that he admitted might be proved wrong after all the evidence was in. The only occasion on which his views appeared in print during his lifetime was in the *Notes on Virginia*. But when he wrote that book he had no idea that he was laying his ideas before the world.

The significance of the *Notes on Virginia* is not that Jefferson presented a brief for black inferiority but that he demanded the extinction of slavery. For the first time, the author of the Declaration of Independence disclosed that the institution of slavery was not set above the principles proclaimed in 1776. Nor did he sanctify slavery under the hallowed rubric of the rights of property. Although a few abolitionists took him to task for giving credit to tall tales about orangutans and denigrating the intelligence of blacks, his opinions on these matters did not occasion general surprise or condemnation. At that time almost everyone believed that blacks were naturally inferior to whites: it would have been remarkable only if Jefferson had asserted that they were equals.

The *Notes on Virginia* did not present a wholly negative view of blacks: Jefferson conceded that they had some redeeming qualities that, had they not had black skin, might have enabled them to remain in the United States. For example, they were musical, their memory was good, and, above all, their moral sense was equal to that of whites. Jefferson defined moral sense as an innate ability to distinguish right from wrong and a propensity to act rightly. Jefferson believed that, without this moral sense, humans could not live together in society; reason alone could not create social harmony. Thus, an all-wise Providence had provided humans with the capabilities necessary to lead a moral life in a social milieu.

Because the doctrine of the universality of the moral sense was to the philosophes a self-evident truth, Jefferson could not have denied this quality to the blacks without denying their humanity. By acknowledging that they possessed the moral sense, Jefferson demonstrated its universality and its durability—it had survived even in slaves. And because blacks were capable of virtuous action—Jefferson attributed such derelictions as lying, stealing, and laziness to their environment—they had a right to the pursuit of happiness. In short, they were free to enjoy all the rights of man—in Africa.

In 1790, Jefferson learned of the existence of a black who understood Euclid. This prodigy was Benjamin Banneker, a free black of mixed race (his grandmother was white) who lived in rural Maryland. Basically self-taught, Banneker had perfected his knowledge of mathematics, astronomy, and almanac making with the aid of his white friends, the Ellicotts of Ellicott's Mills.

On the recommendation of Andrew Ellicott, chief surveyor of the District of Columbia, and on the strength of "a very elegant solution of Geometrical problems" by Banneker, Jefferson appointed him an assistant surveyor for the District. Shortly afterward, he sent a specimen of Banneker's mathematical work to the Marquis de Condorcet, secretary of the French Royal Academy of Science, a prominent philosophe and a firm believer in racial equality; Jefferson described Banneker as "a very worthy and respectable member of society"—terms he did not often apply to free blacks.

Jefferson found in Banneker's life proof of "moral excellence": the son of an African slave had, against great odds, distinguished himself in a field Jefferson regarded as the highest form of knowledge. His mathematical exercises seemed to Jefferson to indicate, when he wrote to the Marquis de Condorcet on 30 August 1791, that the mediocrity of talents he had observed in blacks was "merely the effect of their degraded condition, and not proceeding from any difference in the structure of the parts on which intellect depends." It was a graceful retraction of the hypothesis he had propounded in the *Notes on Virginia*. Few authors or politicians have professed themselves as eager as Jefferson to have their theories disproved by new evidence.

In August 1791, after he had left his surveying job, Banneker, acting on the advice of the abolitionist friends in Philadelphia and Baltimore who had financed his almanac, wrote Jefferson a hectoring, almost insulting letter, criticizing him for holding slaves by "fraud and violence" while pretending to be an enemy of slavery. He reminded Jefferson that while writing the Declaration of Independence, he had held slaves contrary to the will of God and nature "under groaning captivity and cruel oppression." He recommended that Jefferson remove all doubts concerning his sincerity by

acting, not merely writing, against slavery. He felt sure that Jefferson would do so "if he were a friend of liberty . . . if he was a supporter of the rights of human nature," and if he were a genuine enemy of slavery. Left open was the possibility that Jefferson was none of these.

To Banneker's trenchant letter, Jefferson returned a soft, conciliatory answer. In a letter dated 30 August 1791, he assured the black mathematician that "no body wishes more than I do to see such proofs as you exhibit, that nature has given to our black brethren, talents equal to those of the other colors of men, and that the appearance of a want of them is owing merely to the degraded condition of their existence, both in Africa and America" and that "no body wishes more ardently to see a good system commenced for raising the condition both of their body and mind to what it ought to be, as fast as the imbecility of their present existence, and other circumstances which cannot be neglected, will admit."

Again probably influenced by his abolitionist benefactors, Banneker published in his almanac for 1792 his letter to Jefferson and Jefferson's reply. While he hoped, no doubt, thereby to increase the sales of his almanac, he succeeded as well in casting doubt upon Jefferson's sincerity as an opponent of slavery. The almanac was actually a political as well as an antislavery document; in a foreword, Federalist Sen. James McHenry of Maryland declared that Banneker's work conclusively proved, contrary to Jefferson's theory, "that the powers of the mind are disconnected with the colour of the skin."

That Jefferson resented Banneker's breach of confidence in publishing their correspondence was evident in his letter to Joel Barlow dated 8 October 1809, in which he assessed Banneker's character and ability. He now dismissed Banneker's mathematical work as second-rate and suggested that it was probably more the work of Banneker's white friends than of Banneker himself. The letter from Banneker that he had answered courteously in 1791 he now cited as the work of a commonplace mind. He remarked sourly that any ability shown by blacks had a direct correlation with the amount of white "blood" they possessed.

As early as 1785, Jefferson excused himself from further active participation in the antislavery movement on the ground that the final victory over the institution was properly the work of the younger generation to whom he gladly handed the torch. As secretary of state, vice-president, and president, he adhered strictly to that resolution.

After his election to the presidency, Jefferson vowed never to commit his thoughts on slavery to paper and to avoid "every public act or manifestation on the subject." Instead, he devoted his efforts to sweeping deftly the "hideous evil" of slavery under the ample rug of republicanism. He habitually spoke of the United States as though slavery had been abolished and the slaves repatriated in Africa. In his eyes, the American republic was pure and virtuous; "every one has an equal right to judge for himself"; and the people lived under a government "so modelled as to rest continuously on the will of the whole society." It was a land of "equal liberty" and "lovely equality," "a hallowed ark of human hope and happiness," "the solitary republic of the world, the only monument of human rights and the sole depository of the sacred fire of self-government." The Heaven-ordained mission of the United States was to bring light and liberty to Europe by dispelling the "clouds of barbarism and despotism" that hung heavily over that benighted continent.

Such self-congratulatory idealism is the prerogative of every politician, and Jefferson certainly was not the only practitioner of that form of sleight of hand. No one would guess from the speeches of Pericles that Athenian democracy was based upon a large slave population. Still, rhetoric could not hide the fact that the United States was the greatest slave power in the world and that one-fourth of the population was not included among "the people." The opening lines of Rousseau's *Social Contract*—"Man is born free; and everywhere he is in chains"—were actually more applicable to the United States than to Europe.

The Constitution adopted in 1788 prohibited the federal government from interfering in the foreign slave trade for twenty years—a period of grace that Georgia and South Carolina used to increase significantly the slave population of the United States. In 1808, time expired for this commerce in human beings, and on 1 January 1808, the earliest possible moment, the president and Congress declared the trade abolished.

But the abrogation of the slave trade did not prove to be the prelude, as Jefferson hoped, to the extinction of slavery itself. Instead, it put a premium upon increasing the existing slave population by natural increase. It also vastly increased the domestic slave trade, especially to the cotton- and sugar-producing areas of the Gulf and South Atlantic States. Moreover, slaves continued to be sold at public auction within sight of the United States Capitol, and the streets of Washington, D.C., were so crowded with coffles of handcuffed and manacled slaves that they created a traffic problem. Despite the protests of citizens of the District and Alexandria County, neither President Jefferson nor Congress took action. It was not until 1850 that the slave trade was abolished in the District of Columbia.

Ironically, during his presidency, Jefferson was accused of committing the "crime against nature" he most abhorred—miscegenation. The presence of "bright-colored" children had been noted by visitors at Monticello, and Jefferson's political enemies drew the inference that they were Jefferson's progeny, conceived upon Sally Hemings. First heard in the election of 1800, the story was revived and elaborated upon in 1802 by

James Thomson Callender, a British hack journalist who had aided Jefferson in the presidential election by aspersing the moral characters of John Adams and Alexander Hamilton. Having failed to secure from President Jefferson an appointment to a postmastership as a reward for his work as a hatchet man in the election of 1800, he became a disappointed office seeker, the most deadly of all political animals.

Sally Hemings, "Dusky Sally," "the African Venus," or "the wench, Sally," at whose feet Jefferson was alleged to have prostrated himself, was one of the mulatto slaves acquired by Jefferson from his wife's dowry. She and several other members of the Hemings family were probably the illegitimate offspring of Jefferson's late father-in-law, who was given to exercising droit du seigneur over his slave women. The almost-white children born to Sally Hemings were probably fathered by Peter Carr, Jefferson's wayward nephew who enjoyed free rein at Monticello, including the slave quarters.

The hue and cry sounded by Callender was taken up by Federalist politicians and, later, by abolitionists. The American people were told that Jefferson maintained at Monticello a "Congo Harem" and that he deliberately brought children into the world in order that he might sell them and thereby turn his debaucheries to profit. The author of the Declaration of Independence was said to dream of freedom "in a slave's embrace." One of his mulatto daughters was reported to have been sold at public auction in New Orleans. The *New York Evening Post,* a Federalist newspaper, predicted in 1802 that what Nero was to Roman history, Thomas Jefferson would be to the history of the American republic.

Jefferson bore this vilification without public comment. To be accused of being an "atheist, Deist, or devil" seemed to him to be an inescapable part of the presidential office. Public office in the United States, he said, meant serving as a target for "every man's dirt." Answering such calumnies, he thought, would do no good: his enemies would merely dream up something even more heinous. In this instance, moreover, he probably did not wish to involve Peter Carr, a recent bridegroom whose wife might not regard his youthful escapades with an indulgent eye.

The Sally Hemings story can be made credible only by a major suspension of disbelief. Jefferson was reported to have seduced Sally in Paris when she was fifteen years old, under the promise that any children she might bear him would be freed when they reached maturity. In accord with this agreement she produced five children, four of whom survived infancy. Jefferson took no interest in the upbringing of these children; he made no effort to educate them —Sally herself was apparently illiterate—but he did give them their freedom even though they were wholly unprepared for it. Such indifference to the welfare of his own children is incomprehensible in a man who, like Jefferson, took such joy in family life and who was so vitally concerned with education.

Perhaps Jefferson offered the best refutation of this titillating tale of seduction and secret passion when he said in another connection that if a historian or biographer, dealing with a person whose character was "well known and established on satisfactory testimony, imputes to it things incompatible with that character, we reject without hesitation, and assent to that only of what we have better evidence." In other words, Jefferson warned historians and biographers against embracing improbabilities that violated the principle of consistency of character unless the weight of evidence left no other recourse. In the case of Sally Hemings, Jefferson's known character is his strongest defense.

In 1814, after Jefferson had passed his seventieth year, his young friend and neighbor Edward Coles urged him to raise the standard of emancipation and summon the people to rally to his support. By commiting his prestige fully to the struggle against "the greatest of our calamities," Coles told the former president, he would assure himself of immortality as the "revered father of our political and social blessings."

Jefferson once said that there were occasions "when it is a duty to risk all against nothing" but he seldom if ever acted upon that maxim. He did not attain the presidency by espousing lost causes or gambling everything upon a doomed assault. Instead, he followed a very different maxim: politics was the art of the possible, and the business of a politician was to choose wisely between probabilities and improbabilities. Jefferson described himself as "an empiric in natural philosophy"; he was also an empiric in politics. "What is practicable," he said, "must often control what is pure theory; and the habits of the governed determine in a great degree what is practicable."

Applying this maxim to the existing state of public opinion, Jefferson concluded that it would be folly to answer Coles's call to action. For one thing, he felt badly let down by the younger generation: they had had a rendezvous with destiny but had failed to show up for the appointment. Ignoring the warnings of coming disaster he had issued in the *Notes on Virginia,* they remained apathetic, indifferent to the promptings of reason and the moral sense, asking only to make money. He told Coles in a letter of 25 August 1814 that he had the distinction of being the only young man who seemed disposed to join the crusade. As for his own generation, he had given up hope that they would bestir themselves: many of them seemed to believe that slaves were "as legitimate subjects of property as their horses and cattle." The self-interest and avarice of southern slaveholders seemed quite as intractable as that of northern speculators, bankers, and merchants.

Among other reasons for not responding to Coles's appeal, Jefferson might have cited his disillusionment with politics and his desire to spend his last years in *otium cum dignitate*—the ideal of Cicero. Since 1776, he yearned to retire to Monticello; and now he did not want to disturb that hard-won felicity by engaging in a cause certain, he believed, to bring further obloquy upon him. Above all, he hesitated to impair his "usefulness"— the test he always applied to a proposed course of action—in some future crisis.

As for his conscience, he said that it was in excellent shape. He had done all he could to extirpate slavery, and no man could be asked to do more. His thoughts on slavery and his plan for its elimination were a matter of record: he had set it all down in *Notes on Virginia,* and it was up to the American people to respond to the iniquity of slavery as they had earlier responded to British tyranny.

Nor did the fact that he was a slave owner disturb him unduly. He never admitted that slavery had impaired his morals or that he was any the less virtuous because of it; the "boisterous passions" it aroused were experienced by other people, not by him. It is unlikely that the intermittent headaches from which he suffered were caused by contrition and remorse. He was not a Puritan who writhed in agonies of self-loathing and self-abasement, crying out that he was abominable in the sight of God; Jefferson had no quarrel with the Lord and he believed that He had none with him. He saw his and his friends' slaves as unhappy beings "whom fortune has thrown into our hands" —with an assist from George III. He yearned to see his slaves happily bound for Africa, but that event awaited his own emancipation from his debts—a day he never lived to see.

By most of his own slaves (with the exception of those who ran away to join the British during the War of Independence), Jefferson was reckoned a good master. They were not overworked; they were adequately fed, clothed, and housed; and they were given the incentive of reward for industriousness. When he sold slaves he always tried to keep husband and wife together. In his personal relations with blacks, he tried to treat them courteously and preferred to think of them as "servants" rather than as slaves. He liked individual blacks—among his household and personal slaves he had definite favorites —but, unlike Cicero, who loved to converse on philosophical subjects with his Greek slaves, Jefferson established no intellectual rapport with any of his "servants." He valued them chiefly for their obedience, loyalty, and skill in executing the tasks he assigned them. For example, he rejoiced in a "good" slave like Dinah whom he described as "a fine wench of the best disposition in the world." His fears and prejudices came to the fore only when he contemplated blacks as an alien, unwanted, and rebellious race whose presence in the United States was perpetuated by greed and folly. The invidious pronouncements made in the *Notes on Virginia* were delivered under the stresses and anxieties generated by his concern for the future of a racially polarized country that God and nature had designated to serve as an example to mankind of liberty, justice, and equality.

Being the sort of man who hated personal confrontations of any kind, political or social, Jefferson was personally incapable of whipping a slave but not, as his slaves discovered, incapable of ordering a particularly refractory slave to be whipped, even though he preferred to deal with habitual offenders by selling them. When one of his nail boys proved incorrigible, Jefferson directed that he be sold but contrived to make it appear that the boy was "put out of the way by death." Jefferson reasoned that if the other nail boys believed their companion had been killed, they would apply themselves diligently to their nail making. Fundamentally, slaves were ruled by terror, and even

Jefferson found it impossible wholly to dispense with the threat of severe punishment and even death.

In 1819, Jefferson was startled by "a fire-bell in the night" warning that the Union was in danger of expiring in the flames of civil war. With threats of secession voiced by northern and southern spokesmen, Jefferson feared that the "ungovernable passions" of men would create in both sections of the Union such "mutual and mortal hatred as to render separation preferable to eternal discord." Like classical Greece and the Peloponnesian War, the United States might go down in the blood and chaos of a full-blown internecine conflict.

The crisis was precipitated by the territory of Missouri's request for admission to statehood with a proslavery constitution. A bloc of northern representatives and senators opposed acceptance by Congress. They proposed to stop the westward advance of slavery by making the Mississippi River above 36° 30′ latitude (the southern boundary of the state of Missouri) the line of demarcation of slavery. This "containment policy" would have made most of the Louisiana Purchase free soil.

Thirty-five years before the Missouri Controversy, Jefferson had tried to exclude slavery from all the territories of the United States east of the Mississippi River. Since the Ordinance of 1784, however, the power of the general government of the United States had undergone a radical change: no longer a weak, tottering, innocuous government, it had become the dominant force in the Union, overshadowing the states and capable of enacting tariffs, laws, and bounties for the encouragement of manufactures—all of which most southerners regarded as inimical to the interests of their section. Moreover, the North and South were now locked in a struggle for control of the West, which, as the most rapidly growing section of the Union, held the balance of power between the two older sections. This balance hinged upon sectional equality in the United States Senate; therefore southerners and their peculiar institution must be given free access to the West to carve out new states for the "slave interest."

For these reasons, Jefferson completely reversed in 1819–1821 the position he had adopted in 1784. Rather than advocate the denial of slavery to the western territories, he now demanded that they be open to slavery, and that Missouri be admitted as a slave state. Congress, he declared, lacked constitutional authority to prescribe the terms of admission of a state to the Union. In this regard the people of a territory were sovereign.

In the Missouri Controversy Jefferson detected a conspiracy by certain northern politicians to revive the moribund Federalist party on a sectional foundation. Having virtually eliminated the Federalist party as a national force, he now found that the Federalist mind was still alive and well; the "monarchists" had merely been metamorphosed into "consolidationists." By diverting the virtuous feelings of northerners against slavery into a fanatical hatred of the South and southerners, these power-hungry politicians proposed in 1819–1820 to draw a geographical line between two political parties and bid them grapple for control of the general government. Jefferson did not know of a more effective way of dissolving the Union.

If these latter-day Federalists, animated as he supposed by a bitter hatred of the South, came to power, Jefferson feared that they would, for political reasons, try to destroy slavery by an act of Congress or by a fiat from the Supreme Court. To eradicate slavery by such action, Jefferson said, was both unconstitutional and unnecessary. Despite appearances to the contrary, the United States was a consensual society; both southerners and northerners agreed that slavery must go. Such differences as existed had to do merely with timing and by whom the evil

was to be eradicated. Jefferson asked northerners to give the people of the South time to set their house in order; everything would come right in the end, as it always did in the United States, if the people were permitted to reflect and to act in their own good time, in their best interest. If that point were conceded, he felt certain that the states would do what every right-thinking American devoutly wished—emancipate the slaves and send them back to Africa.

Despite his insistence upon majority rule as the essence of republicanism—there could be no departure, he said, from the obligation of "absolute acquiescence in the decisions of the majority"—Jefferson refused to admit that this principle could be applied on a national scale to the subject of slavery. Wherever it was established, that institution was under the exclusive jurisdiction of the states individually and separately; the only function of the federal government was to maintain and protect it. Although this was sound antebellum constitutional doctrine, it precluded the participation of the American people as a whole from the attempt to solve collectively one of the most intractable problems they had ever confronted. It was enough for Jefferson that a majority of the people of Missouri wanted to establish slavery; what the greater majority wished had no bearing upon the matter.

Jefferson not only claimed the right of slavery to go everywhere in the national domain: he asserted that such a "diffusion" of slavery would be a good thing for the blacks, the whites, and the country itself and that it would hasten the disappearance of slavery.

The "diffusionist theory" was neither the last infirmity of a noble mind or a cynical perversion of idealism to serve the purposes of an aggressive "slave interest." Jefferson had observed that slaves were better treated on small farms, where they often worked alongside their masters, than on large plantations where they labored in gangs under overseers whose only objective was "to get out the crop." Moreover—and more important—small slaveowners would be less averse to emancipation for the simple reason that they had less to lose. Thus, he reasoned, humanitarianism and the public good dictated the widest possible diffusion of slavery.

Hitherto, Jefferson had advocated that free citizens be given a stake in the country in the form of land; now he proposed to give them a stake in slavery—a piece of the action, as it were, in the form of ownership of human beings, under the persuasion that their reason and moral sense would be thereby enlisted in the cause of emancipation. The idea was pushed to its logical conclusion in 1859 when an effort was made at the Southern Commercial Convention to reopen the African slave trade in order to involve more people in slave ownership, not, however, with any thought of subverting the institution. Jefferson's plan stood to benefit Virginia, a state with a surplus slave population, by relieving the pressures, including the danger of a servile uprising, generated by the doubling of the slave population every twenty years, and providing at the same time a lucrative market in the West for slaves. Jefferson inadvertently pitted the profit motive against morality and, not unexpectedly, the profit motive prevailed.

In the Missouri Controversy, Jefferson took a political rather than a moral stand. Had he supported the North as his principles seemingly required him to do, he would have certainly forfeited his political "usefulness" in his native state and throughout the South. Among other things, he would have cancelled all hope of establishing the University of Virginia—his "last act of usefulness."

Coincident with the Missouri Controversy, a change began to occur in Jefferson's attitude toward the institution of slavery. He now noted with approval the rapid increase in the slave population of Virginia and the marked improvement in the treatment ac-

corded slaves. From these and other circumstances, he drew the conclusion that while slavery must be abolished, it was not, from the workers' point of view, the worst labor system in the world.

In effect, Jefferson revised the "misery index" of slavery. In the *Notes on Virginia*, he had observed that among the slaves "there is misery enough, God knows," and in 1786 he had marveled that any American patriot could bear to inflict "on their fellow-men a bondage one hour of which is fraught with more misery than ages of that which he rose in rebellion to oppose." But now, in happier, more abundant days for slaves, he rejoiced that they were "better fed, warmer clothed and labored less than the journeymen or day laborers of England." English factory workers, he said, might in one respect at least envy the slaves of the American South: in their old age, the latter were provided for by considerate masters. The South, it appeared, had no monopoly either of misery or of poor people who suffered exploitation. Moreover, he observed, Americans were not alone in depriving men of their freedom and inflicting punishment upon them for neglect of duty; in this respect, the soldiers and sailors of Great Britain were in no better position than the slaves on southern plantations.

After the War of 1812, Jefferson discovered that the breeding of slaves could be profitable. He calculated that a slave woman who brought a child into the world every two years was worth more than the best farm worker. "What she produces," he observed, "is an addition to capital, while his labor disappears in mere consumption." Accordingly, he instructed his overseer to take special care of pregnant slave women. For such women, Jefferson pointed out, "it is not their labor, but their increase which is the first consideration with us." Slave breeding became a preoccupation with the master of Monticello. His solicitude for his "breeding women" was rewarded by the birth of almost one hundred slaves on his plantations from 1810 to 1822. As a result, over half of Jefferson's slaves were women, infants, and adolescents, some of whom were destined for market.

But Jefferson's rejoicing in the fecundity of his slave women proved ill founded; even their heroic efforts could not save him from insolvency. How replenishing the earth with black slaves would hasten the end of slavery, Jefferson did not say; his overriding concern was to save himself from financial ruin. Alexander Hamilton might have observed, as he did on another occasion, that poverty rather than wealth is the real enemy of virtue, that a mean and degrading need for money impels men to act in ways that in more affluent circumstances they would have disdained as dishonorable.

But this more indulgent view of slavery did not weaken Jefferson's conviction that the institution must be destroyed. The Missouri Controversy, and the abyss of disunion and racial war it had opened up for all who looked into the future, added urgency to the emancipation and removal of the slaves. Also, increasing doubts about the capacity of the American of the Colonization Society, organized in 1817 for the removal of "free persons of color" to Liberia, to keep pace with the proliferation of the black population of the United States revealed to Jefferson the hopelessness of private efforts to accomplish the task. The American Colonization Society read its doom in the census returns.

In 1824–1825, with his life drawing to a close, therefore, Jefferson revived the plan he had adumbrated in the *Notes on Virginia* for the gradual abolition of slavery. In this revised version, contained in private letters, one significant difference appeared: instead of the state of Virginia, it was the United States government that was to supervise and pay the cost of emancipating, training, and transporting the slaves to a new homeland. He realized that the task was beyond the resources of the individual states and private enterprise and that therefore an amendment to the Constitution might be necessary.

In his last effort to eradicate slavery and, by so doing, to save the Union, Jefferson proposed that the federal government purchase all slave children, superintend the preparations for their new lives as free men and free women, and, when they reached maturity, ship them to Haiti, the black republic in the Caribbean that Jefferson now preferred over Liberia as a site for colonization. In a benign West Indian environment, to which ultimately all American slaves would be given free passage, Jefferson thought that blacks would have the best chance of proving wrong his "suspicions" of their inferiority. He calculated that the labor of the children—who, before they reached maturity, would be the property of the United States government—would offset the cost to taxpayers of their training and transportation. Additional expense might be defrayed by the proceeds from the sale of western lands.

Jefferson did not doubt that the emancipated adult slaves and the free blacks would eagerly follow the children to the Promised Land in the West Indies rather than remain to enjoy the dubious blessings of liberty in the United States. As he visualized this climactic event, the freed slaves would be dismissed with honor and gratitude by their former masters and he supposed that the blacks would depart with equal thankfulness and good will. Clearly, in his anxiety to remove an evil that he feared would ultimately inflict upon the United States the combined horrors of civil and racial war, Jefferson failed to realize that the expansion of cotton and the cultivation of other staples had utterly destroyed his dream of ridding the country of black workers who had been given their freedom. Cotton, tobacco, rice, and sugar, and the wealth and political power they generated—not the Jeffersonian vision of a racially homogeneous and socially egalitarian society of yeomen farmers—were to determine the course of the American republic.

Many years before, Jefferson had said that the powers of government, wisely used, were "one of the greatest blessings and most powerful instruments for procuring safety and happiness to men collected in large societies." Now, almost at the end of his life, he proposed to use those powers to achieve what he regarded as a great humanitarian goal in the public interest and for the public safety. Here a link was forged between Alexander Hamilton and Thomas Jefferson. In the course of American history, the Hamiltonian state was to be used in ways and for purposes not dreamed of in the philosophy of the first secretary of the treasury.

Jefferson's contribution to the antislavery movement was to bind it authoritatively with the Declaration of Independence. The author himself said that the self-evident truths he had therein proclaimed and the existence of the Union itself required that the slaves be freed. At every crisis of American history when slavery was the issue, the Declaration of Independence was exalted as a charter of freedom and Jefferson was summoned to bear witness against slavery.

Jefferson never doubted that in the long run slavery would cease to exist. "Nothing is more certainly written in the book of fate," he wrote in his *Autobiography,* "than that these people are to be free," and, he added, it was equally certain that they were to leave the United States. Jefferson never despaired; *nil desperandum* might well have been the motto inscribed on the portico of Monticello. It was impossible for Jefferson to believe that slavery could long endure in a country where "Life and Liberty are on steady advance," where education was dispelling ignorance and superstition, and where people were learning to "respect those rights in others which we value in ourselves." Slavery would inevitably wither and die in the American environment of justice, reason, moral values, and free enquiry. "Tyranny and oppression of body and mind will vanish," he prophesied, "like evil spirits at the dawn of day."

Realizing that his own end was near, Jefferson comforted himself with the thought that his ideas would not die with him. The noblest of those ideas have survived to become the canons of American democracy. It is likewise true that the ideas regarding racial inferiority to which he gave utterance did not die with him.

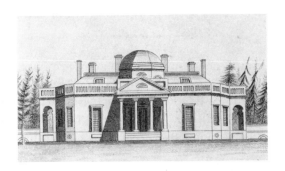

Monticello

JAMES A. BEAR, JR.

THE house that Thomas Jefferson began building about 1770 was partially completed by 1782, remodeled into its present form beginning in 1796, and completed (if it ever was) about 1809. The first house was an academically inspired edifice that fell into disrepair and disfavor during Jefferson's absence in France. Returning from abroad, he decided to rebuild and enlarge it. The seemingly heavy double porticoes were scrapped, and emphasis was placed on privacy and convenience, not magnificence. By his innate virtuosity he created what appeared to be a smaller structure while actually doubling the living area. A dome commanded the west front: it was a house with two fronts and no back. What was once a constrained and tense central mass, joined by flanking terrace walks to balancing outbuildings, was transformed into a seemingly one-story pavilion with the same appendages. The influence was Palladian, the immediate example was French, but viewed from any possible position Monticello was Jeffersonian.

The emphasis of the design was centered on the main, or ground, floor of eleven rooms and two long transverse halls that ran its length in a north-south direction. Entry was from the east portico into a large entrance hall, which contained Jefferson's cabinet of natural history, diverse paintings and pieces of statuary, and a gallery that ran around the upper part of the hallway. This was the first of three public rooms.

Here Jefferson greeted his guests, and from here they passed through the folding glass doors into the parlor, or salon, with its parquet floor and five-sided bow. Family and social activities such as weddings, after-dinner conversations, musical entertainments, and games took place in this room. A pair of large glass doors allowed one to exit to the west lawn and gardens. To the right of the parlor was the dining room, and from there an elliptical archway led into the tea room, designated as Jefferson's "most honorable suite" by the nature of the delineations of American heroes hanging and standing there. The north passageway, also to the right, led past the north square and north octagonal bedrooms and through a piazza to the terrace walk and north out-building.

Jefferson's apartment, which contained a bed–dressing room combination and his library suite, was to the left of the hall. Entry was by invitation only, even for other members of the household. The first small room was dominated by a closet rising above Jefferson's bed and a skylight, one of fourteen in the house. The bed was in a recess, but unlike the other beds in the house it was accessible from both sides. The cabinet, part of the three-room library, was on the other side of the bed alcove. Here Jefferson stationed his specially designed reading and writing apparatus. The cabinet, the connecting area, and the book room made up the library suite that housed, until 1815, one of the finest libraries in America.

The door into the library from the south passageway was kept closed, making a dead end; however, from this hall, as in the north passageway, a very narrow (twenty-four-inch) stairway gave access to the second and third levels or to the basement. The south square room, planned as a bedroom, was used as a nursery, schoolroom, sitting room, and overflow dining area. After 1809 Jefferson seldom went above the first floor, leaving the upper floors to his family and visitors.

There was no mistaking the man of the house as he greeted the many persons who crossed the threshold and passed into the entrance hall. To many he presented an imposing appearance; some said he seemed rather stern looking, while others viewed his countenance as cold. Isaac Jefferson, Monticello's slave chronicler, remembered him to have been as "strait-bodied [a] man as ever you see, right square-shouldered." An 1808 visitor described Jefferson as "a tall thin man not very dignified . . . very agreeable in his manners—his face expressed great good humor." In 1824 Samuel Whitcomb, Jr., a Massachusetts bookdealer, saw him as "tall and very straight excepting his neck which appears limber and inclined to crook." First-time callers may have been surprised at his height: he measured six feet two inches in his stocking feet.

As a youth he might have been referred to as dangerously skinny, but this was misleading since his large and bony frame was well muscled. Middle age brought on a certain stoutness; however, early in retirement his long frame was again thin and spare. As an elderly person he was described as "tall and very thin, a little bent with age."

His head, held high at the apex of a long neck, was of a normal size and shape but perhaps somewhat elongated and seemed set a little forward of his broad and square shoulders, especially when he was conversing. His face was angular, with high cheekbones, not handsome but reflecting dignity and resolution. His blue eyes, "small, very light, and now neither brilliant nor striking," as Daniel Webster wrote in 1824, were set on either side of a prominent nose. His well-formed mouth lost none of its natural shape as he aged, for he kept his own teeth. A female visitor, impressed by their brightness, thought it a pity that his smile was neither frequent nor broad enough to expose them to full advantage. As a youth his hair was a true carrot red; by his sixty-fourth birthday it had become an indistinct straw or sandy color. From his youth through the presidential years he powdered his hair.

When he was a boy his skin was fair and freckled; in his maturity freckles were evident but not in such profusion. His face, particularly over his high cheekbones, was florid and tended to blister and peel after overexposure to the sun and wind. Superficial veins bled at the slightest blow and no doubt were the source of the cutaneous scars commented on by Daniel Webster.

His uncommonly long limbs ended with large feet—surviving footwear attests to this —and large hands. By his seventy-seventh year his wrists were reputed to have become of extraordinary size and the joints of his wrists and fingers had become so stiff that writing was tiring and difficult. This condition was brought on by breaks and what was probably osteoarthritis, not rheumatism as Jefferson so often stated. There was nothing precise in his walk, which exhibited the loose and friendly gait one associates with tall men. As he aged, however, his legs became stiff, severely restricting his mobility.

While seated, Jefferson appeared much shorter than was the case—the result of his sitting in a position described by visitors as "lounging" and by himself as a recumbent posture. Such a stance may be likened to a fraternity, or library, slouch where the sitter's body rests somewhere between the end of his spine and top of his seat. This position may be traced to the osteoarthritis in Jefferson's legs, lower back, and hips, which made an upright and comfortable position at the writing table impossible. Writing was difficult even when he occupied his specially contrived combination reading and writing arrangement of a revolving chair, chaise lounge, and table. Give or take a few pounds, wrinkles, elasticity of gait, angle of stance, or color of hair, this was Thomas Jefferson at almost any age.

Only as a youth, in and about Williamsburg and while serving as America's representative at the court of Louis XVI, was Jefferson particular about his appearance. There is no question that in retirement he hewed to no fashion line. Here he wore what he liked, often mixing items of several styles. Isaac remembered: "Old Master wore Vaginny cloth and a red waistcoat (all the gentlemen wore red waistcoats in dem days) and small clothes; arter dat he used to wear red breeches too." An 1816 visitor, George Flower, said: "His dress, in color and form, was quaint and old-fashioned, plain and neat—a dark pepper-and-salt coat, cut in the old Quaker fashion, with a single row of large metal buttons, knee-breeches, gray-worsted stockings, shoes fashioned by large metal buckles."

Ellen Randolph Coolidge, a granddaughter, gave biographer Henry S. Randall an "official" version:

> His dress was simple, and adapted to his ideas of neatness and comfort. He paid little attention to fashion, wearing whatever he liked best, and sometimes blending the fashions of several different periods. He wore long waistcoats when the mode was for very short, white cambric stocks fastened behind with a buckle, when cravats were universal. He adopted the pantaloon very late in life, because he found it more comfortable and convenient, and cut off his queue for the same reason.

Early pieces of clothing, however unfashionable, carried a special mark stitched in red thread, namely his initials in block letters followed by a number possibly designating either the date of acquisition or the number of the article, thus "T.J. 08."

His riding clothes were as varied as his daily attire. One account has him in a gray straight-bodied coat and a spencer (a short jacket worn by men), both fastened by large pearl buttons. Around his neck he wore a white woolen tippet or sometimes a stock. Black velvet gaiters under his pantaloons covered the tops of leather shoes with pointed toes. A visiting clergyman, writing in 1822, recalled another outfit: "His coat was checked gingham, manufactured in Virginia. . . . The buttons on it were of white metal and nearly the size of a dollar. His pantaloons were of the same fabric. . . . He had no hat on but a lady's parasol, stuck in his coat behind, spread its canopy over his head. . . . Such a great man in such a plain and singular garb."

Thomas Jefferson was a man of habit, and despite visitors or other circumstances, nothing seriously disrupted his daily routine. This "setness" so provoked young George Ticknor that he wrote, "When you know how one day is filled, I suppose you know how it is with the others." Jefferson, who often boasted that the sun never caught him in bed, arose as soon as he could see the hands of the black obelisk-pillared clock stationed at the foot of his sleeping alcove. He scratched at the ashes in his fireplace to rekindle the fire of the night before and copied in his ivory notebook the readings from his thermometers. Once a week he transcribed these readings into separate weather memorandum books. This routine had been well established since the death of his wife, Martha Wayles Skelton, on 6 September 1782.

His morning ablutions were not unlike those performed by most gentlemen of his station. Perhaps his most noteworthy practice was bathing, or soaking, his feet in cold water, a routine that he had followed "every morning, for sixty years." As a result, he claimed, he had "been remarkably exempted from colds (not having had one in every seven years of my life on an average)." Once clothed he devoted himself to the writing table until called to breakfast. The most reliable accounts say a warning bell was sounded at seven o'clock telling all that breakfast would be served in the dining room at eight. Isaac recalled that "Old Master was never seen to come out before breakfast." This repast offered coffee, tea, muffins, hot wheat and corn bread, a cold meat, and butter. Jefferson ate sparingly.

Francis Calley Gray, visiting Monticello in 1815, recalled that on one occasion the company "chatted" at the breakfast table for an hour. However, another visitor remembered that almost immediately after the meal the family went as routine directed: the children to the schoolroom; Jefferson to his quarters; Thomas Mann Randolph, a son-in-law, to Edgehill; and visitors to their chambers, the parlor, gardens, or grounds as inclination led them. There was little effort at this time of day to see to their entertainment.

Within the confines of his bedroom-library suite, his "sanctum sanctorum" as Margaret Bayard Smith called it, Jefferson set about the numerous tasks that faced the owner of a large plantation and an individual of such wide public notice and varied interests. Later, he went outside to visit the workshops and nearby slave quarters along the Mulberry Row and beneath the adjacent terrace walks, to the gardens, or elsewhere as needed. Constant overseeing was a must, since farm operations at Monticello and Poplar Forest were predicated on the system of forced and unskilled labor, in which slaves were mistreated and mishandled more often than not by overseers whose experience, efficiency, honesty, and character varied from individual to individual and plantation to plantation. Jefferson always insisted on efficient, honest, and humane overseers.

At noon, or seldom later than one o'clock, he mounted his horse for visits to the satellite farms of Shadwell, Tufton, and Lego, the Shadwell mills, Milton, Charlottesville, or the University of Virginia, once construction was underway, or wherever his presence was required. He returned from his ride, which sometimes covered as many as fourteen miles but averaged between six to eight, in time to prepare for dinner, which was served sometime between three-thirty and five o'clock. Once again a tocsin was sounded telling the household to gather in the parlor or hall and be prepared to pass promptly into the dining room at the second ringing. Guests and family made their ways into the dining salon "pell-mell." Mrs. Randolph, or later a granddaughter, sat at the head of the table while Jefferson and special guests sat at the foot.

Daniel Webster characterized the bill of fare as half Virginian and half French—proof that Jefferson was not so completely Frenchified that he completely abjured his native victuals, as Patrick Henry had so unkindly pronounced. He had merely added to his cultivated palate a taste for the nuances of French cookery. Meats included pork, ham, lamb, fowl, and beef prepared according to French and American recipes. Even "stalled beef," produced by forced feeding in the confinement of a stall, was tough and overly fat and not the favorite it is today; pork and lamb were preferred. These were accompanied by an array of vegetables, including sea kale, broccoli, eggplant, tomatoes, and various kinds of lettuce including "tennis ball," a French variety not generally seen in Virginia dining rooms.

Although setting a bountiful table, Jefferson was a light eater by the standards of the time. He ate little meat, preferring it in an auxiliary role as a seasoner for vegetables. By admission he preferred vegetables, and if there was a favorite, it was the early spring pea, of which he grew as many as a dozen varieties, including the delicious, if starchy, Hotspurs and Charltons. During meals guests drank malt liquors and cider; no wine was served until the cloth had been removed. Jefferson, a connoisseur and lover of wine, limited himself to no more than three glasses, usually halved with water.

The period between the serving of wine and tea time would vary according to the season, the weather, and the number and attractiveness of the guests. At meal's end the ladies usually left the gentlemen for their own gathering elsewhere in the house— probably the south square room. Occasionally they remained with the gentlemen and entered into the conversation, which Ticknor said never treated subjects beyond their comprehension.

If not further conversing with an engaging guest, Jefferson might supervise his grandchildren's races or games on the west lawn; or all might enjoy a musical entertainment in the parlor featuring Martha Randolph on the harpsichord or her daughter Virginia on the cittern, a tour of the cabinet of natural history in the entrance hall, or a supervised visit to the library. The entire party might troop out to the gardens or make a turn of any of the several roundabouts, the four parallel roads constructed on the mountain's declivities.

No matter what the scene of postdinner activities, guests and members of the household returned to the tea room generally between eight and nine o'clock for tea and conversation. These were the most pleasing of Monticello's social activities. They were easily entered into, always agreeable, and the host carefully channeled them so as to exclude no one. They were never controversial. Jefferson conversed with great ease and animation, even with total strangers, in his distinct, low voice, which many claimed cost him a prominent place on the hustings. He was discursive and particularly loved to talk of things American, such as the accomplishments of Francis Hopkinson, the nation's first composer, or Eli Whitney and his cotton gin; of plows, harrows, the harvest, weather, and like subjects; or, as with the Marquis de Chastellux, of Ossian, classical literature, or the latest inventions. The Duc de La Rochefoucauld-Liancourt stated after a visit that Jefferson possessed a stock of information not inferior to any man. Young, old, women, and children took pleasure in his society and conversations. If the visitors were stimulating and Jefferson felt well, he might remain with the company well past his bedtime; if not, he would make an early departure.

There was every certainty that once in his bedroom, Jefferson would remain undisturbed to read or putter as he wished until the morrow's breakfast bell. His reading here was of the most substantial kind (he seldom read novels, which he once alluded to as a "mass of trash"), and as an older man he limited himself to classical or historically inspired works. He seldom went to sleep without perusing something moral, "whereon to ruminate in the intervals of sleep." Five to eight hours were sufficient, and no matter the length of his repose, the sun failed to catch him in bed. This was ever his boast.

If Jefferson was the centerpiece of life at Monticello, then Monticello and its household were the centerpieces of his existence. His many years of public service ensured lengthy absences from home and fireside, but his thoughts were always there. The many references in his correspondence are sound evidence of his inner feelings. In 1780 he wrote: "Abstracted from home, I know no happiness in this world." Seven years later and in a more poignant vein he stated: "I am as happy nowhere else, and in no other society." And in 1810, a full year into his retirement, his feelings had not changed when he summarized: "I am retired to Monticello, where in the bosom of my family and surrounded by my books, I enjoy a repose to which I have been long a stranger." His hopes were high, and rightly so, that happiness and contentment would ever serve him at Monticello. This had certainly been the case with visits during his eight years in the presidency, and he foresaw nothing to alter this situation in retirement.

Family life in the house on the hill, from the early spring of 1809 on, did see happy times, particularly the several happy weddings of his granddaughters and the births of numerous grandchildren, most of whom bore the names of his friends, such as James Madison, Benjamin Franklin, and Meriwether Lewis. He completed the one-thousand-foot vegetable garden terrace and refurbished the orchard below; constructed his retreat Poplar Forest, seventy miles away in Bedford County; and, most satisfying of all, designed and fathered the "hobby of his old age," the University of Virginia.

The unalloyed happiness of retirement that Jefferson so long anticipated and honestly believed his due was not to be. Events such as the unhappy marriage of granddaughter Anne Cary Randolph to Charles Lewis Bankhead, a confirmed and combative alcoholic, wrought great turmoil and unhappiness almost from its beginning in 1808. The hordes of visitors, most of whom were uninvited, who flocked to see the "saint" and his "shrine" became an impossible burden on his time and finances. His correspondence, which grew yearly, became a mental and physical chore as his wrists and fingers succumbed to the tortures of old injuries and osteoarthritis. Finances that were never as sound as he imagined received their coup de grâce in the default of Wilson Cary Nicholas (his grandson's father-in-law) on two notes of $10,000 each, upon which Jefferson had inscribed his name as first endorser. His health, sound for most of his life, took a turn for the worse after his visit in 1818 to the Warm Springs, where he suffered mercury poisoning. Perhaps it was the irrational stirrings within the family circle that were his major travail: how could he have predicted that his favored son-in-law and friend, Thomas Mann Randolph, would become so alienated by real and supposed situations that he would finally absent himself completely from the fireside?

No matter what transpired within the walls of Monticello or without, happy times or sad ones, the noble structure remained steadfast and solid under the tender care and attention lavished on it by its designer, builder, and first lover.

Life there as it had existed for nearly half a century ceased at fifty minutes past the meridian on 4 July 1826, when Jefferson died in his sanctum sanctorum. Clustered about the alcove bed were the remnants of his once happy society and one outsider—Dr. Robley Dunglison, Jefferson's thirty-fifth physician by count and, according to all reports, his most satisfactory. Included in the deathwatch were Thomas Jefferson Randolph, by then the head of the family; Nicholas Philip Trist, a Philadelphian who had married Virginia Randolph in 1824; Martha Jefferson Randolph, his sole surviving daughter and lifelong companion; probably Mrs. Hastings Marks, a sister; possibly some of the older grandchildren; and most certainly a cluster of devoted and faithful servants that would have included the slaves Wormley, Burwell, and John Hemings. Only

Thomas Mann Randolph was wanting; perhaps had he realized that theirs was a deathwatch he too would have been present.

Jefferson wished his interment to be private and without parade. Consequently, no invitations were issued, but those who came to pay their respects were welcome. Thomas Mann Randolph came up from his North Milton hideout and during the ceremony stood at the head of the grave that had been dug by Wormley. Jefferson Randolph, from whom he was still estranged, faced him from the foot. Others of the family were clustered facing the Reverend Frederick W. Hatch, the Episcopal cleric whose professional services Jefferson had eschewed several days earlier. Just as the last rites were concluded, a large party of students and townspeople arrived at the graveside.

If Jefferson anticipated the vicissitudes that would overtake his house and family after his death, he never so stated. With his grandson and advisor Thomas Jefferson Randolph, he made at least one effort to make his estate solvent—the 1826 lottery. This was called off primarily owing to an early influx of voluntary donations and the hope of more. When these failed to materialize, a halfhearted effort was made to revive the lottery. But after Jefferson's death it was too late.

Those who would have been delighted to have assisted the aging and financially strapped patriot showed little inclination to aid his heirs. Many assumed that the Randolphs, an old and established Virginia family, were financially solvent. The lottery prizes were in vastly overvalued land that could not be disposed of for anything like the announced estimates. Thus by the winter of 1828 Jefferson Randolph again called off the lottery, which at best was not a good solution. He now had to look to the estate's assets—the land, the house, and Jefferson's personal property.

In late 1826 the house and grounds were showing signs of wear, but they still looked much as they had during the preceding seventeen years when they were the centerpieces of Jefferson's cherished family society. The exterior appeared little different to the casual observer than it had when the remodeling was completed in 1809. The dome, with its three plinths, still dominated the central mass of the house on the west and overshadowed the terrace walks. Here, the floors had rotted and fallen in, forcing the erection of an unsightly cover that prevented promenading. Except for this area and the out-of-sight ones such as the roof, which leaked badly at the bases of the skylights (themselves so cracked and broken they had to be covered with shingles), the structure within its sixteen-inch walls was sound.

The interior's thirty-odd rooms needed refurbishing. They had last been painted before Jefferson's retirement, and most of the curtains—some of them veterans of Jefferson's tenure in the President's House—had been hanging since 1809. The furniture was old and odd, good and bad, and much of it unusable; here and there, pieces by John Hemings and other plantation craftsmen stood alongside finer ones purchased in Philadelphia, Paris, New York, and Washington. Some housekeepers would have demanded a thorough cleaning and sorting of the hundreds of objects and artifacts that included "portraits of historical figures, works of art of highly disparate subjects and —presumably—disparate quality, natural history and ethnological specimens, pots, pans, costumes, bones, maps, prints, books, medals; objects of a staggering variety jostling each other in a building that was already crowded with family, servants, friends, and casual visitors." The "variety and indescribableness" of these objects, as Jefferson described them in his will, were not subject to mere good housekeeping tenets. This was no ordinary house, and it had been presided over by no ordinary man. But ordinary men were now in charge of effecting the required changes, which would disperse Jefferson memorabilia halfway around the world and deliver Monticello into alien hands.

The decision to hold an estate sale was made in the fall of 1826 before Martha Randolph's departure, with children Septimia Anne and George Wythe, for a long stay with daughter Ellen and son-in-law Joseph Coolidge in Boston. The issue of what to sell was the subject of a family debate. Jefferson Randolph, the executor, was violently opposed to including the slaves, most of whom he had known since childhood; his mother-in-law, Mrs. Wilson Cary Nicholas, spoke out against selling the furniture, and certainly not that from Jefferson's own bedroom. It was finally decided to sell everything: the slaves, household furnishings, memorabilia, grain, farm animals, and farm equipment. Held back were the paintings, statuary, and books, for it was thought these would bring larger returns if disposed of in an eastern metropolitan center such as Boston or New York. The artworks were sent to Boston and twice offered for sale with very disappointing receipts; the books were put up at auction at Nathaniel P. Poore's Washington rooms in 1829 with unrecorded results.

The vendue at Monticello was advertised in the Richmond *Enquirer* of 8 November 1828 over Thomas Jefferson Randolph's signature. The notice read:

> On the fifteenth of January at Monticello . . . the whole of the residue of the personal property of Thomas Jefferson, dec., consisting of 130 valuable negroes, stock, crops, &c. household and kitchen furniture. The attention of the public is earnestly invited to this property.

Sensing that the public might react with disbelief, Randolph added this assurance: "The sales being unavoidable, it is a sufficient guarantee to the public, that they will take place at the times and places ap-

pointed." The terms were very accommodating; everything was to be sold for cash or at "12 months credit without interest."

The sales went well, particularly the slaves, farm products, and agricultural tools. *Niles' Weekly Register* reported on 19 July 1828 that the executors were able to pay "the sum of $12,840 on account of the interest on the debt, and that of $35,000 in part discharge of it." This was obviously of help, but it failed to solve all the vexing problems incident to a nearly bankrupt estate. Their real emotional problem, the disposition of the Monticello house and land, remained. Finances were still so bad that Martha and her large family could not afford to occupy the property even as a part-time residence.

In the division of duties among Jefferson's executors, the care of the property had been entrusted, rent free, to Virginia and Nicholas Philip Trist. Although they and their children were in residence and presumably looking after things, visitors and vandals continued to come in great numbers. Some were there to see the "shrine" and make their obeisances at Jefferson's tomb; others were seeking a memento of one kind or another of the dead president. Some dug up flowers, roots, fig bushes, vines, or "everything and anything they fancied." This state of affairs caused Jefferson Randolph to run a notice in the Charlottesville *Central Gazette* stating that legal action would be taken to protect the property and peace of mind of the inhabitants if these ruinous trespasses did not cease. It produced only a temporary respite and failed to prevent vandals of firm conviction from chipping away at Jefferson's tomb and gathering other Monticello memorabilia.

In the early spring of 1828 the family resumed their temporary residence at Monticello. One of them wrote to a prospective visitor: "We will exert ourselves to make you as comfortable as we can in this *bare* castle of ours. By a division of bedding we shall continue to have a spare bed to offer any of our friends who love us enough to occupy it, and we can also promise that you shall find a chair to set down in."

Returning members of the family who rejoined the Trists for varying periods of time included Virginia Trist's sisters Cornelia and Mary and her brothers James Madison and Benjamin Franklin Randolph. The younger children Septimia and George Wythe remained in Boston; Meriwether Lewis was probably with brother Jeff at Edgehill. Martha Randolph returned for a brief stay in May, and Thomas Mann Randolph gave up his North Milton residence for the north pavilion at Monticello, where he died in June 1828, finally at peace with his family.

The prime problem facing Jefferson's executors was the disposition of Monticello. In the fall of 1828 Martha Randolph reluctantly acknowledged it would have to be sold. But finding a serious buyer was difficult. The idea of the family's conducting a school on the premises, first advanced in 1827, promised no more success in 1828 and was finally abandoned. A last hope of retaining title lay in a plan of Gen. John Hartwell Cocke, of Bremo, Fluvanna County, a longtime friend of the family, who proposed to occupy the house and a certain number of acres "at a modest rent" for a school for boys. By mid-1829 he gave up the idea. Cocke's failure to rent the property and Mrs. Randolph's "very straightened funds" again brought the family face to face with reality: the house must be sold for whatever price it would bring.

The final exodus began on a "Monday night" in August 1829 when Virginia Trist informed her mother that everything except her grandfather's clothes had been packed. Martha, temporarily at Edgehill, informed Ellen Coolidge in Boston: "We shall carry [to Edgehill] all our bedding some dining tables your press and Virginia's tall chest of drawers . . . and a great many odds and ends." The final vestiges of Jefferson's happy family society would pass off the land by 1 January 1830.

Jefferson Randolph, who knew the condition of the house and estate better than anyone else, wrote brother-in-law Joseph Coolidge that "in a year or two the house would require extensive repairs" and the estate would be "unredeemably insolvent." He had already concluded that "it will be a fortunate thing . . . to give up the house and 900 acres of good land if a buyer could be found."

Randolph had been encouraged by his sale of the Tufton farm that lay just southeast of and continuous to Monticello in May 1829 for $6,300. Eager to "close" the sale of Monticello, he declared in December that he "would take $10,000 for it with 1,000 acres." There were no serious offers and he was desperate until a prospective purchaser finally appeared. Martha, fearing that an early identification might spoil the chance, cautioned a member of the inner circle that she did not wish "it spoken of as yet."

The prospect was James Turner Barclay, of Staunton, then operating an apothecary shop in Charlottesville. Barclay and his new wife were looking for a permanent residence and began treating with Randolph early in the summer of 1831. He wished to include as part of the $7,500 asking price the value of his Charlottesville house, estimated to be $4,500. Randolph, desperately needing cash, was not inclined to accept Barclay's offer, and the negotiations were extended. They finally agreed on terms of $4,500 less the value of Barclay's residence in return for Monticello and 552 acres. The deed, signed 1 November 1831 by Randolph, Martha, and Barclay, reserved "the family graveyard with free access to same" for Martha Randolph and her heirs. Members of the Monticello Association, a family organization, retain and exercise rights of interment.

According to the only available account of this period, "the Barclays came into possession of many relics of Jefferson." In his bedroom they found a lamp, some books, and his herbarium, which contained many rare flowers. His bedstead remained attached at the head and foot of the alcove. The great clock remained in the entrance hall, as well as the folding ladder used to reach its winding stations and a collection of "heathen images," obviously left from Jefferson's cabinet of natural history. The Louis XVI pier mirrors hung on the walls in the parlor, and nearby were remnants of the once "handsome silk damask curtains." In the book room of the library suite one of the executors had left, certainly inadvertently, Jefferson's "adjustable book shelves."

The Barclays were well-to-do, and they brought with them a great deal of handsome furniture that blended in well with those pieces the Randolphs had left behind. Julia Sowers Barclay was an excellent housekeeper who kept the elegant floors in fine shape by constant "waxing and dry rubbing," especially the cherry and beech parquet floor in the parlor. After a visit, Jefferson Randolph is alleged to have said that Mrs. Barclay kept the floors in a far more beautiful condition than they were kept during the lifetime of his grandfather. Other members of the family were not so complimentary of Barclay's preparations for converting the grounds into a site for the culture of silkworms, an agricultural endeavor that somehow eluded Thomas Jefferson. Barclay is accused of felling a number of old and rare trees, digging up shrubbery, and making other drastic adjustments to the landscaping. Barclay family history continues to claim that he kept the property in tip-top shape.

The change of ownership failed to stem the tide of visitors, who were as much of a travail to the Barclays as they had been to Jefferson and the Randolphs. All wanted to see the house, hear about Jefferson, and visit his grave. If permission was not forthcoming from the servants detailed for this purpose, many embarked on their own unguided tours. During a particularly trying day, Barclay's visiting mother-in-law exclaimed: "I wouldn't live at Monticello if you'd give me the place." By October 1833 the Barclays had had their fill, and the house and grounds were put up for sale.

Responses to public notices in the eastern and southern press were not encouraging, and it was nearly a year before a buyer appeared. This was Uriah Phillips Levy, a Jew, an officer in the United States Navy, and a longtime and ardent admirer of Thomas Jefferson. A probable motive for Levy's offer was his veneration of Jefferson as a great American and of his ideas and actions on behalf of religious freedom. This is borne out in a letter he wrote in 1832 to George M. Carr, an attorney retained by the family to represent their Albemarle County interests.

> I consider Thomas Jefferson to be one of the greatest men in history—author of the Declaration and an absolute democrat. He serves as an inspiration to millions of Americans. He did much to mould our Republic in a form in which a man's *religion* does not make him ineligible for political or governmental life. A noble man—yet there is no statue to him in the Capitol in Washington. As a small payment for his determined stand on the side of religious liberty, I am preparing to personally commission a statue of Jefferson.

Another letter to Carr written nearly twenty-five years later on 17 September 1858 from Spezio, Sardinia, where Levy was commanding the U.S.S. *Macedonia,* of the Mediterranean Squadron, is equally revealing of his motives.

> I arrived here day before yesterday, and have received yours of the 11th August and also the Jeffersonian containing an account of the celebration of the 4th of July at Monticello. It must have been a spirited affair, and I am rejoiced

446

that Virginians more and more appreciate the nation's birthday and honor the memory of the man who was among the first, if not the first to call the Nation into being, who guided its infant footsteps aright, and taught its infant tongue to lisp no other sentiments than those which were truly Republican.

There is something appropriate in solemnizing the Nation's Natal day at the tomb of Jefferson and although I was many miles from Monticello I was full of thought of what might be happening there.

Biographers Donovan Fitzpatrick and Saul Sapphire report, probably correctly, that while studying advanced naval tactics in France in 1832, Levy commissioned Pierre Jean David d'Angers, whose atelier was the most celebrated in France, to execute a full-length likeness of Jefferson. During this visit Levy met the Marquis de Lafayette, who on learning of Levy's plan offered the use of his portrait of Jefferson by Thomas Sully as a guide. Lafayette invited Levy to visit him at La Grange, outside Paris, and while entertaining Levy inquired as to the well-being of Martha Jefferson Randolph and Monticello. The latter had no answer but promised to inform Jefferson's old friend as soon as possible. On his return to America, Levy took the first opportunity to visit Monticello and while there summarily decided to purchase the property.

A bargain was struck on 5 April 1834: the house and some acreage for $2,700. Before consummation of the sale, the question arose of exactly how many acres would accompany the house, and when this could not be resolved, Levy sued. The Albemarle County Circuit Court of Law and Chancery held on 8 May 1836 in *Levy* v. *Barclay* that the plaintiff would pay $2,700 for 218 acres. A deed of conveyance was signed 20 May 1836, after which Levy reported, "My heart leaped."

Unfortunately, Levy's main interests lay with his naval career and investments and properties in New York, and he never became more than a part-time resident. During his 1839 visit, his mother, Rachael Phillips Levy, died and was buried along the estate's Mulberry Row. A caretaker and overseer named Joel Wheeler was engaged; a more disastrous move for Monticello could not have been made. In 1858, at the age of sixty-one, Levy married his eighteen-year-old niece, Virginia Lopez. After the marriage, Levy continued his periodic visits, but even so he never was as successful as his nephew would be in assuming a role in Albemarle County life.

Levy died in New York City in 1862. In his will, a compassionate and strange document, Monticello was bequeathed to the United States government for use as an agricultural school to train children of deceased warrant officers of the United States Navy. Alternate benefactors were the Commonwealth of Virginia and then the Hebrew congregations of New York, Philadelphia, and Richmond. The school would be supported by the income of Levy's considerable estate.

But by this time the Civil War was raging. The property was confiscated by the Confederate States of America and sold at auction on 17 November 1864 to Benjamin Ficklin for $80,500 in Confederate currency, despite various efforts before the local courts by George Carr to thwart the confiscation. After the fall of the Confederacy in 1865, the house and its 218 acres were again subject to the vagaries of Levy's will. There were nearly half a hundred heirs scattered from New York to New Orleans to the West Indies. Most had no concern for Monticello; all were interested in breaking the will. Their attempts began in 1863, initiating about twenty years of litigation that proved most harmful to Monticello.

Under the press of wartime conditions and the uncertainty of a ruling on the will by the New York courts, the federal government began to move toward accepting Monticello. There were, however, unanswered questions concerning the legality of the will and the feasibility of the government's interest in the matter. Among the objections were whether the federal government should become involved in the litigation over the will and whether Congress would agree to the terms once they were fully known. The attorney general ruled that the bequest had not been accepted by an Act of Congress and was doubtful of the legality of the government's assuming "execution of a purely charitable trust." The federal government finally decided not to pursue its claims and renounced all rights.

The Commonwealth of Virginia made no move toward accepting the property until after the Civil War. In 1869 its attorney general, acting for the Commonwealth, appealed directly to the state supreme court of appeals for a ruling that would define its rights. Such a move was met with favor by the Levy litigants. The case was not heard until 1873, when the court ruled against the Commonwealth.

Meanwhile at Monticello, Joel Wheeler, a "sour-looking man" with a rasping voice and absolutely no appreciation for the property he was now renting for $260 a year, showed that he was fully aware of the value of the tourist's dollar in post–Civil War central Virginia when he charged a fee of twenty-five cents to see the interior of the house.

There are varying accounts of what visitors saw. Many windowpanes were broken; the roof, bereft of shingles, leaked, especially around the skylights; the steps on the east front were decayed and broken, while those on the west were hidden beneath a layer of dirt, grass, and weeds. The gutters on all sides had rotted, allowing extensive water damage.

On the inside, visitors made their way over and around debris of all sizes and shapes; they saw grain piled in some of the bedrooms, and there was evidence that during the winter season pigs and cattle may have been stabled in the parlor. George Carr gave his clients a brief and somewhat misleading report when he wrote that "the house was in bad order," with "some glass broken." If the truth had been told, Monticello was a sadly desecrated house. There would be no relief for the structure until the courts settled the legal entanglements that would allow a responsible and appreciative individual to assume ownership.

Such an individual was Jefferson Monroe Levy, Uriah's nephew, a well-to-do New York attorney and the only member of the family who possessed his uncle's feelings for the property. He had been working to this end since early in the 1870s and by 1878 controlled a majority of the outstanding shares. At this juncture he attempted to oust Wheeler, a resident of about forty years, who averred he would not leave until the house had been sold at auction. Hoping to force such a sale, Jefferson Levy brought suit in the circuit court of the City of Richmond against the remaining heirs.

In this case, *Levy et al.* v. *Levy et al.,* the court handed down a decree directing a public sale of Monticello and named George Carr as commissioner to oversee it. The sale was held 20 March 1879 at Monticello, and Levy bid in the house and its 218 acres for $10,500. He took possession the day of the sale and summarily removed Wheeler.

Contemporary visitors' accounts reveal the depths from which Jefferson M. Levy would have to raise the property before it would again be habitable. A touring gentleman who journeyed there in 1870 from far southwestern Virginia reported: "We . . . were soon at the mansion, moss-covered, dilapidated and criminally neglected. . . . The upper rooms, small and illy ventilated, were originally lighted [by skylights] from the roof, but shingles having been substituted for glass, the rooms are now as dark and gloomy as the cells of a prison."

In 1875 Frank Woodman, a student at the University of Virginia, wrote, "the house is one of the most curious I ever saw and is in a semi-ruinous state.'' A young lady visitor in 1877 was taken in by the relatively solid appearance of the exterior, which no doubt reflected the stopgap repairs effected by the Levy family before Jefferson Monroe Levy became the sole owner. These included covering the roof with shingles, patching and pointing up brick and stone work, and replacing broken window panes, gutters, and downspouts.

Major repair work—or restoration, as Levy referred to it—did not begin until he gained clear title to the property in 1879. That on the exterior included erection of the dormer windows on the east, north, and south roofs to cover leaking skylights. These blended so well with the structure that they were considered original and not removed until the major restoration work instituted by the Thomas Jefferson Memorial Foundation in 1954. The roof had been covered with a tin roofing material, in keeping with Jefferson's specifications. At about the same time major innovations carried out in the interior made the house more livable. Running water was installed, allowing for the addition of modern bathroom facilities. A kindred facility was the coal-burning furnace which heated water for the numerous radiators placed throughout the house.

Frank Stockton, a writer for national publications, wrote in 1887: ''The whole establishment has been put in excellent order . . . and is now as sound and substantial a country mansion as it ever was. . . . There is a modern air about its furnishings which are not Jeffersonian, but the house is still Monticello.'' Had Stockton or any of the other reporters troubled themselves, they would have seen, particularly in the public rooms, a number of Jefferson's eighteenth- and nineteenth-century pieces alongside Levy's Victorian objects. This strange union of furnishings remained for the next quarter century.

Martha Jefferson Trist, who had been born in the house, left this description after her visit in 1880:

> Jefferson . . . Levy has done a great deal in the way of cleaning both house & grounds, it is so gratifying to see the beloved old place in the hands of a person who appreciates it, & whose wish appears to be, to restore the whole house to its' former condition—he renovated the dining room and over the mantle is hanging a beautiful picture which Mr. Levy calls a Vandyke.

It would be extremely difficult to ferret out and recount in detail the hundreds of things that Levy did to furnish Monticello. A most important step was the location and acquisition of Jefferson heirlooms spread about Albemarle County and elsewhere. Many more were located than acquired; the latter included a pair of Sheraton card tables, a Chippendale marble-topped side table, a silver coffee urn, acquired from a descendant, and the handsome Wedgwood insets in the dining room mantel. These—when viewed in concert with the seven-day calendar clock that had hung over the entrance-hall door since its installation in the early 1800s, the double, folding or ''magic'' doors, between the hall and parlor, and finally the large pier mirrors on the parlor walls—were evidences of success. Thomas L. Rhodes, the longtime and able overseer, summed up Levy's efforts in *The Story of Monticello:* ''Levy spent large sums of money in improvements upon Monticello and refurnishing it. . . . [However,] most of the furnishings of the mansion when he lived there bore relationship to the Levy family.''

Levy, who from 1880 to 1922 spent approximately four months each year (July through October) at Monticello, was able to enjoy his property for about twenty years before his right of ownership was seriously questioned. Long before his first serious encounter with those who, for one reason or another, would relieve him of the property, he continued to allow and even host visiting personalities or groups. Beginning in the 1880s and continuing for a number of years, this notice appeared in *The Jeffersonian* of Charlottesville: "Mr. Jefferson Monroe Levy and family have settled at Monticello for the summer. Visitors . . . will always meet a warm welcome at the hands of its courteous owner." As Monticello became better known and more easily accessible, the number of visitors increased, forcing Levy to institute a new routine. *The Jeffersonian* disseminated it: "Mr. Levy expects to have one day during the week when the citizens of Albemarle County and Charlottesville will be invited to visit historic Monticello. The day will be announced in due time."

Despite Levy's generous visiting policy and the sound condition of the house, there were those who considered the property too important to remain out of the public weal. An early effort was made by William Jennings Bryan, a onetime Democratic candidate for president, who in 1897 inquired of Levy whether he might be willing to dispose of the property to the federal government. Levy was adamant when he exclaimed there was not money enough in the federal treasury to buy it.

It was a visit by another congressman, Amos J. Cummings of New York, that raised the issue in the public press. Cummings had been so disenchanted by being charged admission to the grounds and denied a visit inside the house that he violently attacked Levy in an article, "A National Humiliation," published in the 24 April 1902 issue of the *New York Sun*.

A riposte in the form of a small booklet, *Monticello and Its Preservation* by Alfred Townsend, sought to point out all that was good concerning Levy's ownership of Monticello. Charges that Levy had written the booklet under a pseudonym or that he had underwritten its costs were never proved. It did have the effect of temporarily quieting his foes.

By 1911 a new and more determined figure came on the scene to contest Monticello's private ownership. This was Mrs. Martin W. (Maud) Littleton, the attractive and energetic wife of another congressman from New York. Mrs. Littleton, after residing in the capital for only a short time, learned to her great annoyance that there was no monument of any kind to Jefferson. In lieu of attempting to erect a statue honoring Jefferson, she decided there could be no more fitting memorial than his own house. She had a lengthy and unusual fight with Levy, traced in detail in Charles Hosmer's *The Presence of the Past*. Mrs. Littleton came very close to succeeding and was only denied victory by Congress' preoccupation with World War I.

Following this conflict Levy found himself in severe financial straits, so much so that he was favorably disposed to sell Monticello, which he claimed cost him $40,000 a year to operate. He placed it in the hands of Harry N. Hillery, a Washington, D.C., real-estate agent. Levy intimated that $400,000 was a fair asking price. No individual stepped forward to purchase, preserve, and maintain the house, although Hosmer notes that a number of groups claimed they would like to do so.

The movement to purchase Monticello seemed doomed to failure when renewed interest was generated by Gregory Doyle of Mountain Lake, New Jersey. Doyle had cooperated with several earlier efforts to organize and purchase Monticello and was fully aware of the diverse and difficult problems to be faced. Nevertheless, he took the first step by arranging a small meeting of interested parties in New York City in February 1922. Among those attending was Col. Thomas Jefferson Randolph, a descendant of Jefferson and a representative of the governor of Virginia, E. Lee Trinkle. Also present were several influential New Yorkers, including Stuart Gibboney, an attorney, civic leader, and native-born Virginian. This nameless group had the good sense to name as its head Gibboney, who then appointed a select committee to assist him.

Less than a month later Gibboney and his committee met with John Henry Ranger, Levy's representative, who told those assembled that Levy had to sell. After the conference Gibboney and the others were so encouraged that they decided then and there to organize an association aimed at purchasing Monticello. They named it the Thomas Jefferson Memorial Foundation, and offices were set up at 115 Broadway in New York City, with Jack Slaight, a former editor of the *New York World,* in charge.

The first order of business was to draw up a certificate of incorporation, which was signed by thirty-four incorporators on 13 March 1923. This allowed for the writing and adoption of a constitution, thus laying the groundwork for a working organization. Its aims were simple and commendable. They would purchase, preserve, and maintain the property as a memorial to the high ideals of democracy. They would further foster and preserve the name of Thomas Jefferson as a noble example of democratic simplicity, inculcating and demonstrating a sincere reverence for the noblest patriotic deeds in our past.

Formal announcement of the incorporation was reported in the *New York Times* on 5 April 1923. The foundation was not to become active until 13 April, the 180th anniversary of Jefferson's birth, when it was officially acclaimed at ceremonies held simultaneously in Charlottesville, Virginia, and Albany, New York. The foundation endured many organizational changes and growing pains, and the directors authorized a myriad of events, contests, and activities to raise the $500,000 purchase price.

After the incorporation and the organization in 1923, the directors named a Restoration Committee to counsel them on plans and methods for renovating and restoring the house, gardens, and outbuildings and to furnish the interior. Their plan was to return the estate to Jefferson's concept and execution. They were extremely fortunate in obtaining the services of Fiske Kimball, whose *Thomas Jefferson, Architect* had established him as an authority on Jefferson and his architecture. His presence reassured those who doubted how Monticello might fare at the hands of the New York bankers and attorneys who made up the majority of the board of directors. Before his death in 1955, Kimball had overseen the spending of about half a million dollars for renovation, restoration, and acquisition of furnishings. The appearance and condition of Monticello today are a monument to his efforts.

Before any restoration could be contemplated, the house, the terrace walks and offices below, and the outbuildings had to be stabilized, and the entrance and departure roads simplified. These measures were carried out under Thomas Rhodes's direction with the authorization of Kimball and his committee. A first task was repairing the floors of the terrace walks and pointing up the stonework beneath. The floors of these walks had rotted and fallen in before Jefferson's death and had been a problem for every subsequent owner. Soon the road leading up the hill past the graveyard had been graded and resurfaced; later, as the result of his research, Kimball rerouted the entrance road up the trace of the old South Road, a more direct approach to the house, which is used to the present day. Many trees on the east and west front lawns that had escaped Barclay's hatchet and years of neglect were pruned and tended. The roof was patched and painted, and the rotting cornices and leaking gutters were replaced and painted. A new coat of paint was applied in 1931, probably the first complete one since Jefferson's lifetime.

A very important move by Gibboney was his request to the Garden Club of America for assistance with the restoration of the gardens and grounds. Finally, the Garden Club of Virginia, an affiliate, came into the picture and named a committee to consult with Kimball and Edwin M. Betts, a professor of biology at the University of Virginia and consultant to the foundation in matters of gardens and plantings. In 1940 the gardens on the west and east fronts were fully restored at no cost to the foundation.

With the house stabilized and the adjacent gardens restored, in 1953 the directors authorized a complete structural renovation of Monticello's interior and the installation of climate controls. Thus the dangerous old stoves that were used to heat the house were removed, as were the radiators and the huge coal-fired furnace, the heart of the steam heating system. The sagging original floors were taken up, and steel joists surrounded by fireproof insulation were installed before the floors were relaid. The house was now as fireproof as modern method could make it and would be vastly more comfortable for the thousands of visitors who make their pilgrimages during the summer months. Several years later the dormer windows installed by Jefferson M. Levy over the leaking skylights were removed, and the three step plinths restored to the outside of the dome. Thus after nearly a century and a half, Monticello's exterior appeared much as it had during Jefferson's residence.

It would be as impossible to return the interior to its original appearance as it would be for Jefferson to reappear and greet visitors in the entrance hall. The vast majority of the odd-shaped stones, fossil bones, Indian artifacts, heathen idols, and other curios gathered by Jefferson are unfortunately lost. Reassembling the few paintings, portraits, pieces of statuary, and family memorabilia now at Monticello has proved a long-term and difficult accomplishment. Yet the process goes on, with the recording of occasional successes. In fact, a full re-creation of the house with "the variety and indescribableness" noted in Jefferson's will might strike the modern visitor as exceedingly unhistorical, a far cry from the pristeen "early American" interiors shown in decorators' magazines.

So Monticello stands today much as it did in 1809 when it was completed. Unquestionably, it is in better repair and there are far more visitors than when it was the site of Jefferson's "family society." There can be no doubt that Jefferson would recognize it. Once inside the hall, he might wonder at the high degree of housekeeping and the absence of so many of his ethnological artifacts and objects. But the building stands, after one hundred and fifty years, still as Jefferson's own house and home.

Bibliographic Essay

FRANK SHUFFELTON

It has become almost a convention in recent years for new books on Thomas Jefferson to begin with an apology to the effect that although so much has been written about him, there is still need for another volume. Certainly an extraordinary amount of attention has been paid to him, yet so rich and varied were his interests, so influential his ideas, so significant his role in American history that it seems unlikely that there will be an end to our concern with him for years to come. The preceding essays suggest the range of Jefferson's appeal. For those wishing to read further about Jefferson, this essay offers historical and critical guidance to the most important interpretations of his life, his interests, and his accomplishments. Because Jefferson early became an almost totemic figure in American culture, some of the books and essays noted here are perhaps now more important for what they reveal about the manner in which their writers used Jefferson's image to suit their own needs than for their intrinsic merits. The majority of the works described below, however, offer real insights into the puzzling Thomas Jefferson, a man so complex that the reader will find many writers offering seemingly conflicting views of his life and career.

EDITIONS OF THE WRITINGS

The best place to begin is with the man himself. The first collection of Jefferson's writings appeared three years after his death when his grandson and executor, Thomas Jefferson Randolph, edited four volumes entitled *Memoir, Correspondence, and Miscellanies from the Papers of Thomas Jefferson* (1829). Randolph was aware of the importance of his grandfather's papers both as historical material of the highest significance and as a financial resource for Jefferson's heirs, and he carefully preserved them until 1848, when Congress appropriated $20,000 on the condition "that said T. J. Randolph shall deposit all the said papers and manuscripts of a public nature in the State Department, and execute a conveyance thereof to the United States." Henry Augustine Washington of the College of William and Mary was appointed to edit the papers; working with remarkable speed, he prepared in the next three years nine volumes of *The Writings of Thomas Jefferson* (1853–1854). Three decades later Sarah N. Randolph, Jefferson's great-granddaughter, and Ainsworth R. Spofford, the librarian of Congress, raised serious questions about the quality of Washington's editorial work and called for a new edition, to be done by Randolph under Spofford's general direction. Unfortunately, she died in 1892 before Congress authorized a new edition. The next edition of Jefferson's papers appeared in ten volumes edited by Paul Leicester Ford as *The Writings of Thomas Jefferson* (1892–1899; repr. 1904, as the twelve-volume Federal edition with the title *The Works of Thomas Jefferson*), and this edition has retained some usefulness because of Ford's careful editing. Ford's selection of papers for inclusion, however, emphasized the public and political side of Jefferson's career, and in the course of the nineteenth century a large number of papers were separated from the original holdings for a variety of reasons. Ford's edition was followed by the more extensive collection edited by Andrew A. Lipscomb and Albert Ellery Bergh, published in twenty volumes as *The Writings of Thomas Jefferson* (1903–1904). Because it is the most inclusive, this edition was long the standard, but since many of its texts were based on the Henry A. Washington edition of 1853–1854, it retains many of Washington's errors, elisions, and silent emendations. Independently of these editions the Massachusetts Historical Society printed a selection of its large holdings of Jefferson material in its *Collections,* 7th ser., vol. 1 (1900), and William K. Bixby printed a selection of his large manuscript collection under the title *Thomas Jefferson Correspondence, Printed from the Originals in the Collections of William K. Bixby* (1916).

All of these editions are now being superseded by the Princeton edition under the direction of Julian P. Boyd and his successors, published as *The Papers of Thomas Jefferson* (1950–   ). This edition is appearing in two series, one chronological and the other topical. The chronological series embraces every available letter written by or to Thomas Jefferson, along with messages, speeches, reports, legislative bills, state papers, memoranda, travel journals, resolutions, petitions, advertisements, minutes of proceedings, and other nonepistolary documents written by Jefferson or having a direct relationship to him. The authoritative texts are accompanied by extremely helpful and illuminating notes, some of them extending to essay length. As of 1982, the chronological series has presented twenty volumes containing Jefferson's papers through August 1791, and a twenty-first volume provides an index to the preceding volumes. The topical series is intended to include Jefferson's autobiography, his *Notes on the State of Virginia,* the *Manual of Parliamentary Practice,* his extracts from the Gospels, legal papers, account books, architectural and other drawings, and the farm and garden books, among others. Only one volume in this series has appeared so far, Dickinson W. Adams' edition of *Jefferson's Extracts from the Gospels: "The Philosophy of Jesus" and "The Life and Morals of Jesus"* (1983). An impeccably edited and handsomely printed edition, the *Papers* is one of the monumental scholarly enterprises of our time, and every person seriously interested in Jefferson should attend to it.

For those whose interests are either less scholarly or less advanced and who wish to read a briefer compendium of Jefferson's best writing, a number of convenient anthologies are available. Saul K. Padover's *The Complete Jefferson* (1943) was published in the bicentennial year of Jefferson's birth and has the advantage of including more of his public papers than other one-volume collections. Because the selections are arranged by topic, this volume offers a concise, if hardly complete, guide to the range of Jefferson's thought. The material in Padover's later *A Jefferson Profile as Revealed in His Letters* (1956) pays greater attention to his private life but, as the title suggests, includes only correspondence. John Dewey's *The Living Thoughts of Thomas Jefferson* (1940) excerpts passages from Jefferson's writings and is more interesting as a sign of what Dewey thought Jefferson meant for the American experience than as a guide to Jefferson himself. Adrienne Koch and William Peden edited a useful collection for the Modern Library under the title *The Life and Selected Writings of Thomas Jefferson* (1944). Merrill D. Peterson more recently edited *The Portable Thomas Jefferson* (1975), which includes an informative introduction plus the major texts and most widely quoted letters. Peterson also selected the texts for what is probably the best of all the one-volume collections, the Library of America's *Thomas Jefferson: Writings* (1984), which offers an extensive, informed selection and helpful notes.

A number of important and interesting volumes have appeared containing either a single work by Jefferson or material pertaining to a specific topic or relationship. *Notes on the State of Virginia,* first published in Paris in 1785, was Jefferson's only full-length, original book published in his lifetime; it has gone through numerous editions before his death and since. It is included in most of the one-volume selections noted above; a well-prepared and readily available separate printing with a useful introduction and notes is William Peden's edition (1955). Jefferson maintained record books for both his garden activities and the business of his plantations, and Edwin M. Betts has edited both of these. *Thomas Jefferson's Garden Book* (1944) contains, in addition to a transcript of Jefferson's memorandum book on plantings and harvestings, an enormous amount of supporting material in the form of notes and extracts from letters and account books. *Thomas Jefferson's Farm Book* (1953) is edited

along similar lines, although it offers a photographic facsimile of Jefferson's original memorandum rather than a transcription. Entries Jefferson made in his garden book might sometimes have been made more appropriately in his farm book and vice versa, so anyone interested in Jefferson as agriculturalist or in the management of his plantations should consult both works. The farm book is also notable for its records on the slave population of Jefferson's plantations.

In his youth Jefferson also maintained two commonplace books, notebooks in which he copied out passages from his reading that seemed especially worth remembering. Gilbert Chinard has edited these, one as *The Commonplace Book of Thomas Jefferson: A Repertory of His Ideas on Government* (1926), in which Jefferson extracted material on law and political philosophy from Coke, Kames, Montesquieu, Beccaria, and James Wilson, among others. The subtitle of *The Literary Bible of Thomas Jefferson: His Commonplace Book of Philosophers and Poets* (1928) suggests its contents; it should not be confused with his extracts from the Gospels, which he called "The Life and Morals of Jesus of Nazareth." Chinard also edited several important collections of letters between Jefferson and French friends and acquaintances. *Les amitiés américaines de Madame d'Houdetot, d'après sa correspondance inédite avec Benjamin Franklin et Thomas Jefferson* (1924) and *Trois amitiés françaises de Jefferson, d'après sa correspondance inédite avec Madame de Bréhan, Madame de Tessé et Madame de Corny* (1927) shed light on his social life during his stay in France. *The Letters of Lafayette and Jefferson* (1929) contains introductory material putting the correspondence into historical and biographical context. Three volumes edited by Chinard delineate Jefferson's relations with French intellectuals after 1783: *The Correspondence of Jefferson and Du Pont de Nemours, with an Introduction on Jefferson and the Physiocrats* (1931), *Volney et l'Amérique, d'après des documents inédits et sa correspondance avec Jefferson* (1923), and

Jefferson et les Idéologues, d'après sa correspondance inédite avec Destutt de Tracy, Cabanis, J.-B. Say et Auguste Comte (1925), which are all useful for those who wish to focus on this aspect of Jefferson's intellectual career. Dumas Malone has also edited the *Correspondence Between Thomas Jefferson and Pierre Samuel Du Pont de Nemours, 1798–1817* (1930), which is slightly less complete than Chinard's similar edition but has the advantage of offering translations of the French letters into English. Finally, the most famous correspondence Jefferson maintained with a single person was that with his old friend and sometime rival John Adams. Lester J. Cappon has brought all of these letters together in his two-volume edition of *The Adams-Jefferson Letters: The Complete Correspondence Between Thomas Jefferson and Abigail and John Adams* (1959).

BIOGRAPHICAL STUDIES

Jefferson's life has been a matter of public interest since the period of his service as George Washington's secretary of state, but a considerable portion of the biographical writing responding to this interest has been in the service of one political agenda or another. In the year of Jefferson's retirement from public life, for example, Stephen Cullen Carpenter published anonymously the *Memoirs of the Hon. Thomas Jefferson* (1809), which was not a genuine biography but a Federalist attack on Jefferson that purported to show "the Rise and Progress of French Influence and French Principles" in the United States. The death of both Jefferson and John Adams on 4 July 1826 brought forth a flood of eulogies celebrating the patriot fathers and remarking on the providential significance of their departure on the fiftieth anniversary of the Declaration of Independence. These eulogies can be sampled in *A Selection of Eulogies, Pronounced in the Several States, in Honor of Those Illustrious Patriots

and Statesmen, John Adams and Thomas Jefferson* (1826). Robert P. Hay examines contemporary reactions to the deaths of Adams and Jefferson in "The Glorious Departure of the American Patriarchs," in *Journal of Southern History,* 35 (1969). Randolph's 1829 edition of the papers printed for the first time both Jefferson's own memoirs, later referred to as his autobiography, and the Anas, a collection of notes and comments on public figures and events made during his career in government. This material called forth Henry Lee's *Observations on the Writings of Thomas Jefferson* (1832), an outraged attack on Jefferson for a disparaging reference to General Henry ("Light-Horse Harry") Lee, as well as B. L. Rayner's pro-Jeffersonian *Sketches of the Life, Writings, and Opinions of Thomas Jefferson* (1832). Theodore Dwight, the last and least witty of the Connecticut Wits, also responded with a lengthy attack on Jefferson as secretary of state in his *History of the Hartford Convention* (1833). The debates about Jefferson's life have not yet ended, and Merrill D. Peterson's *The Jefferson Image in the American Mind* (1960) charts the ebb and flow of Jefferson's reputation and is essential reading for those who wish to understand how our sense of Jefferson's life evolved.

The first genuinely significant biography was George Tucker's two-volume *The Life of Thomas Jefferson* (1837). Tucker was the professor of moral philosophy at the University of Virginia, and T. J. Randolph gave him access to the Jefferson papers. Tucker, like the biographer Henry S. Randall, had the advantage of being able to talk with people who had known Jefferson. Randall also received help from Randolph, and he had access to sources not open to Tucker or other earlier writers. His three-volume *The Life of Thomas Jefferson* (1858) is the most important biography of Jefferson written in the nineteenth century and is still of some interest despite a prose style that falls rather short of grace. James Parton's *Life of Thomas Jefferson,*

Third President of the United States (1874) offered a positive view of Jefferson for post–Civil War readers but no new insights. Sarah N. Randolph wrote a charming account of her great-grandfather, *The Domestic Life of Thomas Jefferson* (1871), which has often been reprinted and is still interesting for its family reminiscences. John T. Morse's *Thomas Jefferson* (1883), a volume in the often reprinted American Statesmen series, offered a basically Federalist point of view in a highly critical biography.

At the beginning of the twentieth century, Thomas E. Watson, the Southern populist, used his *Life and Times of Thomas Jefferson* (1903) in part as a reply to Theodore Roosevelt's disparaging comments in *The Winning of the West* (1889); Watson portrayed Jefferson as a courageous fighter against religious bigotry, class despotism, and all other forms of oppression. Albert Jay Nock's *Jefferson* (1926) is not so much a formal biography as a study of character organized along biographical lines. It is often shrewd, sometimes idiosyncratic, and still worth reading. Claude G. Bowers published the first and most influential of three separately issued volumes as *Jefferson and Hamilton: The Struggle for Democracy in America* (1925). This was followed by *Jefferson in Power: The Death Struggle of the Federalists* (1936) and *The Young Jefferson, 1743–1789* (1945). Franklin D. Roosevelt reviewed *Jefferson and Hamilton* in the New York *Evening World* of 3 December 1925, hailing it as an antidote to "the romantic cult which has . . . surrounded the name of Alexander Hamilton." In "Bowers, Roosevelt, and the 'New Jefferson,'" in *Virginia Quarterly Review*, 34 (1958), Merrill Peterson discusses the significance of Bower's apotheosis of Jefferson as the hero of liberal democrats and how Franklin Roosevelt used the refurbished image of Jefferson. Gilbert Chinard's *Thomas Jefferson, the Apostle of Americanism* (1929; rev. ed. 1939) was also influential and argued that the sources for Jefferson's political ideas were in classical and British writers rather than, as had sometimes been supposed, in the French Enlightenment.

In the 1940s the New Deal era's attention to Jefferson combined with the two-hundredth anniversary of his birth and with the wartime need for democratic heroes to produce several major biographical efforts. Bernard Mayo's *Jefferson Himself: The Personal Narrative of a Many-sided American* (1942) skillfully interweaves long selections from Jefferson's own writing with connecting narrative and is still valuable as an introduction to Jefferson's life. Saul K. Padover's *Jefferson* (1942) hailed the philosopher of freedom and happiness. Marie Kimball published three carefully researched volumes covering Jefferson's life before his return from the French mission: *Jefferson: The Road to Glory, 1743–1776* (1943), *Jefferson: War and Peace, 1776 to 1784* (1947), and *Jefferson: The Scene of Europe, 1784 to 1789* (1950), all of which may still be read with some profit. Nathan Schachner's two-volume *Thomas Jefferson* (1951) is an intelligent, balanced study.

For Jefferson biography, 1948 was a landmark year, for it was then that the first volume of Dumas Malone's definitive life of Jefferson was published. The whole work, which eventually filled six volumes, has been published under the general title of *Jefferson and His Time*. The first volume, *Jefferson the Virginian* (1948), covers Jefferson's life up to his departure for France in 1784. *Jefferson and the Rights of Man* (1951) deals with his years in France and his subsequent service as secretary of state. *Jefferson and the Ordeal of Liberty* (1962) portrays his career from 1792 through his term as vice-president under John Adams. The titles of *Jefferson the President: First Term, 1801–1805* (1970) and *Jefferson the President: Second Term, 1805–1809* (1974) signify their contents. *The Sage of Monticello* (1981) portrays Jefferson in retirement. Malone is warmly sympathetic toward his subject, yet he manages to present a balanced view of Jefferson's strengths and weaknesses, straightforwardly offering all the known facts in the case for Jefferson's less happy actions as well as for his successes. Malone offers meliorating explanations for events like Jefferson's near disastrous term as governor of Virginia and the Callender scandals, but his presentation of the facts allows the reader the option of accepting or rejecting the interpretation. He is most apologetic in the fifth volume, on Jefferson's second term as president, in part because Fawn M. Brodie had begun to publish on the purported affair with Sally Hemings, but in the final volume he begins with a masterly critique of Jefferson's successes and failures as president. *Jefferson and His Time* is required reading for anyone seriously interested in Jefferson.

The best one-volume biography is Merrill Peterson's *Thomas Jefferson and the New Nation* (1970), a balanced and comprehensive account. Brodie published *Thomas Jefferson: An Intimate History* (1974) as a study of Jefferson's private and inner life, and it immediately became a succès de scandale for its acceptance as historical truth of a rumored love affair with Sally Hemings, one of the house servants at Monticello. Her study was criticized both on grounds of historical accuracy and psychological method, but her discussion of Jefferson's intense grief over his wife's death and her account of how this experience colored his life are worth some consideration. Page Smith's *Jefferson: A Revealing Biography* (1976) attempts, as Brodie does, to comprehend Jefferson's emotional life, but with less success and no documentation. Carl Binger's *Thomas Jefferson: A Well-Tempered Mind* (1970) claims to demonstrate the inner harmony of Jefferson's mind, and Erik Erikson's *Dimensions of a New Identity* (1974), which is less strictly biographical but still interesting in this regard, argues that Jefferson was a founding personality for a new national identity. Younger readers might be directed to Leonard Wibberley's *Man of Liberty: A Life of Thomas Jefferson*

(1968), which prints in one volume four titles previously issued separately. Merrill Peterson has collected eleven previously published and significant essays in *Thomas Jefferson: A Profile* (1967).

A great many books and articles have focused on particular events and phases in Jefferson's life. On Jefferson's home life and his relations with members of his family, Edwin M. Betts and James A. Bear, Jr., have edited *The Family Letters of Thomas Jefferson* (1966), which provides both firsthand information in the letters and a useful introduction. Jefferson's parents are somewhat shadowy figures, but Ramón I. Harris in "Thomas Jefferson: Female Identification," in *American Imago,* 25 (1968), attempts a psychoanalytic explanation of Jefferson's relations with his mother, although Gisela Tauber's "Reconstruction in Psychoanalytic Biography: Understanding Thomas Jefferson," in *Journal of Psychohistory,* 7 (1979), seems more suggestive. Bernard Mayo covers what is known about *Thomas Jefferson and His Unknown Brother Randolph* (1942). Gordon Langley Hall discusses Martha Wayles Jefferson and the Jefferson daughters, Maria ("Polly") and Martha ("Patsy"), among others, in *Mr. Jefferson's Ladies* (1966), a book marred by sentimentality and occasional inaccuracy. James A. Bear's "Thomas Jefferson and the Ladies," in *Augusta Historical Bulletin,* 6 (1970), is a corrective. Sarah N. Randolph contributed a chapter on her grandmother, Martha Jefferson Randolph, to *Worthy Women of Our First Century,* edited by Mrs. O. J. Wister (1877), and Dumas Malone has written charmingly of Jefferson's other daughter in "Polly Jefferson and Her Father," in *Virginia Quarterly Review,* 7 (1931). Bettie Woodson Weaver's "Mary Jefferson and Eppington," in *Virginia Cavalcade,* 19 (1969), describes Polly's life with her aunt while her father was in Paris. George G. Shackelford edited *Collected Papers to Commemorate Fifty Years of the Monticello Association of the Descendants of Thomas Jefferson*

(1965), which contains essays on the grave-yard at Monticello and on each of Jefferson's children and grandchildren. William H. Gaines, Jr.'s *Thomas Mann Randolph: Jefferson's Son-in-Law* (1966) contains much on family life at Monticello. Marie Kimball's "A Playmate of Thomas Jefferson," in *North American Review*, 213 (1921), discusses his relationship with his granddaughter, Ellen Wayles Randolph, while Barbara Mayo's "Twilight at Monticello," in *Virginia Quarterly Review*, 17 (1941), views Jefferson's last years through the letters of Virginia Randolph, another granddaughter. Jan Lewis in *The Pursuit of Happiness: Family and Values in Jefferson's Virginia* (1983) attempts to portray typical Virginian attitudes about family but specifically discusses the situations of some of Jefferson's grandchildren. A darker side of family life is shown in Joseph C. Vance's "Knives, Whips and Randolphs on the Court House Lawn," in *Magazine of Albemarle County History*, 15 (1956), an account of Charles L. Bankhead's nearly fatal attack on his brother-in-law, Thomas Jefferson Randolph. Boynton Merrill, Jr.'s *Jefferson's Nephews: A Frontier Tragedy* (1976) examines the vicious murder of a slave by Lilburne and Isham Lewis, sons of Jefferson's sister Lucy, and gives incidental information on Jefferson's relations with some of the more far-flung members of his family. Paul Wilstach offers some interesting anecdotes about life at Monticello in *Jefferson and Monticello* (1925), a rather uncritical book aimed at a popular audience. James A. Bear, Jr., has edited two important texts in his *Jefferson at Monticello* (1967): the memoirs of the Monticello slave Isaac Jefferson and Hamilton W. Pierson's edition of the memoirs of Edmund Bacon, overseer at Monticello from 1806 until 1821.

Interest in Jefferson's romantic life has recently centered on his supposed love affair with Sally Hemings. This story originated in the scandals spread by James T. Callender, a disappointed office seeker and onetime yellow journalist in the republican cause. The legend of Jefferson's black children by Sally Hemings never quite died; it was given fictional treatment in the mid-nineteenth century in William Wells Brown's *Clotel; or, The President's Daughter* (1853), and it was given fresh currency by Fawn Brodie's biography and by Barbara Chase-Riboud's novel *Sally Hemings* (1979). Charles A. Jellison's "That Scoundrel Callender," in *Virginia Magazine of History and Biography*, 67 (1959), sketches Callender's unsavory career, and Jerry W. Knudson in "Thomas Jefferson and James Callender," in *Negro History Bulletin*, 32 (1969), explains Callender's animus toward Jefferson. Virginius Dabney's *The Jefferson Scandals* (1981) attempts to refute Brodie and Chase-Riboud, giving an adequate account of the origins of Callender's libels, but it undermines its rebuttal by an almost hysterical tone. The most reasonably argued and best-informed exoneration of Jefferson from the charge of keeping a slave mistress is Douglass Adair's "The Jefferson Scandals" in his *Fame and the Founding Fathers* (1974), in which he cites evidence pointing to one of Jefferson's nephews as Sally Heming's probable lover. Dumas Malone in "Mr. Jefferson's Private Life," in *Proceedings of the American Antiquarian Society*, 84 (1974), prints a letter from Ellen Randolph Coolidge, Jefferson's granddaughter, claiming that Peter and Samuel Carr, his nephews, were the lovers of Sally and Betty Hemings. In "A Note on Evidence: The Personal History of Madison Hemings," in *Journal of Southern History*, 41 (1975), Malone and Steven H. Hochman argue that Madison Hemings' account of his paternity was solicited, edited, and published for political reasons. Garry Wills criticizes Brodie's inaccuracies in "Uncle Thomas's Cabin," in *New York Review of Books*, 18 April 1974.

The one woman Jefferson may well have fallen in love with in addition to his wife was Maria Cosway, the wife of an English portrait painter he met in Paris. Helen D. Bullock's *My Head and My Heart: A Little History of Thomas Jefferson and Maria Cosway* (1945) is a charming if somewhat inconclusive account of this friendship. In "Jefferson's Earliest Note to Maria Cosway with Some New Facts and Conjectures on His Broken Wrist," in *William and Mary Quarterly*, 3rd ser., 5 (1948), Lyman H. Butterfield and Howard C. Rice, Jr., suggest that Jefferson may have broken his wrist while showing off on an expedition with Cosway to see the Desert de Retz. Elizabeth Cometti's "Maria Cosway's Rediscovered Miniature of Jefferson," in *William and Mary Quarterly*, 3rd ser., 9 (1952), discusses the miniature portrait of Jefferson by John Trumbull given to Cosway. Jon Kula, in "Flirtation and *Feux d'Artifices,*" in *Virginia Cavalcade*, 26 (1976), notes that on the day they first met, Jefferson and Mrs. Cosway may have attended a fireworks display by the famed Ruggieris.

JEFFERSON'S ASSOCIATES

Many significant or suggestive studies have been published on Jefferson's particular friendships and working relationships. Bernard Mayo's "A Peppercorn for Mr. Jefferson," in *Virginia Quarterly Review*, 19 (1943), and *Another Peppercorn for Mr. Jefferson* (1977) celebrate Jefferson's capacity for friendship and his social grace. Of Jefferson's many friendships probably the most famous is that with John Adams, and John Murray Allison's *Adams and Jefferson: The Story of a Friendship* (1966) is a pleasant if not especially insightful account of this. More stimulating is Merrill Peterson's *Adams and Jefferson: A Revolutionary Dialogue* (1976), which discusses the friendship between an enlightened Puritan and a man of the Enlightenment. Henry F. May considers Adams and Jefferson as culminating figures of the American Enlightenment in a chapter entitled "The End of the Eighteenth Century" in his book *The Enlightenment in America* (1976), as does Ezra Pound

in his inimitable, cranky manner in "The Jefferson-Adams Correspondence," in *North American Review*, 244 (1938), reprinted in Pound, *Selected Prose* (1973). Edward Dumbauld's "Jefferson and Adams' English Garden Tour," in William Howard Adams, ed., *Jefferson and the Arts* (1976), documents their joint visits to several English country estates. Joyce Appleby gives a perspicacious account of an early sign of the growing distance between the two men in "The Jefferson-Adams Rupture and the First French Translation of John Adams' *Defence,*" in *American Historical Review*, 73 (1968), which shows Jefferson's changing response to Adams' *Defence of the Constitutions.* Lyman Butterfield describes how Benjamin Rush fostered the reconciliation of Adams and Jefferson in "The Dream of Benjamin Rush," in *Yale Review*, 40 (1950). Walter Muir Whitehill notes that Adams was one of the figures who provided a significant New England connection for Jefferson in "The Union of New England and Virginia," in *Virginia Quarterly Review*, 40 (1964), the others being Ellen Randolph Coolidge and George Ticknor. Rush Welter suggests in "The Adams-Jefferson Correspondence, 1812–1826," in *American Quarterly*, 2 (1950), that Adams tended to lead the later correspondence in its somewhat fitful analysis of human nature, civil polity, and human learning, and two essays comment on the shared love of the classics demonstrated in the later letters: Susan Ford's "Thomas Jefferson and John Adams on the Classics," in *Arion*, 6 (1967), and Richard M. Gummere's "Adams and Jefferson," in his *The American Colonial Mind and the Classical Tradition* (1963). Henry Steele Commager distinguishes between Adams' and Jefferson's views of the relationship between history and the present in "The Past as an Extension of the Present," in *Proceedings of the American Antiquarian Society*, 79 (1969). Finally, Judith Pulley's "The Bittersweet Friendship of Thomas Jefferson and Abigail Adams," in *Essex Institute Histori-*

cal Collections, 108 (1972), points out that Jefferson never regained the rapport with Abigail that he did with John.

Jefferson perhaps felt most comfortable in his friendships with fellow Virginians because there he found a stock of shared experience and values. As a student at the College of William and Mary he became intimate with Governor Francis Fauquier, William Small, and George Wythe, older men who were at once mentors and friends. This group is described in William Shands Meacham's "Thomas Jefferson and the Greatest Party of Four," in *Commonwealth, The Magazine of Virginia,* 34 (1967). The impact of William Small, professor of mathematics and natural philosophy, is shown in Herbert L. Ganter's "William Small, Jefferson's Beloved Teacher," in *William and Mary Quarterly,* 3rd ser., 4 (1947), and Dumas Malone's "Jefferson Goes to School in Williamsburg," in *Virginia Quarterly Review,* 33 (1957). Jefferson read law with George Wythe, as did John Marshall, a point made by Dice R. Anderson in "The Teacher of Jefferson and Marshall," in *South Atlantic Quarterly,* 15 (1916). Jefferson was more rival than friend to Patrick Henry, as is clearly shown in Stan V. Henkels' "Jefferson's Recollections of Patrick Henry," in *Pennsylvania Magazine of History and Biography,* 34 (1910). Much of the scholarship on the relationship with James Madison focuses on their political concerns and will be dealt with later in this essay, but their New England vacation trip of 1791 is described in Philip M. Marsh's "The Jefferson-Madison Vacation," in *Pennsylvania Magazine of History and Biography,* 71 (1947), which emphasizes that their purpose was pleasure rather than politics, and in William K. Bottorff's "Mr. Jefferson Tours New England," in *New-England Galaxy,* 20 (1979). In "Madison's Bookish Habits," in *Quarterly Journal of the Library of Congress,* 37 (1980), Robert A. Rutland discusses Jefferson's influence on Madison's reading interests. Irving Brant, Madison's

biographer, argues in "James Madison and His Times" in *American Historical Review,* 57 (1952), that Madison was no mere follower of Jefferson but often led him in policymaking, a point made earlier by Roy J. Honeywell's "President Jefferson and His Successor," in *American Historical Review,* 46 (1940). Adrienne Koch's *Jefferson and Madison: The Great Collaboration* (1950) is an extended study of their working relationship, including political activities, that is well worth reading, although it has a tendency to "Jeffersonize" Madison. Harry Ammon's "James Monroe and the Election of 1808 in Virginia," in *William and Mary Quarterly,* 3rd ser., 20 (1963), discusses the cooling of relations between Jefferson and Monroe that led the latter to become the presidential candidate of the "Old Republicans." Manning J. Dauer distinguishes usefully between two men of the same name, one a supporter, the other an enemy of Jefferson, in "The Two John Nicholases: Their Relationship to Washington and Jefferson," in *American Historical Review,* 45 (1939). A number of remarkable young Virginians served Jefferson as private secretary at some point in their careers. Rochonne Abrams discusses the most famous of these in "Meriwether Lewis: Two Years with Jefferson, the Mentor," in *Missouri Historical Society Bulletin,* 36 (1979), and Yvon Bizardel and Howard C. Rice, Jr., describe the relationship with William Short, his secretary in Paris, in "Poor in Love Mr. Short," in *William and Mary Quarterly,* 3rd ser., 21 (1964). Nicholas Trist, who was Jefferson's last secretary, his grandson-in-law, and a friend of Andrew Jackson, is considered in Robert A. Brent's "Nicholas Philip Trist—A Link Between Jefferson and Jackson?" in *Southern Quarterly,* 1 (1963). Jefferson sent his young friend Francis Gilmer to search for European professors for his university, and their relationship is described in Richard Beale Davis' introduction to his *Correspondence of Thomas Jefferson and Francis Walker Gilmer, 1814–1826* (1946).

Dr. Robley Dunglison became the university's first professor of medicine and Jefferson's physician; their friendship is portrayed in Samuel X. Radbill's "Dr. Robley Dunglison and Jefferson," in *Transactions and Studies of the College of Physicians of Philadelphia*, 27 (1959), and in the introduction to John M. Dorsey's *The Jefferson-Dunglison Letters* (1960).

Correspondence survives documenting Jefferson's many friendly interchanges with Europeans he met at home and abroad. Gilbert Chinard's editions of letters to and from French acquaintances have been noticed above, and Auguste Levasseur's *Lafayette in America in 1824 and 1825* (1829) provides a firsthand account of the reunion of Lafayette and Jefferson at Monticello in 1824. Marie Kimball describes Jefferson's friendship with several Hessian prisoners of war lodged in Albemarle County in 1779 in "Europe Comes to Jefferson," in *American-German Review*, 15 (1949). One of Jefferson's warmest admirers from abroad, and one who caused him some difficulty, was Philip Mazzei, an Italian he had first met in Virginia before the Revolution and with whom he later corresponded. Margherita Marchione's *Philip Mazzei: Jefferson's "Zealous Whig"* (1975) provides biographical background, facsimiles of letters, and a translation of Mazzei's *Historical and Political Enquiries Concerning the United States of America*. Howard R. Marraro earlier published some of the correspondence with annotations, in "Unpublished Correspondence of Jefferson and Adams to Mazzei," in *Virginia Magazine of History and Biography*, 51 (1943), and "Unpublished Mazzei Letters to Jefferson," in *William and Mary Quarterly*, 3rd ser., 1 (1944). Of particular interest is Marraro's "The Four Versions of Jefferson's Letter to Mazzei," in *William and Mary Quarterly*, 2nd ser., 22 (1942), which traces the history of a letter that caused Jefferson much trouble when it was eventually published in America; Marraro shows that the letter became more pro-

vocative as it was translated by various hands successively into Italian, French, and back to English. A less interesting friendship than it might have been is portrayed in Gilbert Chinard's "La correspondance de Madame de Staël avec Jefferson," in *Revue de littérature comparée*, 2 (1922). A more significant friendship was that with Tadeusz Kościuszko, described in Edward P. Alexander's "Jefferson and Kosciuszko: Friends of Liberty and of Man," in *Pennsylvania Magazine of History and Biography*, 92 (1968), and Bogdan Grzelonski's *Jefferson/Kosciuszko Correspondence* (1978). In "A Testamentary Tragedy: Mr. Jefferson and the Wills of General Kosciuszko," in *American Bar Association Journal*, 44 (1958), Louis Ottenberg confirms Jefferson's wisdom in declining to serve as Kościuszko's executor; it took thirty years to settle the estate, in part because there were four separate wills, none of which canceled the others. Another Polish connection was Julien Ursyn-Niemcewicz, described in W. M. Kozlowski's "Niemcewicz en Amérique et sa correspondance inédite avec Jefferson (1797–1810)," in *Revue de littérature comparée*, 8 (1928), and Eugene F. Kusielewicz' "The Jefferson-Niemcewicz Correspondence," in *Polish Review*, 2, no. 4 (1957).

JEFFERSON AND THE LAW

After Jefferson finished reading law under George Wythe, he began his own law practice, and although he maintained this practice for only a relatively brief period, the theory and history of law continued to interest him, perhaps even to guide the forms of his thinking, for the rest of his life. Edward Dumbauld's *Thomas Jefferson and the Law* (1978) is the best full-length study of Jefferson's legal education, his achievements as a lawyer, his work as a lawmaker, and his stature as a legal scholar. Frank L. Dewey has recently published a number of articles based on study of Jefferson's casebook, fee book, and account books, which provide some insight into this opening phase of Jefferson's public life. "Thomas Jefferson's Law Practice," in *Virginia Magazine of History and Biography,* 85 (1977), gives a general overview of Jefferson as a practicing lawyer, and in four other articles Dewey describes specific cases; "Thomas Jefferson and a Williamsburg Scandal: The Case of *Blair* v. *Blair,*" in *Virginia Magazine of History and Biography,* 89 (1981), and "Thomas Jefferson's Notes on Divorce," in *William and Mary Quarterly,* 3rd ser., 39 (1982), explain his actions on behalf of Dr. James Blair, while "The Waterson-Madison Episode: An Incident in Thomas Jefferson's Law Practice," in *Virginia Magazine of History and Biography,* 90 (1982), and "Thomas Jefferson's Law Practice: The Norfolk Anti-Inoculation Riots," in *Virginia Magazine of History and Biography,* 91 (1983), discuss cases involving land speculation and public protests against Dr. Archibald Campbell's inoculation activities. John C. Wyllie notes a later opinion written well after Jefferson ended his law practice in "The Second Mrs. Wayland: An Unpublished Jefferson Opinion on a Case in Equity," in *American Journal of Legal History,* 9 (1965). George M. Curtis discusses Jefferson's legal career and his contributions to the Virginia Law Reports of 1769–1772 in W. Hamilton Bryson, ed., *The Virginia Law Reporters Before 1880* (1977). Julian S. Waterman explains his dislike of William Blackstone's "Mansfieldism" in "Thomas Jefferson and Blackstone's *Commentaries,*" in *Illinois Law Review,* 27 (1933), and Edward Dumbauld describes how his personal library with its collection of valuable legal manuscripts became a resource for Virginia courts in "A Manuscript from Monticello: Jefferson's Library in Legal History," in *American Bar Association Journal,* 38 (1952). Louis M. Sears has shown Jefferson's knowledge of the classic sources of international law in "Jefferson and the Law of Nations," in *American Political Science Review,* 13 (1919),

while Charles M. Wiltse finds a tendency to depart from older natural-law theory in favor of a sociological interpretation of international law in "Thomas Jefferson on the Law of Nations," in *American Journal of International Law,* 29 (1935). Gail M. Beckman's "Three Penal Codes Compared," in *American Journal of Legal History,* 10 (1966), looks at Jefferson's proposed penal code of 1776 for Virginia, comparing it with those of Edward Livingston for Louisiana and David Dudley Field for New York; Beckman contends that Jefferson's was an expression of the Enlightenment that made way for penal code reforms in other states. George Dargo gives a helpful account of Jefferson's efforts to supplant civil law in Louisiana with the common law of the Anglo-American tradition in *Jefferson's Louisiana: Politics and the Clash of Legal Traditions* (1975). John T. Noonan, Jr., claims that Jefferson and George Wythe were blinded to the nature of slavery and of slaves as persons because their legal training taught them that decisions were to be made in terms of the abstract conditions of the law without respect to persons, in a subtly argued study entitled *Persons and Masks of the Law: Cardozo, Holmes, Jefferson, and Wythe as Makers of the Masks* (1976). Morris L. Cohen shows Jefferson in the act of instructing John Minor on how to study for the law in "Thomas Jefferson Recommends a Course of Law Study," in *University of Pennsylvania Law Review,* 119 (1971).

JEFFERSON AND THE AMERICAN REVOLUTION

Jefferson's emergence into public life as a member of the Virginia House of Burgesses and the subsequent revolutionary conventions is best treated in Malone's *Jefferson the Virginian* and Peterson's *Thomas Jefferson and the New Nation* (noted above). His first publication, *A Summary View of the Rights of British America,* brought the young Jefferson to the attention of readers beyond the borders of Virginia. In "Jefferson's Expression of the American Mind," in *Virginia Quarterly Review,* 50 (1974), Julian P. Boyd discusses the conditions under which Jefferson wrote the *Summary View* and hypothesizes that in its earliest form it may have been intended for delivery by Patrick Henry. Anthony M. Lewis' "Jefferson's *Summary View* as a Chart of Political Union," in *William and Mary Quarterly,* 3rd ser., 5 (1948), claims that Jefferson more clearly than any of his contemporaries saw the need for a division of power between the local and imperial sphere. H. Trevor Colbourn describes Jefferson's reading of whig history as a key both to the *Summary View* and his whole career in the chapter "Thomas Jefferson and the Rights of Expatriated Men" in his excellent *The Lamp of Experience: Whig History and the Intellectual Origins of the American Revolution* (1965). Jefferson's first important writing assignment in Congress was to draft a resolution justifying Americans arming themselves against the British, although Congress eventually adopted a more moderate version drafted by John Dickinson. Julian P. Boyd explains the respective roles of Jefferson and Dickinson in "The Disputed Authorship of the Declaration on the Causes and Necessity of Taking up Arms, 1775," in *Pennsylvania Magazine of History and Biography,* 74 (1950).

The scholarship and commentary on Jefferson and the Declaration of Independence is extensive enough to justify a separate bibliography. Readers wishing to study the process of writing the Declaration would profit from Julian P. Boyd's *The Declaration of Independence: The Evolution of the Text* (1945), which prints facsimiles of the known drafts and provides a helpful analysis of changes in successive versions. Boyd also offers intelligent conjecture on the fate of the now missing draft that Congress actually approved in "The Declaration of Independence: The Mystery of the Lost Original," in *Pennsylvania Magazine of History and Biography,* 100

(1976). David Hawke's *A Transaction of Free Men* (1964) is a well-written account for a general audience; it focuses on Jefferson's role in conceiving and drafting the Declaration. John H. Hazelton's *The Declaration of Independence* (1906; repr. 1970) retains some interest as a careful and intensive study of the Declaration and the circumstances of its creation. Carl Becker's *The Declaration of Independence: A Study in the History of Political Ideas* (1922) is a classic analysis of Jefferson's debt to the English-speaking Enlightenment inspired by Locke and Newton, and it remains an important statement on the supposedly Lockean origins of the Declaration. Edward Dumbauld's *The Declaration of Independence and What It Means Today* (1950) explores the intellectual and historical background of the Declaration by means of a useful if not profound phrase-by-phrase analysis. Garry Wills has offered the most important rejoinder to Becker and the Lockeans in his *Inventing America: Jefferson's Declaration of Independence* (1978), where he contends that to read the Declaration correctly we must recognize the primary significance of Francis Hutcheson and the moral-sense philosophers of the Scottish commonsense school. Wills's argument brings a significant influence on Jefferson back into focus, but the position of some of his critics is forcefully stated by Ronald Hamowy in "Jefferson and the Scottish Enlightenment: A Critique of Garry Wills's *Inventing America: Jefferson's Declaration of Independence,*" in *William and Mary Quarterly,* 3rd ser., 36 (1979). Wilbur Samuel Howell's "The Declaration of Independence and Eighteenth-Century Logic," in *William and Mary Quarterly,* 3rd ser., 18 (1961), compares the argumentative structure of the Declaration with the theory of argumentative structure elaborated in the rhetorical guides of Jefferson's time, particularly William Duncan's *The Elements of Logic.* Robert Ginsberg includes his essay "The Declaration as Rhetoric" in the useful collection he edited, *A Casebook on the Declaration of Independence* (1967), and Howard Mumford Jones also points to the rhetorical qualities of the text as he explains what Jefferson meant when he claimed to have given "the common sense of the subject" in "The Declaration of Independence: A Critique," in *Proceedings of the American Antiquarian Society,* 85 (1975). Two suggestive essays demonstrate ways in which the Declaration capitalized on a New England tradition of evangelical rhetoric: David Levin's "Cotton Mather's Declaration of Gentlemen and Thomas Jefferson's Declaration of Independence," in *New England Quarterly,* 50 (1977), and Barry Bell's "Reading and 'Misreading' the Declaration of Independence," in *Early American Literature,* 18 (1983). Charles Warren's "Fourth of July Myths," in *William and Mary Quarterly,* 3rd ser., 2 (1945), explains how Jefferson later misremembered the actual manner of signing the Declaration and how the document was signed by people who were not present for the deliberations and not signed by some who were; Whitfield J. Bell, Jr.'s *The Declaration of Independence: Four 1776 Versions* (1976) provides a convenient account of how the Declaration was printed.

Debate continues on what Jefferson intended when he referred to the inalienable right of the pursuit of happiness. In addition to Becker and Wills, one might consult Arthur M. Schlesinger, who says in a brief note that "pursuit" means the practice of happiness, in "The Lost Meaning of 'The Pursuit of Happiness,' " in *William and Mary Quarterly,* 3rd ser., 21 (1964). Adrienne Koch in "Power and Morals and the Founding Fathers: Jefferson," in *Review of Politics,* 15 (1953), claims it is the right to pursue the life of reason and the fulfillment of human nature, and she furthermore points to Locke's use of the phrase. Caroline Robbins' "The Pursuit of Happiness," in Irving Kristol, ed., *America's Continuing Revolution: An Act of Conservation* (1975), maintains in an appropriately conservative fashion that Jefferson intended not individual but public happiness,

the fulfillment of "the aspirations of the majority." Ursula M. von Eckardt's *The Pursuit of Happiness in the Democratic Creed* (1959) explores the notion as central to Jefferson's political thought as well as to American culture itself.

Uncertainty about the meaning of happiness seems to be a peculiarly twentieth-century problem, but from the nineteenth century on, political thinkers have been exercised by Jefferson's claim that all men are created free and equal, an argument that haunts us yet. The title of R. B. Mayes's "The Divine Legation of Thomas Jefferson —Are All Men Created Free?—Are All Men Created White," in *DeBow's Review,* 30 (1861), suggests the tenor of a number of articles on the Declaration that appeared just before the Civil War in this South Carolina magazine. Forty years later William F. Dana offered an apparently more progressive view by contending in "The Declaration of Independence as Justification for Revolution," in *Harvard Law Review,* 13 (1900), that the Declaration is a political, not a social, statement and must be read in the context of other state papers such as the Virginia Bill of Rights. Daniel Boorstin's "The American Revolution: Revolution Without Dogma," a chapter in his *Genius of American Politics* (1953), tries to convince us that Jefferson had no "rash desire to remake all society and institutions." Bernard Wishy's "John Locke and the Spirit of '76," in *Political Science Quarterly,* 73 (1958); Martin Diamond's "The American Idea of Equality: The View from the Founding," in *Review of Politics,* 38 (1976); and Paul Eidelberg's *On the Silence of the Declaration of Independence* (1976), all offer essentially conservative readings downplaying interpretations of the Declaration as an egalitarian document. However, in "The Contemporary Significance of the American Declaration of Independence," in *Philosophy and Phenomenological Research,* 38 (1978), John Somerville argues that its significance is greater than ever because of Jefferson's recognition of the priority of civil rights and of the people's right to revolution; and Shingo Shibata in "Fundamental Human Rights and the Problem of Freedom," in *Social Praxis,* 3 (1976), thinks that while the Declaration was advanced for its time, its most significant features have been subsumed by Marxism, "the most comprehensive theory of freedom." A more balanced and less contentious statement than any of the above is J. R. Pole's scholarly "The Meanings of a Self-Evident Truth" in his book *The Pursuit of Equality in American History* (1978), in which he describes Jefferson's preamble as "a vulnerable instrument of revolutionary policy" that was later turned against itself. The one other element of the Declaration to receive particular attention is the rejected passage on slavery and the slave trade. Sidney Kaplan discusses this in "The 'Domestic Insurrections' of the Declaration of Independence," in *Journal of Negro History,* 61 (1976); by a rhetorical analysis of the text Edwin Gittleman perceives a central theme of slavery under tyranny that makes the rejected lines an essential element of the Declaration's logic, in "Jefferson's 'Slave Narrative': The Declaration of Independence as a Literary Text," in *Early American Literature,* 8 (1974).

Jefferson's work for political and legal reform in Virginia in the years after the Declaration is well covered by both Malone and Peterson in their biographies, but a number of studies on specific issues are also useful. Dice R. Anderson's "Jefferson and the Virginia Constitution," in *American Historical Review,* 21 (1916), suggests that Jefferson's draft of a constitution was probably too radical for the convention. Elisha P. Douglass claims Jefferson was much less a radical democrat than were some of his Virginia contemporaries in "Thomas Jefferson and Revolutionary Democracy," a chapter in his *Rebels and Democrats* (1955; repr. 1971), and Robert E. Brown and B. Katherine Brown make a similar claim in the chapter "The

Revolution as a Social Movement" in their *Virginia 1705–1786: Democracy or Aristocracy?* (1964), although they allow a possible exception for Jefferson's ideas on education and religion. C. Ray Keim gives an informative account of the reforms touching the transmission of estates in "Primogeniture and Entail in Colonial Virginia," in *William and Mary Quarterly,* 3rd ser., 25 (1968). A great deal has been written on Jefferson as a champion of religious freedom, but for substantive accounts one might turn to Willibald M. Plochl's interesting, if somewhat subjective, "Thomas Jefferson, Author of the Statute of Virginia for Religious Freedom," in *The Jurist,* 3 (1943), which argues for the statute's basis in natural law. Sidney Mead analyzes the consequences of Jefferson's rational defense of religion in "Thomas Jefferson's 'Fair Experiment'— Religious Freedom," in *Religion in Life,* 23 (1954), and Thomas E. Buckley gives the best overview in *Church and State in Revolutionary Virginia, 1776–1787* (1977). Hamilton J. Eckenrode provides a still useful account of Jefferson's governorship in *The Revolution in Virginia* (1916).

JEFFERSON AND FOREIGN POLICY

In 1784, Jefferson departed on his mission to France, initiating his career as a statesman and diplomatist. The best study of Jefferson's political dealings with France, both as minister and after his return to America, is Lawrence S. Kaplan's *Jefferson and France: An Essay on Politics and Political Ideas* (1967), which one might supplement with Kaplan's "Toward Isolationism: The Jeffersonian Republicans and the Franco-American Alliance of 1778," in *Historical Reflections,* 3 (1976), arguing for the seriousness of the isolationist sentiments in Jefferson's first inaugural address. R. R. Palmer's "The Dubious Democrat: Thomas Jefferson in Bourbon France," in *Political Science Quarterly,* 72 (1957), explores Jefferson's attitudes toward the French Revolution and his concern that the French were not yet ready for American-style democracy. William K. Woolery's *The Relation of Thomas Jefferson to American Foreign Policy, 1783–1793* (1927) contends that Jefferson was in effect the guiding genius of American foreign policy in these years, and similarly Samuel Flagg Bemis in the second volume of his *American Secretaries of State and Their Diplomacy* (1927) sees him as the best man of his time to guide American diplomacy, even though he was troubled by his rivalry with Alexander Hamilton and by Hamilton's interference. Paul A. Varg's *Foreign Policies of the Founding Fathers* (1963) points to the economic basis of early national foreign policy and describes Jefferson as an "idealist" in opposition to Hamilton, the "realist." Albert H. Bowman, on the other hand, calls Jefferson the realist in his "Jefferson, Hamilton, and American Foreign Policy," in *Political Science Quarterly,* 71 (1956), because Jefferson was guided by an understanding of the national interest rather than by a vision of what he wanted the nation to become. Lawrence S. Kaplan presents "Thomas Jefferson: The Idealist as Realist" in Frank J. Merli and Theodore A. Wilson, eds., *Makers of American Diplomacy* (1974) as being forced in the 1790s to deal with both Hamilton's Anglophilia and French intransigencies, although in "The Consensus of 1789: Jefferson and Hamilton on American Foreign Policy," in *South Atlantic Quarterly,* 71 (1972), Kaplan claims historians have exaggerated the differences between the two men, particularly for the years 1789–1791.

Merrill Peterson evaluates Jefferson's attempts to use commerce as an instrument of foreign policy in "Thomas Jefferson and Commercial Policy, 1783–1793," in *William and Mary Quarterly,* 3rd ser., 22 (1965). Alexander DeConde emphasizes domestic political rivalries as a major source of American

problems in foreign relations in *Entangling Alliance: Politics and Diplomacy under George Washington* (1958), and Albert H. Bowman's *The Struggle for Neutrality: Franco-American Diplomacy during the Federalist Era* (1974) views American diplomacy as dominated by the need to keep the French at arm's length. Jefferson's great diplomatic success as president was the Louisiana Purchase, well explored in Alexander DeConde's *This Affair of Louisiana* (1976), which describes the underlying expansionist ethos as "a kind of pious imperialism." Clifford L. Egan's *Neither Peace Nor War* (1983) shows Franco-American relations in the years after the Purchase as a series of missed opportunities. Yves Auguste in "Jefferson et Haiti (1804–1810)," in *Revue d'histoire diplomatique,* 86 (1973), portrays Jefferson's changing ideas about Haiti and his attempts to use it as an instrument of foreign policy. Isaac J. Cox's "The Pan-American Policy of Jefferson and Wilkinson," in *Mississippi Valley Historical Review,* 1 (1914); Clifford L. Egan's "United States, France, and West Florida, 1803–1807," in *Florida Historical Quarterly,* 47 (1969); and Jared W. Bradley's "W. C. C. Claiborne and Spain: Foreign Affairs under Jefferson and Madison," in *Louisiana History,* 12 (1971), shed light on Jefferson's efforts to acquire Florida. Louis M. Sears's *Jefferson and the Embargo* (1927) has long been the standard treatment of what is perhaps Jefferson's most significant diplomatic failure, but it should now be supplemented by Burton Spivak's *Jefferson's English Crisis: Commerce, Embargo, and the Republican Revolution* (1979), a thorough examination of the embargo in the context of his long-held animosity toward England. Richard Mannix' "Gallatin, Jefferson, and the Embargo of 1808," in *Diplomatic History,* 3 (1979), contends that Jefferson was not particularly concerned with the embargo and that only Gallatin made a somewhat reluctant effort to manage it. Finally, Reginald C. Stuart's *The Half-Way Pacifist: Thomas Jefferson's View of War* (1978) argues that Jefferson saw violence as an instrument of last resort in foreign policy even though he had a basically "defensive mentality."

THE PARTY LEADER

Jefferson's rivalry with Hamilton had consequences not only for his conduct of foreign policy but also, and more important, for the beginnings of the first party system. This has attracted a wide range of scholarly attention at least since Alexander Everett's "Origin and Character of the Old Parties," in *North American Review*, 39 (1834), which presented the distinction between Jefferson's Republicans as the party of liberty and Hamilton's Federalists as the party of law. Recent scholarship includes Joseph Charles's *The Origins of the American Party System* (1956), which views the party system as a response to divisive issues of the early 1790s, including Jay's Treaty, examined in Jerald A. Combs's *The Jay Treaty: Political Battleground of the Founding Fathers* (1970). Richard Hofstadter includes two chapters tracing Jefferson's and Madison's movement from legitimate opposition to the achievement of power in *The Idea of a Party System* (1969) and explains the early distrust and eventual acceptance of parties. Richard Buel, Jr., shows how the styles of the Federalists and Republicans were a natural outgrowth of their political beliefs in *Securing the Revolution: Ideology in American Politics, 1789–1815* (1972). Dumas Malone's monograph *Thomas Jefferson as Political Leader* (1963) attempts to explain how he became a party leader, and Noble E. Cunningham, Jr.'s *The Jeffersonian Republicans: The Formation of Party Organization, 1789–1801* (1957) and *The Jeffersonian Republicans in Power: Party Operations, 1801–1809* (1963) offer the best studies of the organization and functioning of the Jeffersonian party. Lance Banning's excellent *The Jeffersonian Persuasion: Evolution of a Party Ideology* (1978) argues that the ideology of the Jeffersonians was a continuation of the "country" party position that dominated the thinking of the revolutionary-era patriots. This can be supplemented with John Zvesper's *Political Philosophy and Rhetoric: A Study of the Origins of American Party Politics* (1977) and particularly by Joyce Appleby's *Capitalism and a New Social Order: The Republican Vision of the 1790s* (1984), which rejects the description of Jefferson's politics as a version of the old "country" party, emphasizing instead contemporary economic issues and the importance of Jefferson's support of capitalist expansion on the part of individual farmers and entrepreneurs. In this regard, see also Appleby's "What Is Still American in the Political Philosophy of Thomas Jefferson?" in *William and Mary Quarterly*, 3rd ser., 39 (1982).

The vice-presidency was no more powerful an office when Jefferson held it under John Adams than it would be in ensuing years, but Jefferson's one important vice-presidential contribution was to compile the Senate's manual of parliamentary procedure, which in various revisions has been used ever since. On this, see Giles Wilkeson Gray's "Thomas Jefferson's Interest in Parliamentary Practice," in *Speech Monographs*, 27 (1960). The great domestic issue of the years 1796–1800 was the passage and attempted enforcement of the Alien and Sedition Acts, and scholars have examined Jefferson's responses to this as a point of entry into discussions of his attitudes toward civil rights and into his role in the Kentucky and Virginia Resolutions. For the acts themselves and subsequent efforts to prosecute offenders, James Morton Smith's *Freedom's Fetters: The Alien and Sedition Laws and American Civil Liberties* (1956) is the best and fullest account, but John C. Miller's *Crisis in Freedom* (1951) is also of interest. Linda K. Kerber's *Federalists in Dissent: Imagery and Ideology in Jeffersonian America* (1970) is an excellent account of the Federalist attacks on Jefferson that were one side of the newspaper wars that helped provoke the acts, and Frank L. Mott's *Jefferson and the Press* (1943) portrays Jefferson's growing disappointment with the performance, if not with the principle, of a free press. Adrienne Koch's *Jefferson and Madison: The Great Collaboration,* noted above, portrays Madison as tempering Jefferson's reactions to the Alien and Sedition Acts, and writing with Harry Ammon in "The Virginia and Kentucky Resolutions: An Episode in Jefferson's and Madison's Defense of Civil Liberties," in *William and Mary Quarterly,* 3rd ser., 5 (1948), she concludes that Jefferson and Madison are the only major authors of the resolutions. Joseph McGraw, in " 'To Secure These Rights': Virginia Republicans on the Strategies of Political Opposition, 1788–1800," in *Virginia Magazine of History and Biography,* 91 (1983), discusses Jefferson's Kentucky Resolutions as part of a program to inculcate republican principles. James Morton Smith's "The Grass Roots Origins of the Kentucky Resolutions," in *William and Mary Quarterly,* 3rd ser., 27 (1970), argues for closer attention to events in Kentucky as a balance to historians' concentration on Jefferson as theoretician and author of the resolutions. Leonard W. Levy's *Jefferson and Civil Liberties: The Darker Side* (1963) is an important study that has been criticized for holding Jefferson up to his own highest standards of civil liberty and finding him sometimes to come up short, most notably in his behavior during the Burr trial.

THE PRESIDENCY

Jefferson's victory in the fiercely contested election of 1800 has sometimes been hailed as marking the second American Revolution. Charles O. Lerche, Jr.'s "Jefferson and the Election of 1800: A Case Study in the Political Smear," in *William and Mary Quarterly,* 3rd ser., 5 (1948), and Charles F. O'-Brien's "The Religious Issue in the Presi-

dential Campaign of 1800," in *Essex Institute Historical Collections,* 107 (1971), look at some of the vituperative elements of the election. Daniel Sisson's *The American Revolution of 1800* (1974) suggestively explores the significance of Jefferson's coming to power. Henry Adams' *History of the United States of America During the [First and Second] Administration[s] of Thomas Jefferson* (1889–1890) is a classic of American historical writing, but it must be read critically. Lynton K. Caldwell's *The Administrative Theories of Hamilton and Jefferson* (1944) presents Jefferson's efforts to control the exercise of power by government. Leonard D. White's *The Jeffersonians: A Study in Administrative History, 1801–1829* (1951) finds Jefferson's place in American history less important for his contribution to the art of administration than for his convictions about democracy. Sidney H. Aronson's *Status and Kinship in the Higher Civil Service* (1964) analyzes the social origins of Jefferson's appointees to office and attempts to determine how representative they were of American society as a whole. Two of the most penetrating studies of Jefferson's presidency were published in the same year and agree in crediting a great deal of the success of his administration to Jefferson's talents for organization and to his ability to use his personal prestige: Noble E. Cunningham, Jr.'s *The Process of Government under Jefferson* (1978) emphasizes his skill as an administrator and Robert M. Johnstone, Jr.'s *Jefferson and the Presidency: Leadership in the Young Republic* (1978) points to his success in drawing on extraconstitutional sources of power. Forrest McDonald's *The Presidency of Thomas Jefferson* (1976) surveys Jefferson's handling of the office but perhaps overstates the case when it claims that "just about everything" in Jeffersonian republicanism appears first in Bolingbroke. Ralph Ketcham's "The Transatlantic Background of Thomas Jefferson's Ideas of Executive Power," in *Studies in Eighteenth-Century Culture,* 11 (1982), portrays Jefferson and the other early presidents as torn between Boling-broke's Augustan model of patriot leadership and the new republican politics.

Jefferson's first problem after assuming office was posed by John Adams' last-minute appointment of the "midnight judges," and this affair initiated a series of difficulties with the Supreme Court and Chief Justice John Marshall. Julian P. Boyd's "The Chasm That Separated Thomas Jefferson and John Marshall" in Gottfried Dietze, ed., *Essays on the American Constitution* (1964), and Philip G. Henderson, "Marshall Versus Jefferson: Politics and the Federal Judiciary in the Early Republic," in *Michigan Journal of Politics,* 2 (1983), portray the antagonistic relationship between Jefferson and Marshall. Richard E. Ellis' *The Jeffersonian Crisis: Courts and Politics in the Young Republic* (1971) is an excellent account of the struggles with the courts that were waged by the Jeffersonians. Donald O. Dewey in *Marshall Versus Jefferson: The Political Background of Marbury vs. Madison* (1970) discusses the case that arose out of the midnight-judges episode and that in turn resulted in the establishment of the principle of judicial review. Chief Justice Warren E. Burger gives his account of *Marbury* v. *Madison* in "The Doctrine of Judicial Review: Mr. Marshall, Mr. Jefferson, and Mr. Marbury," in William F. Swindler, ed., *The Constitution and Chief Justice Marshall* (1978). Jerry W. Knudson examines the attempt to impeach Samuel Chase in "The Jeffersonian Assault on the Federalist Judiciary, 1802–1805: Political Forces and Press Reaction," in *American Journal of Legal History,* 14 (1970), and Raoul Berger considers Jefferson's subpoena by Marshall in the Burr case in "The President, Congress, and the Courts," in *Yale Law Review,* 83 (1974). Caleb Perry Patterson offers an overview of Jefferson's ultimate beliefs on the interrelationship of the branches of government in *The Constitutional Principles of Thomas Jefferson* (1953).

Military and defense policy was one area of serious disagreement between Jeffer-son and the Federalists. Donald Jackson's "Jefferson, Meriwether Lewis, and the Reduction of the United States Army," in *Proceedings of the American Philosophical Society,* 124 (1980), and Theodore J. Crackel's "Jefferson, Politics, and the Army: An Examination of the Military Peace Establishment Act of 1802," in *Journal of the Early Republic,* 2 (1982), are informative on Jefferson's efforts to ease Federalists out of the army. Mary P. Adams' "Jefferson's Reaction to the Treaty of San Ildefonso," in *Journal of Southern History,* 21 (1955), examines Jefferson's military policy for defending the Louisiana territory. Julia H. Macleod's "Jefferson and the Navy: A Defense," in *Huntington Library Quarterly,* 8 (1945), gives an overview of his naval policy, arguing that he was in some ways in advance of his time in understanding the strategic use of naval power, but the fullest analysis of Jefferson's attitudes toward the navy is a doctoral dissertation by Joseph G. Henrich, "The Triumph of Ideology: The Jeffersonians and the Navy, 1779–1807" (Duke University, 1971), which contends there was no clear administrative naval policy. James A. Carr's "John Adams and the Barbary Problem: The Myth and the Record," in *American Neptune,* 26 (1966) is a good account of Adams' and Jefferson's support and deployment of the navy, and Eugene S. Ferguson's "Mr. Jefferson's Dry Docks," in *American Neptune,* 11 (1951), explains the scheme to build a covered dry dock large enough to hold twelve Constitution-class frigates. Frederick C. Leiner's "The 'Whimsical Phylosophic President' and His Gunboats," in *American Neptune,* 43 (1983), examines another of Jefferson's naval enthusiasms.

The Louisiana Purchase was the greatest accomplishment of Jefferson's administration; studies of the diplomatic background to this are noted above, but as significant as the purchase itself was Jefferson's prompt dispatch of exploring parties, most notably Lewis and Clark's. The best study of this is Donald Jackson's excellent *Thomas Jefferson and the Stony Mountains: Exploring the West from Monticello* (1981); Jackson has also edited *Letters of the Lewis and Clark Expedition, with Related Documents, 1783–1854* (1962). Focusing on the Lewis and Clark expedition itself but also informative on Jefferson's interest in western exploration is John Logan Allen's *Passage Through the Garden: Lewis and Clark and the Image of the American Northwest* (1975). Milford F. Allen's "Thomas Jefferson and the Louisiana-Arkansas Frontier," in *Arkansas Historical Quarterly,* 20 (1961), and Dan L. Flores' *Jefferson and Southwestern Exploration: The Freeman and Custis Accounts of the Red River Expedition of 1806* (1984) are good introductions to exploration on the southwestern borders of the Purchase. The first chapter of William H. Goetzmann's *When the Eagle Screamed: The Romantic Horizon in American Diplomacy, 1800–1860* (1966) provides a context for Jefferson's views about western expansion, and Goetzmann's *Exploration and Empire: The Explorer and the Scientist in the Winning of the American West* (1966) deals with both the Jeffersonian expeditions and the subsequent history of western exploration in the nineteenth century.

The acquisition of an immense western territory made necessary a comprehensive policy toward native Americans even as it changed the conditions for a possible solution of the Indian problem. The best study of Jefferson's Indian policy is Bernard W. Sheehan's *Seeds of Extinction: Jeffersonian Philanthropy and the American Indian* (1973), which contends that Jefferson's desires to assimilate the Indians were frustrated by his tendency to conceptualize them abstractly. Harold Hellenbrand's "Not 'to Destroy But to Fulfil': Jefferson, Indians, and Republican Dispensation," in *Eighteenth-Century Studies,* 18 (1985), explores some of the complexities of those abstractions. Jared W. Bradley's "William C. C. Claiborne: The Old Southwest and the Development of American Indian Policy," in *Tennessee Historical Quarterly,* 33 (1974), claims Jefferson's policy was in

effect predetermined for him before he took office, and William G. McLoughlin's "Thomas Jefferson and the Beginning of Cherokee Nationalism, 1806 to 1809," in *William and Mary Quarterly,* 3rd ser., 32 (1975), examines the impact of the 1808 proposal to move the tribe west and the alternative offer of assimilation. Reginald Horsman's "American Indian Policy in the Old Northwest, 1783–1812," in *William and Mary Quarterly,* 3rd ser., 18 (1961), portrays a Jefferson torn between concern for the Indians' welfare and "a voracious appetite for their land." William E. Foley and Charles David Rice's "Visiting the President: An Exercise in Jeffersonian Indian Diplomacy," in *American West,* 16 (1979), describe visits of Indian delegations to Washington, and Anthony Hillbruner's "Word and Deed: Jefferson's Addresses to the Indians," in *Speech Monographs,* 30 (1963), examines the rhetorical strategies of the presidential speeches, finding an increasingly paternal tone after 1803.

Highly informative on Jefferson's handling of economic issues and his ideas on economy is Drew R. McCoy's *The Elusive Republic: Political Economy in Jeffersonian America* (1980), the only book-length study of this topic. Richard E. Ellis' "The Political Economy of Thomas Jefferson," in Lally Weymouth, ed., *Thomas Jefferson: The Man, His World, His Influence* (1973), provides a useful summary, and Stuart Bruchey's chapter "Federal Government and Community Will" in his book *The Roots of American Economic Growth, 1607–1861* (1965) minimizes the practical differences between the economic policies of Jefferson and Hamilton. Also useful is William D. Grampp's "A Reexamination of Jeffersonian Economics," in *Southern Economic Journal,* 12 (1946). Merrill Peterson's important article on "Thomas Jefferson and Commercial Policy, 1783–1793," noted in the paragraphs above on foreign policy, is also relevant here, as are the studies of the embargo by Louis M.

Sears and Burton Spivak. Alexander Balinky's *Albert Gallatin: Fiscal Theories and Policies* (1958) is a useful examination of Jefferson's secretary of the Treasury, perhaps the best political appointment he ever made.

THE POLITICAL THINKER

When John F. Kennedy, in addressing a gathering of Nobel laureates, observed that the only previous time so much talent had been seated at a White House table was when Thomas Jefferson dined alone, he implicitly recognized that Jefferson's thinking was as important for American democratic life as his political achievements were. Adrienne Koch's *The Philosophy of Thomas Jefferson* (1943) is a pioneering and still essential study of the ideas that underlay Jefferson's political, religious, scientific, and educational activities. Gilbert Chinard's "Jefferson Among the Philosophers," in *Ethics*, 53 (1943), offers a good brief survey of Jefferson's philosophic background, and in the same bicentennial year of Jefferson's birth, Douglass Adair completed his doctoral dissertation, "The Intellectual Origins of Jeffersonian Democracy: Republicanism, the Class Struggle, and the Virtuous Farmer" (Yale, 1943), an important resource for a generation of scholars interested in Jefferson's political and agrarian thought. Garry Wills's *Inventing America* (1978), noted above in the paragraphs on the Declaration, is a brilliant if somewhat overly contentious discussion of the importance of the Scots commonsense philosophers as an influence on Jefferson. J. David Hoeveler, Jr.'s "Thomas Jefferson and the American 'Provincial' Mind," in *Modern Age*, 25 (1981), and Gilman Ostrander's "Jefferson and Scottish Culture," in *Historical Reflections*, 5 (1978), also look usefully at the Scots connection. Morton White's *Philosophy of the American Revolution* (1978) argues for the extensive influence of the Scots and of

Jean Jacques Burlamaqui on Jefferson and the other founders. James F. Jones, Jr.'s "Montesquieu and Jefferson Revisited: Aspects of a Legacy," in *French Review*, 51 (1978), and David W. Carrithers' "Montesquieu, Jefferson, and the Fundamentals of Eighteenth-Century Republican Theory," in *French-American Review*, 6 (1982), are informative on Jefferson's use of and changing attitudes toward Montesquieu. Merrill D. Peterson's "Thomas Jefferson and the Enlightenment: Reflections on Literary Influence," in *Lex et Scientia*, 11 (1975), suggestively considers his readings of Bolingbroke, Montesquieu, and Beccaria. Jeffrey Barnouw's "The Pursuit of Happiness in Jefferson and Its Background in Bacon and Hobbes," in *Interpretation*, 11 (1983), contends for an often overlooked strain of thought leading through Hobbes. Joyotpaul Chaudhuri's "Jefferson's Unheavenly City," in *American Journal of Economics and Sociology*, 34 (1975), makes some interesting distinctions between Jefferson and Locke. Robert Weyant's "Helvétius and Jefferson: Studies of Human Nature and Government in the Eighteenth Century," in *Journal of the History of the Behavioral Sciences*, 9 (1973), suggestively compares these two thinkers, finding Jefferson's ideas sociocentric rather than egocentric as Helvetius' are.

Charles M. Wiltse's *The Jeffersonian Tradition in American Democracy* (1935) was long a standard description of Jefferson as a liberal political theorist and is still useful. Louis M. Hartz's *The Liberal Tradition in America: An Interpretation of American Political Thought since the Revolution* (1955) is a classic argument for Jefferson as a keystone in the American liberal tradition, but Richard K. Matthews' *The Radical Politics of Thomas Jefferson* (1984) rejects this in favor of seeing his political ideas as fundamentally much more revolutionary. J. W. Cooke's "Jefferson on Liberty," in *Journal of the History of Ideas*, 34 (1973), analyzes his conception of freedom and observes no important change in his basic ideas after 1776. Edmund S. Morgan's *The Meaning of Independence: John Adams, George Washington, Thomas Jefferson* (1976) offers a brief but stimulating discussion of what independence meant for Jefferson. Harris G. Mirkin's "Rebellion, Revolution, and the Constitution: Thomas Jefferson's Theory of Civil Disobedience," in *American Studies,* 13 (1972), sees a tension in Jefferson's thought between the values of revolution and those of constitutional order. Robert E. Shalhope's "Thomas Jefferson's Republicanism and Antebellum Southern Thought," in *Journal of Southern History,* 42 (1976), provides an excellent account of Jefferson's thinking in the last two decades of his life and of his place in the mind of the South before the war. C. William Hill's "Contrasting Themes in the Political Theories of Jefferson, Calhoun, and John Taylor of Caroline," in *Publius,* 6 (1976), offers an interesting if tendentious comparison of the thought of the three most important political thinkers of the antebellum South.

JEFFERSON THE HUMANIST

Jefferson, like many of his contemporaries, read deeply in the classics, and the ideas he found there both shaped his view of the world and brought him comfort in his old age. Meyer Reinhold's *Classica Americana: The Greek and Roman Heritage in the United States* (1984) offers essays on various aspects of the classical tradition in America and includes a bibliography on Jefferson and the classics. Karl Lehmann-Hartleben's *Thomas Jefferson, American Humanist* (1947) considers his humanism as a response to the classical past. Louis B. Wright gives a good overview of the character and range of Jefferson's classical learning in "Thomas Jefferson and the Classics," in *Proceedings of the American Philosophical Society,* 87 (1943). Henry C. Montgomery's "Epicurus at Monticello," in *Classical Studies Presented to Ben Edwin Perry* (1969),

demonstrates the influence of stoicism and Epicureanism on Jefferson's thinking. Douglas Wilson's "The American Agricola: Jefferson's Agrarianism and the Classical Tradition," in *South Atlantic Quarterly,* 80 (1981), is an excellent discussion of the classical roots of Jefferson's agrarianism, and Susan Ford Wiltshire's "Jefferson, Calhoun, and the Slavery Debate: The Classics and the Two Minds of the South," in *Southern Humanities Review,* 11 (1977), distinguishes between two classical traditions in the old South. H. C. Montgomery's "Thomas Jefferson as a Philologist," in *American Journal of Philology,* 65 (1944), describes his interests in classical languages as well as those of the American Indians. In "The Classics in Jefferson's Theory of Education," in *Classical Journal,* 40 (1944), Norbert Sand shows that Jefferson found a place for the classics in a modern education.

The best account of Jefferson's religious beliefs is in Eugene R. Sheridan's introduction to the Jefferson Papers edition of *Jefferson's Extracts from the Gospels* (1983), but also useful is Charles B. Sanford's broad survey *The Religious Life of Thomas Jefferson* (1984). Sidney Mead is always stimulating on Jefferson; his essay on Jefferson and religious freedom has already been noted, but readers should also turn to "The Nation with the Soul of a Church," in *Church History,* 36 (1967), and *The Old Religion in the Brave New World* (1977), the Jefferson Memorial Lectures for 1974. Henry Wilder Foote's *Thomas Jefferson: Champion of Religious Freedom, Advocate of Christian Morals* (1947) tries to claim Jefferson for the Unitarians, while George Knoles's "The Religious Ideas of Thomas Jefferson," in *Mississippi Valley Historical Review,* 30 (1943), portrays him as a rationalist. Sanford Kessler offers an interesting account of a rationalist influence in "Locke's Influence on Jefferson's 'Bill for Establishing Religious Freedom,'" in *Journal of Church and State,* 25 (1983). Donald J. D'Elia's "Jefferson, Rush, and the Limits of

Philosophical Friendship," in *Proceedings of the American Philosophical Society,* 117 (1973), describes Benjamin Rush's efforts to make a more orthodox Christian out of Jefferson, and Constance B. Schulz's " 'Of Bigotry in Politics and Religion': Jefferson's Religion, the Federal Press, and the Syllabus," in *Virginia Magazine of History and Biography,* 91 (1983), examines the impact on Jefferson of the numerous Federalist attacks during his first presidential term. Robert M. Healey is informative on a somewhat specialized topic in "Jefferson on Judaism and the Jews," in *American Jewish History,* 73 (1984), and Healey's *Jefferson on Religion in Public Education* (1962) is the best discussion of his beliefs about the separation of church and state.

One could argue that religion was merely a variety of education for Jefferson, for he was always more interested in public virtue than in otherworldly affairs. Roy J. Honeywell's *The Educational Work of Thomas Jefferson* (1931) has long been a standard work on this subject. It can be usefully supplemented with Robert D. Heslep's *Thomas Jefferson and Education* (1969) and James B. Conant's *Thomas Jefferson and the Development of American Public Education* (1962), which in somewhat different ways stress the importance of Jefferson as a democratic educator. Jefferson's great achievement as an educational activist was the creation of the University of Virginia, and Philip Alexander Bruce's five-volume *History of the University of Virginia, 1819–1919: The Lengthened Shadow of One Man* (1920) is still an excellent source, particularly in the first two volumes. Nicholas Hans's "The Project of Transferring the University of Geneva to America," in *History of Education Quarterly,* 8 (1968), and Richard Beale Davis' edition of the *Correspondence of Thomas Jefferson and Francis Walker Gilmer* (1946) are informative on the problems of staffing the university. Stanley R. Hauer's "Thomas Jefferson and the Anglo-Saxon Language," in *PMLA,* 98 (1983), offers the most comprehensive account of Jefferson's interest in Anglo-Saxon and his efforts to make it part of the university curriculum. Andrew de Jarnette Hart, Jr., discusses Jefferson as a reformer of medical education in "Thomas Jefferson's Influence on the Foundation of Medical Instruction at the University of Virginia," in *Annals of Medical History,* n.s. 10 (1938). Elizabeth Cometti's *Jefferson's Ideas on a University Library* (1950) presents his letters to a Boston bookseller with an informative editorial introduction.

Charles B. Sanford's *Thomas Jefferson and His Library* (1977) provides a good overview of Jefferson's interests in book collecting and library organization. The great and indispensable work of scholarship in this area is E. Millicent Sowerby's five-volume *Catalogue of the Library of Thomas Jefferson* (1952–1959), an annotated catalog of the "great" library that became the foundation of the Library of Congress. Leo E. LaMontagne is informative on Jefferson's scheme to classify his books in *American Library Classification* (1961). Richard Beale Davis' "Jefferson as Collector of Virginiana," in *Studies in Bibliography,* 14 (1961), examines Jefferson's efforts to preserve the history of his state. William Bainter O'Neal's *Jefferson's Fine Arts Library: His Selections for the University of Virginia, Together with His Own Architectural Books* (1976) is a masterly description of this specialized aspect of Jefferson's library. Harry Clemons' *The University of Virginia Library, 1825–1950* (1954) gives a useful account of the library's Jeffersonian origins. Arthur M. Bestor's pages on Jefferson in *Three Presidents and Their Books* (1955) examine his concern for the potential dangers to the republican spirit posed by the ready accessibility of books such as David Hume's *History of England* and Sir William Blackstone's *Commentaries on the Laws of England.*

SCIENTIFIC INTERESTS

A great deal has been written on Thomas Jefferson's scientific interests, but three book-length studies are especially notable:

Edwin T. Martin's *Thomas Jefferson, Scientist* (1952) surveys the range of Jefferson's scientific interests; Daniel Boorstin's *The Lost World of Thomas Jefferson* (1948) is a classic account of the scientific activities and ideas of the Jeffersonians in the American Philosophical Society; John C. Greene's *American Science in the Age of Jefferson* (1984) offers the best contextual study of scientific achievement in Jefferson's time. A number of more specialized studies are also of interest. George Gaylord Simpson's "The Beginnings of Vertebrate Paleontology in North America," in *Proceedings of the American Philosophical Society,* 86 (1942); Howard C. Rice, Jr.'s "Jefferson's Gift of Fossils to the Museum of Natural History in Paris," in *Proceedings of the American Philosophical Society,* 95 (1951); and Julian P. Boyd's "The Megalonyx, the Megatherium, and Thomas Jefferson's Lapse of Memory," in *Proceedings of the American Philosophical Society,* 102 (1958), are all informative on his interests in paleontology. Antonello Gerbi's *The Dispute of the New World: The History of a Polemic, 1750–1900* (1973) gives the fullest account of Buffon's theory about the degeneration of species in the New World and discusses Jefferson's attempts to rebut them in the *Notes on the State of Virginia.* Anna C. Jones's "Antlers for Jefferson," in *New England Quarterly,* 12 (1939), describes amusingly another attempt to counter Buffon. Alexander F. Chamberlain's "Thomas Jefferson's Ethnological Opinions and Activities," in *American Anthropologist,* 9 (1907), surveys Jefferson's interest in Indians as subjects of anthropological study. Karl Lehmann-Hartleben discusses Jefferson as a pioneering field-worker in "Thomas Jefferson, Archaeologist," in *American Journal of Archaeology,* 47 (1943). Rodney H. True's "Thomas Jefferson in Relation to Botany" (*Scientific Monthly,* 3:1916) is still useful. Robert H. Halsey, *How the President, Thomas Jefferson, and Doctor Benjamin Waterhouse Established Vaccination as a Public Health Procedure* (1936), gives the best and fullest account of Jefferson and the introduction of vaccination for smallpox. John S. Spratt's "Thomas Jefferson: The Scholarly Politician and His Influence on Medicine," in *Southern Medical Journal,* 69 (1976), and George Rosen's "Political Order and Human Health in Jeffersonian Thought," in *Bulletin of the History of Medicine,* 26 (1952), offer informative and suggestive discussions of Jefferson as a medical thinker. Jefferson's interest in science always had a practical turn, and any visitor to Monticello comes away fascinated by his enthusiasm for technology. Margaret A. Whiting's "The Father of Gadgets," in *Stone and Webster Journal,* 49 (1932), surveys this; and Silvio A. Bedini's "Godfather of American Invention," in *The Smithsonian Book of Invention* (1978), includes a discussion of Jefferson's administration of the patent office. Bedini has also written a fascinating study, "Thomas Jefferson, Clock Designer," in *Proceedings of the American Philosophical Society,* 108 (1964), which gives an exhaustive account of Jefferson's interests in horology. Bedini's *Thomas Jefferson and His Copying Machines* (1984) studies his encouragement of Charles Willson Peale's efforts to perfect a copying device. M. L. Wilson's "Jefferson and His Moldboard Plow," in *Land,* 3 (1943), is the best readily available account of Jefferson's most notable contribution to agricultural technology.

AGRARIAN AND FARMER

If agriculture was an object of Jefferson's scientific attention, it was also the practical ground of his agrarian thought and the primary term of his self-definition. A. Whitney Griswold's "The Agrarian Democracy of Thomas Jefferson," in *American Political Science Review,* 40 (1946), and his *Farming and Democracy* (1948) argue for the centrality of the agrarian tradition in Jefferson's thinking and for its continuing importance in American society. Chester E. Eisinger's "The Freehold Concept in Eighteenth-Century American Letters," in *William and Mary Quar-*

terly, 3rd ser., 4 (1947), analyzes the Jeffersonian myth of the farmer republican; and Richard Bridgman's "Jefferson's Farmer Before Jefferson," in *American Quarterly,* 14 (1962), compares the myth to the actuality. Joseph Dorfman's "Thomas Jefferson: Commercial Agrarian Democrat," in the first volume of his *The Economic Mind in American Civilization, 1606–1865* (1946), and Joyce Appleby's "Commercial Farming and the 'Agrarian Myth' in the Early Republic," in *Journal of American History,* 68 (1982), assist the understanding of the commercial aspect of Jefferson's agrarianism. Harry V. Jaffa's "Agrarian Virtue and Republican Freedom: An Historical Perspective," in his *Equality and Liberty: Theory and Practice in American Politics* (1965), and Staughton Lynd's "Beard, Jefferson, and the Tree of Liberty," in *Midcontinent American Studies Journal,* 9 (1968), offer stimulating considerations of the ideological origins and political consequences of Jefferson's agrarianism. Everett E. Edwards, ed., *Jefferson and Agriculture: A Sourcebook* (1943) is informative on the practical aspects of Jefferson as a farmer, and M. L. Wilson surveys Jefferson's contributions to agriculture science and education in "Thomas Jefferson—Farmer," in *Proceedings of the American Philosophical Society,* 87 (1943). Hugh H. Bennett's *Thomas Jefferson, Soil Conservationist* (1944) and James E. Ward's "Monticello: An Experimental Farm," in *Agricultural History,* 19 (1945), are also interesting in this regard. Essential for understanding the actual business of farming as Jefferson practiced it are his farm and garden books, noted above in the paragraphs on editions of his writings.

Jefferson's extensive plantations were made possible by the peculiar institution of chattel slavery, and the issue of slavery shadows his whole career. In this essay, for example, notice of the scholarship on Jefferson and the slave question could as well have been attached to the discussions of egalitarianism as expressed in the Declaration, or

slavery could have been discussed as the one important issue Jefferson did not confront in his presidency. The most extensive study of Jefferson's concerns with and about slavery is John C. Miller's judicious *The Wolf by the Ears: Thomas Jefferson and Slavery* (1977). Robert McColley's *Slavery and Jeffersonian Virginia* (1964) portrays Jefferson as a model racist who nevertheless went as far as an elected representative of Virginia could go in attacking slavery. Winthrop D. Jordan's *White over Black: American Attitudes Toward the Negro, 1550–1812* (1968) balances Jefferson's derogation of blacks as inferior against the heritage of his egalitarianism. William Cohen's "Thomas Jefferson and the Problem of Slavery," in *Journal of American History,* 56 (1969), contends that his practical involvement with the system of black bondage was congruent with his racist ideas whereas his libertarian views about slavery tended to become abstractions. David Brion Davis in *Was Thomas Jefferson an Authentic Enemy of Slavery?* (1970) and *The Problem of Slavery in the Age of Revolution, 1770–1823* (1975) explains him as trapped by his loyalty to his class and society. William W. Freehling's "The Founding Fathers and Slavery," in *American Historical Review,* 77 (1972), emphasizes the positive side of Jefferson's opposition to slavery, and William D. Richardson's "Thomas Jefferson and Race: The Declaration and *Notes on the State of Virginia,*" in *Polity,* 16 (1984), claims that while Jefferson allowed blacks to have the same rights as all men, he did not say they should be enabled to become equal partners in the same polity with whites. John P. Diggins' "Slavery, Race, and Equality: Jefferson and the Pathos of the Enlightenment," in *American Quarterly,* 28 (1976), examines the responses of scholars between 1943 and 1975 to Jefferson's reasoning on racial equality, contending that like Jefferson they, too, have been unable to resolve the contradictory inheritance of Enlightenment thought.

That contradictory inheritance is perhaps

nowhere so poignantly obvious as in Monticello, the splendid artifact that stands for a genuinely enlightened, humane vision of life but an artifact built largely by the labor of Jefferson's black retainers. A good beginning for those interested in learning more about Jefferson's house and his life there can be made with Frederick D. Nichols and James A. Bear, Jr.'s *Monticello: A Guidebook* (1982), a model of what a guide to an historical site ought to be. William Howard Adams' *Jefferson's Monticello* (1983), handsomely illustrated with photographs by Langdon Clay of the house and grounds as they are now, includes an informative text. James A. Bear, Jr., was the longtime curator of Monticello, and he knows more about the house and grounds than anyone since Jefferson himself; his *Old Pictures of Monticello* (1957) is an iconographic study showing the changing appearance of the house and grounds over the years. Mary Cable and Annabelle Prager give a brief but informative account of the Levy family's ownership of the property in "The Levys of Monticello," in *American Heritage,* 29 (1978). Bear's *Jefferson at Monticello* (1967) contains the recollections of Isaac Jefferson, a family slave, and Edmund Bacon, Monticello's longtime overseer, and is informative on the daily routines on the estate. Bear's "Mr. Jefferson's Nails," in *Magazine of Albemarle County History,* 16 (1958), is the best account of Monticello's most notable manufacturing enterprise; Bear provides further insights in "Thomas Jefferson—Manufacturer," in *The Iron Worker,* 25 (1961). Walter Muir Whitehill's *The Many Faces of Monticello* (1965) is an informative pamphlet on the architectural evolution of the house and its contents. Charles L. Granquist gives an excellent account of Jefferson's greatest contribution to the bureaucratic style, the swivel chair, in "Thomas Jefferson's 'Whirligig' Chairs," in *Antiques,* 109 (1976). Bear's "The Furniture and Furnishings of Monticello," in *Antiques,* 102 (1972), offers a good account of Jeffer-

son's acquisition of furniture, and his "Thomas Jefferson's Silver," in *Antiques,* 74 (1958), does the same for Monticello's collection of silverware. Julian P. Boyd's "Thomas Jefferson and the Roman Askos of Nîmes," in *Antiques,* 104 (1973), is fascinating not only for its account of Jefferson's commissioning a piece of silver in France but for information on his visit to Nîmes and his relations with Charles-Louis Clérisseau. Edwin M. Betts and Hazlehurst B. Perkins provide a convenient discussion of Jefferson's landscaping in *Thomas Jefferson's Flower Garden at Monticello* (1971). Archaeological investigation of the flower and kitchen gardens continues; a recent interesting account is William M. Kelso's "Jefferson's Garden: Landscape Archaeology at Monticello," in *Archaeology,* 35 (1982).

ARCHITECTURE AND THE ARTS

On Jefferson as an architect, the pioneering work was by Fiske Kimball; "Thomas Jefferson and the First Monument of the Classical Revival in America," in *Journal of the American Institute of Architects,* 3 (1915), was his doctoral dissertation and discusses the historical importance of Jefferson's work on the Virginia capitol in Richmond. Buford Pickens' "Mr. Jefferson as Revolutionary Architect," in *Journal of the Society of Architectural Historians,* 34 (1975), by a recent supporter of Jefferson as an architectural innovator, examines his accomplishment against the limited options offered by the technology of his era. Kimball's *Thomas Jefferson, Architect* (1916) prints over two hundred drawings and related manuscripts; it should preferably be read in the more recent reprint (1968), which includes a significant essay by Frederick D. Nichols correcting some of Kimball's errors. Nichols' edition of *Thomas Jefferson's Architectural Drawings* (1961) is an essential document. Nichols collaborated with Ralph E. Griswold to produce a broad, informative survey, *Thomas Jefferson, Landscape Architect* (1978), which includes discussion of his horticultural interests. Fiske Kimball's two articles on "Jefferson and the Public Buildings of Virginia," in *Huntington Library Quarterly,* 12 (1949), describes drawings for buildings in Williamsburg and Richmond. Paul Foote Norton's doctoral dissertation, "Latrobe, Jefferson, and the National Capitol" (Princeton, 1952), is an excellent account of Jefferson's contributions to the eventual shape of the Capitol; this item has been printed (1977) in Garland Publishing's series of outstanding dissertations in the fine arts. Saul K. Padover's collection *Thomas Jefferson and the National Capital* (1946) provides numerous documents revealing his impact on the design of the city itself. William Hubbard's *Complicity and Conviction: Steps Toward an Architecture of Convention* (1980) and Gérard Le Coat's "Thomas Jefferson et l'architecture métaphorique," in *RACAR: Canadian Art Review,* 3 (1976), offer stimulating analyses of Jefferson's designs for the University of Virginia. William B. O'Neal's *Jefferson's Buildings at the University of Virginia: The Rotunda* (1960) discusses the design and building of the central structure of Jefferson's university, and Joseph Lee Vaughan and Omer Allan Gianniny, Jr.'s *Thomas Jefferson's Rotunda Restored, 1973–1976* (1981) describes subsequent revisions and the recent restoration to what seem to have been Jefferson's original intentions.

Jefferson and the Arts: An Extended View (1976), edited by William Howard Adams, contains essays on Jefferson's interest in architecture as well as in the other fine arts; this wide-ranging collection is an excellent introduction to his activities as a connoisseur, collector, and practitioner of the arts. Adams also edited the catalog of a major bicentennial exhibit at the National Gallery of Art, *The Eye of Thomas Jefferson* (1976), which provides not only a veritable iconography of Jefferson's age but an excellent text

as well. Eleanor Berman's *Thomas Jefferson Among the Arts,* (1947) usefully surveys Jefferson's aesthetic principles but overemphasizes the supposed influence of William Hogarth. Max L. Baeumer's "Simplicity and Grandeur: Winckelmann, French Classicism, and Jefferson," in *Studies in Eighteenth-Century Culture,* 7 (1978), examines the influence of Winckelmann's notion of classical beauty. Lee Quinby's "Thomas Jefferson: The Virtue of Aesthetics and the Aesthetics of Virtue," in *American Historical Review,* 87 (1982), sees a fusion of art and morals in Jefferson's ethics and aesthetics and illuminates connections between his aesthetic and political sensibilities. Noble E. Cunningham, Jr.'s *The Image of Thomas Jefferson in the Public Eye: Portraits for the People, 1800–1809* (1981) is an interesting illustrated study of contemporary representations of Jefferson the president. David Meschutt offers two informative essays on Jefferson's involvement with painters: "Gilbert Stuart's Portraits of Thomas Jefferson," in *American Art Journal,* 13 (1981), and "The Adams-Jefferson Portrait Exchange," in *American Art Journal,* 14 (1982), on the Mather Brown portraits. A number of items have been written on Jefferson's musical activities and interests, but the one substantial and authoritative study is Helen Cripe's *Thomas Jefferson and Music* (1974).

Serious attention to Jefferson as a literary artist has surfaced only in comparatively recent times. William K. Bottorff's *Thomas Jefferson* (1979) is a volume in the Twayne United States Authors series and pays particular attention to Jefferson's literary gifts. Stephen D. Cox's "The Literary Aesthetic of Thomas Jefferson," in J. A. Leo Lemay, ed., *Essays in Early Virginia Literature Honoring Richard Beale Davis* (1977), discusses Jefferson's attraction to the sublime coupled with the need for an ordered lucidity, and in the same volume of essays William J. Scheick's "Chaos and Imaginative Order in Thomas Jefferson's *Notes on the State of Virginia*" perceives an underlying aesthetic vision of "temperate liberty." Clayton W. Lewis' "Style in Jefferson's *Notes on the State of Virginia*," in *Southern Review,* 14 (1978), provides one of the most suggestive readings of Jefferson as a literary artist. Robert A. Ferguson's "'Mysterious Obligation': Jefferson's *Notes on the State of Virginia*," in *American Literature,* 52 (1980), compellingly makes the case for understanding the literary strategy of *Notes* against the tradition of English common law and the great, humanistic legal compendia of the Enlightenment. Leo Marx's discussion of *Notes* in *The Machine in the Garden* (1964) is the classic consideration of Jefferson's implication in the tradition of pastoral, and Lewis P. Simpson suggestively discusses the inherently alienating paradox of a pastoral vision erected on a system of chattel slavery in *The Dispossessed Garden: Pastoral and History in Southern Literature* (1975). James M. Cox makes an impressive claim for Jefferson as a major American writer in "Jefferson's *Autobiography:* Recovering Literature's Lost Ground," in *Southern Review,* 14 (1978).

Jefferson acquired or enlarged many of his interests in the arts, both fine and domestic, while in Europe. Edward Dumbauld's *Thomas Jefferson, American Tourist* (1946) and Howard C. Rice, Jr.'s *Thomas Jefferson's Paris* (1976) offer enjoyable and informative accounts of Jefferson the aesthetic traveler. Jefferson's interest in cooking and fine food is described in Marie Kimball's "The Epicure of the White House," in *Virginia Quarterly Review,* 9 (1933), and Jean Hanvey Hazelton's "Thomas Jefferson, Gourmet," in *American Heritage,* 15 (1964). Marie Kimball has also edited and written an introduction to *Thomas Jefferson's Cook Book* (1976). Jefferson's interest in wine and his efforts in viticulture and oenology are covered in R. de Treville Lawrence, Sr., ed., *Jefferson and Wine* (1976).

There are numerous other excellent articles on special topics pertaining to Jefferson, but space precludes notice of them all. For further information, one might consult Frank Shuffelton's *Thomas Jefferson: A Comprehensive, Annotated Bibliography of Writings About Him, 1826–1980* (1983) for the most complete listing of items. William B. O'Neal's *An Intelligent Interest in Architecture* (1969) is also of interest, for it lists books and articles that mention Jefferson even in passing and includes an iconography of nineteenth-century views of the University of Virginia.

Declaration of Independence

In CONGRESS, July 4, 1776.

The unanimous Declaration of the thirteen united States of America,

When in the Course of human events it becomes necessary for one people to dissolve the political bands which have connected them with another, and to assume among the powers of the earth, the separate and equal station to which the Laws of Nature and of Nature's God entitle them, a decent respect to the opinions of mankind requires that they should declare the causes which impel them to the separation.—We hold these truths to be self-evident, that all men are created equal, that they are endowed by their Creator with certain unalienable Rights, that among these are Life, Liberty and the pursuit of Happiness.—That to secure these rights, Governments are instituted among Men, deriving their just powers from the consent of the governed,—That whenever any Form of Government becomes destructive of these ends, it is the Right of the People to alter or to abolish it, and to institute new Government, laying its foundation on such principles and organizing its powers in such form, as to them shall seem most likely to effect their Safety and Happiness. Prudence, indeed, will dictate that Governments long established should not be changed for light and transient causes; and accordingly all experience hath shewn, that mankind are more disposed to suffer, while evils are sufferable, than to right themselves by abolishing the forms to which they are accustomed. But when a long train of abuses and usurpations, pursuing invariably the same Object evinces a design to reduce them under absolute Despotism, it is their right, it is their duty, to throw off such Government, and to provide new Guards for their future security.—Such has been the patient sufferance of these Colonies; and such is now the necessity which constrains them to alter their former Systems of Government. The history of the present King of Great Britain is a history of repeated injuries and usurpations, all having in direct object the establishment of an absolute Tyranny over these States. To prove this, let Facts be submitted to a candid world.—He has refused his Assent to Laws, the most wholesome and necessary for the public good.—He has forbidden his Governors to pass Laws of immediate and pressing importance, unless suspended in their operation till his Assent should be obtained; and when so suspended, he has utterly neglected to attend to them.—He has refused to pass other Laws for the accommodation of large districts of people, unless those people would relinquish the right of Representation in the Legislature, a right inestimable to them and formidable to tyrants only.—He has called together legislative bodies at places unusual, uncomfortable, and distant from the depository of their public Records, for the sole purpose of fatiguing them into compliance with his measures.—He has dissolved Representative Houses repeatedly, for opposing with manly firmness his invasions on the rights of the people.—He has refused for a long time, after such dissolutions, to cause others to be elected; whereby the Legislative powers, incapable of Annihilation, have returned to the People at large for their exercise; the State remaining in the mean time exposed to all the dangers of invasion from without, and convulsions within.—He has endeavoured to prevent the population of these States; for that purpose obstructing the Laws for Naturalization of Foreigners; refusing to pass others to encourage their migrations hither, and raising the conditions of new Appropriations of Lands.—He has obstructed the Administration of Justice, by refusing his Assent to Laws for establishing Judiciary powers.—He has made Judges dependent on his Will alone, for the tenure of their offices, and the amount and payment of their salaries.—He has erected a multitude of New Offices, and sent hither swarms of Officers to harass our people and eat out their substance.—He has kept among us, in times of peace, Standing Armies without the Consent of our legislatures.—He has affected to render the Military independent of and superior to the Civil power.—He has combined with others to subject us to a jurisdiction foreign to our constitution, and unacknowledged by our laws; giving his Assent to their Acts of pretended Legislation:—For quartering large bodies of armed troops among us:—For protecting them, by a mock Trial, from punishment for any Murders which they should commit on the Inhabitants of these States:—For cutting off our Trade with all parts of the world:—For imposing Taxes on us without our Consent:—For depriving us in many cases, of the benefits of Trial by Jury:—For transporting us beyond Seas to be tried for pretended offences:—For abolishing the free System of English Laws in a neighbouring Province, establishing therein an Arbitrary government, and enlarging its Boundaries so as to render it at once an example and fit instrument for introducing the same absolute rule into these Colonies:—For taking away our Charters, abolishing our most valuable Laws, and altering fundamentally the Forms of our Governments:—For suspending our own Legislatures and declaring themselves invested with power to legislate for us in all cases whatsoever.—He has abdicated Government here, by declaring us out of his Protection and waging War against us.—He has plundered our seas, ravaged our Coasts, burnt our towns, and destroyed the lives of our people.—He is at this time transporting large Armies of foreign Mercenaries to compleat the works of death, desolation and tyranny, already begun with circumstances of Cruelty & perfidy scarcely paralleled in the most barbarous ages, and totally unworthy the Head of a civilized nation.—He has constrained our fellow Citizens taken Captive on the high Seas to bear Arms against their Country, to become the executioners of their friends and Brethren, or to fall themselves by their Hands.—He has excited domestic insurrections amongst us, and has endeavoured to bring on the inhabitants of our frontiers, the merciless Indian Savages, whose known rule of warfare, is an undistinguished destruction of all ages, sexes and conditions. In every stage of these Oppressions We have Petitioned for Redress in the most humble terms: Our repeated Petitions have been answered only by repeated injury. A Prince, whose character is thus marked by every act which may define a Tyrant, is unfit to be the ruler of a free people. Nor have We been wanting in attentions to our Brittish brethren. We have warned them from time to time of attempts by their legislature to extend an unwarrantable jurisdiction over us. We have reminded them of the circumstances of our emigration and settlement here. We have appealed to their native justice and magnanimity, and we have conjured them by the ties of our common kindred to disavow these usurpations, which, would inevitably interrupt our connections and correspondence. They too have been deaf to the voice of justice and of consanguinity. We must, therefore, acquiesce in the necessity, which denounces our Separation, and hold them, as we hold the rest of mankind, Enemies in War, in Peace Friends.—

WE, THEREFORE, the Representatives of the UNITED STATES OF AMERICA, in General Congress, Assembled, appealing to the Supreme Judge of the world for the rectitude of our intentions, do, in the Name, and by Authority of the good People of these Colonies, solemnly publish and declare, That these United Colonies are, and of Right ought to be FREE AND INDEPENDENT STATES; that they are Absolved from all Allegiance to the British Crown, and that all political connection between them and the State of Great Britain, is and ought to be totally dissolved; and that as Free and Independent States, they have full Power to levy War, conclude Peace, contract Alliances, establish Commerce, and to do all other Acts and Things which Independent States may of right do.—And for the support of this Declaration, with a firm reliance on the protection of divine Providence, we mutually pledge to each other our Lives, our Fortunes and our sacred Honor.

List of Contributors

William Howard Adams
THE FINE ARTS

James A. Bear, Jr.
MONTICELLO

Silvio A. Bedini
Smithsonian Institution
MAN OF SCIENCE

Richard R. Beeman
University of Pennsylvania
THE AMERICAN REVOLUTION

A. J. Beitzinger
University of Notre Dame
POLITICAL THEORIST

Noble E. Cunningham, Jr.
University of Missouri
POLITICAL PARTIES

Robert Dawidoff
Claremont Graduate School
MAN OF LETTERS

Richard E. Ellis
State University of New York—Buffalo
CONSTITUTIONALISM

E. S. Gaustad
University of California—Riverside
RELIGION

John Howe
University of Minnesota
REPUBLICANISM

Donald Jackson
THE WEST

Robert M. Johnstone, Jr.
Earlham College
THE PRESIDENCY

Lawrence S. Kaplan
Kent State University
FOREIGN AFFAIRS

Joseph F. Kett
University of Virginia
EDUCATION

Leonard W. Levy
Claremont Graduate School
CIVIL LIBERTIES

Dumas Malone
THE LIFE OF THOMAS JEFFERSON

Henry F. May
THE ENLIGHTENMENT

Drew R. McCoy
Harvard University
POLITICAL ECONOMY

John C. Miller
SLAVERY

Frederick D. Nichols
ARCHITECTURE

Meyer Reinhold
THE CLASSICAL WORLD

Robert E. Shalhope
University of Oklahoma
AGRICULTURE

Bernard W. Sheehan
Indiana University
AMERICAN INDIANS

Frank Shuffelton
University of Rochester
BIBLIOGRAPHIC ESSAY

Douglas L. Wilson
Knox College
JEFFERSON'S LIBRARY

List of Chapter Ornaments

THE LIFE OF THOMAS JEFFERSON (p. 1):
Thomas Jefferson. Detail from *The Presidents of the United States* (1834), engraved by J. W. Casilear from the original portrait painting by Thomas Sully. The New York Public Library, Print Collection (Astor, Lenox and Tilden Foundations).

THE AMERICAN REVOLUTION (p. 25):
Death of Warren. A wood engraving after the original painting, *The Battle of Bunker's Hill* (1786), by John Trumbull. Reproduced from Samuel G. Goodrich, *A Pictorial History of America* (House & Brown, Hartford, 1850). The New York Public Library, General Research Division (Astor, Lenox and Tilden Foundations).

THE ENLIGHTENMENT (p. 47):
Sir Isaac Newton (l.). Detail from an engraving by J. Outrim from the original drawing in the Pepysian Collection at Cambridge. Reproduced from *Correspondence of Sir Isaac Newton and Professor Cotes,* edited by Joseph Edleston (John W. Parker, London, 1850). The New York Public Library, General Research Division (Astor, Lenox and Tilden Foundations).
Sir Francis Bacon (m.). Detail reproduced from *English Men of Letters,* edited by John Morley (Harper & Brothers, New York, 1894). The New York Public Library, General Research Division (Astor, Lenox and Tilden Foundations).

John Locke (r.). Detail from an engraving by J. June after the original portrait painting by Sir Godfrey Kneller. The New York Public Library, Print Collection (Astor, Lenox and Tilden Foundations).

REPUBLICANISM (p. 59):
Arms of Virginia: Thus always with tyrants. Reproduced from the title page of Henry Howe, *Historical Collections of Virginia* (Babcock & Co., Charleston, S.C., 1845). The New York Public Library, General Research Division (Astor, Lenox and Tilden Foundations).

POLITICAL THEORIST (p. 81):
The Drafting Committee, l. to r.: John Adams, Roger Sherman, Robert Livingston, Thomas Jefferson and Benjamin Franklin, present the Declaration of Independence to John Hancock and members of the Second Continental Congress on July 4th 1776. A vignette drawn by E. Purcell after the original painting, *The Declaration of Independence* (1820–1823), by John Trumbull. Engraving by Weekes, reproduced from the title page of Robert Sears, *A New and Popular Pictorial Description of the United States* (John A. Lee & Co., Boston, 1848). The New York Public Library, General Research Division (Astor, Lenox and Tilden Foundations).

POLITICAL ECONOMY (p. 101):
Sowing scene from rural America in the early 19th century. An engraving by Alexander Anderson. The New York

485

Public Library, Print Collection (Astor, Lenox and Tilden Foundations).

CONSTITUTIONALISM (p. 119):
E Pluribus Unum. Reproduced from the title page of *The Autobiography of Colonel John Trumbull*, edited by Theodore Sizer (New Haven, 1953). Courtesy Yale University Press.

THE CLASSICAL WORLD (p. 135):
Homer. Detail from an engraving by Gimber, published by Harper & Brothers. The New York Public Library, Print Collection (Astor, Lenox and Tilden Foundations).

JEFFERSON'S LIBRARY (p. 157):
Mr. Jefferson's chair and writing table. Reproduced from "Thomas Jefferson's Home" in *Century Magazine,* September 1887, Volume XXXIV, No. 5. The New York Public Library, Print Collection (Astor, Lenox and Tilden Foundations).

MAN OF LETTERS (p. 181):
The Natural Bridge over Cedar Creek in Rockbridge County, Virginia. An engraving drawn by W. Goodacre. Reproduced from *The History and Topography of the United States of America,* edited by John Howard Hinton (London Printing & Publishing Co., London, 1850). The New York Public Library, General Research Division (Astor, Lenox and Tilden Foundations).

THE FINE ARTS (p. 199):
Socrates at the moment of taking the hemlock. Detail from an engraving by J. L. Jules David from the original painting, *Death of Socrates* (1787), by Jacques Louis David. Reproduced from *Le Peintre Louis David* (Victor Havard, Paris, 1882). The New York Public Library, Art and Architecture Division (Astor, Lenox and Tilden Foundations).

ARCHITECTURE (p. 215):
The Capitol of Virginia at Richmond. Engraving reproduced from Robert Sears, *A Pictorial Description of the United States* (John A. Lee & Co., Boston, 1873). The New York Public Library, General Research Division (Astor, Lenox and Tilden Foundations).

EDUCATION (p. 233):
A View of the University of Virginia, Taken from the East Side (1856). Detail from an engraving by H. Weber. Reproduced from *Bohn's Album and Autographs of the University of Virginia* (Casimir Bohn, Washington, D.C., 1859). The New York Public Library, General Research Division Annex (Astor, Lenox and Tilden Foundations).

MAN OF SCIENCE (p. 253):
Toe bones of Megalonyx jeffersoni. An engraving by James Akin from chalk drawings by W. S. Jacobs. Reproduced from "A Memoir on the Discovery of Certain Bones of a Quadruped of the Clawed Kind in the western part of Virginia" by Thomas Jefferson, in *Transactions of the American Philosophical Society,* Volume 4, Chapter XXX, 1799. Courtesy of the American Philosophical Society, Philadelphia.

RELIGION (p. 277):
Sermon on the Mount: "Blessed are the pure in heart, for they shall see God." Matth. 5.8. An engraving by W. Baumann, published by G. G. Lange, Darmstadt, Germany. The New York Public Library, General Research Division Annex (Astor, Lenox and Tilden Foundations).

POLITICAL PARTIES (p. 295):
Thomas Jefferson (l.). Detail from an engraving by A. B. Hall from the original portrait painting by Mather Brown. Reproduced from *Appletons' Cyclopaedia of American Biography,* edited by James Grant Wilson and John Fiske (D. Appleton and Company, New York, 1887). The New York Public Library, Rare Books and Manuscripts Division (Astor, Lenox and Tilden Foundations).
Alexander Hamilton (r.). Detail from an engraving by Girsch from the original portrait painting by John Trumbull. Reproduced from *Appletons' Cyclopaedia of American Biography,* edited by James Grant Wilson and John Fiske (D. Appleton and Company, New York, 1888). The New York Public Library, General Research Division (Astor, Lenox and Tilden Foundations).

FOREIGN AFFAIRS (p. 311):
Capt. STERRETT in the Schr. ENTERPRISE paying tribute to TRIPOLI, August 1801. An engraving by M. Corné. Reproduced from Horace Kimball, *American Naval Battles* (J. J. Smith, Jr., Boston, 1831). The New York Public Library, General Research Division Annex (Astor, Lenox and Tilden Foundations).

CIVIL LIBERTIES (p. 331):
The Liberty Bell. Reproduced from Benson J. Lossing, *The American Revolution and the War of 1812* (New York Book Concern, New York, 1875). The New York Public Library, General Research Division (Astor, Lenox and Tilden Foundations).

THE PRESIDENCY (p. 349):
The President's House in Washington (prior to its destruction by the British Army). An aquatint from the original sketch of the White House by C. W. Janson, published

by G. & S. Robinson. Reproduced from *Lady's Magazine,* October 1814, No. 10. The New York Public Library, Print Collection (Astor, Lenox and Tilden Foundations).

THE WEST (p. 369):
Captain Lewis & Clark holding a Council with the Indians. Engraving reproduced from Patrick Gass, *Journal of the Voyages and Travels of a Corps of Discovery, Under the command of Capt. Lewis and Capt. Clark* (printed for Mathew Carey, Philadelphia, 1812). The New York Public Library, Rare Books and Manuscripts Division (Astor, Lenox and Tilden Foundations).

AGRICULTURE (p. 385):
Model of the Mould-Board Plough designed by Thomas Jefferson. Courtesy of the National Museum of American History, Smithsonian Institution.

AMERICAN INDIANS (p. 399):
Chief Logan, of the Mingo Tribe. Reproduced from "Dedication of the Logan Elm" by Miss May Lowe, in the *Ohio Archaeological and Historical Quarterly,* Volume XXII, January 1913, No. 1. The New York Public Library, General Research Division (Astor, Lenox and Tilden Foundations).

SLAVERY (p. 417):
Life in Eastern Virginia. The Home of the Planter. An engraving by Alexander Anderson. The New York Public Library, Print Collection (Astor, Lenox and Tilden Foundations).

MONTICELLO (p. 437):
Sketch of Mr. Jefferson's Seat, Monticello. Detail from an engraving by Asher B. Durand. The New York Public Library, Print Collection (Astor, Lenox and Tilden Foundations).

BIBLIOGRAPHIC ESSAY (p. 453):
Illustration drawn and engraved by W. Croome. Reproduced from John Frost, *The Pictorial History of the United States of America* (Benjamin Walker, Philadelphia, 1844). The New York Public Library, General Research Division (Astor, Lenox and Tilden Foundations).

Index